Middle School 3-1

학교시험 완벽대비

KB100524

1학기 전과정

적중 100 plus

영어 기출문제집

중 3

능률 | 김성곤

Best Collection

구성과 특징

교과서의 주요 학습 내용을 중심으로 학습 영역별 특성에 맞춰 단계별로 다양한 학습 기회를 제공하여 단원별 학습능력 평가는 물론 중간 및 기말고사 시험 등에 완벽하게 대비할 수 있도록 내용을 구성

Words & Expressions

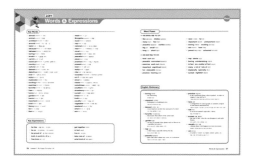

Step1
Key Words 단원별 핵심 단어 설명 및 풀이
Key Expression 단원별 핵심 숙어 및 관용어 설명
Word Power 반대 또는 비슷한 뜻 단어 배우기
English Dictionary 영어로 배우는 영어 단어

Step2
실력평가 단원별 수시평가 대비 주관식, 객관식 문제풀이

Step3
서술형 대비 학업성취도 및 수행능력평가 대비 서술형 문제풀이

Conversation

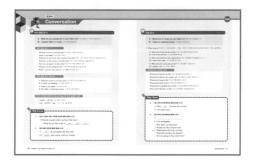

Step1
핵심 의사소통 소통에 필요한 주요 표현 방법 요약
핵심 Check 기본적인 표현 방법 및 활용능력 확인

Step2
대화문 익히기 교과서 대화문 심층 분석 및 확인

Step3
교과서 확인학습 빈칸 채우기를 통한 문장 완성 능력 확인

Step4
기본평가 시험대비 기초 학습 능력 평가

Step5
실력평가 단원별 수시평가 대비 주관식, 객관식 문제풀이

Step6
서술형 대비 학업성취도 및 수행능력평가 대비 서술형 문제풀이

Grammar

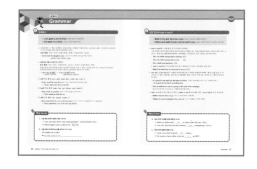

Step1
주요 문법 단원별 주요 문법 사항과 예문을 알기 쉽게 설명
핵심 Check 기본 문법사항에 대한 이해 여부 확인

Step2
기본평가 시험대비 기초 학습 능력 평가

Step3
실력평가 단원별 수시평가 대비 주관식, 객관식 문제풀이

Step4
서술형 대비 학업성취도 및 수행능력평가 대비 서술형 문제풀이

Reading

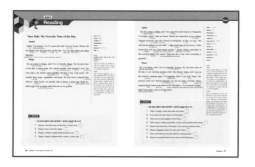

Step1
구문 분석 단원별로 제시된 문장에 대한 구문별 분석과 내용 설명
확인문제 문장에 대한 기본적인 이해와 인지능력 확인

Step2
확인학습A 빈칸 채우기를 통한 문장 완성 능력 확인

Step3
확인학습B 제시된 우리말을 영어로 완성하여 작문 능력 키우기

Step4
실력평가 단원별 수시평가 대비 주관식, 객관식 문제풀이

Step5
서술형 대비 학업성취도 및 수행능력평가 대비 서술형 문제풀이
교과서 구석구석 교과서에 나오는 기타 문장까지 완벽 학습

Composition

|영역별 핵심문제|

단어 및 어휘, 대화문, 문법, 독해 등 각 영역별 기출문제의 출제 유형을 분석하여 실전에 대비하고 연습할 수 있도록 문제를 배열

|단원별 예상문제|

기출문제를 분석한 후 새로운 시험 출제 경향을 더하여 새롭게 출제될 수 있는 문제를 포함하여 시험에 완벽하게 대비할 수 있도록 준비

|서술형 실전 및 창의사고력 문제|

학교 시험에서 점차 늘어나는 서술형 시험에 집중 대비하고 고득점을 취득하는데 만전을 기하기 위한 학습 코너

|단원별 모의고사|

영역별, 단계별 학습을 모두 마친 후 실전 연습을 위한 모의고사

교과서 파헤치기

- **단어Test1~3** 영어 단어 우리말 쓰기, 우리말을 영어 단어로 쓰기, 영영풀이에 해당하는 단어와 우리말 쓰기
- **대화문Test1~2** 대화문 빈칸 완성 및 전체 대화문 쓰기
- **본문Test1~5** 빈칸 완성, 우리말 쓰기, 문장 배열연습, 영어 작문하기 복습 등 단계별 반복 학습을 통해 교과서 지문에 대한 완벽한 습득
- **구석구석지문Test1~2** 지문 빈칸 완성 및 전문 영어로 쓰기

Contents

A Life Full of Experiences

의사소통 기능

- 바람에 대해 묻고 답하기
  A: What would you like to do this year?
  B: I'd like to travel to other countries.

- 만족이나 불만족에 대해 묻기
  How do you like hiking?

언어 형식

- 현재완료진행형
  I **have been writing** my shopping lists in Spanish!

- 관계대명사 what
  Find **what** keeps you motivated.

Words & Expressions

Key Words

- **ask** [æsk] 동 묻다, 요청하다
- **awesome** [ɔ́:səm] 형 엄청난
- **case** [keis] 명 사례, 경우, 상자
- **confident** [kánfədənt] 형 자신 있는
- **creative** [kriéitiv] 형 창조적인
- **culture** [kʌ́ltʃər] 명 문화
- **exactly** [igzǽktli] 부 정확하게
- **experience** [ikspíəriəns] 명 경험
- **finally** [fáinəli] 부 마침내
- **finish** [fíniʃ] 동 끝내다
- **foreign** [fɔ́:rən] 형 외국의
- **furniture** [fɔ́:rnitʃər] 명 가구
- **guess** [ges] 동 추측하다
- **hold** [hould] 동 쥐다, 들다
- **improve** [imprú:v] 동 개선하다, 향상시키다
- **join** [dʒɔin] 동 가입하다
- **meaningful** [mí:niŋfəl] 형 의미 있는, 중요한
- **memorize** [méməraiz] 동 암기하다
- **motivate** [móutəvèit] 동 동기를 부여하다
- **nervous** [nɔ́:rvəs] 형 불안한
- **own** [oun] 형 ~ 자신의 동 소유하다

- **perfect** [pə́:rfikt] 형 완벽한
- **perform** [pərfɔ́:rm] 동 공연하다, 수행하다
- **post** [poust] 동 (웹사이트에 정보·사진을) 올리다[게시하다]
- **recommend** [rèkəménd] 동 추천하다
- **requirement** [rikwáiərmənt] 명 필요조건, 요건
- **responsibility** [rispànsəbíləti] 명 책임감
- **review** [rivjú:] 명 검토, 후기
- **share** [ʃɛər] 동 공유하다
- **shelf** [ʃelf] 명 선반, 책꽂이
- **shopping list** 쇼핑 목록
- **social media** 소셜 미디어
- **spend** [spend] 동 쓰다
- **subtitle** [sʌ́btaitəl] 명 자막
- **talent** [tǽlənt] 명 재능
- **translation** [trænsléiʃən] 명 번역[통역](된 것), 번역문
- **travel** [trǽvəl] 동 여행하다
- **treasure** [tréʒər] 명 보물
- **vocabulary** [voukǽbjulèri] 명 어휘
- **volunteer** [vàləntíər] 명 자원봉사자 동 자원봉사하다
- **weakness** [wí:knis] 명 약점

Key Expressions

- **a review of a match** 경기 논평
- **be good at ~** ~을 잘하다
- **be interested in ~** ~에 관심을 가지다
- **be proud of ~** ~을 자랑스러워하다
- **be related to ~** ~에 관련되다
- **be struck by** ~에 감동받다
- **become familiar with ~** ~에 친숙해지다
- **first of all** 첫째로
- **get better at ~** ~에 능숙해지다
- **get used to ~** ~에 익숙해지다
- **give up** 포기하다

- **go shopping** 쇼핑하러 가다
- **in any case** 어쨌든
- **keep A motivated** A가 계속 의욕을 가지게 하다
- **not ~ at all** 전혀 ~가 아닌
- **run a race** 경주를 하다
- **spend time -ing** ~하면서 시간을 보내다
- **take a swimming class** 수영 수업을 받다
- **take care of** ~을 돌보다
- **try -ing** 시험 삼아 ~해 보다
- **what's most important** 가장 중요한 것
- **would like to ~** ~하고 싶다

Word Power

※ 서로 비슷한 뜻을 가진 어휘

□ **confident** 자신 있는 : **convinced** 확신하는

□ **improve** 개선하다 : **develop** 발달시키다

□ **exactly** 정확하게 : **correctly** 정확하게

□ **travel** 여행하다 : **tour** 여행하다

□ **finally** 마침내 : **at last** 마침내

□ **guess** 추측하다 : **infer** 추론하다

□ **recommend** 추천하다 : **suggest** 제안하다

□ **nervous** 불안한 : **annoyed** 짜증이 난

□ **awesome** 엄청난 : **amazing** 놀랄만한

□ **spend** 쓰다 : **use** 사용하다

□ **finish** 끝내다 : **complete** 완성하다

※ 서로 반대의 뜻을 가진 어휘

□ **confident** 자신 있는 ↔ **unconfident** 자신감이 없는

□ **responsibility** 책임감 ↔ **irresponsibility** 무책임

□ **perfect** 완벽한 ↔ **imperfect** 불완전한

□ **exactly** 정확하게 ↔ **inexactly** 정확하지 않게

□ **weakness** 약점 ↔ **strength** 강점

□ **meaningful** 의미 있는 ↔ **meaningless** 의미 없는

□ **finish** 끝내다 ↔ **begin** 시작하다

English Dictionary

□ **motivate** 동기를 부여하다
→ to make someone want to achieve something and make them willing to work hard in order to do this
누군가가 무엇인가를 이루도록 만들거나 그것을 위하여 열심히 노력하도록 만들다

□ **perfect** 완벽한
→ not having any mistakes, faults, or damage
아무런 실수, 결점 또는 손상이 없는

□ **post** (웹사이트에 정보·사진을) 올리다[게시하다]
→ add a message to an online message board
메시지를 온라인 게시판에 올리다

□ **recommend** 추천하다
→ to advise someone to do something
어떤 사람에게 무엇인가를 하도록 조언하다

□ **requirement** 필요조건, 요건
→ something that someone needs or asks for
누군가가 필요하거나 요구하는 어떤 것

□ **responsibility** 책임감
→ a duty to be in charge of someone or something
어떤 사람 또는 무엇인가를 담당하는 의무

□ **review** 검토
→ a careful examination of a situation or process
어떤 상황이나 과정에 대한 신중한 조사

□ **share** 공유하다
→ to have or use something with other people
다른 사람과 함께 어떤 것을 가지거나 사용하다

□ **shelf** 선반
→ a long flat narrow board attached to a wall
벽에 붙은 길고 평평한 좁은 판자

□ **talent** 재능
→ a natural ability to do something well
어떤 일을 잘 하는 천부적인 능력

□ **treasure** 보물
→ a group of valuable things such as gold, silver, jewels
금, 은, 보석 같은 귀중한 것의 집합

□ **volunteer** 자원봉사자
→ someone who does a job willingly without being paid
보수를 받지 않고 기꺼이 일하는 사람

01 다음 문장의 빈칸에 들어가기에 적절한 것은?

> What's most important is to become familiar with the language first. I suggest watching Spanish movies often. It will help you get _____ to the sound of the language.

① known   ② used   ③ closed

④ learned   ⑤ convinced

02 다음 영영풀이에 해당하는 단어를 고르시오.

> a long flat narrow board attached to a wall

① shelf   ② culture

③ responsibility   ④ subtitle

⑤ door

03 다음 대화의 빈칸에 들어갈 말로 적절한 것을 고르시오.

> B: We are finally on top of the mountain! How do you like hiking?
> G: It isn't easy at all, but now I understand why not _____ up is so important.

① looking   ② running

③ giving   ④ hanging

⑤ filling

04 다음 중 밑줄 친 부분의 뜻풀이가 바르지 않은 것은?

① I'd like to learn how to make my <u>own</u> mobile game. (소유하다)

② What did the girl learn <u>through</u> the experience? (~을 통해서)

③ Many people learn languages for <u>fun</u>. (재미)

④ They are my <u>favorite</u> players. (아주 좋아하는)

⑤ How can I <u>improve</u> my Spanish? (개선하다)

05 다음 중 〈보기〉에 있는 단어를 사용하여 자연스러운 문장을 만들 수 없는 것은?

> ┤ 보기 ├
> match   familiar   suggest   practice

① The best way to learn a new language is to _____ it every day.

② I have _____ the language of my phone to Spanish.

③ What's most important is to become _____ with the language first.

④ I can't wait to see the final _____.

⑤ I _____ watching Spanish movies often.

서답형

06 다음 주어진 단어를 이용해 빈칸을 완성하시오.

> Can you tell me about one of your _____ experiences? (mean)

➡ _____

01 다음 밑줄 친 부분을 알맞은 어형으로 고치시오.

> Furthermore, they had to <u>memory</u> the long poem.

➡ _____

02 다음 우리말에 맞게 빈칸에 알맞은 말을 쓰시오.

(1) 어쨌든, 학생들은 새로운 언어를 배우는 재미있는 방법을 가지고 있다.
　➡ In any _____, students have interesting ways to study new languages.

(2) 나는 무언가를 만들고 난 후에 자신감을 느낀다.
　➡ I feel _____ after I finish making something.

(3) 너를 동기 부여되도록 하는 것을 찾아라. 그러면 배우는 것을 더 즐길 수 있을 거야.
　➡ Find what keeps you _____; then you will enjoy learning more.

(4) 만약 사람들의 말이 너무 빠르면 먼저 스페인 어린이 영화 보기를 시도해 보아라.
　➡ If the people talk too fast, try _____ Spanish children's movies first.

03 주어진 단어를 이용해 빈칸을 완성하시오.

> Many students learn new languages because of school _____s. (require)

➡ _____

04 다음 짝지어진 단어의 관계가 같도록 빈칸에 알맞은 말을 쓰시오. (주어진 철자로 시작할 것)

> exactly : correctly = f_____ : complete

05 빈칸에 공통으로 들어갈 단어를 쓰시오.

> • You have to _____ used to other cultures.
> • Watching Chinese dramas with Chinese subtitles is a good way to _____ better at listening.

06 빈칸에 알맞은 단어를 〈보기〉에서 골라 쓰시오.

> ─┤ 보기 ├─
> experiences　talents　review　joined subtitles

(1) She _____ a skateboarding club last month.
(2) Having new experiences lets us find new _____.
(3) Also, why don't you try writing a _____ of a match in Spanish?
(4) It's also a good idea to print out the _____ and read them first.
(5) I am sure that these new _____ in Jeju Island would help me understand Korea better.

Conversation

1 바람에 대해 묻고 답하기

A What would you like to do this year? 올해 너는 무엇을 할 거니?
B I'd like to travel to other countries. 나는 다른 나라들을 여행하고 싶어.

■ 상대방이 바라는 것에 대해 물을 때는 '~하고 싶다'는 의미인 'would like to'를 써서 'What would you like to ~?'로 나타내거나 'What do you want to ~?' 등의 표현을 쓸 수 있다. 바라는 것은 to do, to drink, to eat 등의 to부정사 형태로 쓴다. 이에 답할 때는 'I'd like to ~.', 'I want to ~.' 등의 표현 또는 'I am going to ~'나 'I'm looking forward to -ing'을 쓸 수 있다.

■ 상대방이 무엇을 하고 싶은지 바라는 것을 물어볼 때, 실현 가능성이 낮은 경우 'I wish I could ~'라고 대답할 수 있다.

바람 묻기

- What would you like to do? 너는 무엇을 하고 싶으니?
- What do you want to eat? 너는 무엇을 먹기를 원하니?
- What are you going to do? 너는 무엇을 할 거니?

바람·소망을 나타내는 여러 표현

- I'm willing to V (기꺼이) …하겠다
- I can't wait to V …하고 싶어 기다릴 수 없다
- I am dying to V …하고 싶어서 죽겠다
- I am eager to V …하고 싶어 하다

- My wish is to V …이 내 바람이다
- I look forward to V-ing …하기를 기대하다
- I hope that … …이기를 바라다

핵심 Check

1. 다음 우리말과 일치하도록 빈칸에 알맞은 말을 쓰시오.

   A: _____ would you _____ to do this year? (올해 무엇을 하고 싶니?)
   B: I would like to learn a new language. (나는 새로운 언어를 배우고 싶어.)

2. 다음 대화의 순서를 바르게 배열하시오.

   B: What are you doing?
   (A) That's nice. What would you like to do this year?
   (B) Well, first of all, I'd like to spend time volunteering with my friends during summer vacation.
   (C) I'm writing a list of things that I want to do this year.

   ➡ _____

2 만족이나 불만족에 관해 묻기

• **How do you like hiking?** 하이킹은 마음에 드니?

■ 'How do you like ~?'는 '~은 어떻습니까?' '~는 마음에 드나요?'의 의미로 상대방이 어떤 대상에 만족하는지 혹은 불만족하는지를 물어보는 표현이다. 'How do you like ~?'는 '(음식 등을) 어떻게 해드릴까요?'의 의미를 나타내기도 한다.

■ 'How do you like ~?'에 대하여 대답할 때는 만족하는지 아닌지를 직접적으로 나타내어 'It is great.', 'It is nice.', 'It wasn't bad.' 등으로 대답하거나 'It isn't easy.' 'It isn't interesting.' 등으로 대답한다.

■ 만족이나 불만족에 대하여 물을 때는 'Are you satisfied with ~?' 또는 'Are you happy with ~?'를 사용하여 '~에 만족하니?'라고 물어보기도 한다. 'Do you like ~?'와 'Is this the one that you want(ed)?'와 같은 표현도 만족이나 불만족을 물어보는 표현이다.

만족이나 불만족에 관해 묻기

• How do you like it? 그것이 마음에 드니?
• Are you satisfied with it? 그것이 만족스럽니?
  = Are you happy with it?

• Do you like it? 너는 그것을 좋아하니?
• Is this what you wanted? 이것이 네가 원한 것이니?
  = Is this the one that you wanted?

만족이나 불만족에 대한 대답

• It is great. = It is nice. 그것은 좋다.

• It wasn't bad. 그것은 나쁘지 않았어.

핵심 Check

3. 다음 대화의 순서가 바르게 배열된 것을 고르시오.

B: Hey, Suji! What are you holding?

G: Hi, Ben. It's a skateboard. I'm going skateboarding.

B: Wow! I didn't know that you could skateboard. How did you learn to skateboard?

(A) It's really fun! It helps me make new friends, too.

(B) I joined a local skateboarding club last month.

(C) I see. So how do you like it?

B: How?

G: I go skateboarding with other members of the club, and we share tips with one another.

① (A) – (C) – (B)　　　② (B) – (A) – (C)　　　③ (B) – (C) – (A)

④ (C) – (A) – (B)　　　⑤ (C) – (B) – (A)

Listen & Talk 1 C

B: What are you doing?

G: I'm writing a list of things ❶that I want to do this year.

B: That's nice. ❷What would you like to do this year?

G: Well, first of all, I'd like to ❸spend time volunteering with my friends during summer vacation.

B: That sounds great.

G: ❹What about you? What would you like to do this year?

B: I'm thinking of ❺taking a swimming class.

G: That's really cool.

B: 너는 무엇을 하고 있니?
G: 올해 하고 싶은 일의 목록을 작성하고 있는 중이야.
B: 멋있다. 너는 올해 무엇을 하기를 원하니?
G: 음. 우선 여름 방학 동안 친구들과 자원봉사를 하면서 시간을 보내고 싶어.
B: 그거 좋겠다.
G: 너는 어떠니? 너는 올해 무엇을 하고 싶어?
B: 나는 수영 수업 받는 것을 생각하고 있어.
G: 그거 정말 멋있구나.

❶ that은 주격 관계대명사로 선행사는 a list of things이다.
❷ 'What would you like to do this year?'는 상대방에게 바람이 무엇인지 물어보는 말이다.
❸ 'spend 시간 -ing'는 '~하면서 시간을 보내다'의 의미이다.
❹ 'What about you?'는 '너는 어떠니?'의 의미로 상대방의 의견을 묻고 있다.
❺ 'take a class'는 '수업을 듣다'의 의미이다.

Check(√) True or False

(1) The girl would like to spend time volunteering this winter. T ☐ F ☐

(2) The boy wants to take a swimming class this year. T ☐ F ☐

Listen & Talk 2 B

B: Hey, Suji! What are you holding?

G: Hi, Ben. It's a skateboard. I'm going skateboarding.

B: Wow! I didn't know ❶that you could skateboard. How did you learn to skateboard?

G: I joined a local skateboarding club last month.

B: I see. So ❷how do you like it?

G: It's really fun! It ❸helps me make new friends, too.

B: How?

G: I go skateboarding with other members of the club, and we share tips with one another.

B: 안녕, 수지야! 들고 있는 것이 뭐니?
G: 안녕, Ben. 그것은 스케이트보드야. 나는 스케이트보드를 타러 가는 중이야.
B: 와우! 네가 스케이트보드를 탈줄 아는지 몰랐어. 스케이트보드는 어떻게 배웠니?
G: 지난달에 지역 스케이트보드 클럽에 가입했어.
B: 알겠다. 너는 그것이 마음에 드니?
G: 정말로 좋아! 그것은 또한 새로운 친구를 사귀도록 도와줘.
B: 어떻게?
G: 나는 클럽의 다른 회원들과 스케이트보드를 타러 가는데, 우리는 서로 방법을 공유해.

❶ that은 동사 know의 목적어가 되는 명사절을 유도하는 접속사이다.
❷ 'how do you like it?'은 만족하는지 여부를 묻는 말로 '그것이 마음에 드니?'의 의미이다.
❸ 동사 help는 목적격보어로 to부정사 또는 원형부정사를 쓴다.

Check(√) True or False

(3) Suji is satisfied with going skateboarding. T ☐ F ☐

(4) Ben joined a local skateboarding club last month. T ☐ F ☐

(5) Going skateboarding helps Ben make new friends. T ☐ F ☐

Listen & Talk 1 B

G: ❶What would you like to do this year?

B: I'd like to learn the guitar. I listened to the song "Cavatina," and I ❷was struck by the sound of the guitar.

G: That's great. ❸Where are you going to learn it?

B: My friend Jinsu is a very good guitar player. I'll ❹ask him to teach me.

❶ 상대방에게 하고 싶어하는 것이 무엇인지 물어보는 표현이다.

❷ be struck by = ~에 감동을 받다

❸ 'Where are you going to learn it?'은 현재진행형을 사용하여 미래의 계획을 묻는 질문이다.

❹ 'ask+목적어+to부정사'로 '~에게 …하도록 요청하다'의 의미이다

Listen & Talk 2 C

G: Did you make this shelf ❶yourself? It's amazing!

B: Thanks. I started making furniture last year.

G: Cool! ❷How do you like it?

B: It was hard at first, but now I love it. I feel so confident after I finish making something.

G: That's great. I think you're really good at it.

B: Thanks. I guess I found a new talent. I think ❸it's good to try new things.

G: Exactly. ❹Having new experiences lets us find new talents.

❶ yourself는 강조 용법의 재귀대명사이다.

❷ '그것이 마음에 드니?'의 의미로 상대방이 만족하는지를 묻고 있다.

❸ 가주어 it, 진주어 to부정사의 구문이다.

❹ 동명사가 주어로 쓰였다.

Listen & Talk 2 D

A: I ❶ran a race last year.

B: How did you like it?

A: I liked it a lot. It helped me ❷build confidence.

❶ run a race = 경주하다, 달리기하다

❷ 동사 help의 목적격보어로 쓰인 원형부정사이다.

Presentation Time Step 1

A: Can you tell me about ❶one of your meaningful experiences?

B: I cooked dinner for my family last Sunday.

A: How did you like it?

B: It was not easy, but I learned ❷that I could ❸make people happy with my cooking.

❶ one of the/소유격+복수명사 = ~ 중의 하나

❷ that은 동사 learned의 목적어 역할을 하는 명사절을 유도하는 접속사이다.

❸ 'make+목적어+목적격보어(형용사)'의 형태로 5형식 구문이다.

Presentation Time Step 3

Our group ❶recommends cooking dinner for your family. It is a meaningful experience ❷because you will learn that cooking for others can make them ❸happy. After this experience, ❹you will feel great.

❶ recommends의 목적어로 동명사가 쓰였다.

❷ because+주어+동사 cf. because of+명사(구)

❸ happy는 목적격보어로 쓰인 형용사이다.

❹ 동사 feel의 보어로 형용사 great를 썼다.

Do It Yourself A

B: My band ❶performed at the school festival yesterday.

G: Cool. ❷How did you like that?

B: It wasn't bad, but I made some mistakes.

G: It's okay. ❸I'm sure you sounded fine.

B: Thanks for ❹saying so. It was my first time playing the drums in front of so many people.

G: How did you feel about that?

B: I was very nervous, but I felt great, too!

G: That's awesome. ❺I'm so proud of you.

❶ perform = 공연하다, 연주하다

❷ '그것이 마음에 들었니?'의 의미로 상대방이 만족하는지 물어보는 표현이다.

❸ 'I'm sure' 뒤에는 접속사 that이 생략되었다.

❹ saying은 전치사의 목적어로 쓰인 동명사이다.

❺ be proud of ~ = ~을 자랑스러워하다. = pride oneself on ~

● 다음 우리말과 일치하도록 빈칸에 알맞은 말을 쓰시오.

Listen & Talk 1 B

G: What _____ you _____ to do this year?

B: I'd _____ to _____ the guitar. I _____ to the song "Cavatina," and I _____ _____ by the _____ of the guitar.

G: That's great. _____ are you _____ to learn it?

B: My friend Jinsu is a very _____ guitar _____. I'll _____ him to teach me.

G: 너는 올해 무엇을 하기를 원하니?
B: 나는 기타를 배우고 싶어. 나는 "Cavatina"라는 노래를 들었는데 기타 소리에 감동을 받았어.
G: 좋겠다. 너는 어디에서 그것을 배울 거니?
B: 내 친구 진수가 기타를 매우 잘 쳐. 나는 그에게 가르쳐 달라고 요청할 거야.

Listen & Talk 1 C

B: _____ are you _____?

G: I'm _____ a list of _____ _____ I want to _____ this year.

B: That's nice. _____ would you _____ to do this year?

G: Well, _____ of all, I'd _____ to _____ time _____ with my friends _____ summer vacation.

B: That _____ great.

G: _____ _____ you? _____ would you _____ to do this year?

B: I'm _____ of _____ a swimming _____.

G: That's really _____.

B: 너는 무엇을 하고 있니?
G: 올해 하고 싶은 일의 목록을 작성하고 있는 중이야.
B: 멋있다. 너는 올해 무엇을 하기를 원하니?
G: 음, 우선 여름 방학 동안 친구들과 자원봉사를 하면서 시간을 보내고 싶어.
B: 그것 좋겠다.
G: 너는 어떠니? 너는 올해 무엇을 하고 싶어?
B: 나는 수영 수업을 받는 것을 생각하고 있어.
G: 그것 정말 멋있구나.

Listen & Talk 2 B

B: Hey, Suji! _____ are you _____?

G: Hi, Ben. It's a _____. I'm going _____.

B: Wow! I didn't _____ _____ you could skateboard. _____ did you _____ to _____?

G: I _____ a _____ skateboarding club _____ _____.

B: I _____. So _____ do you _____ it?

G: It's _____ fun! It _____ me _____ new friends, too.

B: How?

G: I _____ _____ with other _____ of the club, and we _____ _____ with one another.

B: 이런, 수지야! 들고 있는 것이 뭐니?
G: 안녕, Ben. 스케이트보드야. 나는 스케이트보드를 타러 가는 중이야.
B: 와우! 네가 스케이트보드를 탈줄 아는지 몰랐어. 스케이트보드는 어떻게 배웠니?
G: 지난달에 지역 스케이트보드 클럽에 가입했어.
B: 알겠다. 너는 그것이 마음에 드니?
G: 정말 재미있어! 그것은 또한 새로운 친구를 사귀도록 도와줘.
B: 어떻게?
G: 나는 클럽의 다른 회원들과 스케이트보드를 타러 가는데, 우리는 서로 방법을 공유해.

Listen & Talk 2 C

G: Did you _____ this _____ _____? It's _____!

B: Thanks. I _____ _____ _____ last year.

G: Cool! _____ do you _____ it?

B: It was _____ at first, but now I _____ it. I _____ so _____ after I finish _____ something.

G: That's _____. I think you're _____ _____ _____ it.

B: Thanks. I _____ I _____ a new _____. I think it's _____ to _____ new things.

G: _____. _____ new _____ lets us _____ new talents.

Listen & Talk 2 D

A: I _____ a _____ last year.

B: _____ did you _____ it?

A: I _____ it a lot. It _____ me build _____.

Presentation Time Step 1

A: Can you _____ me about _____ of your _____ experiences?

B: I _____ dinner _____ my family last Sunday.

A: _____ did you _____ it?

B: It was _____ _____, but I learned _____ I could _____ people _____ with my _____.

Presentation Time Step 3

Our group _____ _____ dinner for your family. It is a _____ _____ _____ you will learn that _____ for _____ can _____ them happy. After this _____, you will _____ great.

Do It Yourself A

B: My band _____ at the school _____ yesterday.

G: Cool. _____ did you _____ that?

B: It _____ _____, but I _____ some _____.

G: It's okay. I'm sure you _____ _____.

B: Thanks _____ _____ so. It was my first time _____ the drums in _____ of so many people.

G: How did you _____ about that?

B: I was very _____, but I _____ great, too!

G: That's _____. I'm _____ _____ of you.

해석

G: 그 책꽂이를 직접 만들었니? 멋있다!

B: 고마워. 나는 작년에 가구 만들기를 시작했어.

G: 멋있어! 그것이 마음에 드니?

B: 처음에는 어려웠어. 그러나 지금 나는 그것을 아주 좋아해. 무엇인가를 만들고 나면 매우 자신감을 느껴.

G: 좋겠다. 나는 네가 그것을 정말 잘한다고 생각해.

B: 고마워. 나는 새로운 재능을 발견했다고 생각해. 새로운 것을 시도하는 것은 좋다고 생각해.

G: 그렇지. 새로운 경험을 하는 것이 우리에게 새로운 재능을 발견하도록 해.

A: 나는 작년에 달리기를 했어.

B: 그것이 마음에 들었니?

A: 굉장히 좋았어. 그것이 자신감을 가지도록 도와주었어.

A: 너에게 의미 있었던 경험 중 하나를 말해주겠니?

B: 나는 지난 일요일에 가족을 위하여 저녁을 요리했어.

A: 그것이 마음에 들었니?

B: 그것은 쉽지 않았어. 하지만 나는 내가 요리한 것을 가지고 사람을 행복하게 만들 수 있다는 것을 배웠어.

우리 모둠은 여러분의 가족을 위하여 저녁을 요리할 것을 추천합니다. 그것은 여러분이 다른 사람을 위하여 요리하는 것이 그들을 행복하게 만들 수 있다는 것을 배울 것이기 때문에 의미 있는 경험입니다. 이 경험 이후에 여러분은 기분 좋게 느낄 것입니다.

B: 우리 밴드가 어제 학교 축제에서 연주를 했어.

G: 멋있네. 너는 그것이 마음에 들었니?

B: 나쁘지 않았어. 하지만 내가 몇 가지 실수를 저질렀어.

G: 괜찮아. 네 연주는 확실히 좋았어.

B: 그렇게 말해주니 고마워. 그것이 그토록 많은 사람들 앞에서 처음으로 드럼을 연주한 것이었어.

G: 그것에 대하여 어떻게 느꼈니?

B: 나는 매우 불안했어. 그러나 또한 기분 좋기도 했어.

G: 훌륭하구나. 나는 네가 정말 자랑스러워.

01 다음 대화의 밑줄 친 부분이 의도하는 것을 고르시오.

> B: We are finally on top of the mountain! <u>How do you like hiking?</u>
>
> G: It isn't easy at all, but now I understand why not giving up is so important.

① 계획 묻기　　　　　　② 초대하기

③ 취미 묻기　　　　　　④ 하고 싶은 일 권유하기

⑤ 만족이나 불만족에 대해 묻기

[02~03] 다음 대화를 읽고 물음에 답하시오.

> G: What would you like ____(A)____ this year?
>
> B: I'd like to learn the quitar. I listened to the song "Cavatina," and I was (B)strike by the sound of the guitar.
>
> G: That's great. Where are you going to learn it?
>
> B: My friend Jinsu is a very good guitar player. I'll ask him to teach me.

02 위 대화의 빈칸 (A)에 알맞은 것은?

① to do　　　　　　② do

③ doing　　　　　　④ for doing

⑤ to doing

03 위 대화의 밑줄 친 (B)를 알맞은 형으로 고치시오.

➡ _____

04 다음 대화의 문맥상 또는 어법상 어색한 것을 찾아 고치시오.

> A: I took care of my friend's pet.
>
> B: What did you like it?
>
> A: I liked it a lot. It helped me develop responsibility.

_____ ➡ _____

[01~03] 다음 대화를 읽고 물음에 답하시오.

Lina: Can you tell me about one of your meaningful experiences?
Bill: I cooked dinner for my family last Sunday.
Lina: _____(A)_____
Bill: It was not easy, but (B)나는 나의 요리를 가지고 사람들을 행복하게 만들 수 있다는 것을 알게 되었어. (that / I / I / happy / people / learned / could make / with my cooking).

01 빈칸 (A)에 들어가기에 적절하지 <u>않은</u> 것은?

① Were you satisfied with it?
② How did you like it?
③ Do you think it tasted good?
④ Did you like cooking food for your family?
⑤ Were you happy with the experience?

02 주어진 어구를 배열하여 (B)의 밑줄 친 우리말을 영어로 옮길 때 5번째 오는 단어는?

① that　　② could　　③ make
④ people　　⑤ happy

03 위 대화를 읽고 대답할 수 <u>없는</u> 질문은?

① What was Bill's meaningful experience?
② When did Bill cook dinner for his family?
③ How did Bill like his experience?
④ What did Bill learn from his experience?
⑤ Why did Lina ask Bill about meaningful experience?

[04~05] 다음 대화를 읽고 물음에 답하시오.

B: Hey, Suji! What are you ___(A)___?
G: Hi, Ben. It's a skateboard. I'm going skateboarding.
B: Wow! I didn't know that you could skateboard. How did you learn to skateboard?
G: I joined a local skateboarding club last month.
B: I see. So how do you like it?
G: It's really fun! It helps me make new friends, too.
B: How?
G: I go skateboarding with other members of the club, and we share tips with one another.

04 빈칸 (A)에 들어갈 가장 알맞은 말을 고르시오.

① looking at　　② holding
③ going　　④ reading
⑤ driving

05 위 대화의 내용과 일치하는 것은?

① Ben is learning skateboarding.
② Suji learned skateboarding by video.
③ Suji will go skateboarding with Ben.
④ Suji and Bed share tips with each other.
⑤ Ben asks Suji how she learned skateboarding.

06 다음 글의 내용과 일치하지 <u>않는</u> 것은?

Today was my school festival! My band was okay, but I made some mistakes. It was my first time playing the drums in front of so many people! I was very nervous but I felt great, too!

① The writer made some mistakes.

② The writer felt good about his or her band.

③ The writer played the guitar.

④ There were many people at the festival.

⑤ The writer played the drums for the first time in front of so many people.

[07~09] 다음 대화를 읽고 물음에 답하시오.

B: My band performed at the school festival yesterday.

G: Cool. How did you like that?

B: It wasn't bad, but I made some mistakes.

G: It's okay. I'm sure you sounded ___(A)___ .

B: Thanks for saying so. It was my first time playing the drums in front of so many people.

G: How did you feel about that?

B: I was very nervous, but I felt great, too!

G: That's awesome. (B)나는 네가 너무 자랑스러워. (so)

---

07 빈칸 (A)에 들어가기에 가장 적절한 것은?

① terrible ② fine ③ cold

④ slow ⑤ loud

서답형

08 밑줄 친 (B)를 주어진 단어를 써서 영어로 쓰시오.

➡ _____

09 다음 중 위 대화를 읽고 대답할 수 없는 질문은?

① Is the boy a member of the school band?

② Did the girl like the performance?

③ How did the boy feel after the performance?

④ How many times did the boy play the drums in front of many people?

⑤ How many mistakes did the boy make at the festival?

10 다음 빈칸 ⓐ~ⓔ에 들어갈 대화로 어색한 것은?

B: _____ⓐ_____

G: I'm writing a list of things that I want to do this year.

B: That's nice. _____ⓑ_____

G: Well, first of all, I'd like to spend time volunteering with my friends during summer vacation.

B: _____ⓒ_____

G: _____ⓓ_____ What would you like to do this year?

B: I'm thinking of taking a swimming class.

G: _____ⓔ_____

---

① ⓐ What are you doing?

② ⓑ What would you like to do this year?

③ ⓒ That sounds great.

④ ⓓ What about her?

⑤ ⓔ That's really cool.

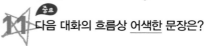

다음 대화의 흐름상 어색한 문장은?

G: Did you make this shelf yourself? It's amazing!

B: Thanks. ⓐI started making furniture last year.

G: Cool! ⓑHow do you like it?

B: It was hard at first, but now I love it. I feel so confident after I finish making something.

G: ⓒThat's too bad. I think you're really good at it.

B: Thanks. ⓓI guess I found a new talent. I think it's good to try new things.

G: Exactly. ⓔHaving new experiences lets us find new talents.

---

① ⓐ ② ⓑ ③ ⓒ ④ ⓓ ⑤ ⓔ

[01~03] 다음 대화를 읽고 물음에 답하시오.

B: Hey, Suji! What are you holding?

G: Hi, Ben. It's a skateboard. I'm going skateboarding.

B: Wow! I didn't know that you could skateboard. ___(A)___ did you learn to skateboard?

G: I joined a local skateboarding club last month.

B: I see. (B)So how do you like it?

G: It's really fun! (C)그것은 또한 새로운 친구를 사귀도록 나에게 도움을 줘. [helps / new friends / too]

B: How?

G: I go skateboarding with other members of the club, and we share tips with one another.

01 빈칸 (A)에 들어갈 의문사를 쓰시오.

➡ _____

중요
02 밑줄 친 (B)와 바꿔 쓸 수 있는 말을 완성하기 위하여 빈칸에 적절한 말을 쓰시오. (주어진 철자로 시작)

➡ So are you s_____ with it?

03 밑줄 친 (C)의 우리말을 영작하시오. (주어진 단어를 반드시 포함)

➡ _____

[04~05] 다음 대화를 읽고 물음에 답하시오.

G: Did you make this shelf yourself? It's amazing!

B: Thanks. I started making furniture last year.

G: Cool! How do you like it?

B: It was hard at first, but now I love it. 나는 무엇인가를 만들고 난 후에 매우 자신감을 느낀다. [so, confident, make, finish, something]

G: That's great. I think you're really good at it.

B: Thanks. I guess I found a new talent. I think it's good to try new things.

G: Exactly. Having new experiences let us find new talents.

04 밑줄 친 우리말을 "I"로 시작하는 영어 문장으로 옮겨 쓰시오. (주어진 단어 포함 및 필요하면 어형 변화)

➡ I _____.

중요
05 위 대화의 문맥상 또는 어법상 어색한 것을 찾아 고치시오.

_____

➡ _____

06 다음 대화의 흐름상 어색한 문장을 찾아 바로잡아 쓰시오.

B: What are you doing?

G: I'm writing a list of things that I want to do this year.

B: That's nice. How would you like to do this year?

G: Well, first of all, I'd like to spend time volunteering with my friends during summer vacation.

B: That sounds great.

G: What about you? What would you like to do this year?

B: I'm thinking of taking a swimming class.

G: That's really cool.

_____

➡ _____

교과서

Grammar

① 현재완료진행형

> • I **have been writing** my shopping lists in Spanish!
> 제가 사야 할 목록을 스페인어로 적어 오고 있어요!
>
> • My brother **has been studying** Spanish since last year.
> 내 남동생은 지난해부터 스페인어를 공부해 오고 있다.

■ 현재완료진행형은 'have[has] been+동사원형-ing'의 형태로 보통 for(~ 동안)나 since(~ 이래로)와 함께 쓰여 '~ 이래로[~ 동안] …해 오고 있다'라고 해석한다.

  • He **has been waiting** for her for two hours. 그는 두 시간 동안 그녀를 기다리고 있다.

■ 현재완료진행형은 어떤 상태나 행위가 과거 어느 때부터 시작되어 현재까지 계속 진행되고 있음을 나타내거나 현재까지 계속적으로 반복되고 있는 것을 나타낸다.

  • Imelda **has been cleaning** her house for 2 hours. Imelda는 두 시간 동안 그녀의 집을 청소하고 있다.

■ 현재완료진행형에서 진행형이 가능한 동사는 현재완료진행형으로 동작의 계속을 표현하고, 진행형으로 쓸 수 없는 동사(have(소유), belong, know, like, hate 등)는 현재완료형으로 상태의 계속을 표현한다. 즉, 현재완료진행은 '상태'가 아닌 '동작'만을 나타낸다.

  • It **has been raining** since yesterday. 어제부터 계속 비가 내리고 있다.: 동작의 계속

  • He **has had** poor crops this year. 그는 올해 적은 농작물을 수확했다.: 상태의 계속

■ **현재완료 / 현재완료진행형**
현재완료는 동작의 결과에 초점을 맞춘다고 생각할 수 있지만, 현재완료진행형은 계속되고 있는 동작 그 자체에 초점을 맞춘다고 생각할 수 있다.

  • She **has done** the dishes. 그녀는 설거지를 했다. → 결과에 초점

  • She **has been doing** the dishes. 그녀는 설거지를 하고 있다. → 동작에 초점

핵심 Check

1. 주어진 어휘를 빈칸에 어법에 맞게 쓰시오.

(1) I have been _____ French for four hours. (study)

(2) Andy has _____ playing soccer since he was eight. (like)

(3) They have been _____ Christmas since 2016. (celebrate)

2 관계대명사 what

> • Find **what** keeps you motivated. 당신에게 계속 동기 부여가 되는 것을 찾아라.
> • This book is **what** I wanted to buy. 이 책은 내가 사고자 원했던 것이다.

■ 관계대명사 what은 다른 관계대명사와 다르게 선행사를 포함하는 관계대명사로 '~하는 것'으로 해석하며, the thing(s) which[that]의 의미이다.

■ 관계대명사 what이 이끄는 절은 명사절로 문장에서 주어, 보어, 목적어의 역할을 한다.

(1) 주어 역할

• **What** you need is something to eat. 당신한테는 먹을 것이 필요해요.

(2) 보어 역할

• This is **what** they said. 이것이 그들이 말한 것이다.

(3) 목적어 역할

• If I do not understand **what** he says, I always ask him.
난 그가 하는 말이 이해가 안 될 때는 언제나 그에게 물어본다. (동사의 목적어)

• Listen to **what** he says on the matter. 그 일에 대해 그가 하는 말을 잘 들어라. (전치사의 목적어)

■ **관계대명사 what의 관용적인 표현**

• They experience **what is called** jet lag. 그들은 시차로 인한 피로라고 불리는 것을 경험합니다.

• I respect him, not for **what he has**, but for **what he is**.
내가 그를 존경하는 것은 그의 재산 때문이 아니라 그의 인격 때문이다.

• **What's worse**, I have a muscle pain. 설상가상으로, 나는 근육통을 겪고 있어.

핵심 Check

2. 다음 빈칸에 들어갈 알맞은 말을 쓰시오.

(1) Michelle은 그녀가 하고 있는 것을 정말 좋아합니다.
➡ Michelle loves _____ she is doing.

(2) 내가 해줄 수 있는 건 이 정도야.
➡ This is _____ I could do for you.

(3) 그녀의 말은 완전히 허튼 소리야.
➡ _____ she says is pure nonsense.

01 다음 두 문장이 같은 의미가 되도록 할 때 빈칸에 알맞은 것은?

> These are the things which she bought.
> = These are _____ she bought.

① how   ② which   ③ who
④ that   ⑤ what

02 다음 괄호 안에서 알맞은 말을 고르시오.

(1) He has been (waiting / waited) for her for an hour.
(2) I (am living / have been living) in Seoul for 10 years.
(3) The book is (what / that) she bought yesterday.
(4) (What / That) he wants to do is to play the guitar.

03 다음 두 문장을 한 문장으로 바꾸어 쓸 때 알맞게 표현한 것을 고르시오.

> • It started snowing the day before yesterday.
> • It is still snowing.

① It is snowing now.
② It snowed two days ago.
③ It has been snowing for three days.
④ It was snowing the day before yesterday.
⑤ It will be snowing tomorrow.

04 다음 우리말에 맞게 주어진 어휘를 바르게 배열하시오.

(1) 네가 어젯밤에 한 것을 내게 말해 줘.
     (you, me, tell, did, night, what, last)
     ➡ _____

(2) 내가 어제 네게 말했던 것을 기억해라.
     (I, you, yesterday, told, remember, what)
     ➡ _____

(3) 요즘은 허리가 영 시원찮다.
     (me, my, back, bothering, been, lately, has)
     ➡ _____

01 다음 중 어법상 올바른 것은?

① He has been planting apple trees for 2010.
② I've been looked for this book for an hour.
③ Megan has been write letters all day long.
④ It has been raining heavily for more than three hours.
⑤ He has been reading the book since about two hours.

02 다음 중 어법상 어색한 것은?

① What Jumi wants to do after school is to go shopping with her friends.
② It made me think what I liked.
③ Do you understand that he says?
④ What I want is something cold to drink.
⑤ What is the things that she brought to the party?

03 다음 빈칸에 알맞은 말이 바르게 짝지어진 것은?

> • She _____ ballet since she was eight.
> • This brush is _____ Kate bought yesterday.

① learns – which
② learned – that
③ is learning – what
④ has learned – that
⑤ has been learning – what

서답형

04 다음 괄호 안에서 알맞은 말을 고르시오.

(1) How long have you (wear / been wearing) this dress?
(2) Mary has been teaching English (since / for) two years.
(3) He has been practicing the violin (since / for) he was a little boy.
(4) The restaurant didn't sell (that / what) I wanted to eat.
(5) He lost all (that / what) he owned.

05 다음 대화의 빈칸에 들어갈 말로 알맞은 것은?

> M: What are you looking for there?
> W: _____ I'm looking for is my smart phone.

① What   ② That
③ This   ④ Which
⑤ It

06 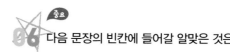 다음 문장의 빈칸에 들어갈 알맞은 것은?

> My wife has been studying Chinese _____ five years.

① since   ② for
③ at   ④ during
⑤ with

07 밑줄 친 부분의 쓰임이 올바른 것은?

① I <u>have been studying</u> Chinese last year.
② They <u>have been knowing</u> her for a long time.
③ We <u>have been meeting</u> them 5 years ago.
④ It <u>has been raining</u> since last Friday.
⑤ Amy <u>have been reading</u> the book for an hour.

서답형

08 다음 문장에서 어법상 **틀린** 부분을 찾아 바르게 고쳐 쓰시오.

Jamie's uncle is that is called a walking dictionary.

_____ ➡ _____

서답형

09 주어진 어휘를 이용하여 다음 우리말을 영작하시오.

가격이 몇 달째 꾸준히 오르고 있다. (7단어)
(months, prices, increase, steadily, for)

➡ _____

10 다음 주어진 문장의 밑줄 친 what과 같은 용법으로 쓰인 것을 **모두** 고르시오.

<u>What</u> I want to experience in Andong is to try Andong-jjimdak.

① I didn't know <u>what</u> to do next.
② Sophie showed me <u>what</u> was in her backpack.
③ <u>What</u> he said on the phone made his mom upset.
④ <u>What</u> are you talking about?
⑤ You don't know <u>what</u> it means to me.

11 다음 우리말에 맞게 빈칸에 알맞은 것을 고르시오.

하루 종일 계속 비가 오고 있다.
→ It _____ all day long.

① rained   ② rains
③ is raining   ④ has been raining
⑤ has been rained

12 다음 빈칸에 들어갈 말이 나머지와 **다른** 하나는?

① I disagree with _____ you say about that matter.
② I think _____ you say is logically wrong.
③ Could you name the person _____ you respect most?
④ She was very passionate about _____ she was doing.
⑤ You'd better just ignore _____ she says.

13 다음 두 문장을 한 문장으로 바르게 연결한 것은?

• Elena told me that she wanted to buy the things.
• They looked nice but cheap.

① Elena told me that she wanted to buy looked nice but cheap.
② Elena told me that she wanted to buy the things looked nice but cheap.
③ Elena told me that she wanted to buy which looked nice but cheap.
④ Elena told me that she wanted to buy that looked nice but cheap.
⑤ Elena told me that she wanted to buy what looked nice but cheap.

05 주어진 두 문장을 what을 이용하여 하나의 문장으로 쓰시오.

(1) • Find the thing.
  • The thing keeps you motivated.
  ⇒ _____

(2) • It made me think the thing.
  • I liked it.
  ⇒ _____

(3) • You said the thing.
  • It made me surprised.
  ⇒ _____

(4) • Something is done.
  • It cannot be undone.
  ⇒ _____

06 다음 문장에서 어법상 어색한 것을 바르게 고치시오.

(1) How long have you been lived in Korea?
  _____ ⇒ _____

(2) Mr. McDonald has been working in the restaurant since 10 years.
  _____ ⇒ _____

(3) Ben has been reading a book for this morning.
  _____ ⇒ _____

(4) That can I do now is to build a strong house.
  _____ ⇒ _____

(5) Let me tell you that I saw last night.
  _____ ⇒ _____

(6) You're the only one what really understands me.
  _____ ⇒ _____

(7) That he did with his wealth was quite unique.
  _____ ⇒ _____

07 현재완료진행형을 사용하여, 주어진 두 문장을 한 문장으로 바꾸시오.

(1) • Harold is reading the book.
  • He started reading the book this morning.
  ⇒ _____

(2) • Taehee started talking on the phone at one p.m.
  • She is still talking on the phone at 3 p.m.
  ⇒ _____

08 다음 우리말을 괄호 안에 주어진 어휘를 이용하여 영작하시오.

(1) 그들은 4대째 계속 여기 살고 있다. (here, four generations, live, for, 8 단어)
  ⇒ _____

(2) 과학자들은 토성의 고리를 연구해 오고 있다. (study, Saturn's rings, 6 단어)
  ⇒ _____

(3) 그 영화는 3개월째 상영되고 있어요. (the movie, show, for, 8 단어)
  ⇒ _____

(4) 일전에 한 약속을 잊지 마라. (forget, promise, the other day, 8 단어)
  ⇒ _____

Reading

Learn a New Language, Find a New World

Why Do People Learn Foreign Languages?

Many students learn new languages because of school requirements.
Many others learn them for fun. In any case, students everywhere
have found interesting ways to study new languages. Let's meet
these students and listen to their ideas.

I Love Soccer!

I'm a big fan of a Spanish soccer team. I want to understand
interviews with my favorite players. However, it's not easy because I
don't know Spanish that well. How can I improve my Spanish?

- Owen, 16

The best way to learn a new language is to practice it every day. I
have changed the language of my phone to Spanish, and I have been
writing my shopping lists in Spanish!

- Julie, 15

---

foreign 외국의, 타국의
requirement 필요 조건, (학교에서의) 필수 수업
case 경우, 상자
interview 인터뷰, 면접
improve 향상시키다, 나아지다
practice 연습하다

확인문제

● 다음 문장이 본문의 내용과 일치하면 T, 일치하지 않으면 F를 쓰시오.

1 Many students learn new languages because of school requirements. ☐

2 Owen wants to have interviews with his favorite soccer players. ☐

3 Owen doesn't know Spanish well. ☐

4 Julie says the best way to learn a new language is to practice it with native speakers. ☐

5 Julie has changed the language of her phone to Spanish. ☐

6 Julie has been writing her homework lists in Spanish. ☐

What's most important is to become familiar with the language first. I suggest watching Spanish movies often. It will help you get used to the sound of the language. If the people talk too fast, try watching Spanish children's movies first. — Inho, 14

Some words are used only in soccer, not in everyday life. Learn some soccer vocabulary and memorize it. Also, why don't you try writing a review of a match in Spanish? It will help you improve your writing skills. — Rohan, 16

No More Subtitles!

DREAM4 is back! I'm so excited to see my favorite Korean boy band perform. Their singing and their dancing are just perfect. I want to understand their songs without subtitles or translations though. Any tips? — Marisa, 14

You should find friends who are interested in DREAM4 and start a club. In my club, we motivate one another. We translate songs and sing together. Doing these things is fun and really improves our Korean! — Lori, 15

---

familiar 익숙한, 친숙한

get used to …에 익숙해지다

vocabulary 어휘

memorize 암기하다

review 후기, 검토

match 경기, 시합

skill 기능, 기술

subtitle 자막

perform 수행하다, 공연하다

perfect 완벽한, 완전한

translation 번역[통역](된 것), 번역문

though 그렇지만, (비록) …이긴 하지만

be interested in …에 관심[흥미]이 있다

motivate 동기를 부여하다

translate 번역[통역]하다, 옮기다

확인문제

● 다음 문장이 본문의 내용과 일치하면 T, 일치하지 않으면 F를 쓰시오.

1 Inho suggests watching Spanish movies often. ☐

2 Inho thinks watching Spanish children's movies isn't good. ☐

3 Rohan suggests learning some soccer vocabulary and memorizing it. ☐

4 Rohan also suggests reading a review of a match in Spanish. ☐

5 Marisa is so excited to see her favorite Korean boy band perform. ☐

6 Lori should find friends who are interested in DREAM4 and start a club. ☐

Follow DREAM4 on social media. They often post short messages
= The members of DREAM4

in Korean about how they are doing. They also post pictures with the
한국어로 / 간접의문문(의문사+주어+동사) / ~와 함께

messages, so you can understand the posts more easily.   - Aishah, 14

I recommend watching Korean dramas. I've been watching Korean
recommend는 목적어로 동명사를 취한다. / 현재완료진행형

dramas for a year, and they're really interesting! You can use Korean
for+숫자(~ 동안)

subtitles for help with listening. It's also a good idea to print out the
가주어 / 진주어

subtitles and read them first.   - Brandon, 16
to print out과 (to) read가 등위접속사 and로 병렬 연결되어 있다.

What Works for You?

There are hundreds of good tips out there, but everyone has their
수백의

own way of learning. Find what keeps you motivated; then you will
동격의 전치사 / 선행사를 포함한 관계대명사 / 동기가 부여된

enjoy learning more. Remember, every language is hard at first, but a
enjoy는 목적어로 동명사를 취한다. / 처음에는

new language can make your world much bigger!
비교급 강조(= even. still. far. a lot)

follow 따르다. (사회관계망 서비스 등에서) 팔로하다

social media 소셜 미디어

post (웹 사이트에 정보 · 사진을) 올리다

recommend 추천하다

print out (프린터로) 출력하다

📎 **확인문제**

● 다음 문장이 본문의 내용과 일치하면 T, 일치하지 <u>않으면</u> F를 쓰시오.

1   The members of DREAM4 often post short messages in Korean about how they are doing. ☐

2   The members of DREAM4 also post pictures with the messages in many foreign languages. ☐

3   Brandon recommends watching Korean dramas. ☐

4   Brandon has been watching Korean dramas for many years. ☐

5   The writer says every language is hard at first. ☐

6   The writer says a new language can make your world much more exciting. ☐

• 우리말을 참고하여 빈칸에 알맞은 말을 쓰시오.

1 Learn _____ _____ _____, Find a New World

2 Why Do People Learn _____ _____?

3 Many students learn new languages _____ _____ _____ _____.

4 Many others learn them _____ _____.

5 _____ _____ _____, students everywhere have found interesting ways to study new languages.

6 Let's meet these students and _____ _____ _____ _____.

7 I _____ Soccer!

8 I'm _____ _____ _____ of a Spanish soccer team.

9 I want to _____ _____ with my favorite players.

10 _____, it's not easy because I don't know _____ _____ _____.

11 How can I _____ _____ _____ _____? - Owen, 16

12 The best way to learn a new language is _____ _____ _____ every day.

13 I _____ _____ _____ _____ of my phone to Spanish, and I _____ _____ _____ my shopping lists in Spanish! - Julie, 15

14 What's most important is to _____ _____ _____ the language first.

1 새로운 언어를 배우고, 새로운 세상을 찾아라

2 왜 사람들은 외국어를 배울까?

3 많은 학생들이 학교 필수 수업이기 때문에 새로운 언어를 배운다.

4 다른 많은 이들은 재미를 위해 그것을 배운다.

5 어떤 경우에도, 모든 곳의 학생들은 새로운 언어를 공부하는 데 흥미로운 방법들을 찾아낸다.

6 이 학생들을 만나서 그들의 생각을 들어보자.

7 저는 축구를 정말 좋아해요!

8 전 스페인 축구 팀의 엄청난 팬이랍니다.

9 저는 제가 정말 좋아하는 선수들의 인터뷰를 이해하고 싶어요.

10 그런데 스페인어를 그렇게 잘 알지 못하기 때문에 그것이 쉽지 않아요.

11 어떻게 하면 제가 스페인어 실력을 늘릴 수 있을까요? – 오언, 16세

12 새로운 언어를 배울 수 있는 가장 좋은 방법은 그 언어를 매일 연습하는 것이랍니다.

13 저는 제 휴대 전화의 설정을 스페인어로 바꿨고, 제가 사야 할 목록을 스페인어로 적어 오고 있어요! – 줄리, 15세

14 가장 중요한 것은 우선 그 언어와 친해지는 것이에요.

15 I _____ _____ Spanish movies often.

16 It will help you _____ _____ _____ the sound of the language.

17 If the people talk too fast, _____ _____ Spanish children's movies first. - Inho, 14

18 Some words _____ _____ only in soccer, not in everyday life.

19 Learn some _____ _____ and _____ it.

20 Also, _____ _____ _____ try writing a review of a match _____ _____?

21 It will help you _____ _____ _____ _____. - Rohan, 16

22 _____ _____ Subtitles!

23 DREAM4 _____ _____!

24 I'm _____ _____ to see my favorite Korean boy band perform.

25 Their singing and their dancing are _____ _____.

26 I want to understand their songs _____ _____ or _____ though.

27 _____ _____? - Marisa, 14

28 You should find friends who _____ _____ _____ DREAM4 and start a club.

29 In my club, we motivate _____ _____.

30 We _____ songs and _____ _____.

15 전 스페인 영화들을 자주 볼 것을 제안하는데요.

16 그것은 당신이 언어의 소리에 익숙해지도록 도울 거예요.

17 만약 사람들이 너무 빨리 말한다면, 어린이를 위한 스페인 영화들을 먼저 보는 것을 시도해 보세요. – 인호, 14세

18 어떤 단어들은 일상생활에서가 아니라 오직 축구에서만 쓰인답니다.

19 몇몇 축구 어휘들을 배우고 기억하세요.

20 또한, 스페인어로 경기에 대한 후기를 써 보는 건 어때요?

21 그것은 당신이 작문 실력을 향상하도록 도울 거예요. – 로한, 16세

22 더는 자막 없이!

23 DREAM4가 돌아왔어요!

24 저는 제가 정말 좋아하는 한국의 젊은 남성 밴드가 공연하는 것을 보는 게 너무 신이 나요.

25 그들의 노래와 춤은 정말 완벽하답니다.

26 그렇지만 자막이나 번역이 없이 그들의 노래를 이해하고 싶어요.

27 어떤 조언들이 있을까요? – 마리사, 14세

28 당신은 DREAM4에 관심이 있는 친구들을 찾아 모임을 시작해야 해요.

29 우리 모임에서 우리는 서로 동기를 부여한답니다.

30 우리는 함께 노래를 번역하고 노래해요.

31 _____ these things is fun and really _____ _____

_____ ! - Lori, 15

32 Follow DREAM4 _____ _____ _____ .

33 They often _____ _____ _____ in Korean about how they

are doing.

34 They also post pictures _____ _____ _____ , so you can

understand the posts _____ _____ .- Aishah, 14

35 I _____ _____ Korean dramas.

36 _____ _____ _____ Korean dramas for a year, and they're

really interesting!

37 You can use Korean subtitles _____ _____ _____

_____ .

38 It's also a good idea to _____ _____ _____ _____ and

read them first. - Brandon, 16

39 What _____ for You?

40 There are _____ _____ good tips out there, but everyone has

_____ _____ _____ of learning.

41 Find _____ keeps you _____ ; then you will enjoy learning

more.

42 Remember, every language is hard _____ _____ , but a new

language can make your world _____ _____ !

31 이런 것들을 하는 것은 재미있고 정말로 우리의 한국어 실력을 향상해요! – 로리, 15세

32 소셜 미디어에서 DREAM4를 팔로하세요.

33 그들은 종종 자신들이 어떻게 지내는지에 대해 한국어로 짧은 메시지를 올려요.

34 그들은 또한 메시지와 함께 사진들을 올려서 당신은 더 쉽게 게시물을 이해할 수 있어요. – 아이샤, 14세

35 저는 한국 드라마들을 볼 것을 추천해요.

36 저는 1년 동안 한국 드라마들을 시청해 왔고, 그것들은 정말 재미있어요!

37 듣기에 도움이 되도록 한국어 자막을 사용할 수 있고요.

38 먼저 자막들을 출력해서 읽는 것도 좋은 생각이랍니다. – 브랜던, 16세

39 무엇이 당신에게 효과가 있는 걸까?

40 세상에는 수백 가지 좋은 조언들이 있지만, 모든 사람이 학습에 대한 그들만의 방법을 가지고 있다.

41 당신에게 계속 동기 부여가 되는 것을 찾아라, 그러면 당신은 학습을 더욱 즐길 것이다.

42 기억해라, 모든 언어는 처음에는 어렵지만, 새로운 언어가 당신의 세상을 더욱 넓혀줄 수 있다!

● 우리말을 참고하여 본문을 영작하시오.

1 새로운 언어를 배우고, 새로운 세상을 찾아라

➡ _____

2 왜 사람들은 외국어를 배울까?

➡ _____

3 많은 학생들이 학교 필수 수업이기 때문에 새로운 언어를 배운다.

➡ _____

4 다른 많은 이들은 재미를 위해 그것을 배운다.

➡ _____

5 어떤 경우에도, 모든 곳의 학생들은 새로운 언어를 공부하는 데 흥미로운 방법들을 찾아낸다.

➡ _____

6 이 학생들을 만나서 그들의 생각을 들어보자.

➡ _____

7 저는 축구를 정말 좋아해요!

➡ _____

8 전 스페인 축구 팀의 엄청난 팬이랍니다.

➡ _____

9 저는 제가 정말 좋아하는 선수들의 인터뷰를 이해하고 싶어요.

➡ _____

10 그런데 스페인어를 그렇게 잘 알지 못하기 때문에 그것이 쉽지 않아요.

➡ _____

11 어떻게 하면 제가 스페인어 실력을 늘릴 수 있을까요? – 오언, 16세

➡ _____

12 새로운 언어를 배울 수 있는 가장 좋은 방법은 그 언어를 매일 연습하는 것이랍니다.

➡ _____

13 저는 제 휴대 전화의 설정을 스페인어로 바꿨고, 제가 사야 할 목록을 스페인어로 적어 오고 있어요!
– 줄리, 15세

➡ _____

_____

14 가장 중요한 것은 우선 언어와 친해지는 것이에요.

➡ _____

15 전 스페인 영화들을 자주 볼 것을 제안하는데요.

➡ _____

16 그것은 당신이 언어의 소리에 익숙해지도록 도울 거예요.

➡ _____

17 만약 사람들이 너무 빨리 말한다면, 어린이를 위한 스페인 영화들을 먼저 보는 것을 시도해 보세요.
– 인호, 14세

➡ _____

18 어떤 단어들은 일상생활에서가 아니라 오직 축구에서만 쓰인답니다.

➡ _____

19 몇몇 축구 어휘들을 배우고 기억하세요.

➡ _____

20 또한, 스페인어로 경기에 대한 후기를 써 보는 건 어때요?

➡ _____

21 그것은 당신이 작문 실력을 향상하도록 도울 거예요. – 로한, 16세

➡ _____

22 더는 자막 없이!

➡ _____

23 DREAM4가 돌아왔어요!

➡ _____

24 저는 제가 정말 좋아하는 한국의 젊은 남성 밴드가 공연하는 것을 보는 게 너무 신이 나요.

➡ _____

25 그들의 노래와 춤은 정말 완벽하답니다.

➡ _____

26 그렇지만 자막이나 번역이 없이 그들의 노래를 이해하고 싶어요.

➡ _____

27 어떤 조언들이 있을까요? – 마리사, 14세

➡ _____

28 당신은 DREAM4에 관심이 있는 친구들을 찾아 모임을 시작해야 해요.

➡ _____

29 우리 모임에서 우리는 서로 동기를 부여한답니다.

➡ _____

30 우리는 함께 노래를 번역하고 노래해요.

➡ _____

31 이런 것들을 하는 것은 재미있고 정말로 우리의 한국어 실력을 향상해요! – 로리, 15세

➡ _____

32 소셜 미디어에서 DREAM4를 팔로하세요.

➡ _____

33 그들은 종종 자신들이 어떻게 지내는지에 대해 한국어로 짧은 메시지를 올려요.

➡ _____

34 그들은 또한 메시지와 함께 사진들을 올려서 당신은 더 쉽게 게시물을 이해할 수 있어요.

– 아이샤, 14세

➡ _____

_____

35 저는 한국 드라마들을 볼 것을 추천해요.

➡ _____

36 저는 1년 동안 한국 드라마들을 시청해 왔고, 그것들은 정말 재미있어요!

➡ _____

37 듣기에 도움이 되도록 한국어 자막을 사용할 수 있고요.

➡ _____

38 맨 먼저 자막들을 출력해서 읽는 것도 좋은 생각이랍니다. – 브랜던, 16세

➡ _____

39 무엇이 당신에게 효과가 있는 걸까?

➡ _____

40 세상에는 수백 가지 좋은 조언들이 있지만, 모든 사람이 학습에 대한 그들만의 방법을 가지고 있다.

➡ _____

41 당신에게 계속 동기 부여가 되는 것을 찾아라, 그러면 당신은 학습을 더욱 즐길 것이다.

➡ _____

42 기억해라, 모든 언어는 처음에는 어렵지만, 새로운 언어가 당신의 세상을 더욱 넓혀줄 수 있다!

➡ _____

[01~03] 다음 글을 읽고 물음에 답하시오.

_____ ⓐ _____ is most important is to become familiar with the language first. I suggest watching Spanish movies often. It will help you get used to the sound of the language. If the people talk too fast, try watching Spanish children's movies first. - Inho, 14

Some words are used only in soccer, not in everyday life. Learn some soccer vocabulary and memorize it. Also, why don't you try writing a review of a match in Spanish? ⓑ그 것은 당신이 작문 실력을 향상하도록 도울 거예요. - Rohan, 16

서답형

01 Fill in the blank ⓐ with the suitable word.

➡ _____

서답형

02 위 글의 밑줄 친 ⓑ의 우리말에 맞게 주어진 어휘를 이용하여 8단어로 영작하시오.

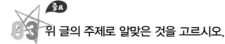
improve, writing skills

➡ _____

03 위 글의 주제로 알맞은 것을 고르시오.

① how to become familiar with Spanish movies

② various ways of improving your Spanish

③ the useful way of watching Spanish children's movies

④ some words used only in sports

⑤ how to write a review of a match in Spanish

[04~06] 다음 글을 읽고 물음에 답하시오.

I Love Soccer!

I'm a big fan of a ①Spanish soccer team. I want to understand interviews with my favorite players. _____ ⓐ _____, it's not easy because I don't know ②Spanish that well. How can I improve my ③Spanish? - Owen, 16

The best way to learn a new language is to practice it every day. I have changed the language of my phone to ④Spanish, and I ⓑhave been writing my shopping lists in ⑤ Spanish! - Julie, 15

04 위 글의 빈칸 ⓐ에 들어갈 알맞은 말을 고르시오.

① Therefore   ② However

③ Besides   ④ In other words

⑤ For instance

05 밑줄 친 ①~⑤ 중에서 단어의 뜻이 나머지 넷과 다른 것은?

①   ②   ③   ④   ⑤

06 위 글의 밑줄 친 ⓑhave been writing과 현재완료의 용법이 같은 것을 모두 고르시오.

① He has watched the movie twice.

② She has been sick since last Friday.

③ I have just finished reading the book.

④ He has lived in Busan for 10 years.

⑤ Have you ever seen a lion?

[07~09] 다음 글을 읽고 물음에 답하시오.

(A)[How / Why] Do People Learn Foreign Languages?

Many students learn new languages (B) [because / because of] school requirements. Many others learn ⓐthem for fun. In any case, students everywhere have (C)[found / founded] interesting ways to study new languages. Let's meet these students and listen to their ideas.

서답형

07 위 글의 괄호 (A)~(C)에서 문맥이나 어법상 알맞은 낱말을 골라 쓰시오.

➡ (A) _____ (B) _____ (C) _____

서답형

08 위 글의 밑줄 친 ⓐthem이 가리키는 것을 본문에서 찾아 쓰시오.

➡ _____

중요

09 위 글의 뒤에 올 내용으로 가장 알맞은 것을 고르시오.

① 새로운 언어를 배우는 이유
② 학교 필수 수업에 해당하는 새로운 언어
③ 전 세계의 재미있는 언어의 종류
④ 새로운 언어를 공부하는 흥미로운 방법들
⑤ 전 세계 학생들이 선호하는 외국어

[10~13] 다음 글을 읽고 물음에 답하시오.

Follow DREAM4 on social media. They often post short messages in Korean about ⓐ자신들이 어떻게 지내는지. They also post pictures with the messages, so you can understand the posts more easily.

— Aishah, 14

I recommend watching Korean dramas. I've been watching Korean dramas for a year, and they're really interesting! You can use Korean subtitles for help with listening. ⓑIt's also a good idea to print out the subtitles and read them first.

— Brandon, 16

서답형

10 위 글의 밑줄 친 ⓐ의 우리말에 맞게 주어진 어휘를 알맞게 배열하시오.

doing / are / they / how

➡ _____

11 위 글의 밑줄 친 ⓑIt과 문법적 쓰임이 같은 것을 고르시오.

① It is 2 miles from here to the airport.
② I make it a rule to get up early.
③ It's Jim who will marry Ann.
④ How's it going with you?
⑤ It's impossible to get there in time.

서답형

12 다음 문장에서 위 글의 내용과 <u>다른</u> 부분을 찾아서 고치시오.

As the members of DREAM4 post comments with the messages, it is possible to understand the posts more easily.

_____ ➡ _____

서답형

13 다음 빈칸 (A)와 (B)에 알맞은 단어를 넣어 한국어를 배우기 위한 아이샤와 브랜던의 조언을 완성하시오.

Aishah recommends (A)_____ DREAM4 on social media and Brandon recommends watching (B)_____ _____.

[14~15] 다음 글을 읽고 물음에 답하시오.

(A)What's most important is to become familiar with the language first. I suggest watching Spanish movies often. It will help you get used to the sound of the language. If the people talk too fast, try watching Spanish children's movies first.　　　- Inho, 14

Some words ___(B)___ only in soccer, not in everyday life. Learn some soccer vocabulary and memorize it. Also, why don't you try writing a review of a match in Spanish? It will help you improve your writing skills.

- Rohan, 16

14 위 글의 밑줄 친 (A)What과 같은 의미로 쓰인 것을 모두 고르시오.

① What kind of music do you like?
② What a genius he is!
③ He will do what he can do for you.
④ I pointed to what looked like a bird.
⑤ What are you looking for?

서답형

15 위 글의 빈칸 (B)에 use를 알맞은 형태로 쓰시오.

➡ _____

[16~18] 다음 글을 읽고 물음에 답하시오.

ⓐ _____

DREAM4 is back! I'm so excited to see my favorite Korean boy band perform. Their singing and their dancing are just perfect. I want to understand their songs without subtitles or translations though. Any tips?

- Marisa, 14

You should find friends who are interested in DREAM4 and start a club. In my club, we motivate one another. We translate songs and sing together. ⓑDoing these things is fun and really improves our Korean!　　　- Lori, 15

중요

16 위 글의 빈칸 ⓐ에 들어갈 제목으로 알맞은 것을 고르시오.

① DREAM4 Is My Favorite Band
② Do You Like Perfect Singing?
③ No More Subtitles!
④ How to Start a Club
⑤ The Easy Way to Master Korean

서답형

17 위 글의 밑줄 친 ⓑ를 다음과 같이 바꿔 쓸 때 빈칸에 들어갈 알맞은 말을 두 단어로 쓰시오.

➡ It is fun and really improves our Korean _____ _____ these things!

중요

18 Which question CANNOT be answered after reading the passage?

① Why is Marisa so excited?
② What's the name of Marisa's favorite Korean boy band?
③ Can Marisa understand her favorite Korean band's songs without subtitles or translations?
④ What does Lori recommend to Marisa?
⑤ How many members are there in Lori's club?

[19~22] 다음 글을 읽고 물음에 답하시오.

 Many students learn new languages because of school requirements. Many others learn them for fun. ⓐIn any case, students everywhere have found interesting ways ⓑto study new languages. Let's meet these students and listen to their ideas.

19 위 글의 밑줄 친 ⓐIn any case와 바꿔 쓸 수 <u>없는</u> 말을 고르시오.

① Anyway   ② Anyhow
③ By the way   ④ At any rate
⑤ At all events

20 위 글의 밑줄 친 ⓑto study와 to부정사의 용법이 같은 것을 <u>모두</u> 고르시오.

① He went abroad to study new languages.
② It's time for you to study new languages.
③ She is clever enough to study new languages.
④ I decided to to study new languages.
⑤ We need the place to study new languages in.

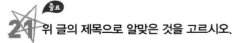

21 위 글의 제목으로 알맞은 것을 고르시오.

① How Do People Learn Foreign Languages?
② Many Kinds of Languages
③ The Difficulty of Learning Foreign Languages
④ Why Do People Learn Foreign Languages?
⑤ Wonderful Ways to Communicate with Foreigners

22 본문의 내용과 일치하도록 다음 빈칸 (A)와 (B)에 알맞은 단어를 쓰시오.

Many students learn new languages because of (A)_____ _____ or (B)_____ _____.

[23~25] 다음 글을 읽고 물음에 답하시오.

I Love Soccer!
 I'm a big fan of a Spanish soccer team. I want to understand interviews with my favorite players. However, it's not easy because I don't know Spanish that well. How can I improve my Spanish?   - Owen, 16
 The best way (A)to learn a new language is (B)to practice it every day. I have changed the language of my phone ___ⓐ___ Spanish, and I have been writing my shopping lists ___ⓑ___ Spanish!   - Julie, 15

23 위 글의 빈칸 ⓐ와 ⓑ에 들어갈 전치사가 바르게 짝지어진 것은?

  ⓐ   ⓑ   ⓐ   ⓑ
① by – in   ② to – in
③ in – from   ④ in – by
⑤ to – by

24 아래 〈보기〉에서 위 글의 밑줄 친 (A)to learn, (B)to practice와 to부정사의 용법이 같은 것을 각각 고르시오.

┌── 보기 ──┐
① I have many friends to talk with.
② It is important to use your time well.
③ He awoke to find himself famous.
④ I want something cold to drink.
⑤ Her dream is to be a doctor.

➡ (A)와 같은 것: _____
   (B)와 같은 것: _____

25 According to the passage, which is NOT true?

① Owen is a big fan of a Spanish soccer team.

② Owen speaks Spanish well enough to understand interviews with his favorite players.

③ According to Julie, the best way to learn a new language is to practice it every day.

④ Julie has changed the language of her phone to Spanish.

⑤ Julie has been writing her shopping lists in Spanish.

[26~28] 다음 글을 읽고 물음에 답하시오.

> I recommend ⓐwatching Korean dramas. I've been ⓑwatching Korean dramas for a year, and they're really interesting! You can use Korean subtitles for help with listening. It's also a good idea to print out the subtitles and read them first. - Brandon, 16
>
> **What Works for You?**
> There are hundreds of good tips out there, but everyone has their own way of learning. ⓒFind what keeps you motivated; then you will enjoy learning more. Remember, every language is hard at first, but a new language can make your world ⓓmuch bigger!

서답형

26 아래 〈보기〉에서 위 글의 밑줄 친 ⓐwatching, ⓑwatching 과 문법적 쓰임이 같은 것을 각각 모두 고르시오.

┌─── 보기 ───
① I like watching Korean dramas.
② Watching Korean dramas makes me happy.
③ She is watching Korean dramas.
④ My hobby is watching Korean dramas.
⑤ I saw him watching Korean dramas.
└───

➡ ⓐ: _____, ⓑ: _____

서답형

27 위 글의 밑줄 친 ⓒ를 다음과 같이 바꿔 쓸 때 빈칸에 들어 갈 알맞은 말을 두 단어로 쓰시오.

➡ _____ _____ find what keeps you motivated, you will enjoy learning more.

28 위 글의 빈칸 ⓓmuch와 바꿔 쓸 수 없는 말을 고르시오.

① still ② a lot ③ far
④ even ⑤ very

[29~30] 다음 글을 읽고 물음에 답하시오.

> **I Love Soccer!**
> I'm a big fan of a ___ⓐ___ soccer team. (①) I want to understand interviews with my favorite players. (②) How can I improve my Spanish? (③) - Owen, 16
> The best way to learn a new language is to practice it every day. (④) I have changed the language of my phone to Spanish, and I have been writing my shopping lists in Spanish! (⑤) - Julie, 15

서답형

29 위 글의 빈칸 ⓐ에 Spain을 알맞은 형태로 쓰시오.

➡ _____

 30 위 글의 흐름으로 보아, 주어진 문장이 들어가기에 가장 적 절한 곳은?

> However, it's not easy because I don't know Spanish that well.

① ② ③ ④ ⑤

[01~03] 다음 글을 읽고 물음에 답하시오.

I Love Soccer!

I'm a big fan of a Spanish soccer team. I want to understand interviews with my favorite players. However, (A)it's not easy because I don't know Spanish that well. How can I improve my Spanish?　　　- Owen, 16

The best way to learn a new language is to practice it every day. I have changed the language of my phone to Spanish, and I _____(B)_____ my shopping lists in Spanish!
　　　　　　　　　　　　　　　- Julie, 15

01 위 글의 밑줄 친 (A)it이 가리키는 것을 본문에서 찾아 쓰시오.

➡ _____

02 Fill in the blanks (B) with suitable words to match the meaning of the sentence below.

> I started to write my shopping lists in Spanish and I am still writing them in Spanish!

➡ _____

03 위 글의 내용을 다음과 같이 정리하고자 한다. 빈칸 (A)~(C)에 들어갈 알맞은 단어를 본문에서 찾아 쓰시오.

How to Learn a New Language	
Interests	Spanish (A)_____ team
Wants	To (B)_____ the players' interviews
Useful Tip	Practice (C)_____ every day.

[04~06] 다음 글을 읽고 물음에 답하시오.

I recommend watching Korean dramas. I've been watching Korean dramas for a year, and they're really (A)[interesting / interested]! You can use Korean subtitles for help with listening. It's also a good idea to print out the subtitles and (B)[read / reading] them first.
　　　　　　　　　　　　　- Brandon, 16

※ You = Marisa

What Works for You?

There are hundreds of good tips out there, but everyone has their own way of learning. Find _____ⓐ_____ keeps you (C)[motivating / motivated]; then you will enjoy learning more. Remember, every language is hard at first, but a new language can make your world much bigger!

04 Fill in the blank ⓐ with a suitable word.

➡ _____

05 위 글의 괄호 (A)~(C)에서 어법상 알맞은 낱말을 골라 쓰시오.

➡ (A) _____ (B) _____ (C) _____

06 다음 빈칸 (A)~(C)에 알맞은 단어를 넣어, 브랜던이 마리사에게 추천하는 한국 드라마들을 보는 방법을 완성하시오.

> He recommends using (A)_____ _____ for help with listening, (B)_____ _____ the subtitles, and (C)_____ them first.

[07~09] 다음 글을 읽고 물음에 답하시오.

What's most important is to become familiar with the language first. ⓐI suggest to watch Spanish movies often. It will help you ⓑ소리에 익숙해지도록 of the language. If the people talk too fast, try watching Spanish children's movies first.　　　　　　　　　- Inho, 14

Some words are used only in soccer, not in everyday life. Learn some soccer vocabulary and memorize it. Also, why don't you try writing a review of a match in Spanish? It will help you improve your writing skills.

　　　　　　　　　- Rohan, 16

　　　　　　　　　※ you = Owen

07 위 글의 밑줄 친 ⓐ에서 어법상 틀린 부분을 찾아 고치시오.

_____ ➡ _____

08 위 글의 밑줄 친 ⓑ의 우리말에 맞게 5단어로 영작하시오.

➡ _____

09 위 글의 내용과 일치하도록 다음 빈칸 (A)와 (B)에 알맞은 단어를 쓰시오.

Rohan suggests that Owen should learn and memorize some (A)_____ _____. Rohan also suggests writing a review of a match (B)_____ _____.

[10~12] 다음 글을 읽고 물음에 답하시오.

No More Subtitles!

DREAM4 (A)[is / are] back! I'm so excited to see my favorite Korean boy band perform. Their singing and their dancing (B)[is / are] just perfect. I want to understand their songs without subtitles or translations though. Any tips?　　　　　　　　　- Marisa, 14

You should find friends who are interested in DREAM4 and start a club. In my club, we motivate one another. We translate songs and sing together. ⓐDoing these things (C)[is / are] fun and really improves our Korean!

　　　　　　　　　- Lori, 15

10 위 글의 괄호 (A)~(C)에서 문맥과 어법상 알맞은 낱말을 골라 쓰시오.

➡ (A) _____ (B) _____ (C) _____

11 위 글의 밑줄 친 ⓐDoing these things가 가리키는 것을 영어로 쓰시오.

➡ _____

12 주어진 영영풀이를 참고하여 아래 빈칸에 철자 m으로 시작하는 단어를 넣어 로리의 모임에 대한 소개를 완성하시오.

영영풀이: provide with a motive

Lori and her friends _____ each club member to learn and improve Korean, and they translate songs and sing together.

After You Read B

A: I want to improve my Chinese. Do you have any tips?
자신이 바라는 것을 표현 = I'd like to ~

B: Learn vocabulary which is related to your interests.
which는 주격 관계대명사이며 선행사는 vocabulary

C: Watching Chinese dramas with Chinese subtitles is a good way to get better
동명사가 문장의 주어이다. 동명사는 단수 취급한다.
at listening.

A: Thanks a lot!

구문해설
· **improve**: 증가시키다, 늘리다   · **subtitle**: 자막
· **a good way to ~**: ~하기 위한 좋은 방법   · **a lot**: 많이, 매우

After You Read C

How to Learn a New Language
의문사+to부정사: 명사적 용법

Interests   Spanish soccer team
스페인의(형용사)

Wants   To understand the players' interviews

Useful Tips   · Practice Spanish every day.
스페인어(명사)
· Become familiar with Spanish.
~와 친해지다
· Learn soccer vocabulary and write a review of a match
축구 어휘   후기   경기
in Spanish.
스페인어로

Find what keeps you motivated; then you will enjoy learning more.
관계대명사   동기가 부여된

구문해설
· **Spanish**: 스페인의(형용사); 스페인어(명사)   · **practice**: 연습하다
· **become familiar with**: ~와 친해지다   · **vocabulary** 어휘   · **motivated**: 동기가 부여된

새로운 언어를 배울 수 있는 방법

관심: 스페인 축구 팀

원하는 것: 선수들의 인터뷰를 이해하기

· 유용한 조언들: 스페인어를 매일 연습해라.

· 스페인어와 친해져라.

· 축구 어휘들을 배우고 스페인어로 경기에 대한 후기를 써 보아라.

당신에게 계속 동기 부여가 되는 것을 찾아라, 그러면 당신은 학습을 더욱 즐길 것이다.

Do It Yourself B

I'm so excited to see my favorite Korean boy band perform. I want to
부정사의 부사적 용법(원인)   지각동사 see의 목적격보어로 동사원형(현재분사형도 가능)
understand their songs without subtitles or translations though. Any tips?
부사: 그러나, 그래도   = Can you give me any tips?

- Marisa

구문해설
· **perform**: 공연[연주]하다   · **translation**: 번역

Words & Expressions

01 다음 짝지어진 단어의 관계가 같도록 빈칸에 들어갈 알맞은 말을 고르시오.

> improve : develop = _____ : finish

① recommend   ② complete
③ practice   ④ translate
⑤ perform

02 다음 문장의 빈칸에 적절한 것은?

> Some words are used only in soccer, not in everyday life. Learn some soccer _____ and memorize it.

① rule   ② idiom   ③ phrase
④ subtitle   ⑤ vocabulary

03 다음 대화의 빈칸에 들어갈 말로 적절한 것을 고르시오.

> A: What _____ you like to do this year?
> B: I'd like to travel to other countries.

① would   ② should
③ could   ④ might
⑤ did

04 다음 우리말에 맞게 빈칸에 알맞은 말을 쓰시오.

(1) 나는 자원봉사하면서 시간을 쓰고 싶어.
➡ I'd like to _____ time volunteering.

(2) 그 경험을 통해서 소녀는 무엇을 배웠나?
➡ What did the girl learn _____ the experience?

Conversation

[05~07] 다음 대화를 읽고 물음에 답하시오.

> B: What are you doing?
> G: I'm writing a list of things that I want to do this year.
> B: That's nice. _____(A)_____
> G: Well, first of all, I'd like to spend time volunteering with my friends during summer vacation.
> B: That sounds great.
> G: _____(B)_____ What would you like to do this year?
> B: (C)나는 수영 수업을 받는 것을 생각하고 있어.(am thinking of, take)
> G: That's really cool.

05 빈칸 (A)에 들어갈 가장 알맞은 말을 고르시오.

① What would you like to do this year?
② What are you looking at right now?
③ What does she want to do?
④ Where do you like to go?
⑤ What does she want to have?

06 Which one is most suitable for the blank (B)?

① Really?
② What about you?
③ Do you think so?
④ How nice!
⑤ Where are you going?

07 주어진 단어를 써서 밑줄 친 (C)에 해당하는 영어 문장을 쓰시오.

➡ _____

[08~10] 다음 대화를 읽고 물음에 답하시오.

> G: __(A)__ would you like to do this year?
> B: I'd like to learn the guitar. I listened to the song "Cavatina," and (B)나는 기타 소리에 감동을 받았어.
> G: That's great. Where are you going to learn it?
> B: My friend Jinsu is a very good guitar player. I'll ask him to teach me.

08 빈칸 (A)에 들어갈 의문사를 쓰시오.

➡ _____

09 밑줄 친 (B)의 우리말을 영작하시오. (was struck, sound 포함)

➡ _____

10 위 대화의 내용과 일치하는 것은?

① The girl plays the guitar very well.
② The boy learned to play the piano.
③ The boy listened to the song "Cavatina."
④ Jinsu is poor at playing the guitar.
⑤ The boy will learn to play the guitar from the girl.

11 다음 대화의 순서가 바르게 배열된 것은?

> A: Can you tell me about one of your meaningful experiences?
> (A) It was not easy, but I learned that I could make people happy with my cooking.
> (B) How did you like it?
> (C) I cooked dinner for my family last Sunday.

① (A) – (C) – (B)   ② (B) – (A) – (C)
③ (B) – (C) – (A)   ④ (C) – (A) – (B)
⑤ (C) – (B) – (A)

12 다음 대화의 빈칸에 들어갈 말로 알맞은 것은?

> B: Hey, Suji! What are you holding?
> G: Hi, Ben. It's a skateboard. I'm going skateboarding.
> B: Wow! I didn't know that you could skateboard. _____
> G: I joined a local skateboarding club last month.
> B: I see. So how do you like it?
> G: It's really fun! It helps me make new friends, too.

① Where did you buy the skateboard?
② Why are you holding the skateboard?
③ How about making some new friends?
④ Who made you join the club?
⑤ How did you learn to skateboard?

13 다음 대화의 흐름상 어색한 문장은?

> B: My band performed at the school festival yesterday.
> G: Cool. ⓐWhy did you like that?
> B: It wasn't bad, but ⓑI made some mistakes.
> G: It's okay. ⓒI'm sure you sounded fine.
> B: Thanks for saying so. It was my first time playing the drums in front of so many people.
> G: ⓓHow did you feel about that?
> B: I was very nervous, but I felt great, too!
> G: That's awesome. ⓔI'm so proud of you.

① ⓐ   ② ⓑ   ③ ⓒ   ④ ⓓ   ⑤ ⓔ

Grammar

14 다음 문장의 빈칸에 알맞은 말이 바르게 짝지어진 것은?

> • My sister has been surfing the Internet _____ 2 hours.
> • My little brother has been taking a swimming class _____ last month.

① for – for
② since – for
③ since – since
④ for – since
⑤ since – during

15 다음 중 <u>어색한</u> 문장을 <u>모두</u> 고르시오.

① Please tell me that you bought for Jane's birthday.
② What Jake wants to do after school is to play soccer with his friends.
③ My mom has been growing vegetables last year.
④ Long time ago, they believed what the earth was flat.
⑤ I have been writing a report for two hours.
⑥ Julie has been teaching French for three years.

16 다음 그림을 참고하여 괄호 안에 주어진 어휘를 이용하여 빈칸에 알맞게 쓰시오.

Mariko _____ _____ _____ _____ an hour. (cook)

17 다음 두 문장의 의미가 같도록 빈칸에 알맞은 말을 쓰시오.

(1) Mina shows me the thing that she painted. (3 단어)
 = Mina shows me _____.
(2) Hugh bought his son something that looked really nice. (6 단어)
 = Hugh bought _____ _____.
(3) Some people believe something that they want to believe. (6 단어)
 = Some people _____ _____.

18 다음 빈칸에 들어갈 말이 나머지와 <u>다른</u> 하나는?

① _____ surprised Taeho was the ending of the movie.
② I know _____ you did something wrong.
③ The students couldn't understand _____ the instructor said.
④ She showed me _____ she had in her bag.
⑤ That is _____ I have been looking for.

19 다음 ⓐ~ⓖ 중 어법상 옳은 것을 <u>모두</u> 고르시오.

> ⓐ I knew what you did it.
> ⓑ Please show me that you will wear to the party.
> ⓒ What I have to do right now is to call my mom.
> ⓓ Do you always believe what you see?
> ⓔ He has been studying science for 1997.
> ⓕ I have been writing my shopping lists in Spanish!
> ⓖ It has been snowing last week.

➡ _____

Reading

[20~21] 다음 글을 읽고 물음에 답하시오.

I Love Soccer!

  I'm a big fan of a Spanish soccer team. I want to understand interviews with my favorite players. However, it's not easy because I don't know Spanish ⓐthat well. How can I improve my Spanish?　　　　- Owen, 16

  ⓑ새로운 언어를 배울 수 있는 가장 좋은 방법은 그 언어를 매일 연습하는 것이랍니다. I have changed the language of my phone to Spanish, and I have been writing my shopping lists in Spanish!　　　　- Julie, 15

20 위 글의 밑줄 친 ⓐthat과 문법적 쓰임이 같은 것을 고르시오.

① What's <u>that</u> over there?
② This is the book <u>that</u> you lent me.
③ I am so tired <u>that</u> I cannot go on.
④ I can't go <u>that</u> far.
⑤ She said <u>that</u> the story was true.

21 위 글의 밑줄 친 ⓑ의 우리말에 맞게 주어진 어휘를 알맞게 배열하시오.

> to practice it / a new language / the best way / every day / is / to learn / .

➡ _____
　_____

[22~24] 다음 글을 읽고 물음에 답하시오.

  What's most important is to become familiar ____ⓐ____ the language first. I suggest (A)watching Spanish movies often. It will help you get used ____ⓑ____ the sound of the language. If the people talk too fast, try watching Spanish children's movies first.
　　　　　　　　　　　　- Inho, 14

  Some words are used only in soccer, not in everyday life. Learn some soccer vocabulary and memorize it. Also, why don't you try writing a review of a match in Spanish? It will help you improve your writing skills.
　　　　　　　　　　　　- Rohan, 16
　　　　　　　　　　　　※ you = Owen

22 위 글의 빈칸 ⓐ와 ⓑ에 들어갈 전치사가 바르게 짝지어진 것은?

	ⓐ	ⓑ		ⓐ	ⓑ
①	with	– to	②	in	– by
③	to	– for	④	with	– by
⑤	in	– to			

23 위 글의 밑줄 친 (A)watching과 문법적 쓰임이 <u>다른</u> 것을 <u>모두</u> 고르시오.

① I know the girl <u>watching</u> TV there.
② He is fond of <u>watching</u> TV.
③ <u>Watching</u> TV always makes me happy.
④ My hobby is <u>watching</u> TV.
⑤ He is <u>watching</u> TV now.

24 According to the passage, which is NOT true?

① Inho says that becoming familiar with Spanish first is the most important.

② Inho recommends watching Spanish movies often as it will help Owen get used to the sound of Spanish.

③ Inho suggests Owen should get used to the fast sound of Spanish before watching a children's movie.

④ Rohan advises Owen to learn some soccer vocabulary and memorize it.

⑤ Rohan advises Owen to write a review of a match in Spanish.

[25~26] 다음 글을 읽고 물음에 답하시오.

No More Subtitles!

DREAM4 is back! I'm so excited ⓐto see my favorite Korean boy band perform. Their singing and their dancing are just perfect. ⓑI want to understand their songs with subtitles or translations though. Any tips? - Marisa, 14

25 아래 〈보기〉에서 위 글의 밑줄 친 ⓐto see와 to부정사의 용법이 다른 것의 개수를 고르시오.

┌─── 보기 ├───
① I need a friend to talk with.
② My dream is to see the band perform.
③ She felt sorry to see what happened.
④ This is the best chance to see the show.
⑤ He ran fast to see the design first.
└─────────────

① 1개   ② 2개   ③ 3개   ④ 4개   ⑤ 5개

26 위 글의 밑줄 친 ⓑ에서 흐름상 어색한 부분을 찾아 고치시오.

_____ ➡ _____

[27~29] 다음 글을 읽고 물음에 답하시오.

Follow DREAM4 on social media. They often post short messages in Korean about how they are doing. They also post pictures with the messages, so you can understand the posts more easily.   - Aishah, 14

I recommend watching Korean dramas. ⓐI've been watching Korean dramas for a year, and ⓑthey're really interesting! You can use Korean subtitles for help with listening. ⓒIt's also a good idea to print out the subtitles and read them first.   - Brandon, 16

27 According to Aishah, why is it possible to understand the posts of DREAM4 more easily? Fill in the blanks below with suitable words.

➡ Because they also post _____ _____

_____ _____.

28 위 글의 밑줄 친 ⓐ를 다음과 같이 바꿔 쓸 때 빈칸에 들어갈 알맞은 말을 두 단어로 쓰시오.

➡ I started to watch Korean dramas a year _____, and I'm still _____ them.

29 위 글의 밑줄 친 ⓑthey와 ⓒIt이 가리키는 것을 각각 본문에서 찾아 쓰시오.

➡ ⓑ _____
  ⓒ _____

출제율 90%

01 짝지어진 단어의 관계가 같도록 빈칸에 알맞은 것은?

> weakness : strength = _____ : forget

① remember   ② realize

③ motivate   ④ join

⑤ convince

출제율 95%

02 다음 단어의 영영풀이가 어색한 것은?

① shelf – a long flat narrow board attached to a wall

② confident – sure that something will happen in the way that you want or expect

③ responsibility – a duty to be in charge of someone or something

④ recommend – to advise someone to do something

⑤ perfect – having some mistakes, faults, or damage

[03~05] 다음 대화를 읽고 물음에 답하시오.

G: Did you make this shelf yourself? It's amazing!

B: Thanks. I started ___(A)___ furniture last year.

G: Cool! How do you like it?

B: It was hard at first, but now I love it. I feel so confident after I finish making something.

G: That's great. (B)나는 네가 그것을 정말 잘한다고 생각해. (really, good)

B: Thanks. I guess I found a new talent. I think it's good to try new things.

G: Exactly. Having new experiences lets us to find new talents.

출제율 95%

03 빈칸 (A)에 들어가기에 적절한 것을 고르시오.

① making   ② buying   ③ moving

④ dealing   ⑤ selling

출제율 85%

04 밑줄 친 (B)에 주어진 단어를 써서 해당하는 영어 문장을 완성하시오.

➡ _____

출제율 90%

05 위 대화에서 어법이 어색한 문장을 찾아 바로 잡으시오.

_____

➡ _____

[06~08] 다음 대화를 읽고 물음에 답하시오.

B: What are you doing?

G: I'm writing a list of things that I want to do this year.

B: That's nice. (A)너는 올해 무엇을 하고 싶니? (would, like)

G: Well, first of all, I'd like to spend time volunteering with my friends during summer vacation.

B: That sounds great.

G: What about you? What would you like to do this year?

B: I'm thinking of taking a swimming class.

G: That's really cool.

출제율 90%

06 밑줄 친 (A)의 우리말을 영어로 옮겨 쓰시오. (주어진 표현 포함)

➡ _____

07 What would the boy like to do this year?

① He would like to write a shopping list.
② He would like to do volunteering.
③ He would like to spend time with his friends.
④ He would like to take a swimming class.
⑤ He would like to go hiking with his family.

08 위 대화를 읽고 대답할 수 있는 것은?

① What will the boy do this week?
② What does the girl plan to do this summer?
③ Why does the boy ask the girl her plan?
④ Where are they talking at the moment?
⑤ How will the girl go volunteering with her friends?

09 다음 빈칸에 알맞은 말이 순서대로 짝지어진 것은?

> • _____ is most important is to become familiar with the language first.
> • He has been talking on the phone _____ 3 p.m.

① What – since
② That – for
③ What – for
④ That – since
⑤ Which – for

10 다음 중 어법상 적절한 문장은? (2개)

① It has been snowed for three days.
② She has been cleaning her room last night.
③ He has been building his house since two months.
④ Anne has been swimming for an hour.
⑤ Tom has been to Paris several times.

11 다음 두 문장이 같도록 할 때 빈칸에 알맞은 말을 쓰시오.

> • Yuna gave me the things that she kept for years.
> = Yuna gave me _____ she kept for years.

12 다음 중 어법상 바르지 않은 것은?

① I have been doing my homework for two hours.
② Cathy has been listening to the music 3 hours ago.
③ Is eating healthy food what they want to do?
④ We have known her since she was a little child.
⑤ That's what is keeping you up so late.

13 다음 문장의 빈칸에 알맞은 말은?

> Grace has been _____ for her daughter since this morning.

① look
② looked
③ looking
④ to look
⑤ to looking

[14~16] 다음 글을 읽고 물음에 답하시오.

What's most important is ⓐto become familiar with ⓑthe language first. I suggest watching Spanish movies often. It will help you get used to the sound of the language. If the people talk too fast, try watching Spanish children's movies first. - Inho, 14

ⓒSome words are used only in soccer, not in everyday life. Learn some soccer vocabulary and memorize ⓓit. Also, why don't you try writing a review of a match in Spanish? It will help you improve your writing skills.
- Rohan, 16

14 아래 〈보기〉에서 위 글의 밑줄 친 ⓐto become과 to부정사의 용법이 같은 것의 개수를 고르시오.

┌─ 보기 ├─
① He wanted me to study English hard.
② He was the last man to tell a lie.
③ I was excited to see the show.
④ This book is easy to read.
⑤ What do you want to be in the future?

① 1개 ② 2개 ③ 3개 ④ 4개 ⑤ 5개

15 위 글의 밑줄 친 ⓑthe language와 ⓓit이 가리키는 것을 본문에서 찾아 쓰시오.

➡ ⓑ _____ ⓓ _____

16 위 글의 밑줄 친 ⓒ를 다음과 같이 바꿔 쓸 때 빈칸에 들어갈 알맞은 단어를 쓰시오.

➡ Some words are used not in everyday life _____ only in soccer.

[17~19] 다음 글을 읽고 물음에 답하시오.

No More Subtitles!

DREAM4 is back! I'm so excited to see my favorite Korean boy band perform. Their singing and their dancing are just perfect. I want to understand their songs without subtitles or translations (A)though. Any tips?
- Marisa, 14

You should find friends __ⓐ__ are interested in DREAM4 and start a club. In my club, we motivate one another. We translate songs and sing together. (B)Doing these things is fun and really improve our Korean! - Lori, 15

17 Fill in the blank ⓐ with a suitable word.

➡ _____

18 위 글의 밑줄 친 (A)though와 같은 의미로 쓰인 것을 고르시오.

① Though it stopped raining, the wind was still blowing.
② He supported his family though he was young.
③ Our team lost. It was a good game though.
④ Though she was tired, she worked hard.
⑤ Though he tried very hard, he failed the course.

19 위 글의 밑줄 친 (B)에서 어법상 틀린 부분을 찾아 고치시오.

_____ ➡ _____

[20~21] 다음 글을 읽고 물음에 답하시오.

Follow DREAM4 on social media. They often post short messages in Korean about how they are doing. They also post pictures with the messages, so you can understand the posts more easily.   - Aishah, 14

I recommend watching Korean dramas. I've been watching Korean dramas for a year, and they're really interesting! You can use Korean subtitles for help with listening. It's also a good idea to print out the subtitles and read them first.   - Brandon, 16

What Works for You?

There are hundreds of good tips out there, but everyone has their own way of learning. Find what keeps you motivated; then you will enjoy learning more. Remember, every language is hard at first, but a new language can make your world much bigger!

✏ 출제율 90%

20 How long has Brandon been watching Korean dramas? Answer in English in a full sentence. (8 words)

➡ _____

✏ 출제율 100%

21 According to the passage, which is NOT true?

① The members of DREAM4 often post short messages in Korean about how they are doing.

② The members of DREAM4 also post pictures with the messages.

③ Brandon recommends watching Korean dramas.

④ Everyone has their own way of learning a new language.

⑤ Every language is easy at first, and a new language can make your world much bigger.

[22~24] 다음 글을 읽고 물음에 답하시오.

What I Want to Experience in Andong

What city do you want to go to in Korea? (①) I want to go to Andong. (②) I'd also like to make my own Hahoe mask and learn how to dance the *talchum*. (③) Also, I want to visit Hahoe Village. (④) I am sure that ⓐthese new experiences in Andong would help me understand Korea better. (⑤)

✏ 출제율 95%

22 위 글의 흐름으로 보아, 주어진 문장이 들어가기에 가장 적절한 곳은?

In Andong, I want to try Andong-jjimdak.

①   ②   ③   ④   ⑤

✏ 출제율 90%

23 위 글의 밑줄 친 ⓐ가 가리키는 것 세 가지를 본문에서 찾아 쓰시오.

➡ (1) _____
   (2) _____
   (3) _____

✏ 출제율 100%

24 위 글을 읽고 알 수 없는 것을 고르시오.

① 한국에서 가 보고 싶은 도시

② 그 도시에서 먹고 싶은 음식

③ 하회탈 만드는 법

④ 그 도시에서 배우고 싶은 춤

⑤ 그 도시에서 방문하고 싶은 마을

[01~02] 다음 대화를 읽고 물음에 답하시오.

> A: I want to ___(A)___ my Chinese. Do you have any tips?
>
> B: Learn vocabulary which is related to your interests.
>
> C: (B)중국어 자막이 있는 중국 드라마를 보는 것이 듣기를 잘하는 좋은 방법이야. (watch, dramas, subtitles, get better)
>
> A: Thanks a lot!

01 빈칸 (A)에 들어갈 알맞은 말을 주어진 철자로 시작하여 쓰시오.

➡ i_____

02 밑줄 친 (B)의 우리말을 영어로 쓰시오. (주어진 단어를 포함할 것)

➡ _____

_____

03 다음 우리말에 맞게 빈칸에 알맞은 말을 쓰시오. (주어진 철자로 시작할 것)

(1) 나는 기타 소리에 감동을 받았어.
➡ I was s_____ by the sound of the guitar.

(2) 나는 수영 수업 듣는 것을 생각하고 있어.
➡ I'm thinking of t_____ a swimming class.

(3) 우리는 서로 방법을 공유하고 있어.
➡ We s_____ tips with one another.

04 관계대명사 what을 사용하여 주어진 두 문장을 한 문장으로 바꾸시오.

(1) • This is something.
   • I wanted to buy it.
   ➡ _____

(2) • I enjoyed the food.
   • You cooked it for me last night.
   ➡ _____

(3) • Do you remember the dress?
   • Bella wore it at the party last night.
   ➡ _____

_____

05 현재완료진행형을 사용하여 주어진 두 문장을 한 문장으로 바꾸시오.

(1) • The alarm started ringing 5 minutes ago.
   • It is still ringing.
   ➡ _____

(2) • Mary began chatting with her friends at two o'clock.
   • She is still chatting.
   ➡ _____

_____

(3) • He is writing a book.
   • He started writing the book last month.
   ➡ _____

06 다음 우리말을 주어진 어휘를 이용하여 영작하시오.

(1) 그 보고서는 내가 알고 싶어했던 것을 보여 주었다. (the report, show, want)
   ➡ _____

(2) 그는 그녀가 한 말의 많은 것에 묵시적으로 동의했다. (much of, silently, agree, had said)
   ➡ _____

(3) 나는 그 신문에서 읽은 것을 전혀 믿지 않는다.
(never, believe, in the newspaper)

➡ _____

(4) 엄마는 몇 주 동안 계속 쇼핑을 하고 계신다.
(mom, weeks, shop, been)

➡ _____

(5) 누군가가 계속해서 부엌에서 사탕을 훔쳐 가
고 있다. (someone, candies, from the
kitchen, steal, been)

➡ _____

(6) 이 영화는 많은 사람들이 기다려 온 것이다.
(this movie, been, what, wait)

➡ _____

[07~09] 다음 글을 읽고 물음에 답하시오.

ⓐ가장 중요한 것은 우선 언어와 친해지는 것이에
요. I suggest watching Spanish movies often.
It will help you get used to the sound of
the language. If the people talk too fast, try
watching Spanish children's movies first.

- Inho, 14

Some words are used only in soccer, not in
everyday life. Learn some soccer vocabulary
and memorize it. Also, ⓑwhy don't you try
writing a review of a match in Spanish? It
will help you improve your writing skills.

- Rohan, 16

07 위 글의 밑줄 친 ⓐ의 우리말에 맞게 주어진 어휘를 이용하
여 11 단어로 영작하시오.

> what's, become familiar with, first

➡ _____
_____

08 위 글의 밑줄 친 ⓑ를 다음과 같이 바꿔 쓸 때 빈칸에 들어
갈 알맞은 말을 두 단어로 쓰시오.

➡ _____ _____ trying

09 위 글의 내용과 일치하도록 다음 빈칸 (A)와 (B)에 알맞은
단어를 쓰시오.

> Inho suggests watching (A)_____
> _____ often because it will be helpful
> in getting used to (B)_____ _____
> of the language.

[10~11] 다음 글을 읽고 물음에 답하시오.

No More Subtitles!

DREAM4 is back! I'm so excited to see
my favorite Korean boy band perform. Their
singing and their dancing are just perfect.
I want to understand their songs without
subtitles or translations though. Any tips?

- Marisa, 14

You should find friends who are interested
in DREAM4 and start a club. In my club, we
motivate one another. We translate songs and
sing together. Doing these things is fun and
really improves our ___ⓐ___! - Lori, 15

10 위 글의 빈칸 ⓐ에 들어갈 알맞은 말을 본문에서 찾아 쓰시오.

➡ _____

11 위 글의 내용을 다음과 같이 정리하고자 한다. 빈칸 (A)와
(B)에 들어갈 알맞은 단어를 본문에서 찾아 쓰시오.

> Marisa asks for advice about the ways
> to understand the songs of DREAM4,
> her favorite Korean boy band, without
> (A)_____ or (B)_____.

01 다음 〈보기 A〉와 〈보기 B〉에서 알맞은 말을 하나씩 골라 완전한 문장을 만드시오.

보기 A	보기 B
• She has been	• working here since 2018.
• I have been	• known her for two years.
• They have	• swimming for half an hour.
• It has been	• raining since last night.

(1) _____

(2) _____

(3) _____

(4) _____

02 A와 B에 주어진 어구를 활용하여, 관계대명사 what이 들어간 문장을 어법에 맞게 3문장 이상 쓰시오.

A	Jumi/want to do	I/bought	he/like the most	I/like
B	take a walk in the park	*the Little Prince*	play the guitar	she gave me

보기
What Jumi wants to do after school is to take a walk in the park with her friends.

(1) _____

(2) _____

(3) _____

03 다음 내용을 바탕으로 특정 지역에 가서 경험해 보고 싶은 일을 계획하는 글을 쓰시오.

Andong
- Food that I want to try: Andong-jjimdak
- Activities that I want to try or learn: – make a Hahoe mask
　　　　　　　　　　　　　　　　　　　　 – learn how to dance the *talchum*
- Place that I want to visit: Hahoe Village

What I Want to Experience in Andong

What city do you want to go to in Korea? I want to go to (A)_____. In Andong, I want to try (B)_____. I'd also like to make my own (C)_____ and learn how to dance (D)_____. Also, I want to visit (E)_____. I am sure that these new experiences in Andong would help me understand Korea better.

12 다음 중 〈보기〉의 문장과 의미가 같은 것을 고르시오.

> **┤ 보기 ├**
>
> Emily is sleeping in her room now. She began sleeping at ten o'clock.

① Emily is sleeping in her room at ten o'clock.

② Emily has been sleeping in her room since ten o'clock.

③ Emily slept in her room at ten o'clock.

④ Emily has slept in her room for ten o'clock.

⑤ Emily had slept in her room since ten o'clock.

13 다음 빈칸에 들어갈 말을 순서대로 묶은 것은?

> • You should be satisfied with _____ you have.
>
> • If the facts are true, that is all _____ counts.

① which – what
② that – that
③ that – what
④ what – that
⑤ what – what

14 다음 문장에서 어법상 어색한 것을 바르게 고쳐 다시 쓰시오.

(1) This ring is that my mom gave me.

➡ _____

(2) You can look up that you need on the computer.

➡ _____

(3) Is this the thing what you were looking for?

➡ _____

(4) Russia has been belonging to such a category.

➡ _____

15 다음 중 어법상 옳은 문장을 모두 고르시오.

① I could not understand that the teacher talked about.

② Judy has been having the hairpin for 10 years.

③ I have been cleaning my room for two hours.

④ This dress is what she bought it last weekend.

⑤ I remember what he did last month.

[16~17] 다음 글을 읽고 물음에 답하시오.

> **I Love Soccer!**
>
> I'm a big fan of a Spanish soccer team. I want to understand interviews with my favorite players. However, it's not easy because I don't know Spanish that well. How can I improve my Spanish?
> - Owen, 16
>
> The best way to learn a new language is to practice it every day. I have changed the language of my phone to Spanish, and I have been writing my shopping lists in Spanish!
> - Julie, 15

16 Why does Owen have difficulty in understanding interviews with his favorite players? Answer in English. (7 words)

➡ _____

17 줄리가 새로운 언어를 매일 연습하기 위해 실천해 온 두 가지를 우리말로 쓰시오.

➡ (1) _____

(2) _____

[18~19] 다음 글을 읽고 물음에 답하시오.

What's most important is to become familiar with the language first. I suggest watching Spanish movies often. ⓐIt will help you get used to the sound of the language. If the people talk too fast, try watching Spanish children's movies first.   - Inho, 14

ⓑSome words are used only in soccer, not in everyday life. Learn some soccer vocabulary and memorize it. Also, why don't you try writing a review of a match in Spanish? ⓒIt will help you improve your writing skills.

- Rohan, 16

18 위 글의 밑줄 친 ⓐIt과 ⓒIt이 가리키는 것을 각각 본문에서 찾아 쓰시오.

➡ ⓐ _____

ⓒ _____

19 위 글의 밑줄 친 ⓑ를 능동태로 고치시오.

➡ _____

[20~21] 다음 글을 읽고 물음에 답하시오.

No More Subtitles!

DREAM4 is back! ⓐI'm so excited to see my favorite Korean boy band to perform. Their singing and their dancing are just perfect. I want to understand their songs without subtitles or translations though. Any tips?

- Marisa, 14

You should find friends who are interested in DREAM4 and start a club. In my club, we motivate one another. We translate songs and sing together. Doing these things is fun and really improves our Korean!   - Lori, 15

20 위 글의 밑줄 친 ⓐ에서 어법상 틀린 부분을 찾아 고치시오.

_____ ➡ _____

21 According to the passage, which is NOT true?

① Marisa's favorite Korean boy band is DREAM4.

② Marisa wants to understand DREAM4's songs without subtitles or translations.

③ Marisa is looking for friends who are interested in DREAM4.

④ Lori and her friends motivate one another in their club.

⑤ Lori and her friends translate songs and sing together.

[22~23] 다음 글을 읽고 물음에 답하시오.

I recommend ___ⓐ___ Korean dramas. I've been watching Korean dramas for a year, and they're really interesting! You can use Korean subtitles for help with listening. It's also a good idea to print out the subtitles and read them first.   - Brandon, 16

22 위 글의 빈칸 ⓐ에 watch를 알맞은 형태로 쓰시오.

➡ _____

23 주어진 영영풀이에 해당하는 단어를 본문에서 찾아 쓰시오.

translation of foreign dialogue of a movie or TV program

➡ _____

Lesson 2

Take Care of Yourself

🔊 의사소통 기능

- 알고 있는지 묻기
  Have you heard the term *body image*?
- 놀람 표현하기
  I'm surprised that this small band can do all that.

🔊 언어 형식

- 관계대명사의 계속적 용법
  Walnuts also have wrinkles, **which** the brain has too.
- 명사의 뒤에서 명사를 수식하는 분사
  We all know that a diet **containing** a variety of food keeps our bodies healthy.

Words & Expressions

Key Words

- **accept** [æksépt] 동 받아들이다
- **active** [ǽktiv] 형 활발한
- **advice** [ædváis] 명 충고
- **awesome** [ɔ́:səm] 형 엄청난
- **beneficial** [bènəfíʃəl] 형 유익한
- **benefit** [bénəfit] 명 이득
- **brain** [brein] 명 뇌
- **cell** [sel] 명 세포
- **check** [tʃek] 동 검토하다
- **chemical** [kémikəl] 명 화학물질
- **chew** [tʃu:] 동 씹다
- **clue** [klu:] 명 단서
- **compared** [kəmpɛ́ərd] 형 비교되는
- **contain** [kəntéin] 동 포함하다
- **convenient** [kənví:njənt] 형 편리한
- **damage** [dǽmidʒ] 동 손상을 주다
- **deep sleep** 숙면
- **diet** [dáiət] 명 음식
- **function** [fʌ́ŋkʃən] 명 기능
- **ginger** [dʒíndʒər] 명 생강
- **healthy** [hélθi] 형 건강한
- **hollow** [hálou] 형 속이 빈
- **however** [hauévər] 부 그러나
- **improve** [imprú:v] 동 개선하다
- **increase** [inkrí:s] 동 증가하다
- **lower** [lóuər] 동 낮추다
- **meaningful** [mí:niŋfəl] 형 의미 있는
- **midnight** [mídnait] 명 자정
- **mirror** [mírər] 동 반사하다
- **moved** [mu:vd] 형 감동받은
- **multiple** [mʌ́ltəpl] 형 복합적인
- **negative** [négətiv] 형 부정적인
- **pillow** [pílou] 명 베개
- **positive** [pázətiv] 형 긍정적인
- **prevent** [privént] 동 방해하다, 가로 막다
- **process** [práses] 동 처리하다
- **productive** [prədʌ́ktiv] 형 생산적인
- **risk** [risk] 명 위험
- **search** [sə:rtʃ] 동 조사하다
- **sensitive** [sénsətiv] 형 민감한
- **similar** [símələr] 형 비슷한
- **slice** [slais] 동 얇게 자르다
- **smart band** 스마트 밴드
- **stomach** [stʌ́mək] 명 위장
- **thirsty** [θə́:rsti] 형 목마른
- **track** [træk] 동 진행과정을 추적하다
- **upset** [ʌ́pset] 형 불편한
- **vision** [víʒən] 명 시력
- **walnut** [wɔ́:lnʌt] 명 호두
- **wrinkle** [ríŋkl] 명 주름

Key Expressions

- **a variety of** 다양한
- **as it is** 있는 그대로
- **as usual** 평소처럼
- **at least** 적어도
- **be divided into** ~로 나뉘어지다
- **be good for ~** ~에 좋다
- **by oneself** 혼자서
- **come to mind** 생각이 떠오르다
- **compare A to B** A를 B에 비교하다
- **feel like -ing** ~하고 싶다
- **for this reason** 이런 이유로
- **from now on** 지금부터
- **give praise** 칭찬하다
- **in addition** 게다가
- **keep -ing** 계속 ~하다
- **look like** ~처럼 보이다
- **move on to** (새로운 일·주제로) 넘어가다
- **not only A but also B** A뿐만 아니라 B도
- **on the other hand** 반면에
- **prevent A from -ing** A가 ~하지 못하게 하다
- **stay healthy** 건강을 유지하다
- **that's why** 그런 이유로
- **throw up** 토하다
- **work out** 운동하다

Word Power

※ 서로 비슷한 뜻을 가진 어휘

□ **contain** 포함하다 : **involve** 포함하다

□ **sensitive** 민감한 : **touchy** 민감한

□ **improve** 개선하다 : **develop** 발전하다

□ **however** 그러나 : **yet** 그러나

□ **convenient** 편리한 : **handy** 편리한

□ **function** 기능 : **role** 역할

□ **hollow** 속이 빈 : **empty** 빈

□ **risk** 위험 : **danger** 위험

□ **damage** 손상을 주다 : **harm** 손상시키다

□ **advice** 충고 : **tip** 충고

□ **positive** 긍정적인 : **affirmative** 긍정적인

□ **check** 검토하다 : **review** 검토하다

□ **awesome** 엄청난 : **amazing** 굉장한

□ **benefit** 이득 : **advantage** 이득

□ **lower** 낮추다 : **reduce** 줄이다

□ **beneficial** 유익한 : **helpful** 도움이 되는

※ 서로 반대의 뜻을 가진 어휘

□ **contain** 포함하다 ↔ **exclude** 제외하다

□ **sensitive** 민감한 ↔ **insensitive** 무감각한

□ **prevent** 가로 막다 ↔ **allow** 허용하다

□ **increase** 증가하다 ↔ **decrease** 감소하다

□ **multiple** 복합적인 ↔ **uniform** 단일한

□ **lower** 낮추다 ↔ **raise** 올리다

□ **healthy** 건강한 ↔ **ill** 아픈, 병든

□ **positive** 긍정적인 ↔ **negative** 부정적인

□ **convenient** 편리한 ↔ **inconvenient** 불편한

□ **similar** 비슷한 ↔ **different** 다른

□ **hollow** 속이 빈 ↔ **full** 꽉 찬

□ **beneficial** 유익한 ↔ **harmful** 해로운

English Dictionary

□ **active** 활발한
→ always busy doing things, especially physical or mental activities
무엇인가를, 특히 육체적인 또는 정신적인 활동을 하느라 언제나 바쁜

□ **brain** 뇌
→ the organ inside your head that controls how you think, feel, and move
머릿속에 있는 생각, 감정, 동작을 조절하는 기관

□ **convenient** 편리한
→ useful to you because it saves you time
시간을 덜어 주어 유용한

□ **hollow** 속이 빈
→ having an empty space inside
내부에 빈 공간을 가진

□ **improve** 개선하다
→ to make something better, or to become better
무엇인가를 더 좋게 만들거나 더 좋아지다

□ **pillow** 베개
→ a cloth bag filled with soft material that you put your head on
머리를 올려놓는 부드러운 물질로 채워진 포대

□ **risk** 위험
→ the possibility that something bad, unpleasant, or dangerous may happen
나쁘거나 불쾌하거나 위험한 일이 일어날 가능성

□ **slice** 얇게 자르다
→ to cut meat, bread, vegetables, etc into thin flat pieces
고기, 빵, 채소를 얇은 조각으로 자르다

□ **thirsty** 목마른
→ feeling that you want or need a drink
음료를 원하거나 필요하다고 느끼는

□ **vision** 시력
→ the ability to see
보는 능력

□ **walnut** 호두
→ a nut that you can eat, shaped like a human brain
인간의 뇌처럼 생긴 먹을 수 있는 견과류

□ **wrinkle** 주름
→ lines on your face and skin that you get when you are old
나이가 들어 얼굴과 피부에 생기는 선

01 다음 대화의 빈칸에 들어갈 말로 적절한 것을 고르시오.

> B: Have you heard that chewing ice is bad for your teeth?
> G: No, I haven't. Why is that?
> B: It can _____ your teeth. It can also make them too sensitive.

① damage
② clean
③ produce
④ lower
⑤ check

 02 다음 중 밑줄 친 부분의 뜻풀이가 바르지 <u>않은</u> 것은?

① A diet <u>containing</u> a variety of foods keeps our bodies healthy. (포함하는)
② Slice open a tomato and <u>compare</u> it with the human heart. (비교하다)
③ Eating tomatoes can <u>lower</u> your risk of heart disease. (낮추다)
④ Walnuts help our brains stay healthy and <u>active</u>. (활발한)
⑤ You may not like ginger's strong <u>taste</u> or smell. (취향)

03 다음 문장의 빈칸에 들어갈 말로 적절한 것을 고르시오.

> To stay _____, you need to exercise regularly.

① harmful
② multiple
③ similar
④ sensitive
⑤ healthy

 04 다음 영영풀이에 해당하는 단어를 고르시오.

> a cloth bag filled with soft material that you put your head on

① pillow
② walnut
③ wrinkle
④ sofa
⑤ furniture

 05 다음 문장에 공통으로 들어갈 말은?

> • Each of these foods looks _____ a certain body part.
> • A walnut is divided into two parts, just _____ the brain.
> • You may not _____ ginger's strong taste or smell.

① as
② for
③ like
④ about
⑤ alike

06 다음 중 〈보기〉에 있는 단어를 사용하여 자연스러운 문장을 만들 수 <u>없는</u> 것은?

> ┤ 보기 ├
> preventing   lower   shape   clue

① Nature, however, gives us a big _____.
② For this _____, ginger can be good for your stomach.
③ They are also good for _____ Alzheimer's disease.
④ Look at the _____ of a walnut.
⑤ Eating tomatoes can _____ your risk of heart disease.

01 주어진 단어를 이용해 빈칸을 완성하시오.

> Can you tell me about one of your _____ experiences?

➡ _____ (mean)

02 다음 짝지어진 단어의 관계가 같도록 빈칸에 알맞은 말을 쓰시오. (주어진 철자로 시작할 것)

> improve : develop = p_____ : profitable

03 빈칸에 알맞은 단어를 〈보기〉에서 골라 쓰시오.

> ┌ 보기 ─────────────────┐
> usual　healthy　advice　what
> └───────────────────────┘

(1) Which picture shows a _____ habit?

(2) What _____ does the boy give the girl?

(3) That's probably _____ is making you tired.

(4) I went to bed after midnight, as _____.

04 다음 우리말에 맞게 빈칸에 알맞은 말을 쓰시오.

(1) 너는 body image라는 용어를 들어본 적이 있니?
　➡ Have you heard the _____ *body image*?

(2) 너는 얼음을 씹는 것이 이에 나쁘다는 것을 들어본 적이 있니?
　➡ Have you heard that _____ ice is bad for your teeth?

(3) 토마토를 얇게 잘라 내서 그것을 인간의 심장과 비교해 보아라.
　➡ Slice open a tomato and _____ it with the human heart.

(4) 그것은 인간의 두뇌 형태와 매우 비슷하다.
　➡ It's very similar to the _____ of the human brain

05 다음 영어 설명에 해당하는 단어를 쓰시오. (주어진 철자로 시작할 것)

> feeling that you want or need a drink

➡ t_____

06 다음 우리말을 주어진 단어를 이용하여 영작하시오.

> 몇몇 음식들은 그 음식이 유익한 신체 부위의 생김새를 반영한다. (mirror, good for)

➡ _____
　_____

07 다음 대화의 빈칸에 들어갈 말로 적절한 말을 쓰시오.

> G: What's this?
> B: It's a smart band. It lets me check my health information on my smartphone.
> G: What kind of information?
> B: It shows how far I _____ during the day and how well I _____ at night.
> G: Interesting. I'm surprised that this small band can do all that.

Conversation

1 알고 있는지 묻기

• **Have you heard the term *body image*?** body image라는 용어를 들어본 적이 있니?

■ 'Have you heard ~?'는 '~을 들어본 적이 있니?'라는 의미로 상대방이 지금 이야기하는 것에 대해 알고 있는지를 물어보는 말이다. '~에 관하여 들어본 적이 있니?'라는 의미로 'Have you heard about ~?' 또는 'Have you heard of ~?'라고 할 수도 있다. 접속사 that을 사용하여 'Have you heard that 주어+동사?' 형태로 말할 수도 있다.

■ 'Have you heard ~?'는 현재완료를 사용하여 어떤 일에 대하여 과거에 들어본 적이 있어서 현재에 그 것을 알고 있는지 물어보는 것으로, 현재완료의 용법 중에서 '경험'에 해당한다. 'Do you know ~?'라고 해도 비슷한 의미의 질문이 될 수 있지만 좀 더 직설적인 느낌을 준다.

■ 'Have you heard ~?'에 대한 대답은 'Yes, I have.' 'No, I haven't.'라고 하여야 하지만 경우에 따라서는 'Have you heard ~?'로 질문하는 경우에 그 의도가 새로운 정보를 전달하는 것일 때도 있기 때문에 'I knew that.' 'I didn't know that.' 등으로 대답하기도 한다.

알고 있는지 묻기

• Have you heard about/of ~? ~에 대하여 들어본 적이 있습니까?

• Have you heard that 주어+동사? ~이라는 것을 들어본 적이 있습니까?

• Do you know that 주어+동사 ~? ~이라는 것을 아십니까?

• Did you know about ~? ~에 대해서 알고 있었습니까?

알고 있는지 대답하기

• Yes, I have. 네, 들어본 적이 있습니다.

• I've never heard of it. 전혀 들어본 적 없어.

• Oh, really? 아, 진짜로?

• I didn't know that. 그건 몰랐어요.

• No, that's new to me. 아니, 그건 처음 들어봐.

• I think I have. 들어본 적 있는 것 같은데.

핵심 Check

1. 다음 대화의 빈칸에 들어갈 말을 고르시오.

B: Have you heard that chewing ice is bad for your teeth?

G: _____ Why is that?

B: It can damage your teeth. It can also make them too sensitive.

① Have you heard?　　　② No, I haven't.

③ Did you know that?　　④ Yes, I did.

⑤ No way.

2 놀람 표현하기

- **I'm surprised that this small band can do all that.**
  이 작은 밴드가 그 모든 것을 할 수 있다니 놀랍다.

- 상대방이 말하는 사실에 대하여 놀라움을 표현할 때는 'I'm surprised that 주어+동사 ~.'의 형태를 사용하여 '~라는 사실에 놀랐다.'라는 의미를 나타낸다. surprised 대신 shocked, amazed를 사용해서 'I'm shocked that ~.' 'I'm amazed that ~.'이라고 할 수도 있다.

- 단순히 상대의 말에 '놀랐다'는 의미로 'I can't believe it.' 'It's amazing.' 등을 사용하기도 한다. '놀랍지 않다' '당연하다'의 의미로는 'No wonder (that) 주어+동사 ~.'를 쓸 수 있다. 'No wonder (that) ~'은 'It is no wonder that ~.'에서 It is를 생략한 것이다.

나는 ~에 놀랐다.

- I'm surprised that ~.
- I'm shocked that ~.
- I'm amazed that ~.

놀람 표현하기

- How could that be possible? 그게 어떻게 가능해?
- It can't be true. 그게 사실일 리 없어.
- I can't believe it. 믿을 수 없어.
- It's[That's] surprising. 놀라워.
- What a surprise! 놀랍다!

믿을 수 없어., 정말이야?, 농담이지?

- You're kidding (me).
- You must be joking.
- You have got to be kidding me.
- Really?

핵심 Check

2. 다음 대화의 빈칸에 들어갈 말로 가장 자연스러운 것은?

   B: It's a smart band. It lets me check my health information on my smartphone.

   G: What kind of information?

   B: It shows how far I walk during the day and how well I sleep at night.

   G: Interesting. _____ this small band can do all that.

   ① No wonder that
   ② I'm surprised that
   ③ It is believed that
   ④ You're surprised that
   ⑤ It is disappointing that

Listen & Talk 1 B

B: You look tired. Did you get enough sleep?

G: Yes, I did. I slept ❶for over seven hours.

B: Okay. When did you go to bed?

G: I went to bed after midnight, ❷as usual.

B: That's probably what is making you tired. Have you heard that ❸when you go to bed is very important?

G: No, I haven't. Why is that?

B: Scientists say that ❹going to bed late can make you feel tired the next day.

G: I didn't know that.

B: On the other hand, going to bed early can improve your memory and help you be more productive. From now on, try to go to bed earlier.

B: 너 피곤해 보인다. 잠은 충분히 잤니?

G: 응. 그래. 나는 일곱 시간 이상 잤어.

B: 알았어. 너는 언제 잠들었니?

G: 평소처럼 자정이 넘어서 잠들었어.

B: 아마 그것이 너를 피곤하게 만드는 것일 거야. 네가 언제 잠드는지가 아주 중요하다는 말을 들어본 적이 있니?

G: 아니. 왜 그렇지?

B: 과학자들은 늦게 잠자리에 드는 것은 그 다음날 피곤함을 느끼게 할 수 있다고 말해.

G: 나는 몰랐어.

B: 반면에 일찍 잠자리에 드는 것은 기억력을 향상시키고, 더 생산적이 되도록 도와줄 수 있어. 지금부터는 일찍 자도록 노력해 봐.

❶ 전치사 for는 기간을 나타내어 '~ 동안'이라는 뜻이다.
❷ as usual = 평소처럼
❸ that절에서 'when you go to bed'가 주어로 쓰였다.
❹ going은 동명사로 can make의 주어 역할을 한다.

Check(√) True or False

(1) The boy advises the girl to go to bed early.　　　　T ☐ F ☐

(2) Going to bed late can help to be more productive.　　T ☐ F ☐

Listen & Talk 2 B

B: What are you doing in the living room?

G: I'm doing yoga.

B: You're working out by yourself?

G: Yes, I'm following this online video. It shows me all the steps.

B: Let me see. Wow, ❶it's been watched two million times! I'm surprised that so many people have watched this video.

G: I know! These kinds of programs are becoming popular right now.

B: It looks very convenient. You don't have to go out to exercise.

G: That's right. ❷That's why I love these programs. You should try them, too.

B: 너 거실에서 무엇을 하고 있니?

G: 나는 요가를 하는 중이야.

B: 혼자서 운동한다는 말이니?

G: 그래. 이 온라인 비디오를 따라하는 중이야. 그것이 나에게 모든 단계를 보여줘.

B: 어디 보자. 와, 2백만 번이나 시청되었구나! 그렇게 많은 사람이 이 비디오를 보았다니 놀라워.

G: 알아! 이런 종류의 프로그램이 지금 인기를 얻는 중이야.

B: 그것은 매우 편리해 보여. 너는 운동하러 밖에 나갈 필요가 없어.

G: 맞아. 그런 이유로 나는 이런 프로그램을 아주 좋아해. 너도 한번 시도해 봐.

❶ 'it's been watched'는 현재완료 수동태이다.
❷ That's why ~. = 그것이 ~하는 이유이다., 그런 이유로 ~하다.

Check(√) True or False

(3) The girl is doing yoga with the boy.　　　　　　T ☐ F ☐

(4) Online video program is becoming popular.　　　T ☐ F ☐

Listen & Talk 1 A

B: Have you heard that ❶chewing ice is bad for your teeth?
G: No, I haven't. Why is that?
B: It can damage your teeth. It can also make them too ❷sensitive.

❶ 'chewing ice'는 is의 주어인 동명사이다.
❷ sensitive는 동사 make의 목적격보어이다.

Listen & Talk 1 C

G: ❶Have you heard the term *body image*? It means "the way you see your own body." A lot of teens have a negative body image. They think they're too fat or too thin ❷compared to others. However, I want you to build a positive body image. Accept your body as it is and give ❸yourself praise every day. Remember, there is only one you, so don't compare yourself to others. Loving yourself can make a big difference in your life.

❶ 상대방이 body image라는 용어를 아는지 묻는 말이다.
❷ compared to = ~와 비교하여
❸ yourself는 재귀 용법의 재귀대명사이다.

Listen & Talk 1 D-1

A: Have you heard that ❶writing by hand is good for your health?
B: Oh, really?
A: Yes, it improves your memory.

❶ 'writing by hand'는 주어 역할을 하는 동명사이다.

Listen & Talk 1 D-2

A: Have you heard that ❶using a cell phone before bed is bad for your health?
B: Oh, really?
A: Yes, ❷it prevents deep sleep.

❶ 'using a cell phone before bed'가 동사 is의 주어인 동명사이다.
❷ it = using a cell phone before bed

Listen & Talk 2 A

G: What's this?
B: It's a smart band. ❶It lets me check my health information on my smartphone.
G: What kind of information?
B: It shows ❷how far I walk during the day and how well I sleep at night.
G: Interesting. I'm surprised that this small band can do all that.

❶ 사역동사 let이 쓰여서 목적격보어 check는 원형부정사이다.
❷ 'how far ~'와 'how well ~'은 간접의문문으로 show의 목적어이다.

Listen & Talk 2 C

B: What is that? It looks nice.
G: This is a magic cup. I carry it everywhere with me.
B: What's special about it?
G: It's awesome. ❶It tells me to drink water every two hours.
B: Really? I'm surprised that it can talk to you.
G: It even asks me questions like "Aren't you thirsty?"
B: That's so cool! But why are you trying to drink more water?
G: Because ❷drinking a lot of water can increase your energy and help your blood flow.
B: That's amazing. I should buy one!

❶ 'tell+목적어+to부정사'의 구문으로 to부정사가 목적격보어이다.
❷ 'drinking a lot of water'는 주어 역할을 하는 동명사구이다.

Do It Yourself A

B: Oh, I'm so hungry.
G: Why don't you eat some snacks before dinner?
B: ❶I don't want to. I'll wait until dinner.
G: Okay, but have you heard that eating little and often is good for your health?
B: Really? I thought eating three meals a day was fine.
G: If you keep waiting until dinner, you will eat too much and too quickly. Eating little and often ❷prevents you from eating like that.
B: I see. Then I'll go eat an apple right now.

❶ 'I don't want to.' 뒤에는 'eat some snacks before dinner'가 생략되었다.
❷ prevent A from -ing= A가 ~하지 못하게 하다

● 다음 우리말과 일치하도록 빈칸에 알맞은 말을 쓰시오.

Listen & Talk 1 A

B: _____ you _____ that _____ ice is bad for your _____?

G: No, I haven't. _____ is that?

B: It can _____ your teeth. It can also _____ them too _____.

Listen & Talk 1 B

B: You _____ tired. Did you _____ _____ sleep?

G: Yes, I did. I _____ _____ _____ seven hours.

B: Okay. _____ _____ you _____ to bed?

G: I _____ _____ _____ after midnight, _____ _____.

B: That's probably _____ is _____ you tired. _____ you heard that _____ you go to bed is very important?

G: No, I haven't. _____ is _____?

B: Scientists say that _____ _____ _____ _____ can make you _____ _____ the next day.

G: I didn't know that.

B: On the _____ hand, going to bed early can _____ your _____ and help you be more _____. From _____ on, try to go to bed earlier.

Listen & Talk 1 D-1

A: _____ you heard that _____ by hand is _____ for your _____?

B: Oh, _____?

A: Yes, it _____ your memory.

Listen & Talk 2 A

G: What's this?

B: It's a _____ band. It lets me _____ my _____ information on my _____.

G: What _____ of information?

B: It shows _____ _____ I walk during the day and _____ _____ I sleep at night.

G: Interesting. I'm _____ that this _____ band can do all that.

해석

B: 너는 얼음을 씹는 것이 이에 나쁘다는 말을 들어보았니?

G: 아니. 왜 그런데?

B: 그것이 이에 손상을 줄 수 있어. 그것은 또한 이를 너무 예민하게 만들 수 있어.

B: 너 피곤해 보인다. 잠은 충분히 잤니?

G: 응, 그래. 나는 일곱 시간 이상 잤어.

B: 알았어. 너는 언제 잠들었니?

G: 평소처럼 자정이 넘어서 잠들었어.

B: 아마 그것이 너를 피곤하게 만드는 것일 거야. 네가 언제 잠자리에 드는지가 아주 중요하다는 말을 들어본 적이 있니?

G: 아니. 왜 그렇지?

B: 과학자들은 늦게 잠자리에 드는 것은 그 다음날 피곤함을 느끼게 할 수 있다고 말해.

G: 나는 몰랐어.

B: 반면에 일찍 잠자리에 드는 것은 기억력을 향상시키고, 더 생산적이 되도록 도와줄 수 있어. 지금부터는 일찍 자도록 노력해 봐.

A: 손으로 글을 쓰는 것이 건강에 좋다는 말을 들어본 적이 있니?

B: 오, 정말?

A: 그래, 그것이 기억력을 높여준데.

G: 이것이 뭐니?

B: 그것은 스마트밴드야. 그것은 나에게 스마트폰으로 건강 정보를 점검할 수 있도록 해줘.

G: 어떤 종류의 정보니?

B: 그것은 내가 낮에 얼마나 멀리 걷는지, 밤에 얼마나 잘 자는지를 보여줘.

G: 흥미롭다. 나는 이 작은 밴드가 그 모든 일을 할 수 있다는 것이 놀라워.

Listen & Talk 2 B

B: _____ are you doing in the _____ room?

G: I'm _____ _____.

B: You're _____ out by _____?

G: Yes, I'm _____ this online video. It shows me all the _____.

B: _____ me see. Wow, it's _____ _____ two million times! I'm _____ that so many people _____ _____ this video.

G: I know! These kinds of _____ are becoming _____ right now.

B: It looks very _____. You don't have to go _____ to _____.

G: That's right. _____ _____ I love these programs. You should _____ them, too.

B: 너 거실에서 무엇을 하고 있니?
G: 나는 요가를 하는 중이야.
B: 혼자서 운동한다는 말이니?
G: 그래, 이 온라인 비디오를 따라하는 중이야. 그것이 나에게 모든 단계를 보여줘.
B: 어디 보자. 와, 2백만 번이나 시청되었구나! 그렇게 많은 사람이 이 비디오를 보았다니 놀라워.
G: 알아! 이런 종류의 프로그램이 지금 인기를 얻는 중이야.
B: 그것은 매우 편리해 보여. 너는 운동하러 밖에 나갈 필요가 없어.
G: 맞아. 그런 이유로 나는 이런 프로그램을 아주 좋아해. 너도 한번 시도해 봐.

Listen & Talk 2 C

B: What is that? It _____ nice.

G: This is a _____ cup. I carry it _____ with me.

B: What's _____ about it?

G: It's _____. It tells me to _____ water _____ two hours.

B: Really? I'm _____ that it can _____ to you.

G: It even _____ me questions like "Aren't you _____?"

B: That's so cool! But _____ are you _____ to drink more water?

G: Because _____ a lot of water can _____ your energy and _____ your blood _____.

B: That's amazing. I should _____ one!

B: 저것이 뭐니? 그것은 좋아 보인다.
G: 이것은 매직 컵이야. 나는 어디든지 그것을 가지고 다녀.
B: 그것은 무엇이 특별하니?
G: 정말 끝내줘. 그것은 두 시간마다 물을 마시라고 나에게 말을 해.
B: 정말? 그것이 너에게 말을 할 수 있다는 것이 놀라워.
G: 심지어 그것은 "목마르지 않니?"와 같은 질문도 해.
B: 정말 멋지구나! 그런데 왜 너는 물을 더 마시려고 애쓰니?
G: 왜냐하면 물을 많이 마시는 것이 에너지를 높여주고, 피가 잘 흐르게 도와줘.
B: 정말 놀랍구나. 하나 사야겠다!

Do It Yourself A

B: Oh, I'm so _____.

G: Why _____ you eat some snacks _____ dinner?

B: I don't _____ to. I'll _____ until dinner.

G: Okay, but have you heard that _____ little and _____ is good for your _____?

B: _____? I thought _____ three meals a day was fine.

G: If you keep _____ until dinner, you will _____ too much and _____ quickly. _____ and _____ prevents you _____ like that.

B: I see. Then I'll go _____ an apple _____ now.

B: 오, 나는 너무 배가 고파.
G: 저녁 먹기 전에 간식을 좀 먹는 것이 어떠니?
B: 나는 그것을 원하지 않아. 나는 저녁 식사까지 기다릴 거야.
G: 알았어. 하지만 너는 조금 자주 먹는 것이 건강에 좋다는 말을 들어본 적이 있니?
B: 정말이니? 나는 하루에 세끼 식사하는 것이 좋다고 생각했는데.
G: 만약 네가 저녁식사까지 계속 기다리면 너무 많이 그리고 너무 빨리 먹을 거야. 조금 자주 먹는 것이 네가 그렇게 먹는 것을 막아 줄 거야.
B: 알았어. 그러면 지금 당장 사과를 먹으러 가야겠다.

01 다음 대화의 빈칸에 들어갈 말로 알맞은 것은?

> A: This running app can track your running course. It can suggest many different training plans, too.
> B: I'm _____ that it can do all that.

① worried   ② disappointed   ③ surprised
④ happy   ⑤ concerned

02 다음 중 밑줄 친 말 대신 쓰기에 <u>어색한</u> 것을 고르시오.

> B: Have you heard that chewing ice is bad for your teeth?
> G: <u>No, I haven't.</u> Why is that?
> B: It can damage your teeth. It can also make them too sensitive.

① I think I have.   ② Oh, really?   ③ I didn't know that.
④ No, that's new to me.   ⑤ No. I've never heard of it.

[03~04] 다음 대화를 읽고 물음에 답하시오.

> B: What are you doing in the living room?
> G: I'm doing yoga.
> B: You're working out by yourself?
> G: Yes, I'm following this online video. It shows me all the steps.
> B: Let me see. Wow, it's been watched two million times! I'm surprised that so many people have watched this video.
> G: I know! These kinds of programs are becoming popular right now.
> B: It looks very convenient. You don't have to go out to exercise.
> G: That's right. <u>그런 이유로 나는 이 프로그램을 아주 좋아해.</u> (that's, these programs, why, love, I) You should try them, too.

03 밑줄 친 우리말 의미에 어울리도록 주어진 단어를 배열하시오.

➡ _____

04 위 대화의 내용과 일치하는 것은?

① The boy and the girl are doing yoga.
② The boy is showing the online video.
③ The girl follows all the steps of the video.
④ The girl didn't know many people watched the video.
⑤ Because of the video, the girl wants to go out.

[01~03] 다음 대화를 읽고 물음에 답하시오.

B: You look tired. Did you get enough sleep?

G: Yes, I did. I slept ___(A)___ over seven hours.

B: Okay. When did you go to bed?

G: I went to bed after midnight, (B)평소처럼.

B: That's probably what is making you tired. Have you heard that when you go to bed is very important?

G: No, I haven't. Why is that?

B: Scientists say that going to bed late can make you feel tired the next day.

G: I didn't know that.

B: On the other hand, going to bed early can improve your memory and help you be more productive. From now on, try to going to bed earlier.

01 빈칸 (A)에 들어갈 전치사를 고르시오.

① with ② on ③ in ④ for ⑤ by

02 밑줄 친 (B)의 우리말을 영어로 쓰시오.

➡ _____

03 위 대화를 읽고 대답할 수 <u>없는</u> 것은?

① Did the girl get enough sleep?

② Why does the girl go to bed late?

③ How many hours did the girl sleep?

④ Why does the girl look tired?

⑤ What does the boy advise the girl to do?

04 밑줄 친 ①~⑤ 중 문맥상이나 어법상 <u>어색한</u> 것을 찾아 고치시오.

B: Oh, ①I'm so hungry.

G: Why don't you eat some snacks before dinner?

B: I don't want to. ②I'll wait until dinner.

G: Okay, but have you heard that ③ <u>eat little and often is good for your health</u>?

B: Really? I thought eating three meals a day was fine.

G: If you keep waiting until dinner, ④ <u>you will eat too much and too quickly</u>. Eating little and often prevents you from eating like that.

B: I see. ⑤<u>Then I'll go eat an apple right now</u>.

➡ _____

05 다음 대화의 빈칸에 들어갈 말을 고르시오.

A: Have you heard that using a cell phone before bed is bad for your health?

B: Oh, really?

A: _____

① Yes, it prevents deep sleep.

② I'm surprised that you know that.

③ Didn't you have a cell phone?

④ Why don't you buy a new cell phone?

⑤ How many hours do you use your cell phone?

서답형

06 다음 문장에서 어법상 어색한 부분을 찾아 올바른 형태로 고치시오.

> Have you heard that swimming is good for your back? Our group made a plan go swimming together every Tuesday and Thursday at World Sports Park. We are sure it will help us stay healthy.

➡ _____

[07~10] 다음 대화를 읽고 물음에 답하시오.

B: What is that? It looks nice.
G: This is a magic cup. I carry it everywhere with me. (ⓐ)
B: What's special about it?
G: It's awesome. (ⓑ)
B: Really? I'm surprised that it can talk to you.
G: It even asks me questions like "Aren't you thirsty?" (ⓒ)
B: That's so cool! But ___(A)___ are you trying to drink more water? (ⓓ)
G: Because drinking a lot of water can ___(B)___ your energy and help your blood flow. (ⓔ)
B: That's amazing. I should buy one!

중요

07 ⓐ~ⓔ 중에서 다음 문장이 들어가기에 적절한 곳은?

> It tells me to drink water every two hours.

① ⓐ   ② ⓑ   ③ ⓒ   ④ ⓓ   ⑤ ⓔ

서답형

08 빈칸 (A)에 들어가기에 적절한 의문사를 쓰시오.

➡ _____

서답형

09 위 대화의 빈칸 (B)에 다음 영영풀이에 해당하는 단어를 철자 i로 시작하여 쓰시오.

> to make something larger or greater in size, amount, number, etc.

➡ _____

10 위 대화의 내용과 일치하지 않는 것은?

① The girl carries a cup everywhere.
② The cup makes the girl drink water every three hours.
③ The boy is surprised that the cup can talk.
④ Drinking a lot of water increases our energy.
⑤ The cup can ask questions like "Aren't you thirsty?"

11 밑줄 친 ⓐ~ⓔ 중 대화의 흐름상 어색한 문장은?

B: What are you doing in the living room?
G: I'm doing yoga.
B: ⓐYou're working out by yourself?
G: Yes, ⓑI'm following this online video. It shows me all the steps.
B: Let me see. Wow, ⓒit's been watched two million times! I'm surprised that so many people have watched this video.
G: I know! ⓓThese kinds of programs are becoming popular right now.
B: It looks very convenient. You don't have to go out to exercise.
G: That's right. That's why I love these programs. ⓔYou should avoid them, too.

① ⓐ   ② ⓑ   ③ ⓒ   ④ ⓓ   ⑤ ⓔ

[01~03] 다음 대화를 읽고 물음에 답하시오.

B: Have you heard that chewing ice is bad ___(A)___ your teeth?

G: No, I haven't. ____(B)____ ?

B: It can damage your teeth. (C)그것은 또한 그것들을 너무 민감하게 만들 수 있어.

01 빈칸 (A)에 들어갈 전치사를 쓰시오.

➡ _____

02 빈칸 (B)에 들어갈 적절한 내용의 의문문을 쓰시오. (that을 포함하는 3단어)

➡ _____

03 밑줄 친 (C)의 우리말을 영작하시오.

➡ _____

04 다음 대화의 빈칸에 들어갈 말을 <보기>에서 골라 순서대로 배열하시오.

> B: Oh, I'm so hungry.
> G: _____
> B: _____
> G: Okay, but have you heard that eating little and often is good for your health?
> B: Really? _____
> G: If you keep waiting until dinner, you will eat too much and too quickly.
> _____
> B: _____

┌─ 보기 ─┐

(A) Eating little and often prevents you from eating like that.

(B) Why don't you eat some snacks before dinner?

(C) I see. Then I'll go eat an apple right now.

(D) I thought eating three meals a day was fine.

(E) I don't want to. I'll wait until dinner.

➡ _____

[05~06] 다음 대화를 읽고 물음에 답하시오.

B: What are you doing in the living room?

G: I'm doing yoga.

B: You're ___(A)___ out by yourself?

G: Yes, I'm following this online video. It shows me all the steps.

B: Let me see. Wow, it's been watched two million times! (B)그렇게 많은 사람들이 이 비디오를 보았다는 사실에 놀랐다. (have watched)

G: I know! These kinds of programs are becoming popular right now.

B: It looks very convenient. You don't have to go out to exercise.

G: That's right. That's why I love these programs. You should try them, too.

05 내용상 (A)에 들어가기에 적절한 말을 쓰시오.

➡ _____

06 밑줄 친 (B)의 우리말을 영어 문장으로 옮겨 쓰시오.

➡ _____

Grammar

① 관계대명사의 계속적 용법

- Walnuts also have wrinkles, **which** the brain has too.
  호두에는 또한 주름이 있는데, 이 주름은 인간의 뇌에도 있다.

- Stadler, **who** is 33 years old, was the 2004 winner. Stadler는 33세인데, 2004년 우승자였다.

■ 관계대명사의 계속적 용법은 관계대명사 앞에 콤마(,)를 붙인 형태로 선행사를 부연 설명한다. 제한적 용법과 마찬가지로 선행사가 사람이면 who, 사물이면 which를 쓴다. 제한적 용법은 관계사가 이끄는 절부터 해석하고, 계속적 용법은 앞에서부터 해석한다.

- He has two daughters **who** are teachers. 그는 교사인 딸이 둘 있다.: 제한적 용법 → 딸이 둘인지 더 있는지 모름.

- He has two daughters, **who** are teachers. 그는 딸이 둘인데, 그들은 교사이다.: 계속적 용법 → 딸이 둘만 있음.

■ 계속적 용법의 관계대명사는 '접속사(and, but, for, though 등)+대명사'로 고쳐 쓸 수 있다.

- I bought a book, **which** was written by Roald Dahl.
  = I bought a book, **and it** was written by Roald Dahl.
  나는 책을 한 권 샀는데 그 책은 Roald Dahl에 의해 씌여진 것이다.

■ 관계대명사 that과 what은 계속적 용법으로 사용할 수 없으며, 관계대명사가 계속적 용법으로 쓰였을 때는 생략하지 않는다.

- The swing, **which** I rode when I was a child, gathered rust. (○)

- The swing, that I rode when I was a child, gathered rust. (×)
  그 그네는 내가 어렸을 때 타고 놀았던 것인데, 녹이 슬었다.

■ which는 선행사로 구나 절을 가질 수도 있다.

- People say that I found my level, **which** I don't agree.
  사람들이 내가 알맞은 곳에 자리잡았다고 하지만, 나는 그렇게 생각하지 않는다.

핵심 Check

1. 빈칸에 알맞은 관계대명사를 쓰시오.
   (1) This story is about a man, _____ had two daughters.
   (2) I was offered another position, _____ I accepted.
   (3) He has a car, _____ is expensive.

2 명사의 뒤에서 명사를 수식하는 분사

- We all know that a diet **containing** a variety of food keeps our bodies healthy. 우리는 모두 다양한 음식을 포함하는 식사가 우리의 몸을 건강하게 유지시켜 준다는 것을 알고 있다.
- Frank took part in a meeting **held** in Seoul. Frank는 서울에서 열린 회의에 참석했다.

■ 분사는 명사의 앞이나 뒤에서 명사를 꾸며 주는 형용사 역할을 한다. 현재분사는 '능동' 이나 '진행'의 의미가 있고, 과거분사는 '수동'이나 '완료'의 의미가 있다.

- There is a baby **sleeping** in the cradle. 요람에서 자고 있는 아기가 있다.: 뒤에서 수식하는 현재분사 '진행'
- The **sleeping** baby is very cute. 자고 있는 그 아기는 매우 귀엽다.: 앞에서 수식하는 현재분사 '진행'
- I met a little girl **named** Lily. 나는 Lily라는 이름의 어린 소녀를 만났다.: 뒤에서 수식하는 과거분사 '수동'
- Many of the **invited** guests will not attend the party.
  초대 받은 손님 중 상당수가 파티에 참석하지 않을 것이다.: 앞에서 수식하는 과거분사 '수동'

■ 분사에 다른 어구(목적어나 보어, 수식어구 등)가 함께 있을 때는 뒤에서 명사를 수식한다.

- Look at the boy **dancing** on the stage. 무대 위에서 춤추는 소년을 보세요.
- I entered the hall **crowded** with people. 나는 사람들이 붐비는 복도로 들어갔다.

■ 명사를 뒤에서 수식하는 경우에는 그 앞에 '주격 관계대명사+be 동사'가 생략된 것으로 생각할 수 있다.

- Look at the boy (who is) **dancing** on the stage.
- I entered the hall (which was) **crowded** with people.

핵심 Check

2. 괄호 안에 주어진 어휘를 이용하여 빈칸을 알맞게 채우시오.

(1) I would love to have a room _____ with books. (fill)

(2) This photo is about a woman _____ a bag. (carry)

(3) There was a young man _____ tea in the living room. (have)

01 다음 빈칸에 들어갈 말로 알맞은 것은?

> Bill had some books, _____ he read again and again.

① who   ② which   ③ how
④ that   ⑤ what

02 다음 괄호 안에서 알맞은 말을 고르시오.

(1) It is a fact (knowing / known) to everybody.

(2) There were some pictures (painting / painted) by herself.

(3) The girl (wearing / worn) a blue hat is my sister.

(4) A bright light brought the (sleeping / slept) baby into view.

03 다음 두 문장을 한 문장으로 바꾸어 쓸 때 알맞게 표현한 것을 고르시오.

> • Ms. Green is an English teacher.
> • She lives in this house.

① Ms. Green, which is an English teacher, lives in this house.

② Ms. Green, what is an English teacher, lives in this house.

③ Ms. Green, who is an English teacher, lives in this house.

④ Ms. Green, whom is an English teacher, lives in this house.

⑤ Ms. Green, that is an English teacher, lives in this house.

04 다음 우리말에 맞게 주어진 어휘를 바르게 배열하시오.

(1) 나는 그 책을 읽기 시작했는데 그것은 매우 재미있었다.

(I, the book, interesting, read, began, was, very, which, to)

➡ _____

(2) TV를 보고 있는 소년은 Jane의 아들입니다.

(the boy, Jane's son, TV, watching, is)

➡ _____

(3) 그는 한국에서 만들어진 스마트폰을 샀다.

(he, Korea, smart phone, bought, made, a, in)

➡ _____

01 다음 중 어법상 어색한 것은?

① Walnuts also have wrinkles, which the brain has too.
② Amy lives in a house, that has a nice pool.
③ These are the books, which I bought yesterday.
④ Mike, who is a thief, is in the jail now.
⑤ The Eiffel Tower, which is made of steel, is in France.

02 다음 중 어법상 바르지 않은 것은?

① The castle attacked by the enemy was finally destroyed.
② There was only one book remaining in the box.
③ Saint Exupery wrote many touched stories.
④ The little girl taking a walk in the park is my daughter.
⑤ We all know that a diet containing a variety of food keeps our bodies healthy.

03 다음 빈칸에 알맞은 말이 바르게 짝지어진 것은?

• The students _____ the movie looked so bored.
• He likes Kate, _____ is very kind.

① watching – who
② watching – that
③ watched – who
④ watched – that
⑤ watch – what

04 다음 괄호 안에서 알맞은 말을 고르시오.

(1) I know Ms. Chalsey, (who / that) is from Canada.
(2) Tom visited his house, (who / which) was in London.
(3) He said nothing, (that / which) made his mom get angrier.
(4) Look at the man (playing / played) the flute.
(5) Can you show me the article (posting / posted) on the site?
(6) Shirley couldn't get into the house because of the fiercely (barking / barked) dog.

05 주어진 문장의 밑줄 친 부분의 쓰임이 나머지 넷과 다른 것은?

① *The Kiss* is a famous picture <u>painted</u> by Klimt.
② Mr. Kim is a Korean artist <u>known</u> to everyone in Korea.
③ Noah read a newspaper <u>written</u> in English.
④ Everyone <u>invited</u> to the party is expected to bring a gift.
⑤ Someone had already <u>made</u> coffee by the time I arrived at my office.

06 다음 밑줄 친 부분을 바꿔 쓸 때, 의미상 가장 적절한 것은?

> This is *The Old Man and the Sea*, which was written by Hemingway.

① as it
② but it
③ or it
④ and it
⑤ because it

07 Which is suitable for the blank?

> Mina is appreciating a painting _____ by Pierre-Auguste Renoir.

① draw
② drew
③ drawn
④ drawing
⑤ to draw

서답형

08 다음 빈칸에 알맞은 관계대명사를 쓰시오.

(1) This is Sarah, _____ is the kindest girl in our school.
(2) Carrots have some chemicals that can make vitamin A, _____ improves your vision.
(3) She went to the party with Hannah, _____ is her best friend.
(4) We visited a museum, _____ is in Jeonju.

09 다음 우리말을 바르게 영작한 것을 고르시오.

> 나를 기다리는 사람들이 있었다.

① There were waiting people for me.
② There were people waiting for me.
③ There were people waited for me.
④ There were waited people for me.
⑤ There were people wait for me.

10 다음 문장의 밑줄 친 부분 중 어법상 어색한 것은?

> This is the picture of Leopard Cat, ⓐthat ⓑis ⓒeasily ⓓfound ⓔin Thailand and Southeast Asia

① ⓐ
② ⓑ
③ ⓒ
④ ⓓ
⑤ ⓔ

11 다음 문장의 빈칸에 들어갈 수 없는 것은?

> *Yesterday* is a famous song _____ by many singers.

① sung
② singing
③ loved
④ which is sung
⑤ which is loved

서답형

12 다음 밑줄 친 부분을 바꿔 쓸 때, 빈칸에 적절한 말을 쓰시오.

> • To buy some food, she went to the store, for it was the cheapest.
> = To buy some food, she went to the store, _____ was the cheapest.

13 다음 문장의 빈칸에 들어갈 수 없는 말은?

> The boy _____ is my friend.

① dancing to music
② invited to the party
③ talking to Sumi
④ reading a book
⑤ wears glasses

14 다음 빈칸에 알맞은 것은?

> Yesterday I met Clare, _____ I haven't seen for long.

① whom
② which
③ that
④ what
⑤ when

 중요

15 다음 빈칸에 알맞은 말이 순서대로 바르게 짝지어진 것을 고르시오.

> • The curry _____ at this restaurant tastes good.
> • The lady _____ a pretty bag is talking on the phone with her friend.

① served – held
② served – holding
③ serves – holds
④ serving – held
⑤ serving – holding

서답형

16 다음 문장에서 어법상 어색한 것을 바르게 고쳐 다시 쓰시오.

(1) I didn't like the students, which ran here and there in the library.

➡ _____

(2) I put the picture on the wall, that made me remember my best friend.

➡ _____

(3) There was a little baby cried on the bed.

➡ _____

(4) People all over the world love to eat food making out of potatoes.

➡ _____

중요

17 다음 중 어법상 어색한 것을 고르시오. (2개)

① Sam liked the present, that Bella gave to her.
② Mick is the boy singing on the stage.
③ I will visit my friend in Suwon, who is a teacher.
④ The woman nicknaming Black Swan is working at the bank.
⑤ I opened the box, which was filled with a lot of books.

18 다음 우리말에 맞게 영작한 것을 고르시오.

> 나는 그 방에서 상자 하나를 발견했는데, 그것은 녹색 천으로 덮여 있었다.

① I discovered a box in the room, that was covered with a green cloth.
② I discovered a box in the room, to cover with a green cloth.
③ I discovered a box in the room, which was covered with a green cloth.
④ I discovered a box in the room, which was covering with a green cloth.
⑤ I discovered a box in the room, covering with a green cloth.

서답형

19 다음 문장에서 생략되어 있는 것을 찾아 어법에 맞게 다시 쓰시오.

(1) Kim Yuna loved by many Koreans was a famous figure skater.

➡ _____

(2) People in Germany want to buy smart phones made in Korea.

➡ _____

01 빈칸에 알맞은 관계대명사를 쓰시오.

(1) Emily, _____ is five years old, can play the flute.

(2) Help yourself to the food, _____ is very delicious.

(3) My best friend, _____ wants to be a B-boy dancer, is Jackson.

(4) Mom let me play computer games, _____ made me surprised.

02 다음 우리말에 맞게 주어진 어구를 바르게 배열하시오.

(1) 무명 작가에 의해 씌여진 그 소설은 작년에 영화로 만들어졌다. (an, author, written, was, the novel, a movie, unknown, made, last year, into, by)

➡ _____

_____

(2) 한국은 10위를 차지했는데 그것은 인도와 브라질보다 앞선 순위였다. (Korea, India and Brazil, ahead, 10th place, ranked, was, which, of)

➡ _____

_____

(3) 개를 산책시키고 있는 그 남자는 내 친구이다. (the man, of, his dog, a friend, walking, is, is, mine, who)

➡ _____

_____

03 다음 문장에서 생략된 것을 넣어 다시 쓰시오.

(1) A lot of people like cars made in Korea.

➡ _____

_____

(2) The man reading a book at the table is my father.

➡ _____

_____

(3) The little girl holding the woman's hand is crying loudly.

➡ _____

_____

04 다음 두 문장을 해석하고 그 차이를 설명하시오.

(1) Jacob has two sons who are farmers.

(2) Jacob has two sons, who are farmers.

➡ 해석: _____

_____

차이: _____

_____

_____

_____

05 괄호 안에 있는 단어를 어법에 맞게 고쳐 쓰시오.

(1) The second story is about a woman (bake) bread.

➡ _____

(2) I got a message (write) in numbers.

➡ _____

06 다음 그림을 보고, 주어진 어휘를 이용하여 빈칸을 알맞게 채우시오.

(1) All the actors _____

make the musical interesting. (sing and dance)

(2) Do not bother the _____ trees. (plant)

07 다음 〈보기〉에 주어진 단어를 이용하여 문맥에 맞게 문장을 완성하시오.

┌── 보기 ┐
│   lie   wrap   │
└───────────────────────┘

(1) Do you see a little box _____ in silver _____ paper?

(2) Look at the big snake _____ in a coil.

08 관계대명사의 계속적 용법을 이용하여 주어진 두 문장을 하나의 문장으로 쓰시오.

(1) • The new library can hold many people.
• And it made them happy.
➡ _____
_____

(2) • Ella carried a box.
• It looked very heavy for her.
➡ _____
_____

(3) • I like Jane.
• I like her, for she is kind and wise.
➡ _____
_____

09 다음 문장에서 어법상 <u>어색한</u> 것을 바르게 고치시오.

(1) Snow White lived in the palace, who had a nice and beautiful garden.
_____ ➡ _____

(2) The owner, which is a scary person, will be angry at you.
_____ ➡ _____

(3) I visited my grandfather, that wasn't home.
_____ ➡ _____

(4) The sleeping in the bed baby is Emma's daughter.
_____ ➡ _____

(5) Frank has a nice car making in Germany.
_____ ➡ _____

(6) The shop sold toy cars became popular.
_____ ➡ _____

Beneficial Foods for Our Bodies

We all know that a diet containing a variety of foods keeps our
<small>that은 명사절을 이끄는 접속사로 생략 가능   현재분사로 앞의 명사 a diet를 수식</small>

bodies healthy. But sometimes we are not sure which foods are good
<small>의문형용사</small>

for which body parts. Nature, however, gives us a big clue. Look at the
<small>= gives a big clue to us (4형식)</small>

following examples. Each of these foods not only looks like a certain
<small>= not merely[just/simply]</small>

body part but is also good for that body part.
<small>not only A but also B = B as well as A: 'A뿐만 아니라 B도</small>

Slice open a tomato and compare it with the human heart. You will
<small>얇게 썰어 열다   compare A with B: A와 B를 비교하다</small>

see that they look similar. They both have multiple hollow spaces and
<small>= a tomato (which is sliced open) and the human heart</small>

are red. Researchers say that the chemicals that make tomatoes red are
<small>선행사 the chemicals를 수식하는 주격 관계대명사</small>

good for your heart and blood. In addition, eating tomatoes can lower
<small>= Besides   동명사 주어</small>

your risk of heart disease.

Look at the shape of a walnut. Do you notice anything? Yes, it's very
<small>= the shape of a walnut</small>

similar to the shape of the human brain! A walnut is divided into two
<small>A is similar to B: A는 B와 유사하다   be divided into: ~로 나뉘다</small>

parts, just like the brain. Walnuts also have wrinkles, which the brain
<small>꼭 ~처럼   콤마(,)와 함께 쓰인 계속적 용법의 목적격 관계대명사</small>

has too. Studies show that walnuts help our brains stay healthy and
<small>help+목적어+원형부정사 또는 to부정사</small>

active. They are also good for preventing Alzheimer's disease.
<small>be good for: ~에 좋다</small>

---

beneficial 유익한, 이로운
diet 식사, 식습관
contain …이 함유되어 있다
a variety of 여러 가지의
nature 자연, 본성
clue 단서, 실마리
slice (얇게) 썰다
compare 비교하다
multiple 많은, 다수의, 다양한
hollow 속이 빈, 텅 빈
researcher 연구원, 조사원
chemical 화학 물질, 화학제품
risk 위험
disease 질병, 병
in addition 게다가, 덧붙여
similar 유사한, 닮은
wrinkle 주름, 주름을 잡다
active 활동적인, 활발한
prevent 예방하다, 막다

📎 **확인문제**

● 다음 문장이 본문의 내용과 일치하면 T, 일치하지 않으면 F를 쓰시오.

1 A diet containing a variety of foods keeps our bodies healthy. ☐

2 We are sure which foods are good for which body parts. ☐

3 A tomato and the human heart have multiple hollow spaces and are red. ☐

4 Eating tomatoes can increase your risk of heart disease. ☐

5 The chemicals that make tomatoes red are good for your heart and blood. ☐

6 Walnuts help our stomach stay healthy and active. ☐

A slice of carrot looks like the human eye. Carrots have some
look like+명사: …인 것처럼 보이다

chemicals that can make vitamin A, which improves your vision. It
선행사 some chemicals를 수식하는 주격 관계대명사   which는 계속적 용법의 주격 관계대명사이며, 선행사 vitamin A를 부연 설명

helps your eyes process light and send a clear image to the brain. So if
help+목적어+원형부정사 또는 to부정사

you want healthy eyes, eat carrots.

Cutting onions is not fun because it makes you cry. But try slicing
동명사 주어   are(×)   사역동사(make)+목적어+원형부정사   잘라 보아라

one anyway. You can see that the inside looks a little like a human cell.
= anyhow = at any rate = in any case = at all events   └ ~처럼 보인다 ┘

Scientists say that onions contain vitamin B, which helps make new,
                    계속적 용법의 주격 관계대명사로, 선행사 vitamin B를 부연 설명   help+원형부정사 또는 to부정사

healthy cells.

Now, let's move on to ginger. What body part comes to mind when
어떤(의문형용사)

you see it? Doesn't it look like a stomach? You may not like ginger's
= ginger   ~하지 않을지도 모른다

strong taste or smell, but these come from a special chemical that
~로부터 나오다

prevents you from feeling sick and throwing up. For this reason, ginger
prevent A from ~ing: A가 ~하는 것을 막다

can be good for your stomach.

Isn't it amazing that some foods mirror the body parts that they
가주어   진주어가 되는 명사적을 이끄는 접속사   목적격 관계대명사

are good for? Interestingly, there are many other such foods. Find
수사의문문: 강한 반어적 표현(It is amazing의 뜻을 더 강하게 표현한 것임.)

as many as you can and try to eat a variety of them.
as+원급+as+주어+can[could] = as+원급+as possible: '가능한 한 …한'

---

improve 개선하다, 향상시키다

vision 시력, 눈

process 과정; 처리하다

cell 작은 방, 세포

move on (새로운 일·주제로) 넘어가다

ginger 생강

come to mind 생각이 떠오르다, 생각 나다

stomach 위, 위장, 복부

throw up 토하다

mirror 거울; 잘 보여주다, 반영하다

📎 **확인문제**

● 다음 문장이 본문의 내용과 일치하면 T, 일치하지 않으면 F를 쓰시오.

1 A slice of carrot is similar to the human eye. ☐

2 Vitamin B helps your eyes process light. ☐

3 It is not fun to cut onions because it makes you cry. ☐

4 Vitamin A in onions helps make new, healthy cells. ☐

5 Ginger looks like a stomach. ☐

6 It isn't amazing that some foods mirror the body parts that they are good for. ☐

● 우리말을 참고하여 빈칸에 알맞은 말을 쓰시오.

1 _____ Foods for Our Bodies

2 We all know that a diet _____ a variety of foods _____ our bodies _____.

3 But sometimes we are not sure which foods _____ _____ _____ which body parts.

4 Nature, however, gives us _____ _____ _____.

5 Look at the _____ examples.

6 Each of these foods _____ _____ looks like a certain body part _____ is _____ good for that body part.

7 Slice open a tomato and _____ it _____ the human heart.

8 You will see that they _____ _____.

9 They both have _____ _____ _____ and are red.

10 Researchers say _____ the chemicals _____ make tomatoes red _____ good for your heart and blood.

11 _____ _____, eating tomatoes can _____ your risk of heart disease.

12 Look at _____ _____ of a walnut.

13 Do you notice _____?

14 Yes, it's very _____ _____ the shape of the human brain!

15 A walnut _____ _____ _____ two parts, just like the brain.

16 Walnuts also have wrinkles, _____ the brain has too.

17 Studies show that walnuts help our brains _____ _____ and active.

---

1 우리 몸에 이로운 음식

2 우리는 다양한 음식을 포함하는 식사가 우리의 몸을 건강하게 유지해 준다는 것을 알고 있다.

3 그러나 때때로 우리는 어떤 음식이 어떤 신체 부위에 좋은지 잘 모를 때가 있다.

4 하지만 자연은 우리에게 확실한 단서를 제시해 준다.

5 다음의 예들을 살펴보자.

6 각각의 이 음식들은 우리 신체의 특정 부분과 비슷해 보일 뿐만 아니라 그 신체 부위에도 좋다.

7 토마토 한 개를 잘라내서 그것을 사람의 심장과 비교해 보자.

8 당신은 그 둘이 비슷해 보인다는 것을 알게 될 것이다.

9 둘 다 여러 개의 빈 공간이 있고 붉은 색이다.

10 연구원들은 토마토를 붉게 만드는 화학 물질이 사람의 심장과 피에 유익하다고 한다.

11 게다가, 토마토를 먹는 것이 심장병에 걸릴 위험성을 낮출 수 있다.

12 호두의 모양을 살펴보자.

13 뭔가를 알아차릴 수 있는가?

14 그렇다. 호두의 모양은 인간의 뇌 형태와 매우 유사하다!

15 호두는 마치 인간의 뇌처럼 두 부분으로 나뉜다.

16 호두에는 또한 주름이 있는데, 이는 인간의 뇌에도 있는 것이다.

17 연구 결과는 호두가 사람의 뇌가 건강하고 활동적인 상태를 유지하는 데 도움을 준다는 것을 보여준다.

18 They are also good for _____ Alzheimer's disease.

19 _____ _____ _____ _____ looks like the human eye.

20 Carrots have some chemicals _____ can make vitamin A, _____ improves your vision.

21 It helps your eyes _____ light and _____ a clear image _____ the brain.

22 So if you want _____ _____, eat carrots.

23 _____ _____ is not fun because it _____ _____ _____.

24 But _____ _____ one anyway.

25 You can see that the inside _____ _____ _____ _____ a human cell.

26 Scientists say that onions contain vitamin B, _____ _____ _____ new, healthy cells.

27 Now, let's _____ _____ _____ ginger.

28 What body part _____ _____ _____ when you see it?

29 _____ it look like a stomach?

30 You may not like ginger's _____ _____ or smell, but these _____ _____ a special chemical that _____ you _____ _____ sick and _____ up.

31 _____ _____ _____, ginger can be good for your stomach.

32 Isn't it amazing that some foods _____ the body parts _____ they are good for?

33 Interestingly, there are _____ _____ _____ _____.

34 Find _____ _____ _____ _____ _____ and try to eat a variety of them.

18 호두는 또한 알츠하이머병을 예방하는 데도 좋다.

19 썰어 놓은 당근의 모양은 사람의 눈과 비슷해 보인다.

20 당근에는 비타민 A를 만들 수 있는 화학 성분이 있는데, 그것이 시력을 개선한다.

21 비타민 A는 눈이 빛을 처리하여 뇌에 선명한 이미지를 보낼 수 있도록 돕는다.

22 그러므로 건강한 눈을 원한다면, 당근을 먹어라.

23 양파를 써는 것은 즐겁지 않은데 왜냐하면 그것이 당신을 울게 만들기 때문이다.

24 그렇지만 어쨌든 하나를 잘라 보아라.

25 당신은 양파의 내부가 약간 인간의 세포처럼 보인다는 것을 알 수 있다.

26 과학자들은 양파가 비타민 B를 함유하는데, 이 비타민 B가 새롭고 건강한 세포를 만드는 데 도움이 된다고 주장한다.

27 이제 생강으로 넘어가 보자.

28 생강을 보면 몸의 어떤 부위가 생각나는가?

29 생강이 마치 위장처럼 생기지 않았는가?

30 당신은 어쩌면 생강의 강한 맛과 냄새를 좋아하지 않을지도 모르지만, 이러한 맛과 냄새는 복통과 구토를 예방하는 생강의 특별한 성분에서 나온다.

31 이러한 이유로 생강은 당신의 위장에 좋을 수 있다.

32 어떤 음식이 그 음식이 유익한 신체 부위의 생김새를 반영하고 있다는 점이 놀랍지 않은가?

33 흥미롭게도 그러한 음식은 상당히 많다.

34 가능한 한 그러한 음식을 많이 찾아서 다양한 음식을 먹도록 하라.

● 우리말을 참고하여 본문을 영작하시오.

1 우리 몸에 이로운 음식
➡ _____

2 우리는 다양한 음식을 포함하는 식사가 우리의 몸을 건강하게 유지해 준다는 것을 알고 있다.
➡ _____

3 그러나 때때로 우리는 어떤 음식이 어떤 신체 부위에 좋은지 잘 모를 때가 있다.
➡ _____

4 하지만 자연은 우리에게 확실한 단서를 제시해 준다.
➡ _____

5 다음의 예들을 살펴보자.
➡ _____

6 각각의 이 음식들은 우리 신체의 특정 부분과 비슷해 보일 뿐만 아니라 그 신체 부위에도 좋다.
➡ _____

7 토마토 한 개를 잘라내서 그것을 사람의 심장과 비교해 보자.
➡ _____

8 당신은 그 둘이 비슷해 보인다는 것을 알게 될 것이다.
➡ _____

9 둘 다 여러 개의 빈 공간이 있고 붉은 색이다.
➡ _____

10 연구원들은 토마토를 붉게 만드는 화학 물질이 사람의 심장과 피에 유익하다고 한다.
➡ _____

11 게다가, 토마토를 먹는 것이 심장병에 걸릴 위험성을 낮출 수 있다.
➡ _____

12 호두의 모양을 살펴보자.
➡ _____

13 뭔가를 알아차릴 수 있는가?
➡ _____

14 그렇다, 호두의 모양은 인간의 뇌 형태와 매우 유사하다!
➡ _____

15 호두는 마치 인간의 뇌처럼 두 부분으로 나뉜다.
➡ _____

16 호두에는 또한 주름이 있는데, 이는 인간의 뇌에도 있는 것이다.
➡ _____

17 연구 결과는 호두가 사람의 뇌가 건강하고 활동적인 상태를 유지하는 데 도움을 준다는 것을 보여준다.
➡ _____

18 호두는 또한 알츠하이머병을 예방하는 데도 좋다.

➡ _____

19 썰어 놓은 당근의 모양은 사람의 눈과 비슷해 보인다.

➡ _____

20 당근에는 비타민 A를 만들 수 있는 화학 성분이 있는데, 그것이 시력을 개선한다.

➡ _____

21 비타민 A는 눈이 빛을 처리하여 뇌에 선명한 이미지를 보낼 수 있도록 돕는다.

➡ _____

22 그러므로 건강한 눈을 원한다면, 당근을 먹어라.

➡ _____

23 양파를 써는 것은 즐겁지 않은데 왜냐하면 그것이 당신을 울게 만들기 때문이다.

➡ _____

24 그렇지만 어쨌든 하나를 잘라 보아라.

➡ _____

25 당신은 양파의 내부가 약간 인간의 세포처럼 보인다는 것을 알 수 있다.

➡ _____

26 과학자들은 양파가 비타민 B를 함유하는데, 이 비타민 B가 새롭고 건강한 세포를 만들어 내는 데 도움이 된다고 주장한다.

➡ _____

27 이제 생강으로 넘어가 보자.

➡ _____

28 생강을 보면 몸의 어떤 부위가 생각나는가?

➡ _____

29 생강이 마치 위장처럼 생기지 않았는가?

➡ _____

30 당신은 어쩌면 생강의 강한 맛과 냄새를 좋아하지 않을지도 모르지만, 이러한 맛과 냄새는 복통과 구토를 예방하는 생강의 특별한 성분에서 나온다.

➡ _____

_____

31 이러한 이유로 생강은 당신의 위장에 좋을 수 있다.

➡ _____

32 어떤 음식이 그 음식이 유익한 신체 부위의 생김새를 반영하고 있다는 점이 놀랍지 않은가?

➡ _____

33 흥미롭게도 그러한 음식은 상당히 많다.

➡ _____

34 가능한 한 그러한 음식을 많이 찾아서 다양한 음식을 먹도록 하라.

➡ _____

[01~03] 다음 글을 읽고 물음에 답하시오.

We all know that a diet ⓐcontaining a variety of foods keeps our bodies healthy. But sometimes we are not sure which foods are good (A)[at / for] which body parts. Nature, however, gives us a big clue. Look at the following examples. Each of these foods not only (B)[look / looks] like a certain body part but (C)[is / are] also good for that body part.

01 위 글의 밑줄 친 ⓐcontaining과 문법적 쓰임이 같은 것을 모두 고르시오.

① I won't give up playing soccer.
② He kept me waiting all day.
③ My job is selling cars.
④ Do you mind opening the window?
⑤ Jane was listening to music.

02 위 글의 괄호 (A)~(C)에서 문맥이나 어법상 알맞은 낱말을 골라 쓰시오.

➡ (A) _____ (B) _____ (C) _____

03 According to the passage, which is NOT true?

① A diet containing various foods keeps our bodies healthy.
② Nobody knows which foods are good for which body parts.
③ Nature gives us a big clue about which foods are good for which body parts.
④ Some foods look like a certain body part.
⑤ Some foods are also good for those body parts.

[04~07] 다음 글을 읽고 물음에 답하시오.

Slice open a tomato and compare it with the human heart. You will see that they look similar. They both have multiple hollow spaces and are red. (A)Researchers say that the chemicals that makes tomatoes red is good for your heart and blood. ____ⓐ____, eating tomatoes can lower your risk of heart disease.

04 위 글의 빈칸 ⓐ에 들어갈 알맞은 말을 고르시오.

① Instead
② However
③ Still
④ On the other hand
⑤ In addition

05 위 글의 밑줄 친 (A)에서 어법상 틀린 부분을 찾아 고치시오. (두 군데)

_____ ➡ _____, _____ ➡ _____

06 위 글의 제목으로 알맞은 것을 고르시오.

① Food Similar to Your Heart Is Good for Your Heart
② Various Foods That Keep Our Bodies Healthy
③ Which Foods Are Good for Which Body Parts?
④ Let's Compare Foods with Our Body Parts
⑤ The Chemicals That Make Tomatoes Red

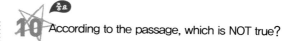

07 Which question CANNOT be answered after reading the passage?

① Which food looks like the human heart?
② What's the similarity between a tomato and the human heart?
③ What chemicals make tomatoes red?
④ Do tomatoes have any chemicals that are good for your heart and blood?
⑤ Can eating tomatoes lower your risk of heart disease?

[08~10] 다음 글을 읽고 물음에 답하시오.

A slice of carrot looks like the human eye. Carrots have some chemicals that can make vitamin A, (A)which improves your _____ⓐ_____. It helps your eyes process light and send a clear image to the brain. So if you want healthy eyes, eat carrots.

08 위 글의 빈칸 ⓐ에 들어갈 알맞은 말을 고르시오.

① heart   ② brain
③ stomach   ④ vision
⑤ hearing

서답형

09 위 글의 밑줄 친 (A)를 다음과 같이 바꿔 쓸 때 빈칸에 들어갈 알맞은 단어를 쓰시오.

➡ Carrots have some chemicals that can make vitamin A, _____ improves your vision.

10 According to the passage, which is NOT true?

① A slice of carrot looks like the human eye.
② There are some chemicals that can lower the effect of vitamin A in carrots.
③ Vitamin A helps your eyes process light.
④ Vitamin A helps your eyes send a clear image to the brain.
⑤ Eating carrots helps you have healthy eyes.

[11~13] 다음 글을 읽고 물음에 답하시오.

Look at the shape of a walnut. (①) Do you notice anything? (②) A walnut is divided into two parts, just like the brain. (③) Walnuts also have wrinkles, which the brain has too. (④) Studies show that walnuts help our brains stay healthy and active. (⑤) ⓐThey are also good for protecting Alzheimer's disease.

11 위 글의 흐름으로 보아, 주어진 문장이 들어가기에 가장 적절한 곳은?

Yes, it's very similar to the shape of the human brain!

①   ②   ③   ④   ⑤

서답형

12 위 글의 밑줄 친 ⓐ에서 흐름상 어색한 부분을 찾아 고치시오.

_____ ➡ _____

서답형

13 다음 빈칸 (A)와 (B)에 알맞은 단어를 넣어 호두와 인간의 뇌의 모양에 있어 서로 유사한 점을 완성하시오.

They are divided into (A)_____ _____ and have (B)_____.

[14~15] 다음 글을 읽고 물음에 답하시오.

Now, let's move on ____ⓐ____ ginger. What body part comes ____ⓐ____ mind when you see it? Doesn't it look like a stomach? You may not like ginger's strong taste or smell, but these come ____ⓑ____ a special chemical that prevents you ____ⓑ____ feeling sick and throwing up. For this reason, ginger can be good for your stomach.

14 위 글의 빈칸 ⓐ와 ⓑ에 각각 공통으로 들어갈 전치사가 바르게 짝지어진 것은?

     ⓐ   ⓑ   ⓐ   ⓑ

① for – from   ② on – in

③ to – from   ④ to – for

⑤ for – in

서답형

15 Why can ginger be good for your stomach? Fill in the blanks (A) and (B) with suitable words.

It's because a (A)_____ _____ of ginger prevents you from feeling sick and (B)_____ _____.

[16~19] 다음 글을 읽고 물음에 답하시오.

Cutting onions is not fun because ⓐit makes you cry. But try slicing one ⓑanyway. You can see that the inside looks a little like a human cell. ⓒScientists say that onions contain vitamin B, which helps make new, healthy cells.

서답형

16 위 글의 밑줄 친 ⓐit이 가리키는 것을 본문에서 찾아 쓰시오.

➡ _____

17 위 글의 밑줄 친 ⓑanyway와 바꿔 쓸 수 없는 말을 고르시오.

① anyhow   ② at any rate

③ by the way   ④ in any case

⑤ at all events

서답형

18 위 글의 밑줄 친 ⓒ를 다음과 같이 바꿔 쓸 때 빈칸에 들어갈 알맞은 말을 두 단어로 쓰시오.

➡ Scientists say that onions contain vitamin B, which helps _____ new, healthy cells.

서답형

19 위 글의 내용을 다음과 같이 정리하고자 한다. 빈칸 ①~③에 들어갈 알맞은 단어를 쓰시오.

Food: ①_____

Similar Body Part: ②_____ _____

_____

Benefit: ③_____ _____ in this food helps make new, healthy cells.

중요

20 주어진 글 다음에 이어질 글의 순서로 가장 적절한 것은?

We all know that a diet containing a variety of foods keeps our bodies healthy.

(A) Nature, however, gives us a big clue. Look at the following examples.

(B) Each of these foods not only looks like a certain body part but is also good for that body part.

(C) But sometimes we are not sure which foods are good for which body parts.

① (A) – (C) – (B)   ② (B) – (A) – (C)

③ (B) – (C) – (A)   ④ (C) – (A) – (B)

⑤ (C) – (B) – (A)

영역별 핵심문제

01 다음 중 밑줄 친 부분의 뜻풀이가 바르지 <u>않은</u> 것은?

① Form now on, <u>try</u> to go to bed earlier. (애쓰다)

② Did you get <u>enough</u> sleep? (충분한)

③ I went to bed after <u>midnight</u>, as usual. (정오)

④ You will see that they look <u>similar</u>. (비슷한)

⑤ So if you want <u>healthy</u> eyes, eat carrots. (건강한)

02 다음 중 〈보기〉에 있는 단어를 사용하여 자연스러운 문장을 만들 수 <u>없는</u> 것은?

┌─ 보기 ─┐
stay   contain   notice   variety

① He didn't even _____ I was sitting here.

② A walnut is _____ into two parts, just like the brain.

③ Walnuts help our brains _____ healthy and active.

④ Scientists say that onions _____ vitamin B.

⑤ Find as many as you can and try to eat a _____ of them.

03 주어진 내용으로 보아 다음 빈칸에 들어갈 말로 적절한 것을 고르시오.

Studies show that walnuts help our brains stay healthy and active. They are also good for _____ Alzheimer's disease.

① preventing   ② giving   ③ producing
④ containing   ⑤ finding

04 다음 밑줄 친 단어와 의미가 같은 단어를 고르시오.

B: Have you heard that chewing ice is bad for your teeth?
G: No, I haven't. Why is that?
B: It can <u>damage</u> your teeth. It can also make them too sensitive.

① harm   ② chew   ③ contain
④ improve   ⑤ compare

05 다음 대화의 순서가 바르게 배열된 것을 고르시오.

B: What are you doing in the living room?
G: I'm doing yoga.
B: You're working out by yourself?
G: Yes, I'm following this online video. It shows me all the steps.
B: Let me see. Wow, it's been watched two million times! I'm surprised that so many people have watched this video.
(A) It looks very convenient. You don't have to go out to exercise.
(B) That's right. That's why I love these programs. You should try them, too.
(C) I know! These kinds of programs are becoming popular right now.

① (A) – (C) – (B)   ② (B) – (A) – (C)
③ (B) – (C) – (A)   ④ (C) – (A) – (B)
⑤ (C) – (A) – (B)

[06~07] 다음 글을 읽고 물음에 답하시오.

G: Have you heard the term *body image*? It means "the way you see your own body." A lot of teens have a negative body image. They think they're too fat or too thin compared __(A)__ others. However, I want you to build a positive body image. Accept your body as (B)it is and give yourself praise every day. Remember, there is only one you, so don't compare yourself __(C)__ others. Loving yourself can make a big difference in your life.

06 위 글의 (A)와 (C)에 공통으로 알맞은 것은?

① at   ② of   ③ to
④ for   ⑤ from

07 위 글의 (B)it이 가리키는 것을 영어로 쓰시오.

➡ _____

08 위 글의 내용과 일치하지 <u>않는</u> 것은?

① The term '*body image*' means 'the way you see your own body.'
② Most teens have a bright body image.
③ Some teens think they are too thin.
④ Some teens think they are too fat.
⑤ You had better not compare yourself to others.

[09~10] 다음 대화를 읽고 물음에 답하시오.

B: Oh, I'm so hungry.
G: Why don't you eat some snacks before dinner?
B: _____(A)_____ I'll wait until dinner.
G: Okay, but have you heard that eating little and often is good for your health?
B: Really? I thought eating three meals a day was fine.
G: If you keep waiting until dinner, you will eat too much and too quickly. Eating little and __(B)__ prevents you from eating like that.
B: I see. Then I'll go eat an apple right now.

09 빈칸 (A)에 들어가기에 적절한 내용을 고르시오.

① Would you give me some?
② I already had some.
③ Let's have some snacks together.
④ I don't want to.
⑤ I'd like to have some snacks.

10 대화의 내용으로 보아 (B)에 들어가기에 적절한 것을 고르시오.

① none   ② often
③ three times   ④ apples
⑤ fruit

[11~12] 다음 대화를 읽고 물음에 답하시오.

G: What's this?
B: It's a smart band. It lets me check my health information on my smartphone.
G: What kind of information?
B: It shows how far I walk during the day and how well I sleep at night.
G: Interesting. I'm surprised that this small band can do all that.

11 위 대화를 읽고 알 수 <u>없는</u> 것은?

① A smart band is related with health.

② A smart band shows health information on the smartphone.

③ A smart band shows us how far we walk during the day.

④ A smart band is a kind of app for the smartphone.

⑤ The smart band lets him know how well he sleeps at night.

12 위 대화에서 a smart band가 구체적으로 하는 일을 우리말로 쓰시오.

➡ _____

_____

13 다음 대화의 빈칸 ⓐ~ⓔ에 들어갈 말로 어색한 것은?

B: You look tired. _____ⓐ_____

G: Yes, I did. I slept for over seven hours.

B: Okay. When did you go to bed?

G: _____ⓑ_____

B: That's probably what is making you tired. Have you heard that when you go to bed is very important?

G: _____ⓒ_____

B: Scientists say that going to bed late can make you feel tired the next day.

G: _____ⓓ_____

B: On the other hand, going to bed early can improve your memory and help you be more productive. _____ⓔ_____

① ⓐ Did you get enough sleep?

② ⓑ I went to bed after midnight, as usual.

③ ⓒ No, I haven't. Why is that?

④ ⓓ I already knew that.

⑤ ⓔ From now on, try to go to bed earlier.

Grammar

14 다음 빈칸에 들어갈 말로 알맞은 것은?

Our art room, _____ is on the third floor, is very big.

① where ② who ③ what
④ that ⑤ which

15 다음 중 어법상 <u>어색한</u> 문장을 <u>모두</u> 고르시오.

① The injured man was lain on the ground.

② Jim gave me the photos taken last week.

③ This is the most expensive car making in England.

④ The place was full of people enjoying themselves at the party.

⑤ I am looking for a girl wearing a blue skirt.

16 다음 그림을 참고하여 빈칸에 알맞게 쓰시오.

I met Jenny and Jack, _____ _____ I picked up garbage.

17 다음 두 문장의 의미가 같도록 빈칸에 알맞은 말을 쓰시오.

(1) Let's pick up the leaves fallen on the pavement.

= Let's pick up the leaves _____ fallen on the pavement.

(2) The boy listening to music is holding a spoon.

= The boy _____ listening to music is holding a spoon.

18 다음 문장을 의미에 맞게 바르게 바꿔 쓴 문장을 고르시오.

> I love Isabella, who is making it very hard for me to do so.

① I love Isabell, for she is making it very hard for me to do so.

② I love Isabella, though she is making it very hard for me to do so.

③ I love Isabella, and she is making it very hard for me to do so.

④ I love Isabella, so she is making it very hard for me to do so.

⑤ I love Isabella unless she is making it very hard for me to do so.

19 다음 ⓐ~ⓖ 중 어법상 옳은 것을 모두 고르시오.

> ⓐ My parents were moved by the letter written by my sister and me.
>
> ⓑ I ate freshly baking bread and jam this morning.
>
> ⓒ Abigail sitting on the sofa is reading a book.
>
> ⓓ Is the girl jumped rope with Daniel Amanda?
>
> ⓔ I'd like to see the movie *The Help*, which many people recommended.

> ⓕ I want to go to the party with Jia, that is a close friend of mine.
>
> ⓖ I know a girl, whose elder sister is a famous singer.

➡ _____

Reading

[20~22] 다음 글을 읽고 물음에 답하시오.

> (A)We all know that a diet containing a variety of foods keeps our bodies healthily. But sometimes we are not sure which foods are good for which body parts. Nature, ___ⓐ___, gives us a big clue. Look at the following examples. Each of these foods (B) not only looks like a certain body part but is also good for that body part.

20 위 글의 빈칸 ⓐ에 들어갈 알맞은 말을 고르시오.

① therefore   ② in addition

③ however   ④ similarly

⑤ for instance

21 위 글의 밑줄 친 (A)에서 어법상 틀린 부분을 찾아 고치시오.

_____ ➡ _____

22 위 글의 밑줄 친 (B)not only와 바꿔 쓸 수 없는 말을 모두 고르시오.

① not just   ② not merely

③ not mainly   ④ not simply

⑤ not mostly

[23~24] 다음 글을 읽고 물음에 답하시오.

Look at the shape of a walnut. Do you notice anything? Yes, it's very similar to the shape of the human brain! A walnut is divided into two parts, just like the brain. ⓐWalnuts also have wrinkles, that the brain has too. Studies show that walnuts help our brains stay healthy and active. They are also good for preventing Alzheimer's disease.

23 위 글의 밑줄 친 ⓐ에서 어법상 틀린 부분을 찾아 고치시오.

⟶

24 Which question canNOT be answered after reading the passage?

① What does the shape of a walnut look like?

② How many parts are a walnut and the human brain divided into?

③ Why do walnuts and the human brain have wrinkles?

④ What food helps our brains stay healthy and active?

⑤ What food is good for preventing Alzheimer's disease?

[25~27] 다음 글을 읽고 물음에 답하시오.

ⓐCutting onions (A)[is / are] not fun because it makes you (B)[cry / to cry]. But ⓑ어쨌든 하나를 잘라 보아라. You can see that the inside looks (C)[a few / a little] like a human cell. Scientists say that onions contain vitamin B, which helps make new, healthy cells.

25 위 글의 밑줄 친 ⓐCutting과 문법적 쓰임이 다른 것을 모두 고르시오.

① I don't like cutting onions.

② Cutting onions needs much patience.

③ She is cutting onions.

④ I saw him cutting onions.

⑤ Are you good at cutting onions?

26 위 글의 괄호 (A)~(C)에서 문맥이나 어법상 알맞은 낱말을 골라 쓰시오.

➡ (A) _____ (B) _____ (C) _____

27 위 글의 밑줄 친 ⓑ의 우리말에 맞게 4단어로 영작하시오.

➡ _____

[28~29] 다음 글을 읽고 물음에 답하시오.

Now, let's move on to ginger. What body part comes to mind when you see it? Doesn't it look like a stomach? You may not like ginger's strong taste or smell, ⓐbut these come from a special chemical that prevents you from feeling sick and overeating. For this reason, ginger can be good for your stomach.

28 위 글의 요지로 알맞은 것을 고르시오.

① Ginger and a stomach have some similarity.

② Ginger that looks like a stomach is good for a stomach.

③ Some people may not like ginger.

④ Ginger has strong taste or smell.

⑤ Ginger has a special chemical.

29 위 글의 밑줄 친 ⓐ에서 문맥상 낱말의 쓰임이 적절하지 않은 것을 찾아 알맞게 고치시오.

➡ _____ ➡ _____

01 다음 짝지어진 단어의 관계가 같도록 빈칸에 알맞은 것은?

> prevent : allow = _____ : refuse

① chew ② contain ③ search
④ accept ⑤ increase

02 다음 중 밑줄 친 단어 대신 쓸 수 있는 것을 모두 고르시오.

> The strong taste or smell of the ginger come from a special chemical that prevents you from feeling sick and throwing up.

① keeps ② tries ③ stops
④ helps ⑤ accepts

03 다음 영영풀이에 해당하는 단어를 고르시오.

> the organ inside your head that controls how you think, feel, and move

① brain ② stomach ③ eye
④ heart ⑤ mouth

04 빈칸에 알맞은 단어를 〈보기〉에서 골라 쓰시오.

> ┌─ 보기 ─┐
> hollow process popular chewing

(1) Have you heard that _____ ice is bad for your teeth?
(2) These kinds of programs are becoming _____ right now.
(3) They both have multiple _____ spaces and are red.
(4) Vitamin A helps your eyes _____ light.

05 다음 빈칸에 들어갈 말이 순서대로 바르게 짝지어진 것은?

> B: You look tired. Did you get __(A)__ sleep?
> G: Yes, I did. I slept for over seven hours.
> B: Okay. __(B)__ did you go to bed?
> G: I went to bed after midnight, as usual.

	(A)	(B)		(A)	(B)
①	enough – What		②	much – How
③	much – Why		④	little – Where
⑤	enough – When			

[06~08] 다음 대화를 읽고 물음에 답하시오.

> B: What is that? It looks nice.
> G: This is a magic cup. I carry it everywhere with me.
> B: _____(A)_____
> G: It's awesome. It tells me to drink water every two hours.
> B: Really? I'm (B)surprised that it can talk to you.
> G: It even asks me questions like "Aren't you thirsty?"
> B: That's so cool! But why are you trying to drink more water?
> G: Because drinking a lot of water can increase your energy and (C)혈액이 흐르는 것을 도와준다. (your blood)
> B: That's amazing. I should buy one!

06 빈칸 (A)에 들어가기에 적절한 것을 고르시오.

① What's the name of this cup?
② What's special about it?
③ How long have you used this?
④ How much does it hold?
⑤ Is it good for your health?

19 위 글의 밑줄 친 ⓐ의 우리말에 맞게 4단어로 영작하시오.
출제율 90%

➡ _____

20 위 글의 밑줄 친 ⓑ를 다음과 같이 바꿔 쓸 때 빈칸에 들어갈 알맞은 말을 각각 두 단어로 쓰시오.
출제율 90%

➡ It helps your eyes _____ light and _____ a clear image to the brain.

21 Fill in the blanks (A) and (B) with suitable words to match the content of the paragraph above.
출제율 90%

> Food: (A)_____
> Similar Body Part: eyes
> Benefits: They help improve your (B)_____.

[22~23] 다음 글을 읽고 물음에 답하시오.

> Isn't (A)it amazing ___ⓐ___ some foods mirror the body parts ___ⓑ___ they are good for? Interestingly, there are many other such foods. Find as many as you can and try to eat a variety of them.

22 위 글의 빈칸 ⓐ와 ⓑ에 공통으로 들어갈 알맞은 단어를 쓰시오.
출제율 90%

➡ _____

23 위 글의 밑줄 친 (A)it과 문법적 쓰임이 같은 것을 고르시오.
출제율 100%

① Did you hear it?
② I find it strange that she doesn't want to go.
③ It's impossible to get there in time.
④ It's ten past twelve.
⑤ Look! It's climbing up that tree.

[24~26] 다음 글을 읽고 물음에 답하시오.

> **Eat Chicken Sandwiches, Be Healthier**
> A chicken sandwich is a healthy food that I recommend. I'd like to talk about some of ⓐits ingredients that are good for our health. First, chicken breast is meat with a lot of protein and little fat. Onions contain lots of vitamin B. Also, walnuts are good for the brain. So ⓑwhy don't you try a chicken sandwich this weekend?

24 위 글의 종류로 알맞은 것을 고르시오.
출제율 100%

① review
② book report
③ summary
④ recommendation
⑤ essay

25 위 글의 밑줄 친 ⓐ에 해당하는 재료 세 가지와 그것들이 건강에 좋은 이유를 우리말로 쓰시오.
출제율 90%

➡ _____
_____
_____

26 위 글의 밑줄 친 ⓑ를 동명사를 사용하여 고치시오.
출제율 90%

➡ _____
_____

[01~03] 다음 대화를 읽고 물음에 답하시오.

> B: It's a smart band. It lets me check my ___(A)___ information on my smartphone.
>
> G: What kind of information?
>
> B: It shows (B)하루 동안 얼마나 걷는지 밤에 잠을 얼마나 잘 자는지.(how far, during the day, at night)
>
> G: Interesting. I'm ___(C)___ that this small band can do all that.

01 위 대화의 내용으로 보아 빈칸 (A)에 들어가기에 적절한 단어를 주어진 철자로 시작하여 쓰시오.

➡ h_____

02 밑줄 친 (B)의 우리말을 영어로 쓰시오. (주어진 단어를 반드시 포함할 것)

➡ _____

_____

03 빈칸 (C)에 들어가기에 적절한 단어를 주어진 철자로 시작하여 쓰시오.

➡ s_____

04 다음 주어진 단어를 이용해 빈칸을 완성하시오.

> A lot of teens have a negative body image. They think they're too fat or too thin _____ to others.

➡ _____ (compare)

05 다음 우리말에 맞게 빈칸에 알맞은 말을 쓰시오.

(1) 호두의 모양을 보아라.

➡ Look at the _____ of a walnut.

(2) 그러나 자연은 우리에게 큰 단서를 준다.

➡ Nature, however, gives us a big _____.

(3) 과학자들은 양파가 비타민 B를 포함하고 있다고 말한다.

➡ Scientists say that onions _____ vitamin B.

06 계속적 용법의 관계대명사를 사용하여 주어진 두 문장을 한 문장으로 바꾸시오.

(1) • I want to meet Jon Kim in person someday.
  • He is my favorite actor.

➡ _____

_____

(2) • Have you read the book, *The Last Leaf*.
  • It was written by O. Henry?

➡ _____

_____

07 다음 문장에서 **틀린** 것을 고쳐 다시 쓰시오.

(1) The men given out flyers are wearing caps.

➡ _____

_____

(2) The soldier injuring in the war was lying on the bed.

➡ _____

_____

(3) Last week I bought a new computer, that I like a lot.

➡ _____

_____

08 다음 우리말을 주어진 어휘를 이용하여 영작하시오.

(1) 그는 Huong과 결혼했는데, 그녀는 베트남 출신이다. (got married, is, Vietnam)

➡ _____

_____

(2) 그녀는 그 옷을 사고 싶어 했는데, 그것은 너무 비쌌다. (the dress, buy, want, too)

➡ _____

_____

(3) 정원에 심겨진 그 꽃은 매우 빠르게 자랐다. (plant, grow up, fast)

➡ _____

_____

[09~11] 다음 글을 읽고 물음에 답하시오.

We all know that a diet containing (A)a variety of foods keeps our bodies healthy. But sometimes we are not sure which foods are good for which body parts. Nature, however, gives us a big ___@___ . Look at the following examples. (B)Each of these foods not only looks like a certain body part but is also good for that body part.

09 주어진 영영풀이를 참고하여 빈칸 @에 철자 c로 시작하는 단어를 쓰시오.

something that helps you to find the answer to a problem or mystery

➡ _____

10 위 글의 밑줄 친 (A)a variety of와 바꿔 쓸 수 있는 단어를 철자 v로 시작하여 쓰시오.

➡ _____

11 위 글의 밑줄 친 (B)를 다음과 같이 바꿔 쓸 때 빈칸에 들어갈 알맞은 말을 세 단어로 쓰시오.

➡ Each of these foods is also good for that body part _____ looks like a certain body part.

[12~14] 다음 글을 읽고 물음에 답하시오.

Slice open a tomato and compare it with the human heart. You will see that they look (A) [different / similar]. They both have multiple hollow spaces and are red. Researchers say that the chemicals (B)[that / what] make tomatoes red are good for your heart and blood. In addition, eating tomatoes can (C) [increase / lower] your risk of heart disease.

12 위 글의 괄호 (A)~(C)에서 문맥이나 어법상 알맞은 낱말을 골라 쓰시오.

➡ (A) _____ (B) _____ (C) _____

13 What do a tomato and a human heart have in common? Fill in the blanks (A) and (B) with suitable words.

They both have multiple (A)_____ _____ and are (B)_____.

14 What makes tomatoes good for your heart and blood? Answer in English. (6 words)

➡ _____

01 Look at the tips about the body image and fill in the blanks.

> **Tips for Building a Positive Body Image**
> • _____ your body as it is. (여러분의 몸을 있는 그대로 받아들여라.)
> • Give yourself _____ every day. (매일 스스로를 칭찬하라.)
> • Don't _____ yourself to others. (자신을 다른 사람들과 비교하지 마라.)

02 다음 주어진 〈보기〉와 같이, 분사를 사용하여 빈칸에 자기 자신의 문장을 쓰시오.

> ┌─ 보기 ─
> I have a scarf <u>made in Italy</u>.

(1) I received a letter _____ from a strange girl.

(2) I'm excited when I walk on a road _____.

(3) I like the lady _____.

03 다음 내용을 바탕으로 반 친구들에게 건강에 좋은 음식을 추천하는 글을 쓰시오.

> **Food:** What food do you recommend?
> — fruit yogurt salad
> **Healthy Ingredients:** What are its healthy ingredients?
> — bananas, blueberries, yogurt
> **Benefits:** Why are these ingredients good for your health?
> — • bananas: plenty of potassium, which helps lower blood pressure
>   • blueberries: lots of vitamin C
>   • yogurt: a lot of calcium, which is good for our bones

> **Eat Fruit Yogurt Salad, Be Healthier**
> (A)_____ is a healthy food that I recommend. I'd like to talk about some of its ingredients that are good for our health. First, (B)_____ have plenty of potassium, which helps (C)_____. Blueberries have lots of (D)_____, and yogurt has a lot of calcium, which is good for our (E)_____. So why don't you try fruit yogurt salad this weekend?

단원별 모의고사

01 다음 문장의 빈칸에 들어갈 말로 적절한 것을 고르시오.

> However, I want you to build a positive body image. Accept your body as it is and give yourself praise every day. Remember, there is only one you, so don't _____ yourself to others. Loving yourself can make a big difference in your life.

① compare ② improve
③ lower ④ check
⑤ prevent

02 다음 대화의 빈칸에 들어갈 말로 적절한 것을 고르시오.

> B: You look tired. Did you get enough sleep?
> G: Yes, I did. I slept for over seven hours.
> B: Okay. When did you go to bed?
> G: I went to bed _____, as usual.

① by myself ② with the light off
③ after midnight ④ in the dark
⑤ regularly

03 다음 영영풀이에 해당하는 단어를 고르시오.

> having an empty space inside

① hollow ② sensitive
③ productive ④ positive
⑤ moved

[04~05] 다음 대화를 읽고 물음에 답하시오.

> B: What are you doing in the living room?
> G: I'm doing yoga.
> B: (A)혼자서 운동하고 있구나?
> G: Yes, I'm following this online video. It shows me all the steps.
> B: Let me see. Wow, it's been watched two million times! I'm surprised that so many people have watched this video.
> G: I know! These kinds of programs are becoming popular right now.
> B: It looks very convenient. You don't have to go out to exercise.
> G: That's right. That's why I love these programs. You should try them, too.

04 밑줄 친 (A)를 영어로 옮길 때 빈칸에 철자 w로 시작하는 단어를 쓰시오.

➡ You're _____ out by yourself?

05 위 대화를 읽고, 다음 질문에 해당하는 대답의 빈칸에 들어가기에 적절한 것을 고르시오.

> Q. Why does the girl love those programs?
> A. Because they are very _____ to follow and she doesn't have to go out to exercise.

① famous ② convenient
③ interesting ④ surprising
⑤ sensitive

06 다음 중 짝지어진 대화가 <u>어색한</u> 것을 고르시오.

① A: This is your birthday gift. It's a new phone.
B: Really? Thanks a lot.
② A: There's no class tomorrow.
B: It can't be true. Tomorrow is Tuesday.
③ A: The book says pigs are smarter than the dog.
B: Really? That's hard to believe.
④ A: It's snowing outside.
B: It's no wonder. It's April now.
⑤ G: Look, Eric. It's raining.
B: I can't believe it. It was completely sunny when I left home.

[07~09] 다음 대화를 읽고 물음에 답하시오.

B: You look tired. Did you get enough sleep?
G: Yes, I did. I slept for over seven hours.
B: Okay. When did you go to bed?
G: I went to bed after midnight, as usual.
B: That's probably that is making you tired. Have you heard that when you go to bed is very important?
G: No, I haven't. Why is that?
B: (A)과학자들은 늦게 자는 것이 너를 다음날 피곤하게 느끼도록 만들 수 있다고 말해. (going to bed, scientists, can, feel, make, say, that, late, tired, you, the next day).
G: I didn't know that.

07 위 대화에서 문맥상 또는 어법상 <u>어색한</u> 것을 찾아 고치시오.

➡ _____ ➡ _____

08 밑줄 친 (A)의 우리말을 주어진 어구를 배열하여 영어로 옮기시오.

➡ _____
_____

09 According to the passage, which one is true?

① The boy didn't get enough sleep.
② The girl slept for over seven hours.
③ The girl went to bed before midnight.
④ When you go to bed isn't important.
⑤ The girl will go to bed late as usual.

10 다음 빈칸 (A)와 (B)에 들어갈 말이 순서대로 바르게 짝지어진 것은?

B: Oh, I'm so hungry.
G: Why don't you eat some snacks before dinner?
B: I don't want to. I'll wait until dinner.
G: Okay, but have you heard that eating ____(A)____ is good for your health?
B: Really? I thought eating three meals a day was fine.
G: If you keep ____(B)____ until dinner, you will eat too much and too quickly. Eating little and often prevents you from eating like that.
B: I see. Then I'll go eat an apple right now.

	(A)	(B)
①	little and often	waiting
②	various foods	counting
③	three times	watching
④	much food	eating
⑤	in the house	suggesting

11 다음 주어진 단어의 형태를 알맞게 바꿔 문장을 완성하시오.

(1) Is the car _____ next to mine Ann's car? (park)

(2) The man _____ his car on the street is my English teacher. (park)

12 다음 빈칸에 들어갈 말을 순서대로 묶은 것은?

- Suyeon is my best friend, _____ works at an animal hospital.
- It is *The Mona Lisa*, _____ was painted by Leonardo da Vinci.

① that – that
② which – who
③ which – which
④ who – who
⑤ who – which

13 다음 밑줄 친 부분과 바꿔 쓸 수 있는 것은?

I broke the promise, <u>and it</u> made Megan upset.

① which
② that
③ what
④ who
⑤ where

14 다음 문장에서 어법상 어색한 것을 바르게 고쳐 다시 쓰시오.

(1) I can't find the books, that Evelyn gave them to me.

➡ _____

(2) She is my friend, Sophia, that is from Hungary.

➡ _____

(3) I got a C in my test, what made my mom disappointed.

➡ _____

(4) The girl who cleaning the room is my sister.

➡ _____
_____

(5) You can find a nice beach covering with white sand.

➡ _____
_____

[15~16] 다음 글을 읽고 물음에 답하시오.

We all know that a diet _____ⓐ_____ a variety of foods keeps our bodies healthy. But sometimes we are not sure ⓑ어떤 음식이 어떤 신체 부위에 좋은지. Nature, however, gives us a big clue. Look at the following examples. Each of these foods not only looks like a certain body part but is also good for that body part.

15 위 글의 빈칸 ⓐ에 contain을 알맞은 형태로 쓰시오.

➡ _____

16 위 글의 밑줄 친 ⓑ의 우리말에 맞게 한 단어를 보충하여, 주어진 어휘를 알맞게 배열하시오.

are / body parts / which / good / foods / which

➡ _____

[17~19] 다음 글을 읽고 물음에 답하시오.

(①) Slice open a tomato and compare it with the human heart. (②) They both have multiple hollow spaces and are red. (③) Researchers say that the chemicals that make tomatoes red are good for your heart and blood. (④) In addition, ⓐeating tomatoes can lower your risk of heart disease. (⑤)

17 위 글의 흐름으로 보아, 주어진 문장이 들어가기에 가장 적절한 곳은?

> You will see that they look similar.

①   ②   ③   ④   ⑤

18 아래 〈보기〉에서 위 글의 밑줄 친 ⓐeating과 문법적 쓰임이 같은 것의 개수를 고르시오.

> ┤ 보기 ├
> ① She left without saying a word.
> ② Look at the smiling girl.
> ③ I heard him speaking English.
> ④ Telling a lie is not good.
> ⑤ Seeing is believing.

① 1개   ② 2개   ③ 3개   ④ 4개   ⑤ 5개

19 위 글의 내용을 다음과 같이 정리하고자 한다. 빈칸 (A)~(C)에 들어갈 알맞은 단어를 본문에서 찾아 쓰시오.

> Food: tomatoes
> Similar Body Part: (A)_____
> Benefit: They are good for the
> (B)_____ and (C)_____.

[20~22] 다음 글을 읽고 물음에 답하시오.

A slice of carrot ⓐlooks like the human eye. Carrots have some chemicals that can make vitamin A, which improves your vision. It helps your eyes ⓑprocess light and send a clear image to the brain. So if you want healthy eyes, eat carrots.

20 위 글의 밑줄 친 ⓐlooks like와 바꿔 쓸 수 있는 말을 모두 고르시오.

① resembles   ② looks for
③ is similar to   ④ is alike
⑤ looks after

21 위 글의 밑줄 친 ⓑprocess와 같은 의미로 쓰인 것을 고르시오.

① It's a normal part of the learning process.
② I want to know the manufacturing process.
③ We're in the process of selling our house.
④ This machine can quickly process the data.
⑤ The process of making steel is complex.

22 Which vitamin helps improve your vision? Answer in English. (3 words)

➡ _____

Always Aware,
Always Prepared

 의사소통 기능

- 궁금증 표현하기
  I'm curious about how that happened.

- 경고하기 · 주의 주기
  Make sure you don't take the elevators in a real fire.

 언어 형식

- 과거완료
  One night in February, after I **had gone** to bed, an earthquake hit.

- 여러 가지 접속사
  Since it was my first time experiencing an earthquake, I didn't know how to react.

Words & Expressions

Key Words

- **actually** [ǽktʃuəli] 부 실제로
- **affect** [əfékt] 동 영향을 주다
- **avoid** [əvɔ́id] 동 ~을 피하다
- **amusement park** 놀이 공원
- **aware** [əwɛ́ər] 형 인식하는
- **cause** [kɔːz] 동 초래하다
- **character** [kǽriktər] 명 등장인물
- **chest** [tʃest] 명 가슴
- **collapse** [kəlǽps] 동 붕괴되다, 무너지다
- **common** [kámən] 형 흔한
- **confusion** [kənfjúːʒən] 명 혼란, 혼동
- **crawl** [krɔːl] 동 기어가다
- **curious** [kjúəriəs] 형 호기심이 많은
- **damage** [dǽmidʒ] 명 손상
- **destroy** [distrɔ́i] 동 파괴하다
- **disaster** [dizǽstər] 명 재난
- **drill** [dril] 명 훈련
- **earthquake** [ɔ́ːrθkweik] 명 지진
- **exactly** [igzǽktli] 부 정확하게
- **exit** [égzit] 동 나가다, 퇴장하다
- **flood** [flʌd] 명 홍수
- **heat wave** 폭염
- **heavy rain** 폭우
- **hit** [hit] 동 치다, 때리다, 부딪치다
- **immediately** [imíːdiətli] 부 즉시
- **include** [inklúːd] 동 포함하다
- **mention** [ménʃən] 동 언급하다
- **missing** [mísiŋ] 형 실종된
- **natural disaster** 자연 재해
- **nervously** [nɔ́ːrvəsli] 부 불안하게
- **occur** [əkɔ́ːr] 동 (일·사건 등이) 일어나다, 발생하다
- **panic** [pǽnik] 명 극심한 공포, 공황
- **perform** [pərfɔ́ːrm] 동 공연하다, 수행하다
- **prepared** [pripɛ́ərd] 형 준비된
- **press** [pres] 동 누르다
- **properly** [prápərli] 부 제대로, 적절하게
- **reaction** [riǽkʃən] 명 반응
- **realize** [ríːəlàiz] 동 깨닫다
- **recently** [ríːsntli] 부 최근에
- **scary** [skɛ́əri] 형 무서운
- **serious** [síəriəs] 형 심각한
- **shake** [ʃéikiŋ] 동 흔들리다, 흔들다
- **smash** [smæʃ] 동 세게 부딪치다
- **special effect** 특수 효과
- **suddenly** [sʌ́dnli] 부 갑자기, 급작스럽게
- **survival kit** 생존 장비
- **swing** [swiŋ] 동 흔들리다, 흔들다
- **tap** [tæp] 동 두들기다
- **urgently** [ɔ́ːrdʒəntli] 부 긴급하게
- **violently** [váiələntli] 부 격렬하게, 심하게
- **weight** [weit] 명 무게
- **whole** [houl] 형 전체의
- **wildfire** [wáildfaiər] 명 들불, 산불
- **worse** [wəːrs] 형 더 나쁜

Key Expressions

- **a large number of** 매우 많은
- **as well** 역시, 또한
- **at any time** 어느 때든지
- **a variety of** 다양한
- **based on ~** ~에 바탕을 둔
- **break into pieces** 산산조각이 나다
- **get a discount** 할인을 받다
- **in case of ~** ~의 경우에
- **in the middle of** ~의 한가운데에
- **keep ~ing** 계속해서 ~하다
- **make one's way** 가다, 나아가다
- **make sure** 확실하게 하다
- **pull over** 길 한쪽으로 차를 대다
- **put in** 집어넣다
- **pull out** 끌어내다
- **roll off** 굴러 떨어지다
- **take ~ seriously** 진지하게 받아들이다
- **tip over** 넘어지다, 기울어지다

Word Power

※ 서로 비슷한 뜻을 가진 어휘

- □ **damage** 손상 : **harm** 손해
- □ **include** 포함하다 : **involve** 포함하다
- □ **exactly** 정확하게 : **correctly** 정확하게
- □ **nervously** 불안하게 : **anxiously** 불안하게

- □ **affect** 영향을 주다 : **influence** 영향을 주다
- □ **properly** 적절하게 : **rightly** 적절하게
- □ **recently** 최근에 : **lately** 최근에
- □ **actually** 실제로 : **really** 실제로

※ 서로 반대의 뜻을 가진 어휘

- □ **aware** 아는, 인식하는 ↔ **unaware** 알지 못하는
- □ **destroy** 파괴하다 ↔ **construct** 건설하다
- □ **exit** 나가다 ↔ **enter** 들어가다
- □ **violently** 격렬하게 ↔ **nonviolently** 비폭력적으로

- □ **common** 흔한 ↔ **rare** 드문
- □ **include** 포함하다 ↔ **exclude** 제외하다
- □ **whole** 전체의 ↔ **partial** 부분적인
- □ **avoid** 피하다 ↔ **face** 마주하다

※ 명사 – 동사

- □ **confuse** 혼란을 주다 – **confusion** 혼란
- □ **weigh** 무게가 나가다 – **weight** 무게

- □ **destroy** 파괴하다 – **destruction** 파괴
- □ **perform** 공연하다 – **performance** 공연, 수행

English Dictionary

- □ **cause** 초래하다
  - → to make something happen, especially something bad
  - 어떤 일, 특히 나쁜 일이 일어나게 만들다
- □ **collapse** 붕괴하다
  - → to break apart and fall down suddenly
  - 갑자기 부서지거나 무너지다
- □ **common** 흔한
  - → happening often and to many people or in many places
  - 너무 많은 사람에게 또는 너무 많은 장소에서 자주 일어나는
- □ **crawl** 기어가다
  - → to move along on your hands and knees with your body close to the ground
  - 바닥에 몸을 가까이 하고 손이나 무릎으로 이동하다
- □ **curious** 호기심이 많은
  - → wanting to know about something
  - 어떤 것에 대해 알기를 원하는
- □ **destroy** 파괴하다
  - → to damage something so badly that it no longer exists or cannot be used or repaired
  - 더 이상 존재하거나 사용할 수 없거나 고칠 수 없도록 심하게 손상시키다

- □ **disaster** 재난
  - → a sudden event such as a flood, storm, or accident which causes great damage or suffering
  - 큰 손상이나 고통을 초래하는 홍수, 폭풍 또는 사고와 같은 갑작스러운 사건
- □ **earthquake** 지진
  - → a sudden shaking of the Earth's surface that often causes a lot of damage
  - 종종 많은 손상을 가져오는 지표면의 갑작스러운 흔들림
- □ **exit** 나가다, 퇴장하다
  - → to leave a place
  - 어떤 장소를 떠나다
- □ **flood** 홍수
  - → a very large amount of water that covers an area that is usually dry
  - 대개는 건조한 한 지역을 덮는 아주 많은 양의 물
- □ **include** 포함하다
  - → to make someone or something part of a larger group
  - 어떤 사람 또는 어떤 것을 더 큰 집단의 구성원이 되도록 만들다
- □ **properly** 적절하게
  - → correctly, or in a way that is considered right
  - 정확하게 또는 올바르다고 여겨지는 방식으로

01 다음 짝지어진 단어의 관계가 같도록 빈칸에 알맞은 말을 고르시오.

> damage : harm = _____ : correct

① exact
② aware
③ serious
④ legal
⑤ worse

02 다음 빈칸에 들어갈 말로 적절한 것은?

> I was driving home when the shaking started. But I _____ immediately. I'm listening to the radio to find out what's going on.

① pulled in
② pulled out
③ pulled down
④ pulled off
⑤ pulled over

03 다음 중 영영풀이가 어색한 것은?

① flood: a very large amount of water that covers an area that is usually dry
② storm: a sudden shaking of the Earth's surface that often causes a lot of damage
③ disaster: a sudden event such as a flood, storm, or accident which causes great damage or suffering
④ common: happening often and to many people or in many places
⑤ exit: to leave a place

04 다음 중 밑줄 친 부분의 뜻풀이가 바르지 않은 것은?

① We nervously made our way down the stairs. (내려갔다)
② What natural disasters have you experienced? (재난)
③ Make sure you place your hands in the middle of the person's chest. (한 가운데에)
④ Make sure that you exit the building immediately. (들어가다)
⑤ Soon the whole room began to shake violently. (전체의)

05 다음 중 〈보기〉에 있는 단어를 사용하여 자연스러운 문장을 만들 수 없는 것은? (대·소문자 무시)

> ┤ 보기 ├
> rang   based   crawling   destroyed

① We started _____ toward the door.
② _____ on the report, earthquakes are fourth.
③ Many houses and building were _____ by the earthquake.
④ Then suddenly the _____ seemed to stop.
⑤ At that moment, my mom's cell phone _____.

서답형

06 다음 밑줄 친 단어와 의미가 같은 단어를 쓰시오. (주어진 철자로 시작할 것)

> Although I had done many earthquake drills in school, I had never thought I'd experience a real earthquake.

➡ t_____

01 다음 주어진 단어를 이용해 빈칸을 완성하시오.

> Performing CPR _____ can save someone's life. Here are the steps for proper CPR.

➡ _____ (proper)

 02 다음 빈칸에 공통으로 들어가기에 적절한 단어를 쓰시오.

> • In case of yellow dust, make sure that you wear a mask when you go _____.
> • I'm listening to the radio right now to find _____ what's going on.

➡ _____

03 다음 문장의 빈칸에 들어가기에 적절한 단어를 주어진 철자로 시작하여 쓰시오.

> 나는 건물이 붕괴될까봐 걱정이 되기 시작했다.
> ➡ I started to worry that the building would c_____.

04 다음 우리말에 맞게 빈칸에 알맞은 말을 쓰시오.

(1) 나는 여전히 정확하게 무엇이 일어나고 있는지 몰랐다.
   ➡ I still didn't know what _____ was happening.
(2) 엄마는 나와 동생을 침대 밖으로 끌어내셨다.
   ➡ My mom _____ me and my brother _____ _____ bed.
(3) 화재가 났을 경우에는 무엇을 해야 할까요?
   ➡ _____ _____ _____ a fire, what should I do?

05 다음 짝지어진 단어의 관계가 같도록 빈칸에 알맞은 말을 쓰시오.

> destroy : construct = _____ : exclude

 06 빈칸에 알맞은 단어를 〈보기〉에서 골라 쓰시오.

> ┤ 보기 ├
> scared   seriously   prepared
> made our way

(1) We nervously _____ down the stairs and outside.
(2) I still get _____ when I remember that night.
(3) After that night, I began to take earthquake drills _____.

07 다음 영영풀이에 해당하는 단어를 주어진 철자로 쓰시오.

> to damage something so badly that it no longer exists or cannot be used or repaired

➡ d_____

08 밑줄 친 단어의 반대말을 쓰시오. (주어진 철자로 시작할 것)

> A: In case of a fire, what should I do?
> B: Make sure that you cover your mouth with a wet cloth.
> A: Anything else?
> B: Make sure that you <u>exit</u> the building immediately.

➡ e_____

Conversation

1 궁금증 표현하기

- **I'm curious about how that happened.** 나는 어떻게 그것이 일어났는지 궁금하다.

■ 'curious'는 '호기심이 생기는, 궁금한'이라는 뜻이다. 상대방에게 궁금한 것을 질문으로 표현하는 대신 '나는 ~에 관하여 호기심이 생긴다, ~에 관하여 궁금하다'라는 뜻으로 'I'm curious about ~'의 형태로 궁금증이나 호기심을 표현할 수 있다. '나는 ~이 궁금하다.'라는 뜻의 'I wonder ~.' 또는 'I would like to know ~.'를 쓸 수도 있다.

■ '나는 ~에 대하여 궁금하다'의 의미는 '나는 ~을 알고 싶다'의 의미로 'I want to know ~'의 의미이기 도 하다. 좀 더 직접적으로 'Do you know ~?'라는 형태로 물어볼 수도 있다. 보통 '~에 대하여 궁금하 다.'는 표현을 들었을 때 그 내용을 알면 자세한 설명을 해주고 그렇지 않을 때는 '같이 알아보자'는 표 현 등이 따라 온다.

궁금증 표현하기

- I am curious about ~. 나는 ~이 궁금하다.
- I wonder ~. 나는 ~인지 궁금하다.
- I would like/want to know ~. 나는 ~이 알고 싶다.

궁금증을 나타내는 유사 표현

- Do you know ~? 너는 ~을 알고 있니?
- I'd be very interested to know ~. 나는 ~이 알고 싶다.
- Can you tell me about ~? ~에 대해 말해 줄 수 있니?

핵심 Check

1. 다음 대화의 순서를 바르게 배열하시오.

A: I heard that there have been many wildfires in Korea.

(A) I'm curious about when it happened.

(B) Yes. There was a big one in Yangyang.

(C) It happened in 2005.

① (A) – (C) – (B) ② (B) – (A) – (C)
③ (B) – (C) – (A) ④ (C) – (A) – (B)
⑤ (C) – (B) – (A)

② 경고하기 · 주의 주기

> • Make sure you don't take the elevators in a real fire.
> 실제 화재에서는 절대로 엘리베이터를 타지 않도록 해라.

■ 상대방에게 주의 사항을 알려주어서 경고할 때는 'Make sure ~'를 사용한다. 'make sure ~'는 '반드시 ~하도록 하다' '~임을 확인하다'의 의미로 상대에게 '반드시 확인하라.'의 의미로 경고하는 경우에 자주 쓰인다. 'Be sure ~'도 마찬가지 의미가 될 수 있다. 우리말로 해석할 때는 '~을 확실하게 해라' '반드시 ~해라'가 된다.

■ 'Make sure' 또는 'Be sure' 뒤에는 접속사 that이 이끄는 절이 온다. 그래서 'Make sure that 주어+동사 ~', 'Be sure that 주어+동사 ~'의 형태가 되지만 접속사 that은 대부분 생략하고 'Make sure 주어+동사 ~', 'Be sure 주어+동사 ~'의 형태가 된다.

■ 보통 상대방에게 직접적인 경고를 할 때는 '~을 조심해라.'의 의미로 'Watch out for ~', 'Look out for ~'를 쓴다. 'Make sure you don't ~' 'Be sure you don't ~'은 '절대로 ~하지 마라'의 의미이다.

경고하기 · 주의하기 표현

• Make sure (that) ~. : 반드시 ~해라.

• Watch out for ~. : ~을 조심해라.

• Make sure you don't ~. : ~하지 않도록 명심해라.

• You need to keep in mind that ~ : ~라는 사실을 명심해라.

• Be sure (that) ~. : ~을 확실하게 해라.

• Look out for ~. : ~을 잘 살펴라.

• Be careful not to ~. : ~하지 않도록 조심해라.

핵심 Check

2. 다음 대화의 밑줄 친 말 대신 쓸 수 있는 것을 고르시오.

B: Mom, what else do we need to put in the natural disaster survival kit?

W: Well, we need water, some food, and radio.

B: Anything else, Mom?

W: Oh, <u>make</u> sure that you include batteries for the radio.

① be   ② keep   ③ need   ④ watch   ⑤ look

3. 우리말과 일치하도록 주어진 어구를 배열하여 문장을 만드시오.

A: In case of yellow dust, what should I do?

B: _____ (밖에 나갈 때는 반드시 마스크를 착용하도록 해라.)

(that / make / you / you / sure / a mask / when / wear / go out)

Listen & Talk 1 B

G: There seem to be many natural disasters in Korea these days.

B: I agree. There was an earthquake in the south last week. Also a storm is coming this week.

G: I'm curious about ❶which type of natural disaster causes the most damage in Korea.

B: Actually I read a report yesterday about the damage from each type of natural disaster. Number one is storms.

G: I see. I guess earthquakes are second.

B: No, second is heavy rain, and third is heavy snow.

G: What about earthquakes?

B: Based on the report, earthquakes are fourth. But the damage from earthquakes ❷has been increasing recently because they have been happening more often in Korea.

G: I see. It seems like we have to be prepared for a variety of natural disasters in Korea.

G: 요즘 한국에서 많은 자연 재해가 있는 것 같아.

B: 동의해. 지난주에 남부에서 지진이 있었어. 또한 이번 주에는 태풍이 올 거야.

G: 나는 어떤 종류의 자연 재해가 한국에서 가장 큰 피해를 주는지 궁금해.

B: 사실 나는 어제 각 유형의 자연 재해로 인한 피해에 관한 보고서를 읽었어. 첫 번째가 폭풍이야.

G: 그렇구나. 지진이 두 번째인 것 같아.

B: 아니야. 두 번째는 폭우이고 세 번째는 폭설이야.

G: 지진은?

B: 보고서에 따르면, 지진은 네 번째야. 하지만 최근 한국에서 지진이 더 자주 일어나기 때문에 지진으로 인한 피해가 증가하고 있어.

G: 그렇구나. 한국에서는 다양한 자연 재해에 대비를 해야 할 것 같아.

---

❶ 'which type of ~'는 간접의문문으로 전치사 about의 목적어이다.

❷ 'has been increasing'은 현재완료진행형으로 과거로부터 시작해서 지금도 계속되는 일을 나타낸다.

Check(√) True or False

(1) Storms cause the most damage in Korea.　　　　　　　　　　T ☐ F ☐

(2) The damage from heavy rain is increasing recently.　　　　　T ☐ F ☐

Listen & Talk 2 B

W: Performing ❶CPR properly can save someone's life. Here are the steps for proper CPR. First, check that the person needs help. Tap the person and shout, "Are you okay?" If there's no reaction, call 119 for help. Second, ❷listen, look, and feel for breathing. If the person's not breathing, begin CPR. Make sure you place your hands in the middle of the person's chest. Use your body weight to press harder on the chest. After 30 presses, give the person two breaths. ❸Keep doing CPR until help arrives.

W: 제대로 심폐소생술을 수행하는 것은 누군가의 생명을 구할 수 있습니다. 여기 적절한 심폐소생술을 위한 단계가 있습니다. 첫째, 그 사람이 도움을 필요로 하는지 확인하십시오. 그 사람을 두드리며 "괜찮으세요?"라고 큰소리로 외치세요. 반응이 없으면 119에 전화를 걸어 도움을 요청하세요. 둘째, 호흡을 하는지 듣고, 보고, 느끼세요. 그 사람이 숨을 쉬지 않으면 심폐소생술을 시작하세요. 손을 반드시 그 사람의 가슴 가운데에 놓도록 하세요. 가슴을 더 세게 누르기 위해 체중을 이용하세요. 30번 누른 후, 그 사람에게 두 번 바람을 불어 넣으시오. 도움이 올 때까지 심폐소생술을 계속하세요.

---

❶ CPR = 심폐소생술 (cardiopulmonary resuscitation)

❷ 호흡이 있는지 살피라는 의미로 귀, 눈, 촉감을 모두 동원해서 확인한다는 의미로 'listen, look, feel'을 사용했다.

❸ keep ~ing = ~을 계속하다

Check(√) True or False

(3) When someone needs help, first begin CPR.　　　　　　　　T ☐ F ☐

(4) You should place your hands in the middle of the person's chest to perform CPR.　　T ☐ F ☐

Listen & Talk 1 A

B: There was a big flood in Europe. Did you hear about it?
G: No, I didn't. But floods aren't that common in winter, ❶are they? I'm curious about how that happened.
B: ❷Me too. Let's do some online research.

❶ be동사가 있는 문장의 부가의문문이다.
❷ Me too. = I agree.

 Listen & Talk 1 C

B: Hey, did you hear about the big fires in California?
G: No, I didn't. How serious are they?
B: They've destroyed ❶a large number of houses and other buildings.
G: Are the fires still going on?
B: Yes, actually the wind has made the fires worse. I hope all the people ❷living there are okay.
G: ❸So do I. I'm curious about how many people had to leave their homes.
B: Actually more than 20,000 people had to leave their homes, and about 400 people are missing in that area.
G: That's terrible. I hope they're somewhere safe.

❶ 'a number of'를 강조하여 'a large number of'라고 했다.
❷ 현재분사 living은 people을 뒤에서 수식한다.
❸ 'So do I.'는 '나도 마찬가지야.'의 의미로 'Me, too.' 또는 'I agree.'에 해당한다.

 Listen & Talk 1 D

A: I heard that there have been many wildfires in Korea.
B: Yes. There was a big ❶one in Yangyang.
A: I'm curious about ❷when it happened.
B: It happened in 2005.

❶ one = wildfire
❷ 전치사 about의 목적어로 간접의문문이다.

 Listen & Talk 2 A

B: Mom, what else do we need to put in the natural disaster survival kit?
W: Well, we need water, some food, and a radio.
B: ❶Anything else, Mom?
W: Oh, ❷make sure that you include batteries for the radio.

❶ Anything else? = Is there anything else?
❷ 접속사 that은 생략 가능하다.

 Listen & Talk 2 D

A: ❶In case of a fire, what should I do?
B: Make sure that you cover your mouth with a wet cloth.
A: Anything else?
B: Make sure that you exit the building immediately.

❶ In case of ~ = ~의 경우에

 Do It Yourself A

G: Did you hear that earthquakes ❶are occurring more often in Korea than before?
B: Oh, really? I've never felt an earthquake in Korea.
G: They usually occur in the southern part of Korea, but now they are occurring in other places as well.
B: I didn't know that. I'm curious about ❷why earthquakes have occurred so often in Korea recently.
G: ❸Why don't we do some research to find out?
B: Sounds good, but where do we look first?
G: How about asking our science teacher first? I think she can help us.
B: Okay. ❹Let's go and find her.

❶ 현재진행시제를 사용하여 현재에 계속되는 일을 나타내고 있어서 시제 일치를 시키지 않았다.
❷ 전치사 about의 목적어가 되는 간접의문문이다.
❸ Why don't we ~? = ~하는 게 어때?
❹ go and find = go to find

● 다음 우리말과 일치하도록 빈칸에 알맞은 말을 쓰시오.

Listen & Talk 1 A

B: There _____ a big _____ in Europe. Did you _____ about it?

G: No, I didn't. But _____ aren't that _____ in winter, _____ they? I'm _____ about _____ that happened.

B: Me too. Let's do some online _____.

Listen & Talk 1 B

G: There _____ to be many _____ _____ in Korea _____ days.

B: I agree. There was an _____ in the _____ last week. Also a _____ is coming this week.

G: I'm _____ about _____ type of _____ _____ causes the _____ _____ in Korea.

B: Actually I read a _____ yesterday about the _____ from _____ _____ of natural disaster. Number one is storms.

G: I see. I _____ earthquakes are _____.

B: No, second is _____ rain, and third is heavy _____.

G: _____ about earthquakes?

B: _____ on the report, _____ are fourth. But the _____ from earthquakes has _____ _____ recently _____ they have _____ happening more often in Korea.

G: I see. It _____ _____ we have to be _____ for a _____ of _____ _____ in Korea.

Listen & Talk 1 C

B: Hey, did you _____ _____ the big _____ in California?

G: No, I didn't. How _____ are they?

B: They've _____ a large number of _____ and _____ buildings.

G: _____ the fires still _____ _____?

B: Yes, _____ the wind has made the fires _____. I hope all the people _____ _____ are okay.

G: _____ _____ I. I'm _____ about how many people had to _____ their homes.

B: _____ more than 20,000 people had to _____ their homes, and about 400 people are _____ in that area.

G: That's _____. I hope they're _____ safe.

해석

B: 유럽에 큰 홍수가 있었어. 그것에 대해 들었니?

G: 아니. 하지만 겨울에는 홍수가 그렇게 흔하지 않아, 그렇지 않니? 나는 어떻게 그런 일이 일어났는지 궁금해.

B: 나도 그래. 온라인 검색을 해보자.

G: 요즈음 한국에서 많은 자연 재해가 있는 것 같아.

B: 동의해. 지난주에 남부에서 지진이 있었어. 또한 이번 주에는 태풍이 올 거야.

G: 나는 어떤 종류의 자연 재해가 한국에서 가장 큰 피해를 주는지 궁금해.

B: 사실 나는 어제 각 유형의 자연 재해로 인한 피해에 관한 보고서를 읽었어. 첫 번째가 폭풍이야.

G: 그렇구나. 지진이 두 번째인 것 같아.

B: 아니야. 두 번째는 폭우이고 세 번째는 폭설이야.

G: 지진은?

B: 보고서에 따르면, 지진은 네 번째야. 하지만 최근 한국에서 지진이 더 자주 일어나기 때문에 지진으로 인한 피해가 증가하고 있어.

G: 그렇구나. 한국에서는 다양한 자연 재해에 대비를 해야 할 것 같아.

B: 안녕. 너 캘리포니아에서 일어난 큰 화재에 대해 들었니?

G: 아니. 얼마나 심각하니?

B: 많은 집들과 다른 건물들을 파괴했어.

G: 아직도 화재가 진행되고 있니?

B: 그래. 사실 바람이 화재를 더 악화시켰어. 나는 거기 사는 모든 사람들이 괜찮기를 바라.

G: 나도 그래. 얼마나 많은 사람들이 집을 떠나야 했는지 궁금해.

B: 사실 2만 명 이상이 집을 떠나야 했고, 약 400명이 실종되었어.

G: 끔찍하구나. 나는 그들이 안전한 곳에 있기를 바라.

[01~03] 다음 대화를 읽고 물음에 답하시오.

G: There seem to be many natural disasters in Korea these days.

B: I agree. There was an earthquake in the south last week. Also a storm is coming this week.

G: (A)나는 궁금하다 which type of natural disaster causes the most damage in Korea.

B: Actually I read a report yesterday about the damage from each type of natural disaster. Number one is storms.

G: I see. I guess earthquakes are second.

B: No, second is heavy rain, and third is heavy snow.

G: (B)   earthquakes?

B: Based on the report, earthquakes are fourth. But the damage from earthquakes has been increasing recently because they have been happening more often in Korea.

G: I see. (C)한국에서는 다양한 자연 재해에 대하여 준비가 되어야 할 것 같다.(it, like, seems, have to, prepared for, be, we, natural disasters, a variety of, in Korea)

01 밑줄 친 (A)의 우리말에 맞게 영어로 쓰시오. (about 포함)

➡ _____

02 대화의 내용으로 보아 빈칸 (B)에 들어가기에 적절한 말을 2단어로 쓰시오.

➡ _____

03 밑줄 친 (C)의 우리말을 주어진 어구를 배열하여 영작하시오.

➡ _____
_____

[04~06] 다음 글을 읽고 물음에 답하시오.

W: Performing CPR properly can save someone's life. Here are the steps for proper CPR. First, check that the person needs help. Tap the person and shout, "Are you okay?" If there's no   (A) , call 119 for help. Second, listen, look, and feel for breathing. If the person's not breathing, begin CPR. (B)반드시 그 사람의 가슴 가운데에 손을 놓도록 하세요.(sure, place, your hands, you, make, the person's chest, in the middle of). Use your body weight to press harder on the chest. After 30 presses, give the person two breaths. Keep doing CPR until help arrives.

04 빈칸 (A)에 들어가기에 적절한 단어를 쓰시오.

➡ _____

05 주어진 어구를 배열하여 밑줄 친 (B)의 우리말을 영작하시오.

➡ _____
_____

06 When should we start CPR on the person? Answer in English. (9 words)

➡ _____
_____

Grammar
교과서

① 과거완료

> * One night in February, after I **had gone** to bed, an earthquake hit.
>   2월 어느 날 밤, 내가 잠자리에 든 후에 지진이 일어났다.
> * It was more beautiful than I **had imagined**. 그건 내가 상상했던 것보다 더 아름답더군요.

■ 과거완료는 과거 이전에 일어난 일이 과거의 어느 시점까지 영향을 미칠 때 쓰며, 'had+과거분사'의 형태로 쓴다. 과거완료도 현재완료처럼 완료, 계속, 경험, 결과의 용법이 있다. 또한 과거의 어느 시점보다 먼저 일어난 일이나 상태를 나타낼 때도 쓰이며 이것을 보통 '대과거'라고 한다.

* I **had** just **finished** my homework when he called me. 〈완료〉 그가 내게 전화했을 때 나는 막 숙제를 마쳤다.

* She **had cleaned** her house for two hours before I visited her. 〈계속〉
  그녀는 내가 그녀를 방문하기 전에 2시간 동안 그녀의 집을 청소했다.

* He **had** never **seen** a live tiger before.. 〈경험〉 그는 전에 살아 있는 호랑이를 한 번도 본 적이 없었다.

* He **had gone** to Seoul when I visited him. 〈결과〉 내가 그를 방문했을 때 그는 서울로 가고 없었다.

* He realized that he **had met** her before. 〈대과거〉 그는 전에 그녀를 만난 적이 있다는 것을 깨달았다. 〈대과거〉

■ 한 문장에 두 가지 과거의 일이 나올 때, 두 동작이 거의 동시에 일어났거나 시간차가 거의 없이 연속적으로 일어났을 경우에는 단순과거로 표현한다. 또, 접속사 after나 before가 쓰여 두 동작의 전후 관계가 명백할 때도 단순과거로 표현할 수 있다.

* I **showed** them how to do it and they **tried**. 나는 그들에게 그것을 어떻게 하는지 보여주었고, 그들은 해 보았다.
  〈시간차가 거의 없는 연속 동작〉

* The village **was** quiet before they **came**. 그들이 오기 전에는 마을이 조용했다. 〈전후 관계가 명백함〉

핵심 Check

1. 다음 괄호 안에서 알맞은 말을 고르시오.
   (1) When she came home, her husband (had done / does) the dishes already.
   (2) Judy knew that Megan (had finished / finished) her homework the previous day.
   (3) The train (has / had) just left when I arrived at the station.

② 여러 가지 접속사

> • **Since** it was my first time experiencing an earthquake, I didn't know how to react. 지진을 경험한 것이 처음이었기 때문에, 나는 어떻게 반응해야 할지 몰랐다.

■ 접속사란 단어와 단어, 구와 구, 절과 절을 연결시켜 주는 말이다.

(1) 이유를 나타내는 since

■ since는 '~이기 때문에'라는 의미로 이유를 나타내는 접속사로 쓰인다. since가 이끄는 부사절이 이유를 나타내고, 주절이 그 결과를 나타내며, 이때의 since는 as나 because로 바꿔 쓸 수 있다.

- He couldn't go out **since** he was sick. 그는 아파서 나갈 수 없었다.
  = He couldn't go out **as[because]** he was sick.

cf. since와 같은 의미인 due to나 because of 등은 뒤에 (대)명사나 동명사가 온다.

- He quit the job **because of** his health. 그는 건강상의 이유로 직장을 그만 두었다.

■ since는 이외에도 전치사나 접속사로 '~한 이래로'의 뜻으로 쓰인다.

- He has worked **since** he left school. 그는 학교를 나온 이래 일하고 있다.

(2) 양보절을 이끄는 although

■ although는 '비록 ~일지라도'라는 의미로 양보절을 이끌며 이끄는 절의 내용과 주절의 내용은 서로 상반되고 even though나 though로 바꿔 쓸 수 있다.

- **Although** he is rich, he is not happy. 그는 부자지만 행복하지는 않다.

cf. although와 비슷한 의미인 despite는 전치사이므로 뒤에 (대)명사나 동명사가 나온다.

- He is very strong **despite** his age. 그는 노령임에도 불구하고 매우 정정하다.

cf. even if는 '만일 ~라고 할지라도(가정)' 정도의 뜻이다.

■ **기타 접속사**

(1) 시간 관계를 나타내는 접속사: after, before, as soon as, when, while, until 등
(2) 조건을 나타내는 접속사: if, unless, in case (that), in the event (that) 등
(3) 목적을 나타내는 접속사: so that, in order that 등

핵심 Check

2. 다음 빈칸에 들어갈 말을 〈보기〉에서 골라 쓰시오.

> ─ 보기 ─
> although   after   since

(1) _____ I'm broke, I don't need your help.

(2) We don't worry _____ we are armed with effective tools.

(3) Several years _____ they'd split up, they met again by chance in Paris.

01 다음 빈칸에 들어갈 말로 알맞은 것은?

I recognized her at once as I _____ her before.

① see   ② saw   ③ seen
④ have seen   ⑤ had seen

02 다음 괄호 안에서 알맞은 말을 고르시오.

(1) When I called, he (already started / had already started).

(2) I admitted to her that I (lied / had lied) to her.

(3) (Although / When) the sun was shining, it wasn't very warm.

(4) I was here a bit early (after / since) my watch gained time.

03 다음 두 문장을 한 문장으로 바꾸어 쓸 때 알맞게 표현한 것을 고르시오.

• Mike is not honest.
• I don't believe him.

① Although Mike is not honest, I don't believe him.
② Mike is not honest although I don't believe him.
③ Since Mike is not honest, I don't believe him.
④ Mike is not honest since I don't believe him.
⑤ Mike is not honest after I don't believe him.

04 다음 우리말에 맞게 주어진 어휘를 바르게 배열하시오.

(1) 작년까지 Linda는 Paris를 방문한 적이 전혀 없었다. (until로 시작할 것)
   (year, Linda, Paris, had, last, until, visited, never)
   ➡ _____

(2) 그는 부자였지만, 사람들은 그가 가난한 줄 알았다. (접속사로 시작할 것)
   (he, he, people, was, was, thought, poor, rich, although)
   ➡ _____

(3) 나는 간밤에 너무 무서워서 잠을 잘 수 없었다. ('주절+종속절'의 구조로 쓸 것)
   (I, I, night, couldn't, afraid, sleep, was, last, so, since)
   ➡ _____

01 다음 중 어법상 어색한 것은?

① Our little friends had finished the shoes when we got up.
② They talked about the accident that happened there a few hours before.
③ When I arrived at the bus stop, the bus had already left.
④ He had never been abroad before he became thirty.
⑤ The plane had already taken off when I reached the airport.

02 다음 중 어법상 바르지 않은 것은?

① Although we have to say goodbye for now, we can meet next year.
② Though it rained heavily, we played outside.
③ Even though she had an umbrella, she got wet in the rain.
④ It started to rain though we decided to leave.
⑤ Though I bought it only yesterday, I'll give it to you.

03 다음 빈칸에 알맞은 말이 바르게 짝지어진 것은?

• _____ he was born in England, he is a Korean boy.
• It was more beautiful than I _____.

① Even though – had imagined
② Since – had imagined
③ Even though – imagined
④ Since – imagined
⑤ Because – have imagined

서답형

04 다음 괄호 안에서 알맞은 말을 고르시오.

(1) When he came home, his son had (finish / finished) homework.
(2) I realized that I (had made / made) a big mistake.
(3) I (had prepared / prepared) to be a musician since I was a kid.
(4) (Although / Because) he was tall, he couldn't touch the ceiling.
(5) (Since / Although) I didn't have lunch today, I had a big dinner.
(6) (Despite / Though) I love snow, I hope it will stop snowing.

05 주어진 문장의 틀린 부분을 찾아, 올바르게 고친 것을 고르시오.

When I reached home, my brother go to bed and only Mom was awake.

① When I reached home, my brother went to bed and only Mom was awake.
② When I reached home, my brother has gone to bed and only Mom was awake.
③ When I reached home, my brother had gone to bed and only Mom was awake.
④ When I have reached home, my brother went to bed and only Mom was awake.
⑤ When I had reached home, my brother had gone to bed and only Mom was awake.

06 다음 문장의 밑줄 친 부분 중 어법상 어색한 것은?

> ⓐAlthough she ⓑhas been ill ⓒfor a long time, it still ⓓcame as a shock when she eventually ⓔdied.

① ⓐ ② ⓑ ③ ⓒ ④ ⓓ ⑤ ⓔ

07 빈칸 (A)와 (B)에 알맞은 것으로 바르게 짝지어진 것은?

> Eric was late for the meeting ___(A)___ he ___(B)___ the bus.

	(A)	(B)
①	since	has missed
②	though	missed
③	because	has missed
④	though	had missed
⑤	because	had missed

서답형

08 〈보기〉에서 알맞은 접속사를 골라 다음 빈칸을 채우시오.

> ┌ 보기 ┐
> when   though   after   since   unless

(1) You'll miss the bus _____ you walk more quickly.

(2) He achieved success _____ he made lots of efforts.

(3) She hasn't phoned, _____ she said she would.

(4) I still get scared _____ I remember that night.

(5) Yesterday he stayed home from work _____ he got a really bad flu.

09 다음 문장의 빈칸에 알맞은 말은?

> _____ their house was not so nice, they looked happy.

① After ② Unless
③ If ④ Though
⑤ Since

10 다음 우리말을 바르게 영작한 것을 고르시오.

> 그 진주는 진짜같이 보여도 가짜예요.

① The pearls are fake, so they look real.
② The pearls are fake, though they look real.
③ The pearls are fake, unless they look real.
④ The pearls are fake since they look real.
⑤ The pearls are fake as they look real.

11 다음 문장의 빈칸에 들어갈 알맞은 말은?

> Isabelle _____ in Rome for 15 years when I met her.

① lives ② lived
③ living ④ has lived
⑤ had lived

서답형

12 다음 두 문장을 한 문장으로 바꿔 쓰고자 한다. 빈칸에 들어갈 알맞은 말을 쓰시오.

> • Brian started to learn Korean in the year of 2015.
> • Brian gave a speech in Korean at the meeting last weekend.
> = Brian gave a speech in Korean at the meeting last weekend as he _____ it since 2015.

13 다음 밑줄 친 과거완료의 용법이 〈보기〉와 같은 것은?

— 보기 —

Janet <u>had been</u> ill in bed for three days when I visited her.

① When she got to the station, the train <u>had</u> just <u>left</u> for London.
② Herold <u>had</u> never <u>seen</u> such a big animal till then.
③ Christine <u>had lived</u> in Boston since she got married.
④ I thought that he <u>had lost</u> his bag on the train to New York.
⑤ She asked her to feel the eggs that <u>had become</u> hard.

서답형

14 다음 문장에서 문맥상 어색한 접속사를 바르게 고쳐 다시 쓰시오.

(1) I missed the first bus because I got up early in the morning.

➡ _____

_____

(2) Although I am a student, I will get a discount.

➡ _____

_____

(3) David was doing the dishes since Monica called him.

➡ _____

_____

(4) All of them look tired before they worked hard.

➡ _____

_____

(5) I'll take the job if the pay is much too low.

➡ _____

_____

[15~16] 다음 우리말에 맞게 영작한 것을 고르시오.

15 비록 그것이 사실일지라도, 그는 그것을 믿지 않았다.

① Since it was true, he didn't believe it.
② Since he didn't believe it, it was true.
③ Though it was true, he didn't believe it.
④ It was true, though he didn't believe it.
⑤ As though it was true, he didn't believe it.

16 그때 이전에 바다에서 고래를 본 적이 있었니?

① Do you ever see a whale in the sea before then?
② Did you ever see a whale in the sea before then?
③ Have you ever seen a whale in the sea before then?
④ Have you ever been seeing a whale in the sea before then?
⑤ Had you ever seen a whale in the sea before then?

17 다음 중 어법상 어색한 것을 고르시오. (2개)

① Since it's very hot outside, I will play soccer.
② Our teacher will edit our video after we finish recording it.
③ I had never been in such a situation, so my face got really red.
④ I remembered that I met him at the party.
⑤ When I arrived at school, class had already begun.

Grammar **133**

01 시간 흐름에 따른 사건 전개에 맞게 빈칸을 채워 문장을 완성하시오.

> (1) Mom bought a smart phone for me last week.
> → I lost the phone yesterday.
> → I don't have the phone now.
> (2) Kyle bought a flower vase last month.
> → He broke the vase by mistake today.
> → His mom knew the fact later.

(1) Yesterday I lost the smart phone that _____ last week.

(2) Today Kyle's mom knew that Kyle broke the vase by mistake that _____ last month.

02 다음을 when을 이용하여 한 문장으로 연결할 때 빈칸을 알맞게 채우시오. (시제에 유의할 것.)

(1) I wanted to go to Seoul. I arrived at the station. The train already left for Seoul.
➡ When I arrived at the station to go to Seoul, the train _____ for Seoul.

(2) I promised to meet Tom at the bookstore. I went there quite late. He was there but went back to work. So, I couldn't meet him.
➡ When I went to the bookstore to meet Tom, _____ to work.

03 다음 우리말에 맞게 주어진 어구를 바르게 배열하시오.

(1) 비록 집은 파괴되었지만 아무도 다치지 않았습니다. (one, the house, even, no, was, was, hurt, destroyed, though) (접속사로 시작할 것)
➡ _____
_____

(2) 설사 그것이 너의 것이 아니라도 낭비하지 마라. (things, they, yours, even, don't, not, are, waste, if) ('주절+종속절'의 구문으로 작성할 것)
➡ _____
_____

(3) 그는 완전히 새로운 인종을 발견했다는 것을 깨달았다. (he, he, human species, a, discovered, realized, had, whole, new, that)
➡ _____
_____

(4) 나는 그가 왜 그런 어리석은 짓을 했는지 의아했다. (I, he, done, wondered, had, a, thing, stupid, such, why)
➡ _____
_____

04 다음 문장에서 내용에 맞게 <u>잘못된</u> 어휘를 알맞게 고치시오.

(1) Because animals do not speak like humans, some of them actually have a "language."
_____ ➡ _____

(2) As though they are so poor, they seem happy together.
_____ ➡ _____

(3) Despite he often talks big, I love him so much.
_____ ➡ _____

05 그림을 보고, 주어진 어휘를 이용하여 빈칸을 알맞게 채우시오.

(1) I noticed that my sister _____ my glasses. (break)

(2) Molly cleaned her living room this afternoon. At night, Mom arrived home. When Mom came home from work, Molly _____ her house. (already, clean)

06 알맞은 접속사를 이용하여 주어진 두 문장을 하나의 문장으로 쓰시오. ((1), (3)은 '주절+종속절'의 구문, (2)는 접속사로 시작할 것)

(1) • Horses sleep just like us.
 • They do so in a different way.

➡ _____

_____

(2) • The Earth is rotating.
 • Two tides occur each day.

➡ _____

_____

(3) • We had lunch.
 • We had ice cream as dessert.

➡ _____

_____

07 다음 문장에서 어법상 어색한 것을 바르게 고쳐 다시 쓰시오.

(1) Bella has already done the dishes when he came back home.

➡ _____

_____

(2) Dave never visited Paris until then.

➡ _____

_____

(3) She told me why she left him.

➡ _____

_____

(4) The boy disappeared during walking home from school.

➡ _____

_____

(5) He made his choice, although regretted it later.

➡ _____

_____

(6) Anne was fond of Tim, despite he often annoyed her.

➡ _____

_____

08 다음 두 문장을 알맞은 접속사를 이용하여 한 문장으로 연결하되, 두 사건의 시간차가 드러나도록 쓰시오. ('주절+종속절'의 구문으로 작성할 것)

• Kay didn't recognize any of them.
• She heard of their names.

➡ _____

_____

Reading

Waking Up to an Earthquake

One night in February, after I had gone to bed, an earthquake hit. I
<small>지진이 일어난 것보다 잠자리에 든 것이 먼저 일어난 일이기 때문에 과거완료로 씀.</small>

woke up suddenly because my bed was shaking. I thought my brother

was shaking my bed as a joke. But then I heard the mirror on my desk
<small>장난으로   지각동사</small>

fall to the floor and break into pieces. I knew it wasn't my brother then,
<small>지각동사(heard)+목적어+목적격보어(원형부정사)</small>

but I still didn't know what exactly was happening.
<small>부정의 조동사 앞에 위치   know의 목적어(간접의문문)</small>

Soon the whole room began to shake violently, and my confusion
<small>= Before long   = shaking</small>

turned to panic. My mom shouted that it was an earthquake and ran
<small>명사절을 이끄는 접속사</small>

into my room. Since it was my first time experiencing an earthquake, I
<small>= Because[As]   be one's first time+-ing: ~하는 게 처음이다</small>

didn't know how to react. I just kept saying, "What should I do?"
<small>= how I should react   keep ~ing: 계속해서 ~하다</small>

My mom pulled me and my brother out of bed. We ran to the kitchen
<small>~의 밖으로</small>

and crawled under the table.

---

suddenly 갑자기, 급작스럽게

shake 흔들다, 흔들리다

break into pieces 산산조각이 나다

exactly 정확하게

happen (사건이) 일어나다

violently 격렬하게, 심하게

confusion 혼란, 혼동

panic 극심한 공포, 공황

react 반응하다, 반응을 보이다

crawl 기어가다

확인문제

● 다음 문장이 본문의 내용과 일치하면 T, 일치하지 <u>않으면</u> F를 쓰시오.

1   The writer woke up suddenly because her bed was shaking. ☐

2   The writer's brother was shaking her bed as a joke. ☐

3   The mirror on the writer's desk fell to the floor and broke into pieces. ☐

4   The writer's brother shouted that it was an earthquake. ☐

5   The writer didn't experience an earthquake before. ☐

6   The writer pulled her brother out of bed. ☐

I could see the light swinging violently and books falling to the floor.
지각동사(see)+목적어+현재분사   목적어+현재분사

Our family picture dropped from the wall and the glass covering it
앞에 있는 명사 the glass를 수식

broke. A cup tipped over and rolled off the kitchen table. Every second,
= Every moment

I could hear something else in the apartment break. I started to worry
다른 어떤 것   = worrying

that the building would collapse.

Then the shaking seemed to stop. We started crawling toward the
= it seemed that the shaking stopped

door. At that moment, my mom's cell phone rang. It was my dad, who
전화를 한 사람   = and he

was coming home from work.

He shouted, "It stopped! Get out of the building! Take the stairs!
= The shaking

Don't take the elevator! Hurry!" "Where are you? Are you okay?" my

mom asked urgently. My dad answered, "Don't worry. I'm okay. I was

driving home when the shaking started. But I pulled over immediately.
to home(×)   = at once

I'm listening to the radio right now to find out what's going on."
to부정사의 부사적 용법(목적)   = happening

swing 흔들다, 흔들리다
drop 떨어지다, 쓰러지다
cover 가리다, 덮다
tip over 넘어뜨리다, 넘어지다
roll 굴러가다
collapse 붕괴되다, 무너지다
seem to V …인 것 같다
urgently 긴급하게, 급히
pull over 길 한쪽으로 차를 대다
immediately 즉시, 당장

📎 확인문제

● 다음 문장이 본문의 내용과 일치하면 T, 일치하지 않으면 F를 쓰시오.

1 The writer could see the light swinging violently and books falling to the floor. ☐

2 The writer's family picture dropped from the table and the glass covering it broke. ☐

3 The writer started to worry that the building would collapse. ☐

4 When the shaking seemed to be violent, the writer's family started crawling toward the door. ☐

5 The writer's dad was driving home when the shaking started. ☐

6 The writer's mom was listening to the radio to find out what was going on. ☐

We nervously <u>made our way down</u> the stairs and outside. I looked
make one's way: 나아가다, 가다

around. Parts of buildings <u>had fallen</u> and <u>had smashed</u> several cars. We
밖으로 나가기 전에 건물의 일부분이 떨어져 나갔고 몇몇 차들은 박살이 난 것이므로 과거완료로 씀.

went to an open space <u>to avoid</u> more falling pieces. How could all this
to부정사의 부사적 용법(목적)

have happened <u>in a few minutes</u>?
몇 분 만에

Although I <u>had done</u> many earthquake drills in school, I <u>had never</u>
과거(지진이 일어났던 상황)보다 더 이전에 지진 훈련을 했었기 때문에 과거완료로 씀.   과거(지진이 일어났던 상황)보다 더 이전에 지진을 겪으
리라고는 생각해 본 적 없었기 때문에 과거완료로 씀.

<u>thought</u> I'd experience a real earthquake. I still get scared when I

remember that night. I can't forget the <u>panic I felt</u> when the <u>furniture</u>
the panic과 I 사이에 목적격 관계대명사 that[which]이 생략   furnitures(×):
항상 단수로 쓰는 집합명사

was shaking and things were falling to the floor. After that night, I

began <u>to take</u> earthquake drills seriously. I realized <u>that</u> I should be
= taking   목적어를 이끄는 접속사(생략 가능함.)

prepared for the next earthquake, <u>which</u> can occur <u>at any time</u>.
that(×)   언제든

 확인문제

● 다음 문장이 본문의 내용과 일치하면 T, 일치하지 <u>않으면</u> F를 쓰시오.

1 The writer's family nervously made their way down the stairs and outside. ☐

2 All the buildings had fallen and had smashed several cars. ☐

3 The writer's family went to an open space to avoid more falling pieces. ☐

4 The writer had never done an earthquake drill in school. ☐

5 The writer had never thought she would experience a real earthquake. ☐

6 The writer realized that she should be prepared for the next earthquake, though it

seldom occurs. ☐

nervously 신경질적으로, 초조하게

smash 박살내다, 때려 부수다

avoid …을 피하다

drill 훈련

seriously 심각하게, 진지하게

occur (일·사건 등이) 일어나다, 발생하
다

● 우리말을 참고하여 빈칸에 알맞은 말을 쓰시오.

1 _____ _____ to an Earthquake

2 One night in February, after I _____ _____ _____ _____, an earthquake hit.

3 I woke up suddenly because my bed _____ _____.

4 I thought my brother was shaking my bed _____ _____ _____.

5 But then I heard the mirror on my desk _____ _____ _____ and _____ _____ _____.

6 I knew it wasn't my brother then, but I still didn't know _____ _____ _____ _____.

7 Soon the whole room began to shake violently, and my confusion _____ _____ _____.

8 My mom shouted that it was an earthquake and _____ _____ my room.

9 Since it was _____ _____ _____ _____ an earthquake, I didn't know how to react.

10 I just _____ _____, "What should I do?"

11 My mom pulled me and my brother _____ _____ _____.

12 We ran to the kitchen and _____ _____ the table.

13 I could see the light _____ violently and books _____ to the floor.

1	지진에 눈을 뜨는 것
2	2월 어느 날 밤, 내가 잠자리에 든 후에 지진이 일어났다.
3	침대가 흔들렸기 때문에 나는 갑자기 잠에서 깼다.
4	나는 남동생이 장난으로 침대를 흔들고 있다고 생각했다.
5	하지만 그때 나는 내 책상 위에 있던 거울이 바닥으로 떨어져 산산조각이 나는 소리를 들었다.
6	그때 나는 남동생이 그런 것이 아니라는 것을 알았지만, 정확히 무슨 일이 일어나고 있었는지를 여전히 알지 못했다.
7	머지않아 방 전체가 심하게 흔들리기 시작했고 혼란스러움은 공포로 변했다.
8	엄마가 지진이라고 소리를 지르며 내 방으로 뛰어 들어왔다.
9	지진을 경험한 것이 처음이었기 때문에, 나는 어떻게 반응해야 할지 몰랐다.
10	나는 그저 "어떻게 해야 하지?"라는 말을 반복했다.
11	엄마는 나와 남동생을 침대 밖으로 잡아끌었다.
12	우리는 주방으로 달려가서 식탁 아래로 기어들어 갔다.
13	나는 전등이 심하게 흔들리는 것과 책이 바닥으로 떨어지는 것을 볼 수 있었다.

14 Our family picture dropped from the wall and the glass _____
_____ _____.

15 A cup _____ _____ and _____ _____ the kitchen table.

16 _____ _____, I could hear something else in the apartment break.

17 I started _____ _____ that the building would _____.

18 Then the shaking _____ _____ _____.

19 We started _____ _____ the door.

20 _____ _____ _____, my mom's cell phone rang.

21 It was my dad, who was _____ _____ _____ _____.

22 He shouted, "_____ _____!

23 Get _____ _____ the building!

24 _____ the stairs!

25 _____ _____ the elevator!

26 _____!"

27 "_____ are you?

28 Are you okay?" my mom asked _____.

29 My dad answered, "_____ _____.

30 I'm _____.

---

14 우리 가족 사진이 벽에서 떨어졌고 사진을 덮고 있던 유리가 깨졌다.

15 컵이 넘어지고 식탁에서 굴러 떨어졌다.

16 매 순간, 나는 아파트에 있는 다른 어떤 것들이 부서지는 소리를 들을 수 있었다.

17 나는 건물이 무너지지는 않을까 하는 걱정이 들기 시작했다.

18 그때 흔들림이 멈추는 것 같았다.

19 우리는 문으로 기어가기 시작했다.

20 그 순간, 엄마의 휴대 전화가 울렸다.

21 전화를 한 사람은 바로 아빠였는데, 직장에서 퇴근하던 중이었다.

22 아빠는 소리쳤다. "지진이 멈췄어요!

23 건물 밖으로 나와요!

24 계단을 이용해요!

25 엘리베이터를 타면 안 돼요!

26 서둘러요!"

27 "어디예요?

28 괜찮아요?"라고 엄마가 다급하게 물었다.

29 아빠가 대답했다. "걱정 말아요.

30 나는 괜찮아요.

31 I _____ _____ _____ when the shaking started.

32 But I _____ _____ immediately.

33 I'm listening to the radio _____ _____ to find out what's _____ _____."

34 We nervously _____ _____ _____ down the stairs and outside.

35 I looked _____.

36 Parts of buildings _____ _____ and _____ _____ several cars.

37 We went to an open space _____ _____ more falling pieces.

38 How _____ all this _____ _____ in a few minutes?

39 Although I had done many _____ _____ in school, I had never thought I'd experience _____ _____ _____.

40 I still _____ _____ when I remember that night.

41 I can't forget _____ _____ _____ _____ when the furniture was shaking and things were falling to the floor.

42 After that night, I began to _____ earthquake _____ _____.

43 I realized that I should _____ _____ _____ the next earthquake, which can occur _____ _____ _____.

31 진동이 시작할 때 운전해서 집으로 가던 중이었어요.

32 하지만 즉시 차를 길 한쪽에 댔어요.

33 무슨 일이 일어나는지 알기 위해 지금 라디오를 듣고 있어요."

34 우리는 초조한 마음으로 계단을 내려가서 밖으로 나갔다.

35 나는 주변을 둘러보았다.

36 건물의 일부분이 떨어져 나갔고 몇몇 차들은 박살이 났다.

37 우리는 추가적인 낙하물을 피하기 위해 공터로 갔다.

38 어떻게 이런 일이 몇 분 만에 일어날 수 있단 말인가?

39 비록 학교에서 많은 지진 대피 훈련을 해 왔지만, 내가 실제 지진을 겪으리라고는 전혀 생각해 보지 않았었다.

40 그날 밤을 기억하면 나는 여전히 두려워진다.

41 가구가 흔들리고 물건들이 바닥으로 떨어졌을 때 내가 느꼈던 공포심을 나는 잊을 수가 없다.

42 그날 밤 이후, 나는 지진 대피 훈련에 진지하게 임하기 시작했다.

43 나는 언제든 발생할 수 있는 다음 지진을 대비해야 한다는 것을 깨달았다.

● 우리말을 참고하여 본문을 영작하시오.

1 지진에 눈을 뜨는 것

➡ _____

2 2월 어느 날 밤, 내가 잠자리에 든 후에 지진이 일어났다.

➡ _____

3 침대가 흔들렸기 때문에 나는 갑자기 잠에서 깼다.

➡ _____

4 나는 남동생이 장난으로 침대를 흔들고 있다고 생각했다.

➡ _____

5 하지만 그때 나는 내 책상 위에 있던 거울이 바닥으로 떨어져 산산조각이 나는 소리를 들었다.

➡ _____

6 그때 나는 남동생이 그런 것이 아니라는 것을 알았지만, 정확히 무슨 일이 일어나고 있었는지를 여전히 알지 못했다.

➡ _____

7 머지않아 방 전체가 심하게 흔들리기 시작했고 혼란스러움은 공포로 변했다.

➡ _____

8 엄마가 지진이라고 소리를 지르며 내 방으로 뛰어 들어왔다.

➡ _____

9 지진을 경험한 것이 처음이었기 때문에, 나는 어떻게 반응해야 할지 몰랐다.

➡ _____

10 나는 그저 "어떻게 해야 하지?"라는 말을 반복했다.

➡ _____

11 엄마는 나와 남동생을 침대 밖으로 잡아끌었다.

➡ _____

12 우리는 주방으로 달려가서 식탁 아래로 기어들어 갔다.

➡ _____

13 나는 전등이 심하게 흔들리는 것과 책이 바닥으로 떨어지는 것을 볼 수 있었다.

➡ _____

14 우리 가족 사진이 벽에서 떨어졌고 사진을 덮고 있던 유리가 깨졌다.

➡ _____

15 컵이 넘어지고 식탁에서 굴러 떨어졌다.

➡ _____

16 매 순간, 나는 아파트에 있는 다른 어떤 것들이 부서지는 소리를 들을 수 있었다.

➡ _____

17 나는 건물이 무너지지는 않을까 하는 걱정이 들기 시작했다.

➡ _____

18 그때 흔들림이 멈추는 것 같았다.

➡ _____

19 우리는 문으로 기어가기 시작했다.

➡ _____

20 그 순간, 엄마의 휴대 전화가 울렸다.

➡ _____

21 전화를 한 사람은 바로 아빠였는데, 직장에서 퇴근하던 중이었다.

➡ _____

22 아빠는 소리쳤다, "지진이 멈췄어요!

➡ _____

23 건물 밖으로 나와요!

➡ _____

24 계단을 이용해요!

➡ _____

25 엘리베이터를 타면 안 돼요!

➡ _____

26 서둘러요!"

➡ _____

27 "어디예요?

➡ _____

28 괜찮아요?"라고 엄마가 다급하게 물었다.

➡ _____

29 아빠가 대답했다, "걱정 말아요.

➡ _____

30 나는 괜찮아요.

➡ _____

31 진동이 시작할 때 운전해서 집으로 가던 중이었어요.

➡ _____

32 하지만 즉시 차를 길 한쪽에 댔어요.

➡ _____

33 무슨 일이 일어나는지 알기 위해 지금 라디오를 듣고 있어요."

➡ _____

34 우리는 초조한 마음으로 계단을 내려가서 밖으로 나갔다.

➡ _____

35 나는 주변을 둘러보았다.

➡ _____

36 건물의 일부분이 떨어져 나갔고 몇몇 차들은 박살이 났다.

➡ _____

37 우리는 추가적인 낙하물을 피하기 위해 공터로 갔다.

➡ _____

38 어떻게 이런 일이 몇 분 만에 일어날 수 있단 말인가?

➡ _____

39 비록 학교에서 많은 지진 대피 훈련을 해 왔지만, 내가 실제 지진을 겪으리라고는 전혀 생각해
보지 않았었다.

➡ _____

_____

40 그날 밤을 기억하면 나는 여전히 두려워진다.

➡ _____

41 가구가 흔들리고 물건들이 바닥으로 떨어졌을 때 내가 느꼈던 공포심을 나는 잊을 수가 없다.

➡ _____

42 그날 밤 이후, 나는 지진 대피 훈련에 진지하게 임하기 시작했다.

➡ _____

43 나는 언제든 발생할 수 있는 다음 지진을 대비해야 한다는 것을 깨달았다.

➡ _____

[01~04] 다음 글을 읽고 물음에 답하시오.

One night in February, after I (A)had gone to bed, an earthquake hit. (①) I woke up suddenly because my bed was shaking. (②) But then I heard the mirror on my desk fall to the floor and break ___ⓐ___ pieces. (③) I knew it wasn't my brother then, but I still didn't know what exactly was happening. (④) Soon the whole room began to shake violently, and my confusion turned ___ⓑ___ panic. (⑤) My mom shouted that it was an earthquake and ran into my room. Since it was my first time experiencing an earthquake, I didn't know how to react. I just kept saying, "What should I do?"

01 위 글의 빈칸 ⓐ, ⓑ에 들어갈 말이 바르게 짝지어진 것은?

	ⓐ	ⓑ		ⓐ	ⓑ
①	by	– into	②	into	– by
③	for	– by	④	for	– into
⑤	into	– to			

02 위 글의 흐름으로 보아, 주어진 문장이 들어가기에 가장 적절한 곳은?

> I thought my brother was shaking my bed as a joke.

①　　②　　③　　④　　⑤

03 위 글의 밑줄 친 (A)had gone과 과거완료의 용법이 같은 것을 고르시오.

① I did not tell him at first, for I <u>had</u> never <u>seen</u> him before.

② I <u>had</u> just <u>finished</u> my homework when she came.

③ I couldn't buy it as I <u>had lost</u> my purse.

④ He <u>had been</u> to France twice before he was twenty years old.

⑤ When I visited her, she <u>had been</u> ill for a week.

04 According to the passage, which is NOT true?

① One night in February, the writer had gone to bed before an earthquake hit.

② The writer's brother was shaking the writer's bed as a joke.

③ Before long the whole room began to shake violently.

④ The writer had never experienced an earthquake before.

⑤ The writer didn't know how to react to the earthquake.

[05~07] 다음 글을 읽고 물음에 답하시오.

My mom pulled me and my brother out of bed. We ran to the kitchen and crawled under the table. ⓐ<u>I could see the light to swing violently and books to fall to the floor.</u> Our family picture dropped from the wall and the glass covering ⓑ<u>it</u> broke. A cup tipped over and rolled off the kitchen table. Every second, I could hear something else in the apartment break. I started to worry that the building would collapse.

05 위 글의 밑줄 친 ⓐ에서 어법상 틀린 부분을 찾아 고치시오. (두 군데)

_____ ➡ _____

_____ ➡ _____

06 위 글의 밑줄 친 ⓑit이 가리키는 것을 본문에서 찾아 쓰시오.

➡ _____

07 다음 중 위 글의 지진 때문에 일어난 일이 <u>아닌</u> 것을 고르시오.

① 전등이 심하게 흔들렸다.
② 책이 바닥으로 떨어졌다.
③ 가족 사진이 벽에서 떨어졌다.
④ 컵이 넘어지고 식탁에서 굴러 떨어졌다.
⑤ 아파트 건물이 무너졌다.

[08~10] 다음 글을 읽고 물음에 답하시오.

Then the shaking seemed to stop. We started crawling toward the door. At that moment, my mom's cell phone rang. It was my dad, who was coming home from work.

He shouted, "It stopped! Get out of the building! Take the stairs! Don't take the elevator! Hurry!" "Where are you? Are you okay?" my mom asked urgently. My dad answered, "Don't worry. I'm okay. I was driving home when the shaking started. But I pulled over immediately. I'm listening to the radio right now ⓐto find out what's going on."

08 아래 〈보기〉에서 위 글의 밑줄 친 ⓐto find와 to부정사의 용법이 같은 것의 개수를 고르시오.

┌─── 보기 ───┐
① He tried to stop smoking.
② There's nothing to stop you from doing it.
③ The policeman ran to stop the flight.
④ I wanted the baby to stop crying.
⑤ You must be crazy to stop the car in the middle of the street.
└───────────┘

① 1개   ② 2개   ③ 3개   ④ 4개   ⑤ 5개

09 위 글의 분위기로 가장 알맞은 것을 고르시오.

① exciting   ② urgent   ③ touching
④ fantastic   ⑤ boring

서답형
10 주어진 영영풀이에 해당하는 단어를 본문에서 찾아 쓰시오.

┌─────────────────────────────┐
moved to the side of the road and stopped
└─────────────────────────────┘

➡ _____

[11~14] 다음 글을 읽고 물음에 답하시오.

We nervously made our way down the stairs and outside. I looked around. ⓐParts of buildings fell and smashed several cars. We went to an open space to avoid more falling pieces. ⓑHow could all this have happened in a few minutes?

Although I had done many earthquake drills in school, I had never thought I'd experience a real earthquake. I still get scared when I remember that night. ⓒ가구가 흔들리고 물건들이 바닥으로 떨어졌을 때 내가 느꼈던 공포심을 나는 잊을 수가 없다. After that night, I began to take earthquake drills seriously. I realized that I should be prepared for the next earthquake, which can occur at any time.   <I: a girl>

서답형
11 위 글의 밑줄 친 ⓐ에서 어법상 <u>틀린</u> 부분을 찾아 고치시오. (두 군데)

_____ ➡ _____
_____ ➡ _____

12 위 글의 밑줄 친 ⓑ에서 알 수 있는 글쓴이의 심경으로 가장 알맞은 것을 고르시오.

① excited   ② ashamed
③ disappointed   ④ puzzled
⑤ depressed

13 위 글의 밑줄 친 ⓒ의 우리말에 맞게 주어진 어휘를 알맞게 배열하시오.

> were falling / when / I / the furniture / can't forget / to the floor / felt / things / and / I / was shaking / the panic / .

➡ _____

_____

14 위 글에 어울리는 속담으로 가장 알맞은 것을 고르시오.

① A friend in need is a friend indeed.
② Prevention is better than cure.
③ Every cloud has a silver lining.
④ Look before you leap.
⑤ Make hay while the sun shines.

15 주어진 글 다음에 이어질 글의 순서로 가장 적절한 것은?

> One night in February, after I had gone to bed, an earthquake hit. I woke up suddenly because my bed was shaking.
>
> (A) I knew it wasn't my brother then, but I still didn't know what exactly was happening. Soon the whole room began to shake violently, and my confusion turned to panic.
>
> (B) I thought my brother was shaking my bed as a joke. But then I heard the mirror on my desk fall to the floor and break into pieces.
>
> (C) My mom shouted that it was an earthquake and ran into my room. Since it was my first time experiencing an earthquake, I didn't know how to react. I just kept saying, "What should I do?"

① (A) – (C) – (B)
② (B) – (A) – (C)
③ (B) – (C) – (A)
④ (C) – (A) – (B)
⑤ (C) – (B) – (A)

[16~17] 다음 글을 읽고 물음에 답하시오.

> Then the shaking seemed to stop. We started crawling toward the door. At that moment, my mom's cell phone rang. It was my dad, who was coming home from work.
>
> He shouted, "It stopped! Get out of the building! Take the stairs! Don't take the elevator! Hurry!" "Where are ①you? Are ②you okay?" ③my mom asked urgently. My dad answered, "Don't worry. I'm okay. ④I was driving home when the shaking started. But I pulled over immediately. ⑤I'm listening to the radio right now to find out what's going on."

16 밑줄 친 ①~⑤ 중에서 가리키는 대상이 나머지 넷과 다른 것은?

①   ②   ③   ④   ⑤

17 According to the passage, which is NOT true?

① When the shaking seemed to stop, the writer started crawling toward the door.
② The writer's dad was coming home from work.
③ The writer's dad told the writer's mom to take the elevator.
④ The writer's mom didn't know where the writer's dad was.
⑤ The writer's dad was listening to the radio to find out what was going on.

[18~20] 다음 글을 읽고 물음에 답하시오.

My mom pulled me and my brother out of bed. We ran to the kitchen and crawled under the table. I could see the light swinging violently and books falling to the floor. Our family picture dropped from the wall and the glass ⓐcovering it broke. A cup tipped over and rolled off the kitchen table. Every second, I could hear something else in the apartment break. I started to worry that the building would collapse. <I: a girl>

18 위 글의 밑줄 친 ⓐ를 관계대명사를 사용하여 두 단어로 고치시오.

➡ _____

서답형
19 주어진 영영풀이에 해당하는 단어를 본문에서 찾아 쓰시오.

> to fall down very suddenly

➡ _____

중요
20 위 글을 읽고 질문에 답할 수 <u>없는</u> 것을 고르시오.

① What did the writer's mom do?
② Where did the writer take refuge with her mom and her brother?
③ What could the writer see during the earthquake?
④ How long did the earthquake last?
⑤ Why did the writer start to worry that the building would collapse?

[21~23] 다음 글을 읽고 물음에 답하시오.

One night in February, after I ___ⓐ___ to bed, an earthquake hit. I woke up suddenly because my bed was shaking. I thought my brother was shaking my bed as a joke. But then I heard the mirror on my desk fall to the floor and break into pieces. I knew it wasn't my brother then, but I still didn't know what exactly was happening.

Soon the whole room began to shake violently, and my confusion turned to panic. My mom shouted that it was an earthquake and ran into my room. ⓑ지진을 경험한 것이 처음이었기 때문에, I didn't know how to react. I just kept saying, "What should I do?"

21 위 글의 빈칸 ⓐ에 들어갈 알맞은 말을 <u>모두</u> 고르시오.

① have gone
② would go
③ had gone
④ go
⑤ went

서답형
22 위 글의 밑줄 친 ⓑ의 우리말에 맞게 주어진 어휘를 이용하여 9단어로 영작하시오.

> since, experiencing

➡ _____

_____

23 위 글의 제목으로 알맞은 것을 고르시오.

① Have You Experienced an Earthquake?
② My Brother Likes to Play Jokes on Me
③ Waking Up to an Earthquake
④ Wow! My Room Began Shaking Violently!
⑤ My Mom Ran into My Room in Panic!

[24~26] 다음 글을 읽고 물음에 답하시오.

One night in February, after I had gone to bed, an earthquake hit. I woke up suddenly because my bed was shaking. I thought my brother was shaking my bed as a joke. ⓐBut then I heard the mirror on my desk to fall to the floor and to break into pieces. I knew it wasn't my brother then, but I still didn't know what exactly was happening.

Soon the whole room began to shake violently, and my confusion turned to panic. My mom shouted that it was an earthquake and ran into my room. ⓑSince it was my first time experiencing an earthquake, I didn't know how to react. I just kept saying, "What should I do?"   <I: a girl>

서답형

24 위 글의 밑줄 친 ⓐ에서 어법상 틀린 부분을 찾아 고치시오. (두 군데)

_____ ➡ _____

_____ ➡ _____

25 아래 〈보기〉에서 위 글의 밑줄 친 ⓑSince와 같은 의미로 쓰인 것의 개수를 고르시오.

┌─ 보기 ─┐

① She has moved house six times since she came here.

② Let's do our best since we can expect no help from others.

③ He has written to me once since he left here.

④ Since we're not very busy just now, I can get away from the office.

⑤ Since we live in the computer era, you should get used to personal computers.

① 1개   ② 2개   ③ 3개   ④ 4개   ⑤ 5개

26 Why didn't the writer know how to react to the earthquake? Answer in English. (9 words)

➡ _____

[27~29] 다음 글을 읽고 물음에 답하시오.

Although I had done many earthquake drills in school, I ⓐhad never thought I'd experience a real earthquake. I still get (A) [scaring / scared] when I remember that night. I can't forget the panic I felt when the furniture was shaking and things were falling to the floor. After that night, I began to take earthquake drills (B)[serious / seriously]. I realized that I should be prepared for the next earthquake, (C)[that / which] can occur at any time.   <I: a girl>

27 위 글의 밑줄 친 ⓑhad never thought와 현재완료의 용법이 같은 것을 모두 고르시오.

① I have eaten Pad thai twice.

② They have lived in Seoul since 1998.

③ How many times have you been to Europe?

④ He has not finished his homework yet.

⑤ Have you ever seen such a wonderful scene before?

서답형

28 위 글의 괄호 (A)~(C)에서 문맥이나 어법상 알맞은 낱말을 골라 쓰시오.

➡ (A) _____ (B) _____ (C) _____

서답형

29 다음 빈칸에 알맞은 단어를 넣어 글쓴이가 이번 지진으로 깨달은 점을 완성하시오.

The writer realized that she should be _____ _____ the next earthquake, which can occur at any time.

[01~03] 다음 글을 읽고 물음에 답하시오.

One night in February, after I had gone to bed, an earthquake hit. I woke up suddenly because my bed was shaking. I thought my brother was shaking my bed as a joke. But then I heard the mirror on my desk fall to the floor and break into pieces. ⓐI knew it wasn't my brother then, but I still didn't know what exactly was happened.

Soon the whole room began to shake violently, and my confusion turned to panic. My mom shouted that it was an earthquake and ran into my room. Since it was my first time experiencing an earthquake, I didn't know ⓑhow to react. I just kept saying, "What should I do?" <I: a girl>

01 Why did the writer wake up suddenly one night in February? Answer in English. (5 words)

➡ _____

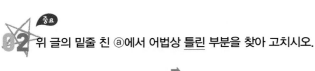
위 글의 밑줄 친 ⓐ에서 어법상 틀린 부분을 찾아 고치시오.

_____ ➡ _____

03 위 글의 밑줄 친 ⓑhow to react를 다음과 같이 바꿔 쓸 때 빈칸에 들어갈 알맞은 말을 두 단어로 쓰시오.

➡ how _____ _____ react

[04~06] 다음 글을 읽고 물음에 답하시오.

My mom (A)[pulled / pushed] me and my brother out of bed. We ran to the kitchen and crawled under the table. ⓐ나는 전등이 심하게 흔들리는 것과 책이 바닥으로 떨어지는 것을 볼 수 있었다. Our family picture dropped from the

wall and the glass (B)[covering / covered] it broke. A cup tipped over and rolled off the kitchen table. Every second, I could hear something else in the apartment (C)[break / to break]. I started to worry that the building would collapse. <I: a girl>

04 위 글의 괄호 (A)~(C)에서 문맥이나 어법상 알맞은 낱말을 골라 쓰시오.

➡ (A) _____ (B) _____ (C) _____

05 위 글의 밑줄 친 ⓐ의 우리말에 맞게 주어진 어휘를 알맞게 배열하시오.

violently / the light / and / I / books / to the floor / see / swinging / falling / could / .

➡ _____
_____

06 다음 빈칸 (A)와 (B)에 알맞은 단어를 넣어 글쓴이의 가족이 지진이 났을 때 취한 행동을 완성하시오.

The writer ran to (A)_____ _____ and (B)_____ under the table with her mom and her brother.

[07~10] 다음 글을 읽고 물음에 답하시오.

ⓐThen the shaking seemed to stop. We started crawling toward the door. At that moment, my mom's cell phone rang. It was my dad, who was coming home from work.

He shouted, "ⓑIt stopped! Get out of the building! Take the stairs! Don't take the elevator! Hurry!" "Where are you? Are you okay?" my mom asked urgently. My dad answered, "Don't worry. I'm okay. I was driving home when the shaking started. But I pulled over ⓒimmediately. I'm listening to the radio right now to find out what's going on."

07 위 글의 밑줄 친 ⓐ를 다음과 같이 바꿔 쓸 때 빈칸에 들어갈 알맞은 단어를 쓰시오.

➡ Then _____ seemed that the shaking stopped.

08 위 글의 밑줄 친 ⓑit이 가리키는 것을 본문에서 찾아 쓰시오.

➡ _____

09 위 글의 밑줄 친 ⓒimmediately와 바꿔 쓸 수 있는 말을 쓰시오. (두 단어)

➡ _____ 또는 _____

10 다음 빈칸 (A)와 (B)에 알맞은 단어를 넣어 글쓴이의 아빠에 대한 소개를 완성하시오.

The writer's dad was (A)_____
_____ when the shaking started, but he pulled over immediately. He was (B)_____ _____ _____ _____ right then to find out what was going on.

[11~14] 다음 글을 읽고 물음에 답하시오.

We nervously made our way down the stairs and outside. I looked around. Parts of buildings had fallen and had smashed several cars. We went to an open space to avoid more falling pieces. (A)어떻게 이런 일이 몇 분 만에 일어날 수 있단 말인가?

Although I ___ⓐ___ many earthquake drills in school, I had never thought I'd experience a real earthquake. I still get scared when I remember that night. I can't forget the panic I felt when the furniture was shaking and things were falling to the floor. After that night, I began to take earthquake drills seriously. (B)I realized that I should be prepared for the next earthquake, which can be occurred at any time.   <I: a girl>

11 위 글의 빈칸 ⓐ에 do를 알맞은 형태로 쓰시오.

➡ _____

12 위 글의 밑줄 친 (A)의 우리말에 맞게 주어진 어휘를 이용하여 10 단어로 영작하시오.

how, could, all, have, in

➡ _____

13 위 글의 밑줄 친 (B)에서 어법상 틀린 부분을 찾아 고치시오.

_____ ➡ _____

14 How does the writer feel when she remembers that night? Fill in the blanks (A) and (B) with suitable words.

She still (A)_____ _____, and she can't forget (B)_____ _____ she felt when the furniture was shaking and things were falling to the floor.

After You Read B

R: How did you feel when the earthquake occurred?
접속사 when은 "~할 때"의 의미로 시간의 부사절이다.

W: I began to panic because the whole room was shaking violently.

R: How scary! What did you do next?
How+형용사+(주어+동사)의 형태로 감탄문이다.

W: We all crawled under the table after my mom got us out of bed.
get A out of B A를 B에서 끌어내다

R: What was happening at the moment?

W: Lots of things were falling to the floor. I heard many things in the
= Many
apartment break.
지각동사 heard의 목적격보어

R: What did you realize after that night?

W: I realized that I should be prepared for the next earthquake. It can occur
at any time!
어느 때고

구문해설 • **occur** 발생하다 • **violently** 격렬하게 • **scary** 무서운 • **crawl** 기어가다
• **realize** 깨닫다

R: 지진이 일어났을 때 어떻게 느끼셨습니까?

W: 방 전체가 심하게 흔들렸기 때문에 공포에 사로잡히기 시작했어요.

R: 얼마나 무서웠을까! 그 다음에 무엇을 했나요?

W: 어머니가 우리를 침대에서 끌어내린 후, 우리는 모두 식탁 아래로 기어갔어요.

R: 그 순간에 무슨 일이 일어나고 있었나요?

W: 많은 것들이 바닥으로 떨어지고 있었어요. 나는 아파트 안에 있는 많은 것들이 깨지는 소리를 들었어요.

R: 그날 밤 이후에 무엇을 깨달았나요?

W: 나는 내가 다음 지진에 대비해야 한다는 것을 깨달았어요. 지진은 언제든지 일어날 수 있어요!

Think & Write Step 3

San Andreas

I would like to tell you about the movie *San Andreas*. This movie is set in Los
want to의 공손한 표현   배경으로 하고 있다
Angeles and San Francisco in 2014. The main character, a search-and-rescue
                                              └   동격   ┘
pilot, must search for his missing family during an earthquake. The special
                        missed(×)
effects used in the disaster scenes are very good. The movie is a little sad
        which[that] are used   a few(×)
at times, but the story is very interesting. I give *San Andreas* four stars. Go
= sometimes
and watch it!

구문해설 • **would like to:** ~하고 싶다 • **main character:** 주인공
• **search-and-rescue pilot:** 수색구조 조종사 • **missing:** 행방불명된
• **at times:** 가끔(=sometimes)

San Andreas

저는 영화 **San Andreas**에 대해 말하고 싶습니다. 이 영화의 배경은 2014년 **Los Angeles**와 **San Francisco**입니다. 수색구조 조종사인 주인공은 지진이 일어난 동안 행방불명된 그의 가족을 찾아야 합니다. 재난 장면에 사용된 특수효과는 매우 좋습니다. 이 영화는 가끔 약간 슬프지만, 이야기는 매우 재미있습니다. 저는 **San Andreas**에게 별 4개를 줍니다. 가서 보세요!

01 다음 두 문장에 공통으로 알맞은 것을 고르시오.

> • I read a report yesterday _____ the damage from each type of natural disaster.
> • I'm curious _____ how that happened.

① at   ② about   ③ in
④ of   ⑤ for

02 다음 문장의 빈칸에 알맞은 단어를 고르시오.

> Soon the whole room began to shake _____, and my confusion turned to panic.

① violently   ② properly   ③ recently
④ actually   ⑤ exactly

03 다음 대화의 빈칸에 들어갈 말로 적절한 것을 고르시오.

> B: There was a big flood in Europe. Did you hear about it?
> G: No, I didn't. But floods aren't that _____ in winter, are they? I'm curious about how that happened.
> B: Me too. Let's do some online research.

① aware   ② missing   ③ exact
④ proper   ⑤ common

04 다음 영영풀이에 해당하는 단어를 주어진 철자로 시작하여 쓰시오.

> to break apart and fall down suddenly

➡ c_____

[05~07] 다음 대화를 읽고 물음에 답하시오.

> B: Hey, did you hear about the big fires in California?
> G: _____ (A) _____
> B: They've destroyed a large number of houses and other buildings.
> G: Are the fires still going on?
> B: Yes, actually the wind has made the fires worse. I hope all the people living there are okay.
> G: So do I. (B)나는 얼마나 많은 사람들이 집을 떠나야 했는지 궁금하다. (curious, had to, how many, leave, I'm, people, about, their homes)
> B: Actually more than 20,000 people had to leave their homes, and about 400 people are missing in that area.
> G: That's terrible. I hope they're somewhere safe.

05 위 대화의 빈칸 (A)에 적절한 것은?

① Really? How did it start?
② Yes. It's not so serious.
③ Well, they stopped at the moment.
④ No, I didn't. How serious are they?
⑤ Of course. I don't know much.

06 밑줄 친 (B)의 우리말에 맞게 주어진 단어를 바르게 배열하시오.

➡ _____

_____

07 위 대화의 내용과 일치하지 <u>않는</u> 것은?

① The fires destroyed a large house.
② The fires are still going on.
③ The fires got worse due to the wind.
④ A lot of people had to leave their homes.
⑤ People missing in that area are about 400.

[08~09] 다음 대화를 읽고 물음에 답하시오.

G: Did you hear that earthquakes are ___(A)___ more often in Korea than before?
B: Oh, really? I've never felt an earthquake in Korea.
G: They usually occur in the southern part of Korea, but now they are ___(B)___ in other places as well.
B: I didn't know that. I'm curious about why earthquakes have occurred so often in Korea recently.
G: Why don't we do some research to find out?
B: Sounds good, but where do we look first?
G: How about asking our science teacher first? I think she can help us.
B: Okay. Let's go and find her.

08 빈칸 (A)와 (B)에 공통으로 들어가기에 적절한 것은?

① watching   ② increasing
③ occurring   ④ researching
⑤ finding

09 According to the dialogue, what does the boy want to know?

① the time when earthquakes occurred
② the places where earthquakes have occurred
③ the reason why earthquakes have occurred so often in Korea recently
④ the way they do some research
⑤ the person who can help them

[10~11] 다음 대화를 읽고 물음에 답하시오.

G: There seem to be many natural disasters in Korea these days.
B: I agree. ⓐThere was an earthquake in the south last week. ⓑAlso a storm is coming this week.
G: ⓒI'm curious about which type of natural disaster causes the most damage in Korea.
B: ⓓActually I read a report yesterday about the damage from each type of natural disaster. Number one is storms.
G: I see. I guess earthquakes are second.
B: ⓔNo, second is earthquakes, and third is heavy snow.

10 위 대화의 ⓐ~ⓔ 중 흐름상 어색한 문장은?

① ⓐ   ② ⓑ   ③ ⓒ   ④ ⓓ   ⑤ ⓔ

11 위 대화의 내용과 일치하지 <u>않는</u> 것은?

① The girl and the boy think natural disasters are occurring more often in Korea.
② The boy read a report about natural disasters.
③ The girl thinks storms cause the second most damage.
④ The boy says heavy snow causes the third most damage.
⑤ The girl wants to know which type of natural disaster causes the most damage.

[12~13] 다음 대화를 읽고 물음에 답하시오.

B: Mom, what else do we need to put in the ___(A)___ survival kit?
W: Well, we need water, some food, and radio.
B: ___(B)___, Mom?
W: Oh, make sure that you include batteries for the radio.

12 빈칸 (A)에 들어가기에 적절한 두 단어를 쓰시오.

➡ _____

13 빈칸 (B)에 적절한 말을 두 단어로 쓰시오.

➡ _____

14 다음 두 문장이 뜻이 비슷하도록 빈칸에 들어갈 알맞은 것은?

> Sinclare was young but he was regarded as their leader by them.
> = _____, he was regarded as their leader by them.

① Although Sinclare was young
② Since Sinclare was young
③ While Sinclare was young
④ As Sinclare was young
⑤ Unless Sinclare was young

15 다음 문장 중에서 어법상 어색한 것을 고르시오.

① After you say goodbye today, don't ever come back here.
② When I got home, my daughter had finished her homework.
③ When he had arrived at home, they already ate dinner.
④ Mom had gone to work when I woke up.
⑤ Claudia lost the camera that her boy friend had bought for her.

16 다음 그림을 참고하여 빈칸에 알맞은 말을 쓰시오.

_____ my dad went to work by car this morning, he came back home on foot.

17 다음 문장의 빈칸에 들어갈 수 <u>없는</u> 것은?

> When Monica went back home, he _____.

① had finished cleaning the house
② had walked the dog
③ had already dinner alone
④ had just gone to bed
⑤ had watered the plants

18 다음 두 문장을 since 또는 although를 이용해 한 문장으로 만드시오. (접속사로 시작할 것)

(1) • It's very hot outside.
    • I will walk my dog.
    ➡ _____

(2) • They had to paint quickly to capture the effect of light.
    • They did not sketch their paintings in advance.
    ➡ _____
       _____

(3) • Most people recognize it as a jewel.
    • The diamond most directly affects our daily lives as a tool.
    ➡ _____
       _____

19 다음 ⓐ~ⓕ 중 어법상 옳은 것을 <u>모두</u> 고르시오.

> ⓐ I had never eaten *pho* until I have visited Vietnam.
> ⓑ I was wearing the dress that my mom had made for me.
> ⓒ When I had got home, the TV was turned on.
> ⓓ I knew Francesca well since I had seen her before.
> ⓔ While playing basketball, Mike broke his leg.
> ⓕ Since they are rich, they don't seem happy at all.

➡ _____

Reading

[20~22] 다음 글을 읽고 물음에 답하시오.

One night in February, after I had gone to bed, an earthquake hit. I woke up suddenly because my bed was shaking. I thought my brother was shaking my bed as a joke. But then I heard the mirror on my desk fall to the floor and (A)산산조각이 나다. I knew it wasn't my brother then, but I still didn't know what exactly was happening.

Soon the whole room began to shake violently, and my confusion turned to panic. My mom shouted that it was an earthquake and ran into my room. ___ⓐ___ it was my first time experiencing an earthquake, I didn't know how to react. I just kept saying, "What should I do?"

20 위 글의 빈칸 ⓐ에 들어갈 알맞은 접속사를 고르시오.

① Though ② While ③ Even if
④ Whereas ⑤ Since

21 위 글의 밑줄 친 (A)의 우리말에 맞게 3 단어로 영작하시오.

➡ _____

22 위 글에서 알 수 있는 글쓴이의 심경 변화로 가장 알맞은 것을 고르시오.

① bored → scared
② nervous → satisfied
③ puzzled → frightened
④ pleased → upset
⑤ confused → bored

[23~24] 다음 글을 읽고 물음에 답하시오.

Then the shaking seemed (A)[to stop / stopping]. We started crawling toward the door. At that moment, my mom's cell phone rang. It was my dad, (B)[that / who] was coming home from work.

He shouted, "It stopped! Get out of the building! Take the stairs! Don't take the elevator! Hurry!" "Where are you? Are you okay?" my mom asked urgently. My dad answered, "Don't worry. I'm okay. I was driving (C)[home / to home] when the shaking started. But I pulled over immediately. I'm listening to the radio right now to find out what's ⓐgoing on."

23 위 글의 괄호 (A)~(C)에서 어법상 알맞은 낱말을 골라 쓰시오.

➡ (A) _____ (B) _____ (C) _____

24 위 글의 밑줄 친 ⓐgoing on과 바꿔 쓸 수 있는 한 단어를 h로 시작하여 쓰시오.

➡ _____

[25~26] 다음 글을 읽고 물음에 답하시오.

We nervously made our way down the stairs and outside. I looked around. Parts of buildings had fallen and had smashed several cars. We went to an open space ⓐto avoid more falling pieces. How could all this have happened in a few minutes?

Although I had done many earthquake drills in school, I had never thought I'd experience a real earthquake. I still get scared when I remember that night. I can't forget the panic I felt when the furniture was shaking and things were falling to the floor. After that night, I began to take earthquake drills seriously. I realized that I should be prepared for the next earthquake, which can occur at any time.

<I: a girl>

25 위 글의 밑줄 친 ⓐto avoid와 to부정사의 용법이 다른 것을 모두 고르시오.

① It is good to get up early in the morning.
② Do you have anything delicious to eat?
③ She went to the store to buy some pens.
④ His job is to take pictures.
⑤ He can't be rich to ask me for some money.

26 위 글을 읽고 알 수 없는 것을 고르시오.

① What did the writer see when she made her way down the stairs and outside?
② Where did the writer's family go after they got out of the building?
③ How many earthquake drills had the writer done in school?
④ Had the writer thought she'd experience a real earthquake?
⑤ What did the writer realize after this earthquake?

[27~29] 다음 글을 읽고 물음에 답하시오.

San Andreas
I would like ①telling you about ⓐthe movie *San Andreas*. This movie ②is set in Los Angeles and San Francisco in 2014. The main character, a search-and-rescue pilot, must search for his ③missing family during an earthquake. The special effects ④used in the disaster scenes are very good. The movie is a little sad ⑤at times, but the story is very interesting. I give *San Andreas* four stars. Go and watch it!

27 위 글의 밑줄 친 ①~⑤ 중 어법상 틀린 것을 찾아 고치시오.

_____ 번 ➡ _____

28 위 글의 종류로 알맞은 것을 고르시오.

① article   ② essay   ③ review
④ book report   ⑤ biography

29 위 글을 읽고 ⓐthe movie에 대해 알 수 없는 것을 고르시오.

① 제목   ② 배경
③ 주인공의 직업   ④ 주인공의 나이
⑤ 간략한 줄거리

01 짝지어진 단어의 관계가 같도록 빈칸에 들어갈 알맞은 말을 고르시오.

> destroy : damage = _____ : lately

① recently   ② properly   ③ urgently
④ nervously   ⑤ exactly

02 다음 빈칸에 들어갈 말로 적절한 것은?

> One night in February, after I had gone to bed, _____ hit. I woke up suddenly because my bed was shaking.

① a yellow dust   ② an earthquake
③ a heavy rain   ④ a heat wave
⑤ a wildfire

03 다음 문장에 공통으로 들어가기에 적절한 것은?

> • A cup tipped over and rolled _____ the kitchen table. Every second, I could hear something else in the apartment break.
> • Never put _____ until tomorrow what you can do.

① around   ② under   ③ over
④ off   ⑤ below

04 주어진 우리말에 맞게 빈칸을 채우시오. (철자가 주어진 경우 그 철자로 시작할 것)

(1) 우리 가족 사진이 벽에서 떨어지고 그것을 덮고 있던 유리가 깨졌다.
    ➡ Our family picture dropped from the wall and the glass c_____ it broke.

(2) 우리는 초조한 마음으로 계단을 내려가서 밖으로 나갔다.
    ➡ We nervously _____ _____ _____ down the stairs and outside.

[05~07] 다음 대화를 읽고 물음에 답하시오.

G: There seem to be many natural disasters in Korea these days. (ⓐ)
B: I agree. There was an earthquake in the south last week. Also a storm is coming this week. (ⓑ)
G: I'm curious about _____ (A) _____ causes the most damage in Korea. (ⓒ)
B: Actually I read a report yesterday about the damage from each type of natural disaster. Number one is storms.
G: I see. (ⓓ)
B: No, second is heavy rain, and third is heavy snow.
G: What about earthquakes? (ⓔ)
B: Based on the report, earthquakes are fourth. But the damage from earthquakes has been increasing recently because they have been happening more often in Korea.
G: I see. It seems like we have to be prepared for a variety of natural disasters in Korea.

05 ⓐ~ⓔ 중에서 다음 문장이 들어가기에 적절한 곳은?

> I guess earthquakes are second.

① ⓐ   ② ⓑ   ③ ⓒ   ④ ⓓ   ⑤ ⓔ

06 위 대화의 빈칸 (A)에 들어가기에 적절한 것은?

① what kind of earthquakes
② which type of natural disaster
③ which season of the year
④ whose report on the disaster
⑤ how many natural disasters

07 위 대화의 내용으로 보아 대답할 수 없는 것은?

① What natural disaster was there last week?

② Which type of natural disaster causes the most damage in Korea?

③ How has the damage from earthquakes been recently?

④ How much damage have storms caused?

⑤ Why has the damage from earthquakes been increasing?

[08~09] 다음 대화를 읽고 물음에 답하시오.

R: How did you feel when the earthquake occurred?

W: ⓐI began to panic because the whole room was shaking violently.

R: ⓑHow scary! What did you do next?

W: ⓒWe all crawled over the table after my mom got us out of bed.

R: What was happening at the moment?

W: ⓓLots of things were falling to the floor. I heard many things in the apartment break.

R: ⓔWhat did you realize after that night?

W: I realized that I should be prepared for the next earthquake. It can occur at any time!

08 밑줄 친 ⓐ~ⓔ 중에서 대화의 흐름으로 보아 어색한 문장을 고르시오.

① ⓐ　　② ⓑ　　③ ⓒ　　④ ⓓ　　⑤ ⓔ

09 다음 중 위 대화에서 기자가 질문하지 않은 것은?

① What was the feeling of the woman when the earthquake occurred?

② How scary was the earthquake?

③ What did the woman do after the panic?

④ What was happening when the woman crawled?

⑤ What did the woman realize after that night?

10 다음 중 어법상 적절한 문장은?

① After she finished her homework, she had gone to bed.

② I had known the story because I have read the book.

③ I couldn't get in the room because I had forget my key.

④ Jin told me how hard he had prepared for the match.

⑤ He carried out all the responsibilities I gave to him.

11 빈칸에 알맞은 접속사를 〈보기〉에서 골라 써 넣으시오.

┌─ 보기 ├─

though　when　before　if　since

(1) _____ it was snowing heavily, I stayed home all day.

(2) _____ it is against the law, poor villagers chop down the trees and sell them to make a living.

(3) I can't forget the panic I felt _____ the furniture was shaking and things were falling to the floor.

12 다음 〈보기〉에 주어진 단어를 이용하여 문맥에 맞게 문장을 완성하시오. 출제율 100%

보기
happen   take   practice

(1) The teacher notified his students of their results from the test they _____ a few days earlier.

(2) He ran as he _____ and finally won the race.

(3) A reporter asked the man what _____.

13 다음 빈칸에 들어갈 말을 순서대로 묶은 것은? 출제율 95%

• They achieved more than they _____ at first.
• _____ he was new to his firm, people didn't know him.

① had expected – Though
② had expected – Since
③ expected – Since
④ expected – Though
⑤ expected – When

[14~16] 다음 글을 읽고 물음에 답하시오.

One night in February, after I had gone to bed, an earthquake hit. I woke up suddenly because my bed was shaking. I thought my brother was shaking my bed as a joke. But then I heard the mirror on my desk fall to the floor and break into pieces. I knew it wasn't my brother then, but ⓐ정확히 무슨 일이 일어나고 있었는지를 여전히 알지 못했다.

ⓑSoon the whole room began to shake violently, and my confusion turned to comfort. My mom shouted that it was an earthquake and ran into my room. Since it was my first time experiencing an earthquake, I didn't know how to react. I just kept saying, "What should I do?"

14 위 글의 밑줄 친 ⓐ의 우리말에 맞게 주어진 어휘를 알맞게 배열하시오. 출제율 95%

what / still / know / I / was happening / didn't / exactly

➡ _____

_____

15 위 글의 밑줄 친 ⓑ에서 흐름상 어색한 부분을 찾아 고치시오. 출제율 90%

_____ ➡ _____

16 Which question CANNOT be answered after reading the passage? 출제율 100%

① When did the earthquake occur?
② Was the writer still awake when an earthquake hit?
③ What was the writer's brother doing when the earthquake hit?
④ Did the writer experience an earthquake before?
⑤ Did the writer know how to react to an earthquake?

[17~19] 다음 글을 읽고 물음에 답하시오.

(①) We nervously made our way down the stairs and outside. (②) Parts of buildings had fallen and had smashed several cars. (③) We went to an open space to avoid more falling pieces. (④) How could all this have happened ____ⓐ____ a few minutes? (⑤) Although I had done many earthquake drills in school, I had never thought I'd experience a real earthquake. I still get scared when I remember that night. I can't forget the panic I felt when the furniture was shaking and things were falling to the floor. After that night, I began to take earthquake drills seriously. I realized that I should be prepared ____ⓑ____ the next earthquake, which can occur at any time.

출제율 90%

17 위 글의 빈칸 ⓐ와 ⓑ에 들어갈 전치사가 바르게 짝지어진 것은?

① at – for ② at – to
③ in – for ④ for – to
⑤ in – on

출제율 100%

18 위 글의 흐름으로 보아, 주어진 문장이 들어가기에 가장 적절한 곳은?

I looked around.

① ② ③ ④ ⑤

출제율 95%

19 위 글의 주제로 알맞은 것을 고르시오.

① We should know how to avoid more falling pieces.
② We should go to an open space when an earthquake occurs.
③ What could happen in a few minutes?
④ An ounce of prevention is worth a pound of cure.
⑤ We should remember the panic of an earthquake.

[20~21] 다음 글을 읽고 물음에 답하시오.

Haeundae

I would like to tell you about the movie *Haeundae*. This movie is set in Busan, South Korea in 2009. It is a movie about a tsunami that hits the city of Busan. A tsunami researcher warns people, but everyone believes that Korea is safe. Eventually, people realize ⓐthe deadly wave is coming in only ten minutes. It is one of the few South Korean natural disaster movies. It offers some great shots of Haeundae Beach. The best shot in the film is the moment the wave reaches Diamond Bridge near Gwangalli Beach. The movie is full of good special effects! I give *Haeundae* three stars. Go and watch it!

출제율 100%

20 위 글의 밑줄 친 ⓐthe deadly wave가 가리키는 것을 본문에서 찾아 쓰시오.

➡ _____

출제율 95%

21 According to the passage, which is NOT true?

① *Haeundae* is set in Busan, South Korea in 2009.
② *Haeundae* is a movie about a tsunami that hits the city of Busan.
③ *Haeundae* is one of the few South Korean natural disaster movies.
④ The best shot in the film is the moment the wave reaches Diamond Bridge near Haeundae Beach.
⑤ *Haeundae* is full of good special effects.

[01~02] 다음 대화를 읽고 물음에 답하시오.

B: There was a big flood in Europe. Did you hear about it?
G: No, I didn't. But floods aren't that common in winter, are they? I'm _____(A)_____ how that happened.
B: (B)Me too. Let's do some online research.

01 빈칸 (A)에 들어가기에 적절한 말을 두 단어로 쓰시오.

➡ _____

02 밑줄 친 (B)와 바꿔 쓸 수 있는 말을 쓰시오. (3단어)

➡ _____

03 빈칸에 알맞은 단어를 〈보기〉에서 골라 쓰시오.

┌─ 보기 ─────────────────────┐
│ get   cover   damage   hands │
└────────────────────────────┘

(1) I'm curious about which type of natural disaster causes the most _____ in Korea.
(2) I still _____ scared when I remember that night.
(3) Make sure you place your _____ in the middle of the person's chest.
(4) Make sure that you _____ your mouth with a wet cloth.

04 다음 문장에서 틀린 것을 고쳐 다시 쓰시오.

(1) David has lost his glasses, so he couldn't read anything.

➡ _____
_____

(2) After he moves to a new city, he joined the company baseball team.

➡ _____
_____

(3) In summer, food is easily spoiled because it is kept well.

➡ _____
_____

(4) Our feet remain firmly on the earth since our planet is spinning on its axis.

➡ _____
_____

*spin: 돌다, 뱅뱅 돌다 *axis: 축

05 주어진 단어를 활용하여 빈칸을 완성하시오.

(1) I was shocked to hear that he _____ his job. (quit)
(2) Linda began to tell him that she _____ to a salesman. (marry)
(3) Though _____ it, you must do it. (like)

06 다음 우리말을 주어진 어휘를 이용하여 영작하시오.

(1) 한 남자가 자신의 가게에 강도가 들었다고 경찰에 신고했다. (a man, his store, the police, notify, rob, that)

➡ _____

(2) 비록 손은 없지만, 그녀가 할 수 없는 일은 없습니다. (there, nothing, hands, have, do, cannot, even, 13 단어)

➡ _____
_____

One night in February, after I had gone to bed, an earthquake hit. I (A)[fell asleep / woke up] suddenly (B)[because / because of] my bed was shaking. I thought my brother was shaking my bed as a joke. But then I heard the mirror on my desk fall to the floor and break into pieces. I knew it wasn't my brother then, but I still didn't know what exactly was happening.

Soon the whole room began to shake violently, and my confusion turned to panic. My mom shouted that it was an earthquake and ran into my room. ⓐSince it was my first time experiencing an earthquake, I didn't know (C)[how / what] to react. I just kept saying, "What should I do?"   <I: a girl>

07 위 글의 괄호 (A)~(C)에서 문맥이나 어법상 알맞은 낱말을 골라 쓰시오.

➡ (A) _____ (B) _____ (C) _____

08 위 글의 밑줄 친 ⓐ를 다음과 같이 바꿔 쓸 때 빈칸에 알맞은 단어를 쓰시오.

➡ Since it was the first time that I _____ an earthquake

= Since _____ _____ an earthquake for the first time

09 위 글의 내용과 일치하도록 다음 빈칸 (A)와 (B)에 알맞은 단어를 쓰시오.

When the writer heard the mirror on her desk fall to the floor and break into pieces, she could know that her bed had shaken because of some other reason, not because of (A)_____ _____, but she wasn't sure what was (B)_____.

Then the shaking seemed to stop. We started crawling toward the door. At that moment, my mom's cell phone rang. It was my dad, who was coming home from work.

He shouted, "It stopped! Get out of the building! Take the stairs! ⓐ엘리베이터를 타면 안 돼요! Hurry!" "Where are you? Are you okay?" my mom asked urgently. My dad answered, "Don't worry. I'm okay. I was driving home when the shaking started. But I pulled over immediately. I'm listening to the radio right now ⓑto find out what's going on."   <I: a girl>

10 위 글의 밑줄 친 ⓐ의 우리말에 맞게 4 단어로 영작하시오.

➡ _____

11 위 글의 밑줄 친 ⓑ를 다음과 같이 바꿔 쓸 때 빈칸에 들어갈 알맞은 말을 쓰시오.

➡ _____ _____ _____ find out what's going on

= _____ _____ _____ find out what's going on

= _____ _____ _____ I _____ find out what's going on

= _____ _____ I _____ find out what's going on

12 What did the writer do when the shaking seemed to stop? Answer in English. (6 words)

➡ _____

01 다음 〈보기〉의 표현과 접속사 though를 이용하여 예시와 같이 문장을 완성하시오.

> **보기**
>
> be twins   eat fast food   like English
>
> play soccer   study hard   rain heavily
>
> →Tony and Tom are twins though they look different.

(1) I _____ .

(2) He _____ .

(3) She _____ .

(4) They _____ .

02 다음 내용을 바탕으로 영화 비평문을 쓰시오.

> *Title: Haeundae*
>
> Time and Place: Busan, South Korea in 2009
>
> Story: It is a movie about a tsunami that hits the city of Busan. A tsunami researcher warns people, but everyone believes that Korea is safe. Eventually, people realize the deadly wave is coming in only ten minutes.
>
> Reviews: It is one of the few South Korean natural disaster movies. It offers some great shots of Haeundae Beach. The best shot in the film is the moment the wave reaches Diamond Bridge near Gwangalli Beach. The movie is full of good special effects!
>
> Rate the movie! ★ ★ ★ ☆ ☆

> *Haeundae*
>
> I would like to tell you about the movie *Haeundae*. This movie (A)_____ in Busan, South Korea in 2009. It is a movie about (B)_____ that hits the city of Busan. A tsunami researcher warns people, but everyone believes that Korea is safe. Eventually, people realize the deadly wave is coming (C)_____. It is one of the few South Korean (D)_____. It offers some great shots of Haeundae Beach. The best shot in the film is the moment the wave reaches Diamond Bridge near Gwangalli Beach. The movie is full of good (E)_____! I give *Haeundae* three stars. Go and watch it!

단원별 모의고사

01 다음 짝지어진 단어의 관계가 같도록 빈칸에 알맞은 것을 고르시오.

> whole : partial = _____ : rare

① aware　　　　② prepared
③ common　　　④ serious
⑤ worse

02 다음 중 각 단어의 영영풀이로 어색하게 짝지어진 것은?

① curious: wanting to know about something
② flood: a very large amount of snow that covers an area that is usually dry
③ common: happening often and to many people or in many places
④ cause: to make something happen, especially something bad
⑤ wildfire: a fire that moves quickly and cannot be controlled

03 다음 중 〈보기〉의 단어를 사용하여 자연스러운 문장을 만들 수 없는 것은?

> ┤ 보기 ├
> made　collapse　react　joke

① I thought my brother was shaking my bed as a _____.
② Soon the whole room began to shake _____.
③ Since it was my first time experiencing an earthquake, I didn't know how to _____.
④ I started to worry that the building would _____.
⑤ We nervously _____ our way down the stairs and outside.

04 다음 문장에 공통으로 들어가기에 적절한 말을 쓰시오.

> • I pulled _____ immediately.
> • He said that _____ 20,000 people had to leave their homes.
> • A cup tipped _____ and rolled off the kitchen table.

➡ _____

[05~06] 다음 대화를 읽고 물음에 답하시오.

A: In case of a heat wave, what should I do?
B: Make sure that you drink more water than usual.
A: _____(A)_____
B: Make sure that you __(B)__ a cool building immediately.

05 빈칸 (A)에 들어가기에 적절한 말을 고르시오.

① What is it?　　　② Anything else?
③ Really?　　　　④ How about you?
⑤ Is it necessary?

06 위 대화의 내용으로 보아, 빈칸 (B)에 들어가기에 적절한 것은?

① leave　　　　② exit
③ cause　　　　④ destroy
⑤ move into

[07~09] 다음 대화를 읽고 물음에 답하시오.

> B: Hey, did you hear about the big fires in California?
>
> G: No, I didn't. ⓐ<u>How serious are they?</u>
>
> B: They've destroyed a large number of houses and other buildings.
>
> G: ⓑ<u>Are the fires over now?</u>
>
> B: ⓒ<u>Yes, actually the wind has made the fires worse.</u> I hope all the people living there are okay.
>
> G: (A)나도 마찬가지야. ⓓ<u>I'm curious about how many people had to leave their homes.</u>
>
> B: Actually more than 20,000 people had to leave their homes, and about 400 people are missing in that area.
>
> G: ⓔ<u>That's terrible.</u> I hope they're somewhere safe.

07 밑줄 친 (A)에 해당하는 말을 so를 포함하여 3단어의 영어로 쓰시오.

➡ _____

08 위 대화의 ⓐ~ⓔ 중 문맥상 어색한 것은?

① ⓐ ② ⓑ ③ ⓒ ④ ⓓ ⑤ ⓔ

09 위 대화의 내용과 일치하지 <u>않는</u> 것은?

① The boy and the girl are talking about the big fires in California.

② The fires destroyed many houses and buildings.

③ Due to the wind, the fire got worse.

④ More than 20,000 people had to leave their homes.

⑤ About 400 people were found in that area.

10 Which is grammatically WRONG?

① Although Mina knew the right answer, she didn't let us know.

② Family members gather even though they may live far apart.

③ I had to go and greet him since I didn't want to.

④ When in Rome, do as the Romans do.

⑤ Some dogs have a long tail, while others have a short one.

11 다음 빈칸에 들어갈 말을 순서대로 묶은 것은?

> • I found out that I _____ my purse at the restaurant.
>
> • Don't eat too much fast food _____ you love them.

① left – when ② have left – since

③ have left – though ④ had left – since

⑤ had left – though

12 다음 문장에서 어법상 <u>어색한</u> 것을 바르게 고쳐 다시 쓰시오.

(1) Despite it rained a lot, we enjoyed our holiday.

➡ _____

(2) As though it was cold, I felt very happy today.

➡ _____

(3) Though Laura is very kind, she is loved by all of them.

➡ _____

(4) He learned that he has been chosen to play Harry Potter.

➡ _____

(5) The play already started when we arrived.

➡ _____

13 다음 중 어법상 옳은 문장을 모두 고르시오.

① Winter can have negative effects on many people since it is cold.

② Soon I realized that I left my report at home.

③ Because I had done many earthquake drills in school, I had never thought I'd experience a real earthquake.

④ After I finish the exam, I will go to an amusement park.

⑤ I woke up suddenly though my bed was shaking.

14 위 글의 빈칸 ⓐ에 say를 알맞은 형태로 쓰시오.

➡ _____

15 위 글의 밑줄 친 (A)as와 같은 의미로 쓰인 것을 고르시오.

① They did as I had asked.

② The news came as a shock.

③ He sat watching her as she got ready.

④ As one grows older, one becomes more silent.

⑤ You're as tall as your father.

[14~15] 다음 글을 읽고 물음에 답하시오.

One night in February, after I had gone to bed, an earthquake hit. I woke up suddenly because my bed was shaking. I thought my brother was shaking my bed (A)as a joke. But then I heard the mirror on my desk fall to the floor and break into pieces. I knew it wasn't my brother then, but I still didn't know what exactly was happening.

Soon the whole room began to shake violently, and my confusion turned to panic. My mom shouted that it was an earthquake and ran into my room. Since it was my first time experiencing an earthquake, I didn't know how to react. I just kept ___ⓐ___, "What should I do?"

[16~17] 다음 글을 읽고 물음에 답하시오.

My mom pulled me and my brother out of bed. We ran to the kitchen and crawled under the table. I could see the light ①swinging violently and books ②falling to the floor. Our family picture dropped from the wall and the glass covering it broke. A cup ⓐ tipped over and rolled off the kitchen table. Every ③second, I could hear something else in the apartment ④break. I started ⑤ to worry that the building would collapse.

16 위 글의 밑줄 친 ①~⑤와 바꿔 쓸 수 있는 말로 옳지 않은 것을 고르시오.

① swing   ② fall   ③ moment

④ broken   ⑤ worrying

17 위 글의 밑줄 친 ⓐtip과 같은 의미로 쓰인 것을 고르시오.

① It is in the northern tip of the island.

② I need a useful tip on how to save money.

③ It isn't allowed to leave a tip over $5.

④ He gave the waiter a generous tip.

⑤ The machine may tip over and break the dishes.

[18~19] 다음 글을 읽고 물음에 답하시오.

Then the shaking seemed to stop. We started crawling toward the door. At that moment, my mom's cell phone rang. It was my dad, ⓐwho was coming home from work.

He shouted, "It stopped! Get out of the building! Take the stairs! Don't take the elevator! Hurry!" "Where are you? Are you okay?" my mom asked urgently. My dad answered, "Don't worry. I'm okay. I was driving home when the shaking started. But I pulled over immediately. I'm listening to the radio right now to find out what's going on."

18 위 글의 밑줄 친 ⓐwho를 다음과 같이 바꿔 쓸 때 빈칸에 들어갈 알맞은 말을 두 단어로 쓰시오.

➡ _____

19 위 글의 내용과 일치하도록 다음 빈칸 (A)와 (B)에 알맞은 단어를 쓰시오.

The writer's dad called her mom and told her to get out of the building and take (A)_____ _____ instead of (B)_____.

[20~21] 다음 글을 읽고 물음에 답하시오.

We nervously made our way down the stairs and outside. I looked around. Parts of buildings had fallen and had smashed several cars. We went to an open space to avoid more falling pieces. How could all this have happened in a few minutes?

_____ⓐ_____ I had done many earthquake drills in school, I had never thought I'd experience a real earthquake. I still get scared when I remember that night. I can't forget the panic I felt when the furniture was shaking and things were falling to the floor. After that night, I began to take earthquake drills seriously. I realized that I should be prepared for the next earthquake, which can occur at any time.

<I: a girl>

20 위 글의 빈칸 ⓐ에 들어갈 알맞은 접속사를 고르시오.

① Although   ② Because   ③ As

④ If   ⑤ Since

21 According to the passage, which is NOT true?

① The writer's family nervously made their way down the stairs and outside.

② Parts of buildings had fallen and had smashed several cars.

③ The writer had done many earthquake drills in school.

④ The writer still gets scared when she remembers that night.

⑤ The writer had taken earthquake drills seriously before he experienced a real earthquake.

My Roles in Society

🎤 의사소통 기능

- 고민이나 불만족의 원인에 대해 묻기
  What's the matter?

- 확실성 정도 표현하기
  I have no doubt that you will take some
  wonderful pictures.

🎤 언어 형식

- 접속사 *if/whether*
  I suddenly started to wonder **if[whether]** these
  are the only qualities that make a good leader.

- 조동사의 수동태
  I don't think a person like me **can be called** a
  leader.

Words & Expressions

Key Words

- **ability** [əbíləti] 몡 능력
- **achieve** [ətʃíːv] 동 성취하다, 이루다
- **analyst** [ǽnəlist] 몡 분석가
- **analyze** [ǽnəlàiz] 동 분석하다
- **approach** [əpróutʃ] 동 접근하다
- **check** [tʃek] 동 점검하다
- **clear** [kliər] 형 명확한, 뚜렷한
- **confident** [kánfədənt] 형 자신감 있는
- **contact** [kántækt] 몡 접촉
- **create** [kriéit] 동 창조하다
- **decide** [disáid] 동 결정하다
- **decorate** [dékərèit] 동 장식하다
- **deliver** [dilívər] 동 배달하다
- **determine** [ditə́ːrmin] 동 결정하다, 결심하다
- **director** [diréktər] 몡 감독
- **discover** [diskʌ́vər] 동 발견하다, 찾다
- **divide** [diváid] 동 나누다, 분리하다
- **edit** [édit] 동 편집하다
- **effective** [iféktiv] 형 효과적인
- **election** [ilékʃən] 몡 선거
- **ensure** [inʃúər] 동 반드시 ~하게 하다, 보장하다
- **environment** [inváiərənmənt] 몡 환경
- **friendly** [fréndli] 형 친절한
- **goal** [goul] 몡 목적, 목표
- **hands-off** [hǽndzɔ̀ːf] 형 불간섭주의의, 자유방임의
- **instead** [instéd] 부 대신에
- **leadership** [líːdərʃip] 몡 지도력, 리더십
- **logical** [ládʒikəl] 형 논리적인, 타당한, 사리에 맞는
- **material** [mətíəriəl] 몡 자료, 소재, 재료
- **misunderstanding** [mìsʌndərstǽndiŋ] 몡 오해
- **motivate** [móutəvèit] 동 동기를 부여하다
- **outgoing** [áutgouiŋ] 형 외향적인, 사교적인
- **positive** [pázətiv] 형 긍정적인
- **prepare** [pripέər] 동 준비하다
- **presentation** [prèzəntéiʃən] 몡 발표
- **properly** [prápərli] 부 적절히, 제대로
- **quality** [kwáləti] 몡 질, 우수함, 자질
- **realize** [ríːəlàiz] 동 깨닫다
- **reasoning** [ríːzniŋ] 몡 추리, 추론
- **relieved** [rilíːvd] 형 안심이 되는
- **representative** [rèprizéntətiv] 몡 대표(자)
- **research** [risə́ːrtʃ] 몡 조사, 연구
- **responsibility** [rispànsəbíləti] 몡 책임, 의무
- **return** [ritə́ːrn] 동 돌아오다, 반납하다
- **role** [roul] 몡 역할
- **run** [rʌn] 동 달리다, (선거에) 입후보하다
- **seem** [siːm] 동 ~인 것 같다
- **step** [step] 몡 단계
- **strict** [strikt] 형 엄격한
- **supporter** [səpɔ́ːrtər] 몡 지지자
- **switch** [switʃ] 동 바꾸다, 전환하다
- **translate** [trænsléit] 동 해석하다
- **valued** [vǽljuːd] 형 귀중한, 존중 받는
- **vision** [víʒən] 몡 통찰력, 비전, 시력

Key Expressions

- **be good at** ~을 잘하다
- **be in charge of** ~을 담당하다, 책임지다
- **be responsible for** ~에 책임이 있다
- **be stuck in** ~에 갇히다
- **belong to** ~에 속하다
- **call for** ~을 필요로 하다, 요구하다
- **come up** 발생하다, 생기다
- **come up with** ~을 생각해 내다, 내놓다
- **deal with** 다루다, 처리하다
- **field trip** 견학, 체험 학습
- **get along** 잘 지내다, 사이좋게 지내다
- **hang out** 어울려 밖에서 시간을 보내다
- **lead by example** 솔선수범하다, 모범을 보이다
- **let down** 기대를 저버리다, ~을 실망시키다
- **meet the needs** 필요를 채워주다
- **no way** 절대로 아니다
- **on time** 정각에
- **run for** 출마하다
- **take care of** ~을 처리하다, ~을 돌보다
- **take sides** 편들다
- **turn out** (일·진행·결과가 특정 방식으로) 되다
- **work on** 공들여 일하다
- **work out** 해결하다
- **would love to** ~하고 싶다

Word Power

※ 서로 비슷한 뜻을 가진 어휘

- **ability** 능력 : **capability** 능력
- **actually** 실제로 : **really** 실제로
- **choose** 선택하다 : **select** 선택하다
- **environment** 환경 : **surrounding** 환경

- **achieve** 성취하다 : **accomplish** 성취하다
- **approach** 접근하다 : **access** 접근하다
- **decide** 결정하다 : **determine** 결정하다
- **goal** 목적, 목표 : **target** 목표

※ 서로 반대의 뜻을 가진 어휘

- **effective** 효과적인 ↔ **ineffective** 효과 없는
- **positive** 긍정적인 ↔ **negative** 부정적인

- **logical** 논리적인, 타당한 ↔ **illogical** 비논리적인
- **relieved** 안심이 되는 ↔ **worried** 걱정이 되는

※ 명사 – 형용사

- **confidence** 확신 – **confident** 자신 있는
- **decision** 결심 – **decisive** 결정적인
- **effect** 효과 – **effective** 효과적인

- **creation** 창조하다 – **creative** 창조적인
- **doubt** 의심 – **doubtful** 의심스러운
- **environment** 환경 – **environmental** 환경의

※ 동사 – 명사

- **achieve** 성취하다 – **achievement** 성취
- **choose** 선택하다 – **choice** 선택
- **decorate** 장식하다 – **decoration** 장식
- **discover** 발견하다 – **discovery** 발견
- **prepare** 준비하다 – **preparation** 준비

- **analyze** 분석하다 – **analysis** 분석
- **decide** 결정하다 – **decision** 결심
- **determine** 결정하다 – **determination** 결정
- **motivate** 동기를 부여하다 – **motivation** 동기
- **translate** 해석하다 – **translation** 해석

English Dictionary

- **analyze** 분석하다
  → to deeply study every piece of something to understand it 이해하기 위해 무언가의 모든 부분을 깊이 연구하다
- **approach** 접근하다
  → to come close to someone or something
  누군가나 무언가에 가까이 가다
- **confident** 자신감 있는
  → sure that one has the ability to do things well
  일을 잘하는 능력을 갖고 있음을 확신하는
- **effective** 효과적인
  → successful, and working in the way that was intended 성공적인 그리고 의도된 대로 작동하는
- **hands-off** 불간섭주의의, 자유방임의
  → letting people do what they want, without telling them what to do
  무엇을 하도록 말하지 않고 원하는 대로 하도록 허용하는

- **leadership** 지도력, 리더십
  → ability to lead 이끄는 능력
- **logical** 논리적인, 타당한
  → making sense; being reasonable 타당한; 합리적인
- **motivate** 동기를 부여하다
  → to provide with a reason to do something
  무엇인가를 할 이유를 제공하다
- **representative** 대표(자)
  → somebody who has been chosen to speak, or make decisions on behalf of a group
  그룹을 대신해 말하거나 결정하도록 선택된 사람
- **run** (선거에) 입후보하다
  → to compete as a candidate in an election
  선거에서 입후보자로 나서다
- **task** 일, 과업, 과제
  → a piece of work that must be done 처리되어야 하는 일

01 다음 영영풀이가 가리키는 것을 고르시오.

> someone who has been chosen to speak, or make decisions for someone else

① representative
② supporter
③ editor
④ director
⑤ analyst

02 다음 중 밑줄 친 부분의 뜻풀이가 바르지 <u>않은</u> 것은?

① When are you planning to <u>return</u> the books? (되돌아가다)
② There is no <u>doubt</u> about that fact. (의심)
③ Fortunately, she completed her <u>task</u> before deadline. (일, 과업)
④ Mom wants to <u>divide</u> the pizza into eight slices. (나누다)
⑤ Jaemin seems to enjoy <u>editing</u> the school magazine. (편집하다)

03 다음 주어진 문장의 밑줄 친 <u>vision</u>과 같은 의미로 쓰인 것은?

> My grandfather is a man with a great <u>vision</u>.

① Cats have good night <u>vision</u>.
② Have you ever had a <u>vision</u> of great wealth?
③ The scene was beyond my <u>vision</u>.
④ I have normal <u>vision</u>, so I don't need glasses.
⑤ My grandfather has poor <u>vision</u>, so it is dangerous for him to go outside at night.

서답형

04 다음 우리말에 맞게 빈칸에 알맞은 말을 쓰시오. (철자가 주어진 경우 그 철자로 시작할 것.)

(1) 나는 이번 주 금요일에 영어 대회를 준비해야 한다.
➡ I need to _____ the English contest this Friday.

(2) 나는 마지막 시험이 끝난 후 안도감을 느꼈다.
➡ I felt r_____ after finishing the final exam.

(3) James는 영어 기사를 한국어로 번역한다.
➡ James _____ the English article into Korean.

(4) 우리는 환경을 보호하기 위해 쓰레기를 줄여야 한다.
➡ We should r_____ the trash to protect the environment.

05 다음 문장의 (A)와 (B)에 공통으로 들어갈 말이 바르게 짝지어진 것은?

> • If you _____(A)_____ sides, I'll be disappointed with you.
> • My brothers __(A)__ care of patients at the hospital.
> • I don't know how to __(B)__ out his situation.
> • You can't imagine how I __(B)__ on this project.

	(A)	(B)
①	take	come
②	take	work
③	lead	work
④	lead	come
⑤	come	deal

01 다음 짝지어진 단어의 관계가 같도록 빈칸에 알맞은 말을 쓰시오.

> confident : confidence = creative : _____

 02 다음 우리말에 맞게 빈칸에 알맞은 말을 쓰시오.

(1) 당신이 만약 우리의 제품을 사용한다면 절대 실망하지 않을 것이다.
➡ You will never be _____ _____ if you use our product.

(2) 파티가 시작되었을 때, 나는 교통체증에 갇혀 있었다.
➡ When the party began, I _____ _____ _____ a traffic jam.

(3) 기회는 매일 생기지 않는다, 그래서 당신은 기회를 잡아야 한다.
➡ The chances don't _____ _____ every day, so you have to take them.

03 다음 문장의 빈칸에 들어갈 말을 〈보기〉에서 골라 쓰시오.

> ┤ 보기 ├
> analyze   logical   ensure
> valued   reasoning

(1) This method will _____ her success.
(2) I'm a _____ person at my workplace.
(3) It was the most _____ thing to do in that situation.
(4) We can understand his _____ about the case.
(5) Could you _____ the test results in details?

04 다음 우리말과 일치하도록 주어진 단어를 모두 배열하여 영작하시오.

(1) 반 대표에 입후보하는 게 어때?
(don't / class / run / representative / why / you / for)
➡ _____

(2) 만약 네가 입후보한다면 당선될 거라고 믿어 의심치 않아.
(no / that / I / if / you / elected / be / you / have / doubt / will / run)
➡ _____

(3) 나는 발표 자료를 만드는 일을 담당한다.
(materials / making / I'm / of / the / charge / in / presentation)
➡ _____

(4) 많은 사람들이 최고의 지도자들은 솔선수범한다고 믿는다.
(that / people / lead / the / leaders / example / believe / best / many / by)
➡ _____

05 다음 우리말을 주어진 단어를 이용하여 영작하시오.

(1) 형제들이 서로 잘 지낸다. (get, with)
➡ _____

(2) 왕은 솔선수범하기를 원한다. (would, example)
➡ _____

(3) 수질 오염을 끝내기 위한 새로운 아이디어를 생각해 보자. (up, end, pollution)
➡ _____

Conversation

1 고민이나 불만족의 원인에 대해 묻기

• **What's the matter?** 무슨 일 있니?

■ 상대방이 뭔가에 불만족하거나 실망하고 있어 보이거나 걱정스러운 표정일 때, 그 원인을 묻는 말로 'What's the matter (with you)?(무슨 일 있니?)'가 있다. 이와 비슷한 표현으로 'What's wrong?(뭐가 잘못됐니?)', 혹은 'What's the problem?(무슨 문제가 있니?)' 등이 있다.

■ 상대방이 안 좋아 보여서 무슨 문제가 있는지 물어볼 때는 'Is something wrong?(뭐가 잘못되었니?)' 또는 'What's wrong (with you)?(뭐가 잘못됐나요?)'와 같은 표현을 쓸 수도 있다. 고민이나 불만족의 원인을 물을 때는 'Why are you sad?(왜 속상한가요?)', 'Why are you disappointed?(왜 실망스러운가요?)', 'What are you worried/concerned/anxious about?(무엇에 대해 걱정/고민/근심하나요?)' 등의 표현을 쓴다.

■ 고민이나 불만족의 원인을 물어볼 때는 'Is something worrying you?(무슨 걱정거리가 있나요?)' 또는 'Is there something bothering you?(뭔가 걸리는 일이 있나요?)', 'Is there anything wrong?(뭐 잘못된 일 있니?)', 'What happened?(무슨 일 있니?)'와 같은 표현을 사용하기도 한다.

고민이나 불만족의 원인을 묻는 표현

• What's wrong? 뭐가 잘못됐나요?

• Why are you sad? 왜 속상한가요?

• Why are you disappointed? 왜 실망스러운가요?

• What are you worried/concerned/anxious about? 무엇에 대해 걱정/고민/근심하나요?

• Is something worrying you? 무슨 걱정거리가 있나요?

• Is there something bothering you? 뭔가 걸리는 일이 있나요?

• Is there anything wrong? 뭐 잘못된 일 있니?

• What happened? 무슨 일 있니?

핵심 Check

1. 다음 대화의 빈칸에 들어가기에 적절하지 <u>않은</u> 것은?

G: Mom, we've got a problem.

W: _____

G: We're going to have dinner with Grandma this Saturday, right? But I just realized that Sujin's birthday party is on Saturday evening. She's my best friend. What should I do?

W: That sounds like a difficult decision. Let's talk about it with your dad.

① What's wrong?　　　　② What's the matter?

③ Why are you worried?　④ Is there anything wrong?

⑤ What's so interesting?

2 확실성의 정도 표현하기

> • I have no doubt that you will take some wonderful pictures.
> 나는 네가 멋진 사진들을 찍을 것을 확신해.

■ 앞으로 일어날 일에 대하여 상대방에게 확신을 주는 말로, 원하는 것이나 좋은 일이 일어날 것이 확실함을 나타낼 때 'I have no doubt that ~.'이라는 표현을 사용한다. 이 표현은 '~할 거라고 믿는다, ~할 거라고 확신한다.'라는 의미이다.

■ 확실성 정도를 나타내는 표현에는 sure(확실한), certain(확신하는), positive(긍정적인) 등을 사용하여 'I'm sure/certain/positive about[that] ~.(~에 대해 확신하다.)'라고 할 수 있다. '확실하다'라는 의미로 'I'm 100 percent sure.(나는 100% 장담해.)' 또는 'It is obvious/clear that ~.(~가 분명하다.)'를 쓰기도 한다. 'bet'은 '내기를 걸다, 틀림없다'의 뜻으로 'I bet that ~.'이라고 하면 '틀림없이 ~이다.'라는 뜻이 된다. 상대방의 말에 '당연하지.'라고 할 때는 'You bet.'이라고 한다.

■ 상대에게 확신을 물어볼 때는 'Are you sure about ~?(~에 대해 확신하나요?)' 또는 'How sure are you that ~?(~에 대해 얼마나 확신하나요?)'이라고 한다.

확실성의 정도 표현하기

• I have no doubt that ~. ~할 거라고 믿는다.

• I'm sure/certain/positive about[that] ~. ~에 대해 확신하다.

• I bet that ~. 틀림없이 ~이다.　　　　　• Are you sure about ~? ~에 대해 확신하나요?

• How sure are you that ~? ~에 대해 얼마나 확신하나요?

• I'm 100 percent sure. 나는 100% 장담해.　　• It is obvious/clear that ~. ~은 확실하다.

핵심 Check

2. 다음 우리말과 일치하도록 주어진 표현을 포함하여 빈칸에 알맞은 말을 쓰시오.

A: What do you want to do for our class?

B: I want to make a student contact information list.

A: That sounds good. _____ (doubt, helpful)
(나는 그것이 매우 도움이 될 것이라고 믿어.)

3. 다음 대화의 순서를 바르게 배열하시오.

(A) That's great. You are really good at taking photos. I have no doubt that you will take some wonderful pictures.

(B) Sports Day is coming. How do you want to help out?

(C) I want to take photos for Sports Day.

➡ _____

 Listen & Talk 1 A

G: Mom, we've got a problem.

W: ❶What's the matter?

G: We're going to have dinner with Grandma this Saturday, right? But I just realized ❷that Sujin's birthday party is on Saturday evening. She's my best friend. What should I do?

W: That sounds like a difficult ❸decision. Let's talk about it with your dad.

G: Okay, Mom. I'd love to see Grandma, but I don't want to miss my best friend's birthday party.

소녀: 엄마, 우리에게 문제가 생겼어요.
여성: 무슨 일이니?
소녀: 이번 주 토요일에 할머니와 저녁 식사를 하기로 했잖아요. 그렇죠? 그런데 수진이의 생일 파티가 토요일 저녁이라는 것을 방금 깨달았어요. 수진이는 저와 가장 친한 친구예요. 저 어떡하죠?
여성: 결정하기 힘든 문제인 것 같구나. 네 아빠와 함께 이야기해 보자.
소녀: 네, 엄마. 할머니를 정말 뵙고 싶지만, 가장 친한 친구의 생일 파티에 빠지고 싶지는 않아요.

❶ 고민이나 불만족의 원인에 대해 묻는 표현으로 'What's wrong?', 'What's the problem?' 등으로 바꾸어 쓸 수 있다.
❷ 목적어 역할을 하는 명사절을 이끄는 접속사 that이다.　　❸ decision: 결정

Check(√) True or False

(1) The girl is going to see her grandma this Saturday.　　T ☐ F ☐

(2) The girl does not want to attend Sujin's birthday party.　　T ☐ F ☐

 Listen & Talk 1 B

M: Junsu, are you okay? What's the matter?

B: Hello, Mr. Smith. I have a problem.

M: What happened?

B: You know Jaewoo, Yunho, and I are best friends, right? They ❶had a fight, and now ❷I'm stuck in the middle. I don't know what to do.

M: That sounds hard. Do you know why ❸they had a fight?

B: Yes, but it doesn't sound like a big deal to me. I guess they had some kind of ❹misunderstanding.

M: Why don't you all meet together and talk about it? I think they'll listen to you.

B: That's a good idea. They're both good friends of mine. I can't ❺take sides.

M: I understand. I hope everything works out.

남자: 준수야, 괜찮니? 무슨 일이야?
소년: 안녕하세요, Smith 선생님. 저에게 문제가 생겼어요.
남자: 무슨 일인데?
소년: 재우와 윤호, 그리고 제가 서로 가장 친한 사이라는 거 아시죠. 그렇죠? 그 둘이 싸웠고, 저는 이제 중간에 끼어버린 상태예요. 어떻게 해야 할지 모르겠어요.
남자: 힘들겠구나. 그 둘이 왜 싸웠는지는 아니?
소년: 네, 하지만 제가 보기에는 그다지 대단한 일도 아닌 것 같아요. 아무래도 그 둘 사이에 어떤 오해가 생긴 것 같아요.
남자: 너희 모두 다 같이 만나서 그것에 대해 이야기해 보는 게 어떠니? 그 둘이 네 말은 들을 것 같구나.
소년: 그거 좋은 생각이네요. 두 명 모두 저에게는 좋은 친구들이에요. 저는 누구의 편도 들 수 없어요.
남자: 이해한다. 모두 잘 해결되기를 바란다.

❶ have a fight with: ~와 싸우다　　❷ be stuck in: ~에 갇히다　　❸ they는 재우와 윤호를 가리킨다.
❹ misunderstanding: 오해　　❺ take sides: 편들다

Check(√) True or False

(3) Junsu had a fight with Jaewoo and Yunho.　　T ☐ F ☐

(4) Junsu thinks there was some misunderstanding between Jaewoo and Yunho.　　T ☐ F ☐

Listen & Talk 1 C

B: Hey, Mandy. What's the matter?
G: I don't know what to do, Nick. My brother asked me to help him with his homework this Wednesday, but I told him I can't. I have so many things to do ❶that day.
B: What do you have to do this Wednesday?
G: I need to go to the library to ❷return some books. Then I have to meet you to work on our presentation. After that, I have to prepare for an exam at night.
B: Oh, you ❸do have a lot to do.
G: Yes. But my brother seemed ❹let down, so I feel bad.
B: Well, then ❺how about meeting on Thursday instead for our presentation? Then you can do everything and also help your brother on Wednesday.
G: That would help me out so much! Thanks for understanding, Nick!

❶ that day는 수요일을 가리킨다.
❷ return: 반납하다
❸ do는 have를 강조한다.
❹ let down: 실망하다
❺ 'How about ~?: ~하는 게 어때?'를 의미하며 'Why don't we ~?'로 바꾸어 쓸 수 있다.

Listen & Talk 2 A

G: Sports Day is coming. How do you want to help out?
B: I want to take photos for Sports Day.
G: That's great. You ❶are really good at taking photos. ❷I have no doubt that you will take some wonderful pictures.

❶ be good at ~: ~을 잘하다
❷ I have no doubt that ~.: ~할 거라고 확신한다.

Listen & Talk 2 B

B: In the Send Our Stories project, we are going to make a picture book for children in other countries. We've ❶divided everyone into three groups. Each group will ❷be responsible for a different task. Group A will ❸translate a Korean story into English. Group B will make drawings for the book and ❹edit it. After copies of the book are printed, Group C will ❺be in charge of sending them to the children. It won't be easy, but I have no doubt that the children who receive these books will really enjoy them.

❶ divide: 나누다
❷ be responsible for ~: ~에 책임을 갖다
❸ translate: 번역하다
❹ edit: 편집하다
❺ be in charge of: ~을 담당하다, 책임지다

Listen & Talk 2 C

B: I'm so excited about our museum ❶field trip.
G1: Me too. Let's check our ❷tasks. Yen, what are you in charge of?
G2: I'm in charge of taking pictures.
G1: Okay. Sejin, are you going to do some research on the museum?
B: Yes, I am. Are you going to write our field trip report, Emma?
G1: That's right. I think we're ready.
G2: Good. I have no doubt that our project will ❸turn out well.

❶ field trip: 견학, 체험 학습
❷ task: 일, 업무
❸ turn out: (일·진행·결과가 특정 방식으로) 되다

Do It Yourself A

Sujin: What's the matter? You ❶look worried.
Minsu: You know I'm going to be giving a presentation on our team's research. But I feel very nervous when I talk ❷in front of many people.
Sujin: Oh, I didn't know that you got nervous. Actually, I also have a problem.
Minsu: What's wrong?
Sujin: I'm in charge of making the presentation materials, but I'm not good at ❸it.
Minsu: You're not? I thought you were good at ❸it.
Sujin: No, I'm not. Hey, then what about switching roles? I've given presentations many times before, so I ❹don't get nervous at all.
Minsu: Really? That would be great. I think I am good at making presentation materials, and I like making ❺them!
Sujin: That's good. Let's talk to the other team members.
Minsu: Cool. I feel so relieved now.

❶ look+형용사: ~하게 보이다
❷ in front of: ~ 앞에
❸ it은 making the presentation materials를 가리킨다.
❹ not ~ at all: 전혀 ~ 아니다
❺ them은 presentation materials를 가리킨다.

● 다음 우리말과 일치하도록 빈칸에 알맞은 말을 쓰시오.

Listen & Talk 1 A

G: Mom, we've got a _____.

W: What's the _____?

G: We're going to have dinner with Grandma this Saturday, right? But I just realized that Sujin's birthday party is _____ _____ _____. She's my best friend. _____ _____ _____ _____?

W: That sounds like a difficult _____. Let's talk about it with your dad.

G: Okay, Mom. I'd love to see Grandma, but I don't want to _____ my best friend's birthday party.

Listen & Talk 1 B

M: Junsu, are you okay? _____ _____ _____?

B: Hello, Mr. Smith. I have a problem.

M: What _____?

B: You know Jaewoo, Yunho, and I are best friends, right? They _____ _____ _____, and now I'm _____ _____ the middle. I don't know _____ _____ _____.

M: That sounds hard. Do you know _____ they had a fight?

B: Yes, but it doesn't sound like a _____ _____ to me. I guess they had _____ kind of _____.

M: _____ _____ you all meet together and talk about it? I think they'll listen to you.

B: That's a good idea. They're both good friends of mine. I _____ _____ _____.

M: I understand. I hope everything _____ _____.

Listen & Talk 1 C

B: Hey, Mandy. _____ _____ _____?

G: I don't know what to do, Nick. My brother _____ _____ _____ _____ _____ with his homework this Wednesday, but I told him I can't. I have so many things to do that day.

B: What do you have to do this Wednesday?

G: I need to go to the library to _____ _____ _____. Then I have to meet you to work on our _____. After that, I have to _____ for an exam at night.

해석

소녀: 엄마, 우리에게 문제가 생겼어요.

여성: 무슨 일이니?

소녀: 이번 주 토요일에 할머니와 저녁 식사를 하기로 했잖아요, 그렇죠? 그런데 수진이의 생일 파티가 토요일 저녁이라는 것을 방금 깨달았어요. 수진이는 저의 가장 친한 친구예요. 저 어떡하죠?

여성: 결정하기 힘든 문제인 것 같구나. 네 아빠와 함께 이야기해 보자.

소녀: 네, 엄마. 할머니를 정말 뵙고 싶지만, 가장 친한 친구의 생일 파티에 빠지고 싶지는 않아요.

남자: 준수야, 괜찮니? 무슨 일이야?

소년: 안녕하세요, Smith 선생님. 저에게 문제가 생겼어요.

남자: 무슨 일인데?

소년: 재우와 윤호, 그리고 제가 서로 가장 친한 사이라는 거 아시죠, 그렇죠? 그 둘이 싸웠고, 저는 이제 중간에 끼어버린 상태예요. 어떻게 해야 할지 모르겠어요.

남자: 힘들겠구나. 그 둘이 왜 싸웠는지는 아니?

소년: 네, 하지만 제가 보기에는 그다지 대단한 일도 아닌 것 같아요. 아무래도 그 둘 사이에 어떤 오해가 생긴 것 같아요.

남자: 너희 모두 다 같이 만나서 그것에 대해 이야기해 보는 게 어떠니? 그들이 네 말은 들을 것 같구나.

소년: 그거 좋은 생각이네요. 두 명 모두 저에게는 좋은 친구들이에요. 저는 누구의 편도 들 수 없어요.

남자: 이해한단다. 모두 잘 해결되기를 바란다.

남: 어이, Mandy. 무슨 일이야?

여: 어떻게 해야 할지 모르겠어, Nick. 내 동생이 이번 주 수요일에 숙제를 도와달라고 했는데, 도와줄 수 없다고 했어. 나는 그날 해야 할 일이 너무 많아.

남: 이번 주 수요일에 무엇을 해야 하는데?

여: 책을 반납하러 도서관에 가야 해. 그런 다음 우리의 발표 준비를 위해 너를 만나야 하고. 그다음에, 밤에는 시험 준비를 해야 해.

B: Oh, you _____ have a lot to do.

G: Yes. But my brother seemed _____ _____, so I feel bad.

B: Well, then _____ _____ _____ on Thursday instead for our presentation? Then you can do _____ and also _____ your brother on Wednesday.

G: That would _____ _____ _____ so much! Thanks for understanding, Nick!

Listen & Talk 2 A

G: _____ _____ is coming. How do you want to help out?

B: I want to take photos for Sports Day.

G: That's great. You are really _____ _____ _____ _____. I _____ _____ _____ _____ you will take some wonderful pictures.

Listen & Talk 2 B

B: In the Send Our Stories project, we are going to make a picture book for children in other countries. We've _____ everyone _____ three groups. Each group will _____ _____ _____ a different task. Group A will _____ a Korean story into English. Group B will make drawings for the book and _____ it. After copies of the book are printed, Group C will be _____ _____ _____ sending them to the children. It won't be easy, but _____ _____ _____ _____ the children _____ receive these books will really enjoy them.

Listen & Talk 2 C

B: I'm so _____ about our museum _____ _____.

G1: Me too. Let's check our tasks. Yen, what are you _____ _____ _____?

G2: I'm in charge of _____ _____.

G1: Okay. Sejin, are you going to do _____ _____ on the museum?

B: Yes, I am. Are you going to _____ _____ _____ _____ _____ _____, Emma?

G1: That's right. I think we're ready.

G2: Good. I _____ _____ _____ _____ our project will _____ _____ well.

남: 아, 너 정말로 할 일이 많구나.

여: 응. 하지만 내 동생이 실망한 것처럼 보여서, 기분이 좋지가 않아.

남: 음, 그럼 우리 발표를 위해 목요일에 대신 만나는 건 어때? 그러면 너는 수요일에 모든 일을 하고 네 동생도 도와줄 수 있어.

여: 그러면 정말 큰 도움이 될 거야! 이해해 줘서 고마워, Nick!

여: 곧 있으면 운동회야. 어떻게 돕고 싶니?

남: 나는 운동회 날 사진을 찍고 싶어.

여: 그거 좋다. 너는 정말 사진을 잘 찍잖아. 나는 네가 운동회 날에 멋진 사진들을 찍을 것이라는 것을 확신해.

남: Send Our Stories 프로젝트에서 우리는 외국의 아이들을 위한 그림책을 만들 예정입니다. 우리는 모두를 세 그룹으로 나누었습니다. 각 그룹은 서로 다른 작업을 담당할 것입니다. A 그룹은 한국어 이야기를 영어로 번역할 것입니다. B 그룹은 이 책의 그림을 그리고 편집을 할 것입니다. 책들이 인쇄되면, C 그룹은 이 책들을 아이들에게 보내는 일을 맡게 될 것입니다. 쉽지는 않겠지만, 저는 이 책을 받는 어린이들이 이 책을 정말로 좋아할 것이라고 확신합니다.

남: 우리의 박물관 견학이 정말 기대돼.

여1: 나도 그래. 각자 맡은 일을 확인해 보자. Yen, 너는 무엇을 담당하지?

여2: 나는 사진 촬영 담당이야.

여1: 그래. 세진아, 너는 박물관 조사를 할 거지?

남: 응, 맞아. 너는 견학 보고서를 작성할 거지, Emma?

여1: 맞아. 이제 우리는 준비가 된 것 같아.

여2: 좋아. 우리 프로젝트가 잘될 거라는 데 의심의 여지가 없어.

[01~02] 다음 대화를 읽고 물음에 답하시오.

Sejin: I'm so excited about our museum field trip.

Emma: (A)Me too. Let's check our tasks. Yen, what are you in charge of?

Yen: I'm in charge of taking pictures.

Emma: Okay. Sejin, are you going to do some research on the museum?

Sejin: Yes, I am. Are you going to write our field trip report, Emma?

Emma: That's right. I think we're ready.

Yen: Good. I have no ___(B)___ that our project will turn out well.

01 위 대화의 밑줄 친 (A)와 바꾸어 쓸 수 있는 것은?

① So do I. ② So am I. ③ Neither do I.
④ Neither am I. ⑤ Me neither.

02 위 대화의 빈칸 (B)에 알맞은 말을 쓰시오.

➡ _____

03 다음 대화의 내용과 일치하지 <u>않는</u> 것은?

Jisu: Mom, we've got a problem.

Mom: What's the matter?

Jisu: We're going to have dinner with Grandma this Saturday, right? But I just realized that Sujin's birthday party is on Saturday evening. She's my best friend. What should I do?

Mom: That sounds like a difficult decision. Let's talk about it with your dad.

Jisu: Okay, Mom. I'd love to see Grandma, but I don't want to miss my best friend's birthday party.

① 지수는 이번 주 토요일에 할머니와 저녁을 먹을 예정이다.
② 지수의 가장 친한 친구의 생일 파티가 토요일 저녁에 있다.
③ 지수는 할머니도 보고 싶고, 친구의 생일 파티도 놓치고 싶지 않다.
④ 엄마는 지수에게 아빠와 이야기해 볼 것을 조언했다.
⑤ 토요일에 지수는 할머니와의 저녁식사 대신 수진이의 생일 파티에 참석할 것이다.

[01~02] 다음 대화를 읽고 물음에 답하시오.

Jisu: Mom, we've got a problem.

Mom: (A)What's the matter?

Jisu: We're going to have dinner with Grandma this Saturday, right? But I just realized that Sujin's birthday party is on Saturday evening. She's my best friend. What should I do?

Mom: That sounds like a difficult decision. Let's talk about it with your dad.

Jisu: Okay, Mom. I'd love to see Grandma, but I don't want to miss my best friend's birthday party.

01 위 대화의 밑줄 친 (A)와 바꾸어 쓸 수 있는 것은?

① How are you doing?

② Where have you been?

③ Is there something wrong?

④ Can you tell me how to do it?

⑤ How were your holidays?

02 위 대화를 읽고 대답할 수 <u>없는</u> 것은?

① When is Jisu going to have dinner with her grandma?

② When is Sujin's birthday party?

③ What's the matter with Jisu?

④ What are Jisu and her mom going to talk about with her dad?

⑤ What is Jisu going to do on Saturday?

서답형

03 다음 대화에서 밑줄 친 우리말을 <보기>에 주어진 단어를 모두 배열하여 영작하시오.

G: Sports Day is coming. How do you want to help out?

B: I want to take photos for Sports Day.

G: That's great. You are really good at taking photos. 나는 네가 멋진 사진들을 찍을 것이라는 것을 확신해.

┤ 보기 ├

wonderful / no / that / I / you / some / will / have / pictures / doubt / take

➡ _____

[04~06] 다음 대화를 읽고 물음에 답하시오.

Mr. Smith: Junsu, are you okay? What's the matter?

Junsu: ⓐ Hello, Mr. Smith. I have a problem.

Mr. Smith: ⓑ What happened?

Junsu: ⓒ You know Jaewoo, Yunho, and I are best friends, right? They had a fight, and now I'm stuck in the middle. I don't know what to do.

Mr. Smith: ⓓ Do you know why they (A)[had a fight / made up with]?

Junsu: ⓔ Yes, but it doesn't sound like a big deal to me. I guess they had some kind of misunderstanding.

Mr. Smith: Why don't you all meet together and talk about it? I think they'll listen to you.

Junsu: That's a good idea. They're both good friends of mine. I can't (B)[take part / take sides].

Mr. Smith: I understand. I hope everything (C)[works out / works on].

중요

04 위 대화의 ⓐ~ⓔ 중 주어진 문장이 들어가기에 가장 적절한 곳은?

That sounds hard.

① ⓐ ② ⓑ ③ ⓒ ④ ⓓ ⑤ ⓔ

05 위 대화의 (A)~(C)에 알맞은 말이 바르게 짝지어진 것은?

	(A)	(B)	(C)
①	had a fight	take part	works out
②	had a fight	take sides	works on
③	had a fight	take sides	works out
④	made up with	take sides	works on
⑤	made up with	take part	works out

06 위 대화를 읽고 대답할 수 <u>없는</u> 것은?

① What's the matter with Junsu?

② Who are Junsu's best friends?

③ When did Jaewoo and Yunho have a fight?

④ What is Mr. Smith's advice?

⑤ Does Junsu know why Jaewoo and Yunho had a fight?

[07~09] 다음 대화를 읽고 물음에 답하시오.

Sejin: I'm so excited about our museum field trip.

Emma: Me too. Let's check our tasks. Yen, what are you in charge of?

Yen: I'm in charge of taking pictures.

Emma: Okay. Sejin, are you going to do some research on the museum?

Sejin: Yes, I am. Are you going to write our field trip report, Emma?

Emma: That's right. I think we're ready.

Yen: Good.

서답형

07 위 대화의 빈칸에 들어갈 말을 〈보기〉에 주어진 단어들을 모두 배열하여 완성하시오.

┌─ 보기 ─────────────────────┐
that / out / our / no / I / doubt / project / have / well / will / turn
└──────────────────────────┘

➡ _____

서답형

08 What is Sejin going to do for the museum field trip?

➡ _____

서답형

09 Who will be in charge of writing the field trip report?

➡ _____

_____

[10~11] 다음 글을 읽고 물음에 답하시오.

B: In the Send Our Stories project, we are going to make a picture book for children in other countries. ⓐWe've divided everyone into three groups. Each group will be responsible for a different task. Group A will translate a Korean story into English. Group B will make drawings for the book and ⓑedit it. After copies of the book ⓒprinted, Group C will be in charge of ⓓsending them to the children. It won't be easy, but I have no doubt that the children ⓔwho receive these books will really enjoy them.

10 위 글의 밑줄 친 ⓐ~ⓔ 중 어법상 <u>어색한</u> 것을 골라 바르게 고치시오.

_____ ➡ _____

11 위 글의 내용과 일치하지 <u>않는</u> 것은?

① Send Our Stories 프로젝트에서 외국의 아이들을 위한 그림책을 만들 예정이다.

② 모두를 세 그룹으로 나누어 각 그룹은 서로 다른 작업을 담당할 것이다.

③ A 그룹은 영어 이야기를 한국어로 번역할 것이다.

④ B 그룹은 이 책의 그림을 그리고 편집을 할 것이다.

⑤ C 그룹은 이 책들을 아이들에게 보내는 일을 맡게 될 것이다.

[01~03] 다음 글을 읽고 물음에 답하시오.

B: In the Send Our Stories project, we are going to make a picture book for children in other countries. We've divided everyone into three groups. Each group will be responsible for a different task. Group A will translate a Korean story into English. Group B will make drawings for the book and edit it. After copies of the book are printed, Group C will be in charge of sending them to the children. It won't be easy, but I have no doubt that the children who receive these books will really enjoy them.

01 What are they going to do in the Send Our Stories project?

➡ _____

_____

_____

02 What is Group B in charge of?

➡ _____

_____

03 What do students have to do after copies of the book are printed?

➡ _____

04 다음 대화의 내용과 일치하도록 Mandy의 일기를 완성하시오.

Nick: Hey, Mandy. What's the matter?
Mandy: I don't know what to do, Nick. My brother asked me to help him with his homework this Wednesday,

but I told him I can't. I have so many things to do that day.
Nick: What do you have to do this Wednesday?
Mandy: I need to go to the library to return some books. Then I have to meet you to work on our presentation. After that, I have to prepare for an exam at night.
Nick: Oh, you do have a lot to do.
Mandy: Yes. But my brother seemed let down, so I feel bad.
Nick: Well, then how about meeting on Thursday instead for our presentation? Then you can do everything and also help your brother on Wednesday.
Mandy: That would help me out so much! Thanks for understanding, Nick!

Mandy's Diary

Mon, June 22, 2020
Today, I really appreciated Nick. When my brother asked me to (A)_____

_____ this Wednesday, I said I couldn't help him. My brother seemed (B)_____, so I felt so sorry. In fact, I had lots of things to do this Wednesday. I have to go to the library (C)_____

_____, and (D)_____

_____. After that, (E)_____

_____. When I talked about it to Nick, he suggested putting off our meeting schedule. He understood me, so we decided to meet (F)_____

for our presentation. How kind he was! Thanks to Nick, I can help my brother.

Grammar
교과서

1 접속사 if/whether

> • I suddenly started to wonder **if**[**whether**] these are the only qualities that make a good leader. 나는 갑자기 이것들이 좋은 리더를 만드는 유일한 자질들인지 궁금해하기 시작했다.

■ '~인지 (아닌지)'라는 의미의 접속사로 불확실하거나 의문시되는 사실을 나타낼 때 쓰이며, 'if[whether]＋주어＋동사'의 형태로, 주로 ask, be not sure, find out, know, see, tell, wonder 등과 같은 동사의 목적어 역할을 하는 명사절을 이끈다. if 뒤에 오는 절은 의문사가 없는 간접의문문이며 문장 마지막에 or not을 함께 써서 '~ 아닌지'의 의미를 확실하게 전달할 수 있다.

- I'm not sure **if** I should take this job. 이 일을 맡아야 할지 모르겠어. 〈목적어〉
- **Whether** he will fight or run away is his option. 싸우거나 도망하거나 그 사람 마음대로다. 〈주어〉
- What is at issue is **whether** she was responsible for her actions. 쟁점이 되고 있는 것은 그녀가 자기 행동에 대해 책임을 져야 했느냐는 점이다. 〈보어〉

■ whether와 if는 보통 다음과 같은 차이가 있다.

(1) whether는 문장의 맨 처음에 나와 주어를 이끌 수 있지만 if는 그럴 수 없다.

- **Whether** he will carry out his plan (or not) is not confirmed. 그가 계획을 실행할지는 확인되지 않는다.

(2) whether는 전치사의 목적어를 이끌 수 있지만 if는 그럴 수 없다.

- Keep track of **whether** the screensaver has become active (or not). 화면 보호기의 활성화 여부를 추적하세요.

(3) whether는 to부정사와 함께 쓰일 수 있지만 if는 그럴 수 없다.

- He seemed to try to decide **whether** to say something or not. 그는 무슨 말을 할까 말까 결정하려는 듯이 보였다.

(4) whether는 'or not'이 바로 뒤에 나올 때 쓰일 수 있지만 if는 그럴 수 없다. 'whether[if] ~ or not'의 형태로는 쓸 수 있다.

- I don't know **whether** or not it was true. 나는 그것이 사실이었는지 아닌지 모른다.
- I don't know **whether**[**if**] he'll be promoted or not. 나는 그가 승진할지 여부를 모른다.

(5) whether는 be동사의 보어로 쓰일 수 있지만 if는 그럴 수 없다.

- The question is **whether** he is ready for it. 문제는 그가 그것에 준비가 되었느냐는 것이다.

핵심 Check

1. 다음 괄호 안에서 알맞은 말을 고르시오.

(1) Please tell me (if / that) you need anything.

(2) I asked (that / whether) he believed the rumor.

2 조동사의 수동태

> • I don't think a person like me **can be called** a leader.
> 나 같은 사람이 리더로 불릴 수 있다고 생각하지 않아.
>
> • She begged that she **should be allowed** to go. 그녀는 가도록 허락해 달라고 간청했다.

■ 수동태는 행위자보다는 행위의 대상에 중점을 두고 말할 때 쓰며, 조동사가 있는 문장의 수동태는 '조동사+be+과거분사'의 형태로 나타내며, 수동태 문장에 조동사의 뜻을 더하여 해석한다.

- We must take down the sign. 우리는 그 표지판을 치워야 한다.

  → The sign **must be taken** down. 그 표지판은 치워져야 한다.

■ 부정문은 '조동사+not+be+과거분사'의 형태로, 의문문은 '조동사+주어+be+과거분사 ~?'의 형태로 쓴다.

- Applications received after 1 July **will not be counted**. 7월 1일 이후에 접수된 원서는 인정되지 않는다.

- **Can** it **be proved** that he did commit these offences? 그가 정말 이 범행들을 저질렀다는 것을 입증할 수 있을까요?

cf. 1. 수동태 구문에서 행위자가 일반인이거나 강조할 필요가 없을 때에는 'by+행위자'를 생략하고 쓸 수 있다.

- This tool **can be used** in a variety of ways. 이 도구는 갖가지 방식으로 이용될 수 있다.

2. 수동태로 쓰지 않는 동사

자동사는 목적어가 없으므로 수동태로 쓸 수 없으며 '상태'나 '소유'를 나타내는 타동사도 수동태로 쓰이지 않음에 주의해야 한다.

- The idea **occurred** to him in a dream. 그 아이디어는 꿈속에서 그에게 떠오른 것이었다.

  The idea was occurred to him in a dream. (×)

- She **has** a good singing voice. 그녀는 노래하는 목소리가 곱다.

  A good singing voice is had by her. (×)

핵심 Check

2. 다음 우리말과 일치하도록 주어진 어휘를 이용하여 빈칸에 알맞게 쓰시오.

(1) 그 회의는 Glasgow에서 열릴 것이다. (will, hold)

➡ The conference ＿＿＿＿ ＿＿＿＿ ＿＿＿＿ in Glasgow.

(2) 그것은 조심스럽게 처리되어야 한다. (should, handle)

➡ It ＿＿＿＿ ＿＿＿＿ ＿＿＿＿ carefully.

Grammar 시험대비 기본평가

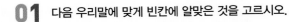

01 다음 우리말에 맞게 빈칸에 알맞은 것을 고르시오.

> 그가 집에 있을지 모르겠다.
> = I wonder _____ he is at home.

① that   ② what   ③ which
④ if   ⑤ unless

02 다음 문장을 수동태로 고쳤을 때 알맞은 것은?

> We can purchase uniforms from the school.

① Uniforms can be purchased from the school.
② Uniforms are purchased from the school.
③ Uniforms be purchased from the school.
④ Uniforms can purchase from the school.
⑤ Uniforms can are purchased from the school.

03 다음 중 어법상 <u>어색한</u> 것은?

① Please check if the rumor is true.
② I wonder if she likes me.
③ I was not sure that she would come.
④ Will you ask him if he will participate in the party?
⑤ I don't know whether there is a library around here.

04 다음 괄호 안의 어휘를 바르게 배열하시오.

(1) The letter (tomorrow, by me, sent, be, will).
   ➡ _____

(2) The pain of the victims (forgotten, be, not, must).
   ➡ _____

(3) How else (it, done, can, be)?
   ➡ _____

01 다음 중 어법상 올바른 것은?

① I don't want to know that something happened.
② I wonder if we can win the soccer game.
③ Matthew asked Vivian if or not she wanted to go back home.
④ I'm not sure that Ted won the speech contest.
⑤ Let me know if she brings some food.

02 다음 중 어법상 바르지 않은 것은?

① The cloth should be laid flat on the table.
② This essay will have to completely rewritten.
③ Nothing could be done without her help.
④ This problem must be solved right now.
⑤ The money will be used to help babies.

03 다음 대화의 빈칸에 들어갈 말로 알맞은 것은?

> M: I want to take photos for Sports Day.
> B: That's great. Some wonderful pictures _____ .

① take   ② are take
③ will take   ④ will taken
⑤ will be taken

서답형
04 다음 괄호 안에서 알맞은 말을 고르시오.

(1) Please let me know (if / that) you will make it or not.
(2) He should decide (whether / that) he will run or not.
(3) It remains to be seen (if / whether) or not this idea can be put into practice.
(4) I doubt if she (is / will be) present at the meeting tomorrow.
(5) They (can are / can be) cooked separately.
(6) I (will be not / will not be) finished for another hour.
(7) The cartoon characters should only (appear / be appeared) on healthy foods.
(8) So many hotels (resemble / are resembled) each other.

서답형
05 다음 우리말에 맞게 괄호 안에 주어진 어휘를 이용하여 영작하시오.

> 나는 그녀가 이탈리아의 음식을 좋아하는지 아닌지 모른다. (she, know, Italian food, if, or, like, not)

➡ _____

서답형

06 다음 우리말과 일치하도록 빈칸에 알맞게 쓰시오. (어휘가 주어진 경우, 그 어휘를 활용할 것.)

(1) 그는 나에게 자기가 암에 걸렸다고 생각하느냐고 물었다.
→ He asked me _____ I thought he had cancer.

(2) 우화는 여러 가지 관점에서 이해될 수 있다. (can, understand)
→ Fables _____ _____ _____ on various levels.

(3) 그녀가 반드시 그 규칙을 지키게 해야 한다. (must, make)
→ She _____ _____ _____ to comply with the rules.

07 다음 빈칸에 알맞은 말이 바르게 짝지어진 것은?

• Will you see _____ you can pick me out in this photo?
• Schools should _____ only on exam results.

① that   – not be judged
② if   – be not judged
③ if   – not be judged
④ whether – be not judged
⑤ whether – judged not be

08 다음 우리말에 맞도록 빈칸에 들어갈 알맞은 것은?

그것은 쉽게 끝마칠 수 있다.
= It _____ with ease.

① can be finished   ② can finish
③ can finished   ④ finishes
⑤ can be finish

09 다음 우리말을 바르게 영작한 것을 고르시오.

나는 비가 오는지 눈이 오는지 궁금해하고 있었다.

① I was wondering that it was raining or snowing.
② I was wondering whether raining or snowing.
③ I was wondering whether it was raining or snowing.
④ I was wondering if raining or snowing.
⑤ I was wondering if it was raining and snowing.

서답형

10 주어진 어휘를 이용하여 다음 우리말을 영작하시오.

그 계획은 비용 때문에 연기되어야만 했다. (the plan, cost, had, because, postpone, to, of)

→ _____
_____

11 다음 두 문장을 한 문장으로 연결할 때 가장 적절한 것은?

• Would you please check?
• Did I fill out this card right?

① Would you please check if I filled out this card right?
② Would you please check if or not I filled out this card right?
③ Would you please check how I filled out this card right?
④ Would you please check that I filled out this card right?
⑤ Would you please check what I filled out this card right?

12 다음 문장을 수동태로 바르게 바꾼 것을 고르시오.

> We may change the prices without prior notice.

① We may be changed the prices without prior notice.

② We may have changed the prices without prior notice.

③ The prices may change without prior notice.

④ The prices may have changed without prior notice.

⑤ The prices may be changed without prior notice.

13 중요 다음 빈칸에 들어갈 말이 나머지와 <u>다른</u> 하나는?

① Check _____ the seat is set at the right height.

② Do you know _____ she has any personal problems?

③ They can decide _____ they like it or not.

④ I am not sure _____ or not he will come tonight

⑤ John asked Peter _____ he could close the window.

14 다음 문장의 빈칸에 들어갈 말로 알맞은 말은?

> Jake wanted to know _____ Angelina liked to watch a movie with him.

① which   ② what   ③ that
④ if   ⑤ unless

15 중요 다음 중 어법상 <u>어색한</u> 것을 고르시오. (2개)

① Personal calls must be taken outside of the office area.

② Very little of the house may be remained after the fire.

③ Art may be used as a vehicle for advertisements.

④ Do you know if will Cathy come home soon?

⑤ Can you tell me if you are going shopping tonight?

서답형

16 다음 문장에서 어법상 <u>어색한</u> 것을 바르게 고쳐 다시 쓰시오.

(1) Joan asked that I want to go to the party.

➡ _____

_____

(2) It depends on if it applies directly to your job.

➡ _____

_____

(3) You'll have to choose if to buy it or not.

➡ _____

_____

(4) The beautiful clothes will put on right now.

➡ _____

_____

(5) Problems will be occurred as a result of human life.

➡ _____

_____

01 다음을 수동태 문장으로 바꿔 쓰시오.

(1) About a million people may watch the final match.

➡ _____

_____

(2) We should not underestimate the value of regular exercise.

➡ _____

_____

(3) We can make the robots work faster in the future.

➡ _____

_____

(4) No one can solve this math problem.

➡ _____

_____

02 주어진 두 문장을 〈보기〉처럼 하나의 문장으로 쓰시오.

┌─── 보기 ───┐
- He asked me.
- He didn't know if Jane had been to Rome.
- → He asked me if[whether] Jane had been to Rome.
└─────────┘

- Ask her.
- You don't know if she watches TV every night.

➡ _____

_____

03 그림을 보고, 주어진 어휘를 이용하여 빈칸을 알맞게 채우시오.

(1)

Susan wonders _____

better than her. (a picture, Jake, draw)

(2)

I have no doubt that some wonderful pictures for Sports Day _____. (will, take)

04 괄호 안에 주어진 말을 이용하여 어법에 맞게 문장을 완성하시오.

(1) I wonder _____ this food. (like, you)

(2) I don't know _____. (I, respond, should, how)

05 if를 이용하여 다음 두 문장을 한 문장으로 바꿔 쓰시오.

(1) • I want to know.
  • Are my study plans effective?
  ➡ _____
  _____

(2) • I want to check.
  • Can I view the content of the site?
  ➡ _____
  _____

(3) • I'm not sure.
  • Does she run fast enough?
  ➡ _____
  _____

06 다음 문장에서 어법상 <u>어색한</u> 것을 바르게 고쳐 다시 쓰시오.

(1) If I believe you or not is important.
  ➡ _____
  _____

(2) My heart raced, not knowing if or not my son was alive.
  ➡ _____
  _____

(3) He seemed undecided if to go or stay.
  ➡ _____
  _____

(4) My lost card might use illegally.
  ➡ _____
  _____

(5) Ghosts can be appeared in visible form in the world of the living.
  ➡ _____
  _____

(6) The tree was had to saw down.
  ➡ _____
  _____

07 다음에 주어진 어휘를 이용하여 문장을 완성하시오.

(1) (may, affect)
  ➡ Manufacturing processes _____ by the purpose of the product.

(2) (will, release)
  ➡ The new model _____ in July.

08 다음 우리말에 맞게 주어진 단어에 한 단어를 추가하여 바르게 배열하시오.

(1) 그는 내가 그의 가방을 봤는지 나에게 물어보았다. (he, his, I, me, backpack, asked, saw)
  ➡ _____
  _____

(2) 아무도 그가 진심인지 아닌지 알 수 없다. (he, one, can, is, tell, no, not, serious, or)
  ➡ _____
  _____

(3) 저 집에 누가 살고 있는지 보자. (let's, anyone, lives, see, that house, in)
  ➡ _____
  _____

(4) 그 방은 오후 2시까지는 청소되지 않을 것이다. (won't, cleaned, until 2 p.m., the room)
  ➡ _____
  _____

(5) 여기서 그들의 목소리를 들을 수 있다. (heard, voices, can, here, their, from)
  ➡ _____
  _____

(6) 우리 모두 그분이 그리울 겁니다. (shall, be, missed, he, us all)
  ➡ _____
  _____

We Are All Leaders

Brian: The election is coming up. <u>Why don't you run</u> for class
= How[What] about running
representative, Yumi?

Yumi: <u>No way.</u> I'm not the right person for that position. <u>I've never</u>
= Definitely not. = Never.
<u>thought</u> about running.
현재완료 용법(경험). 현재완료 경험은 주로 ever, never, before, once 등의 부사와 함께 쓰인다.

Brian: <u>Why not?</u>
Why?(×)

Yumi: Come on, Brian. Leaders have special qualities. I don't think a
person like me <u>can be called</u> a leader.
조동사 can을 써서 나타낸 조동사의 수동태 문장.

Brian: What do you mean? I <u>think you</u> have very good leadership
think와 you 사이에 접속사 that이 생략되어 있음.
qualities. You're really friendly and outgoing. You also help
people <u>get</u> along. I have no doubt that you will be elected <u>if you</u>
= to get   조건을 나타내는 접속사: 만약 ~한다면
run.

Brian told me this afternoon <u>that</u> I have good leadership qualities.
접속사(생략가능)
No one has ever told me <u>that</u> before. Why does he think <u>so</u>? Maybe he
= I have good leadership qualities.   = I have good leadership qualities.
was just trying to be nice. When he said <u>that</u> to me, however, I started
= I have good leadership qualities.
<u>to think.</u> Can I really become a leader?
= thinking

election 선거

run (선거에) 입후보하다

representative 대표(자)

quality 질, 우수함, 자질

leadership 지도력, 리더십

outgoing 외향적인, 사교적인

get along 잘 지내다, 어울려 지내다

확인문제

● 다음 문장이 본문의 내용과 일치하면 T, 일치하지 <u>않으면</u> F를 쓰시오.

1 Yumi says that she is not the right person for class representative. ☐

2 Yumi thinks she has special qualities. ☐

3 Brian thinks Yumi has very good leadership qualities. ☐

4 Brian has no doubt that Yumi will be elected if she runs. ☐

5 Brian told Yumi this afternoon that he has good leadership qualities. ☐

I don't know. I think leaders should have a vision, clear goals, and the ability to motivate others. I don't have any of those things.
= I have none of those things. not ~ any: 아무것도 … 아니다(전체 부정)

Then I suddenly started to wonder if these are the only qualities
접속사: ~인지 아닌지
that make a good leader. Maybe I'm wrong. Maybe there are other
선행사 'the only qualities'를 수식하는 주격 관계대명사. 선행사에 the only가 있으면 주로 관계대명사로 that을 쓴다.
leadership qualities. So I decided to do some research online.
decide는 to부정사를 목적어로 취한다.

Here's what I found!
= the thing which[that]

GREEN LEADERS: "Team Builders"

• Ensure that the team feels valued
= Make sure
• Create a positive environment
↔ negative
• Are friendly and easy to talk to
to talk(×)

RED LEADERS: "Logical Analysts"

• Have good reasoning skills

• Analyze problems and situations

• Think of the most effective ways to achieve the team's goals
형용사적 용법의 to부정사

PURPLE LEADERS: "Hands-Off Managers"

• Allow others to work on their own
allow+목적어+to부정사   on one's own: 혼자서, 단독으로
• Do not try to control people
try to 부정사: ~하려고 노력하다
• Give advice only when it is needed
= advice

vision 시력, 비전
clear 명확한, 뚜렷한
goal 목적, 목표
motivate 동기를 부여하다
ensure 반드시 ~하게 하다, 보장하다
valued 귀중한, 존중 받는
logical 논리적인, 타당한
reasoning 추리, 추론
analyze 분석하다
effective 효과적인
achieve 성취하다, 이루다
hands-off 불간섭주의의, 자유방임의

확인문제

● 다음 문장이 본문의 내용과 일치하면 T, 일치하지 않으면 F를 쓰시오.

1 Yumi thinks leaders should have a vision, clear goals, and the ability to motivate others. ☐

2 Green leaders are "logical analysts." ☐

3 Green leaders make sure that the team feels valued. ☐

4 Red leaders are friendly and easy to talk to. ☐

5 Purple leaders allow others to work on their own. ☐

6 Purple leaders give advice at any time. ☐

ORANGE LEADERS: "Strict Directors"

- Make everyone's role clear
  clearly(×)
- Make sure everything is finished on time
  = Ensure   시간을 어기지 않고, 정각에
- Ensure each step is done properly
  = Make sure

YELLOW LEADERS: "Quiet Supporters"

- Lead by example
- Let the team members shine instead
  to shine(×)
- Meet the team members' needs
  = Satisfy

BLUE LEADERS: "Creative Thinkers"

- Approach problems in new ways
  Approach to(×)
- Come up with fresh ideas
- Deal with tasks differently from others
  = Treat = Handle

I was surprised that there are actually many different leadership styles, but soon I realized the reason.

We belong to many different groups, and many different situations
are belonged to(×)
can come up in our lives. They all call for different leadership styles.
= Many different groups and (many different) situations
Each group's unique situation determines the best leadership style.

"I am a part of many different groups, and I have different responsibilities in each group."

After reading everything, I became more confident. I discovered that
= I read
I have some of the qualities of a "green leader." If my classmates think
조건을 나타내는 접속사: 만약 ~한다면
a green leader would make our class better, they might pick me to be class representative! Okay, let's try it!

---

properly 적절히, 제대로

lead by example 솔선수범하다

approach 접근하다

come up with 찾아내다, 내놓다

deal with 다루다, 처리하다

belong to ~에 속하다

come up 나오다, 발생하다

call for ~을 필요로 하다

determine 결정하다, 결심하다

responsibility 책임, 의무

confident 자신 있는

discover 발견하다, 찾다

📎 **확인문제**

● 다음 문장이 본문의 내용과 일치하면 T, 일치하지 <u>않으면</u> F를 쓰시오.

1 Orange leaders ensure everything is finished on time. ☐

2 Blue leaders let the team members shine instead. ☐

3 The writer was surprised that there are actually many different leadership styles. ☐

4 Many different situations all call for the same leadership styles. ☐

5 Each group's unique situation determines the best leadership style. ☐

6 After reading everything, the writer lost confidence. ☐

• 우리말을 참고하여 빈칸에 알맞은 말을 쓰시오.

1 _____ _____ _____ Leaders

2 Brian: The election is _____ _____.

3 _____ _____ _____ run for class representative, Yumi?

4 Yumi: _____ _____.

5 I'm not the _____ _____ for that position.

6 I've never _____ _____ running.

7 Brian: _____ _____?

8 Yumi: _____ _____, Brian.

9 Leaders have _____ _____.

10 I don't think a person like me _____ _____ _____ a leader.

11 Brian: _____ do you mean?

12 I think you have very _____ _____ _____.

13 You're really _____ and _____.

14 You also help people _____ _____.

15 I have no doubt that you _____ _____ _____ if you run.

16 Brian told me this afternoon that I have _____ _____ _____.

17 No one _____ _____ _____ me that before.

18 _____ does he think so?

19 Maybe he was just _____ _____ _____ nice.

20 When he said that to me, _____, I started to think.

1 우리는 모두 리더들이다

2 Brian: "선거가 다가오고 있어.

3 유미야, 반 대표에 입후보하는 게 어때?"

4 유미: "아니.

5 나는 그 자리에 적절한 사람이 아니야.

6 나는 입후보하는 것에 대해 생각해 본 적이 없어."

7 Brian: "왜?"

8 유미: "이봐, Brian.

9 리더들은 특별한 자질을 갖추고 있어.

10 나 같은 사람이 리더로 불릴 수 있다고 생각하지 않아."

11 Brian: "무슨 말이야?"

12 내 생각에 너는 매우 좋은 지도력 자질들을 갖추고 있어.

13 너는 정말 친절하고 외향적이잖아.

14 또 너는 사람들이 어울리도록 도와주기도 해.

15 만약 네가 입후보한다면 당선될 거라고 믿어 의심치 않아."

16 Brian은 오늘 오후에 내게 내가 좋은 지도력 자질들을 갖추고 있다고 말했다.

17 이전에는 아무도 내게 그런 말을 한 적이 없었다.

18 왜 그는 그렇게 생각했을까?

19 아마도 그는 그저 친절하려고 했을 것이다.

20 그러나 그가 내게 그렇게 말했을 때, 나는 생각하기 시작했다.

21 Can I really _____ _____ _____?

22 I _____ _____.

23 I think leaders should have _____ _____, clear goals, and the ability _____ _____ _____.

24 I don't have _____ _____ _____ _____.

25 Then I suddenly started to _____ _____ these are the only qualities that make a good leader.

26 Maybe I'm _____.

27 Maybe there are _____ _____ _____.

28 So I decided to _____ _____ _____ _____.

29 Here's _____ I found!

30 **GREEN LEADERS:** "Team _____"

31 Ensure that the team _____ _____

32 Create a _____ _____

33 Are friendly and easy _____ _____ _____

34 **RED LEADERS:** "_____ _____"

35 Have good _____ _____

36 _____ problems and situations

37 Think of the most effective ways to _____ _____ _____ _____

38 **PURPLE LEADERS:** "_____ _____"

39 Allow others to work _____ _____ _____

40 Do not _____ _____ _____ people

41 Give advice only when _____ _____ _____

21 내가 정말 리더가 될 수 있을까?

22 나는 모르겠다.

23 나는 리더가 비전, 명확한 목표, 그리고 다른 사람들에게 동기를 부여할 능력을 가지고 있어야 한다고 생각한다.

24 나는 그러한 것들 중 어느 것도 가지고 있지 않다.

25 그때 나는 갑자기 이것들이 좋은 리더를 만드는 유일한 자질들인지 궁금해하기 시작했다.

26 아마도 내가 틀린지도 모른다.

27 어쩌면 다른 지도력 자질들이 있는지도 모른다.

28 그래서 나는 온라인으로 조사해 보기로 결심했다.

29 여기에 내가 찾은 것이 있다!

30 〈녹색 리더〉 '팀 조직자'

31 팀이 반드시 가치 있다고 느끼게 한다

32 긍정적인 환경을 조성한다

33 친절하고 말을 걸기 쉽다

34 〈빨간색 리더〉 '논리적 분석가'

35 좋은 추론 기술을 갖고 있다

36 문제와 상황들을 분석한다

37 팀의 목표를 성취하는 가장 효과적인 방법들을 생각한다

38 〈보라색 리더〉 '방임적 관리자'

39 다른 사람들이 스스로 일하도록 해 준다

40 사람들을 통제하려고 하지 않는다

41 필요할 때만 조언한다

42 ORANGE LEADERS: "_____ _____"

43 Make _____ _____ clear

44 Make sure everything is finished _____ _____

45 Ensure _____ _____ is done properly

46 YELLOW LEADERS: "_____ _____"

47 Lead _____ _____

48 Let the team members _____ _____

49 _____ the team members' _____

50 BLUE LEADERS: "_____ _____"

51 _____ problems in new ways

52 _____ _____ _____ fresh ideas

53 Deal with tasks _____ _____ others

54 I was surprised that there are actually many different leadership styles, but soon I _____ _____ _____.

55 We _____ _____ many different groups, and many different situations can _____ _____ in our lives.

56 They all _____ _____ different leadership styles.

57 Each group's _____ _____ determines the best leadership style.

58 "I am a part of many different groups, and I have _____ _____ in each group."

59 After reading everything, I became _____ _____.

60 I discovered that I have _____ _____ _____ _____ of a "green leader."

61 If my classmates think a green leader would make our class better, they might _____ _____ to be class representative!

62 Okay, _____ _____ it!

---

42 〈주황색 리더〉 '엄격한 감독관'

43 모두의 역할을 분명하게 해 준다

44 모든 일을 제때 끝날 것을 확실히 한다

45 각 단계가 적절히 이행되도록 한다

46 〈노란색 리더〉 '조용한 지지자'

47 솔선수범한다

48 팀원들이 대신 빛나도록 해 준다

49 팀원들의 요구 사항을 충족한다

50 〈파란색 리더〉 '창조적 사상가'

51 새로운 방식으로 문제들에 접근한다

52 신선한 아이디어를 떠올린다

53 다른 사람들과 다르게 일을 처리한다

54 나는 실제로 서로 다른 많은 지도력 유형들이 있어서 놀랐지만, 곧 그 이유를 깨달았다.

55 우리는 서로 다른 여러 집단에 속하고, 우리 인생에서 서로 다른 많은 상황들이 발생할 수 있다.

56 그것들은 모두 서로 다른 지도력 유형들을 요구한다.

57 각 집단의 독특한 상황이 최고의 지도력 유형을 결정한다.

58 "나는 서로 다른 많은 집단의 일부이고, 각 집단에서 각각 다른 책임을 갖고 있어."

59 모든 것을 읽고 나서, 나는 더 자신감이 생겼다.

60 나는 '녹색 리더'의 자질들 중 일부분을 가지고 있다는 것을 알게 되었다.

61 만약 나의 반 친구들이 녹색 리더가 우리 학급을 더 좋게 만들 거라고 생각한다면, 그들은 학급 대표로 나를 뽑을지도 모른다!

62 좋아, 시도해 보자!

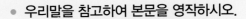

● 우리말을 참고하여 본문을 영작하시오.

1 우리는 모두 리더들이다
➡ _____

2 Brian: "선거가 다가오고 있어.
➡ _____

3 유미야, 반 대표에 입후보하는 게 어때?"
➡ _____

4 유미: "아니.
➡ _____

5 나는 그 자리에 적절한 사람이 아니야.
➡ _____

6 나는 입후보하는 것에 대해 생각해 본 적이 없어."
➡ _____

7 Brian: "왜?"
➡ _____

8 유미: "이봐, Brian.
➡ _____

9 리더들은 특별한 자질을 갖추고 있어.
➡ _____

10 나 같은 사람이 리더로 불릴 수 있다고 생각하지 않아."
➡ _____

11 Brian: "무슨 말이야?
➡ _____

12 내 생각에 너는 매우 좋은 지도력 자질들을 갖추고 있어.
➡ _____

13 너는 정말 친절하고 외향적이잖아.
➡ _____

14 또 너는 사람들이 어울리도록 도와주기도 해.
➡ _____

15 만약 네가 입후보한다면 당선될 거라고 믿어 의심치 않아."
➡ _____

16 Brian은 오늘 오후에 내게 내가 좋은 지도력 자질들을 갖추고 있다고 말했다.
➡ _____

17 이전에는 아무도 내게 그런 말을 한 적이 없었다.
➡ _____

18 왜 그는 그렇게 생각했을까?
➡ _____

19 아마도 그는 그저 친절하려고 했을 것이다.
➡ _____

20 그러나 그가 내게 그렇게 말했을 때, 나는 생각하기 시작했다.
➡ _____

21 내가 정말 리더가 될 수 있을까?
➡ _____

22 나는 모르겠다.
➡ _____

23 나는 리더가 비전, 명확한 목표, 그리고 다른 사람들에게 동기를 부여할 능력을 가지고 있어야
한다고 생각한다.
➡ _____

24 나는 그러한 것들 중 어느 것도 가지고 있지 않다.
➡ _____

25 그때 나는 갑자기 이것들이 좋은 리더를 만드는 유일한 자질들인지 궁금해하기 시작했다.
➡ _____

26 아마도 내가 틀린지도 모른다.
➡ _____

27 어쩌면 다른 지도력 자질들이 있는지도 모른다.
➡ _____

28 그래서 나는 온라인으로 조사해 보기로 결심했다.
➡ _____

29 여기에 내가 찾은 것이 있다!
➡ _____

30 〈녹색 리더〉 '팀 조직자'
➡ _____

31 팀이 반드시 가치 있다고 느끼게 한다
➡ _____

32 긍정적인 환경을 조성한다
➡ _____

33 친절하고 말을 걸기 쉽다
➡ _____

34 〈빨간색 리더〉 '논리적 분석가'
➡ _____

35 좋은 추론 기술을 갖고 있다
➡ _____

36 문제와 상황들을 분석한다
➡ _____

37 팀의 목표를 성취하는 가장 효과적인 방법들을 생각한다
➡ _____

38 〈보라색 리더〉 '방임적 관리자'
➡ _____

39 다른 사람들이 스스로 일하도록 해 준다
➡ _____

40 사람들을 통제하려고 하지 않는다
➡ _____

41 필요할 때만 조언한다
➡ _____

42 〈주황색 리더〉 '엄격한 감독관'
➡ _____

43 모두의 역할을 분명하게 해 준다
➡ _____

44 모든 일을 제때 끝날 것을 확실히 한다
➡ _____

45 단계가 적절히 이행되도록 한다
➡ _____

46 〈노란색 리더〉 '조용한 지지자'
➡ _____

47 솔선수범한다
➡ _____

48 팀원들이 대신 빛나도록 해 준다
➡ _____

49 팀원들의 요구 사항을 충족한다
➡ _____

50 〈파란색 리더〉 '창조적 사상가'
➡ _____

51 새로운 방식으로 문제들에 접근한다
➡ _____

52 신선한 아이디어를 떠올린다
➡ _____

53 다른 사람들과 다르게 일을 처리한다
➡ _____

54 나는 실제로 서로 다른 많은 지도력 유형들이 있어서 놀랐지만, 곧 그 이유를 깨달았다.
➡ _____

55 우리는 서로 다른 여러 집단에 속하고, 우리 인생에서 서로 다른 많은 상황들이 발생할 수 있다.
➡ _____

56 그것들은 모두 서로 다른 지도력 유형들을 요구한다.
➡ _____

57 각 집단의 독특한 상황이 최고의 지도력 유형을 결정한다.
➡ _____

58 "나는 서로 다른 많은 집단의 일부이고, 각 집단에서 각각 다른 책임을 갖고 있어."
➡ _____

59 모든 것을 읽고 나서, 나는 더 자신감이 생겼다.
➡ _____

60 나는 '녹색 리더'의 자질들 중 일부분을 가지고 있다는 것을 알게 되었다.
➡ _____

61 만약 나의 반 친구들이 녹색 리더가 우리 학급을 더 좋게 만들 거라고 생각한다면, 그들은 학급 대표로 나를 뽑을지도 모른다!
➡ _____

62 좋아, 시도해 보자!
➡ _____

[01~03] 다음 글을 읽고 물음에 답하시오.

Brian: The election is coming up. Why (A)[do / don't] you run for class representative, Yumi?

Yumi: No way. I'm not the right person for that position. ⓐI've never thought about running.

Brian: (B)[Why / Why not]?

Yumi: Come on, Brian. Leaders have special qualities. I don't think a person like me can be called a leader.

Brian: What do you mean? I think you have very good leadership qualities. You're really friendly and outgoing. You also help people get along. I have no doubt that you will be elected (C)[if / whether] you run.

서답형

01 위 글의 괄호 (A)~(C)에서 문맥이나 어법상 알맞은 낱말을 골라 쓰시오.

➡ (A) _____ (B) _____ (C) _____

02 아래 〈보기〉에서 위 글의 밑줄 친 문장 ⓐ에 쓰인 현재완료와 용법이 같은 것의 개수를 고르시오.

┌─── 보기 ───
① How long have you studied English?
② She has just finished doing her homework.
③ How many times have you read the book?
④ Yumi has been sick since yesterday.
⑤ Have you ever met each other before?
└─

① 1개 ② 2개 ③ 3개 ④ 4개 ⑤ 5개

03 According to the passage, which is NOT true?

① Brian proposes that Yumi should run for class representative.
② Yumi rejects Brian's proposal saying that she isn't the right person for class representative.
③ Yumi has never thought about running for class representative.
④ Brian doesn't think a person like him can be called a leader.
⑤ Brian thinks Yumi has very good leadership qualities.

[04~06] 다음 글을 읽고 물음에 답하시오.

I was surprised that there are actually many different leadership styles, but soon I realized the reason.

We belong to many different groups, and many different situations can come up in our lives. They all ⓐcall for different leadership styles. Each group's unique situation determines the best leadership style.

"I am a part of many different groups, and I have different responsibilities in each group."

ⓑAfter reading everything, I became more confident. I discovered that I have some of the qualities of a "green leader." If my classmates think a green leader would make our class better, they might pick me to be class representative! Okay, let's try it!

04 위 글의 밑줄 친 ⓐcall for와 바꿔 쓸 수 없는 말을 고르시오.

① require ② stand for
③ need ④ demand
⑤ want

서답형

05 위 글의 밑줄 친 ⓑ를 다음과 같이 바꿔 쓸 때 빈칸에 들어갈 알맞은 말을 두 단어로 쓰시오.

➡ After _____ _____ everything

서답형

06 What determines the best leadership style? Fill in the blanks with suitable words.

The _____ _____ of each group determines it.

[07~10] 다음 글을 읽고 물음에 답하시오.

(A)Here's which I found!
GREEN LEADERS: " ⓐ "
• Ensure that the team feels valued
• Create a positive environment
• Are friendly and easy to talk to
RED LEADERS: "Logical Analysts"
• Have good reasoning skills
• Analyze problems and situations
• Think of the most effective ways to achieve the team's goals
PURPLE LEADERS: "Hands-Off Managers"
• Allow others to work on their own
• Do not try to control people
• Give advice only when it is needed

07 위 글의 빈칸 ⓐ에 들어갈 알맞은 말을 고르시오.

① Strict Directors   ② Team Builders
③ Quiet Supporters   ④ Creative Thinkers
⑤ Carefree Directors

서답형

08 위 글의 밑줄 친 (A)에서 어법상 틀린 부분을 찾아 고치시오.

_____ ➡ _____

서답형

09 What can we call the leaders who analyze problems and situations? Fill in the blanks with suitable words.

They are _____ _____.

➡ _____ 또는 _____

서답형

10 다음 빈칸 (A)~(C)에 알맞은 단어를 넣어 '보라색 리더들'의 특징을 완성하시오.

They let others work (A)_____ _____ _____, don't try to (B)_____ people, and give advice only when (C)_____ _____ _____.

[11~13] 다음 글을 읽고 물음에 답하시오.

Brian told me this afternoon that I have good leadership qualities. No one has ever told me that before. Why does he think so? Maybe he was just trying to be nice. When he said that to me, ⓐ_____, I started to think. ⓑCan I really become a leader? ⓒI don't know. I think leaders should have a vision, clear goals, and the ability to motivate others. I don't have any of those things.

Then I suddenly started to wonder if these are the only qualities that make a good leader. Maybe I'm wrong. Maybe there are other leadership qualities. So I decided to do some research online.

중요

11 위 글의 빈칸 ⓐ에 들어갈 알맞은 말을 고르시오.

① for example   ② in addition
③ furthermore   ④ however
⑤ that is

서답형

12 위 글의 밑줄 친 ⓑ와 ⓒ를 합쳐 다음과 같이 한 문장으로 고칠 때 빈칸에 들어갈 알맞은 단어를 쓰시오.

➡ I don't know _____ I can really become a leader.

13 위 글의 주제로 알맞은 것을 고르시오.

① the best way to be a good leader
② the chance to strengthen leadership
③ a program for leadership qualities
④ a crisis that requires strong leadership
⑤ the qualities leaders should have

[14~17] 다음 글을 읽고 물음에 답하시오.

Here's what I found!
ORANGE LEADERS: "(A)Strict Directors"
• Make everyone's role clear
• Make sure everything is finished on time
• Ensure each step is done properly
YELLOW LEADERS: "Quiet Supporters"
• Lead by example
• (B)Let the team members to shine instead
• Meet the team members' needs
BLUE LEADERS: "Creative Thinkers"
• Approach problems in new ways
• Come up ___ⓐ___ fresh ideas
• Deal ___ⓑ___ tasks differently from others

서답형

14 위 글의 빈칸 ⓐ와 ⓑ에 공통으로 들어갈 알맞은 전치사를 쓰시오.

➡ _____

15 위 글의 밑줄 친 (A)Strict와 바꿔 쓸 수 없는 말을 고르시오.

① Stern   ② Easy-going
③ Severe   ④ Rigid
⑤ Rigorous

서답형

16 위 글의 밑줄 친 (B)에서 어법상 틀린 부분을 찾아 고치시오.

_____ ➡ _____

서답형

17 다음 '주황색 리더들'의 특징에 대한 설명 중, 위 글의 내용과 다른 부분을 찾아서 고치시오.

They are strict directors who make everyone's role clear, don't mind whether everything is finished on time, and make sure each step is done properly.

_____ ➡ _____

[18~21] 다음 글을 읽고 물음에 답하시오.

I was surprised that there are actually many different leadership styles, but soon I realized the reason.

We belong ___ⓐ___ many different groups, and many different situations can come up in our lives. They all call for different leadership styles. Each group's unique situation determines the best leadership style.

"I am a part of many different groups, and I have different responsibilities in each group."

After reading everything, I became more ___ⓑ___ . I discovered that I have some of the qualities of a "green leader." If my classmates think a green leader would make our class better, they might pick me to be class representative! Okay, let's try it!

18 위 글의 빈칸 ⓐ에 알맞은 전치사를 쓰시오.

➡ _____

19 위 글의 빈칸 ⓑ에 들어갈 알맞은 말을 고르시오.

① generous ② modest
③ confident ④ anxious
⑤ selfish

20 Why are there actually many different leadership styles? Fill in the blanks (A)~(C) with suitable words.

> That's because many different situations which call for (A)_____ _____ _____ can come up in our lives, and the (B)_____ situation of each group we are in determines the (C)_____ _____ _____.

21 위 글의 제목으로 알맞은 것을 고르시오.

① How Many Leadership Styles Are There?
② Which Group Do You Want to Choose?
③ Many Different Situations Can Happen in Our Lives
④ Wow! I Have the Qualities of a "Green Leader!"
⑤ The Best Leadership Style Depends on the Situation

[22~24] 다음 글을 읽고 물음에 답하시오.

  Brian told me this afternoon that I have good leadership qualities. No one has ever told me that before. Why does he think so? Maybe he was just trying to be nice. (①) When he said that to me, however, I started to think. (②) Can I really become a leader? (③) I think leaders should have a vision, clear goals, and the ability to motivate others. (④) I don't have any of ⓐthose things. (⑤)

  Then I suddenly started to wonder if these are the only qualities that make a good leader. Maybe I'm wrong. Maybe there are other leadership qualities. So I decided to do some research online.   <I: Yumi>

22 위 글의 흐름으로 보아, 주어진 문장이 들어가기에 가장 적절한 곳은?

> I don't know.

①   ②   ③   ④   ⑤

23 위 글의 밑줄 친 ⓐthose things가 가리키는 것을 본문에서 찾아 쓰시오.

➡ _____
_____

24 위 글의 뒤에 올 내용으로 가장 알맞은 것을 고르시오.

① the reason why Brian told Yumi to run for class representative
② Brian's thought about Yumi's leadership qualities
③ some research Yumi did online about leadership qualities
④ the importance of searching for the necessary information online
⑤ the effective way to do some research online

[25~27] 다음 글을 읽고 물음에 답하시오.

Brian: The election is coming up. Why don't you (A)run for class representative, Yumi?
Yumi: No way. (B)나는 그 자리에 적절한 사람이 아니야. I've never thought about running.

Brian: Why not?

Yumi: Come on, Brian. Leaders have special qualities. I don't think a person like me can be called a leader.

Brian: What do you mean? I think you have very good leadership qualities. You're really friendly and outgoing. You also help people get along. I have no doubt that you will ___ⓐ___ if you run.

서답형

25 위 글의 빈칸 ⓐ에 elect를 알맞은 형태로 쓰시오.

➡ _____

26 위 글의 밑줄 친 (A)run과 같은 의미로 쓰인 것을 고르시오.

① Why did you <u>run</u> for the doctor?

② The buses <u>run</u> every ten minutes.

③ When did he <u>run</u> a factory?

④ She wanted to <u>run</u> in the election.

⑤ The show had a record-breaking <u>run</u> in the London theatre.

서답형

27 위 글의 밑줄 친 (B)의 우리말에 맞게 주어진 어휘를 이용하여 8 단어로 영작하시오.

> right, position

➡ _____

[28~31] 다음 글을 읽고 물음에 답하시오.

Here's what I found!

ORANGE LEADERS: "Strict Directors"

• Make everyone's role clear

• (A)<u>Make sure</u> everything is finished on time

• Ensure each (B)<u>step</u> is done properly

YELLOW LEADERS: "Quiet ___ⓐ___"

• Lead by example

• Let the team members shine instead

• Meet the team members' needs

BLUE LEADERS: "Creative Thinkers"

• Approach problems in new ways

• Come up with fresh ideas

• Deal with tasks differently from others

28 위 글의 빈칸 ⓐ에 들어갈 알맞은 말을 고르시오.

① Competitors   ② Opponents

③ Supporters   ④ Challengers

⑤ Rivals

서답형

29 위 글의 밑줄 친 (A)Make sure와 바꿔 쓸 수 있는 말을 본문에서 찾아 쓰시오.

➡ _____

30 위 글의 밑줄 친 (B)step과 같은 의미로 쓰인 것을 고르시오.

① He took a <u>step</u> towards the door.

② She walked with a quick light <u>step</u>.

③ Why did you <u>step</u> on my foot?

④ When you complete the first stage, you can move on to <u>step</u> 2.

⑤ He sat on the bottom <u>step</u>.

서답형

31 다음 빈칸 (A)~(C)에 알맞은 단어를 넣어 '파란색 리더들'의 특징을 완성하시오.

> Blue leaders are "(A)_____ _____" who approach problems in new ways, think of (B)_____ _____, and treat tasks (C)_____ _____ others.

[01~03] 다음 글을 읽고 물음에 답하시오.

> Brian: The election is coming up. ⓐ<u>Why don't you run for class representative, Yumi?</u>
>
> Yumi: No way. I'm not the right person for ⓑ <u>that position</u>. I've never thought about running.
>
> Brian: Why not?
>
> Yumi: Come on, Brian. Leaders have special qualities. I don't think a person like me can be called a leader.
>
> Brian: What do you mean? I think you have very good leadership qualities. You're really friendly and outgoing. You also help people get along. I have no doubt that you will be elected if you run.

01 위 글의 밑줄 친 ⓐ를 다음과 같이 바꿔 쓸 때 빈칸에 들어갈 알맞은 말을 두 단어로 쓰시오.

➡ _____ _____ running for class representative, Yumi?

02 위 글의 밑줄 친 ⓑthat position이 가리키는 것을 본문에서 찾아 쓰시오.

➡ _____

03 본문의 내용과 일치하도록 다음 빈칸 (A)와 (B)에 알맞은 단어를 쓰시오.

> Yumi says that leaders have (A)_____ _____ and that she is not a suitable person for (B)_____ _____.

[04~06] 다음 글을 읽고 물음에 답하시오.

> Here's what I found!
> **ORANGE LEADERS:** "Strict Directors"
> • Make everyone's role (A)[clear / clearly]
> • Make sure everything is finished on time
> • Ensure each step is done (B)[proper / properly]
> **YELLOW LEADERS:** "Quiet Supporters"
> • Lead by example
> • Let the team members shine instead
> • Meet the team members' needs
> **BLUE LEADERS:** "Creative Thinkers"
> • (C)[Approach / Approach to] problems in new ways
> • Come up with fresh ideas
> • Deal with tasks differently from others

04 위 글의 괄호 (A)~(C)에서 문맥이나 어법상 알맞은 낱말을 골라 쓰시오.

➡ (A) _____ (B) _____ (C) _____

05 다음 빈칸 (A)~(C)에 알맞은 단어를 넣어 주황색 리더들의 특징을 완성하시오.

> Orange leaders are "(A)_____ _____" who make everyone's role clear, make sure everything is finished (B)_____ _____, and ensure each step is done (C)_____.

06 다음 '노란색 리더들'의 특징에 대한 설명 중, 위 글의 내용과 <u>다른</u> 부분을 찾아서 고치시오.

> They are creative thinkers who lead by example, let the team members shine instead, and meet the team members' needs.

➡ _____ ➡ _____

[07~09] 다음 글을 읽고 물음에 답하시오.

Brian told me this afternoon that I have good leadership qualities. No one has ever told me that before. Why does he think so? Maybe he was just trying to be nice. When he said that to me, however, I started to think. Can I really become a leader? I don't know. I think leaders should have a vision, clear goals, and the ability to motivate others. ⓐI don't have any of those things.

ⓑThen I suddenly started to wonder that these are the only qualities that make a good leader. Maybe I'm wrong. Maybe there are other leadership qualities. So I decided to do some research online.　　　　<I: Yumi>

07 위 글의 밑줄 친 ⓐ를 다음과 같이 바꿔 쓸 때 빈칸에 들어갈 알맞은 단어를 쓰시오.

➡ I have _____ of those things.

08 위 글의 밑줄 친 ⓑ에서 어법상 틀린 부분을 찾아 고치시오.

_____ ➡ _____

09 What qualities does Yumi think leaders should have? Answer in English in a full sentence.

➡ _____

_____

[10~12] 다음 글을 읽고 물음에 답하시오.

I was surprised that there are actually many different leadership styles, but soon I realized the reason.

We belong to many different groups, and many different situations can come up in our lives. They all call for different leadership styles. ⓐ각 집단의 독특한 상황이 최고의 지도력 유형을 결정한다.

"I am a part of many different groups, and I have different responsibilities in each group."

After reading everything, I became more confident. I discovered that I have some of the qualities of a "green leader." If my classmates think a green leader would make our class better, they might pick me to be class representative! Okay, let's try it!　　<I: Yumi>

10 위 글의 밑줄 친 ⓐ의 우리말에 맞게 주어진 어휘를 이용하여 9 단어로 영작하시오.

each, unique situation, determines, style

➡ _____

_____

11 After reading everything, what did Yumi discover about her leadership style? Fill in the blanks with suitable words.

She discovered that she has some of the qualities of a "_____ _____."

12 주어진 영영풀이에 해당하는 단어를 본문에서 찾아 쓰시오.

a person who has been chosen to act or make decisions on behalf of another person or a group of people

➡ _____

해석

Presentation Time Step 3

Our group chose tasks to prepare for our class birthday party. I will buy a
부사의 형용사적 용법(tasks 수식) (부사적 용법으로 볼 수도 있음.)

cake. Woojin and Taeho will decorate the classroom. Yeji will play birthday

party songs. I have no doubt that our birthday party will be a lot of fun!
접속사(동격의 명사절을 이끎)   = much

구문해설 · **prepare**: 준비하다[시키다] · **decorate**: 장식하다, 꾸미다
· **doubt**: 의심, 의혹; 의심하다, 의문[의혹]을 갖다, 확신하지 못하다
· **make[have] no doubt of[that]**: ~을 확신하다, 틀림없이 ~하다

우리 모둠은 우리 학급 생일 파티를 준비하기 위한 과제를 선정했다. 나는 케이크를 살 것이다. 우진이와 태호는 교실을 장식할 것이다. 예지는 생일 파티 노래를 연주할 것이다. 나는 우리의 생일 파티가 아주 재미있을 것이라고 확신한다.

After You Read B

1. Hi, I'm Jennifer. I try to lead by example and take care of others' needs. The
= care for

   important thing is that the members of my team shine.
   보어를 이끄는 접속사

2. Hello, I'm Heejin. I enjoy approaching problems in new ways. I try my best
   to approach(×)

   to come up with new ideas.
   to부정사의 부사적 용법(목적)

3. Hi, I'm Chris. I analyze my team's problems and situations, and then I

   look for the most effective ways to achieve our goals.
   ~을 찾다   to부정사의 형용사적 용법

구문해설 · **take care of**: 돌보다 · **shine**: 빛나다 · **approach**: 접근하다 · **come up with**: 생각해 내다
· **analyze**: 분석하다 · **effective**: 효과적인 · **achieve**: 성취하다

1. 안녕, 나는 Jennifer야. 나는 솔선수범하며 다른 사람들의 요구를 해결하려고 노력해. 중요한 것은 우리 팀 구성원들이 빛나는 거야.

2. 안녕, 나는 희진이야. 나는 문제에 새로운 방법으로 접근하는 것이 즐거워. 나는 최선을 다해서 새로운 아이디어를 제시해.

3. 안녕, 나는 Chris야. 나는 우리 팀의 문제점과 상황을 분석해. 그런 다음 우리의 목표를 달성하기 위한 가장 효과적인 방법들을 찾아.

Do it Yourself B

Brian: Why don't you run for class representative, Yumi?
~하는 게 어때? = How about ~? = What about ~?

Yumi: No way. I've never thought about running.
have p.p.: 현재완료

Brian: Why not?

Yumi: Leaders have special qualities. I don't think a person like me can be
= ~처럼(전치사)

called a leader.

Brian: What do you mean? You're really friendly and outgoing. You also help

people get along. I have no doubt that you will be elected if you run.
= 어울리다

구문해설 · **representative**: 대표 · **run**: 입후보하다 · **quality**: 자질 · **outgoing**: 외향적인

Brian: 유미야, 반 대표에 입후보하는 게 어때?
Yumi: 아니. 나는 입후보하는 것에 대해 생각해 본 적이 없어.
Brian: 왜?
Yumi: 리더들은 특별한 자질을 갖추고 있어. 나 같은 사람이 리더로 불릴 수 있다고 생각하지 않아.
Brian: 무슨 말이야? 너는 정말 친절하고 외향적이잖아. 또 너는 사람들이 어울리도록 도와주기도 해. 만약 네가 입후보한다면 당선될 거라고 믿어 의심치 않아.

23 위 글의 밑줄 친 ⓑThey가 가리키는 것을 본문에서 찾아 쓰시오.

➡ _____

24 위 글의 밑줄 친 ⓒ의 우리말에 맞게 주어진 어휘를 알맞게 배열하시오.

> our class / make / think / a green leader / better / my classmates / if / would

➡ _____

_____

[25~27] 다음 글을 읽고 물음에 답하시오.

> Here's what I found!
> **ORANGE LEADERS:** "Strict Directors"
> • Make everyone's role clear
> • Make sure everything is finished on time
> • Ensure each step is done properly
> **YELLOW LEADERS:** "Quiet Supporters"
> • Lead by example
> • Let the team members shine instead
> • Meet the team members' needs
> **BLUE LEADERS:** "Creative Thinkers"
> • Approach problems in new ways
> • Come up with fresh ideas
> • ⓐDeal with tasks differently from others

25 위 글의 밑줄 친 ⓐDeal with와 바꿔 쓸 수 있는 말을 <u>모두</u> 고르시오.

① Treat   ② Attend to   ③ Carry
④ Handle   ⑤ Deal in

26 What is Chris's leadership style? Fill in the blank with a suitable word.

> Hi, I'm Chris. I try to lead by example and care for others' needs. The important thing is that the members of my team shine.

➡ Chris's leadership style is _____ leader.

27 According to the passage, which is NOT true?

① Orange leaders make everyone's role clear.
② Orange leaders are 'Strict Directors' who ensure everything is finished on time.
③ Yellow leaders are 'Quiet Supporters' who satisfy the team members' needs.
④ Blue leaders approach problems in the same ways.
⑤ Blue leaders are 'Creative Thinkers' who handle tasks differently from others.

[28~29] 다음 글을 읽고 물음에 답하시오.

> **Yuna: A Wonderful Leader**
> I think my partner Yuna is a yellow leader because ⓐshe leads the group by example. I noticed it last Friday when we were cleaning the classroom. No one wanted to separate the recycling, but Yuna came over and separated it ⓑherself. I was impressed, so I started helping her. I think she is a wonderful leader.

28 위 글의 밑줄 친 ⓐ의 예를 본문에서 찾아 우리말로 쓰시오.

➡ _____

_____

29 위 글의 밑줄 친 ⓑherself와 문법적 쓰임이 같은 것을 고르시오.

① She absented <u>herself</u> from school.
② I went there by <u>myself</u>.
③ I <u>myself</u> did it.
④ She finished the work for <u>herself</u>.
⑤ He talked to <u>himself</u>.

01 다음 문장의 빈칸에 들어갈 말을 〈보기〉에서 골라 올바른 형태로 쓰시오.

┌─ 보기 ├──
approach / confident / determine / wonder / properly
└────────

(1) This machine works _____ with solar power.

(2) The referee was _____ the player.

(3) I _____ who the Nobel Prize winner is.

(4) What _____ the price of service in a market?

(5) Be _____ in your potential.

02 다음 대화가 자연스럽게 이어지도록 순서대로 배열하시오.

Sejin: I'm so excited about our museum field trip.

(A) Okay. Sejin, are you going to do some research on the museum?

(B) That's right. I think we're ready.

(C) I'm in charge of taking pictures.

(D) Yes, I am. Are you going to write our field trip report, Emma?

(E) Me too. Let's check our tasks. Yen, what are you in charge of?

➡ _____

[03~05] 다음 대화를 읽고 물음에 답하시오.

Sujin: What's the matter? You look worried.

Minsu: ⓐ You know I'm going to be giving a presentation on our team's research. But I feel very nervous when I talk in front of many people.

Sujin: ⓑ Oh, I didn't know that you got nervous. Actually, I also have a problem.

Minsu: ⓒ What's wrong?

Sujin: I'm in charge of making the presentation materials, but I'm not good at it.

Minsu: You're not? I thought you were good at it.

Sujin: ⓓ No, I'm not. Hey, then what about switching roles? I've given presentations many times before, so I don't get nervous at all.

Minsu: ⓔ I think I am good at making presentation materials, and I like making them!

Sujin: That's good. Let's talk to the other team members.

Minsu: Cool. I feel so __(A)__ now.

03 위 대화의 ⓐ~ⓔ 중 주어진 문장이 들어가기에 적절한 곳은?

┌──────────────────────────┐
│ Really? That would be great. │
└──────────────────────────┘

① ⓐ   ② ⓑ   ③ ⓒ   ④ ⓓ   ⑤ ⓔ

04 위 대화의 빈칸 (A)에 들어갈 말로 적절한 것은?

① relieved   ② worried   ③ nervous
④ disappointed   ⑤ upset

05 위 대화를 읽고 대답할 수 없는 것은?

① What's wrong with Minsu?

② What is Minsu in charge of?

③ What isn't Sujin good at?

④ What is Sujin's suggestion?

⑤ How many times has Sujin given presentations?

[06~07] 다음 글을 읽고 물음에 답하시오.

B: In the Send Our Stories project, we are going to make a picture book for children in other countries. ⓐ Each group will be (A)[responded / responsible] for a different task. ⓑ Group A will (B)[translate / transfer] a Korean story into English. ⓒ Group B will make drawings for the book and edit it. ⓓ After copies of the book are printed, Group C will be in charge of sending them to the children. ⓔ It won't be easy, but I have no doubt that the children who (C)[send / receive] these books will really enjoy them.

출제율 100%

06 위 글의 ⓐ~ⓔ 중 주어진 문장이 들어가기에 적절한 곳은?

> We've divided everyone into three groups.

① ⓐ   ② ⓑ   ③ ⓒ   ④ ⓓ   ⑤ ⓔ

출제율 90%

07 위 글의 (A)~(C)에 들어갈 말이 바르게 짝지어진 것은?

	(A)	(B)	(C)
①	responded	translate	send
②	responded	transfer	receive
③	responsible	translate	receive
④	responsible	transfer	send
⑤	responsible	translate	send

[08~10] 다음 대화를 읽고 물음에 답하시오.

Nick: Hey, Mandy. What's the matter?

Mandy: I don't know what to do, Nick. My brother asked me to help him with his homework this Wednesday, but I told him I can't. I have so many things to do that day.

Nick: What do you have to do this Wednesday?

Mandy: I need to go to the library to return some books. Then I have to meet you to work on our presentation. After that, I have to prepare for an exam at night.

Nick: Oh, you do have a lot to do.

Mandy: Yes. But my brother seemed let down, so I feel bad.

Nick: Well, then how about meeting on Thursday instead for our presentation? Then you can do everything and also help your brother on Wednesday.

Mandy: That would help me out so much! Thanks for understanding, Nick!

출제율 95%

08 What did Mandy's brother ask her to do this Wednesday?

➡ _____

출제율 90%

09 What was Mandy supposed to do after going to the library this Wednesday?

➡ _____

출제율 90%

10 What did Nick suggest for their presentation?

➡ _____
_____

출제율 95%

11 다음 빈칸에 알맞은 말이 순서대로 짝지어진 것은?

> • Before you leave, you should check _____ you turned off the light.
> • These books must _____ by next Tuesday.

① that – returned   ② if – return
③ if – be returned   ④ whether – returning
⑤ whether – have returned

12 다음 중 어법상 올바른 문장은? 출제율 95%

① They will check that stores in school zones sell unhealthy food to children.
② I was anxious about if I failed the exam or not.
③ Try this product for a week and decide if or not you want to buy it.
④ The judge is going to decide if he is guilty or not.
⑤ I wonder that you are going to attend the meeting.

13 수동태로 바꾼 문장 중 틀린 것은? 출제율 95%

① They might pick me to be class representative.
→ I might be picked to be class representative by them.
② We will belong to many different groups.
→ Many different groups will be belonged by us.
③ The girl must wear a black skirt with white spots.
→ A black skirt with white spots must be worn by the girl.
④ They will fix the elevator this afternoon.
→ The elevator will be fixed this afternoon.
⑤ You can order the lunch special only from 11 a.m. to 1 p.m.
→ The lunch special can be ordered only from 11 a.m. to 1 p.m.

[14~15] 다음 글을 읽고 물음에 답하시오.

Brian told me this afternoon that I have good leadership qualities. No one has ever told me that before. Why does he think so? Maybe he was just trying to be nice. When he said that to me, however, I started to think. Can I really become a leader? I don't know. I think leaders should have a vision, clear goals, and the ability to motivate others. ⓐ나는 그러한 것들 중 어느 것도 가지고 있지 않다.
Then I suddenly started to wonder if these are the only qualities that make a good leader. Maybe I'm wrong. Maybe there are other leadership qualities. So I decided to do some research online. <I: Yumi>

14 위 글의 밑줄 친 ⓐ의 우리말에 맞게 7 단어로 영작하시오. 출제율 90%

➡ _____

15 According to the passage, which is NOT true? 출제율 100%

① This afternoon, Brian told Yumi that she has good leadership qualities.
② Brian was the first person that told Yumi that she has good leadership qualities.
③ Yumi thinks she can't become a leader.
④ Yumi thinks that there may be other leadership qualities.
⑤ Yumi decided to do some research on leadership qualities online.

[16~18] 다음 글을 읽고 물음에 답하시오.

Here's what I found!
ORANGE LEADERS: "Strict Directors"
• Make everyone's role clear
• Make sure everything is finished on time
• Ensure each step is done properly

YELLOW LEADERS: "Quiet Supporters"
- Lead by example
- Let the team members shine instead
- ⓐMeet the team members' needs

BLUE LEADERS: "Creative Thinkers"
- Approach problems in new ways
- Come up with fresh ideas
- Deal with tasks differently from others

출제율 95%

16 위 글의 밑줄 친 ⓐMeet와 같은 의미로 쓰인 것을 고르시오.

① Maybe we'll meet again some time.
② Where does this road meet the highway?
③ Others didn't meet similar problems.
④ I will meet your wishes.
⑤ Did you meet anyone in town?

출제율 90%

17 What is Jennifer's leadership style? Fill in the blank with a suitable word.

Hello, I'm Jennifer. I try my best to think of new ideas and I treat tasks in a different way from others.

➡ Jennifer's leadership style is _____ leader.

출제율 100%

18 위 글을 읽고 답할 수 없는 질문을 고르시오.

① How do orange leaders make everyone's role clear?
② What can we call the leaders who make sure that each step is done properly?
③ Do yellow leaders lead by example?
④ What is another name for blue leaders?
⑤ How do blue leaders approach problems?

[19~21] 다음 글을 읽고 물음에 답하시오.

I was surprised that there are actually many different leadership styles, but soon I realized the reason. (①)
We belong to many different groups, and many different situations can come up in our lives. (②) Each group's unique situation determines the best leadership style. (③)
After reading everything, I became more confident. (④) I discovered that I have some of the qualities of a "green leader." (⑤) If my classmates think a green leader would make our class better, they might pick me to be class representative! Okay, let's try it! <I: Yumi>

출제율 95%

19 위 글의 흐름으로 보아, 주어진 문장이 들어가기에 가장 적절한 곳은?

They all call for different leadership styles.

①　　　②　　　③　　　④　　　⑤

출제율 95%

20 위 글의 주제로 알맞은 것을 고르시오.

① There are many different leadership styles.
② We belong to many different groups.
③ Many different situations can come up in our lives.
④ The unique situation of each group determines the best leadership style.
⑤ Yumi has some of the qualities of a "green leader."

출제율 95%

21 Why was Yumi surprised? Answer in English beginning with "Because".

➡ _____
_____

[01~03] 다음 대화를 읽고 물음에 답하시오.

Mr. Smith: Junsu, are you okay? What's the matter?

Junsu: Hello, Mr. Smith. I have a problem.

Mr. Smith: What happened?

Junsu: You know Jaewoo, Yunho, and I are best friends, right? They had a fight, and now I'm stuck in the middle. I don't know what to do.

Mr. Smith: That sounds hard. Do you know why they had a fight?

Junsu: Yes, but it doesn't sound like a big deal to me. I guess they had some kind of misunderstanding.

Mr. Smith: Why don't you all meet together and talk about it? I think they'll listen to you.

Junsu: That's a good idea. They're both good friends of mine. I can't take sides.

Mr. Smith: I understand. I hope everything works out.

01 Why did Jaewoo and Yunho have a fight?

➡ _____

02 What does Mr. Smith recommend Junsu to do?

➡ _____
_____

03 Why can't Junsu take sides?

➡ _____
_____

04 다음 문장을 수동태는 능동태로, 능동태는 수동태로 바꾸어 쓰시오.

(1) People must make reservations through the online system.

➡ _____
_____

(2) They can use this item in a variety of ways.

➡ _____
_____

(3) Who can make the most beautiful clothes for me?

➡ _____
_____

(4) Some diseases cannot be cured by medicine.

➡ _____
_____

(5) They can be seen only by wise people.

➡ _____
_____

05 if를 이용하여 다음 두 문장을 한 문장으로 바꿔 쓰시오.

(1) • Before you leave, you should check.
    • Did you turn off the tap?

➡ _____

(2) • My mom asked me.
    • Will you have dinner?

➡ _____
_____

(3) • I don't know.
    • Is he strong?

➡ _____
_____

06 다음 문장에서 어법상 **틀린** 부분을 찾아 바르게 고쳐 다시 쓰시오.

> I want to know if or not I will get taller.

➡ _____

_____

[07~09] 다음 대화를 읽고 물음에 답하시오.

Brian: The election is coming up. Why don't you run for class representative, Yumi?

Yumi: ___ⓐ___ I'm not the right person for that position. I've never thought about running.

Brian: Why not?

Yumi: Come on, Brian. Leaders have special qualities. ⓑ나 같은 사람이 리더로 불릴 수 있다고 생각하지 않아.

Brian: What do you mean? I think you have very good leadership qualities. You're really friendly and outgoing. You also help people get along. I have no doubt that you will be elected if you run.

07 위 대화의 빈칸 ⓐ에 주어진 영영풀이에 해당하는 어구를 두 단어로 쓰시오.

> definitely not, never

➡ _____

08 위 대화의 밑줄 친 ⓑ의 우리말에 맞게 주어진 어휘를 알맞게 배열하시오.

> a leader / like / called / I / be / a person / don't / me / can / think

➡ _____

_____

09 위 대화의 내용과 일치하도록 다음 빈칸 (A)와 (B)에 알맞은 단어를 쓰시오.

> Brian is sure that Yumi will (A)_____ _____ if she runs for class representative because he thinks Yumi has very good (B)_____ _____.

[10~11] 다음 글을 읽고 물음에 답하시오.

Here's what I found!
GREEN LEADERS: "Team Builders"
• Ensure that the team feels valued
• Create a positive environment
• Are friendly and easy to talk to
RED LEADERS: "Logical Analysts"
• Have good reasoning skills
• Analyze problems and situations
• Think of the most effective ways to achieve the team's goals
PURPLE LEADERS: "Hands-Off Managers"
• Allow others to work on their own
• Do not try to control people
• Give advice only when ⓐit is needed

10 위 글의 밑줄 친 ⓐit이 가리키는 것을 본문에서 찾아 쓰시오.

➡ _____

11 What do we call the leaders who let others work on their own? Fill in the blanks with suitable words.

> They are _____ _____.

➡ _____ 또는 _____

창의사고력 서술형 문제

01 다음 대화의 내용과 일치하도록 준수의 일기를 완성하시오.

Mr. Smith: Junsu, are you okay? What's the matter?

Junsu: Hello, Mr. Smith. I have a problem.

Mr. Smith: What happened?

Junsu: You know Jaewoo, Yunho, and I are best friends, right? They had a fight, and now I'm stuck in the middle. I don't know what to do.

Mr. Smith: That sounds hard. Do you know why they had a fight?

Junsu: Yes, but it doesn't sound like a big deal to me. I guess they had some kind of misunderstanding.

Mr. Smith: Why don't you all meet together and talk about it? I think they'll listen to you.

Junsu: That's a good idea. They're both good friends of mine. I can't take sides.

Mr. Smith: I understand. I hope everything works out.

Today I was worried about Jaewoo and Yunho. They had a fight, so I was (A)_____ in the middle. I didn't know (B)_____, so I talked about it with Mr. Smith. I knew the reason why they had a fight. It didn't sound like a big deal to me, but I guessed (C)_____. After listening to me, Mr. Smith advised me to (D)_____. I agreed with him, so I decided to do so soon. Because (E)_____, I couldn't take sides. I hope everything works out soon.

---

02 다음 그림을 보고, 괄호 안에 주어진 어휘를 배열하여 능동태의 문장을 쓰고 그것을 수동태의 문장으로 바꿔 쓰시오.

(the boxes / they / be / unpacking / will)

(1) _____ (능동태)

(2) _____ (수동태)

단원별 모의고사

01 다음 짝지어진 단어의 관계가 같도록 빈칸에 알맞은 말을 쓰시오.

> wide : narrow = negative : _____

02 다음 영영풀이가 가리키는 것을 고르시오.

> to deeply study every piece of something to understand it

① analyze   ② translate   ③ return
④ prepare   ⑤ motivate

03 다음 우리말에 맞게 주어진 단어를 사용하여 영작하시오.

(1) 학생들을 향한 그의 메시지는 매우 명확했다. (clear, very)

➡ _____

(2) 나의 목표는 그저 경주를 마치는 것이다. (just, to)

➡ _____

(3) 선생님은 우리에게 동기를 부여하기 위해 어떤 이야기를 해주셨다. (told, us)

➡ _____

[04~06] 다음 대화를 읽고 물음에 답하시오.

Jisu: (A) Mom, we've got a problem.
Mom: (B) What's the matter?
Jisu: (C) We're going to have dinner with Grandma this Saturday, right? But I just realized that Sujin's birthday party is on Saturday evening. She's my best friend. What should I do?
Mom: (D) Let's talk about it with your dad.
Jisu: (E) Okay, Mom. I'd love to see Grandma, but I don't want to miss my best friend's birthday party.

04 위 대화의 (A)~(E) 중 주어진 문장이 들어가기에 적절한 곳은?

> That sounds like a difficult decision.

① (A)   ② (B)   ③ (C)   ④ (D)   ⑤ (E)

05 What doesn't Jisu want to miss?

➡ _____
_____

06 What does Jisu's mom advise her to do?

➡ _____

[07~09] 다음 대화를 읽고 물음에 답하시오.

Mr. Smith: Junsu, are you okay? What's the matter?
Junsu: Hello, Mr. Smith. I have a problem.
Mr. Smith: What happened?
Junsu: You know Jaewoo, Yunho, and I are best friends, right? They had a fight, and now (a)저는 중간에 끼어버린 상태예요. I don't know what to do.
Mr. Smith: That sounds hard. Do you know why they had a fight?
Junsu: Yes, but it doesn't sound like a big deal to me. I guess they had some kind of misunderstanding.
Mr. Smith: _____(A)_____ I think they'll listen to you.
Junsu: That's a good idea. They're both good friends of mine. I can't take sides.
Mr. Smith: I understand. I hope everything works out.

07 위 대화의 빈칸 (A)에 들어갈 말로 적절하지 <u>않은</u> 것은?

① How about meeting all together and talking about it?

② Why don't you all meet together and talk about it?

③ I think you all should meet together and talk about it.

④ I advise you all to meet together and talk about it.

⑤ I doubt if you all should meet together and talk about it.

08 위 대화의 밑줄 친 (a)의 우리말을 5 단어를 사용하여 영작하시오.

➡ _____

09 위 대화에서 나타난 준수의 심경 변화로 적절한 것은?

① excited → confused

② worried → relieved

③ lonely → worried

④ relaxed → horrified

⑤ relieved → excited

[10~12] 다음 대화를 읽고 물음에 답하시오.

Nick: Hey, Mandy. (A)<u>What's the matter?</u>

Mandy: I don't know what to do, Nick. My brother asked me to help him with his homework this Wednesday, but I told him I can't. I have so many things to do that day.

Nick: What do you have to do this Wednesday?

Mandy: I need to go to the library to return some books. Then I have to meet you to work on our presentation. After that, I have to prepare for an exam at night.

Nick: Oh, you do have a lot to do.

Mandy: Yes. But (B)<u>내 동생이 실망한 것처럼 보였어</u>(seem, let), so I feel bad.

Nick: Well, then how about meeting on Thursday instead for our presentation? Then you can do everything and also help your brother on Wednesday.

Mandy: That would help me out so much! Thanks for understanding, Nick!

10 위 대화의 밑줄 친 (A)와 바꾸어 쓰기가 <u>어색한</u> 것은?

① Is there something bothering you?

② Is something worrying you?

③ What are you worried about?

④ What's wrong?

⑤ How do you like the matter?

11 위 대화의 밑줄 친 우리말 (B)를 주어진 단어를 활용하여 영작하시오.

➡ _____

12 위 대화의 내용과 일치하지 <u>않는</u> 것은?

① Mandy의 남동생이 이번 주 수요일에 그의 숙제를 도와 달라고 했다.

② Mandy는 수요일에 책을 반납하러 도서관에 가야 한다.

③ Mandy는 수요일 밤에 시험 준비를 해야 한다.

④ Mandy와 Nick은 함께 발표 준비를 할 예정이다.

⑤ Mandy는 남동생의 숙제를 목요일에 도와줄 예정이다.

13 다음 중 어법상 올바른 문장을 <u>모두</u> 고르시오.

① I want to know that there are ghosts in the world.

② I doubt whether the new computer will be any better.

③ Some friends have asked me if or not I'd write a novel.

④ Membership fees should be pay to the secretary.

⑤ The boy group's title song will be released tonight.

14 다음 중 어법상 <u>어색한</u> 것을 고르시오.

① He wants to know if the meeting is canceled.

② Before you leave, you should check if you cleaned the living room.

③ Jack may know if or not Andy will come to the meeting.

④ The teacher tried to check whether his students understood the question.

⑤ Your body temperature can differ by two or three degrees, depending on whether you wear a tie.

15 다음 밑줄 친 부분 중 어법상 <u>어색한</u> 것은?

① They announced that the flight <u>would be delayed</u>.

② The button <u>should be pushed</u> right now.

③ Girls <u>will be allowed</u> to wear shorts and pants starting this year.

④ Everything <u>can't be had</u> only by you.

⑤ This artwork <u>may not be touched</u>.

16 다음 우리말을 괄호 안에 주어진 어휘를 이용하여 영작하시오.

(1) 너는 화요일까지 그 일을 해야만 한다. (the job, by Tuesday, must, do, 9 단어)

➡ _____

(2) 이 책은 모든 사람이 읽어야 한다. (this book, should, everyone, 7 단어)

➡ _____

(3) 나는 네가 입후보하면 당선될 것이라고 믿어 의심치 않는다. (I, doubt, elect, run, will, have, that, no, if, 12 단어)

➡ _____

_____

(4) 나는 우리가 이 쿠폰을 쓸 수 있는지 잘 모르겠다. (sure, can, this coupon, if, 9 단어)

➡ _____

_____

(5) 당신은 그 기계가 작동하는지 어떻게 알 수 있나요? (the machine, tell, work, whether, how, 9 단어)

➡ _____

_____

(6) 그 소년은 그 괴물이 살았는지 죽었는지 확인하고 싶었다. (alive or dead, the boy, the monster, want, check, if, 12 단어)

➡ _____

_____

17 다음 중 어법상 올바르지 <u>않은</u> 것을 <u>모두</u> 고르시오.

① I suddenly started to wonder if these are the only qualities that make a good leader.

② I wonder if you've seen my backpack.

③ You should check if or not you locked the door.

④ Beth wants to know if the problem can solve.

⑤ I was wondering if this cake can be sent to my house.

[18~19] 다음 글을 읽고 물음에 답하시오.

Brian told me this afternoon that I have good leadership qualities. No one has ever told me ⓐthat before. Why does he think ⓑso? Maybe he was just trying to be nice. When he said ⓒthat to me, however, I started to think. Can I really become a leader? I don't know. I think leaders should have a vision, clear goals, and the ability to motivate others. I don't have any of ⓓthose things.

Then I suddenly started to wonder if ⓔthese are the only qualities (A)that make a good leader. Maybe I'm wrong. Maybe there are ⓕother leadership qualities. So I decided to do some research online.   <I: Yumi>

18 위 글의 밑줄 친 ⓐ~ⓕ 중에서 가리키는 것이 서로 다른 것을 고르시오.

① ⓐ – ⓑ   ② ⓐ – ⓒ   ③ ⓑ – ⓒ
④ ⓓ – ⓔ   ⑤ ⓔ – ⓕ

19 위 글의 밑줄 친 (A)that과 문법적 쓰임이 다른 것을 고르시오.

① It's the best novel that I've ever read.
② The watch that you gave me keeps perfect time.
③ The people that I spoke to were very helpful.
④ The rumor that the actress was married wasn't right.
⑤ Where's the book that you bought yesterday?

[20~23] 다음 글을 읽고 물음에 답하시오.

Here's what I found!
GREEN LEADERS: "Team Builders"
• Ensure that the team feels valued

• Create a positive environment
• Are friendly and easy to talk to
RED LEADERS: "Logical Analysts"
• Have good reasoning skills
• Analyze problems and situations
• Think of the most effective ways (A)to achieve the team's goals
PURPLE LEADERS: "Hands-Off Managers"
• Allow others to work on their own
• Do not try to control people
• Give advice only when it ___ⓐ___

20 위 글의 빈칸 ⓐ에 need를 알맞은 형태로 쓰시오.

➡ _____

21 위 글의 밑줄 친 (A)to achieve와 to부정사의 용법이 같은 것을 고르시오.

① You must work hard to achieve the team's goals.
② He is the only person to achieve the team's goals.
③ Is it difficult to achieve the team's goals?
④ Teamwork is needed to achieve the team's goals.
⑤ I don't know how to achieve the team's goals.

22 다음 빈칸 (A)~(C)에 알맞은 단어를 넣어 '녹색 리더들'의 특징을 완성하시오.

Green leaders are "(A)_____ _____" who make sure that the team feels valued, create a (B)_____ _____, and are (C)_____ and easy to talk to.

23 다음 '빨간색 리더들'의 특징에 대한 설명 중, 위 글의 내용과 <u>다른</u> 부분을 찾아서 고치시오.

> They are logical analysts who have good reasoning skills and think of the most impressive ways to achieve the team's goals.

_____ ➡ _____

[24~25] 다음 글을 읽고 물음에 답하시오.

I was surprised that there are actually many different leadership styles, but soon I realized the reason.

We belong ____ⓐ____ many different groups, and many different situations can come up in our lives. They all call ____ⓑ____ different leadership styles. Each group's unique situation determines the best leadership style.

🗣 "I am a part of many different groups, and I have different responsibilities in each group."

After reading everything, I became more confident. I discovered that I have some of the qualities of a "green leader." If my classmates think a green leader would make our class better, they might pick me to be class representative! Okay, let's try it!   <I: Yumi>

24 위 글의 빈칸 ⓐ와 ⓑ에 들어갈 전치사가 바르게 짝지어진 것은?

	ⓐ	ⓑ			ⓐ	ⓑ
①	to – for			②	in – on	
③	to – on			④	in – to	
⑤	on – for					

25 According to the passage, which is NOT true?

① Yumi was surprised that there are actually many different leadership styles.

② Yumi couldn't realize the reason why there are actually many different leadership styles.

③ Lots of different situations can come up in our lives.

④ The best leadership style is determined by each group's unique situation.

⑤ After Yumi read everything, she became more confident.

[26~27] 다음 글을 읽고 물음에 답하시오.

Sumin: A Wonderful Leader

I think my partner Sumin is an orange leader because ⓐ<u>he gave the other classmates clear roles</u>. I noticed ⓑ<u>it</u> last Wednesday when we were all enjoying our school sports day. After the event was over, no one knew what to do to clean up, but Sumin gave each of us a different cleaning task after the event. I was grateful, so I started to pick up the trash around us. I think Sumin is a wonderful leader.

26 위 글의 밑줄 친 ⓐ의 예를 본문에서 찾아 쓰시오.

➡ _____

_____

27 위 글의 밑줄 친 ⓑit이 가리키는 것을 본문에서 찾아 쓰시오.

➡ _____

MEMO

MEMO

MEMO

Middle School 3-1
학교시험 완벽 대비

1학기 전과정
적중100 plus
영어 기출문제집

영어 중 3

능률 | 김성곤

Best Collection

내용문의 중등영어발전소 적중100 편집부 TEL 070-4416-3636

INSIGHT
on the textbook

교과서 파헤치기

영어 기출 문제집

적중 100 plus

1학기 전과정

영어 중 3

능률 | 김성곤

INSIGHT
on the textbook

교과서 파헤치기

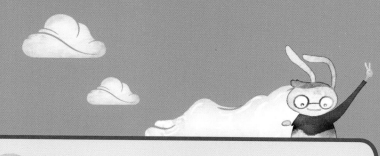

※ 다음 영어를 우리말로 쓰시오.

01 motivate _____

02 confident _____

03 exactly _____

04 perform _____

05 foreign _____

06 furniture _____

07 guess _____

08 own _____

09 treasure _____

10 awesome _____

11 nervous _____

12 improve _____

13 creative _____

14 perfect _____

15 case _____

16 meaningful _____

17 subtitle _____

18 volunteer _____

19 memorize _____

20 culture _____

21 post _____

22 social media _____

23 recommend _____

24 experience _____

25 finally _____

26 responsibility _____

27 talent _____

28 finish _____

29 review _____

30 translation _____

31 vocabulary _____

32 requirement _____

33 weakness _____

34 shelf _____

35 be related to ~ _____

36 get used to ~ _____

37 in any case _____

38 first of all _____

39 take care of _____

40 be struck by _____

41 be proud of ~ _____

42 give up _____

43 spend time -ing _____

※ 다음 우리말을 영어로 쓰시오.

01 (웹사이트에 정보·사진을) 게시하다 _____

02 보물 _____

03 선반, 책꽂이 _____

04 자막 _____

05 암기하다 _____

06 동기를 부여하다 _____

07 어휘 _____

08 쥐다, 들다 _____

09 자신 있는 _____

10 검토, 후기 _____

11 경험 _____

12 마침내 _____

13 문화 _____

14 추측하다 _____

15 창조적인 _____

16 가구 _____

17 필요조건, 요건 _____

18 재능 _____

19 개선하다, 향상시키다 _____

20 엄청난 _____

21 사례, 경우, 상자 _____

22 의미 있는 _____

23 외국의 _____

24 불안한 _____

25 ~ 자신의; 소유하다 _____

26 완벽한 _____

27 정확하게 _____

28 번역된 것, 번역문 _____

29 공연하다, 수행하다 _____

30 자원봉사자 _____

31 공유하다 _____

32 약점 _____

33 책임감 _____

34 추천하다 _____

35 포기하다 _____

36 ~에 친숙해지다 _____

37 ~을 자랑스러워하다 _____

38 첫째로 _____

39 ~에 익숙해지다 _____

40 ~을 돌보다 _____

41 어쨌든 _____

42 전혀 ~가 아닌 _____

43 ~에 관련되다 _____

※ 다음 영영풀이에 알맞은 단어를 <보기>에서 골라 쓴 후, 우리말 뜻을 쓰시오.

1 _____ : a natural ability to do something well: _____

2 _____ : to entertain an audience by singing, acting, etc.: _____

3 _____ : to advise someone to do something: _____

4 _____ : add a message to an online message board: _____

5 _____ : a long flat narrow board attached to a wall: _____

6 _____ : not having any mistakes, faults, or damage: _____

7 _____ : to have or use something with other people: _____

8 _____ : something that someone needs or asks for: _____

9 _____ : to learn something carefully so that you can remember it exactly:
_____

10 _____ : a group of valuable things such as gold, silver, jewels: _____

11 _____ : a duty to be in charge of someone or something: _____

12 _____ : a careful examination of a situation or process: _____

13 _____ : chairs, tables, beds, etc., that are used to make a room ready for use:
_____

14 _____ : someone who does a job willingly without being paid: _____

15 _____ : feeling sure about your own ability to do things and be successful:
_____

16 _____ : to make someone want to achieve something and make them willing to
work hard in order to do this: _____

보기			
confident	motivate	shelf	volunteer
furniture	talent	perfect	recommend
post	requirement	memorize	treasure
share	perform	responsibility	review

※ 다음 우리말과 일치하도록 빈칸에 알맞은 말을 쓰시오.

해석

Listen & Talk 1 B

G: What _____ you _____ to do _____ _____?

B: I'd _____ to _____ the guitar. I _____ to the song "Cavatina," and I _____ _____ _____ the _____ of the guitar.

G: That's great. _____ are you _____ _____ _____ it?

B: My friend Jinsu is a very _____ guitar _____. I'll _____ _____ _____ _____ me.

G: 너는 올해 무엇을 하기를 원하니?
B: 나는 기타를 배우고 싶어. 나는 "Cavatina"라는 노래를 들었는데 기타 소리에 감동을 받았어.
G: 좋겠다. 너는 어디에서 그것을 배울 거니?
B: 내 친구 진수가 기타를 매우 잘 쳐. 나는 그에게 가르쳐 달라고 요청할 거야.

Listen & Talk 1 C

B: _____ are you _____?

G: I'm _____ a list of _____ _____ I _____ _____ _____ this year.

B: That's nice. _____ would you _____ _____ do this year?

G: Well, _____ of all, I'd _____ to _____ _____ _____ with my friends _____ summer vacation.

B: That _____ great.

G: _____ _____ you? _____ _____ you _____ _____ _____ this year?

B: I'm _____ of _____ a _____ _____.

G: That's really _____.

B: 너는 무엇을 하고 있니?
G: 올해 하고 싶은 일의 목록을 작성하고 있는 중이야.
B: 멋있다. 너는 올해 무엇을 하기를 원하니?
G: 음, 우선 여름 방학 동안 친구들과 자원봉사를 하면서 시간을 보내고 싶어.
B: 그거 좋겠다.
G: 너는 어떠니? 너는 올해 무엇을 하고 싶어?
B: 나는 수영 수업 받는 것을 생각하고 있어.
G: 그거 정말 멋있구나.

Listen & Talk 2 B

B: Hey, Suji! _____ are you _____?

G: Hi, Ben. It's a _____. I'm _____ _____.

B: Wow! I didn't _____ _____ you could _____. _____ did you _____ to _____?

G: I _____ a _____ skateboarding club _____ _____.

B: I _____. So _____ do you _____ it?

G: It's _____ fun! It _____ me _____ new friends, _____.

B: How?

G: I _____ _____ with _____ _____ of the club, and we _____ _____ with _____ _____.

B: 안녕, 수지야! 들고 있는 것이 뭐니?
G: 안녕, Ben. 스케이트보드야. 나는 스케이트보드를 타러 가는 중이야.
B: 와우! 네가 스케이트보드를 탈줄 아는지 몰랐어. 스케이트보드는 어떻게 배웠니?
G: 지난달에 지역 스케이트보드 클럽에 가입했어.
B: 알겠어. 너는 그것이 마음에 드니?
G: 정말 재미있어! 그것은 또한 새로운 친구를 사귀도록 도와줘.
B: 어떻게?
G: 나는 클럽의 다른 회원들과 스케이트보드를 타러 가는데, 우리는 서로 방법을 공유해.

Listen & Talk 2 C

G: Did you _____ this _____ _____? It's _____!

B: Thanks. I _____ _____ _____ _____ _____.

G: Cool! _____ do you _____ it?

B: It was _____ _____ _____, but now I _____ it. I _____ so _____ _____ I _____ something.

G: That's _____. I think you're _____ _____ _____ it.

B: Thanks. I _____ I _____ a new _____. I think it's _____ _____ _____ new things.

G: _____. _____ new _____ lets us _____ new _____.

Listen & Talk 2 D

A: I _____ a _____ last year.

B: _____ you _____ it?

A: I _____ it _____ _____. It _____ me build _____.

Presentation Time Step 1

A: Can you _____ me about _____ of your _____ experiences?

B: I _____ dinner _____ my family last Sunday.

A: _____ did you _____ it?

B: It was _____ _____, but I _____ _____ I could _____ people _____ _____ my _____.

Presentation Time Step 3

Our group _____ _____ dinner for your family. It is a _____ _____ _____ you will learn that _____ for _____ can _____ them happy. After this _____, you will _____ great.

Do It Yourself A

B: My band _____ at the school _____ yesterday.

G: Cool. _____ did you _____ that?

B: It _____ _____, but I _____ some _____.

G: It's okay. I'm _____ you _____ _____.

B: Thanks _____ _____ so. It was my first time _____ the drums _____ _____ so many people.

G: _____ did you _____ _____ that?

B: I was very _____, but I _____ great, _____!

G: That's _____. I'm _____ _____ you.

G: 그 책꽂이를 직접 만들었니? 멋있다!

B: 고마워. 나는 작년에 가구 만들기를 시작했어.

G: 멋있어! 그것이 마음에 드니?

B: 처음에는 어려웠어. 그러나 지금 나는 그것을 아주 좋아해. 무엇인가를 만들고 나면 매우 자신감을 느껴.

G: 좋겠다. 나는 네가 그것을 정말 잘한다고 생각해.

B: 고마워. 나는 새로운 재능을 발견했다고 생각해. 새로운 것을 시도하는 것은 좋다고 생각해.

G: 그렇지. 새로운 경험을 하는 것은 우리에게 새로운 재능을 발견하도록 해.

A: 나는 작년에 달리기를 했어.

B: 그것이 마음에 들었니?

A: 굉장히 좋았어. 그것이 자신감을 가지도록 도와주었어.

A: 너에게 의미 있었던 경험 중 하나를 말해주겠니?

B: 나는 지난 일요일에 가족을 위하여 저녁을 요리했어.

A: 그것이 마음에 들었니?

B: 그것은 쉽지 않았어. 하지만 나는 내가 요리한 것을 가지고 사람을 행복하게 만들 수 있다는 것을 배웠어.

우리 모둠은 여러분의 가족을 위해 저녁을 요리할 것을 추천합니다. 그것은 여러분이 다른 사람을 위해 요리하는 것이 그들을 행복하게 만들 수 있다는 것을 배울 것이기 때문에 의미 있는 경험입니다. 이 경험 이후에 여러분은 기분 좋게 느낄 것입니다.

B: 우리 밴드가 어제 학교 축제에서 연주를 했어.

G: 멋있네. 너는 그것이 마음에 들었니?

B: 나쁘지 않았어. 하지만 내가 몇 가지 실수를 저질렀어.

G: 괜찮아. 네 연주는 확실히 좋았어.

B: 그렇게 말해주니 고마워. 그것이 그토록 많은 사람들 앞에서 처음으로 드럼을 연주한 것이었어.

G: 그것에 대하여 어떻게 느꼈니?

B: 나는 매우 불안했어. 그러나 또한 기분 좋기도 했어.

G: 훌륭하구나. 나는 네가 정말 자랑스러워.

Step2

※ 다음 우리말에 맞도록 대화를 영어로 쓰시오.

Listen & Talk 1 B

G: _____

B: _____

_____

G: _____

B: _____

해석

G: 너는 올해 무엇을 하기를 원하니?
B: 나는 기타를 배우고 싶어. 나는 "Cavatina"라는 노래를 들었는데 기타 소리에 감동을 받았어.
G: 좋겠다. 너는 어디에서 그것을 배울 거니?
B: 내 친구 진수가 기타를 매우 잘 쳐. 나는 그에게 가르쳐 달라고 요청할 거야.

Listen & Talk 1 C

B: _____

G: _____

B: _____

G: _____

_____

B: _____

G: _____

B: _____

G: _____

B: 너는 무엇을 하고 있니?
G: 올해 하고 싶은 일의 목록을 작성하고 있는 중이야.
B: 멋있다. 너는 올해 무엇을 하기를 원하니?
G: 음, 우선 여름 방학 동안 친구들과 자원봉사를 하면서 시간을 보내고 싶어.
B: 그거 좋겠다.
G: 너는 어떠니? 너는 올해 무엇을 하고 싶어?
B: 나는 수영 수업 받는 것을 생각하고 있어.
G: 그거 정말 멋있구나.

Listen & Talk 2 B

B: _____

G: _____

B: _____

_____

G: _____

B: _____

G: _____

B: _____

G: _____

_____

B: 안녕, 수지야! 들고 있는 것이 뭐니?
G: 안녕, Ben. 스케이트보드야. 나는 스케이트보드를 타러 가는 중이야.
B: 와우! 네가 스케이트보드를 탈줄 아는지 몰랐어. 스케이트보드는 어떻게 배웠니?
G: 지난달에 지역 스케이트보드 클럽에 가입했어.
B: 알겠다. 너는 그것이 마음에 드니?
G: 정말 재미있어! 그것은 또한 새로운 친구를 사귀도록 도와줘.
B: 어떻게?
G: 나는 클럽의 다른 회원들과 스케이트보드를 타러 가는데, 우리는 서로 방법을 공유해.

Listen & Talk 2 C

G: _____

B: _____

G: _____

B: _____

_____

G: _____

B: _____

G: _____

Listen & Talk 2 D

A: _____

B: _____

A: _____

Presentation Time Step 1

A: _____

B: _____

A: _____

B: _____

Presentation Time Step 3

_____

_____

_____

Do It Yourself A

B: _____

G: _____

B: _____

G: _____

B: _____

G: _____

B: _____

G: _____

G: 그 책꽂이를 직접 만들었니? 멋있다!

B: 고마워. 나는 작년에 가구 만들기를 시작했어.

G: 멋있어! 그것이 마음에 드니?

B: 처음에는 어려웠어. 그러나 지금 나는 그것을 아주 좋아해. 무엇인가를 만들고 나면 매우 자신감을 느껴.

G: 좋겠다. 나는 네가 그것을 정말 잘한다고 생각해.

B: 고마워. 나는 새로운 재능을 발견했다고 생각해. 새로운 것을 시도하는 것은 좋다고 생각해.

G: 그렇지. 새로운 경험을 하는 것은 우리에게 새로운 재능을 발견하도록 해.

A: 나는 작년에 달리기를 했어.

B: 그것이 마음에 들었니?

A: 굉장히 좋았어. 그것이 자신감을 가지도록 도와주었어.

A: 너에게 의미 있었던 경험 중 하나를 말해주겠니?

B: 나는 지난 일요일에 가족을 위하여 저녁을 요리했어.

A: 그것이 마음에 들었니?

B: 그것은 쉽지 않았어. 하지만 나는 내가 요리한 것을 가지고 사람을 행복하게 만들 수 있다는 것을 배웠어.

우리 모둠은 여러분의 가족을 위해 저녁을 요리할 것을 추천합니다. 그것은 여러분이 다른 사람을 위해 요리하는 것이 그들을 행복하게 만들 수 있다는 것을 배울 것이기 때문에 의미 있는 경험입니다. 이 경험 이후에 여러분은 기분 좋게 느낄 것입니다.

B: 우리 밴드가 어제 학교 축제에서 연주를 했어.

G: 멋있네. 너는 그것이 마음에 들었니?

B: 나쁘지 않았어. 하지만 내가 몇 가지 실수를 저질렀어.

G: 괜찮아. 네 연주는 확실히 좋았어.

B: 그렇게 말해주니 고마워. 그것이 그토록 많은 사람들 앞에서 처음으로 드럼을 연주한 것이었어.

G: 그것에 대하여 어떻게 느꼈니?

B: 나는 매우 불안했어. 그러나 또한 기분 좋기도 했어.

G: 훌륭하구나. 나는 네가 정말 자랑스러워.

※ 다음 우리말과 일치하도록 빈칸에 알맞은 것을 골라 쓰시오.

1 _____ a New _____, _____ a New World

A. Language　　B. Learn　　C. Find

2 _____ Do People Learn _____ _____?

A. Foreign　　B. Why　　C. Languages

3 _____ students learn new languages _____ _____ school _____.

A. requirements　　B. because　　C. many　　D. of

4 Many _____ learn them _____ _____.

A. fun　　B. others　　C. for

5 _____ any _____, students everywhere have _____ interesting ways to _____ new languages.

A. case　　B. found　　C. study　　D. in

6 _____ _____ these students and _____ to their _____.

A. ideas　　B. let's　　C. listen　　D. meet

7 I _____ _____!

A. Soccer　　B. Love

8 I'm a _____ _____ of a Spanish soccer _____.

A. fan　　B. team　　C. big

9 I want to _____ _____ with my _____ players.

A. interviews　　B. favorite　　C. understand

10 _____, it's not _____ _____ I don't know Spanish that _____.

A. because　　B. however　　C. well　　D. easy

11 _____ can I _____ my _____? - Owen, 16

A. Spanish　　B. how　　C. improve

12 The best _____ to learn a new language is _____ _____ it _____ day.

A. to　　B. every　　C. way　　D. practice

13 I _____ _____ the language of my phone to Spanish, and I have _____ _____ my shopping lists in Spanish! - Julie, 15

A. been　　B. changed　　C. writing　　D. have

14 _____ most important is to _____ _____ _____ the language first.

A. familiar　　B. what's　　C. with　　D. become

---

1 새로운 언어를 배우고, 새로운 세상을 찾아라

2 왜 사람들은 외국어를 배울까?

3 많은 학생들이 학교 필수 수업이기 때문에 새로운 언어를 배운다.

4 다른 많은 이들은 재미를 위해 그것을 배운다.

5 어떤 경우에도, 모든 곳의 학생들은 새로운 언어를 공부하는 데 흥미로운 방법들을 찾아낸다.

6 이 학생들을 만나서 그들의 생각을 들어보자.

7 저는 축구를 정말 좋아해요!

8 전 스페인 축구 팀의 엄청난 팬이랍니다.

9 저는 제가 정말 좋아하는 선수들의 인터뷰를 이해하고 싶어요.

10 그런데 스페인어를 그렇게 잘 알지 못하기 때문에 그것이 쉽지 않아요.

11 어떻게 하면 제가 스페인어 실력을 늘릴 수 있을까요? – 오언, 16세

12 새로운 언어를 배울 수 있는 가장 좋은 방법은 그 언어를 매일 연습하는 것이랍니다.

13 저는 제 휴대 전화의 설정을 스페인어로 바꿨고, 제가 사야 할 목록을 스페인어로 적어 오고 있어요! – 줄리, 15세

14 가장 중요한 것은 우선 그 언어와 친해지는 것이에요.

15 I _____ _____ Spanish movies _____.

    A. watching   B. suggest   C. often

16 It will _____ you get _____ _____ the _____ of the language.

    A. sound   B. used   C. help   D. to

17 _____ the people talk _____ fast, _____ _____ Spanish children's movies first. - Inho, 14

    A. try   B. if   C. watching   D. too

18 Some words _____ _____ only in soccer, not in _____ _____.

    A. every   B. used   C. are   D. day

19 _____ some soccer _____ and _____ it.

    A. vocabulary   B. learn   C. memorize

20 Also, _____ _____ you try writing a _____ of a match _____ Spanish?

    A. don't   B. in   C. review   D. why

21 It will _____ you _____ your _____ skills. - Rohan, 16

    A. writing   B. help   C. improve

22 _____ More _____!

    A. Subtitles   B. No

23 DREAM4 _____ _____!

    A. back   B. is

24 I'm _____ _____ to see my favorite Korean boy band _____.

    A. perform   B. excited   C. so

25 Their _____ and their dancing are _____ _____.

    A. just   B. singing   C. perfect

26 I want to understand their songs _____ _____ or _____ though.

    A. without   B. translations   C. subtitles

27 _____ _____? - Marisa, 14

    A. tips   B. any

28 You _____ _____ friends who are _____ _____ DREAM4 and start a club.

    A. find   B. interested   C. should   D. in

29 In my club, we _____ _____ _____.

    A. one   B. motivate   C. another

30 We _____ songs and _____ _____.

    A. sing   B. together   C. translate

---

15 전 스페인 영화들을 자주 볼 것을 제안하는데요.

16 그것은 당신이 언어의 소리에 익숙해지도록 도울 거예요.

17 만약 사람들이 너무 빨리 말한다면, 어린이를 위한 스페인 영화들을 먼저 보는 것을 시도해 보세요. – 인호, 14세

18 어떤 단어들은 일상생활에서가 아니라 오직 축구에서만 쓰인답니다.

19 몇몇 축구 어휘들을 배우고 기억하세요.

20 또한, 스페인어로 경기에 대한 후기를 써 보는 건 어때요?

21 그것은 당신이 작문 실력을 향상하도록 도울 거예요. – 로한, 16세

22 더는 자막 없이!

23 DREAM4가 돌아왔어요!

24 저는 제가 정말 좋아하는 한국의 젊은 남성 밴드가 공연하는 것을 보는 게 너무 신이 나요.

25 그들의 노래와 춤은 정말 완벽하답니다.

26 그렇지만 자막이나 번역이 없이 그들의 노래를 이해하고 싶어요.

27 어떤 조언들이 있을까요? – 마리사, 14세

28 당신은 DREAM4에 관심이 있는 친구들을 찾아 모임을 시작해야 해요.

29 우리 모임에서 우리는 서로 동기를 부여한답니다.

30 우리는 함께 노래를 번역하고 노래해요.

31 _____ these _____ is fun and really _____ our Korean! - Lori, 15

A. improves   B. doing   C. things

32 _____ DREAM4 _____ _____ media.

A. on   B. follow   C. social

33 They often _____ short _____ in Korean about _____ they are _____.

A. how   B. post   C. doing   D. messages

34 They also post pictures _____ the _____, so you can _____ the posts more _____.- Aishah, 14

A. easily   B. with   C. messages   D. understand

35 I _____ _____ Korean _____.

A. watching   B. recommend   C. dramas

36 I've _____ _____ Korean dramas for a _____, and they're really interesting!

A. watching   B. year   C. been

37 You can use Korean subtitles _____ _____ _____ _____.

A. help   B. listening   C. with   D. for

38 It's _____ a good idea to _____ _____ the _____ and read them first. - Brandon, 16

A. subtitles   B. print   C. also   D. out

39 _____ _____ for You?

A. Works   B. What

40 There are _____ _____ good tips out there, but everyone has their _____ _____ of learning.

A. of   B. way   C. hundreds   D. own

41 Find _____ keeps you _____; then you will _____ _____ more.

A. what   B. learning   C. motivated   D. enjoy

42 Remember, every language is hard _____ _____, but a new language can make your world _____ _____!

A. first   B. bigger   C. at   D. much

31 이런 것들을 하는 것은 재미있고 정말로 우리의 한국어 실력을 향상해요! – 로리, 15세

32 소셜 미디어에서 DREAM4를 팔로하세요.

33 그들은 종종 자신들이 어떻게 지내는지에 대해 한국어로 짧은 메시지를 올려요.

34 그들은 또한 메시지와 함께 사진들을 올려서 당신은 더 쉽게 게시물을 이해할 수 있어요. – 아이샤, 14세

35 저는 한국 드라마들을 볼 것을 추천해요.

36 저는 1년 동안 한국 드라마들을 시청해 왔고, 그것들은 정말 재미있어요!

37 듣기에 도움이 되도록 한국어 자막을 사용할 수 있고요.

38 먼저 자막들을 출력해서 읽는 것도 좋은 생각이랍니다. – 브랜던, 16세

39 무엇이 당신에게 효과가 있는 걸까?

40 세상에는 수백 가지 좋은 조언들이 있지만, 모든 사람이 학습에 대한 그들만의 방법을 가지고 있다.

41 당신에게 계속 동기 부여가 되는 것을 찾아라, 그러면 당신은 학습을 더욱 즐길 것이다.

42 기억해라, 모든 언어는 처음에는 어렵지만, 새로운 언어가 당신의 세상을 더욱 넓혀줄 수 있다!

※ 다음 우리말과 일치하도록 빈칸에 알맞은 것을 골라 쓰시오.

1 Learn _____ _____ _____, _____ a New World

2 _____ Do People _____ _____ _____?

3 Many students _____ new languages _____ _____ _____ _____.

4 Many _____ learn them _____ _____.

5 _____ _____ _____, students everywhere have found interesting _____ _____ _____ new languages.

6 _____ meet these students and _____ _____ _____ _____.

7 I _____ _____!

8 I'm _____ _____ _____ _____ of a _____ soccer team.

9 I want to _____ _____ _____ my favorite players.

10 _____, it's not easy _____ I don't know _____ _____.

11 _____ can I _____ _____ _____? - Owen, 16

12 _____ _____ _____ to learn a new language is _____ _____ _____ every day.

13 I _____ _____ _____ _____ of my phone to Spanish, and I _____ _____ _____ my shopping lists in Spanish! - Julie, 15

14 What's _____ _____ _____ _____ _____ _____ the language first.

1 새로운 언어를 배우고, 새로운 세상을 찾아라

2 왜 사람들은 외국어를 배울까?

3 많은 학생들이 학교 필수 수업이기 때문에 새로운 언어를 배운다.

4 다른 많은 이들은 재미를 위해 그것을 배운다.

5 어떤 경우에도, 모든 곳의 학생들은 새로운 언어를 공부하는 데 흥미로운 방법들을 찾아낸다.

6 이 학생들을 만나서 그들의 생각을 들어보자.

7 저는 축구를 정말 좋아해요!

8 전 스페인 축구 팀의 엄청난 팬이랍니다.

9 저는 제가 정말 좋아하는 선수들의 인터뷰를 이해하고 싶어요.

10 그런데 스페인어를 그렇게 잘 알지 못하기 때문에 그것이 쉽지 않아요.

11 어떻게 하면 제가 스페인어 실력을 늘릴 수 있을까요? – 오언, 16세

12 새로운 언어를 배울 수 있는 가장 좋은 방법은 그 언어를 매일 연습하는 것이랍니다.

13 저는 제 휴대 전화의 설정을 스페인어로 바꿨고, 제가 사야 할 목록을 스페인어로 적어 오고 있어요! – 줄리, 15세

14 가장 중요한 것은 우선 그 언어와 친해지는 것이에요.

15 I _____ _____ _____ movies often.

16 It _____ _____ you _____ _____ _____ the sound of the language.

17 If the people talk _____ _____, _____ _____ _____ Spanish children's movies first. - Inho, 14

18 Some words _____ _____ _____ in soccer, _____ in everyday life.

19 _____ some _____ _____ and _____ it.

20 Also, _____ _____ _____ _____ _____ a review of a match _____ _____?

21 It _____ _____ you _____ _____ _____ _____ _____. - Rohan, 16

22 _____ _____ Subtitles!

23 DREAM4 _____ _____!

24 I'm _____ _____ to see my favorite Korean boy band _____.

25 Their singing and their dancing are _____ _____.

26 I want to understand their songs _____ _____ or _____ _____.

27 _____ _____? - Marisa, 14

28 You _____ _____ friends who _____ _____ _____ DREAM4 and start a club.

29 In my club, we _____ _____ _____.

30 We _____ songs and _____ _____.

15 전 스페인 영화들을 자주 볼 것을 제안하는데요.

16 그것은 당신이 언어의 소리에 익숙해지도록 도울 거예요.

17 만약 사람들이 너무 빨리 말한다면, 어린이를 위한 스페인 영화들을 먼저 보는 것을 시도해 보세요. – 인호, 14세

18 어떤 단어들은 일상생활에서가 아니라 오직 축구에서만 쓰인답니다.

19 몇몇 축구 어휘들을 배우고 기억하세요.

20 또한, 스페인어로 경기에 대한 후기를 써 보는 건 어때요?

21 그것은 당신이 작문 실력을 향상하도록 도울 거예요. – 로한, 16세

22 더는 자막 없이!

23 DREAM4가 돌아왔어요!

24 저는 제가 정말 좋아하는 한국의 젊은 남성 밴드가 공연하는 것을 보는 게 너무 신이 나요.

25 그들의 노래와 춤은 정말 완벽하답니다.

26 그렇지만 자막이나 번역이 없이 그들의 노래를 이해하고 싶어요.

27 어떤 조언들이 있을까요? – 마리사, 14세

28 당신은 DREAM4에 관심이 있는 친구들을 찾아 모임을 시작해야 해요.

29 우리 모임에서 우리는 서로 동기를 부여한답니다.

30 우리는 함께 노래를 번역하고 노래해요.

31 _____ these things is fun and really _____ _____ _____! - Lori, 15

32 _____ DREAM4 _____ _____ _____.

33 They often _____ _____ _____ in Korean about _____ they _____ _____.

34 They also _____ pictures _____ _____ _____, so you can understand the posts _____ _____.- Aishah, 14

35 I _____ _____ Korean dramas.

36 _____ _____ _____ Korean dramas _____ a year, and they're really interesting!

37 You can use _____ _____ _____ _____ _____.

38 It's also a good idea _____ _____ _____ _____ _____ and read them first. - Brandon, 16

39 What _____ _____ You?

40 There are _____ _____ good tips out there, but everyone has _____ _____ _____ of _____.

41 Find _____ _____ you _____; then you will _____ _____ more.

42 Remember, every language is _____ _____ _____, but a new language can _____ your world _____ _____!

31 이런 것들을 하는 것은 재미있고 정말로 우리의 한국어 실력을 향상해요! – 로리, 15세

32 소셜 미디어에서 DREAM4를 팔로하세요.

33 그들은 종종 자신들이 어떻게 지내는지에 대해 한국어로 짧은 메시지를 올려요.

34 그들은 또한 메시지와 함께 사진들을 올려서 당신은 더 쉽게 게시물을 이해할 수 있어요. – 아이샤, 14세

35 저는 한국 드라마들을 볼 것을 추천해요.

36 저는 1년 동안 한국 드라마들을 시청해 왔고, 그것들은 정말 재미있어요!

37 듣기에 도움이 되도록 한국어 자막을 사용할 수 있고요.

38 먼저 자막들을 출력해서 읽는 것도 좋은 생각이랍니다. – 브랜던, 16세

39 무엇이 당신에게 효과가 있는 걸까?

40 세상에는 수백 가지 좋은 조언들이 있지만, 모든 사람이 학습에 대한 그들만의 방법을 가지고 있다.

41 당신에게 계속 동기 부여가 되는 것을 찾아라, 그러면 당신은 학습을 더욱 즐길 것이다.

42 기억해라, 모든 언어는 처음에는 어렵지만, 새로운 언어가 당신의 세상을 더욱 넓혀줄 수 있다!

※ 다음 문장을 우리말로 쓰시오.

1 ▶ Learn a New Language, Find a New World

➡ _____

2 ▶ Why Do People Learn Foreign Languages?

➡ _____

3 ▶ Many students learn new languages because of school requirements.

➡ _____

4 ▶ Many others learn them for fun.

➡ _____

5 ▶ In any case, students everywhere have found interesting ways to study new languages.

➡ _____

6 ▶ Let's meet these students and listen to their ideas.

➡ _____

7 ▶ I Love Soccer!

➡ _____

8 ▶ I'm a big fan of a Spanish soccer team.

➡ _____

9 ▶ I want to understand interviews with my favorite players.

➡ _____

10 ▶ However, it's not easy because I don't know Spanish that well.

➡ _____

11 ▶ How can I improve my Spanish? - Owen, 16

➡ _____

12 ▶ The best way to learn a new language is to practice it every day.

➡ _____

13 ▶ I have changed the language of my phone to Spanish, and I have been writing my shopping lists in Spanish! - Julie, 15

➡ _____

14 ▶ What's most important is to become familiar with the language first.

➡ _____

15 I suggest watching Spanish movies often.

➡ _____

16 It will help you get used to the sound of the language.

➡ _____

17 If the people talk too fast, try watching Spanish children's movies first. - Inho, 14

➡ _____

18 Some words are used only in soccer, not in everyday life.

➡ _____

19 Learn some soccer vocabulary and memorize it.

➡ _____

20 Also, why don't you try writing a review of a match in Spanish?

➡ _____

21 It will help you improve your writing skills. - Rohan, 16

➡ _____

22 No More Subtitles!

➡ _____

23 DREAM4 is back!

➡ _____

24 I'm so excited to see my favorite Korean boy band perform.

➡ _____

25 Their singing and their dancing are just perfect.

➡ _____

26 I want to understand their songs without subtitles or translations though.

➡ _____

27 Any tips? - Marisa, 14

➡ _____

28 You should find friends who are interested in DREAM4 and start a club.

➡ _____

29 In my club, we motivate one another.

➡ _____

30 We translate songs and sing together.

➡ _____

31 Doing these things is fun and really improves our Korean! - Lori, 15

➡ _____

32 Follow DREAM4 on social media.

➡ _____

33 They often post short messages in Korean about how they are doing.

➡ _____

34 They also post pictures with the messages, so you can understand the posts more easily.
- Aishah, 14

➡ _____

35 I recommend watching Korean dramas.

➡ _____

36 I've been watching Korean dramas for a year, and they're really interesting!

➡ _____

37 You can use Korean subtitles for help with listening.

➡ _____

38 It's also a good idea to print out the subtitles and read them first. - Brandon, 16

➡ _____

39 What Works for You?

➡ _____

40 There are hundreds of good tips out there, but everyone has their own way of learning.

➡ _____

41 Find what keeps you motivated; then you will enjoy learning more.

➡ _____

42 Remember, every language is hard at first, but a new language can make your world much bigger!

➡ _____

※ 다음 괄호 안의 단어들을 우리말에 맞도록 바르게 배열하시오.

1 (a / Learn / Language, / New / a / Find / World / New)
➡ _____

2 (Do / Why / Learn / People / Languages? / Foreign)
➡ _____

3 (students / many / new / learn / because / language / school / requirements. / of)
➡ _____

4 (others / many / them / learn / fun. / for)
➡ _____

5 (any / case, / in / everywhere / students / found / have / ways / interesting / study / to / languages. / new)
➡ _____

6 (meet / let's / students / these / and / to / listen / ideas. / their)
➡ _____

7 (Love / I / Soccer!)
➡ _____

8 (a / I'm / fan / big / of / Spanish / a / team. / soccer)
➡ _____

9 (want / I / to / understand / with / interviews / favorite / my / players.)
➡ _____

10 (it's / however, / not / because / easy / don't / I / Spanish / know / well. / that)
➡ _____

11 (can / how / improve / I / Spanish? / my / - / 16 / Owen,)
➡ _____

12 (best / the / to / way / learn / new / a / language / to / is / it / practice / day. / every)
➡ _____

13 (have / I / the / changed / language / my / of / to / phone / Spanish, / and / have / I / writing / been / shopping / my / in / lists / Spanish! / - / 15 / Julie,)
➡ _____

14 (most / what's / important / to / is / familiar / become / with / language / the / first.)
➡ _____

1 새로운 언어를 배우고, 새로운 세상을 찾아라

2 왜 사람들은 외국어를 배울까?

3 많은 학생들이 학교 필수 수업이기 때문에 새로운 언어를 배운다.

4 다른 많은 이들은 재미를 위해 그것을 배운다.

5 어떤 경우에도, 모든 곳의 학생들은 새로운 언어를 공부하는 데 흥미로운 방법들을 찾아낸다.

6 이 학생들을 만나서 그들의 생각을 들어보자.

7 저는 축구를 정말 좋아해요!

8 전 스페인 축구 팀의 엄청난 팬이랍니다.

9 저는 제가 정말 좋아하는 선수들의 인터뷰를 이3해하고 싶어요.

10 그런데 스페인어를 그렇게 잘 알지 못하기 때문에 그것이 쉽지 않아요.

11 어떻게 하면 제가 스페인어 실력을 늘릴 수 있을까요? – 오언, 16세

12 새로운 언어를 배울 수 있는 가장 좋은 방법은 그 언어를 매일 연습하는 것이랍니다.

13 저는 제 휴대 전화의 설정을 스페인어로 바꿨고, 제가 사야 할 목록을 스페인어로 적어 오고 있어요! – 줄리, 15세

14 가장 중요한 것은 우선 그 언어와 친해지는 것이에요.

15 (suggest / I / watching / movies / often. / Spanish)
➡ _____

16 (will / it / help / get / you / used / the / to / sound / the / of / language.)
➡ _____

17 (the / if / talk / people / fast, / too / watching / try / children's / Spanish / first. / movies / - / 14 / Inho,)
➡ _____
_____

18 (words / some / used / are / in / only / soccer, / in / not / life. / everyday)
➡ _____

19 (some / learn / vocabulary / soccer / and / it. / memorize)
➡ _____

20 (why / also, / don't / try / you / a / writing / review / a / of / match / Spanish? / in)
➡ _____

21 (will / it / you / help / your / improve / skills. / wrting / - / 16 / Rohan,)
➡ _____

22 (More / No / Subtitles!)
➡ _____

23 (is / DREAM4 / back!)
➡ _____

24 (so / I'm / to / excited / see / favorite / my / boy / Korean / perform. / band)
➡ _____

25 (singing / their / and / dancing / their / are / perfect. / just)
➡ _____

26 (want / I / to / their / understand / songs / subtitles / without / or / though. / translations)
➡ _____

27 (tips? / any / - / 14 / Marisa,)
➡ _____

28 (should / you / friends / find / who / interested / are / in / and / DREAM4 / a / club. / start)
➡ _____

29 (my / in / club, / motivate / we / another. / one)
➡ _____

30 (translate / we / songs / and / together. / sing)
➡ _____

15 전 스페인 영화들을 자주 볼 것을 제안하는데요.

16 그것은 당신이 언어의 소리에 익숙해지도록 도울 거예요.

17 만약 사람들이 너무 빨리 말한다면, 어린이를 위한 스페인 영화들을 먼저 보는 것을 시도해 보세요. – 인호, 14세

18 어떤 단어들은 일상생활에서가 아니라 오직 축구에서만 쓰인답니다.

19 몇몇 축구 어휘들을 배우고 기억하세요.

20 또한, 스페인어로 경기에 대한 후기를 써 보는 건 어때요?

21 그것은 당신이 작문 실력을 향상하도록 도울 거예요. – 로한, 16세

22 더는 자막 없이!

23 DREAM4가 돌아왔어요!

24 저는 제가 정말 좋아하는 한국의 젊은 남성 밴드가 공연하는 것을 보는 게 너무 신이 나요.

25 그들의 노래와 춤은 정말 완벽하답니다.

26 그렇지만 자막이나 번역이 없이 그들의 노래를 이해하고 싶어요.

27 어떤 조언들이 있을까요? – 마리사, 14세

28 당신은 DREAM4에 관심이 있는 친구들을 찾아 모임을 시작해야 해요.

29 우리 모임에서 우리는 서로 동기를 부여한답니다.

30 우리는 함께 노래를 번역하고 노래해요.

31 (these / doing / things / fun / is / and / improves / really / Korean! / our / - / 15 / Lori,)

➡ _____

32 (DREAM4 / follow / social / on / media.)

➡ _____

33 (often / they / post / messages / short / Korean / in / how / about / are / they / doing.)

➡ _____

34 (also / they / pictures / post / with / messages, / the / you / so / understand / can / posts / the / easily. / more / - / 14 / Aishah,)

➡ _____

_____

35 (recommend / I / watching / dramas. / Korean)

➡ _____

36 (been / I've / watching / dramas / Korean / a / for / year, / and / really / they're / interesting!)

➡ _____

_____

37 (can / you / Korean / use / for / subtitles / help / listening. / with)

➡ _____

38 (also / it's / good / a / to / idea / out / print / the / and / subtitles / and / them / first. / read / - 16, / Brandon,)

➡ _____

_____

39 (Works / What / You? / for)

➡ _____

40 (are / there / of / hundreds / good / tips / there, / out / everyone / but / their / has / way / own / learning. / of)

➡ _____

_____

41 (what / find / you / keeps / motivated; / you / then / enjoy / will / more. / learning)

➡ _____

_____

42 (every / remember, / language / hard / is / first, / at / but / new / a / language / make / can / world / your / bigger! / much)

➡ _____

_____

31 이런 것들을 하는 것은 재미있고 정말로 우리의 한국어 실력을 향상해요! – 로리, 15세

32 소셜 미디어에서 DREAM4를 팔로하세요.

33 그들은 종종 자신들이 어떻게 지내는지에 대해 한국어로 짧은 메시지를 올려요.

34 그들은 또한 메시지와 함께 사진들을 올려서 당신은 더 쉽게 게시물을 이해할 수 있어요. – 아이샤, 14세

35 저는 한국 드라마들을 볼 것을 추천해요.

36 저는 1년 동안 한국 드라마들을 시청해 왔고, 그것들은 정말 재미있어요!

37 듣기에 도움이 되도록 한국어 자막을 사용할 수 있고요.

38 먼저 자막들을 출력해서 읽는 것도 좋은 생각이랍니다. – 브랜던, 16세

39 무엇이 당신에게 효과가 있는 걸까?

40 세상에는 수백 가지 좋은 조언들이 있지만, 모든 사람이 학습에 대한 그들만의 방법을 가지고 있다.

41 당신에게 계속 동기 부여가 되는 것을 찾아라, 그러면 당신은 학습을 더욱 즐길 것이다.

42 기억해라, 모든 언어는 처음에는 어렵지만, 새로운 언어가 당신의 세상을 더욱 넓혀줄 수 있다!

※ 다음 우리말을 영어로 쓰시오.

1 새로운 언어를 배우고, 새로운 세상을 찾아라

➡ _____

2 왜 사람들은 외국어를 배울까?

➡ _____

3 많은 학생들이 학교 필수 수업이기 때문에 새로운 언어를 배운다.

➡ _____

4 다른 많은 이들은 재미를 위해 그것을 배운다.

➡ _____

5 어떤 경우에도, 모든 곳의 학생들은 새로운 언어를 공부하는 데 흥미로운 방법들을 찾아낸다.

➡ _____

6 이 학생들을 만나서 그들의 생각을 들어보자.

➡ _____

7 저는 축구를 정말 좋아해요!

➡ _____

8 전 스페인 축구 팀의 엄청난 팬이랍니다.

➡ _____

9 저는 제가 정말 좋아하는 선수들의 인터뷰를 이해하고 싶어요.

➡ _____

10 그런데 스페인어를 그렇게 잘 알지 못하기 때문에 그것이 쉽지 않아요.

➡ _____

11 어떻게 하면 제가 스페인어 실력을 늘릴 수 있을까요? – 오언, 16세

➡ _____

12 새로운 언어를 배울 수 있는 가장 좋은 방법은 그 언어를 매일 연습하는 것이랍니다.

➡ _____

13 저는 제 휴대 전화의 설정을 스페인어로 바꿨고, 제가 사야 할 목록을 스페인어로 적어 오고 있어요!
– 줄리, 15세

➡ _____

_____

14 가장 중요한 것은 우선 언어와 친해지는 것이에요.

➡ _____

15 전 스페인 영화들을 자주 볼 것을 제안하는데요.

➡ _____

16 그것은 당신이 언어의 소리에 익숙해지도록 도울 거예요.

➡ _____

17 만약 사람들이 너무 빨리 말한다면, 어린이를 위한 스페인 영화들을 먼저 보는 것을 시도해 보세요.
– 인호, 14세

➡ _____

18 어떤 단어들은 일상생활에서가 아니라 오직 축구에서만 쓰인답니다.

➡ _____

19 몇몇 축구 어휘들을 배우고 기억하세요.

➡ _____

20 또한, 스페인어로 경기에 대한 후기를 써 보는 건 어때요?

➡ _____

21 그것은 당신이 작문 실력을 향상하도록 도울 거예요. – 로한, 16세

➡ _____

22 더는 자막 없이!

➡ _____

23 DREAM4가 돌아왔어요!

➡ _____

24 저는 제가 정말 좋아하는 한국의 젊은 남성 밴드가 공연하는 것을 보는 게 너무 신이 나요.

➡ _____

25 그들의 노래와 춤은 정말 완벽하답니다.

➡ _____

26 그렇지만 자막이나 번역이 없이 그들의 노래를 이해하고 싶어요.

➡ _____

27 어떤 조언들이 있을까요? – 마리사, 14세

➡ _____

28 당신은 DREAM4에 관심이 있는 친구들을 찾아 모임을 시작해야 해요.

➡ _____

29 우리 모임에서 우리는 서로 동기를 부여한답니다.

➡ _____

30 우리는 함께 노래를 번역하고 노래해요.

➡ _____

31 이런 것들을 하는 것은 재미있고 정말로 우리의 한국어 실력을 향상해요! – 로리, 15세

➡ _____

32 소셜 미디어에서 DREAM4를 팔로하세요.

➡ _____

33 그들은 종종 자신들이 어떻게 지내는지에 대해 한국어로 짧은 메시지를 올려요.

➡ _____

34 그들은 또한 메시지와 함께 사진들을 올려서 당신은 더 쉽게 게시물을 이해할 수 있어요.

　　– 아이샤, 14세

➡ _____

_____

35 저는 한국 드라마들을 볼 것을 추천해요.

➡ _____

36 저는 1년 동안 한국 드라마들을 시청해 왔고, 그것들은 정말 재미있어요!

➡ _____

37 듣기에 도움이 되도록 한국어 자막을 사용할 수 있고요.

➡ _____

38 맨 먼저 자막들을 출력해서 읽는 것도 좋은 생각이랍니다. – 브랜던, 16세

➡ _____

39 무엇이 당신에게 효과가 있는 걸까?

➡ _____

40 세상에는 수백 가지 좋은 조언들이 있지만, 모든 사람이 학습에 대한 그들만의 방법을 가지고 있다.

➡ _____

41 당신에게 계속 동기 부여가 되는 것을 찾아라, 그러면 당신은 학습을 더욱 즐길 것이다.

➡ _____

42 기억해라, 모든 언어는 처음에는 어렵지만, 새로운 언어가 당신의 세상을 더욱 넓혀줄 수 있다!

➡ _____

※ 다음 우리말과 일치하도록 빈칸에 알맞은 말을 쓰시오.

After You Read B

1. A: I _____ _____ _____ my Chinese. Do you _____ _____ _____?

2. B: Learn _____ _____ _____ _____ _____ your interests.

3. C: _____ Chinese dramas _____ _____ _____ is a good _____ _____ _____ _____ listening.

4. A: Thanks _____ _____!

1. A: 나는 중국어 실력을 늘리고 싶어. 좋은 방법이 있니?
2. B: 관심있는 것들과 관련된 어휘를 배워.
3. C: 중국어 자막이 있는 중국 드라마를 보는 것이 듣기를 잘하게 하는 좋은 방법이야.
4. A: 정말 고마워!

After You Read C

1. _____ _____ _____ a New Language

2. _____: _____ soccer team

3. Wants: _____ _____ the players' _____

4. Useful Tips: • Practice _____ _____ _____.

5. • _____ _____ _____ Spanish.

6. • Learn _____ _____ and write a _____ of a _____ _____ _____.

7. Find _____ keeps you _____; then you will _____ _____ _____.

1. 새로운 언어를 배울 수 있는 방법
2. 관심: 스페인 축구 팀
3. 원하는 것: 선수들의 인터뷰를 이해하기
4. 유용한 조언들: • 스페인어를 매일 연습해라.
5. • 스페인어와 친해져라.
6. • 축구 어휘들을 배우고 스페인어로 경기에 대한 후기를 써 보아라.
7. 당신에게 계속 동기 부여가 되는 것을 찾아라, 그러면 당신은 학습을 더욱 즐길 것이다.

Do It Yourself B

1. I'm _____ _____ _____ _____ my favorite Korean boy band _____.

2. I want to understand their songs _____ _____ or _____ _____.

3. Any _____? - Marisa

1. 나는 내가 가장 좋아하는 한국의 소년 밴드가 공연하는 것을 보아서 매우 신나요.
2. 그러나 나는 자막이나 번역이 없이 그들의 노래를 이해하고 싶어요.
3. 어떤 조언들이 있을까요? –Marisa

※ 다음 우리말을 영어로 쓰시오.

After You Read B

1. A: 나는 중국어 실력을 늘리고 싶어. 좋은 방법이 있니?
   ➡ _____

2. B: 관심있는 것들과 관련된 어휘를 배워.
   ➡ _____

3. C: 중국어 자막이 있는 중국 드라마를 보는 것이 듣기를 잘하게 하는 좋은 방법이야.
   ➡ _____

4. A: 정말 고마워!
   ➡ _____

After You Read C

1. 새로운 언어를 배울 수 있는 방법
   ➡ _____

2. 관심: 스페인 축구 팀
   ➡ _____

3. 원하는 것: 선수들의 인터뷰를 이해하기
   ➡ _____

4. 유용한 조언들: ·스페인어를 매일 연습해라.
   ➡ _____

5. ·스페인어와 친해져라.
   ➡ _____

6. ·축구 어휘들을 배우고 스페인어로 경기에 대한 후기를 써 보아라.
   ➡ _____

7. 당신에게 계속 동기 부여가 되는 것을 찾아라, 그러면 당신은 학습을 더욱 즐길 것이다.
   ➡ _____

Do It Yourself B

1. 나는 내가 가장 좋아하는 한국의 소년 밴드가 공연하는 것을 보아서 매우 신나요.
   ➡ _____

2. 그러나 나는 자막이나 번역이 없이 그들의 노래를 이해하고 싶어요.
   ➡ _____

3. 어떤 조언들이 있을까요? – Marisa
   ➡ _____

※ 다음 영어를 우리말로 쓰시오.

01	positive	_____
02	awesome	_____
03	beneficial	_____
04	convenient	_____
05	similar	_____
06	brain	_____
07	cell	_____
08	damage	_____
09	deep sleep	_____
10	compared	_____
11	walnut	_____
12	prevent	_____
13	ginger	_____
14	risk	_____
15	search	_____
16	track	_____
17	benefit	_____
18	contain	_____
19	process	_____
20	clue	_____
21	vision	_____

22	increase	_____
23	multiple	_____
24	wrinkle	_____
25	lower	_____
26	mirror	_____
27	hollow	_____
28	improve	_____
29	moved	_____
30	negative	_____
31	sensitive	_____
32	chemical	_____
33	function	_____
34	productive	_____
35	a variety of	_____
36	in addition	_____
37	from now on	_____
38	at least	_____
39	on the other hand	_____
40	come to mind	_____
41	not only A but also B	_____
42	be divided into	_____
43	prevents A from -ing	_____

※ 다음 우리말을 영어로 쓰시오.

01 세포

02 유익한

03 처리하다

04 속이 빈

05 호두

06 부정적인

07 엄청난

08 복합적인

09 베개

10 반사하다

11 비교되는

12 긍정적인

13 감동받은

14 손상을 주다

15 주름

16 조사하다

17 단서

18 기능

19 시력

20 화학물질

21 씹다

22 생강

23 생산적인

24 비슷한

25 증가하다

26 건강한

27 이득

28 포함하다

29 뇌

30 개선하다

31 방해하다, 가로 막다

32 낮추다

33 편리한

34 민감한

35 지금부터

36 운동하다

37 게다가

38 반면에

39 계속 ~하다

40 다양한

41 ~로 나뉘어지다

42 A뿐만 아니라 B도

43 생각이 떠오르다

※ 다음 영영풀이에 알맞은 단어를 <보기>에서 골라 쓴 후, 우리말 뜻을 쓰시오.

1 _____ : feeling that you want or need a drink: _____

2 _____ : having an empty space inside: _____

3 _____ : useful to you because it saves you time: _____

4 _____ : the ability to see: _____

5 _____ : a nut that you can eat, shaped like a human brain: _____

6 _____ : to cut meat, bread, vegetables, etc into thin flat pieces: _____

7 _____ : a cloth bag filled with soft material that you put your head on: _____

8 _____ : always busy doing things, especially physical or mental activities: _____

9 _____ : lines on your face and skin that you get when you are old: _____

10 _____ : the organ inside your head that controls how you think, feel, and move: _____

11 _____ : the possibility that something bad, unpleasant, or dangerous may happen: _____

12 _____ : to become or to make something greater in amount, number, value, etc.: _____

13 _____ : to make something better, or to become better: _____

14 _____ : to bite food into small pieces in your mouth with your teeth to make it easier to swallow: _____

15 _____ : an object, a piece of evidence, or some information that helps the police solve a crime: _____

16 _____ : an advantage that something gives you; a helpful and useful effect that something has: _____

보기			
wrinkle	improve	clue	pillow
chew	thirsty	slice	brain
active	hollow	convenient	risk
vision	increase	walnut	benefit

대화문 Test

※ 다음 우리말과 일치하도록 빈칸에 알맞은 말을 쓰시오.

Listen & Talk 1 A

B: _____ you _____ that _____ ice is _____ _____ your
_____?

G: No, I _____. _____ is that?

B: It can _____ your teeth. It can also _____ them too _____.

Listen & Talk 1 B

B: You _____ _____. Did you _____ _____ sleep?

G: Yes, I did. I _____ _____ _____ seven hours.

B: Okay. _____ _____ you _____ _____ _____?

G: I _____ _____ _____ after midnight, _____ _____.

B: That's _____ _____ is _____ you _____. _____ you
_____ that _____ you go to bed is very important?

G: No, I haven't. _____ is _____?

B: Scientists say that _____ _____ _____ _____ can
_____ you _____ _____ the next day.

G: I didn't know that.

B: On the _____ _____, going to bed early can _____ your
_____ and help you be more _____. From _____ _____,
_____ go to bed _____.

Listen & Talk 1 D-1

A: _____ you _____ that _____ by hand is _____ for your
_____?

B: Oh, _____?

A: Yes, it _____ your _____.

Listen & Talk 2 A

G: What's this?

B: It's a _____ band. It lets me _____ my _____ _____ on
my _____.

G: _____ _____ _____ information?

B: It shows _____ _____ I walk _____ the day and
_____ I sleep at night.

G: Interesting. I'm _____ that this _____ band can do all that.

B: 너는 얼음을 씹는 것이 이에 나쁘다는 말을 들어보았니?

G: 아니. 왜 그런데?

B: 그것이 이에 손상을 줄 수 있어. 그것은 또한 이를 너무 예민하게 만들 수 있어.

B: 너 피곤해 보인다. 잠은 충분히 잤니?

G: 응, 그래. 나는 일곱 시간 이상 잤어.

B: 알았어. 너는 언제 잠들었니?

G: 평소처럼 자정이 넘어서 잠들었어.

B: 아마 그것이 너를 피곤하게 만드는 것일 거야. 네가 언제 잠자리에 드는지가 아주 중요하다는 말을 들어본 적이 있니?

G: 아니. 왜 그렇지?

B: 과학자들은 늦게 잠자리에 드는 것은 그 다음날 피곤함을 느끼게 할 수 있다고 말해.

G: 나는 몰랐어.

B: 반면에 일찍 잠자리에 드는 것은 기억력을 향상시키고, 더 생산적이 되도록 도와줄 수 있어. 지금부터는 일찍 자도록 노력해 봐.

A: 손으로 글을 쓰는 것이 건강에 좋다는 말을 들어본 적이 있니?

B: 오, 정말?

A: 그래, 그것이 기억력을 높여주는데.

G: 이것이 뭐니?

B: 그것은 스마트밴드야. 그것은 나에게 스마트폰으로 건강 정보를 점검할 수 있도록 해줘.

G: 어떤 종류의 정보니?

B: 그것은 내가 낮에 얼마나 멀리 걷는지, 밤에 얼마나 잘 자는지를 보여줘.

G: 흥미롭다. 나는 이 작은 밴드가 그 모든 일을 할 수 있다는 것이 놀라워.

Listen & Talk 2 B

B: _____ are you _____ in the _____ _____?

G: I'm _____ _____.

B: You're _____ out _____ _____?

G: Yes, I'm _____ this online video. It shows me all the _____.

B: _____ me _____. Wow, it's _____ two _____ _____! I'm _____ that so many people _____ _____ this video.

G: I know! These kinds of _____ are becoming _____ right now.

B: It looks very _____. You _____ _____ _____ go _____ to _____.

G: That's right. _____ _____ I love these programs. You should _____ them, _____.

Listen & Talk 2 C

B: What is that? It _____ nice.

G: This is a _____ cup. I _____ it _____ with me.

B: What's _____ _____ it?

G: It's _____. It tells me _____ _____ water _____ two hours.

B: Really? I'm _____ that it can _____ to you.

G: It even _____ me questions _____ "Aren't you _____?"

B: That's so cool! But _____ are you _____ to drink more water?

G: Because _____ a lot of water can _____ your energy and _____ your _____ _____.

B: That's amazing. I should _____ one!

Do It Yourself A

B: Oh, I'm so _____.

G: _____ _____ you eat some snacks _____ dinner?

B: I don't _____ to. I'll _____ _____ dinner.

G: Okay, but _____ you _____ that _____ _____ and is good for your _____?

B: _____? I thought _____ _____ _____ a day was fine.

G: If you keep _____ until dinner, you will _____ too much and _____ quickly. _____ _____ and _____ _____ you _____ like that.

B: I see. Then I'll _____ _____ an apple _____ _____.

B: 너 거실에서 무엇을 하고 있니?
G: 나는 요가를 하는 중이야.
B: 혼자서 운동한다는 말이니?
G: 그래, 이 온라인 비디오를 따라하는 중이야. 그것이 나에게 모든 단계를 보여줘.
B: 어디 보자. 와, 2백만 번이나 시청되었구나! 그렇게 많은 사람이 이 비디오를 보았다니 놀라워.
G: 알아! 이런 종류의 프로그램이 지금 인기를 얻는 중이야.
B: 그것은 매우 편리해 보여. 너는 운동하러 밖에 나갈 필요가 없어.
G: 맞아. 그런 이유로 나는 이런 프로그램을 아주 좋아해. 너도 한번 시도해 봐.

B: 저것이 뭐니? 그것은 좋아 보인다.
G: 이것은 매직 컵이야. 나는 어디든지 그것을 가지고 다녀.
B: 그것은 무엇이 특별하니?
G: 정말 끝내줘. 그것은 두 시간마다 물을 마시라고 나에게 말을 해.
B: 정말? 그것이 너에게 말을 할 수 있다는 것이 놀라워.
G: 심지어 그것은 "목마르지 않니?"와 같은 질문도 해.
B: 정말 멋지구나! 그런데 왜 너는 물을 더 마시려고 애쓰니?
G: 왜냐하면 물을 많이 마시는 것이 에너지를 높여주고, 피가 잘 흐르게 도와줘.
B: 정말 놀랍구나. 하나 사야겠다!

B: 오, 나는 너무 배가 고파.
G: 저녁 먹기 전에 간식을 좀 먹는 것이 어떠니?
B: 나는 그것을 원하지 않아. 나는 저녁 식사까지 기다릴 거야.
G: 알았어. 하지만 너는 조금 자주 먹는 것이 건강에 좋다는 말을 들어본 적이 있니?
B: 정말이니? 나는 하루에 세끼 식사하는 것이 좋다고 생각했는데.
G: 만약 네가 저녁식사까지 계속 기다리면 너무 많이 그리고 너무 빨리 먹을 거야. 조금 자주 먹는 것이 네가 그렇게 먹는 것을 막아 줄 거야.
B: 알았어. 그러면 지금 당장 사과를 먹으러 가야겠다.

※ 다음 우리말에 맞도록 대화를 영어로 쓰시오.

해석

Listen & Talk 1 A

B: _____

G: _____

B: _____

B: 너는 얼음을 씹는 것이 이에 나쁘다는 말을 들어보았니?
G: 아니. 왜 그런데?
B: 그것이 이에 손상을 줄 수 있어. 그것은 또한 이를 너무 예민하게 만들 수 있어.

Listen & Talk 1 B

B: _____

G: _____

B: _____

G: _____

B: _____

_____

G: _____

B: _____

G: _____

B: _____

_____

B: 너 피곤해 보인다. 잠은 충분히 잤니?
G: 응, 그래. 나는 일곱 시간 이상 잤어.
B: 알았어. 너는 언제 잠들었니?
G: 평소처럼 자정이 넘어서 잠들었어.
B: 아마 그것이 너를 피곤하게 만드는 것일 거야. 네가 언제 잠자리에 드는지가 아주 중요하다는 말을 들어본 적이 있니?
G: 아니. 왜 그렇지?
B: 과학자들은 늦게 잠자리에 드는 것은 그 다음날 피곤함을 느끼게 할 수 있다고 말해.
G: 나는 몰랐어.
B: 반면에 일찍 잠자리에 드는 것은 기억력을 향상시키고, 더 생산적이 되도록 도와줄 수 있어. 지금부터는 일찍 자도록 노력해 봐.

Listen & Talk 1 D-1

A: _____

B: _____

A: _____

A: 손으로 글을 쓰는 것이 건강에 좋다는 말을 들어본 적이 있니?
B: 오, 정말?
A: 그래, 그것이 기억력을 높여주는데.

Listen & Talk 2 A

G: _____

B: _____

G: _____

B: _____

G: _____

G: 이것이 뭐니?
B: 그것은 스마트밴드야. 그것은 나에게 스마트폰으로 건강 정보를 점검할 수 있도록 해줘.
G: 어떤 종류의 정보니?
B: 그것은 내가 낮에 얼마나 멀리 걷는지, 밤에 얼마나 잘 자는지를 보여줘.
G: 흥미롭다. 나는 이 작은 밴드가 그 모든 일을 할 수 있다는 것이 놀라워.

Listen & Talk 2 B

B: _____

G: _____

B: _____

G: _____

B: _____

_____

G: _____

B: _____

G: _____

B: 너 거실에서 무엇을 하고 있니?

G: 나는 요가를 하는 중이야.

B: 혼자서 운동한다는 말이니?

G: 그래, 이 온라인 비디오를 따라하는 중이야. 그것이 나에게 모든 단계를 보여줘.

B: 어디 보자. 와, 2백만 번이나 시청되었구나! 그렇게 많은 사람이 이 비디오를 보았다니 놀라워.

G: 알아! 이런 종류의 프로그램이 지금 인기를 얻는 중이야.

B: 그것은 매우 편리해 보여. 너는 운동하러 밖에 나갈 필요가 없어.

G: 맞아. 그런 이유로 나는 이런 프로그램을 아주 좋아해. 너도 한번 시도해 봐.

Listen & Talk 2 C

B: _____

G: _____

B: _____

G: _____

B: _____

G: _____

B: _____

G: _____

B: _____

B: 저것이 뭐니? 그것은 좋아 보인다.

G: 이것은 매직 컵이야. 나는 어디든지 그것을 가지고 다녀.

B: 그것은 무엇이 특별하니?

G: 정말 끝내줘. 그것은 두 시간마다 물을 마시라고 나에게 말을 해.

B: 정말? 그것이 너에게 말을 할 수 있다는 것이 놀라워.

G: 심지어 그것은 "목마르지 않니?"와 같은 질문도 해.

B: 정말 멋지구나! 그런데 왜 너는 물을 더 마시려고 애쓰니?

G: 왜냐하면 물을 많이 마시는 것이 에너지를 높여주고, 피가 잘 흐르게 도와줘.

B: 정말 놀랍구나. 하나 사야겠다!

Do It Yourself A

B: _____

G: _____

B: _____

G: _____

B: _____

G: _____

B: _____

B: 오, 나는 너무 배가 고파.

G: 저녁 먹기 전에 간식을 좀 먹는 것이 어떠니?

B: 나는 그것을 원하지 않아. 나는 저녁 식사까지 기다릴 거야.

G: 알았어. 하지만 너는 조금 자주 먹는 것이 건강에 좋다는 말을 들어본 적이 있니?

B: 정말이니? 나는 하루에 세끼 식사하는 것이 좋다고 생각했는데.

G: 만약 네가 저녁식사까지 계속 기다리면 너무 많이 그리고 너무 빨리 먹을 거야. 조금 자주 먹는 것이 네가 그렇게 먹는 것을 막아 줄 거야.

B: 알았어. 그러면 지금 당장 사과를 먹으러 가야겠다.

※ 다음 우리말과 일치하도록 빈칸에 알맞은 것을 골라 쓰시오.

1 _____ _____ for Our _____
   A. Bodies   B. Foods   C. Beneficial

2 We all know that a diet _____ a _____ of foods _____ our bodies _____.
   A. keeps   B. containing   C. healthy   D. variety

3 But sometimes we are not sure _____ foods are _____ which body _____.
   A. for   B. which   C. good   D. parts

4 Nature, _____, gives us a _____ _____.
   A. big   B. however   C. clue

5 _____ at the _____ _____.
   A. following   B. look   C. examples

6 Each of these foods _____ _____ looks like a certain body part _____ is _____ good for that body part.
   A. but   B. not   C. also   D. only

7 Slice open a tomato and _____ it _____ the human _____.
   A. with   B. heart   C. compare

8 You will see _____ they _____ _____.
   A. that   B. similar   C. look

9 They both have _____ _____ _____ and are red.
   A. hollow   B. multiple   C. spaces

10 Researchers say _____ the _____ make tomatoes red _____ good for your heart and _____.
   A. blood   B. chemicals   C. are   D. that

11 _____ _____, eating tomatoes can _____ your risk of heart _____.
   A. addition   B. disease   C. lower   D. in

12 _____ at the _____ of a _____.
   A. shape   B. walnut   C. look

13 Do you _____ _____?
   A. anything   B. notice

14 Yes, it's very _____ the _____ of the human _____!
   A. to   B. brain   C. similar   D. shape

15 A walnut is _____ _____ two parts, _____ _____ the brain.
   A. like   B. divided   C. just   D. into

16 Walnuts also have _____, _____ the _____ has too.
   A. brain   B. wrinkles   C. which

17 Studies show that walnuts _____ our brains and _____.
   A. stay   B. help   C. active   D. healthy

1 우리 몸에 이로운 음식

2 우리는 다양한 음식을 포함하는 식사가 우리의 몸을 건강하게 유지해 준다는 것을 알고 있다.

3 그러나 때때로 우리는 어떤 음식이 어떤 신체 부위에 좋은지 잘 모를 때가 있다.

4 하지만 자연은 우리에게 확실한 단서를 제시해 준다.

5 다음의 예들을 살펴보자.

6 각각의 이 음식들은 우리 신체의 특정 부분과 비슷해 보일 뿐만 아니라 그 신체 부위에도 좋다.

7 토마토 한 개를 잘라내서 그것을 사람의 심장과 비교해 보자.

8 당신은 그 둘이 비슷해 보인다는 것을 알게 될 것이다.

9 둘 다 여러 개의 빈 공간이 있고 붉은 색이다.

10 연구원들은 토마토를 붉게 만드는 화학 물질이 사람의 심장과 피에 유익하다고 한다.

11 게다가, 토마토를 먹는 것이 심장병에 걸릴 위험성을 낮출 수 있다.

12 호두의 모양을 살펴보자.

13 뭔가를 알아차릴 수 있는가?

14 그렇다. 호두의 모양은 인간의 뇌 형태와 매우 유사하다!

15 호두는 마치 인간의 뇌처럼 두 부분으로 나뉜다.

16 호두에는 또한 주름이 있는데, 이는 인간의 뇌에도 있는 것이다.

17 연구 결과는 호두가 사람의 뇌가 건강하고 활동적인 상태를 유지하는 데 도움을 준다는 것을 보여준다.

18 They are also _____ for _____ Alzheimer's _____.
    A. disease   B. good   C. preventing

19 A _____ of carrot _____ _____ the human eye.
    A. like   B. slice   C. looks

20 Carrots have some _____ that can make vitamin A, _____ _____ your _____.
    A. improves   B. chemicals   C. which   D. vision

21 It helps your eyes _____ light and _____ a clear _____ to the _____.
    A. send   B. process   C. brain   D. image

22 So _____ you want _____ _____, eat carrots.
    A. eyes   B. if   C. healthy

23 _____ onions is not fun _____ it _____ you _____.
    A. makes   B. cutting   C. cry   D. because

24 But _____ _____ one _____.
    A. anyway   B. slicing   C. try

25 You can see that the inside _____ _____ _____ _____ a human cell.
    A. a   B. like   C. looks   D. little

26 Scientists say that onions contain vitamin B, _____ _____ new, healthy _____.
    A. cells   B. helps   C. make   D. which

27 Now, let's _____ _____ _____ ginger.
    A. on   B. move   C. to

28 What body part _____ _____ _____ when you see it?
    A. to   B. comes   C. mind

29 _____ it _____ _____ a stomach?
    A. look   B. doesn't   C. like

30 You may not like ginger's strong _____ or smell, but these come from a special chemical that _____ you from _____ sick and _____ up.
    A. feeling   B. taste   C. throwing   D. prevents

31 _____ this _____, ginger can be _____ for your _____.
    A. stomach   B. reason   C. good   D. for

32 Isn't it _____ that some foods _____ the body parts _____ they are _____ for?
    A. mirror   B. amazing   C. good   D. that

33 Interestingly, there are _____ _____ _____ _____.
    A. other   B. many   C. foods   D. such

34 Find _____ _____ as you can and _____ to eat a _____ of them.
    A. variety   B. many   C. try   D. as

---

18 호두는 또한 알츠하이머병을 예방하는 데도 좋다.

19 썰어 놓은 당근의 모양은 사람의 눈과 비슷해 보인다.

20 당근에는 비타민 A를 만들 수 있는 화학 성분이 있는데, 그것이 시력을 개선한다.

21 비타민 A는 눈이 빛을 처리하여 뇌에 선명한 이미지를 보낼 수 있도록 돕는다.

22 그러므로 건강한 눈을 원한다면, 당근을 먹어라.

23 양파를 써는 것은 즐겁지 않은데 왜냐하면 그것이 당신을 울게 만들기 때문이다.

24 그렇지만 어쨌든 하나를 잘라보아라.

25 당신은 양파의 내부가 약간 인간의 세포처럼 보인다는 것을 알 수 있다.

26 과학자들은 양파가 비타민 B를 함유하는데, 이 비타민 B가 새롭고 건강한 세포를 만드는 데 도움이 된다고 주장한다.

27 이제 생강으로 넘어가 보자.

28 생강을 보면 몸의 어떤 부위가 생각나는가?

29 생강이 마치 위장처럼 생기지 않았는가?

30 당신은 어쩌면 생강의 강한 맛과 냄새를 좋아하지 않을지도 모르지만, 이러한 맛과 냄새는 복통과 구토를 예방하는 생강의 특별한 성분에서 나온다.

31 이러한 이유로 생강은 당신의 위장에 좋을 수 있다.

32 어떤 음식이 그 음식이 유익한 신체 부위의 생김새를 반영하고 있다는 점이 놀랍지 않은가?

33 흥미롭게도 그러한 음식은 상당히 많다.

34 가능한 한 그러한 음식을 많이 찾아서 다양한 음식을 먹도록 하라.

※ 다음 우리말과 일치하도록 빈칸에 알맞은 말을 쓰시오.

1 _____ Foods for Our _____

2 We all know _____ a diet _____ a _____ of foods _____ our bodies _____.

3 But sometimes we are not sure which foods _____ _____ which _____ _____.

4 Nature, _____, gives us _____ _____ _____.

5 _____ _____ the _____ examples.

6 _____ _____ these foods _____ _____ looks like a certain body part _____ is _____ good for that body part.

7 _____ open a tomato and _____ it _____ the human heart.

8 You will see _____ they _____ _____.

9 They both have _____ _____ _____ and _____ _____.

10 Researchers say _____ the chemicals _____ make tomatoes red _____ good for your _____ and _____.

11 _____ _____, eating tomatoes can _____ your risk of _____ _____.

12 Look at _____ _____ of a _____.

13 Do you _____ _____?

14 Yes, it's very _____ _____ the _____ of the human brain!

15 A walnut _____ _____ _____ two parts, just _____ the brain.

16 Walnuts also have _____, _____ the brain has too.

17 Studies show that walnuts help our brains _____ _____ and _____.

1	우리 몸에 이로운 음식
2	우리는 다양한 음식을 포함하는 식사가 우리의 몸을 건강하게 유지해 준다는 것을 알고 있다.
3	그러나 때때로 우리는 어떤 음식이 어떤 신체 부위에 좋은지 잘 모를 때가 있다.
4	하지만 자연은 우리에게 확실한 단서를 제시해 준다.
5	다음의 예들을 살펴보자.
6	각각의 이 음식들은 우리 신체의 특정 부분과 비슷해 보일 뿐만 아니라 그 신체 부위에도 좋다.
7	토마토 한 개를 잘라내서 그것을 사람의 심장과 비교해 보자.
8	당신은 그 둘이 비슷해 보인다는 것을 알게 될 것이다.
9	둘 다 여러 개의 빈 공간이 있고 붉은 색이다.
10	연구원들은 토마토를 붉게 만드는 화학 물질이 사람의 심장과 피에 유익하다고 한다.
11	게다가, 토마토를 먹는 것이 심장병에 걸릴 위험성을 낮출 수 있다.
12	호두의 모양을 살펴보자.
13	뭔가를 알아차릴 수 있는가?
14	그렇다. 호두의 모양은 인간의 뇌 형태와 매우 유사하다!
15	호두는 마치 인간의 뇌처럼 두 부분으로 나뉜다.
16	호두에는 또한 주름이 있는데, 이는 인간의 뇌에도 있는 것이다.
17	연구 결과는 호두가 사람의 뇌가 건강하고 활동적인 상태를 유지하는 데 도움을 준다는 것을 보여준다.

18 They are also good for _____ Alzheimer's _____.

19 _____ _____ _____ _____ looks like the human eye.

20 Carrots have some chemicals _____ can make vitamin A, _____ _____ your _____.

21 It _____ your eyes _____ light and _____ a clear image _____ the brain.

22 So _____ you want _____ _____, eat carrots.

23 _____ _____ is not fun _____ it _____ _____ _____.

24 But _____ _____ one _____.

25 You can see that the inside _____ _____ _____ _____ a _____ _____.

26 Scientists say that onions _____ vitamin B, _____ _____ _____ new, healthy cells.

27 Now, let's _____ _____ _____ _____.

28 What body part _____ _____ _____ when you see it?

29 _____ it _____ _____ a stomach?

30 You may not like ginger's _____ _____ or smell, but these _____ _____ a special chemical that _____ you _____ _____ sick and _____ _____.

31 _____ _____ _____, ginger can _____ _____ your stomach.

32 _____ it amazing that some foods _____ the body parts _____ they are good for?

33 Interestingly, there are _____ _____ _____ _____.

34 Find _____ _____ _____ _____ _____ and try to eat _____ _____ _____ them.

---

18 호두는 또한 알츠하이머병을 예방하는 데도 좋다.

19 썰어 놓은 당근의 모양은 사람의 눈과 비슷해 보인다.

20 당근에는 비타민 A를 만들 수 있는 화학 성분이 있는데, 그것이 시력을 개선한다.

21 비타민 A는 눈이 빛을 처리하여 뇌에 선명한 이미지를 보낼 수 있도록 돕는다.

22 그러므로 건강한 눈을 원한다면, 당근을 먹어라.

23 양파를 써는 것은 즐겁지 않은데 왜냐하면 그것이 당신을 울게 만들기 때문이다.

24 그렇지만 어쨌든 하나를 잘라보아라.

25 당신은 양파의 내부가 약간 인간의 세포처럼 보인다는 것을 알 수 있다.

26 과학자들은 양파가 비타민 B를 함유하는데, 이 비타민 B가 새롭고 건강한 세포를 만드는 데 도움이 된다고 주장한다.

27 이제 생강으로 넘어가 보자.

28 생강을 보면 몸의 어떤 부위가 생각나는가?

29 생강이 마치 위장처럼 생기지 않았는가?

30 당신은 어쩌면 생강의 강한 맛과 냄새를 좋아하지 않을지도 모르지만, 이러한 맛과 냄새는 복통과 구토를 예방하는 생강의 특별한 성분에서 나온다.

31 이러한 이유로 생강은 당신의 위장에 좋을 수 있다.

32 어떤 음식이 그 음식이 유익한 신체 부위의 생김새를 반영하고 있다는 점이 놀랍지 않은가?

33 흥미롭게도 그러한 음식은 상당히 많다.

34 가능한 한 그러한 음식을 많이 찾아서 다양한 음식을 먹도록 하라.

※ 다음 문장을 우리말로 쓰시오.

1 Beneficial Foods for Our Bodies

➡ _____

2 We all know that a diet containing a variety of foods keeps our bodies healthy.

➡ _____

3 But sometimes we are not sure which foods are good for which body parts.

➡ _____

4 Nature, however, gives us a big clue.

➡ _____

5 Look at the following examples.

➡ _____

6 Each of these foods not only looks like a certain body part but is also good for that body part.

➡ _____

7 Slice open a tomato and compare it with the human heart.

➡ _____

8 You will see that they look similar.

➡ _____

9 They both have multiple hollow spaces and are red.

➡ _____

10 Researchers say that the chemicals that make tomatoes red are good for your heart and blood.

➡ _____

11 In addition, eating tomatoes can lower your risk of heart disease.

➡ _____

12 Look at the shape of a walnut.

➡ _____

13 Do you notice anything?

➡ _____

14 Yes, it's very similar to the shape of the human brain!

➡ _____

15 A walnut is divided into two parts, just like the brain.

➡ _____

16 Walnuts also have wrinkles, which the brain has too.

➡ _____

17 Studies show that walnuts help our brains stay healthy and active.

➡ _____

18 ▶ They are also good for preventing Alzheimer's disease.
➡ _____

19 ▶ A slice of carrot looks like the human eye.
➡ _____

20 ▶ Carrots have some chemicals that can make vitamin A, which improves your vision.
➡ _____

21 ▶ It helps your eyes process light and send a clear image to the brain.
➡ _____

22 ▶ So if you want healthy eyes, eat carrots.
➡ _____

23 ▶ Cutting onions is not fun because it makes you cry.
➡ _____

24 ▶ But try slicing one anyway.
➡ _____

25 ▶ You can see that the inside looks a little like a human cell.
➡ _____

26 ▶ Scientists say that onions contain vitamin B, which helps make new, healthy cells.
➡ _____

27 ▶ Now, let's move on to ginger.
➡ _____

28 ▶ What body part comes to mind when you see it?
➡ _____

29 ▶ Doesn't it look like a stomach?
➡ _____

30 ▶ You may not like ginger's strong taste or smell, but these come from a special chemical that prevents you from feeling sick and throwing up.
➡ _____
_____

31 ▶ For this reason, ginger can be good for your stomach.
➡ _____

32 ▶ Isn't it amazing that some foods mirror the body parts that they are good for?
➡ _____

33 ▶ Interestingly, there are many other such foods.
➡ _____

34 ▶ Find as many as you can and try to eat a variety of them.
➡ _____

※ 다음 괄호 안의 단어들을 우리말에 맞도록 바르게 배열하시오.

1 (Foods / Beneficial / Our / for / Bodies)
➡ _____

2 (all / we / that / know / diet / a / containing / variety / a / foods / of / keeps / bodies / our / healthy.)
➡ _____
_____

3 (sometimes / but / are / we / sure / not / foods / which / are / for / good / body / which / parts.)
➡ _____
_____

4 (however, / nature, / us / gives / big / clue. / a)
➡ _____

5 (at / look / the / examples. / following)
➡ _____

6 (of / each / foods / these / only / not / like / looks / certain / a / body / but / part / also / is / good / that / for / part. / body)
➡ _____
_____

7 (open / slice / tomato / a / and / it / compare / the / with / heart. / human)
➡ _____

8 (will / you / that / see / they / similar. / look)
➡ _____

9 (both / they / multiple / have / spaces / hollow / and / red. / are)
➡ _____

10 (say / researchers / that / chemicals / the / that / tomatoes / make / are / red / for / good / heart / your / blood. / and)
➡ _____
_____

11 (addition, / in / tomatoes / eating / lower / can / risk / your / heart / of / disease.)
➡ _____
_____

12 (at / look / shape / the / of / walnut. / a)
➡ _____

13 (you / do / anything? / notice)
➡ _____

14 (yes, / very / it's / to / similar / the / of / shape / the / brain! / human)
➡ _____

15 (walnut / a / divided / is / two / into / parts, / like / just / brain. / the)
➡ _____

16 (also / walnuts / wrinkles, / have / the / which / has / brain / too.)
➡ _____

17 (show / studies / that / help / walnuts / brains / our / healthy / stay / active. / and)
➡ _____
_____

1 우리 몸에 이로운 음식

2 우리는 다양한 음식을 포함하는 식사가 우리의 몸을 건강하게 유지해 준다는 것을 알고 있다.

3 그러나 때때로 우리는 어떤 음식이 어떤 신체 부위에 좋은지 잘 모를 때가 있다.

4 하지만 자연은 우리에게 확실한 단서를 제시해 준다.

5 다음의 예들을 살펴보자.

6 각각의 이 음식들은 우리 신체의 특정 부분과 비슷해 보일 뿐만 아니라 그 신체 부위에도 좋다.

7 토마토 한 개를 잘라내서 그것을 사람의 심장과 비교해 보자.

8 당신은 그 둘이 비슷해 보인다는 것을 알게 될 것이다.

9 둘 다 여러 개의 빈 공간이 있고 붉은 색이다.

10 연구원들은 토마토를 붉게 만드는 화학 물질이 사람의 심장과 피에 유익하다고 한다.

11 게다가, 토마토를 먹는 것이 심장병에 걸릴 위험성을 낮출 수 있다.

12 호두의 모양을 살펴보자.

13 뭔가를 알아차릴 수 있는가?

14 그렇다. 호두의 모양은 인간의 뇌 형태와 매우 유사하다!

15 호두는 마치 인간의 뇌처럼 두 부분으로 나뉜다.

16 호두에는 또한 주름이 있는데, 이는 인간의 뇌에도 있는 것이다.

17 연구 결과는 호두가 사람의 뇌가 건강하고 활동적인 상태를 유지하는 데 도움을 준다는 것을 보여준다.

18 (are / they / good / also / preventing / for / disease. / Alzheimer's)
➡ _____

19 (slice / a / carrot / of / like / looks / human / eye. / the)
➡ _____

20 (have / carrots / chemicals / some / can / that / vitamin / make / A, / improves / which / vision. / your)
➡ _____
_____

21 (helps / it / eyes / your / light / process / and / a / send / image / clear / to / brain. / the)
➡ _____
_____

22 (if / so / want / you / eyes, / healthy / carrots. / eat)
➡ _____

23 (onions / cutting / not / is / because / fun / makes / it / cry. / you)
➡ _____

24 (try / but / one / slicing / anyway.)
➡ _____

25 (can / you / see / the / that / looks / inside / like / little / a / cell. / human / a)
➡ _____

26 (say / scientists / onions / that / vitamin / contain / B, / helps / which / new, / make / cells. / healthy)
➡ _____
_____

27 (let's / now / on / move / ginger. / to)
➡ _____

28 (body / what / comes / part / mind / to / you / when / it? / see)
➡ _____

29 (it / doesn't / like / look / stomach? / a)
➡ _____

30 (may / you / like / not / strong / ginger's / taste / smell, / or / but / come / these / from / special / a / chemical / prevents / that / from / you / feeling / and / sick / up. / throwing)
➡ _____
_____
_____

31 (this / for / reason, / can / ginger / be / for / good / stomach. / your)
➡ _____

32 (it / isn't / that / amazing / foods / some / mirror / body / the / parts / they / that / good / for? / are)
➡ _____
_____

33 (there / interestingly / many / are / other / foods. / such)
➡ _____

34 (as / find / many / you / as / can / try / and / eat / to / a / of / them. / variety)
➡ _____
_____

18 호두는 또한 알츠하이머병을 예방하는 데도 좋다.

19 썰어 놓은 당근의 모양은 사람의 눈과 비슷해 보인다.

20 당근에는 비타민 A를 만들 수 있는 화학 성분이 있는데, 그것이 시력을 개선한다.

21 비타민 A는 눈이 빛을 처리하여 뇌에 선명한 이미지를 보낼 수 있도록 돕는다.

22 그러므로 건강한 눈을 원한다면, 당근을 먹어라.

23 양파를 써는 것은 즐겁지 않은데 왜냐하면 그것이 당신을 울게 만들기 때문이다.

24 그렇지만 어쨌든 하나를 잘라 보아라.

25 당신은 양파의 내부가 약간 인간의 세포처럼 보인다는 것을 알 수 있다.

26 과학자들은 양파가 비타민 B를 함유하는데, 이 비타민 B가 새롭고 건강한 세포를 만드는 데 도움이 된다고 주장한다.

27 이제 생강으로 넘어가 보자.

28 생강을 보면 몸의 어떤 부위가 생각나는가?

29 생강이 마치 위장처럼 생기지 않았는가?

30 당신은 어쩌면 생강의 강한 맛과 냄새를 좋아하지 않을지도 모르지만, 이러한 맛과 냄새는 복통과 구토를 예방하는 생강의 특별한 성분에서 나온다.

31 이러한 이유로 생강은 당신의 위장에 좋을 수 있다.

32 어떤 음식이 그 음식이 유익한 신체 부위의 생김새를 반영하고 있다는 점이 놀랍지 않은가?

33 흥미롭게도 그러한 음식은 상당히 많다.

34 가능한 한 그러한 음식을 많이 찾아서 다양한 음식을 먹도록 하라.

※ 다음 우리말을 영어로 쓰시오.

1 우리 몸에 이로운 음식

➡ _____

2 우리는 다양한 음식을 포함하는 식사가 우리의 몸을 건강하게 유지해 준다는 것을 알고 있다.

➡ _____

3 그러나 때때로 우리는 어떤 음식이 어떤 신체 부위에 좋은지 잘 모를 때가 있다.

➡ _____

4 하지만 자연은 우리에게 확실한 단서를 제시해 준다.

➡ _____

5 다음의 예들을 살펴보자.

➡ _____

6 각각의 이 음식들은 우리 신체의 특정 부분과 비슷해 보일 뿐만 아니라 그 신체 부위에도 좋다.

➡ _____

7 토마토 한 개를 잘라내서 그것을 사람의 심장과 비교해 보자.

➡ _____

8 당신은 그 둘이 비슷해 보인다는 것을 알게 될 것이다.

➡ _____

9 둘 다 여러 개의 빈 공간이 있고 붉은 색이다.

➡ _____

10 연구원들은 토마토를 붉게 만드는 화학 물질이 사람의 심장과 피에 유익하다고 한다.

➡ _____

11 게다가, 토마토를 먹는 것이 심장병에 걸릴 위험성을 낮출 수 있다.

➡ _____

12 호두의 모양을 살펴보자.

➡ _____

13 뭔가를 알아차릴 수 있는가?

➡ _____

14 그렇다, 호두의 모양은 인간의 뇌 형태와 매우 유사하다!

➡ _____

15 호두는 마치 인간의 뇌처럼 두 부분으로 나뉜다.

➡ _____

16 호두에는 또한 주름이 있는데, 이는 인간의 뇌에도 있는 것이다.

➡ _____

17 연구 결과는 호두가 사람의 뇌가 건강하고 활동적인 상태를 유지하는 데 도움을 준다는 것을 보여준다.

➡ _____

18 ▶ 호두는 또한 알츠하이머병을 예방하는 데도 좋다.

➡ _____

19 ▶ 썰어 놓은 당근의 모양은 사람의 눈과 비슷해 보인다.

➡ _____

20 ▶ 당근에는 비타민 A를 만들 수 있는 화학 성분이 있는데, 그것이 시력을 개선한다.

➡ _____

21 ▶ 비타민 A는 눈이 빛을 처리하여 뇌에 선명한 이미지를 보낼 수 있도록 돕는다.

➡ _____

22 ▶ 그러므로 건강한 눈을 원한다면, 당근을 먹어라.

➡ _____

23 ▶ 양파를 써는 것은 즐겁지 않은데 왜냐하면 그것이 당신을 울게 만들기 때문이다.

➡ _____

24 ▶ 그렇지만 어쨌든 하나를 잘라 보아라.

➡ _____

25 ▶ 당신은 양파의 내부가 약간 인간의 세포처럼 보인다는 것을 알 수 있다.

➡ _____

26 ▶ 과학자들은 양파가 비타민 B를 함유하는데, 이 비타민 B가 새롭고 건강한 세포를 만들어 내는 데 도움이 된다고 주장한다.

➡ _____

27 ▶ 이제 생강으로 넘어가 보자.

➡ _____

28 ▶ 생강을 보면 몸의 어떤 부위가 생각나는가?

➡ _____

29 ▶ 생강이 마치 위장처럼 생기지 않았는가?

➡ _____

30 ▶ 당신은 어쩌면 생강의 강한 맛과 냄새를 좋아하지 않을지도 모르지만, 이러한 맛과 냄새는 복통과 구토를 예방하는 생강의 특별한 성분에서 나온다.

➡ _____

_____

31 ▶ 이러한 이유로 생강은 당신의 위장에 좋을 수 있다.

➡ _____

32 ▶ 어떤 음식이 그 음식이 유익한 신체 부위의 생김새를 반영하고 있다는 점이 놀랍지 않은가?

➡ _____

33 ▶ 흥미롭게도 그러한 음식은 상당히 많다.

➡ _____

34 ▶ 가능한 한 그러한 음식을 많이 찾아서 다양한 음식을 먹도록 하라.

➡ _____

※ 다음 우리말과 일치하도록 빈칸에 알맞은 말을 쓰시오.

Presentation Time

1. _____ you _____ that swimming _____ _____ _____ your back?

2. Our group _____ _____ _____ _____ _____ swimming together _____ _____ and _____ at World Sports Park.

3. We are _____ it will _____ _____ _____ _____.

1. 수영을 하는 것이 허리에 좋다는 말을 들어본 적이 있니?
2. 우리 모둠은 매주 화요일과 목요일에 World Sports Park에 함께 수영을 가기로 계획을 세웠어.
3. 우리는 그것이 우리가 건강하게 지내는 데 도움이 될 것이라고 확신하고 있어.

Wrap Up READING

1. Eat Chicken Sandwiches, _____ _____

2. A chicken sandwich is a _____ _____ _____ I _____.

3. I'd _____ _____ _____ _____ some of its ingredients that _____ _____ _____ our health.

4. First, chicken breast is meat _____ a lot of _____ and _____ _____.

5. Onions _____ _____ _____ vitamin B.

6. Also, walnuts _____ _____ _____ _____ _____ _____.

7. So _____ _____ _____ _____ a chicken sandwich this weekend?

1. 치킨 샌드위치를 먹고 더 건강해 지세요
2. 치킨 샌드위치는 제가 추천하는 건강에 좋은 음식입니다.
3. 저는 건강에 좋은 그것의 재료 몇 가지에 대해 이야기하고 싶습니다.
4. 먼저 닭 가슴살은 많은 단백질을 가지고 있고 지방은 거의 없는 고기입니다.
5. 양파는 비타민 B를 많이 포함하고 있습니다.
6. 또한, 호두는 뇌에 좋습니다.
7. 그러니, 이번 주말에 치킨 샌드위치를 드시는 것이 어떠세요?

Culture Link

1. Yoga _____ _____

2. Indian people _____ yoga _____ _____ _____ their minds, bodies, _____, and _____.

3. They use it _____ _____ themselves _____ _____ _____ _____.

1. 인도의 요가
2. 인도 사람들은 그들의 마음, 신체, 생각과 감정을 더 잘 이해하기 위해 요가를 한다.
3. 그들은 자신들을 더 건강한 삶으로 인도하기 위해 그것을 사용한다.

구석구석 지문 Test

※ 다음 우리말을 영어로 쓰시오.

Presentation Time

1. 수영을 하는 것이 허리에 좋다는 말을 들어본 적이 있니?

   ➡ _____

2. 우리 모둠은 매주 화요일과 목요일에 World Sports Park에 함께 수영을 가기로 계획을 세웠어.

   ➡ _____

3. 우리는 그것이 우리가 건강하게 지내는 데 도움이 될 것이라고 확신하고 있어.

   ➡ _____

Wrap Up READING

1. 치킨 샌드위치를 먹고 더 건강해 지세요

   ➡ _____

2. 치킨 샌드위치는 제가 추천하는 건강에 좋은 음식입니다.

   ➡ _____

3. 저는 건강에 좋은 그것의 재료 몇 가지에 대해 이야기하고 싶습니다.

   ➡ _____

4. 먼저 닭 가슴살은 많은 단백질을 가지고 있고 지방은 거의 없는 고기입니다.

   ➡ _____

5. 양파는 비타민 B를 많이 포함하고 있습니다.

   ➡ _____

6. 또한, 호두는 뇌에 좋습니다.

   ➡ _____

7. 그러니, 이번 주말에 치킨 샌드위치를 드시는 것이 어떠세요?

   ➡ _____

Culture Link

1. 인도의 요가

   ➡ _____

2. 인도 사람들은 그들의 마음, 신체, 생각과 감정을 더 잘 이해하기 위해 요가를 한다.

   ➡ _____

3. 그들은 자신들을 더 건강한 삶으로 인도하기 위해 그것을 사용한다.

   ➡ _____

※ 다음 영어를 우리말로 쓰시오.

01	recently	22	whole
02	aware	23	crawl
03	cause	24	flood
04	panic	25	immediately
05	collapse	26	include
06	smash	27	natural disaster
07	damage	28	mention
08	exit	29	tap
09	avoid	30	confusion
10	serious	31	urgently
11	wildfire	32	occur
12	worse	33	reaction
13	properly	34	violently
14	common	35	based on~
15	affect	36	as well
16	nervously	37	get a discount
17	missing	38	a variety of
18	earthquake	39	in case of ~
19	exactly	40	a large number of
20	destroy	41	tip over
21	heavy rain	42	pull over
		43	break into pieces

※ 다음 우리말을 영어로 쓰시오.

01 격렬하게	_____	22 극심한 공포	_____
02 초래하다	_____	23 정확하게	_____
03 반응	_____	24 포함하다	_____
04 혼란, 혼동	_____	25 특수 효과	_____
05 더 나쁜	_____	26 갑자기	_____
06 제대로, 적절하게	_____	27 나가다, 퇴장하다	_____
07 최근에	_____	28 영향을 주다	_____
08 파괴하다	_____	29 두들기다	_____
09 흔한	_____	30 긴급하게	_____
10 손상	_____	31 즉시	_____
11 실종된	_____	32 실제로	_____
12 가슴	_____	33 폭우	_____
13 붕괴되다, 무너지다	_____	34 심각한	_____
14 불안하게	_____	35 길 한쪽으로 차를 대다	_____
15 재난	_____	36 ~의 한 가운데	_____
16 홍수	_____	37 다양한	_____
17 지진	_____	38 넘어지다, 기울어지다	_____
18 (일·사건 등이) 발생하다	_____	39 ~의 경우에	_____
19 기어가다	_____	40 ~에 바탕을 둔	_____
20 세게 부딪치다	_____	41 매우 많은	_____
21 폭염	_____	42 집어넣다	_____
		43 굴러 떨어지다	_____

※ 다음 영영풀이에 알맞은 단어를 <보기>에서 골라 쓴 후, 우리말 뜻을 쓰시오.

1 _____ : to leave a place: _____

2 _____ : wanting to know about something: _____

3 _____ : correctly, or in a way that is considered right: _____

4 _____ : happening often and to many people or in many places: _____

5 _____ : to hit something violently and very hard: _____

6 _____ : to break apart and fall down suddenly: _____

7 _____ : a fire that moves quickly and cannot be controlled: _____

8 _____ : to make something happen, especially something bad: _____

9 _____ : a very large amount of water that covers an area that is usually dry: _____

10 _____ : to make someone or something part of a larger group: _____

11 _____ : a sudden shaking of the Earth's surface that often causes a lot of damage: _____

12 _____ : to move along on your hands and knees with your body close to the ground: _____

13 _____ : to move backward or forward or from side to side while hanging from a fixed point: _____

14 _____ : to do an action or activity that usually requires training or skill: _____

15 _____ : to damage something so badly that it no longer exists or cannot be used or repaired: _____

16 _____ : a sudden event such as a flood, storm, or accident which causes great damage or suffering: _____

보기

smash	earthquake	properly	exit
cause	include	collapse	wildfire
destroy	common	crawl	disaster
perform	curious	flood	swing

※ 다음 우리말과 일치하도록 빈칸에 알맞은 말을 쓰시오.

Listen & Talk 1 A

B: There _____ a big _____ in Europe. Did you _____ _____ it?

G: No, I didn't. But _____ aren't that _____ in winter, _____ they? I'm _____ about _____ that _____.

B: Me too. _____ do some online _____.

B: 유럽에 큰 홍수가 있었어. 그것에 대해 들었니?
G: 아니. 하지만 겨울에는 홍수가 그렇게 흔하지 않아, 그렇지 않니? 나는 어떻게 그런 일이 일어났는지 궁금해.
B: 나도 그래. 온라인 검색을 해보자.

Listen & Talk 1 B

G: There _____ _____ _____ many _____ _____ in Korea _____ _____.

B: I agree. There was an _____ in the _____ last week. Also a _____ is coming this week.

G: I'm _____ about _____ _____ _____ _____ _____ _____ causes the _____ _____ in Korea.

B: Actually I read a _____ yesterday about the _____ from _____ _____ of _____ _____. Number one is _____.

G: I see. I _____ earthquakes are _____.

B: No, second is _____ rain, and third is _____ _____.

G: _____ about earthquakes?

B: _____ _____ the report, _____ are fourth. But the _____ from earthquakes has _____ _____ recently _____ they have _____ _____ more often in Korea.

G: I see. It _____ _____ we have to be _____ for a _____ of _____ _____ in Korea.

G: 요즈음 한국에서 많은 자연 재해가 있는 것 같아.
B: 동의해. 지난주에 남부에서 지진이 있었어. 또한 이번 주에는 태풍이 올 거야.
G: 나는 어떤 종류의 자연 재해가 한국에서 가장 큰 피해를 주는지 궁금해.
B: 사실 나는 어제 각 유형의 자연 재해로 인한 피해에 관한 보고서를 읽었어. 첫 번째가 폭풍이야.
G: 그렇구나. 지진이 두 번째인 것 같아.
B: 아니야. 두 번째는 폭우이고 세 번째는 폭설이야.
G: 지진은?
B: 보고서에 따르면, 지진은 네 번째야. 하지만 최근 한국에서 지진이 더 자주 일어나기 때문에 지진으로 인한 피해가 증가하고 있어.
G: 그렇구나. 한국에서는 다양한 자연 재해에 대비를 해야 할 것 같아.

Listen & Talk 1 C

B: Hey, did you _____ _____ the big _____ in California?

G: No, I didn't. _____ _____ are they?

B: They've _____ a large _____ _____ _____ and _____ _____.

G: _____ the fires still _____ _____?

B: Yes, _____ the wind has made the fires _____. I hope all the people _____ _____ are okay.

G: _____ _____ I. I'm _____ _____ how many people had to _____ their homes.

B: _____ _____ _____ 20,000 people had to _____ their _____, and about 400 people are _____ in that area.

G: That's _____. I hope they're _____ _____.

B: 안녕. 너 캘리포니아에서 일어난 큰 화재에 대해 들었어?
G: 아니. 얼마나 심각하니?
B: 많은 집들과 다른 건물들을 파괴했어.
G: 아직도 화재가 진행되고 있니?
B: 그래. 사실 바람이 화재를 더 악화시켰어. 나는 거기 사는 모든 사람들이 괜찮기를 바라.
G: 나도 그래. 얼마나 많은 사람들이 집을 떠나야 했는지 궁금해.
B: 사실 2만 명 이상이 집을 떠나야 했고, 약 400명이 실종되었어.
G: 끔찍하구나. 나는 그들이 안전한 곳에 있기를 바라.

Listen & Talk 2 A

B: Mom, _____ _____ do we _____ _____ _____ _____ the _____ _____ _____ _____?

W: Well, we need _____, some food, and _____.

B: _____ _____, Mom?

W: Oh, _____ _____ that you _____ _____ for the _____.

Listen & Talk 2 B

W: _____ CPR _____ can _____ someone's life. _____ are the _____ for _____ CPR. First, check that the person _____ help. _____ the person and shout, "_____ you okay?" If there's no _____, call 119 for help. Second, _____, look, and _____ _____ _____. If the person's not _____, begin CPR. Make _____ you _____ your _____ _____ the middle of the person's _____. Use your body _____ to press _____ on the chest. After 30 presses, give the person two _____. _____ _____ CPR _____ _____ _____.

Listen & Talk 2 D

A: _____ _____ _____ a fire, _____ should I _____?

B: _____ _____ that you _____ your mouth with a _____ _____.

A: Anything _____?

B: _____ _____ _____ you _____ the building _____.

Do It Yourself A

G: Did you _____ that earthquakes are _____ more _____ in Korea than _____?

B: Oh, _____? I've _____ _____ an earthquake in Korea.

G: They _____ _____ in the _____ part of Korea, but now they are occurring in _____ _____ _____ _____.

B: I didn't know that. I'm _____ about _____ earthquakes have _____ so often in Korea _____.

G: _____ _____ we do some _____ to find out?

B: Sounds good, but where _____ we look first?

G: _____ _____ _____ our science teacher first? I think she can _____ us.

B: Okay. _____ go and _____ her.

B: 엄마, 자연 재해 생존 장비에 무엇을 더 넣어야 할까요?

W: 글쎄. 우리는 물, 약간의 식량 그리고 라디오가 필요해.

B: 다른 것은요, 엄마?

W: 오, 라디오 건전지를 반드시 포함하도록 해.

W: 제대로 심폐소생술을 수행하는 것은 누군가의 생명을 구할 수 있습니다. 여기 적절한 심폐소생술을 위한 단계가 있습니다. 첫째, 그 사람이 도움을 필요로 하는지 확인하십시오. 그 사람을 두드리며 "괜찮으세요?'라고 큰소리로 외치세요. 반응이 없으면 119에 전화를 걸어 도움을 요청하세요. 둘째, 호흡을 하는지 듣고, 보고, 느끼세요. 그 사람이 숨을 쉬지 않으면 심폐소생술을 시작하세요. 손을 반드시 그 사람의 가슴 가운데에 놓도록 하세요. 가슴을 더 세게 누르기 위해 체중을 이용하세요. 30번 누른 후, 그 사람에게 두 번 바람을 불어 넣으시오. 도움이 올 때까지 심폐소생술을 계속하세요.

A: 화재가 발생하면 어떻게 해야 하나요?

B: 반드시 젖은 천으로 입을 가리도록 해.

A: 다른 것은 뭐가 있을까요?

B: 즉시 건물 밖으로 나가도록 해야 해.

G: 한국에서 지진이 전보다 자주 일어나고 있다는 말을 들었니?

B: 오, 정말? 나는 한국에서 지진을 느껴본 적이 없어.

G: 보통 지진이 한국의 남부에서 발생하지만, 이제는 다른 지역에서도 발생하고 있어.

B: 그건 몰랐어. 나는 왜 최근에 한국에서 지진이 그렇게 자주 발생하는지 궁금해.

G: 알아내기 위해 조사를 해보는 게 어떨까?

B: 좋은 것 같아. 하지만 먼저 어디에서 찾아야 하지?

G: 먼저 과학 선생님께 여쭤보면 어떨까? 나는 선생님께서 우리를 도울 수 있을 거라고 생각해.

B: 알았어. 가서 선생님을 찾아보자.

※ 다음 우리말에 맞도록 대화를 영어로 쓰시오.

Listen & Talk 1 A

B: _____

G: _____

_____

B: _____

B: 유럽에 큰 홍수가 있었어. 그것에 대해 들었니?
G: 아니. 하지만 겨울에는 홍수가 그렇게 흔하지 않아, 그렇지 않니? 나는 어떻게 그런 일이 일어났는지 궁금해.
B: 나도 그래. 온라인 검색을 해보자.

Listen & Talk 1 B

G: _____

B: _____

_____

G: _____

_____

B: _____

_____

G: _____

B: _____

G: _____

B: _____

_____

_____

G: _____

G: 요즈음 한국에서 많은 자연 재해가 있는 것 같아.
B: 동의해. 지난주에 남부에서 지진이 있었어. 또한 이번 주에는 태풍이 올 거야.
G: 나는 어떤 종류의 자연 재해가 한국에서 가장 큰 피해를 주는지 궁금해.
B: 사실 나는 어제 각 유형의 자연 재해로 인한 피해에 관한 보고서를 읽었어. 첫 번째가 폭풍이야.
G: 그렇구나. 지진이 두 번째인 것 같아.
B: 아니야. 두 번째는 폭우이고 세 번째는 폭설이야.
G: 지진은?
B: 보고서에 따르면, 지진은 네 번째야. 하지만 최근 한국에서 지진이 더 자주 일어나기 때문에 지진으로 인한 피해가 증가하고 있어.
G: 그렇구나. 한국에서는 다양한 자연 재해에 대비를 해야 할 것 같아.

Listen & Talk 1 C

B: _____

G: _____

B: _____

G: _____

B: _____

_____

G: _____

B: _____

_____

G: _____

B: 안녕. 너 캘리포니아에서 일어난 큰 화재에 대해 들었니?
G: 아니. 얼마나 심각하니?
B: 많은 집들과 다른 건물들을 파괴했어.
G: 아직도 화재가 진행되고 있니?
B: 그래. 사실 바람이 화재를 더 악화시켰어. 나는 거기 사는 모든 사람들이 괜찮기를 바라.
G: 나도 그래. 얼마나 많은 사람들이 집을 떠나야 했는지 궁금해.
B: 사실 2만 명 이상이 집을 떠나야 했고, 약 400명이 실종되었어.
G: 끔찍하구나. 나는 그들이 안전한 곳에 있기를 바라.

Listen & Talk 2 A

B: _____

W: _____

B: _____

W: _____

Listen & Talk 2 B

W: _____
_____
_____
_____
_____
_____
_____

Listen & Talk 2 D

A: _____

B: _____

A: _____

B: _____

Do It Yourself A

G: _____

B: _____

G: _____
_____

B: _____
_____

G: _____

B: _____

G: _____

B: _____

B: 엄마, 자연 재해 생존 장비에 무엇을 더 넣어야 할까요?

W: 글쎄. 우리는 물, 약간의 식량 그리고 라디오가 필요해.

B: 다른 것은요, 엄마?

W: 오, 라디오 건전지를 반드시 포함하도록 해.

W: 제대로 심폐소생술을 수행하는 것은 누군가의 생명을 구할 수 있습니다. 여기 적절한 심폐소생술을 위한 단계가 있습니다. 첫째, 그 사람이 도움을 필요로 하는지 확인하십시오. 그 사람을 두드리며 "괜찮으세요?"라고 큰소리로 외치세요. 반응이 없으면 119에 전화를 걸어 도움을 요청하세요. 둘째, 호흡을 하는지 듣고, 보고, 느끼세요. 그 사람이 숨을 쉬지 않으면 심폐소생술을 시작하세요. 손을 반드시 그 사람의 가슴 가운데에 놓도록 하세요. 가슴을 더 세게 누르기 위해 체중을 이용하세요. 30번 누른 후, 그 사람에게 두 번 바람을 불어 넣으시오. 도움이 올 때까지 심폐소생술을 계속하세요.

A: 화재가 발생하면 어떻게 해야 하나요?

B: 반드시 젖은 천으로 입을 가리도록 해.

A: 다른 것은 뭐가 있을까요?

B: 즉시 건물 밖으로 나가도록 해야 해.

G: 한국에서 지진이 전보다 자주 일어나고 있다는 말을 들었니?

B: 오, 정말? 나는 한국에서 지진을 느껴본 적이 없어.

G: 보통 지진이 한국의 남부에서 발생하지만, 이제는 다른 지역에서도 발생하고 있어.

B: 그건 몰랐어. 나는 왜 최근에 한국에서 지진이 그렇게 자주 발생하는지 궁금해.

G: 알아내기 위해 조사를 해보는 게 어떨까?

B: 좋은 것 같아. 하지만 먼저 어디에서 찾아야 하지?

G: 먼저 과학 선생님께 여쭤보면 어떨까? 나는 선생님께서 우리를 도울 수 있을 거라고 생각해.

B: 알았어. 가서 선생님을 찾아보자.

※ 다음 우리말과 일치하도록 빈칸에 알맞은 것을 골라 쓰시오.

1 _____ _____ to an _____
   A. Up   B. Waking   C. Earthquake

2 One night _____ February, after I _____ _____ to bed, an earthquake _____.
   A. hit   B. gone   C. in   D. had

3 I _____ _____ suddenly _____ my bed was _____.
   A. because   B. up   C. shaking   D. woke

4 I _____ my brother was _____ my bed _____ a _____.
   A. as   B. joke   C. shaking   D. thought

5 But then I _____ the mirror on my desk _____ to the floor and _____ into _____.
   A. break   B. fall   C. pieces   D. heard

6 I knew it wasn't my brother then, but I still didn't know _____ _____ _____ _____.
   A. exactly   B. what   C. happening   D. was

7 Soon the _____ room began to shake _____, and my confusion _____ to _____.
   A. violently   B. whole   C. panic   D. turned

8 My mom _____ that it was an _____ and _____ _____ my room.
   A. into   B. shouted   C. ran   D. earthquake

9 _____ it was my first time _____ an earthquake, I didn't know _____ to _____.
   A. how   B. since   C. react   D. experiencing

10 I _____ _____ _____, "What should I do?"
   A. saying   B. kept   C. just

11 My mom _____ me and my brother _____ _____ _____.
   A. out   B. pulled   C. of   D. bed

12 We _____ to the kitchen and _____ _____ the table.
   A. crawled   B. ran   C. under

13 I could see the light _____ violently and books _____ to the _____.
   A. falling   B. swinging   C. floor

1 지진에 눈을 뜨는 것

2 2월 어느 날 밤, 내가 잠자리에 든 후에 지진이 일어났다.

3 침대가 흔들렸기 때문에 나는 갑자기 잠에서 깼다.

4 나는 남동생이 장난으로 침대를 흔들고 있다고 생각했다.

5 하지만 그때 나는 내 책상 위에 있던 거울이 바닥으로 떨어져 산산조각이 나는 소리를 들었다.

6 그때 나는 남동생이 그런 것이 아니라는 것을 알았지만, 정확히 무슨 일이 일어나고 있었는지를 여전히 알지 못했다.

7 머지않아 방 전체가 심하게 흔들리기 시작했고 혼란스러움은 공포로 변했다.

8 엄마가 지진이라고 소리를 지르며 내 방으로 뛰어 들어왔다.

9 지진을 경험한 것이 처음이었기 때문에, 나는 어떻게 반응해야 할지 몰랐다.

10 나는 그저 "어떻게 해야 하지?"라는 말을 반복했다.

11 엄마는 나와 남동생을 침대 밖으로 잡아끌었다.

12 우리는 주방으로 달려가서 식탁 아래로 기어들어 갔다.

13 나는 전등이 심하게 흔들리는 것과 책이 바닥으로 떨어지는 것을 볼 수 있었다.

14 Our family picture _____ from the wall and the glass _____ it _____.

A. covering　　　B. dropped　　　C. broke

15 A cup _____ _____ and _____ _____ the kitchen table.

A. off　　　B. tipped　　　C. rolled　　　D. over

16 _____ _____, I could hear _____ _____ in the apartment break.

A. second　　　B. else　　　C. every　　　D. something

17 I started _____ _____ that the building would _____.

A. to　　　B. collapse　　　C. worry

18 Then the shaking _____ _____ _____.

A. to　　　B. seemed　　　C. stop

19 We started _____ _____ the _____.

A. door　　　B. toward　　　C. crawling

20 _____ that _____, my mom's cell phone _____.

A. moment　　　B. rang　　　C. at

21 It was my dad, who was _____ _____ _____ _____.

A. home　　　B. work　　　C. coming　　　D. from

22 He _____, "It _____!

A. stopped　　　B. shouted

23 _____ _____ _____ the building!

A. out　　　B. get　　　C. of

24 _____ the _____!

A. stairs　　　B. take

25 _____ _____ the elevator!

A. take　　　B. don't

26 Hurry!"

27 "_____ _____ you?

A. are　　　B. where

28 Are you _____?" my mom _____ _____.

A. urgently　　　B. okay　　　C. asked

29 My dad _____, "_____ _____.

A. worry　　　B. answered　　　C. don't

30 _____ _____.

A. okay　　　B. I'm

14 우리 가족 사진이 벽에서 떨어졌고 사진을 덮고 있던 유리가 깨졌다.

15 컵이 넘어지고 식탁에서 굴러 떨어졌다.

16 매 순간, 나는 아파트에 있는 다른 어떤 것들이 부서지는 소리를 들을 수 있었다.

17 나는 건물이 무너지지는 않을까 하는 걱정이 들기 시작했다.

18 그때 흔들림이 멈추는 것 같았다.

19 우리는 문으로 기어가기 시작했다.

20 그 순간, 엄마의 휴대 전화가 울렸다.

21 전화를 한 사람은 바로 아빠였는데, 직장에서 퇴근하던 중이었다.

22 아빠는 소리쳤다. "지진이 멈췄어요!

23 건물 밖으로 나와요!

24 계단을 이용해요!

25 엘리베이터를 타면 안 돼요!

26 서둘러요!"

27 "어디예요?

28 괜찮아요?"라고 엄마가 다급하게 물었다.

29 아빠가 대답했다. "걱정 말아요.

30 나는 괜찮아요.

31 I was _____ _____ when the _____ started.

    A. home   B. shaking   C. driving

32 But I _____ _____ _____ .

    A. over   B. pulled   C. immediately

33 I'm listening to the radio _____ _____ to find out what's _____ _____ ."

    A. now   B. on   C. right   D. going

34 We nervously _____ our _____ _____ the stairs and _____ .

    A. way   B. outside   C. made   D. down

35 I _____ _____ .

    A. around   B. looked

36 _____ of buildings had _____ and _____ _____ several cars.

    A. smashed   B. fallen   C. parts   D. had

37 We went to an _____ space to _____ more _____ _____ .

    A. falling   B. open   C. avoid   D. pieces

38 How _____ all this _____ _____ in a _____ minutes?

    A. few   B. have   C. happened   D. could

39 _____ I had done many earthquake _____ in school, I had never _____ I'd experience a _____ earthquake.

    A. real   B. drills   C. thought   D. although

40 I still _____ _____ when I _____ that night.

    A. scared   B. remember   C. get

41 I can't _____ the _____ I _____ when the furniture was shaking and things were _____ to the floor.

    A. falling   B. felt   C. panic   D. forget

42 After that night, I began to _____ earthquake _____ _____ .

    A. drills   B. take   C. seriously

43 I _____ that I should be _____ for the next earthquake, which can _____ at any _____ .

    A. occur   B. prepared   C. realized   D. time

---

31 진동이 시작할 때 운전해서 집으로 가던 중이었어요.

32 하지만 즉시 차를 길 한쪽에 댔어요.

33 무슨 일이 일어나는지 알기 위해 지금 라디오를 듣고 있어요."

34 우리는 초조한 마음으로 계단을 내려가서 밖으로 나갔다.

35 나는 주변을 둘러보았다.

36 건물의 일부분이 떨어져 나갔고 몇몇 차들은 박살이 났다.

37 우리는 추가적인 낙하물을 피하기 위해 공터로 갔다.

38 어떻게 이런 일이 몇 분 만에 일어날 수 있단 말인가?

39 비록 학교에서 많은 지진 대피 훈련을 해 왔지만, 내가 실제 지진을 겪으리라고는 전혀 생각해 보지 않았었다.

40 그날 밤을 기억하면 나는 여전히 두려워진다.

41 가구가 흔들리고 물건들이 바닥으로 떨어졌을 때 내가 느꼈던 공포심을 나는 잊을 수가 없다.

42 그날 밤 이후, 나는 지진 대피 훈련에 진지하게 임하기 시작했다.

43 나는 언제든 발생할 수 있는 다음 지진을 대비해야 한다는 것을 깨달았다.

※ 다음 우리말과 일치하도록 빈칸에 알맞은 말을 쓰시오.

1 _____ _____ to an _____

2 One night _____ February, after I _____ _____ _____ _____, an earthquake _____.

3 I woke up suddenly because my bed _____ _____.

4 I thought my brother _____ _____ my bed _____ _____ _____.

5 But then I _____ the mirror on my desk _____ _____ _____ and _____ _____ _____.

6 I knew it wasn't my brother _____, but I _____ know _____ _____ _____ _____.

7 Soon the whole room began _____ _____ _____, and my _____ _____ _____ _____.

8 My mom _____ _____ it was an earthquake and _____ _____ my room.

9 Since it was _____ _____ _____ _____ an earthquake, I didn't know _____ _____ _____.

10 I just _____ _____, "What should I do?"

11 My mom _____ me and my brother _____ _____ _____.

12 We _____ _____ the kitchen and _____ _____ the table.

13 I could _____ the light _____ _____ and books _____ _____ the floor.

1 지진에 눈을 뜨는 것

2 2월 어느 날 밤, 내가 잠자리에 든 후에 지진이 일어났다.

3 침대가 흔들렸기 때문에 나는 갑자기 잠에서 깼다.

4 나는 남동생이 장난으로 침대를 흔들고 있다고 생각했다.

5 하지만 그때 나는 내 책상 위에 있던 거울이 바닥으로 떨어져 산산조각이 나는 소리를 들었다.

6 그때 나는 남동생이 그런 것이 아니라는 것을 알았지만, 정확히 무슨 일이 일어나고 있었는지를 여전히 알지 못했다.

7 머지않아 방 전체가 심하게 흔들리기 시작했고 혼란스러움은 공포로 변했다.

8 엄마가 지진이라고 소리를 지르며 내 방으로 뛰어 들어왔다.

9 지진을 경험한 것이 처음이었기 때문에, 나는 어떻게 반응해야 할지 몰랐다.

10 나는 그저 "어떻게 해야 하지?" 라는 말을 반복했다.

11 엄마는 나와 남동생을 침대 밖으로 잡아끌었다.

12 우리는 주방으로 달려가서 식탁 아래로 기어들어 갔다.

13 나는 전등이 심하게 흔들리는 것과 책이 바닥으로 떨어지는 것을 볼 수 있었다.

14 Our family picture _____ from the wall and the glass _____ _____ _____.

15 A cup _____ _____ and _____ _____ the kitchen table.

16 _____ _____, I could _____ something else in the apartment _____.

17 I started _____ _____ that the building would _____.

18 Then the _____ _____ _____ _____.

19 We started _____ _____ the door.

20 _____ _____ _____, my mom's cell phone _____.

21 It was my dad, who was _____ _____ _____ _____.

22 He _____, "_____ _____!

23 _____ _____ _____ the building!

24 _____ the _____!

25 _____ _____ the elevator!

26 _____!"

27 "_____ are you?

28 Are you _____?" my mom _____ _____.

29 My dad _____, "_____ _____.

30 I'm _____.

14 우리 가족 사진이 벽에서 떨어졌고 사진을 덮고 있던 유리가 깨졌다.

15 컵이 넘어지고 식탁에서 굴러 떨어졌다.

16 매 순간, 나는 아파트에 있는 다른 어떤 것들이 부서지는 소리를 들을 수 있었다.

17 나는 건물이 무너지지는 않을까 하는 걱정이 들기 시작했다.

18 그때 흔들림이 멈추는 것 같았다.

19 우리는 문으로 기어가기 시작했다.

20 그 순간, 엄마의 휴대 전화가 울렸다.

21 전화를 한 사람은 바로 아빠였는데, 직장에서 퇴근하던 중이었다.

22 아빠는 소리쳤다. "지진이 멈췄어요!

23 건물 밖으로 나와요!

24 계단을 이용해요!

25 엘리베이터를 타면 안 돼요!

26 서둘러요!"

27 "어디예요?

28 괜찮아요?"라고 엄마가 다급하게 물었다.

29 아빠가 대답했다. "걱정 말아요.

30 나는 괜찮아요.

31 I _____ _____ _____ when the _____ started.

32 But I _____ _____ _____.

33 I'm listening to the radio _____ _____ to _____ _____ what's _____ _____."

34 We _____ _____ _____ _____ down the stairs and _____.

35 I _____ _____.

36 _____ _____ buildings _____ _____ and _____ _____ several cars.

37 We went to an open space _____ _____ more _____ _____.

38 How _____ all this _____ _____ in _____ _____ minutes?

39 _____ I had done many _____ _____ in school, I had never thought I'd _____ _____ _____ _____.

40 I still _____ _____ when I _____ that night.

41 I _____ _____ _____ _____ _____ when the furniture was shaking and things _____ _____ _____ the floor.

42 _____ that night, I began to _____ earthquake _____ _____.

43 I _____ that I should _____ _____ _____ the next earthquake, which can _____ _____ _____ _____.

---

31 진동이 시작할 때 운전해서 집으로 가던 중이었어요.

32 하지만 즉시 차를 길 한쪽에 댔어요.

33 무슨 일이 일어나는지 알기 위해 지금 라디오를 듣고 있어요."

34 우리는 초조한 마음으로 계단을 내려가서 밖으로 나갔다.

35 나는 주변을 둘러보았다.

36 건물의 일부분이 떨어져 나갔고 몇몇 차들은 박살이 났다.

37 우리는 추가적인 낙하물을 피하기 위해 공터로 갔다.

38 어떻게 이런 일이 몇 분 만에 일어날 수 있단 말인가?

39 비록 학교에서 많은 지진 대피 훈련을 해 왔지만, 내가 실제 지진을 겪으리라고는 전혀 생각해 보지 않았다.

40 그날 밤을 기억하면 나는 여전히 두려워진다.

41 가구가 흔들리고 물건들이 바닥으로 떨어졌을 때 내가 느꼈던 공포심을 나는 잊을 수가 없다.

42 그날 밤 이후, 나는 지진 대피 훈련에 진지하게 임하기 시작했다.

43 나는 언제든 발생할 수 있는 다음 지진을 대비해야 한다는 것을 깨달았다.

※ 다음 문장을 우리말로 쓰시오.

1 ▶ Waking Up to an Earthquake

➡ _____

2 ▶ One night in February, after I had gone to bed, an earthquake hit.

➡ _____

3 ▶ I woke up suddenly because my bed was shaking.

➡ _____

4 ▶ I thought my brother was shaking my bed as a joke.

➡ _____

5 ▶ But then I heard the mirror on my desk fall to the floor and break into pieces.

➡ _____

6 ▶ I knew it wasn't my brother then, but I still didn't know what exactly was happening.

➡ _____

7 ▶ Soon the whole room began to shake violently, and my confusion turned to panic.

➡ _____

8 ▶ My mom shouted that it was an earthquake and ran into my room.

➡ _____

9 ▶ Since it was my first time experiencing an earthquake, I didn't know how to react.

➡ _____

10 ▶ I just kept saying, "What should I do?"

➡ _____

11 ▶ My mom pulled me and my brother out of bed.

➡ _____

12 ▶ We ran to the kitchen and crawled under the table.

➡ _____

13 ▶ I could see the light swinging violently and books falling to the floor.

➡ _____

14 Our family picture dropped from the wall and the glass covering it broke.

➡ _____

15 A cup tipped over and rolled off the kitchen table.

➡ _____

16 Every second, I could hear something else in the apartment break.

➡ _____

17 I started to worry that the building would collapse.

➡ _____

18 Then the shaking seemed to stop.

➡ _____

19 We started crawling toward the door.

➡ _____

20 At that moment, my mom's cell phone rang.

➡ _____

21 It was my dad, who was coming home from work.

➡ _____

22 He shouted, "It stopped!

➡ _____

23 Get out of the building!

➡ _____

24 Take the stairs!

➡ _____

25 Don't take the elevator!

➡ _____

26 Hurry!"

➡ _____

27 "Where are you?

➡ _____

28 Are you okay?" my mom asked urgently.

➡ _____

29 My dad answered, "Don't worry.

➡ _____

30 I'm okay.

➡ _____

31 I was driving home when the shaking started.

➡ _____

32 But I pulled over immediately.

➡ _____

33 I'm listening to the radio right now to find out what's going on."

➡ _____

34 We nervously made our way down the stairs and outside.

➡ _____

35 I looked around.

➡ _____

36 Parts of buildings had fallen and had smashed several cars.

➡ _____

37 We went to an open space to avoid more falling pieces.

➡ _____

38 How could all this have happened in a few minutes?

➡ _____

39 Although I had done many earthquake drills in school, I had never thought I'd experience

a real earthquake.

➡ _____

40 I still get scared when I remember that night.

➡ _____

41 I can't forget the panic I felt when the furniture was shaking and things were falling to the floor.

➡ _____

42 After that night, I began to take earthquake drills seriously.

➡ _____

43 I realized that I should be prepared for the next earthquake, which can occur at any time.

➡ _____

※ 다음 괄호 안의 단어들을 우리말에 맞도록 바르게 배열하시오.

1 (Up / Walking / to / Earthquake / an)
➡ _____

2 (night / one / February, / in / I / after / gone / had / bed, / to / an / hit. / earthquake)
➡ _____

3 (woke / I / up / because / suddenly / bed / my / shaking. / was)
➡ _____

4 (thought / I / brother / my / shaking / was / bed / my / a / as / joke.)
➡ _____

5 (then / but / heard / I / mirror / the / my / on / desk / to / fall / floor / the / and / into / pieces. / break)
➡ _____

6 (knew / I / wasn't / it / brother / my / then, / I / but / still / know / didn't / exactly / what / happening. / was)
➡ _____

7 (the / soon / whole / began / room / shake / to / violently, / and / confusion / my / to / turned / panic.)
➡ _____

8 (mom / my / that / shouted / was / it / earthquake / an / and / into / ran / room. / my)
➡ _____

9 (it / since / was / first / my / time / an / experiencing / earthquake, / didn't / I / how / know / react. / to)
➡ _____
_____

10 (just / I / saying, / kept / should / "what / do?" / I)
➡ _____

11 (mom / my / me / pulled / and / brother / my / of / out / bed.)
➡ _____

12 (ran / we / the / to / kitchen / and / under / crawled / table. / the)
➡ _____

13 (could / I / the / see / swinging / light / and / violently / books / to / falling / floor. / the)
➡ _____

---

1 지진에 눈을 뜨는 것

2 2월 어느 날 밤. 내가 잠자리에 든 후에 지진이 일어났다.

3 침대가 흔들렸기 때문에 나는 갑자기 잠에서 깼다.

4 나는 남동생이 장난으로 침대를 흔들고 있다고 생각했다.

5 하지만 그때 나는 내 책상 위에 있던 거울이 바닥으로 떨어져 산산조각이 나는 소리를 들었다.

6 그때 나는 남동생이 그런 것이 아니라는 것을 알았지만, 정확히 무슨 일이 일어나고 있었는지를 여전히 알지 못했다.

7 머지않아 방 전체가 심하게 흔들리기 시작했고 혼란스러움은 공포로 변했다.

8 엄마가 지진이라고 소리를 지르며 내 방으로 뛰어 들어왔다.

9 지진을 경험한 것이 처음이었기 때문에. 나는 어떻게 반응해야 할지 몰랐다.

10 나는 그저 "어떻게 해야 하지?" 라는 말을 반복했다.

11 엄마는 나와 남동생을 침대 밖으로 잡아끌었다.

12 우리는 주방으로 달려가서 식탁 아래로 기어들어 갔다.

13 나는 전등이 심하게 흔들리는 것과 책이 바닥으로 떨어지는 것을 볼 수 있었다.

14 (family / our / dropped / picture / the / from / wall / and / glass / the / covering / broke. / it)

➡ _____

15 (cup / a / over / tipped / and / off / rolled / kitchen / the / table.)

➡ _____

16 (second, / every / could / I / something / hear / else / the / in / break. / apartment)

➡ _____

17 (started / I / worry / to / the / that / building / collapse. / would)

➡ _____

18 (the / then / seemed / shaking / stop. / to)

➡ _____

19 (started / we / toward / crawling / door. / the)

➡ _____

20 (that / at / moment, / mom's / my / phone / cell / rang.)

➡ _____

21 (was / it / dad, / my / was / who / home / coming / work. / from)

➡ _____

22 (shouted, / he / stopped! / "it)

➡ _____

23 (out / get / the / of / building!)

➡ _____

24 (the / take / stairs!)

➡ _____

25 (take / don't / elevator! / the)

➡ _____

26 (hurry!")

➡ _____

27 (are / "where / you?)

➡ _____

28 (you / are / okay?" / mom / my / urgently. / asked)

➡ _____

29 (dad / my / "don't / answered, / worry)

➡ _____

30 (okay. / I'm)

➡ _____

14 우리 가족 사진이 벽에서 떨어졌고 사진을 덮고 있던 유리가 깨졌다.

15 컵이 넘어지고 식탁에서 굴러떨어졌다.

16 매 순간, 나는 아파트에 있는 다른 어떤 것들이 부서지는 소리를 들을 수 있었다.

17 나는 건물이 무너지지는 않을까 하는 걱정이 들기 시작했다.

18 그때 흔들림이 멈추는 것 같았다.

19 우리는 문으로 기어가기 시작했다.

20 그 순간, 엄마의 휴대 전화가 울렸다.

21 전화를 한 사람은 바로 아빠였는데, 직장에서 퇴근하던 중이었다.

22 아빠는 소리쳤다, "지진이 멈췄어요!

23 건물 밖으로 나와요!

24 계단을 이용해요!

25 엘리베이터를 타면 안 돼요!

26 서둘러요!"

27 "어디예요?

28 괜찮아요?"라고 엄마가 다급하게 물었다.

29 아빠가 대답했다, "걱정 말아요.

30 나는 괜찮아요.

31 (was / I / home / driving / when / shaking / the / started.)

➡ _____

32 (I / but / over / pulled / immediately.)

➡ _____

33 (listening / I'm / the / to / right / radio / now / find / to / out / going / what's / on.")

➡ _____

34 (nervously / we / our / made / down / way / stairs / the / outside. / and)

➡ _____

35 (looked / I / around.)

➡ _____

36 (of / parts / buildings / fallen / had / and / smashed / had / cars. / several)

➡ _____

37 (went / we / an / to / open / to / space / avoid / falling / more / pieces.)

➡ _____

38 (could / how / this / all / happened / have / a / in / few / minutes?)

➡ _____

39 (I / although / done / had / earthquake / many / in / drills, / school, / had / I / thought / never / experience. / I'd / real / a / earthquake.)

➡ _____

40 (still / I / scared / get / I / when / that / remember / night.)

➡ _____

41 (can't / I / the / forget / panic / felt / I / the / when / was / furniture / shaking / and / were / things / to / falling / floor. / the)

➡ _____

42 (that / after / night, / began / I / take / to / drills / earthquake / seriously.)

➡ _____

43 (realized / I / that / I / be / should / prepared / the / for / earthquake, / next / can / which / at / occur / time. / any)

➡ _____

31 진동이 시작할 때 운전해서 집으로 가던 중이었어요.

32 하지만 즉시 차를 길 한쪽에 댔어요.

33 무슨 일이 일어나는지 알기 위해 지금 라디오를 듣고 있어요."

34 우리는 초조한 마음으로 계단을 내려가서 밖으로 나갔다.

35 나는 주변을 둘러보았다.

36 건물의 일부분이 떨어져 나갔고 몇몇 차들은 박살이 났다.

37 우리는 추가적인 낙하물을 피하기 위해 공터로 갔다.

38 어떻게 이런 일이 몇 분 만에 일어날 수 있단 말인가?

39 비록 학교에서 많은 지진 대피 훈련을 해 왔지만, 내가 실제 지진을 겪으리라고는 전혀 생각해 보지 않았었다.

40 그날 밤을 기억하면 나는 여전히 두려워진다.

41 가구가 흔들리고 물건들이 바닥으로 떨어졌을 때 내가 느꼈던 공포심을 나는 잊을 수가 없다.

42 그날 밤 이후, 나는 지진 대피 훈련에 진지하게 임하기 시작했다.

43 나는 언제든 발생할 수 있는 다음 지진을 대비해야 한다는 것을 깨달았다.

※ 다음 우리말을 영어로 쓰시오.

1 지진에 눈을 뜨는 것

➡ _____

2 2월 어느 날 밤, 내가 잠자리에 든 후에 지진이 일어났다.

➡ _____

3 침대가 흔들렸기 때문에 나는 갑자기 잠에서 깼다.

➡ _____

4 나는 남동생이 장난으로 침대를 흔들고 있다고 생각했다.

➡ _____

5 하지만 그때 나는 내 책상 위에 있던 거울이 바닥으로 떨어져 산산조각이 나는 소리를 들었다.

➡ _____

6 그때 나는 남동생이 그런 것이 아니라는 것을 알았지만, 정확히 무슨 일이 일어나고 있었는지를 여전히 알지 못했다.

➡ _____

7 머지않아 방 전체가 심하게 흔들리기 시작했고 혼란스러움은 공포로 변했다.

➡ _____

8 엄마가 지진이라고 소리를 지르며 내 방으로 뛰어 들어왔다.

➡ _____

9 지진을 경험한 것이 처음이었기 때문에, 나는 어떻게 반응해야 할지 몰랐다.

➡ _____

10 나는 그저 "어떻게 해야 하지?"라는 말을 반복했다.

➡ _____

11 엄마는 나와 남동생을 침대 밖으로 잡아끌었다.

➡ _____

12 우리는 주방으로 달려가서 식탁 아래로 기어들어 갔다.

➡ _____

13 나는 전등이 심하게 흔들리는 것과 책이 바닥으로 떨어지는 것을 볼 수 있었다.

➡ _____

14 우리 가족 사진이 벽에서 떨어졌고 사진을 덮고 있던 유리가 깨졌다.

➡ _____

15 컵이 넘어지고 식탁에서 굴러 떨어졌다.

➡ _____

16 매 순간, 나는 아파트에 있는 다른 어떤 것들이 부서지는 소리를 들을 수 있었다.

➡ _____

17 나는 건물이 무너지지는 않을까 하는 걱정이 들기 시작했다.

➡ _____

18 그때 흔들림이 멈추는 것 같았다.

➡ _____

19 우리는 문으로 기어가기 시작했다.

➡ _____

20 그 순간, 엄마의 휴대 전화가 울렸다.

➡ _____

21 전화를 한 사람은 바로 아빠였는데, 직장에서 퇴근하던 중이었다.

➡ _____

22 아빠는 소리쳤다, "지진이 멈췄어요!

➡ _____

23 건물 밖으로 나와요!

➡ _____

24 계단을 이용해요!

➡ _____

25 엘리베이터를 타면 안 돼요!

➡ _____

26 서둘러요!"

➡ _____

27 "어디예요?

➡ _____

28 괜찮아요?"라고 엄마가 다급하게 물었다.

➡ _____

29 아빠가 대답했다, "걱정 말아요.

➡ _____

30 나는 괜찮아요.

➡ _____

31 진동이 시작할 때 운전해서 집으로 가던 중이었어요.

➡ _____

32 하지만 즉시 차를 길 한쪽에 댔어요.

➡ _____

33 무슨 일이 일어나는지 알기 위해 지금 라디오를 듣고 있어요."

➡ _____

34 우리는 초조한 마음으로 계단을 내려가서 밖으로 나갔다.

➡ _____

35 나는 주변을 둘러보았다.

➡ _____

36 건물의 일부분이 떨어져 나갔고 몇몇 차들은 박살이 났다.

➡ _____

37 우리는 추가적인 낙하물을 피하기 위해 공터로 갔다.

➡ _____

38 어떻게 이런 일이 몇 분 만에 일어날 수 있단 말인가?

➡ _____

39 비록 학교에서 많은 지진 대피 훈련을 해 왔지만, 내가 실제 지진을 겪으리라고는 전혀 생각해 보지 않았었다.

➡ _____

_____

40 그날 밤을 기억하면 나는 여전히 두려워진다.

➡ _____

41 가구가 흔들리고 물건들이 바닥으로 떨어졌을 때 내가 느꼈던 공포심을 나는 잊을 수가 없다.

➡ _____

42 그날 밤 이후, 나는 지진 대피 훈련에 진지하게 임하기 시작했다.

➡ _____

43 나는 언제든 발생할 수 있는 다음 지진을 대비해야 한다는 것을 깨달았다.

➡ _____

※ 다음 우리말과 일치하도록 빈칸에 알맞은 말을 쓰시오.

After You Read B

1. R: How did you feel _____ the _____ _____?

2. W: I _____ _____ panic _____ the whole room _____ _____ _____.

3. R: _____ _____! What did you do next?

4. W: We _____ _____ under the table after my mom _____ _____ _____ _____ _____.

5. R: What was _____ _____ _____ _____ _____?

6. W: _____ _____ things _____ _____ to the floor. I _____ many things in the apartment _____.

7. R: What _____ you _____ after that night?

8. W: I realized that I _____ _____ _____ _____ the next earthquake. It _____ _____ _____ _____ _____!

1. R: 지진이 일어났을 때 어떻게 느끼셨습니까?

2. W: 방 전체가 심하게 흔들렸기 때문에 공포에 사로잡히기 시작했어요.

3. R: 얼마나 무서웠을까! 그 다음에 무엇을 했나요?

4. W: 어머니가 우리를 침대에서 끌어내린 후, 우리는 식탁 아래로 기어갔어요.

5. R: 그 순간에 무슨 일이 일어나고 있었나요?

6. W: 많은 것들이 바닥으로 떨어지고 있었어요. 나는 아프트 안에 있는 많은 것들이 깨지는 소리를 들었어요.

7. R: 그날 밤 이후에 무엇을 깨달았나요?

8. W: 나는 내가 다음번 지진에 대비해야 한다는 것을 깨달았어요. 지진은 언제든지 일어날 수 있어요!

Think & Write Step 3

San Andreas

1. I _____ _____ _____ _____ you about the movie *San Andreas*.

2. This movie _____ _____ _____ Los Angeles and San Francisco _____ 2014.

3. The _____ _____, a search-and-rescue _____, must search for his _____ family _____ an earthquake.

4. The _____ _____ _____ in the _____ _____ are very good.

5. The movie is _____ _____ sad _____ _____, but the story is very interesting.

6. I give *San Andreas* four stars. _____ and _____!

San Andreas

1. 저는 영화 San Andreas에 대해 말하고 싶습니다.

2. 이 영화의 배경은 2014년 Los Angeles와 San Francisco입니다.

3. 수색구조 조종사인 주인공은 지진이 일어난 동안 행방불명된 그의 가족을 찾아야 합니다.

4. 재난 장면에 사용된 특수효과는 매우 좋습니다.

5. 이 영화는 가끔 약간 슬프지만, 이야기는 매우 재미있습니다.

6. 저는 San Andreas에게 별 4개를 줍니다. 가서 보세요!

※ 다음 우리말을 영어로 쓰시오.

After You Read B

1. R: 지진이 일어났을 때 어떻게 느끼셨습니까?
➡ _____

2. W: 방 전체가 심하게 흔들렸기 때문에 공포에 사로잡히기 시작했어요.
➡ _____

3. R: 얼마나 무서웠을까! 그 다음에 무엇을 했나요?
➡ _____

4. W: 어머니가 우리를 침대에서 끌어내린 후, 우리는 식탁 아래로 기어갔어요.
➡ _____

5. R: 그 순간에 무슨 일이 일어나고 있었나요?
➡ _____

6. W: 많은 것들이 바닥으로 떨어지고 있었어요. 나는 아프트 안에 있는 많은 것들이 깨지는 소리를 들었어요.
➡ _____

7. 그날 밤 이후에 무엇을 깨달았나요?
➡ _____

8. W: 나는 내가 다음번 지진에 대비해야 한다는 것을 깨달았어요. 지진은 언제든지 일어날 수 있어요!
➡ _____

Think & Write Step 3

San Andreas

1. 저는 영화 *San Andreas*에 대해 말하고 싶습니다.
➡ _____

2. 이 영화의 배경은 2014년 Los Angeles와 San Francisco입니다.
➡ _____

3. 수색구조 조종사인 주인공은 지진이 일어난 동안 행방불명된 그의 가족을 찾아야 합니다.
➡ _____

4. 재난 장면에 사용된 특수효과는 매우 좋습니다.
➡ _____

5. 이 영화는 가끔 약간 슬프지만, 이야기는 매우 재미있습니다.
➡ _____

6. 저는 *San Andreas*에게 별 4개를 줍니다. 가서 보세요!
➡ _____

※ 다음 영어를 우리말로 쓰시오.

01	strict	22	vision
02	achieve	23	determine
03	ensure	24	approach
04	supporter	25	hands-off
05	reasoning	26	analyst
06	confident	27	motivate
07	analyze	28	return
08	logical	29	outgoing
09	misunderstanding	30	presentation
10	deliver	31	realize
11	positive	32	relieved
12	divide	33	switch
13	edit	34	research
14	contact	35	be stuck in
15	ability	36	lead by example
16	decorate	37	come up with
17	election	38	be in charge of
18	translate	39	work out
19	valued	40	get along
20	representative	41	call for
21	effective	42	deal with
		43	hang out

※ 다음 우리말을 영어로 쓰시오.

01 분석가 _____

02 자신감 있는 _____

03 긍정적인 _____

04 귀중한, 존중 받는 _____

05 배달하다 _____

06 접근하다 _____

07 접촉 _____

08 오해 _____

09 조사, 연구 _____

10 동기를 부여하다 _____

11 외향적인, 사교적인 _____

12 지지자 _____

13 바꾸다, 전환하다 _____

14 해석하다 _____

15 안심이 되는 _____

16 나누다, 분리하다 _____

17 추리, 추론 _____

18 편집하다 _____

19 효과적인 _____

20 능력 _____

21 대표(자) _____

22 준비하다 _____

23 성취하다, 이루다 _____

24 발표 _____

25 (선거에) 입후보하다 _____

26 선거 _____

27 결정하다, 결심하다 _____

28 분석하다 _____

29 논리적인, 타당한 _____

30 목적, 목표 _____

31 대신에 _____

32 엄격한 _____

33 적절히, 제대로 _____

34 통찰력, 비전, 시력 _____

35 편들다 _____

36 ～을 생각해 내다 _____

37 사이좋게 지내다 _____

38 ～을 실망시키다 _____

39 ～에 속하다 _____

40 공들여 일하다 _____

41 ～을 처리하다, ～을 돌보다 _____

42 ～을 담당하다, 책임지다 _____

43 다루다, 처리하다 _____

※ 다음 영영풀이에 알맞은 단어를 <보기>에서 골라 쓴 후, 우리말 뜻을 쓰시오.

1 _____ : ability to lead: _____

2 _____ : to compete as a candidate in an election: _____

3 _____ : a piece of work that must be done: _____

4 _____ : the power or skill to do something: _____

5 _____ : making sense; being reasonable: _____

6 _____ : to make a change from one thing to another: _____

7 _____ : to come close to someone or something: _____

8 _____ : to prepare something written to be published or used: _____

9 _____ : a person who supports a political party, an idea, etc.: _____

10 _____ : to provide with a reason to do something: _____

11 _____ : to deeply study every piece of something to understand it: _____

12 _____ : sure that one has the ability to do things well: _____

13 _____ : successful, and working in the way that was intended: _____

14 _____ : letting people do what they want, without telling them what to do:

_____

15 _____ : somebody who has been chosen to speak, or make decisions on behalf of

a group: _____

16 _____ : the process of choosing a person or a group of people for a position,

especially a political position, by voting: _____

보기

representative	analyze	switch	ability
supporter	run	election	edit
motivate	hands-off	approach	effective
logical	confident	task	leadership

※ 다음 우리말과 일치하도록 빈칸에 알맞은 말을 쓰시오.

Listen & Talk 1 A

G: Mom, we've got a _____.

W: What's the _____?

G: We're _____ _____ have dinner with Grandma this Saturday, _____? But I _____ _____ that Sujin's birthday party is _____ _____ _____. She's my best friend. _____ _____ _____ _____?

W: That sounds _____ a difficult _____. _____ talk about it _____ your dad.

G: Okay, Mom. I'd love to see Grandma, but I don't want to _____ my _____ _____ _____ party.

Listen & Talk 1 B

M: Junsu, are you okay? _____ _____ _____?

B: Hello, Mr. Smith. I have a _____.

M: What _____?

B: You know Jaewoo, Yunho, and I are best friends, right? They _____ _____ _____, and now I'm _____ _____ the middle. I don't know _____ _____ _____.

M: That sounds hard. Do you know _____ they _____ _____?

B: Yes, but it doesn't sound like a _____ _____ to me. I guess they had _____ _____ _____ _____.

M: _____ _____ you all meet together and talk about it? I think they'll _____ _____ you.

B: That's a good idea. They're both good _____ _____ _____. I _____ _____ _____.

M: I understand. I hope everything _____ _____.

Listen & Talk 1 C

B: Hey, Mandy. _____ _____ _____ _____?

G: I don't know _____ _____ _____, Nick. My brother _____ _____ _____ _____ _____ with his homework this Wednesday, but I told him I can't. I have so many _____ _____ _____ that day.

B: What do you _____ _____ do this Wednesday?

G: I need to go to the library to _____ _____ _____. Then I have to meet you to work on our _____. After that, I _____ _____ _____ an exam at night.

해석

소녀: 엄마, 우리에게 문제가 생겼어요.

여성: 무슨 일이니?

소녀: 이번 주 토요일에 할머니와 저녁 식사를 하기로 했잖아요, 그렇죠? 그런데 수진이의 생일 파티가 토요일 저녁이라는 것을 방금 깨달았어요. 수진이는 저의 가장 친한 친구예요. 저 어떡하죠?

여성: 결정하기 힘든 문제인 것 같구나. 네 아빠와 함께 이야기해 보자.

소녀: 네, 엄마. 할머니를 정말 뵙고 싶지만, 가장 친한 친구의 생일 파티에 빠지고 싶지는 않아요.

남자: 준수야, 괜찮니? 무슨 일이야?

소년: 안녕하세요, Smith 선생님. 저에게 문제가 생겼어요.

남자: 무슨 일인데?

소년: 재우와 윤호, 그리고 제가 서로 가장 친한 사이라는 거 아시죠, 그렇죠? 그 둘이 싸웠고, 저는 이제 중간에 끼어버린 상태예요. 어떻게 해야 할지 모르겠어요.

남자: 힘들겠구나. 그 둘이 왜 싸웠는지는 아니?

소년: 네, 하지만 제가 보기에는 그다지 대단한 일도 아닌 것 같아요. 아무래도 그 둘 사이에 어떤 오해가 생긴 것 같아요.

남자: 너희 모두 다 같이 만나서 그것에 대해 이야기해 보는 게 어떠니? 그 둘이 네 말은 들을 것 같구나.

소년: 그거 좋은 생각이네요. 두 명 모두 저에게는 좋은 친구들이에요. 저는 누구의 편도 들 수 없어요.

남자: 이해한단다. 모두 잘 해결되기를 바란다.

남: 어이, Mandy. 무슨 일이야?

여: 어떻게 해야 할지 모르겠어, Nick. 내 동생이 이번 주 수요일에 숙제를 도와달라고 했는데, 도와줄 수 없다고 했어. 나는 그날 해야 할 일이 너무 많아.

남: 이번 주 수요일에 무엇을 해야 하는데?

여: 책을 반납하러 도서관에 가야 해. 그런 다음 우리의 발표 준비를 위해 너를 만나야 하고, 그다음에, 밤에는 시험 준비를 해야 해.

B: Oh, you _____ have _____ _____ to do.

G: Yes. But my brother _____ _____ _____, so I feel bad.

B: Well, then _____ _____ _____ on Thursday _____ for our presentation? Then you can do _____ and also _____ your brother on Wednesday.

G: That would _____ _____ _____ so much! Thanks for _____, Nick!

남: 아, 너 정말로 할 일이 많구나.

여: 응. 하지만 내 동생이 실망한 것처럼 보여서, 기분이 좋지가 않아.

남: 음, 그럼 우리 발표를 위해 목요일에 대신 만나는 건 어때? 그러면 너는 수요일에 모든 일을 하고 네 동생도 도와줄 수 있어.

여: 그러면 정말 큰 도움이 될 거야! 이해해 줘서 고마워, Nick!

Listen & Talk 2 A

G: _____ _____ is coming. How do you want to _____ _____?

B: I want _____ _____ _____ for Sports Day.

G: That's great. You are really _____ _____ _____ _____. I _____ _____ _____ _____ you will take some wonderful pictures.

여: 곧 있으면 운동회야. 어떻게 돕고 싶니?

남: 나는 운동회 날 사진을 찍고 싶어.

여: 그거 좋다. 너는 정말 사진을 잘 찍잖아. 나는 네가 운동회 날에 멋진 사진들을 찍을 것이라는 것을 확신해.

Listen & Talk 2 B

B: In the Send Our Stories project, we are going to make a picture book for children in other countries. We've _____ everyone _____ three groups. Each group will _____ _____ _____ a different task. Group A will _____ a Korean story _____ English. Group B will make drawings for the book and _____ it. After copies of the book _____ _____, Group C will be _____ _____ _____ sending them to the children. It won't be easy, but _____ _____ _____ _____ _____ the children _____ _____ these books will really enjoy them.

남: Send Our Stories 프로젝트에서 우리는 외국의 아이들을 위한 그림책을 만들 예정입니다. 우리는 모두를 세 그룹으로 나누었습니다. 각 그룹은 서로 다른 작업을 담당할 것입니다. A 그룹은 한국어 이야기를 영어로 번역할 것입니다. B 그룹은 이 책의 그림을 그리고 편집을 할 것입니다. 책들이 인쇄되면, C 그룹은 이 책들을 아이들에게 보내는 일을 맡게 될 것입니다. 쉽지는 않겠지만, 저는 이 책을 받는 어린이들이 이 책을 정말로 좋아할 것이라고 확신합니다.

Listen & Talk 2 C

B: I'm so _____ about our museum _____ _____.

G1: Me too. _____ _____ our tasks. Yen, what are you _____ _____ _____?

G2: I'm in charge of _____ _____.

G1: Okay. Sejin, are you going to do _____ _____ on the museum?

B: Yes, I am. Are you going to _____ _____ _____ _____ _____, Emma?

G1: That's right. I think we're _____.

G2: Good. I _____ _____ _____ _____ our project will _____ _____ well.

남: 우리의 박물관 견학이 정말 기대돼.

여1: 나도 그래. 각자 맡은 일을 확인해 보자. Yen, 너는 무엇을 담당하지?

여2: 나는 사진 촬영 담당이야.

여: 그래. 세진아, 너는 박물관 조사를 할 거지?

남: 응, 맞아. 너는 견학 보고서를 작성할 거지, Emma?

여1: 맞아. 이제 우리는 준비가 된 것 같아.

여2: 좋아. 우리 프로젝트가 잘될 거라는 데 의심의 여지가 없어.

※ 다음 우리말에 맞도록 대화를 영어로 쓰시오.

Listen & Talk 1 A

G: _____

W: _____

G: _____

_____

W: _____

G: _____

_____

소녀: 엄마, 우리에게 문제가 생겼어요.
여성: 무슨 일이니?
소녀: 이번 주 토요일에 할머니와 저녁 식사를 하기로 했잖아요, 그렇죠? 그런데 수진이의 생일 파티가 토요일 저녁이라는 것을 방금 깨달았어요. 수진이는 저의 가장 친한 친구예요. 저 어떡하죠?
여성: 결정하기 힘든 문제인 것 같구나. 네 아빠와 함께 이야기해 보자.
소녀: 네, 엄마. 할머니를 정말 뵙고 싶지만, 가장 친한 친구의 생일 파티에 빠지고 싶지는 않아요.

Listen & Talk 1 B

M: _____

B: _____

M: _____

B: _____

_____

M: _____

B: _____

_____

M: _____

B: _____

M: _____

남자: 준수야, 괜찮니? 무슨 일이야?
소년: 안녕하세요, Smith 선생님. 저에게 문제가 생겼어요.
남자: 무슨 일인데?
소년: 재우와 윤호, 그리고 제가 서로 가장 친한 사이라는 거 아시죠, 그렇죠? 그 둘이 싸웠고, 저는 이제 중간에 끼어버린 상태예요. 어떻게 해야 할지 모르겠어요.
남자: 힘들겠구나. 그 둘이 왜 싸웠는지는 아니?
소년: 네, 하지만 제가 보기에는 그다지 대단한 일도 아닌 것 같아요. 아무래도 그 둘 사이에 어떤 오해가 생긴 것 같아요.
남자: 너희 모두 다 같이 만나서 그것에 대해 이야기해 보는 게 어떠니? 그 둘이 네 말은 들을 것 같구나.
소년: 그거 좋은 생각이네요. 두 명 모두 저에게는 좋은 친구들이에요. 저는 누구의 편도 들 수 없어요.
남자: 이해한단다. 모두 잘 해결되기를 바란다.

Listen & Talk 1 C

B: _____

G: _____

_____

_____

B: _____

G: _____

남: 어이, Mandy. 무슨 일이야?
여: 어떻게 해야 할지 모르겠어, Nick. 내 동생이 이번 주 수요일에 숙제를 도와달라고 했는데, 도와줄 수 없다고 했어. 나는 그날 해야 할 일이 너무 많아.
남: 이번 주 수요일에 무엇을 해야 하는데?
여: 책을 반납하러 도서관에 가야 해. 그런 다음 우리의 발표 준비를 위해 너를 만나야 하고. 그다음에, 밤에는 시험 준비를 해야 해.

B: _____

G: _____

B: _____

G: _____

여: 아, 너 정말로 할 일이 많구나.

여: 응. 하지만 내 동생이 실망한 것처럼 보여서, 기분이 좋지가 않아.

남: 음, 그럼 우리 발표를 위해 목요일에 대신 만나는 건 어때? 그러면 너는 수요일에 모든 일을 하고 네 동생도 도와줄 수 있어.

여: 그러면 정말 큰 도움이 될 거야! 이해해 줘서 고마워, Nick!

Listen & Talk 2 A

G: _____

B: _____

G: _____
_____

여: 곧 있으면 운동회야. 어떻게 돕고 싶니?

남: 나는 운동회 날 사진을 찍고 싶어.

여: 그거 좋다. 너는 정말 사진을 잘 찍잖아. 나는 네가 운동회 날에 멋진 사진들을 찍을 것이라는 것을 확신해.

Listen & Talk 2 B

B: _____
_____
_____
_____
_____
_____

남: Send Our Stories 프로젝트에서 우리는 외국의 아이들을 위한 그림책을 만들 예정입니다. 우리는 모두를 세 그룹으로 나누었습니다. 각 그룹은 서로 다른 작업을 담당할 것입니다. A 그룹은 한국어 이야기를 영어로 번역할 것입니다. B 그룹은 이 책의 그림을 그리고 편집을 할 것입니다. 책들이 인쇄되면, C 그룹은 이 책들을 아이들에게 보내는 일을 맡게 될 것입니다. 쉽지는 않겠지만, 저는 이 책을 받는 어린이들이 이 책을 정말로 좋아할 것이라고 확신합니다.

Listen & Talk 2 C

B: _____

G1: _____

G2: _____

G1: _____

G2: _____

B: _____

G1: _____

G2: _____

남: 우리의 박물관 견학이 정말 기대돼.

여1: 나도 그래. 각자 맡은 일을 확인해 보자. Yen, 너는 무엇을 담당하지?

여2: 나는 사진 촬영 담당이야.

여1: 그래. 세진아, 너는 박물관 조사를 할 거지?

남: 응, 맞아. 너는 견학 보고서를 작성할 거지, Emma?

여1: 맞아. 이제 우리는 준비가 된 것 같아.

여2: 좋아. 우리 프로젝트가 잘될 거라는 데 의심의 여지가 없어.

※ 다음 우리말과 일치하도록 빈칸에 알맞은 것을 골라 쓰시오.

1 _____ Are _____ _____
A. All   B. We   C. Leaders

2 Brian: The _____ is _____ _____.
A. coming   B. election   C. up

3 _____ _____ _____ _____ for class representative, Yumi?
A. don't   B. why   C. run   D. you

4 Yumi: _____ _____.
A. way   B. no

5 I'm not the _____ _____ for that _____.
A. right   B. position   C. person

6 I've _____ _____ about _____.
A. thought   B. never   C. running

7 Brian: _____ _____?
A. not   B. why

8 Yumi: _____ _____, Brian.
A. on   B. come

9 Leaders have _____ _____.
A. qualities   B. special

10 I don't think a person _____ me _____ _____ _____ a leader.
A. can   B. called   C. like   D. be

11 Brian: _____ do you _____?
A. mean   B. what

12 I think you have very _____ _____ _____.
A. leadership   B. good   C. qualities

13 You're _____ _____ and _____.
A. outgoing   B. friendly   C. really

14 You _____ _____ people _____ _____.
A. get   B. help   C. along   D. also

15 I have _____ _____ that you will _____ _____ if you run.
A. be   B. doubt   C. elected   D. no

16 Brian told me this afternoon _____ I have _____ _____ _____.
A. good   B. that   C. qualities   D. leadership

17 _____ one _____ _____ _____ me that before.
A. ever   B. no   C. told   D. has

18 _____ does he _____ _____?
A. think   B. why   C. so

19 Maybe he was _____ _____ _____ _____ nice.
A. to   B. just   C. be   D. trying

20 _____ he said that to me, _____, I started to _____.
A. however   B. when   C. think

---

1 우리는 모두 리더들이다

2 Brian: "선거가 다가오고 있어.

3 유미야, 반 대표에 입후보하는 게 어때?"

4 유미: "아니.

5 나는 그 자리에 적절한 사람이 아니야.

6 나는 입후보하는 것에 대해 생각해 본 적이 없어."

7 Brian: "왜?"

8 유미: "이봐, Brian.

9 리더들은 특별한 자질을 갖추고 있어.

10 나 같은 사람이 리더로 불릴 수 있다고 생각하지 않아."

11 Brian: "무슨 말이야?

12 내 생각에 너는 매우 좋은 지도력 자질들을 갖추고 있어.

13 너는 정말 친절하고 외향적이잖아.

14 또 너는 사람들이 어울리도록 도와주기도 해.

15 만약 네가 입후보한다면 당선될 거라고 믿어 의심치 않아."

16 Brian은 오늘 오후에 내게 내가 좋은 지도력 자질들을 갖추고 있다고 말했다.

17 이전에는 아무도 내게 그런 말을 한 적이 없었다.

18 왜 그는 그렇게 생각했을까?

19 아마도 그는 그저 친절하려고 했을 것이다.

20 그러나 그가 내게 그렇게 말했을 때, 나는 생각하기 시작했다.

21 _____ I really _____ a _____ ?
　　A. become　　　　B. can　　　　　C. leader

22 I _____ _____ .
　　A. know　　　　　B. don't

23 I think leaders should have a _____ , clear _____ , and the _____ to _____ others.
　　A. vision　　　　B. motivate　　　C. goals　　　D. ability

24 I don't have _____ _____ _____ _____ .
　　A. those　　　　　B. any　　　　　C. things　　　D. of

25 Then I _____ started to _____ _____ these are the only _____ that make a good leader.
　　A. wonder　　　　B. qualities　　　C. suddenly　　D. if

26 _____ I'm _____ .
　　A. wrong　　　　　B. maybe

27 Maybe there are _____ _____ _____ .
　　A. leadership　　　B. other　　　　C. qualities

28 So I _____ to _____ some _____ .
　　A. online　　　　　B. decided　　　C. research　　D. do

29 Here's _____ I _____ !
　　A. found　　　　　B. what

30 **GREEN LEADERS: "_____ _____ "**
　　A. Builders　　　　B. Team

31 _____ that the team _____
　　A. valued　　　　　B. ensure　　　　C. feels

32 _____ a _____ _____
　　A. environment　　B. create　　　　C. positive

33 Are _____ and easy to _____
　　A. to　　　　　　　B. friendly　　　C. talk

34 **RED LEADERS: "_____ _____ "**
　　A. Analysts　　　　B. Logical

35 _____ good _____
　　A. skills　　　　　B. have　　　　　C. reasoning

36 _____ problems and _____
　　A. situations　　　B. analyze

37 Think of the most _____ ways to _____ the team's _____
　　A. achieve　　　　B. effective　　　C. goals

38 **PURPLE LEADERS: "_____ _____ "**
　　A. Managers　　　　B. Hands-Off

39 _____ others to work _____ their _____
　　A. own　　　　　　B. allow　　　　　C. on

40 Do not _____ _____ _____ people
　　A. control　　　　　B. to　　　　　C. try

41 Give _____ only _____ it is _____
　　A. needed　　　　　B. advice　　　　C. when

21 내가 정말 리더가 될 수 있을까?

22 나는 모르겠다.

23 나는 리더가 비전, 명확한 목표, 그리고 다른 사람들에게 동기를 부여할 능력을 가지고 있어야 한다고 생각한다.

24 나는 그러한 것들 중 어느 것도 가지고 있지 않다.

25 그때 나는 갑자기 이것들이 좋은 리더를 만드는 유일한 자질들인지 궁금해하기 시작했다.

26 아마도 내가 틀린지도 모른다.

27 어쩌면 다른 지도력 자질들이 있는지도 모른다.

28 그래서 나는 온라인으로 조사해 보기로 결심했다.

29 여기에 내가 찾은 것이 있다!

30 〈녹색 리더〉 '팀 조직자'

31 팀이 반드시 가치 있다고 느끼게 한다

32 긍정적인 환경을 조성한다

33 친절하고 말을 걸기 쉽다

34 〈빨간색 리더〉 '논리적 분석가'

35 좋은 추론 기술을 갖고 있다

36 문제와 상황들을 분석한다

37 팀의 목표를 성취하는 가장 효과적인 방법들을 생각한다

38 〈보라색 리더〉 '방임적 관리자'

39 다른 사람들이 스스로 일하도록 해 준다

40 사람들을 통제하려고 하지 않는다

41 필요할 때만 조언한다

42 **ORANGE LEADERS:** "_____ _____"
A. Directors   B. Strict

43 _____ everyone's _____ _____
A. clear   B. make   C. role

44 _____ _____ everything is finished _____
A. time   B. sure   C. on   D. make

45 _____ each _____ is done _____
A. properly   B. step   C. ensure

46 **YELLOW LEADERS:** "_____ _____"
A. Supporters   B. Quiet

47 Lead _____ _____
A. example   B. by

48 _____ the team members _____ _____
A. instead   B. let   C. shine

49 _____ the team _____ _____
A. needs   B. meet   C. members'

50 **BLUE LEADERS:** "_____ _____"
A. Thinkers   B. Creative

51 _____ problems _____ new _____
A. in   B. approach   C. ways

52 _____ _____ _____ fresh ideas
A. up   B. come   C. with

53 _____ _____ tasks _____ _____ others
A. from   B. deal   C. differently   D. with

54 I was _____ that there are actually many _____ leadership styles, but soon I _____ the _____.
A. realized   B. different   C. reason   D. surprised

55 We _____ _____ many different groups, and many different situations can _____ _____ in our lives.
A. up   B. belong   C. to   D. come

56 They all _____ _____ different leadership _____.
A. for   B. styles   C. call

57 _____ group's _____ _____ the best leadership style.
A. situation   B. each   C. determines   D. unique

58 "I am a _____ of many different groups, and I have _____ _____ in each _____."
A. responsibilities   B. part   C. different   D. group

59 _____ _____ everything, I became _____ _____.
A. more   B. reading   C. confident   D. after

60 I _____ that I have _____ _____ the _____ of a "green leader."
A. some   B. discovered   C. qualities   D. of

61 If my classmates think a green leader would _____ our class _____, they might _____ me to be class _____!
A. better   B. pick   C. make   D. representative

62 Okay, _____ _____ it!
A. try   B. let's

---

42 〈주황색 리더〉 '엄격한 감독관'

43 모두의 역할을 분명하게 해 준다

44 모든 일을 제때 끝날 것을 확실히 한다

45 각 단계가 적절히 이행되도록 한다

46 〈노란색 리더〉 '조용한 지지자'

47 솔선수범한다

48 팀원들이 대신 빛나도록 해 준다

49 팀원들의 요구 사항을 충족한다

50 〈파란색 리더〉 '창조적 사상가'

51 새로운 방식으로 문제들에 접근한다

52 신선한 아이디어를 떠올린다

53 다른 사람들과 다르게 일을 처리한다

54 나는 실제로 서로 다른 많은 지도력 유형들이 있어서 놀랐지만, 곧 그 이유를 깨달았다.

55 우리는 서로 다른 여러 집단에 속하고, 우리 인생에서 서로 다른 많은 상황들이 발생할 수 있다.

56 그것들은 모두 서로 다른 지도력 유형들을 요구한다.

57 각 집단의 독특한 상황이 최고의 지도력 유형을 결정한다.

58 "나는 서로 다른 많은 집단의 일부이고, 각 집단에서 각각 다른 책임을 갖고 있어."

59 모든 것을 읽고 나서, 나는 더 자신감이 생겼다.

60 나는 '녹색 리더'의 자질들 중 일부분을 가지고 있다는 것을 알게 되었다.

61 만약 나의 반 친구들이 녹색 리더가 우리 학급을 더 좋게 만들 거라고 생각한다면, 그들은 학급 대표로 나를 뽑을지도 모른다!

62 좋아, 시도해 보자!

※ 다음 우리말과 일치하도록 빈칸에 알맞은 말을 쓰시오.

1 _____ _____ _____ Leaders

2 Brian: The _____ is _____ _____.

3 _____ _____ _____ run for class _____, Yumi?

4 Yumi: _____ _____.

5 I'm not the _____ _____ for that _____.

6 I've never _____ _____ _____.

7 Brian: _____ _____?

8 Yumi: _____ _____, Brian.

9 Leaders have _____ _____.

10 I don't think a person _____ me _____ _____ _____ a leader.

11 Brian: _____ do you _____?

12 I think you have very _____ _____ _____.

13 You're really _____ and _____.

14 You _____ _____ people _____ _____.

15 I have _____ _____ that you _____ _____ _____ if you run.

16 Brian told me this afternoon that I have _____ _____ _____.

17 No one _____ _____ _____ me that before.

18 _____ does he _____ _____?

19 Maybe he was just _____ _____ _____ nice.

20 When he said that to me, _____, I started _____ _____.

1 우리는 모두 리더들이다

2 Brian: "선거가 다가오고 있어.

3 유미야, 반 대표에 입후보하는 게 어때?"

4 유미: "아니.

5 나는 그 자리에 적절한 사람이 아니야.

6 나는 입후보하는 것에 대해 생각해 본 적이 없어."

7 Brian: "왜?"

8 유미: "이봐, Brian.

9 리더들은 특별한 자질을 갖추고 있어.

10 나 같은 사람이 리더로 불릴 수 있다고 생각하지 않아."

11 Brian: "무슨 말이야?

12 내 생각에 너는 매우 좋은 지도력 자질들을 갖추고 있어.

13 너는 정말 친절하고 외향적이잖아.

14 또 너는 사람들이 어울리도록 도와주기도 해.

15 만약 네가 입후보한다면 당선될 거라고 믿어 의심치 않아."

16 Brian은 오늘 오후에 내게 내가 좋은 지도력 자질들을 갖추고 있다고 말했다.

17 이전에는 아무도 내게 그런 말을 한 적이 없었다.

18 왜 그는 그렇게 생각했을까?

19 아마도 그는 그저 친절하려고 했을 것이다.

20 그러나 그가 내게 그렇게 말했을 때, 나는 생각하기 시작했다.

21 Can I really _____ _____ _____?

22 I _____ _____.

23 I think leaders should have _____ _____, clear _____, and the ability _____ _____ _____.

24 I don't have _____ _____ _____ _____.

25 Then I suddenly started to _____ _____ these are the only _____ that make a good leader.

26 Maybe I'm _____.

27 Maybe there are _____ _____ _____.

28 So I decided to _____ _____ _____ _____.

29 Here's _____ I _____!

30 **GREEN LEADERS:** "Team _____"

31 Ensure that the team _____ _____

32 Create a _____ _____

33 Are friendly and easy _____ _____ _____

34 **RED LEADERS:** "_____ _____"

35 Have good _____ _____

36 _____ problems and _____

37 Think of the most _____ _____ to _____ _____ _____ _____

38 **PURPLE LEADERS:** "_____ _____"

39 _____ others to work _____ _____ _____

40 Do not _____ _____ _____ people

41 Give _____ only when _____ _____ _____

21 내가 정말 리더가 될 수 있을까?

22 나는 모르겠다.

23 나는 리더가 비전, 명확한 목표, 그리고 다른 사람들에게 동기를 부여할 능력을 가지고 있어야 한다고 생각한다.

24 나는 그러한 것들 중 어느 것도 가지고 있지 않다.

25 그때 나는 갑자기 이것들이 좋은 리더를 만드는 유일한 자질들인지 궁금해하기 시작했다.

26 아마도 내가 틀린지도 모른다.

27 어쩌면 다른 지도력 자질들이 있는지도 모른다.

28 그래서 나는 온라인으로 조사해 보기로 결심했다.

29 여기에 내가 찾은 것이 있다!

30 〈녹색 리더〉'팀 조직자'

31 팀이 반드시 가치 있다고 느끼게 한다

32 긍정적인 환경을 조성한다

33 친절하고 말을 걸기 쉽다

34 〈빨간색 리더〉'논리적 분석가'

35 좋은 추론 기술을 갖고 있다

36 문제와 상황들을 분석한다

37 팀의 목표를 성취하는 가장 효과적인 방법들을 생각한다

38 〈보라색 리더〉'방임적 관리자'

39 다른 사람들이 스스로 일하도록 해 준다

40 사람들을 통제하려고 하지 않는다

41 필요할 때만 조언한다

42 **ORANGE LEADERS: "_____ _____"**

43 Make _____ _____ _____

44 _____ _____ everything is finished _____ _____

45 Ensure _____ _____ is done _____

46 **YELLOW LEADERS: "_____ _____"**

47 Lead _____ _____

48 Let the team members _____ _____

49 _____ the team members' _____

50 **BLUE LEADERS: "_____ _____"**

51 _____ problems _____

52 _____ _____ _____ fresh ideas

53 _____ _____ tasks _____ _____ others

54 I was surprised that there are actually many different leadership styles, but soon I _____ _____ _____.

55 We _____ _____ many different groups, and many different situations can _____ _____ in our lives.

56 They all _____ _____ different leadership styles.

57 Each group's _____ _____ _____ the best leadership style.

58 "I am _____ _____ _____ many different groups, and I have _____ _____ in each group."

59 After reading everything, I became _____ _____.

60 I discovered that I have _____ _____ _____ _____ of a "green leader."

61 If my classmates think a green leader would make our class better, they might _____ _____ to be _____ _____!

62 Okay, _____ _____ it!

42 〈주황색 리더〉 '엄격한 감독관'

43 모두의 역할을 분명하게 해 준다

44 모든 일을 제때 끝날 것을 확실히 한다

45 각 단계가 적절히 이행되도록 한다

46 〈노란색 리더〉 '조용한 지지자'

47 솔선수범한다

48 팀원들이 대신 빛나도록 해 준다

49 팀원들의 요구 사항을 충족한다

50 〈파란색 리더〉 '창조적 사상가'

51 새로운 방식으로 문제들에 접근한다

52 신선한 아이디어를 떠올린다

53 다른 사람들과 다르게 일을 처리한다

54 나는 실제로 서로 다른 많은 지도력 유형들이 있어서 놀랐지만, 곧 그 이유를 깨달았다.

55 우리는 서로 다른 여러 집단에 속하고, 우리 인생에서 서로 다른 많은 상황들이 발생할 수 있다.

56 그것들은 모두 서로 다른 지도력 유형들을 요구한다.

57 각 집단의 독특한 상황이 최고의 지도력 유형을 결정한다.

58 "나는 서로 다른 많은 집단의 일부이고, 각 집단에서 각각 다른 책임을 갖고 있어."

59 모든 것을 읽고 나서, 나는 더 자신감이 생겼다.

60 나는 '녹색 리더'의 자질들 중 일부분을 가지고 있다는 것을 알게 되었다.

61 만약 나의 반 친구들이 녹색 리더가 우리 학급을 더 좋게 만들 거라고 생각한다면, 그들은 학급 대표로 나를 뽑을지도 모른다!

62 좋아, 시도해 보자!

※ 다음 문장을 우리말로 쓰시오.

1 We Are All Leaders
➡ _____

2 Brian: The election is coming up.
➡ _____

3 Why don't you run for class representative, Yumi?
➡ _____

4 Yumi: No way.
➡ _____

5 I'm not the right person for that position.
➡ _____

6 I've never thought about running.
➡ _____

7 Brian: Why not?
➡ _____

8 Yumi: Come on, Brian.
➡ _____

9 Leaders have special qualities.
➡ _____

10 I don't think a person like me can be called a leader.
➡ _____

11 Brian: What do you mean?
➡ _____

12 I think you have very good leadership qualities.
➡ _____

13 You're really friendly and outgoing.
➡ _____

14 You also help people get along.
➡ _____

15 I have no doubt that you will be elected if you run.
➡ _____

16 Brian told me this afternoon that I have good leadership qualities.
➡ _____

17 No one has ever told me that before.
➡ _____

18 Why does he think so?
➡ _____

19 Maybe he was just trying to be nice.
➡ _____

20 When he said that to me, however, I started to think.
➡ _____

21 Can I really become a leader?
➡ _____

22 I don't know.
➡ _____

23 I think leaders should have a vision, clear goals, and the ability to motivate others.
➡ _____

24 I don't have any of those things.
➡ _____

25 Then I suddenly started to wonder if these are the only qualities that make a good leader.
➡ _____

26 Maybe I'm wrong.
➡ _____

27 Maybe there are other leadership qualities.
➡ _____

28 So I decided to do some research online.
➡ _____

29 Here's what I found!
➡ _____

30 GREEN LEADERS: "Team Builders"
➡ _____

31 Ensure that the team feels valued
➡ _____

32 Create a positive environment
➡ _____

33 Are friendly and easy to talk to
➡ _____

34 RED LEADERS: "Logical Analysts"
➡ _____

35 Have good reasoning skills
➡ _____

36 Analyze problems and situations
➡ _____

37 Think of the most effective ways to achieve the team's goals
➡ _____

38 PURPLE LEADERS: "Hands-Off Managers"
➡ _____

39 Allow others to work on their own
➡ _____

40 Do not try to control people
➡ _____

41 Give advice only when it is needed
➡ _____

42 ORANGE LEADERS: "Strict Directors"
➡️ _____

43 Make everyone's role clear
➡️ _____

44 Make sure everything is finished on time
➡️ _____

45 Ensure each step is done properly
➡️ _____

46 YELLOW LEADERS: "Quiet Supporters"
➡️ _____

47 Lead by example
➡️ _____

48 Let the team members shine instead
➡️ _____

49 Meet the team members' needs
➡️ _____

50 BLUE LEADERS: "Creative Thinkers"
➡️ _____

51 Approach problems in new ways
➡️ _____

52 Come up with fresh ideas
➡️ _____

53 Deal with tasks differently from others
➡️ _____

54 I was surprised that there are actually many different leadership styles, but soon I realized the reason.
➡️ _____

55 We belong to many different groups, and many different situations can come up in our lives.
➡️ _____

56 They all call for different leadership styles.
➡️ _____

57 Each group's unique situation determines the best leadership style.
➡️ _____

58 "I am a part of many different groups, and I have different responsibilities in each group."
➡️ _____

59 After reading everything, I became more confident.
➡️ _____

60 I discovered that I have some of the qualities of a "green leader."
➡️ _____

61 If my classmates think a green leader would make our class better, they might pick me to be class representative!
➡️ _____

62 Okay, let's try it!
➡️ _____

※ 다음 괄호 안의 단어들을 우리말에 맞도록 바르게 배열하시오.

1 (Are / We / Leaders / All)
➡ _____

2 (Brian: / election / the / coming / is / up.)
➡ _____

3 (don't / why / run / you / class / for / Yumi? / representative,)
➡ _____

4 (Yumi: / way. / no)
➡ _____

5 (not / I'm / right / the / for / person / position. / that)
➡ _____

6 (never / I've / thought / running. / about)
➡ _____

7 (Brain: / not? / why)
➡ _____

8 (Yumi: / on, / come / Brian.)
➡ _____

9 (have / leaders / qualities. / special)
➡ _____

10 (don't / I / a / think / like / person / me / be / can / called / leader. / a)
➡ _____

11 (Brian: / do / what / mean? / you)
➡ _____

12 (think / I / have / you / very / leadership / good / qualities.)
➡ _____

13 (really / you're / outgoing. / and / friendly)
➡ _____

14 (also / you / people / help / along. / get)
➡ _____

15 (have / I / doubt / no / you / that / be / will / elected / if / run. / you)
➡ _____

16 (told / Brian / this / me / afternoon / I / that / have / leadership / good / qualities.)
➡ _____

17 (one / no / ever / has / me / told / before. / that)
➡ _____

18 (does / why / think / he / so?)
➡ _____

19 (he / maybe / just / was / to / trying / nice. / be)
➡ _____

20 (he / when / that / said / me, / to / however, / started / I / think. / to)
➡ _____

1 우리는 모두 리더들이다

2 Brian: "선거가 다가오고 있어.

3 유미야, 반 대표에 입후보하는 게 어때?"

4 유미: "아니.

5 나는 그 자리에 적절한 사람이 아니야.

6 나는 입후보하는 것에 대해 생각해 본 적이 없어."

7 Brian: "왜?"

8 유미: "이봐, Brian.

9 리더들은 특별한 자질을 갖추고 있어.

10 나 같은 사람이 리더로 불릴 수 있다고 생각하지 않아."

11 Brian: "무슨 말이야?

12 내 생각에 너는 매우 좋은 지도력 자질들을 갖추고 있어.

13 너는 정말 친절하고 외향적이잖아.

14 또 너는 사람들이 어울리도록 도와주기도 해.

15 만약 네가 입후보한다면 당선될 거라고 믿어 의심치 않아."

16 Brian은 오늘 오후에 내게 내가 좋은 지도력 자질들을 갖추고 있다고 말했다.

17 이전에는 아무도 내게 그런 말을 한 적이 없었다.

18 왜 그는 그렇게 생각했을까?

19 아마도 그는 그저 친절하려고 했을 것이다.

20 그러나 그가 내게 그렇게 말했을 때, 나는 생각하기 시작했다.

21 (I / can / really / become / leader? / a)
➡ _____

22 (know. / don't / I)
➡ _____

23 (think / I / should / leaders / a / have / vision, / goals, / clear / and / ability / the / motivate / to / others.)
➡ _____

24 (don't / I / any / have / those / of / things.)
➡ _____

25 (I / then / started / suddenly / wonder / to / these / if / the / are / qualities / only / make / that / a / leader. / good)
➡ _____

26 (I'm / maybe / wrong.)
➡ _____

27 (there / maybe / other / are / qualities. / leadership)
➡ _____

28 (I / so / to / decided / some / do / online. / research)
➡ _____

29 (what / here's / found! / I)
➡ _____

30 (LEADERS: / GREEN / Builders" / "Team)
➡ _____

31 (that / ensure / the / feels / team / valued)
➡ _____

32 (a / creative / environment / positive)
➡ _____

33 (friendly / are / easy / and / talk / to / to)
➡ _____

34 (LEADERS: / RED / Analysts" / "Logical)
➡ _____

35 (good / have / skills / reasoning)
➡ _____

36 (problems / analyze / situations / and)
➡ _____

37 (of / think / most / the / effective / to / ways / the / achieve / goals / team's)
➡ _____

38 (LEADERS: / PURPLE / Managers" / "Hands-Off)
➡ _____

39 (others / allow / work / to / their / on / own)
➡ _____

40 (not / do / to / try / people / control)
➡ _____

41 (advice / give / when / only / is / it / needed.)
➡ _____

21 내가 정말 리더가 될 수 있을까?

22 나는 모르겠다.

23 나는 리더가 비전, 명확한 목표, 그리고 다른 사람들에게 동기를 부여할 능력을 가지고 있어야 한다고 생각한다.

24 나는 그러한 것들 중 어느 것도 가지고 있지 않다.

25 그때 나는 갑자기 이것들이 좋은 리더를 만드는 유일한 자질들인지 궁금해하기 시작했다.

26 아마도 내가 틀린지도 모른다.

27 어쩌면 다른 지도력 자질들이 있는지도 모른다.

28 그래서 나는 온라인으로 조사해 보기로 결심했다.

29 여기에 내가 찾은 것이 있다!

30 〈녹색 리더〉 '팀 조직자'

31 팀이 반드시 가치 있다고 느끼게 한다

32 긍정적인 환경을 조성한다

33 친절하고 말을 걸기 쉽다

34 〈빨간색 리더〉 '논리적 분석가'

35 좋은 추론 기술을 갖고 있다

36 문제와 상황들을 분석한다

37 팀의 목표를 성취하는 가장 효과적인 방법들을 생각한다

38 〈보라색 리더〉 '방임적 관리자'

39 다른 사람들이 스스로 일하도록 해 준다

40 사람들을 통제하려고 하지 않는다

41 필요할 때만 조언한다

42 (LEADERS: / ORANGE / Directors" / "Strict)
➡ _____

43 (everyone's / make / clear / role)
➡ _____

44 (sure / make / is / everything / on / finished / time)
➡ _____

45 (each / ensure / is / step / properly / done)
➡ _____

46 (LEADERS: / YELLOW / Supporters" / "Quiet)
➡ _____

47 (by / lead / example)
➡ _____

48 (the / let / members / team / instead / shine)
➡ _____

49 (the / meet / members's / team / needs)
➡ _____

50 (LEADERS: / BLUE / Thinkers" / "Creative)
➡ _____

51 (problems / approach / new / in / ways)
➡ _____

52 (up / come / fresh / with / ideas)
➡ _____

53 (with / deal / differently / tasks / others / from)
➡ _____

54 (was / I / surprised / there / that / actually / are / different / many / styles, / leadership / soon / but / realized / I / reason. / the)
➡ _____

55 (belong / we / many / to / groups, / different / many / and / situations / different / come / can / in / up / lives. / our)
➡ _____

56 (all / they / for / call / leadership / different / styles.)
➡ _____

57 (group's / each / situation / unique / the / determines / best / style. / leadership)
➡ _____

58 (am / "I / part / a / of / different / many / groups, / I / and / have / responsibilities / different / in / group." / each)
➡ _____

59 (reading / after / everything, / became / I / confident. / more)
➡ _____

60 (discovered / I / that / have / I / of / some / qualities / the / a / of / leader." / "green)
➡ _____

61 (my / if / think / classmates / green / a / would / leader / our / make / better, / class / might / they / me / pick / be / to / representative! / class)
➡ _____

62 (let's / okay, / it! / try)
➡ _____

본문 **Test 87**

※ **다음 우리말을 영어로 쓰시오.**

1 우리는 모두 리더들이다
➡ _____

2 Brian: "선거가 다가오고 있어.
➡ _____

3 유미야, 반 대표에 입후보하는 게 어때?"
➡ _____

4 유미: "아니.
➡ _____

5 나는 그 자리에 적절한 사람이 아니야.
➡ _____

6 나는 입후보하는 것에 대해 생각해 본 적이 없어."
➡ _____

7 Brian: "왜?"
➡ _____

8 유미: "이봐, Brian.
➡ _____

9 리더들은 특별한 자질을 갖추고 있어.
➡ _____

10 나 같은 사람이 리더로 불릴 수 있다고 생각하지 않아."
➡ _____

11 Brian: "무슨 말이야?
➡ _____

12 내 생각에 너는 매우 좋은 지도력 자질들을 갖추고 있어.
➡ _____

13 너는 정말 친절하고 외향적이잖아.
➡ _____

14 또 너는 사람들이 어울리도록 도와주기도 해.
➡ _____

15 만약 네가 입후보한다면 당선될 거라고 믿어 의심치 않아."
➡ _____

16 Brian은 오늘 오후에 내게 내가 좋은 지도력 자질들을 갖추고 있다고 말했다.
➡ _____

17 이전에는 아무도 내게 그런 말을 한 적이 없었다.
➡ _____

18 왜 그는 그렇게 생각했을까?
➡ _____

19 아마도 그는 그저 친절하려고 했을 것이다.
➡ _____

20 그러나 그가 내게 그렇게 말했을 때, 나는 생각하기 시작했다.
➡ _____

21 내가 정말 리더가 될 수 있을까?
➡ _____

22 나는 모르겠다.
➡ _____

23 나는 리더가 비전, 명확한 목표, 그리고 다른 사람들에게 동기를 부여할 능력을 가지고 있어야 한다고 생각한다.
➡ _____

24 나는 그러한 것들 중 어느 것도 가지고 있지 않다.
➡ _____

25 그때 나는 갑자기 이것들이 좋은 리더를 만드는 유일한 자질들인지 궁금해하기 시작했다.
➡ _____

26 아마도 내가 틀린지도 모른다.
➡ _____

27 어쩌면 다른 지도력 자질들이 있는지도 모른다.
➡ _____

28 그래서 나는 온라인으로 조사해 보기로 결심했다.
➡ _____

29 여기에 내가 찾은 것이 있다!
➡ _____

30 〈녹색 리더〉 '팀 조직자'
➡ _____

31 팀이 반드시 가치 있다고 느끼게 한다
➡ _____

32 긍정적인 환경을 조성한다
➡ _____

33 친절하고 말을 걸기 쉽다
➡ _____

34 〈빨간색 리더〉 '논리적 분석가'
➡ _____

35 좋은 추론 기술을 갖고 있다
➡ _____

36 문제와 상황들을 분석한다
➡ _____

37 팀의 목표를 성취하는 가장 효과적인 방법들을 생각한다
➡ _____

38 〈보라색 리더〉 '방임적 관리자'
➡ _____

39 다른 사람들이 스스로 일하도록 해 준다
➡ _____

40 사람들을 통제하려고 하지 않는다
➡ _____

41 필요할 때만 조언한다
➡ _____

42 〈주황색 리더〉 '엄격한 감독관'
➡ _____

43 모두의 역할을 분명하게 해 준다
➡ _____

44 모든 일을 제때 끝날 것을 확실히 한다
➡ _____

45 단계가 적절히 이행되도록 한다
➡ _____

46 〈노란색 리더〉 '조용한 지지자'
➡ _____

47 솔선수범한다
➡ _____

48 팀원들이 대신 빛나도록 해 준다
➡ _____

49 팀원들의 요구 사항을 충족한다
➡ _____

50 〈파란색 리더〉 '창조적 사상가'
➡ _____

51 새로운 방식으로 문제들에 접근한다
➡ _____

52 신선한 아이디어를 떠올린다
➡ _____

53 다른 사람들과 다르게 일을 처리한다
➡ _____

54 나는 실제로 서로 다른 많은 지도력 유형들이 있어서 놀랐지만, 곧 그 이유를 깨달았다.
➡ _____

55 우리는 서로 다른 여러 집단에 속하고, 우리 인생에서 서로 다른 많은 상황들이 발생할 수 있다.
➡ _____

56 그것들은 모두 서로 다른 지도력 유형들을 요구한다.
➡ _____

57 각 집단의 독특한 상황이 최고의 지도력 유형을 결정한다.
➡ _____

58 "나는 서로 다른 많은 집단의 일부이고, 각 집단에서 각각 다른 책임을 갖고 있어."
➡ _____

59 모든 것을 읽고 나서, 나는 더 자신감이 생겼다.
➡ _____

60 나는 '녹색 리더'의 자질들 중 일부분을 가지고 있다는 것을 알게 되었다.

61 만약 나의 반 친구들이 녹색 리더가 우리 학급을 더 좋게 만들 거라고 생각한다면, 그들은 학급 대표로 나를 뽑을지도 모른다!
➡ _____
_____

62 좋아, 시도해 보자!
➡ _____

※ 다음 우리말과 일치하도록 빈칸에 알맞은 말을 쓰시오.

Presentation Time Step 3

1. Our group _____ _____ _____ _____ _____ our class birthday party.

2. I _____ _____ a cake.

3. Woojin and Taeho _____ _____ _____ _____.

4. Yeji _____ _____ birthday _____ _____.

5. I have _____ _____ _____ our birthday party _____ _____ _____ _____ _____ fun!

After You Read B

1. Hi, I'm Jennifer. I try _____ _____ _____ _____ and _____ _____ _____ _____ _____.

2. The _____ _____ is _____ the members of my team _____.

3. Hello, I'm Heejin. I _____ _____ problems _____ _____ _____.

4. I _____ _____ _____ to _____ _____ _____ new ideas.

5. Hi, I'm Chris. I _____ my team's problems and _____, and then I _____ _____ the most _____ _____ _____ _____ _____ _____.

Do It Yourself B

1. Brian: _____ _____ _____ _____ _____ for class representative, Yumi?

2. Yumi: No way. I've _____ _____ _____ _____ _____.

3. Brian: _____ _____?

4. Yumi: Leaders _____ _____ _____.

5. I don't think _____ _____ _____ me _____ a leader.

6. Brian: _____ _____ you _____?

7. You're _____ _____ and _____.

8. You also _____ _____ _____ _____ _____.

9. I have _____ _____ that you _____ _____ _____ _____ if you _____.

1. 우리 모둠은 우리 학급 생일 파티를 준비하기 위한 과제를 선정했다.
2. 나는 케이크를 살 것이다.
3. 우진이와 태호는 교실을 장식할 것이다.
4. 예지는 생일 파티 노래를 연주할 것이다.
5. 나는 우리의 생일 파티가 아주 재미있을 것을 확신한다.

1. 안녕, 나는 Jennifer야. 나는 솔선수범하며 다른 사람들의 요구를 해결하려고 노력해.
2. 중요한 것은 우리 팀 구성원들이 빛나는 거야.
3. 안녕, 나는 희진이야. 나는 문제에 새로운 방법으로 접근하는 것이 즐거워.
4. 나는 최선을 다해서 새로운 아이디어를 제시해.
5. 안녕, 나는 Chris야. 나는 우리 팀의 문제점과 상황을 분석해. 그런 다음 우리의 목표를 달성하기 위한 가장 효과적인 방법들을 찾아.

1. Brian: 유미야, 반 대표에 입후보하는 게 어때?
2. Yumi: 아니. 나는 입후보하는 것에 대해 생각해 본 적이 없어.
3. Brian: 왜?
4. Yumi: 리더들은 특별한 자질을 갖추고 있어.
5. 나 같은 사람이 리더로 불릴 수 있다고 생각하지 않아.
6. Brian: 무슨 말이야?
7. 너는 정말 친절하고 외향적이잖아.
8. 또 너는 사람들이 어울리도록 도와주기도 해.
9. 만약 네가 입후보한다면 당선될 거라고 믿어 의심치 않아.

구석구석 지문 Test

※ **다음 우리말을 영어로 쓰시오.**

Presentation Time Step 3

1. 우리 모둠은 우리 학급 생일 파티를 준비하기 위한 과제를 선정했다.
   ➡ _____

2. 나는 케이크를 살 것이다.
   ➡ _____

3. 우진이와 태호는 교실을 장식할 것이다.
   ➡ _____

4. 예지는 생일 파티 노래를 연주할 것이다.
   ➡ _____

5. 나는 우리의 생일 파티가 아주 재미있을 것을 확신한다.
   ➡ _____

After You Read B

1. 안녕, 나는 Jennifer야. 나는 솔선수범하며 다른 사람들의 요구를 해결하려고 노력해.
   ➡ _____

2. 중요한 것은 우리 팀 구성원들이 빛나는 거야.
   ➡ _____

3. 안녕, 나는 희진이야. 나는 문제에 새로운 방법으로 접근하는 것이 즐거워.
   ➡ _____

4. 나는 최선을 다해서 새로운 아이디어를 제시해.
   ➡ _____

5. 안녕, 나는 Chris야. 나는 우리 팀의 문제점과 상황을 분석해. 그런 다음 우리의 목표를 달성하기 위한 가장 효과적인 방법들을 찾아.
   ➡ _____
   _____

Do It Yourself B

1. Brian: 유미야, 반 대표에 입후보하는 게 어때?
   ➡ _____

2. Yumi: 아니. 나는 입후보하는 것에 대해 생각해 본 적이 없어.
   ➡ _____

3. Brian: 왜?
   ➡ _____

4. Yumi: 리더들은 특별한 자질을 갖추고 있어.
   ➡ _____

5. 나 같은 사람이 리더로 불릴 수 있다고 생각하지 않아.
   ➡ _____

6. Brian: 무슨 말이야?
   ➡ _____

7. 너는 정말 친절하고 외향적이잖아.
   ➡ _____

8. 또 너는 사람들이 어울리도록 도와주기도 해.
   ➡ _____

9. 만약 네가 입후보한다면 당선될 거라고 믿어 의심치 않아.
   ➡ _____

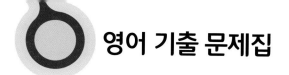

영어 기출 문제집

1학기

정답 및 해설

능률 | 김성곤

중 3

Lesson 1

A Life Full of Experiences

시험대비 실력평가
p.08

01 ②　　02 ①　　03 ③　　04 ①
05 ②　　06 meaningful

01 내용상 '~에 익숙해지다'에 해당하는 'get used to'가 적절하다.

02 '벽에 붙은 길고 평평한 좁은 판자'는 '선반(shelf)'을 가리킨다.

03 산꼭대기까지 올라가는 것은 중간에 포기하지 않는 것을 의미한다. look up 찾아보다 run up 늘리다 give up 포기하다 hang up 전화를 끊다 fill up 채우다

04 'own'은 '자기 자신의'라는 의미로 소유격을 강조한다.

05 ① practice 연습하다 ② changed 바꾸다 ③ familiar 친숙한 ④ match 경기, 시합 ⑤ suggest 제안하다

06 명사 experiences를 수식하는 형용사 meaningful이 적절하다.

서술형 시험대비
p.09

01 memorize　02 (1) case　(2) confident
(3) motivated　(4) watching　03 requirement
04 (f)inish　05 get
06 (1) joined　(2) talents　(3) review　(4) subtitles
(5) experiences

01 memory: 기억 memorize: 암기하다

02 (1) 어쨌든 = in any case (2) confident 자신감 있는 (3) 동기 부여된 = motivated (4) ~을 시도해 보다 = try ~ing

03 학생들은 '학교의 요구 사항' 때문에 새로운 언어를 배운다. require 요구하다 requirements 요구 사항, 의무

04 주어진 단어는 동의어 관계이다. finish 끝내다 complete 완성하다

05 • 너는 다른 문화에 익숙해져야 한다. get used to ~ ~에 익숙해지다 • 중국어 자막이 있는 중국 드라마를 보는 것은 듣기를 더 잘하게 되는 좋은 방법이다. get better at ~ ~을 더 잘하게 되다

06 (1) 가입했다 = joined (2) 재능 = talent (3) 평론 = review (4) 자막 = subtitle (5) 새로운 경험 new experiences

📕교과서 Conversation

핵심 Check
p.10~11

1 What, like　　2 (C) → (A) → (B)
3 ③

03 '스케이트보드를 어떻게 배웠느냐?'는 질문에 (B) 클럽에 가입해서 배웠다고 대답하고 (C) '그것이 마음에 드니?'라고 물어보자 (A) '그것이 재미있고 친구를 사귀는 데 도움이 된다.'고 대답한다.

교과서 대화문 익히기

Check(√) True or False
p.12

1 F　2 T　3 T　4 F　5 F

교과서 확인학습
p.14~15

Listen & Talk 1 B
would, like / like, learn, listened, was struck, sound / Where, going, good, player, ask

Listen & Talk 1 C
What, doing / writing, things that, do / What, like / first, like, spend, volunteering, during / sounds / What about, What, like / thinking, taking, class / cool

Listen & Talk 2 B
What, holding / skateboard, skateboarding / know that, How, learn, skateboard / joined, local, last month / see, how, like / really, helps, make / go skateboarding, members, share tips

Listen & Talk 2 C
make, shelf yourself, amazing / started making furniture / How, like / hard, love, feel, confident, making / great, really good at / guess, found, talent, good, try / Exactly, Having, experiences, find

Listen & Talk 2 D
ran, race / How, like / liked, helped, confidence

Presentation Time Step 1
tell, one, meaningful / cooked, for / How, like / not easy, that, make, happy, cooking

Presentation Time Step 3
recommends cooking, meaningful experience because, cooking, others, make, experience, feel

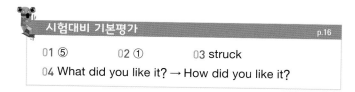

Do It Yourself A

performed, festival / How, like / wasn't bad, made, mistakes / sounded fine / for saying, playing, front / feel / nervous, felt / awesome, so proud

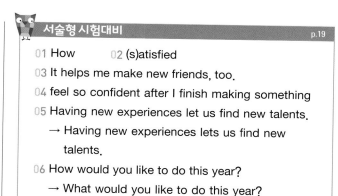

서술형 시험대비   p.19

01 How   02 (s)atisfied

03 It helps me make new friends, too.

04 feel so confident after I finish making something

05 Having new experiences let us find new talents.
   → Having new experiences lets us find new talents.

06 How would you like to do this year?
   → What would you like to do this year?

01 스케이트보드를 배운 방법을 묻고 있어서 how가 적절하다.

02 만족을 물어보는 'How do you like it?'은 'Are you satisfied with it?'으로 바꾸어 쓸 수 있다.

03 새로운 친구를 사귀다 = make new friends

04 매우 자신감을 느낀다 = feel so confident 무엇인가를 만들고 난 후 = after I finish making something

05 주어가 동명사이므로 단수 동사로 받는다.

06 상대가 바라는 것을 물어볼 때는 'What would you like to do?'라고 물어본다.

시험대비 기본평가   p.16

01 ⑤   02 ①   03 struck

04 What did you like it? → How did you like it?

01 밑줄 친 부분은 상대방에게 만족이나 불만족에 대해 묻는 표현이다.

02 would you like 다음에는 to부정사가 온다.

03 수동태이므로 strike의 과거분사 struck가 적절하다.

04 만족을 물어볼 때는 'How did you like it?'이라고 한다.

시험대비 실력평가   p.17~18

01 ③   02 ②   03 ⑤   04 ②

05 ⑤   06 ③   07 ②

08 I'm so proud of you.   09 ⑤   10 ④

11 ③

01 Bill이 요리한 경험을 만족스러워하는지를 물어보는 것이 이어지는 대답과 자연스럽게 연결된다.

02 주어진 문장은 'I learned that I could make people happy with my cooking.'이다.

03 ⑤ Lina가 Bill에게 질문한 이유는 이 대화에서 언급되지 않았다.

04 자신이 가지고 있는 것이 skateboard라고 소개하는 것으로 보아 '들고 있는 것'에 대한 질문이 있었다고 생각할 수 있다.

05 ① skateboarding을 배우는 것은 수지이고, 수지는 club에서 배워서, 클럽 회원들과 tip을 공유한다.

06 이 글의 필자는 학교 축제에서 드럼을 연주했다.

07 앞에 나온 내용에 대하여 감사하다는 반응을 보이는 것으로 보아 칭찬하는 내용이 적절하다.

08 자랑스러워하다 = be proud of, take pride in

09 소년이 연주에서 실수를 했다는 것은 나와 있지만 정확하게 몇 번인지는 나와 있지 않다.

10 ④ 상대방의 의견이나 의도를 물어보는 말로 'What about you?'가 자연스럽다.

11 상대방이 잘한다고 생각하면서 '안됐다.'고 말하는 것은 어색하다. 'That's great.'가 적절하다.

교과서

Grammar

핵심 Check   p.20~21

1 (1) studying   (2) liked   (3) celebrating
2 (1) what   (2) what   (3) What

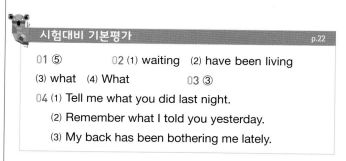

시험대비 기본평가   p.22

01 ⑤   02 (1) waiting   (2) have been living
(3) what   (4) What   03 ③

04 (1) Tell me what you did last night.
   (2) Remember what I told you yesterday.
   (3) My back has been bothering me lately.

01 the thing(s) which[that]는 선행사를 포함하는 관계대명사 what으로 바꿔 쓸 수 있다.

02 (1) 한 시간 동안 계속 그녀를 기다리고 있는 것이므로 현재완료진행형이 적절하다. (2) 10년 동안 살아오고 있는 것이므로 현재완료진행형이 적절하다. (3) is의 보어와 bought의 목적어 역할을 할 수 있는 what이 적절하다. (4) do의 목적어와 is의 주어 역할을 할 수 있는 what이 적절하다.

03 그저께부터 눈이 오기 시작하여 현재까지 계속 진행되고 있으므로 현재완료진행형이 적절하다.

04 (1), (2) the thing(s) which[that]로 쓰일 수 있는 선행사를 포함하는 관계대명사 what을 이용한다. (3) 과거의 어느 때부터 시작되어 현재까지 계속 진행되고 있음을 나타내는 현재완료진행형을 이용한다.

01 ④   **02** ③   **03** ⑤

04 (1) been wearing   (2) for   (3) since   (4) what
     (5) that   **05** ①

06 ②   **07** ④   **08** that → what

09 Prices have been increasing steadily for months.

10 ②, ③   **11** ④   **12** ③   **13** ⑤

14 ③

15 (1) The man has been taking care of the children for a few years.
     (2) Melina taught English at the school two years ago.
     (3) She has been reading a book since 3 p.m..
     (4) Ron has been watching the play for two hours.
     (5) This is the movie which[that] I want to see.
     (6) Let me look at what you took with your camera in Canada.

16 ④   **17** ②, ③   **18** ⑤

01 ① He has been planting apple trees since 2010. ② I've been looking for this book for an hour. ③ Megan has been writing letters all day long. ⑤ He has been reading the book for about two hours.

02 understand와 says의 목적어 역할을 할 수 있도록 that을 what으로 고쳐야 한다.

03 8살 이래로 계속 발레를 배워 오고 있는 것이므로 현재완료진행형이 적절하다. 동사 is의 보어와 bought의 목적어 역할을 할 수 있는 것은 what이다.

04 (1) 현재완료진행형은 'have[has] been+동사원형-ing'의 형태이다. (2), (3) 현재완료진행형에서 since는 '시간'을 나타내는 명사(구)와 함께 쓰이고 for는 '기간'을 나타내는 명사(구)와 함께 쓰인다. (4) eat의 목적어가 없으므로 what이 이끄는 절이 sell의 목적어가 되도록 해야 한다. (5) 선행사 all이 있으므로 관계대명사 that이 적절하다. all을 없애고, what만 써도 어법상 바른 문장이다.

05 for의 목적어와 is의 주어 역할을 할 수 있는 What이 적절하다.

06 현재완료진행형에서 since는 '시간'을 나타내는 명사(구)와 함께

쓰이고, for는 '기간'을 나타내는 명사(구)와 함께 쓰인다.

07 현재완료진행형은 'have[has] been+동사원형-ing'의 형태이며 과거를 나타내는 어구와 함께 쓰이지 않는다. ②번은 know가 진행형으로 쓰이지 않는 동사임에 유의한다.

08 what is called: 소위, 이른바

09 현재완료진행형을 이용하여 쓴다.

10 what이 관계대명사인지 의문사인지 구분하는 문제로 보통 의문사 what은 '무엇을, 무엇이 ~인(한)지'로, 관계대명사 what은 '~하는 것'으로 해석한다. ① 의문대명사 ② 관계대명사 ③ 관계대명사 ④ 의문대명사 ⑤ 의문대명사

11 과거 어느 때부터 시작되어 현재까지 계속 진행되고 있음을 나타내는 현재완료진행형이 적절하다.

12 ③번은 선행사(the person)가 있으므로 who나 that이 들어가야 하고, 나머지는 선행사가 없으므로 what이 적절하다.

13 the things which[that]의 역할을 하는 what을 이용하여 나타내도록 한다.

14 내용상 현재완료진행형(have[has] been+동사원형-ing)을 이용한다.

15 (1) 현재완료진행형은 'have[has] been+동사원형-ing'의 형태이다. (2) 현재완료진행형은 과거를 나타내는 어구와 함께 쓰이지 않는다. (3), (4) 현재완료진행형에서 since는 '시간'을 나타내는 명사(구)와 함께 쓰이고 for는 '기간'을 나타내는 명사(구)와 함께 쓰인다. (5) the movie가 선행사로 나왔으므로 what이 아니라 which나 that을 써야 한다. (6) look at과 took의 목적어 역할을 할 수 있는 what으로 고쳐야 한다.

16 ① 현재완료진행형은 과거를 나타내는 어구와 함께 쓰이지 않는다. ④ the book이라는 선행사가 있으므로 what을 that으로 고쳐야 한다.

17 understand와 said의 목적어 역할을 할 수 있는 what이 적절하며 what은 the thing(s) that으로 바꿔 쓸 수 있다.

18 선행사가 없고 to의 목적어와 is의 주어 역할을 해야 하므로 관계대명사 what이 적절하다.

01 (1) Oliver has been waiting for his friend since one o'clock.
     (2) James has been doing yoga for an hour.
     (3) I have been taking tennis lessons over the last 5 years.

02 (1) You don't think that I know what you're doing.
     (2) What I want to do most is to go to a concert.
     (3) They have been thinking of him as an Italian for years.

03 (1) What she wants to receive
   (2) what I want to
04 (1) for   (2) since
05 (1) Find what keeps you motivated.
   (2) It made me think what I liked.
   (3) What you said made me surprised.
   (4) What is done cannot be undone.
06 (1) lived → living   (2) since → for   (3) for → since
   (4) That → What   (5) that → what   (6) what → that
   (7) That → What
07 (1) Harold has been reading the book since this
   morning.
   (2) Taehee has been talking on the phone for two
   hours.
08 (1) They have been living here for four
   generations.
   (2) Scientists have been studying Saturn's rings.
   (3) The movie has been showing for three months.
   (4) Don't forget what you promised the other day.

01 과거에 시작하여 지금까지 계속되고 있는 것이므로 현재완료진
   행형을 이용한다.
02 (1)~(2) 선행사를 포함하는 관계대명사 what을 이용하여 배열
   한다. what이 선행사를 포함하므로 문장에서 두 가지의 역할을
   함에 유의한다. (3) 과거 어느 때부터 시작되어 현재까지 계속
   진행되고 있음을 나타내는 현재완료진행형 구문을 이용한다.
03 선행사를 포함하는 관계대명사 what을 이용한다.
04 (1) 현재완료진행형에서 since는 '시간'을 나타내는 명사(구)와
   함께 쓰이고, for는 '기간'을 나타내는 명사(구)와 함께 쓰인다.
05 the thing(s) which[that]의 역할을 하는 what을 이용하여
   하나의 문장으로 쓴다.
06 (1) 계속 살아오고 있는 것이므로 현재완료진행형으로 나타낸다.
   (2), (3) 현재완료진행형에서 since는 '시간'을 나타내는 명사(구)
   와 함께 쓰이고 for는 '기간'을 나타내는 명사 (구)와 함께 쓰인다.
   (4) do의 목적어와 is의 주어 역할을 해야 하므로 That을 What
   으로 고친다. (5) tell의 직접목적어와 saw의 목적어 역할을 할 수
   있도록 that을 what으로 고친다. (6) the only one이라는 선행
   사가 있으므로 what을 that으로 고친다. (7) did의 목적어와 was
   의 주어 역할을 해야 하므로 That을 What으로 고친다.
07 과거 어느 때부터 시작되어 현재까지 계속 진행되고 있음을 나
   타내는 현재완료진행형으로 쓰고, 현재완료진행형에서 since는
   '시간'을 나타내는 명사(구)와 함께 쓰이고 for는 '기간'을 나타
   내는 명사(구)와 함께 쓰인다.
08 (1)~(3) 과거 어느 때부터 시작되어 현재까지 계속 진행되고 있
   음을 나타내는 현재완료진행형을 이용한다. (4) forget의 목적
   어와 promise의 목적어 역할을 할 수 있는 what을 이용한다.

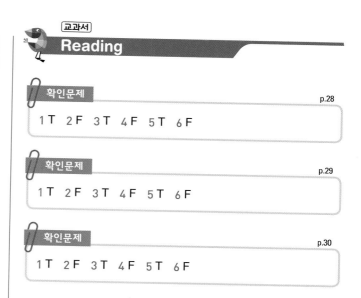

Reading

확인문제   p.28
1 T   2 F   3 T   4 F   5 T   6 F

확인문제   p.29
1 T   2 F   3 T   4 F   5 T   6 F

확인문제   p.30
1 T   2 F   3 T   4 F   5 T   6 F

교과서 확인학습 A   p.31~33

01 a New Language   02 Foreign Languages
03 because of school requirements
04 for fun   05 In any case
06 listen to their ideas   07 Love
08 a big fan
09 understand interviews
10 However, Spanish that well
11 improve my Spanish   12 to practice it
13 have changed the language, have been writing
14 become familiar with   15 suggest watching
16 get used to   17 try watching
18 are used
19 soccer vocabulary, memorize
20 why don't you, in Spanish
21 improve your writing skills
22 No More   23 is back
24 so excited   25 just perfect
26 without subtitles, translations
27 Any tips   28 are interested in
29 one another
30 translate, sing together
31 Doing, improves our Korean
32 on social media   33 post short messages
34 with the messages, more easily
35 recommend watching   36 I've been watching
37 for help with listening 38 print out the subtitles
39 Works
40 hundreds of, their own way
41 what, motivated
42 at first, much bigger

1 Learn a New Language, Find a New World

2 Why Do People Learn Foreign Languages?

3 Many students learn new languages because of school requirements.

4 Many others learn them for fun.

5 In any case, students everywhere have found interesting ways to study new languages.

6 Let's meet these students and listen to their ideas.

7 I Love Soccer!

8 I'm a big fan of a Spanish soccer team.

9 I want to understand interviews with my favorite players.

10 However, it's not easy because I don't know Spanish that well.

11 How can I improve my Spanish? – Owen, 16

12 The best way to learn a new language is to practice it every day.

13 I have changed the language of my phone to Spanish, and I have been writing my shopping lists in Spanish! – Julie, 15

14 What's most important is to become familiar with the language first.

15 I suggest watching Spanish movies often.

16 It will help you get used to the sound of the language.

17 If the people talk too fast, try watching Spanish children's movies first. – Inho, 14

18 Some words are used only in soccer, not in everyday life.

19 Learn some soccer vocabulary and memorize it.

20 Also, why don't you try writing a review of a match in Spanish?

21 It will help you improve your writing skills. – Rohan, 16

22 No More Subtitles!

23 DREAM4 is back!

24 I'm so excited to see my favorite Korean boy band perform.

25 Their singing and their dancing are just perfect.

26 I want to understand their songs without subtitles or translations though.

27 Any tips? – Marisa, 14

28 You should find friends who are interested in DREAM4 and start a club.

29 In my club, we motivate one another.

30 We translate songs and sing together.

31 Doing these things is fun and really improves our Korean! – Lori, 15

32 Follow DREAM4 on social media.

33 They often post short messages in Korean about how they are doing.

34 They also post pictures with the messages, so you can understand the posts more easily. – Aishah, 14

35 I recommend watching Korean dramas.

36 I've been watching Korean dramas for a year, and they're really interesting!

37 You can use Korean subtitles for help with listening.

38 It's also a good idea to print out the subtitles and read them first. – Brandon, 16

39 What Works for You?

40 There are hundreds of good tips out there, but everyone has their own way of learning.

41 Find what keeps you motivated; then you will enjoy learning more.

42 Remember, every language is hard at first, but a new language can make your world much bigger!

01 What

02 It will help you improve your writing skills.

03 ②   04 ②   05 ①   06 ②, ④

07 (A) Why (B) because of (C) found

08 new languages   09 ④

10 how they are doing   11 ⑤

12 comments → pictures

13 (A) following (B) Korean dramas   14 ③, ④

15 are used   16 ③   17 to do   18 ⑤

19 ③   20 ②, ⑤   21 ④

22 (A) school requirements (B) for fun

23 ②   24 ①, ④ / ②, ⑤   25 ②

26 ⓐ: ①, ②, ④ ⓑ: ③, ⑤   27 If you   28 ⑤

29 Spanish   30 ②

01 선행사를 포함한 관계대명사 What을 쓰는 것이 적절하다.

02 help는 5형식 문장에서 목적격보어에 to부정사나 원형부정사를 둘 다 쓸 수 있는 준사역동사이지만, 8단어로 영작하라고 했으므로 원형부정사를 쓰는 것이 적절하다.

03 이 글은 스페인어 구사 능력을 향상시키는 법에 관해 조언하는 글이므로, 주제로는 ②번이 적절하다.

04 앞에 나오는 내용과 상반되는 내용이 뒤에 이어지므로

However가 가장 적절하다. ① 그러므로, ③ 게다가, ④ 즉, 다시 말해, ⑤ 예를 들어

05 ①: 스페인의(형용사), ②~⑤: 스페인어(명사)

06 ⓑ와 ②, ④: 계속 용법, ①, ⑤: 경험 용법, ③: 완료 용법

07 (A) 이 글은 사람들이 외국어를 배우는 이유를 설명하는 글이므로, '왜' 사람들은 외국어를 배우는가 적절하다. (B) because+절(주어+동사), because of+명사구, (C) 흥미로운 방법들을 '찾아낸다'고 해야 하므로 found가 적절하다. find-found-found: 찾다, found-founded-founded: 설립하다

08 '새로운 언어들'을 가리킨다.

09 '모든 곳의 학생들은 새로운 언어를 공부하는 데 흥미로운 방법들을 찾아낸다. 이 학생들을 만나서 그들의 생각을 들어보자.'라고 했으므로, ④번이 적절하다.

10 간접의문문(의문사+주어+동사)의 순서로 쓰는 것이 적절하다.

11 ⓐ와 ⑤: 가주어, ① 비인칭 주어(거리), ② 가목적어, ③ 문장의 어떤 부분을 강조할 때 쓰는 대명사, ④ 비인칭 주어(막연한 상황)

12 DREAM4의 멤버들은 메시지와 함께 '사진들'을 올려서 당신은 더 쉽게 게시물을 이해할 수 있다. comment: 논평, 해설, 설명

13 아이샤는 소셜 미디어에서 DREAM4를 '팔로할' 것을 추천하고, 브랜던은 '한국 드라마들'을 볼 것을 추천한다. recommend는 동명사를 목적어로 취한다.

14 (A)와 ③, ④: 관계대명사, ① 의문형용사(무슨), 어떤, ② 감탄문에 쓰인 의문형용사(얼마나), ⑤ 의문대명사(무엇)

15 어떤 단어들은 일상생활에서가 아니라 오직 축구에서만 '쓰인다'고 해야 하므로, 수동태로 쓰는 것이 적절하다.

16 이 글은 마리사가 자막이나 번역이 없이 DREAM4의 노래를 이해하려고 조언을 구하는 내용이므로, 제목으로는 ③번 '더는 자막 없이!'가 적절하다.

17 진주어를 to부정사로 바꿔 쓰는 것이 적절하다.

18 로리의 모임에 몇 명의 회원이 있는지는 대답할 수 없다. ① Because she can see her favorite Korean boy band perform. ② DREAM4. ③ No. ④ She recommends that Marisa should start a club with friends who are also interested in DREAM4.

19 ⓐ와 ①, ②, ④, ⑤: 어쨌든, ③ by the way: 그런데(대화에서 화제를 바꿀 때 씀)

20 ⓑ와 ②, ⑤: 형용사적 용법, ①, ③: 부사적 용법, ④: 명사적 용법

21 이 글은 사람들이 외국어를 배우는 이유를 설명하는 글이므로, 제목으로는 ④번 '왜 사람들은 외국어를 배울까?'가 적절하다.

22 많은 학생들이 '학교 필수 수업'이기 때문에 혹은 '재미를 위해' 새로운 언어를 배운다.

23 ⓐ change A to B: A를 B로 바꾸다, ⓑ in: 언어, 재료 등을 나타냄

24 (A)와 ①, ④: 형용사적 용법, (B)와 ②, ⑤: 명사적 용법, ③: 부사적 용법

25 오언은 자신이 정말 좋아하는 선수들의 인터뷰를 이해하고 싶지만, 스페인어를 그렇게 잘 알지 못하기 때문에 그것이 쉽지 않다고 했다.

26 ⓐ와 ①, ②, ④: 동명사, ⓑ와 ③, ⑤: 현재분사

27 명령문, and ~ = If you …로 고칠 수 있다. ⓒ의 경우, 세미콜론이 and의 뜻을 나타낸다.

28 very는 원급을 강조하는 말이고, 나머지는 다 비교급을 강조한다.

29 soccer team을 수식하는 형용사 Spanish로 쓰는 것이 적절하다. Spanish: 스페인의(형용사)

30 주어진 문장의 However에 주목한다. ②번 앞에 나오는 내용과 상반되는 내용이 However 뒤에 이어지므로 ②번이 적절하다.

🦉 서술형 시험대비   p.42~43

01 to understand interviews with my favorite players
02 have been writing
03 (A) soccer   (B) understand   (C) Spanish
04 what
05 (A) interesting   (B) read   (C) motivated
06 (A) Korean subtitles   (B) printing out   (C) reading
07 to watch → watching   08 get used to the sound
09 (A) soccer vocabulary   (B) in Spanish
10 (A) is   (B) are   (C) is
11 Translating songs and singing together
12 motivate

01 '내가 정말 좋아하는 선수들의 인터뷰를 이해하는 것'을 가리킨다.

02 과거에 시작된 일이 현재에도 계속 진행 중임을 나타낼 때 쓰이는 현재완료 진행형으로 쓰는 것이 적절하다.

03 흥미: 스페인 '축구' 팀, 원하는 것: 선수들의 인터뷰를 '이해하기', 유용한 조언: 매일 '스페인어'를 연습하기

04 선행사를 포함한 관계대명사 what을 쓰는 것이 적절하다.

05 (A) 감정을 나타내는 동사는 감정을 유발할 때 현재분사를 쓰는 것이 적절하므로 interesting이 적절하다. (B) 진주어 to print와 병렬 구문이 되도록 (to) read로 쓰는 것이 적절하다. (C) 당신이 계속 '동기 부여가 되는 것'이므로 motivated가 적절하다.

06 그는 듣기에 도움이 되도록 '한국어 자막'을 사용할 것과 맨 먼저 자막들을 '출력해서' '읽을' 것을 추천한다.

07 suggest는 목적어로 to부정사가 아니라 동명사를 취하는 동사이다.

08 get used to: ~에 익숙해지다

09 로한은 오언에게 몇몇 '축구 어휘들'을 배우고 기억할 것을 제안한다. 로한은 또한 '스페인어로' 경기에 대한 후기를 써 볼 것을

7

제안한다.

10 (A) DREAM4는 밴드의 이름이므로 단수 취급하여 is가, (B) 주어가 Their singing and their dancing이므로 are가, (C) 주어가 동명사 Doing이므로 is가 적절하다.

11 '함께 노래를 번역하고 노래하는 것'을 가리킨다. Doing에 맞춰 동명사 형태로 답하는 것이 적절하다.

12 로리와 그녀의 친구들은 한국어를 배우고 실력을 향상시키려고 각각의 모임 친구에게 '동기를 부여하고', 함께 노래를 번역하고 노래한다. 영영풀이: 동기를 제공하다

영역별 핵심문제
p.45~49

01 ②   02 ⑤   03 ①
04 (1) spend   (2) through   05 ①   06 ②
07 I'm thinking of taking a swimming class.
08 What
09 I was struck by the sound of the guitar.
10 ③   11 ⑤   12 ⑤   13 ①
14 ④   15 ①, ③, ④   16 has been cooking for
17 (1) what she painted
    (2) his son what looked really nice
    (3) believe what they want to believe
18 ②   19 ⓒ, ⓓ, ⓕ   20 ④
21 The best way to learn a new language is to
    practice it every day.
22 ①   23 ①, ⑤   24 ③   25 ③
26 with → without
27 pictures with the messages
28 ago, watching
29 ⓑ Korean dramas
    ⓒ to print out the subtitles and read them first

01 주어진 단어는 동의어 관계이다. improve 개선하다 – develop 발달시키다 complete 완성하다 finish 끝내다 recommend 추천하다 translate 번역하다 perform 공연하다

02 새로운 언어를 배우는 방법으로 축구를 좋아하는 경우 축구에 사용되는 어휘를 배워서 그것을 암기하는 것이다.

03 바람을 물어보는 표현은 'would like to'를 사용하는 것이 자연스럽다.

04 (1) (시간을) 쓰다 = spend (2) ~을 통해서 = through

05 이어지는 대답에 앞으로 할 일이 나와 있는 것으로 보아 앞으로의 바람이나 계획을 묻는 질문이 적절하다.

06 자신의 바람을 말하고 이어서 상대의 바람을 묻는 대화이므로 '너는 어떠니?'에 해당하는 'What about you?'가 적절하다.

07 나는 ~을 생각하고 있다: I am thinking of ~, 수영 수업을 받는 것: taking a swimming class

08 앞으로의 바람을 묻는 질문은 'What would you like to ~?' 이다.

09 나는 ~에 감동을 받았다. = I was struck by ~., 기타 소리 = the sound of the guitar

10 ③ 소년이 듣고 감동을 받은 노래는 'Cavatina'이었다.

11 (C) 의미 있는 경험을 묻는 말에 요리한 경험으로 대답하고, (B) 그 대답을 듣고 만족하는지를 묻고 (A) 거기에 대한 대답으로 자신이 배운 것을 말한다.

12 스케이트보드 클럽에 가입했다는 내용으로 보아 스케이트보드 타는 방법을 어떻게 배웠는지를 묻는 질문이 적절하다.

13 상대방이 마음에 드는지를 물어볼 때는 'How did you like that?'이라고 한다.

14 현재완료진행형에서 since는 '시간'을 나타내는 명사(구)와 함께 쓰이고, for는 '기간'을 나타내는 명사(구)와 함께 쓰인다.

15 ① Please tell me what you bought for Jane's birthday. ③ My mom has been growing vegetables since last year. 또는 My mom grew vegetables last year. ④ Long time ago, they believed that the earth was flat.

16 과거 어느 때부터 시작되어 현재까지 계속 진행되고 있음을 나타내는 현재완료진행형을 이용한다. '기간'을 나타내는 an hour 가 있으므로 for를 쓴다.

17 선행사를 포함한 관계대명사 what(= the thing(s) which[that])을 이용한다.

18 ②에는 know의 목적어가 되는 명사절을 이끄는 that이 적절하다. 나머지는 모두 what이 적절하다.

19 ⓐ what → that ⓑ that → what ⓔ for → since ⓖ has been snowing → snowed 또는 last week → since last week

20 ⓐ와 ④: 지시부사(수량·정도를 나타내는 형용사·부사를 수식한다.) ① 지시대명사, ② 관계대명사, ③, ⑤: 접속사

21 The best way를 주어로 해서 쓰는 것이 적절하다.

22 ⓐ become familiar with: ~와 친해지다 ⓑ get used to: ~에 익숙해지다

23 (A)와 ②, ③, ④: 동명사, ①, ⑤: 현재분사

24 만약 사람들이 너무 빨리 말한다면, 어린이를 위한 스페인 영화들을 먼저 보는 것을 시도해 보라고 했다.

25 ⓐ와 ③, ⑤: 부사적 용법, ①, ④: 형용사적 용법, ②: 명사적 용법

26 자막이나 번역이 '없이' 그들의 노래를 이해하고 싶다고 해야 하므로 without이 적절하다.

27 그들은 또한 '메시지와 함께 사진들을' 올려서 당신은 더 쉽게 게시물을 이해할 수 있다.

28 현재완료진행형은 과거에 시작된 일이 현재에도 계속 진행 중임을 나타낼 때 쓴다.

29 ⓑ '한국 드라마들', ⓒ It은 가주어로서 진주어인 to부정사 이하의 내용을 가리킨다.

01 ①   **02** ⑤   **03** ①

04 I think you're really good at it.

05 Having new experiences lets us to find new talents. → Having new experiences lets us find new talents.

06 What would you like to do this year?   **07** ④

08 ②   **09** ①   **10** ④, ⑤   **11** what

12 ②   **13** ③   **14** ②

15 ⓑ Spanish   ⓓ some soccer vocabulary

16 but   **17** who[that]   **18** ③

19 improve → improves

20 He has been watching them for a year.

21 ⑤   **22** ②

23 (1) to try Andong-jjimdak

(2) to make my own Hahoe mask and learn how to dance the *talchum*

(3) to visit Hahoe Village

24 ③

01 주어진 단어는 반의어 관계이다. weakness 약점 strength 강점 remember 기억하다 forget 잊어버리다 realize 깨닫다 motivate 동기부여하다 join 가입하다 convince 확신시키다

02 ⑤ 'having some mistakes, faults, or damage'는 '실수, 결점, 손상이 있는'이라는 뜻으로 '불완전한'에 해당한다.

03 G의 물음을 보아 이 대화에서는 가구 만들기가 주제인 것을 알 수 있다.

04 be good at ~ = ~을 잘하다

05 사역동사 let의 목적격보어는 원형부정사이다.

06 '무엇을 하고 싶니?' = 'What would you like to do?'

07 "I'm thinking of taking a swimming class."를 보면 소년은 올해 수영을 배우고 싶어한다는 것을 알 수 있다.

08 ① 이번 주에 소년이 무엇을 할지는 언급되지 않았다. ② 소녀는 여름 방학에 자원봉사를 가려고 한다. ③ 소년이 소녀의 계획을 묻는 이유는 나오지 않았다. ④ 대화의 장소는 알 수 없다. ⑤ 자원봉사 가는 방법은 언급되지 않았다.

09 첫 번째 문장에서는 두 개의 is의 주어 역할을 할 수 있는 관계대명사 what이 적절하다. 두 번째 문장에서는 3 p.m.이라는 시간을 나타내는 명사가 있으므로 since가 적절하다.

10 ① It has been snowing for three days. ② She cleaned her room last night. ③ He has been building his house for two months.

11 관계대명사 what은 선행사를 포함한 관계대명사로 the thing(s) which[that]를 나타낸다.

12 현재완료진행형은 과거의 명백한 시점을 나타내는 ago와 함께 쓰이지 않는다.

13 현재완료진행형은 'have[has] been+동사원형-ing'의 형태로 어떤 상태나 행위가 과거 어느 때부터 시작되어 현재까지 계속 진행되고 있음을 나타내거나, 현재까지 계속적으로 반복되고 있다는 것을 나타낸다.

14 ⓐ와 ①, ⑤: 명사적 용법, ②: 형용사적 용법, ③, ④: 부사적 용법

15 ⓑ '스페인어', ⓓ '몇몇의 축구 어휘'를 가리킨다.

16 not A but B = B, not A: A가 아니라 B

17 선행사 friends를 수식하는 주격 관계대명사 who[that]를 쓰는 것이 적절하다.

18 (A)와 ③: (문장 끝이나 중간에서 단독으로) 그렇지만[하지만] (부사), 나머지는 모두 접속사이다

19 주어가 동명사 Doing이므로 improves로 고치는 것이 적절하다.

20 브랜던은 '1년' 동안 한국 드라마들을 시청해 왔다.

21 모든 언어는 처음에는 '어렵지만', 새로운 언어가 당신의 세상을 더욱 넓혀줄 수 있다.

22 ②번 다음 문장의 also에 주목한다. 주어진 문장에 이어 추가 설명을 하는 것이므로 ②번이 적절하다.

23 (1) 안동 찜닭 먹기, (2) 하회탈을 만들고 탈춤 추는 법을 배우기, (3) 하회 마을 방문하기

24 ③ '하회탈 만드는 법'은 알 수 없다. ① 안동, ② 안동 찜닭, ④ 탈춤, ⑤ 하회 마을

01 (i)mprove

02 Watching Chinese dramas with Chinese subtitles is a good way to get better at listening.

03 (1) (s)truck   (2) (t)aking   (3) (s)hare

04 (1) This is what I wanted to buy.

(2) I enjoyed what you cooked for me last night.

(3) Do you remember what Bella wore at the party last night?

05 (1) The alarm has been ringing for 5 minutes.

(2) Mary has been chatting with her friends since two o'clock.

(3) He has been writing a book since last month.

06 (1) The report showed what I wanted to know.

(2) He silently agreed with much of what she had said.

(3) I never believe what I read in the newspaper.

(4) Mom has been shopping for weeks.

(5) Someone has been stealing candies from the kitchen.

(6) This movie is what many people have been waiting for.

07 What's most important is to become familiar with the language first.

08 how[what] about

09 (A) Spanish movies   (B) the sound

10 Korean   11 (A) subtitles   (B)translations

---

01 이어지는 대화 내용에서 중국어를 잘하도록 방법을 설명하는 것으로 보아 중국어를 잘할 수 있도록 하는 방법을 물어보았다는 것을 알 수 있다.

02 중국어 자막이 있는 중국 드라마 보는 것 = watching Chinese dramas with Chinese subtitles 듣기를 잘하다 = get better at listening

03 (1) 감동 받다 = be struck (2) 수업을 듣다 = take a class (3) 공유하다 = share

04 what은 선행사를 포함한 관계대명사로 '~하는 것'으로 해석하며, the thing(s) which[that]를 나타낸다.

05 현재완료진행형에서 since는 '시간'을 나타내는 명사(구)와 함께 쓰이고 for는 '기간'을 나타내는 명사(구)와 함께 쓰인다.

06 (1)~(3) 선행사를 포함한 관계대명사 what을 이용한다. (4)~(6) 어떤 상태나 행위가 과거 어느 때부터 시작되어 현재까지 계속 진행되고 있음을 나타내거나, 현재까지 계속적으로 반복되고 있다는 것을 나타내는 현재완료진행형을 이용한다.

07 선행사를 포함한 관계대명사 What을 주어로 해서 쓰는 것이 적절하다.

08 why don't you+동사원형 ~? = how[what] about ~ing?: ~하는 게 어때?

09 인호는 스페인 영화들을 보는 것이 그 언어의 '소리'에 익숙해지는 것에 도움이 될 것이기 때문에 '스페인 영화들'을 자주 볼 것을 제안한다.

10 Korean: 한국어(명사), 한국의(형용사)

11 마리사는 자신이 정말 좋아하는 한국의 젊은 남성 밴드인 DREAM4의 노래를 '자막'이나 '번역'이 없이 이해할 수 있는 방법에 대한 조언을 구한다.

창의사고력 서술형 문제   p.56

|모범답안|

01 (1) She has been swimming for half an hour.

(2) I have been working here since 2018.

(3) They have known her for two years.

(4) It has been raining since last night.

---

02 (1) What I bought at the bookstore was the Little Prince.

(2) What he likes the most is to play the guitar.

(3) I like what she gave me yesterday.

03 (A) Andong   (B) Andong-jjimdak

(C) Hahoe mask   (D) the *talchum*

(E) Hahoe Village

---

01 과거에서 현재까지 진행 중인 일에는 현재완료진행형을 사용한다. 단, 진행형이 불가능한 know와 같은 상태 동사의 경우 현재완료(have/has known)를 사용한다. 또한 날씨를 나타낼 때는 비인칭 주어 it을 사용한다.

단원별 모의고사   p.57~60

01 ③   02 (i)mperfect   03 ④

04 Learn vocabulary what is related to your interests.
 → Learn vocabulary which[that] is related to your interests.

05 ①

06 Having new experiences lets us find new talents.

07 ③   08 (C) → (A) → (D) → (B)

09 ④   10 ⑤

11 (1) has been listening to the music for 2 hours

(2) has been cooking bulgogi since 6:00 p.m.

12 ②   13 ④

14 (1) This ring is what my mom gave me.

(2) You can look up what you need on the computer.

(3) Is this the thing that you were looking for?

(4) Russia has belonged to such a category.

15 ③, ⑤

16 Because he doesn't know Spanish that well.

17 (1) 휴대 전화의 설정을 스페인어로 바꿨다.

(2) 사야 할 목록을 스페인어로 적어 오고 있다.

18 ⓐ Watching Spanish movies often
 ⓒ Writing a review of a match in Spanish

19 People use some words only in soccer

20 to perform → perform   21 ③

22 watching   23 subtitles

---

01 ① how to ~ = 어떻게 ~하는지 ② a very good guitar player = 뛰어난 기타 연주자 ③ take a swimming class = 수영 수업을 듣다 ④ go camping = 캠핑을 가다 ⑤ understand 이해하다

02 주어진 단어는 반의어 관계이다. perfect 완벽한 imperfect 불완전한

03 ④ 여기서 'talent'는 '재능'이라는 뜻이다.

04 관계대명사 what은 선행사가 없을 때 사용한다. 선행사 vocabulary가 있을 때 관계대명사는 which 또는 that을 쓴다.

05 앞에 나온 'It was hard'와 대조적으로 만들기는 어려웠다는 내용과는 상반되는 내용이 들어가야 한다.

06 새로운 경험을 하는 것 = having new experiences 우리에게 ~을 발견하도록 해준다. = lets us find ~

07 'I think it's good to try new things.'를 보면 가구 만들기에 대하여 긍정적인 태도를 가지고 있다는 것을 알 수 있다.

08 (C) 금년에 무엇을 할 것이냐는 질문을 하고 자원봉사를 하면서 시간을 보내겠다는 말에 (A) 좋은 일이라고 응답한다. (D) 상대방은 어떤 계획을 가지고 있는지 묻고 (B) 수영을 하겠다는 바람을 나타낸다.

09 ④ 그것이 마음에 들었느냐는 질문에 많이 좋아할 것이라는 대답은 어색하다.

10 금년에 무엇을 할 것이냐는 질문에 (C) 기타를 배우고 싶다고 대답하자 (B) 어디서 배울 것이냐는 물음에 (A) 친구에게 배울 것이라고 대답한다.

11 현재완료진행형에서 since는 '시간'을 나타내는 명사(구)와 함께 쓰이고 for는 '기간'을 나타내는 명사(구)와 함께 쓰인다.

12 과거 어느 때부터 시작되어 현재까지 계속 진행되고 있음을 나타내는 현재완료진행형을 이용한다.

13 첫 번째 빈칸에는 with의 목적어와 have의 목적어 역할을 할 수 있는 what이 적절하고 두 번째 빈칸에는 all이라는 선행사가 있으므로 that이 적절하다.

14 (1) that을 is의 주어와 gave의 직접목적어 역할을 할 수 있는 what으로 고치는 것이 적절하다. (2) that을 look up과 need의 목적어 역할을 할 수 있는 what으로 고치는 것이 적절하다. (3) what = the thing that[which] (4) 진행형으로 쓸 수 없는 동사인 belong은 현재완료형으로 상태의 계속을 표현한다.

15 ① I could not understand what the teacher talked about. ② Judy has had the hairpin for 10 years. ④ This dress is what she bought last weekend.

16 오언은 '스페인어를 그렇게 잘 알지 못하기 때문에' 그가 정말 좋아하는 선수들의 인터뷰를 이해하는 데 어려움을 겪는다.

17 줄리는 '휴대 전화의 설정을 스페인어로 바꿨고 사야 할 목록을 스페인어로 적어 오고 있다.'

18 ⓐ 스페인 영화들을 자주 보는 것, ⓒ 스페인어로 경기에 대한 후기를 써 보는 것

19 생략되어 있는 by people의 people을 주어로 해서 능동태로 고치는 것이 적절하다.

20 지각동사 see+목적어+원형부정사 또는 현재분사

21 'DREAM4에 관심이 있는 친구들을 찾는 것'은 로리가 조언을 한 내용이다.

22 recommend는 동명사를 목적어로 취한다.

23 subtitle: [주로 복수로] (영화나 텔레비전 화면의) 자막, 영화나 TV 프로그램의 외국어 대화의 번역

Lesson **2**

Take Care of Yourself

시험대비 실력평가
p.64

01 ①	02 ⑤	03 ⑤	04 ①
05 ③	06 ②		

01 얼음이 이를 너무 민감하게 하는 것은 손상을 주는 것으로 damage가 적절하다. clean 깨끗하게 하다 produce 생산하다 lower 낮추다 check 검토하다

02 ⑤ "taste or smell"은 "맛이나 냄새"라는 뜻이다.

03 '건강을 유지하기 위하여 너는 규칙적으로 운동을 할 필요가 있다.'가 적절하다.

04 '머리를 올려놓는 부드러운 물질로 채워진 포대'는 'pillow 베개'이다.

05 (1) look like ~처럼 보이다 (2) just like 마치 ~처럼 (3) like 좋아하다

06 ① clue 단서 ② reason 이유 ③ preventing 예방하는 것 ④ shape 형태 ⑤ lower 낮추다

서술형 시험대비
p.65

01 meaningful
02 (p)roductive
03 (1) healthy (2) advice (3) what (4) usual
04 (1) term (2) chewing (3) compare (4) shape
05 (t)hirsty
06 Some foods mirror the body parts that they are good for.
07 walk, sleep

01 명사 experiences를 수식하는 형용사가 필요하다. mean 의미하다 meaningful 의미 있는

02 주어진 단어는 동의어 관계이다. improve 개선하다 develop 발전하다 productive 생산적인 – profitable 이득이 되는

03 (1) healthy 건강한 (2) advice 충고 (3) what ~인 것 (4) as usual 평소처럼

04 (1) 용어 term (2) 씹는 것 chewing (3) 비교하다 compare (4) 형태 shape

05 '음료를 원하거나 필요하다고 느끼는' 것은 '목마른 thirsty'이다.

06 몇몇 음식들은 ~ 신체 부위의 생김새를 반영한다 Some foods mirror the body parts ~

07 문맥상 낮에 측정하는 것은 걷기이고, 밤에 측정하는 것은 잠이다.

교과서 Conversation

핵심 Check
p.66~67

1 ②	2 ②

01 상대방이 알고 있는지 물어보는 사실에 대하여 왜 그러냐고 다시 묻는 것으로 보아. 상대방이 물어본 사실을 모르고 있었다는 것을 알 수 있다.

02 작은 스마트 밴드가 여러 가지 역할을 하는 것에 대하여 놀라움을 나타내는 표현이 적절하다.

교과서 대화문 익히기

Check(√) True or False
p.68

1 T 2 F 3 F 4 T

교과서 확인학습
p.70~71

Listen & Talk 1 A
Have, heard, chewing, teeth / Why / damage, make, sensitive

Listen & Talk 1 B
look, get enough / slept for over / When did, go / went to bed, as usual / what, making, Have, when / Why, that / going to bed late, feel tired / other, improve, memory, productive, now

Listen & Talk 1 D-1
Have, writing, good, health / really / improves

Listen & Talk 2 A
smart, check, health, smartphone / kind / how far how well / surprised, small

Listen & Talk 2 B
What, living / doing yoga / working, yourself / following, steps / Let, been watched, surprised, have watched / programs, popular / convenient, out, exercise / That's why, try

Listen & Talk 2 C
looks / magic, everywhere / special / awesome, drink, every / surprised, talk / asks, thirsty / why, trying / drinking, increase, help, flow / buy

Do It Yourself A
hungry / don't, before / want, wait / eating, often, health / Really, eating / waiting, eat, too, Eating little, often, from eating / eat, right

08 뒤에 비타민 A는 눈이 빛을 처리하여 뇌에 선명한 이미지를 보낼 수 있도록 돕는다는 말이 이어지므로, 비타민 A가 '시력'을 개선한다고 하는 것이 적절하다.

09 which는 계속적 용법의 주격 관계대명사로, and it으로 바꿔 쓸 수 있다.

10 '당근에 비타민 A의 효능을 낮출 수 있는 화학 성분이 있다'는 말은 위 글의 내용과 일치하지 않는다.

11 주어진 문장의 Yes에 주목한다. ②번 앞 문장의 질문에 대한 답에 해당하므로 ②번이 적절하다.

12 알츠하이머병을 '예방하는 데'도 좋다고 해야 하므로, preventing으로 고쳐야 한다. protect: 보호하다, prevent: 예방하다, 막다

13 그것들은 '두 부분'으로 나뉘어 있고, '주름'이 있다.

14 ⓐ move on to: (새로운 일·주제로) 넘어가다, come to mind: 생각이 떠오르다, 생각나다, ⓑ come from: ~에서 나오다, prevent A from ~ing: A가 ~하는 것을 막다

15 생강의 '특별한 성분'이 복통과 '구토'를 예방하기 때문이다.

16 '양파를 써는 것'을 가리킨다..

17 ③: 그런데(대화에서 화제를 바꿀 때 씀), ⓑ와 나머지 모두: '어쨌든'

18 help+원형부정사 또는 to부정사

19 음식: '양파', 유사한 신체 부위: '인간의 세포', 혜택: 이 음식 안의 '비타민 B'가 새롭고 건강한 세포를 만드는 것을 돕는다.

20 (A)의 however가 (C)의 내용과 상반되는 내용을 이끄는 것이므로 (C) 다음에 (A)가 이어지고 (B)의 these foods가 (A)의 the following examples의 음식들을 가리키는 것이므로 (A) 다음에 (B)가 와야 한다. 그러므로 (C)-(A)-(B)의 순서가 적절하다.

21 as+원급+as+주어+can: 가능한 ~한

22 '어떤 음식들'을 가리킨다.

23 (B)와 ②, ③: 명사적 용법, ①, ⑤: 부사적 용법, ④: 형용사적 용법

24 keep+목적어+목적격보어(형용사)

25 우리 신체의 특정 부분과 '비슷해 보이는' 몇몇 음식들은 그 신체 부위들에 '좋다.'

26 '생강의 강한 맛과 냄새'를 가리킨다.

27 어떻게 특별한 성분이 복통과 구토를 예방하는지는 알 수 없다. ① A stomach. ② Yes. ③ Yes. ④ It comes from a special chemical.

🦉 **서술형 시험대비**   p.94~95

01 which[that] contains   02 (A) similar   (B) good
03 looks → looks like   04 mirror
05 possible   06 carrots   07 brain → eye

08 (A) improves   (B) process light   (C) clear image
09 ⓐ to   ⓑ into   10 and, them
11 (A) Walnuts   (B) our brains
12 ⓐ feeling   ⓑ throwing
13 strong taste, smell
14 (A) a[the] tomato   (B) human heart
15 the chemicals that make tomatoes red are good for your heart and blood

01 주격 관계대명사 which 또는 that을 사용하는 것이 적절하다.

02 어떤 음식들의 모양들은 그 음식들이 '유익한' 우리 신체의 특정 부분의 모양들과 자연적으로 '유사'하다. be good for: ~에 좋다

03 뒤에 명사가 있으므로 looks like로 고쳐야 한다. look+형용사, look like+명사

04 '그 음식이 유익한 신체 부위의 생김새를 반영하고 있는 몇몇 음식'을 가리킨다.

05 as + 원급 + as + 주어 + can[could] = as + 원급 + as possible: 가능한 한 …한

06 당근에 있는 화학 성분이 비타민 A를 만들고 그것이 시력을 개선한다고 했으므로, 건강한 눈을 원한다면, '당근'을 먹으라고 하는 것이 적절하다.

07 썰어 놓은 당근의 모양은 사람의 '눈'과 비슷해 보인다.

08 비타민 A는 시력을 '개선하고', 눈이 '빛을 처리하여' 뇌에 '선명한 이미지'를 보낼 수 있도록 돕는다.

09 ⓐ be similar to: ~와 유사하다, ⓑ be divided into: ~로 나뉘다

10 which는 계속적 용법의 목적격 관계대명사로, and ~ them으로 바꿔 쓸 수 있다.

11 '호두'는 알츠하이머병을 예방하는 데도 좋을 뿐만 아니라 '사람의 뇌'가 건강하고 활동적인 상태를 유지하는 데 도움을 준다.

12 전치사 from 다음에 동명사로 쓰는 것이 적절하다.

13 생강의 '강한 맛'이나 '냄새' 때문이다.

14 잘라낸 '토마토'와 '사람의 심장'을 가리킨다.

15 관계대명사 that[which]을 보충하면 된다.

🦉 **영역별 핵심문제**   p.97~101

01 ③   02 ②   03 ①   04 ①
05 ⑤   06 ③   07 your body
08 ②   09 ④   10 ②   11 ④
12 소년이 낮에 얼마나 멀리 걷는지 그리고 밤에 얼마나 잘 자는지 보여준다.
13 ④   14 ⑤   15 ①, ③
16 with whom
17 (1) which are   (2) who is   18 ②

01 ③ midnight = 자정

02 ① 알아차리다 notice ② ~으로 나뉘다 be divided into ③ 유지하다 stay ④ 포함하다 contain ⑤ 다양한 a variety of

03 호두는 뇌를 건강하게 한다고 했으므로 알츠하이머를 예방하는 데 유익하다고 해야 한다.

04 damage 손상을 주다 harm 손상시키다 chew 씹다 contain 포함하다 improve 개선하다 compare 비교하다

05 (C) 이백만 번을 보았다는 사실에 알고 있다는 대답과 그 이유를 덧붙인다. (A) 비디오의 장점으로 밖에 나갈 필요가 없다는 언급에 (B) 동의하는 표현이 따라온다.

06 compared to: ~와 비교하여 compare A to B: A를 B에 비교하다

07 it은 인칭대명사로 앞에 언급된 단수명사를 받는다.

08 ② 'A lot of teens have a negative body image.'를 보면 청소년들은 자신에 대한 부정적인 신체 이미지를 가지고 있다는 것을 알 수 있다.

09 'I'll wait until dinner.'라고 말하는 것으로 보아 먹고 싶지 않다는 내용이 들어가야 한다.

10 하루 세 번 식사하는 것보다는 조금씩 자주 먹는 것이 낫다는 내용이다.

11 ④ 이 대화에서는 a smart band가 별도의 장치인지 smartphone에 탑재되어 있는 앱인지가 밝혀지지 않았다.

13 ④ 이어지는 설명으로 보았을 때 'I didn't know that.'이 적절하다.

14 Our art room을 선행사로 하는 계속적 용법의 주격 관계대명사 which가 와야 한다. that은 계속적 용법의 관계대명사로 쓸 수 없다.

15 ① The injured man was lying on the ground. ③ This is the most expensive car made in England.

16 앞에 콤마(,)가 있는 관계대명사의 계속적 용법을 이용한다. 함께 쓰레기를 주운 것이므로 전치사 with와 목적격이므로 whom을 쓴다.

17 분사가 명사를 뒤에서 수식하는 경우에는 그 앞에 '주격 관계대명사+be동사'가 생략된 것으로 생각할 수 있다.

18 계속적 용법의 관계대명사는 '접속사(and, but, for, though 등)+대명사'로 고쳐 쓸 수 있다. 여기서는 though이 적절하다.

19 ⓑ baking → baked ⓓ jumped → jumping ⓕ that → who

20 앞에 나오는 내용과 상반되는 내용이 뒤에 이어지므로 however가 가장 적절하다. ① 그러므로, ② 게다가, ④ 비슷하게, ⑤ 예를 들어

21 keeps의 목적격보어이므로, 형용사 healthy로 고치는 것이 적절하다. healthily: 건강하게(부사), healthy: 건강한

22 not only[just/merely/simply] A but also B: A뿐만 아니라 B도, ③ mainly: 주로, ⑤ mostly: 주로

23 관계대명사 that은 계속적 용법으로 쓸 수 없으므로 which로 바꾸는 것이 적절하다.

24 호두와 인간의 뇌에 주름이 있는 이유는 대답할 수 없다. ① The shape of the human brain. ② They are divided into two parts. ④ A walnut. ⑤ A walnut.

25 ⓐ와 ①, ②, ⑤: 동명사, ③, ④: 현재분사

26 (A) 동명사 Cutting이 주어이므로 is가 적절하다. (B) '사역동사 make+목적어+원형부사'이므로 cry가 적절하다. (C) a few 뒤에는 셀 수 있는 명사 복수가 와야 하므로 a little이 적절하다.

27 try ~ing: 시험 삼아 ~해 보다

28 이 글은 위장과 유사하게 생긴 생강의 효능을 설명한 글이므로, 요지로는 ②번 '위장과 닮은 생강이 위장에 좋다'가 적절하다.

29 '구토'를 예방한다고 해야 하므로, throwing up으로 고치는 것이 적절하다. overeat: 과식하다, throw up: …을 토하다

01 주어진 단어는 반의어 관계이다. prevent 가로 막다 allow 허용하다 accept 받아들이다 refuse 거부하다

02 "prevent A from ~ing"는 "keep A from ~ing" "stop A from ~ing"로 "A가 ~하지 못하게 막다"는 뜻이다.

03 '생각, 느낌, 행동을 조절하는 머릿속에 있는 기관'은 'brain 뇌'이다.

04 (1) 씹는 것 chewing (2) 인기 있는 popular (3) 속이 빈 hollow (4) 처리하다 process

05 (A) 이어지는 대답으로 7시간 잔다는 것을 통해서 잠의 양에 대

한 질문임을 알 수 있다. (B) 대답에 'after midnight'는 시간을 가리킨다.

06 이어지는 설명에 그 기능이 나와 있으므로 질문은 기능이나 특징을 물어보는 것이어야 한다.

07 놀라움을 나타낼 수 있는 amazed가 적절하다. worried 걱정하는 pleased 즐거워하는 frightened 겁먹은 convinced 확신하는

08 'help+목적어+(to) 부정사'의 구문이 되어야 한다.

09 'so many people have watched this video.'를 보면 앞에 나온 말을 많은 사람이 시청한 것과 어울리는 "Wow, it's been watched two milion times!"가 되어야 한다.

10 놀라움을 나타내는 "I'm surprised that ~."은 "How could it be possible that ~?" "I can't believe that ~." "It's surprising ~."으로 바꿔 쓸 수 있다.

11 모두 관계대명사 who가 적절하지만 ④번은 선행사가 앞선 절 전체이므로 which가 적절하다.

12 ① I found a box filled with many letters at the basement. ② I bought a new laptop manufactured in Korea. ④ Mom bought me a new camera, with which I took lots of photos. ⑤ Sumin loves her new cap, which she bought on sale. basement: 지하실

13 계속적 용법의 관계대명사는 '접속사(and, but, for, though 등)+대명사'로 바꿔 쓸 수 있다. in good shape: (몸의) 상태가 좋은

14 소나기를 만나서 늦은 것이므로 수동의 뜻을 갖는 과거분사가 적절하다. shower: 소나기

15 첫 번째 문장에서는 "iron horse"라고 불리는 것이므로 과거분사가 적절하다. 두 번째 문장에서는 선행사가 사물이고 계속적 용법이므로 which가 적절하다. consecutive: 연속적인

16 토마토를 붉게 만드는 화학 물질이 사람의 심장과 피에 유익하다고 했으므로, 토마토를 먹는 것이 '심장병'에 걸릴 위험성을 낮출 수 있다고 하는 것이 적절하다. ① 복통

17 hollow 속이 빈, 텅 빈, ① vacant: 빈

18 (B)와 ②, ⑤: 접속사, (C)와 ①, ③, ④: 주격 관계대명사

19 a slice of: 한 조각

20 help+목적어+원형부정사 또는 to부정사

21 음식: '당근', 유사한 신체 부위: 눈, 혜택: 그들은 '시력'을 개선한다.

22 ⓐ에는 접속사 that, ⓑ에는 관계대명사 that이 적절하다.

23 (A)와 ③: 가주어, ①, ⑤: 앞에 이미 언급되었거나 현재 이야기되고 있는 것을 가리키는 인칭대명사(그것), ② 가목적어, ④ 비인칭 주어

24 위 글은 ④ '추천하는 글'이다. ① (책·연극·영화 등에 대한) 논평[비평], 감상문, ② 독후감, ③ 요약, 개요, ⑤ 수필

25 ⓐ 다음의 내용을 쓰면 된다.

26 why don't you+동사원형 ~? = how[what] about ~ing?: ~하는 게 어때?

01 (h)ealth
02 how far I walk during the day and how well I sleep at night
03 (s)urprised   04 compared
05 (1) shape (2) clue (3) contain
06 (1) I want to meet Jon Kim, who is my favorite actor, in person someday.
  (2) Have you read the book, *The Last Leaf*, which was written by O. Henry?
07 (1) The men giving out flyers are wearing caps.
  (2) The soldier injured in the war was lying on the bed.
  (3) Last week I bought a new computer, which I like a lot.
08 (1) He got married to Huong, who is from Vietnam.
  (2) She wanted to buy the dress, which was too expensive.
  (3) The flower planted in the garden grew up very fast.
09 clue   10 various   11 as well as
12 (A) similar (B) that (C) lower
13 (A) hollow spaces (B) red
14 The chemicals that make tomatoes red.

01 하루 동안 걷는 거리와 밤에 잠을 잘 자는지 등의 정보는 건강(health) 정보이다.

02 동사 shows에 이어지는 목적어로 간접의문문이 되어서 'how far ~ and how well ~'의 형태가 되어야 한다.

03 놀라움을 나타내는 surprised가 적절하다.

04 주어진 문장의 청소년이 다른 사람과 비교되는 상황을 나타내므로 과거분사 compared가 적절하다.

05 (1) 모양 shape (2) 단서 clue (3) 포함하다 contain

06 (1) 선행사가 사람이므로 who를 이용한다. (2) 선행사가 사물이므로 which를 이용한다.

07 (1) 전단지(flyers)를 주는 것이므로 현재분사가 적절하다. (2) 수동의 의미이므로 과거분사가 적절하다. (3) 계속적 용법에는 that을 사용하지 않는다. which가 적절하다.

08 (1), (2) 계속적 용법의 관계대명사를 이용한다. (3) 꽃이 심겨진 것이므로 과거분사를 이용한다.

09 clue: 단서, 실마리, 문제나 수수께끼에 대한 답을 발견하도록 도와주는 것

10 a variety of = various: 여러 가지의, 각양각색의, 다양한

11 not only A but also B = B as well as A: A뿐만 아니라 B도

12 (A) 그 둘이 '비슷해' 보인다고 해야 하므로 similar가 적절하다. (B) 선행사(the chemicals)가 있으므로 that이 적절하다. (C) 심장병에 걸릴 위험성을 '낮출 수 있다'고 해야 하므로

lower가 적절하다.

13 둘 다 여러 개의 '빈 공간'이 있고 '붉은 색'이다.

14 토마토를 사람의 심장과 피에 유익하게 만드는 것은 '토마토를 붉게 만드는 화학 물질'이다.

창의사고력 서술형 문제　　　　　　　　　　p.108

|모범답안|

01 Accept / praise / compare

02 (1) written in English
　 (2) covered with fallen leaves
　 (3) sitting on the corner

03 (A) Fruit yogurt salad　(B) bananas
　 (C) lower blood pressure　(D) vitamin C
　 (E) bones

01 accept 수용하다, 받아들이다 compare 비교하다

단원별 모의고사　　　　　　　　　　p.109~112

01 ①　　　02 ③　　　03 ①

04 working　05 ②　　　06 ④

07 that is making you tired → what is making you tired

08 Scientists say that going to bed late can make you feel tired the next day.

09 ②　　　10 ①

11 (1) parked　(2) parking　12 ⑤　　　13 ①

14 (1) I can't find the books, which Evelyn gave to me.
　 (2) She is my friend, Sophia, who is from Hungary.
　 (3) I got a C in my test, which made my mom disappointed.
　 (4) The girl cleaning the room is my sister. 또는 The girl who is cleaning the room is my sister.
　 (5) You can find a nice beach covered with white sand.

15 containing

16 which foods are good for which body parts

17 ②　　　18 ③

19 (A) heart　(B) heart　(C) blood

20 ①, ③　　　21 ④　　　22 Vitamin A does.

01 compare 비교하다 improve 향상시키다 lower 낮추다 check 검토하다 prevent 가로막다

02 질문의 내용이 잠이 든 시간이기 때문에 대답도 잠잔 시간을 나타내는 말이 적절하다.

03 '내부에 빈 공간을 가진'에 해당하는 단어는 'hollow 속이 빈'이다. sensitive 민감한 productive 생산적인 positive 긍정적

인 moved 감동 받은

04 "운동하다"는 "work out"이고 be동사에 이어지는 현재분사를 써서 "~하고 있다"에 해당하는 현재진행시제가 되도록 하여야 한다.

05 "That's why I love these programs."를 보면 위 질문에 대한 대답은 "It looks very convenient. You don't have to go out to exercise."에서 찾을 수 있다.

06 ④ "It's no wonder."는 당연함을 나타내는 말로 "4월에 눈이 온다."고 할 때는 놀라움을 나타내는 "It's surprising."이 어울린다.

07 '너를 피곤하게 만드는 것'은 'what is making you tired'라고 한다. 선행사 없이 명사절을 유도하는 what이 적절하다.

08 과학자들이 ~라고 말한다 = Scientists say that ~, 늦게 자는 것 = going to bed late, 너를 다음날 피곤하게 느끼도록 만들 수 있다 = can make you feel tired the next day

09 ① 소년이 충분한 잠을 자는지는 알 수 없다. ③ 소녀는 자정 이후에 잠들었다. ④ 언제 자는 가는 중요하다. ⑤ 소년의 말은 듣고 소녀는 일찍 자려고 할 것이다.

10 (A) 하루 세 번 먹는 것과 대조적으로 조금씩 자주 먹는 것이 되어야 한다. (B) 하루 세 번 먹으려고 배가 고파도 계속 기다리면 나중에는 과식을 하게 된다는 내용이 자연스럽다.

11 (1) 차가 주차된 것이므로 수동의 뜻을 갖는 과거분사를 이용한다. (2) 차를 주차하는 것이므로 능동의 뜻을 갖는 현재분사를 이용한다.

12 관계대명사의 계속적 용법으로 첫 번째 빈칸에는 선행사가 사람이므로 who를 이용하고, 두 번째 빈칸에는 선행사가 사물이므로 which를 이용한다.

13 which는 앞 문장 전체를 선행사로 받을 수 있으므로 접속사 and와 it 대신에 쓸 수 있다.

14 (1) 관계대명사의 계속적 용법으로 that을 쓰지 않으며 관계대명사는 접속사와 대명사의 역할을 하므로 목적어로 쓰인 them을 삭제해야 한다. (2) 계속적 용법이므로 that을 who로 고치는 것이 적절하다. (3) 관계대명사의 계속적 용법으로 what을 쓰지 않으며 앞에 나오는 절을 선행사로 받는 which가 적절하다. (4) 현재분사가 뒤에서 명사를 수식하도록 하거나 '주격 관계대명사+be동사'가 되도록 해야 한다. (5) 해변이 모래로 덮인 것이므로 과거분사가 적절하다.

15 앞의 명사 a diet를 수식하는 현재분사 containing이 적절하다.

16 for를 보충하면 된다.

17 주어진 문장의 they에 주목한다. ②번 앞 문장의 it과 the human heart를 가리키므로 ②번이 적절하다.

18 ②, ③ 현재분사, ⓐ와 ①, ④, ⑤는 동명사

19 음식: 토마토, 유사한 신체 부위: '심장', 혜택: 그들은 '심장'과 '피'에 유익하다.

20 (A)와 ①, ③: ~와 닮다, ~와 비슷[유사]하다, ② ~을 찾다, ④ A slice of carrot and the human eye are alike.라고 쓸 수 있다. ⑤ ~을 돌보다

21 ⓑ와 ④: 처리하다(동사), 나머지는 다 '과정'(명사)

22 시력을 개선하도록 돕는 비타민은 '비타민 A'이다.

1 Waking Up to an Earthquake

2 One night in February, after I had gone to bed, an earthquake hit.

3 I woke up suddenly because my bed was shaking.

4 I thought my brother was shaking my bed as a joke.

5 But then I heard the mirror on my desk fall to the floor and break into pieces.

6 I knew it wasn't my brother then, but I still didn't know what exactly was happening.

7 Soon the whole room began to shake violently, and my confusion turned to panic.

8 My mom shouted that it was an earthquake and ran into my room.

9 Since it was my first time experiencing an earthquake, I didn't know how to react.

10 I just kept saying, "What should I do?"

11 My mom pulled me and my brother out of bed.

12 We ran to the kitchen and crawled under the table.

13 I could see the light swinging violently and books falling to the floor.

14 Our family picture dropped from the wall and the glass covering it broke.

15 A cup tipped over and rolled off the kitchen table.

16 Every second, I could hear something else in the apartment break.

17 I started to worry that the building would collapse.

18 Then the shaking seemed to stop.

19 We started crawling toward the door.

20 At that moment, my mom's cell phone rang.

21 It was my dad, who was coming home from work.

22 He shouted, "It stopped!

23 Get out of the building!

24 Take the stairs!

25 Don't take the elevator!

26 Hurry!"

27 "Where are you?

28 Are you okay?" my mom asked urgently.

29 My dad answered, "Don't worry.

30 I'm okay.

31 I was driving home when the shaking started.

32 But I pulled over immediately.

33 I'm listening to the radio right now to find out what's going on."

34 We nervously made our way down the stairs and outside.

35 I looked around.

36 Parts of buildings had fallen and had smashed several cars.

37 We went to an open space to avoid more falling pieces.

38 How could all this have happened in a few minutes?

39 Although I had done many earthquake drills in school, I had never thought I'd experience a real earthquake.

40 I still get scared when I remember that night.

41 I can't forget the panic I felt when the furniture was shaking and things were falling to the floor.

42 After that night, I began to take earthquake drills seriously.

43 I realized that I should be prepared for the next earthquake, which can occur at any time.

시험대비 실력평가

01 ⑤　　　02 ②　　　03 ③　　　04 ②

05 to swing → swing 또는 swinging,
　 to fall → fall 또는 falling

06 our family picture　　07 ⑤　　　08 ②

09 ②　　　　10 pulled over

11 fell → had fallen, smashed → had smashed

12 ④

13 I can't forget the panic I felt when the furniture was shaking and things were falling to the floor.

14 ②　　　15 ②　　　16 ③　　　17 ③

18 which[that] covered　　19 collapse

20 ④　　　21 ③, ⑤

22 Since it was my first time experiencing an earthquake　　23 ③

24 to fall → fall[falling], to break → break[breaking]

25 ③

26 Because it was her first time experiencing an earthquake.

27 ①, ③, ⑤　　28 (A) scared　(B) seriously　(C) which

29 prepared for

01 ⓐ break into pieces: 산산조각이 나다, ⓑ turn to: (바람·조수·형세 등이) ~으로 변하다, 방향을 바꾸다

02 주어진 문장의 'my brother was shaking my bed'에 주목한다. ②번 앞 문장의 'my bed was shaking'의 원인을 설명하는 것이므로 ②번이 적절하다.

03 (A)와 ③: 대과거 용법(결과 용법으로 보는 것도 가능함), ①, ④: 경험 용법, ②: 완료 용법, ⑤: 계속 용법

04 글쓴이는 처음에는 남동생이 장난으로 침대를 흔들고 있다고 생각했지만, 곧 '남동생이 그런 것이 아니라는 것을 알았다'고 했다.

05 지각동사(see)+목적어+현재분사(원형부정사도 가능함.)

06 '우리 가족 사진'을 가리킨다.

07 '나는 건물이 무너지지는 않을까 하는 걱정이 들기 시작했다.'라고만 되어 있다.

08 ⓐ와 ③, ⑤: 부사적 용법, ①, ④: 명사적 용법, ②: 형용사적 용법

09 ② 긴급한, ① 신나는, 흥미진진한, ③ 감동적인, ④ 환상적인, ⑤ 지루한

10 pull over: (차량·운전자가) (정차하거나 다른 차가 지나가도록) 길 한쪽으로 빠지다[차를 대다]

11 건물의 일부분이 떨어져 나갔고 몇몇 차들이 박살이 난 것이 계단을 내려가서 밖으로 나간 것보다 먼저 일어난 일이므로 과거완료로 쓰는 것이 적절하다.

12 '어떻게 이런 일이 몇 분 만에 일어날 수 있단 말인가?'에서, 글쓴이의 혼란스럽고 어리둥절한 심경을 알 수 있다. puzzled: 어리둥절해하는, 얼떨떨한, ② 부끄러운, ③ 실망한, ⑤ 우울한

13 the panic과 I felt 사이에 목적격 관계대명사 that[which]이 생략되어 있다.

14 이 글은 글쓴이가 지진을 겪은 뒤에 언제든 발생할 수 있는 다음 지진을 대비해야 한다는 것을 깨달았다는 내용의 글이므로, 어울리는 속담으로는 ②번 '예방이 치료보다 낫다.'가 적절하다. ① 어려울 때 친구가 진정한 친구이다. ③ 모든 구름의 뒤편은 은빛으로 빛난다.(괴로움 뒤에는 기쁨이 있다.) ④ 잘 생각해 보고 행동하라(돌다리도 두드려 보고 건너라). ⑤ 해가 비칠 때 건초를 말려라.(기회를 잘 이용하라.)

15 (A)의 'I knew it wasn't my brother then'은 (B)의 첫 문장에 대한 글쓴이의 생각을 바로잡는 것이므로 (B) 다음에 (A)가 이어지고 (C)에서 엄마의 지진이라는 소리에 글쓴이가 상황을 알게 되는 것이므로 (A) 다음에 (C)가 와야 한다. 그러므로 (B)-(A)-(C)의 순서가 적절하다.

16 ③은 글쓴이의 엄마를 가리키고, 나머지는 다 글쓴이의 아빠를 가리킨다.

17 필자의 아빠는 엘리베이터를 타면 안 된다고 말했다.

18 주격 관계대명사 which[that]를 사용하여 과거시제로 고치는 것이 적절하다.

19 지진이 얼마나 오래 계속되었는지는 알 수 없다. ① She pulled the writer and her brother out of bed. ② They took refuge under the kitchen table. take refuge 피난하다, 대피하다, ③ She could see the light swinging violently and books falling to the floor. ⑤ Because every second, she could hear something else in the apartment break.

21 지진이 일어나기 전에 잠자리에 든 것이 먼저 일어난 일이기 때

문에 과거완료로 쓰는 것이 적절하다. 또한, after처럼 시간의 전후 관계를 분명히 알 수 있는 접속사가 있는 경우에는 과거완료 대신 과거시제로 써도 무방하다.

22 be one's first time+-ing: ~하는 게 처음이다

23 위 글은 글쓴이가 처음 겪는 지진 때문에 잠에서 깨어 공포를 느끼는 내용이므로, 제목으로는 '지진에 눈을 뜨는 것'이 적절하다. ② play a joke on: ~에게 장난을 치다, ⑤ in panic: 당황하여

24 지각동사(heard)+목적어+원형부정사(현재분사도 가능함.)

25 ⓑ와 ②, ④, ⑤: [이유를 나타내어] …이므로, …이니까, ①, ③: …한 이래로

26 '지진을 경험한 것이 처음이었기' 때문이다.

27 ⓑ와 ①, ③, ⑤: 경험 용법, ② 계속 용법, ④ 완료 용법

28 (A) 감정을 나타내는 동사는 수식받는 명사가 감정을 느끼게 되는 경우에 과거분사를 써야 하므로 scared가 적절하다. (B) take를 수식하므로 부사 seriously가 적절하다. (C) 관계대명사 that은 계속적용법으로 쓸 수 없으므로 which가 적절하다.

29 글쓴이는 언제든 발생할 수 있는 다음 지진을 '대비해야 한다'는 것을 깨달았다.

서술형 시험대비
p.150~151

01 Because her bed was shaking.
02 happened → happening   03 I should
04 (A) pulled   (B) covering   (C) break
05 I could see the light swinging violently and books falling to the floor.
06 (A) the kitchen   (B) crawled   07 it
08 the shaking   09 at once, right away
10 (A) driving home   (B) listening to the radio
11 had done
12 How could all this have happened in a few minutes?
13 be occurred → occur
14 (A) gets scared   (B) the panic

01 '침대가 흔들렸기 때문에' 갑자기 잠에서 깼다.

02 happen은 수동태로 쓸 수 없으므로 happening으로 고치는 것이 적절하다.

03 의문사+to부정사 = 의문사+'주어+should'+동사원형으로 바꿔 쓸 수 있다.

04 (A) 침대 밖으로 '잡아끌었다'고 해야 하므로 pulled가 적절하다. pull: 끌다, 당기다, push: 밀다, (B) 사진을 '덮고 있던' 유리라고 해야 하므로 covering이 적절하다. (C) '지각동사(hear)+목적어+원형부정사'로 써야 하므로 break가 적절하다.

05 지각동사(see)+목적어+현재분사

06 글쓴이는 엄마와 남동생과 함께 '주방'으로 달려가서 식탁 아래

로 '기어들어 갔다.'

07 'seemed to부정사'를 'it seemed that 주어+동사'로 바꿔 쓸 수 있다.

08 '흔들림'을 가리킨다.

09 immediately = at once = right away: 즉시, 당장, 현재시제 일 때는 right now도 가능함.

10 글쓴이의 아빠는 진동이 시작할 때 '운전해서 집으로 가던' 중이 었지만, 즉시 차를 길 한쪽에 댔다. 그는 무슨 일이 일어나는지 알기 위해 바로 그 때 '라디오를 듣고 있었다.'

11 과거(지진이 일어났던 상황)보다 더 이전에 지진 훈련을 했었기 때문에 과거완료로 쓰는 것이 적절하다.

12 이런 일이 일어난 것이 공터로 간 것보다 먼저 일어난 일이므로 과거완료로 써야 하는데, 가능성을 나타내기 위해 쓰인 could 뒤에서 have happened로 바뀐 것이다.

13 occur는 수동태로 쓸 수 없으므로, be occurred를 occur로 고치는 것이 적절하다.

14 그녀는 여전히 '두려워지고', 가구가 흔들리고 물건들이 바닥으 로 떨어졌을 때 그녀가 느꼈던 '공포심'을 잊을 수가 없다.

영역별 핵심문제
p.153~157

01 ②   02 ①   03 ⑤
04 (c)ollapse   05 ④
06 I'm curious about how many people had to leave
   their homes
07 ①   08 ③   09 ③   10 ⑤
11 ③   12 natural disaster
13 Anything else   14 ①   15 ③
16 Though[Although, Even though]   17 ③
18 (1) Although it's very hot outside, I will walk my
       dog.
   (2) Since they had to paint quickly to capture the
       effect of light, they did not sketch their
       paintings in advance.
   (3) Although most people recognize it as a jewel,
       the diamond most directly affects our daily
       lives as a tool.
19 ⓑ, ⓓ, ⓔ   20 ⑤   21 break into pieces
22 ③   23 (A) to stop   (B) who   (C) home
24 happening   25 ①, ②, ④
26 ③   27 ①, to tell   28 ③   29 ④

01 a report about: ~에 관한 보고서 be curious about ~에 관 하여 궁금하다

02 violently 격렬하게 properly 적절하게 recently 최근에 actually 실제로 exactly 정확히

03 aware 인식하는 missing 실종된 exact 정확한 proper 적절

한 common 흔한

04 '갑자기 부서지거나 무너지다'에 해당하는 것은 '붕괴하다 collapse'이다.

05 이어지는 대화로 보아 소녀는 산불에 대해 알고 있지 않아서 산 불에 대해 질문을 하는 상황이 적절하다.

06 '나는 ~에 대해 궁금하다'는 'I'm curious about ~'이다. 얼마 나 많은 사람이 집을 떠나야 했는지 = how many people had to leave their homes

07 ① 'a large number of houses'는 '매우 많은 주택'이라는 뜻 으로 '하나의 큰 주택'은 아니다.

08 지진의 발생에 관한 글로 "발생하다"는 뜻의 occur를 현재진행 의 시제에 맞게 "occurring"으로 써야 한다.

09 "I'm curious about why earthquakes have occurred so often in Korea recently."를 보면 소년은 한국에서 지진이 최 근에 더 자주 발생하는 원인에 대하여 궁금증을 가지고 있다는 것을 알 수 있다.

10 ⑤ 지진이 두 번째라는 추측에 대하여 아니라고 대답했으므로 지진이 아닌 다른 것을 언급해야 한다.

11 "I guess earthquakes are second."를 통해서 소녀는 지진이 두 번째로 많은 피해를 야기시킨다고 추측하고 있다는 것을 알 수 있다.

12 비상 상황에 사용할 물품을 준비하는 것으로 보아 자연 재난 상 황에 사용할 생존 장비를 꾸리는 것을 알 수 있다.

13 반드시 건전지를 포함하라는 것으로 보아 앞에 나온 것에 대하 여 추가로 준비할 것에 대한 질문이 있었음을 알 수 있다.

14 although로 이끌리는 절은 주절과 상반되는 내용이 나온다.

15 When he arrived at home, they had already eaten dinner. 도착하기 전에 이미 먹은 것이므로 도착한 것은 과거 로, 먹은 것은 과거완료로 써야 한다.

16 아침에 차로 갔다가 걸어서 집에 돌아온 그림이므로 양보절을 이끄는 접속사가 적절하다.

17 already로 보아 과거완료가 나와야 한다.

18 내용에 맞게 (1), (3)에는 서로 상반되는 내용이 나오므로 although를, (2)에는 이유를 나타내고 있으므로 since를 이용 한다.

19 ⓐ have visited → visited ⓒ had got → got, was → had been ⓕ Since → Though

20 지진을 경험한 것이 처음이었기 '때문에', 나는 어떻게 반응해야 할지 몰랐다고 하는 것이 적절하다. since는 이유를 나타내는 부사절을 이끄는 접속사로 '… 때문에'라는 의미이다. ③ …에 도 불구하고, ④ 그런데, …한데, …에 반해서

21 break into pieces: 산산조각이 나다

22 후반부의 'my confusion turned to panic(혼란스러움은 공 포로 변했다)'을 통해 'puzzled'와 'frightened'를 찾을 수 있 다. puzzled: 어리둥절해하는, frightened: 겁먹은, 무서워

하는, ① scared: 겁먹은, ② nervous: 초조한, satisfied: 만족한, ④ pleased: 기쁜, 기뻐하는, upset: 속상한, ⑤ confused: 혼란스러워 하는

23 (A) seem to부정사: ~인 것 같다. (B) that은 계속적 용법으로 쓸 수 없으므로 who가 적절하다. (C) home은 부사이므로 to 없이 쓰는 것이 적절하다.

24 What's going on? = What's happening?: 무슨 일이야?

25 ⓐ와 ③, ⑤: 부사적 용법, ①, ④: 명사적 용법, ②: 형용사적 용법

26 글쓴이가 학교에서 지진 대피 훈련을 몇 번 했는지는 알 수 없다. ① She saw that parts of buildings had fallen and had smashed several cars. ② They went to an open space. ④ No. ⑤ She realized that she should be prepared for the next earthquake, which can occur at any time.

27 would like to부정사: ~하고 싶다

28 위 글은 '영화 비평문'이다. review (책·연극·영화 등에 대한) 논평[비평], 감상문, ① (신문·잡지의) 글, 기사, ② 수필, ④ 독후감, ⑤ 전기

29 '주인공의 나이'는 알 수 없다. ① San Andreas. ② Los Angeles and San Francisco in 2014. ③ A search-and-rescue pilot. ⑤ It's about the search for the missing family during an earthquake.

단원별 예상문제　　　　　　　p.158~161

01 ①　　　02 ②　　　03 ④
04 (1) (c)overing　(2) made our way
05 ④　　　06 ②　　　07 ④　　　08 ③
09 ②　　　10 ④
11 (1) Since　(2) Though　(3) when
12 (1) had taken　(2) had practiced
　　(3) had happened　　　　　13 ②
14 I still didn't know what exactly was happening
　또는 I still didn't know exactly what was
　happening
15 comfort → panic　　16 ③　　　17 ③
18 ②　　　19 ④　　　20 a tsunami
21 ④

01 주어진 단어는 동의어 관계이다. destroy 파괴하다 damage 손상을 입히다 recently 최근에 lately 최근에

02 침대가 흔들리는 것으로 보아 지진이 난 것을 알 수 있다.

03 컵이 넘어지고, 식탁에서 물건이 떨어지는 등의 상황에서 "굴러 떨어지다"는 "roll off"가 적절하다. 오늘 할 일을 내일로 미루지 마라 put off 미루다

04 (1) covering 덮고 있는 (2) make one's way 가다

05 'No, second is heavy rain'은 제시문의 추측이 잘못되었음을 알려주는 것이므로 주어진 문장은 ⓓ가 적절하다.

06 이어지는 설명에 피해를 입히는 자연재해의 종류가 나열되어 있는 것으로 보아 자연재해의 종류에 대하여 궁금해하는 것이 적절하다.

07 ④ 태풍이 가져온 손해가 얼마나 큰지는 소개되지 않았다.

08 지진이 났을 때는 탁자 밑으로 대피를 해야 하기 때문에 "over the table"을 "under the table"로 바꾸어야 한다.

09 대화 속의 "How scary!"는 놀라움에 공감하는 의미의 감탄문으로 질문의 내용은 아니다.

10 ① After she (had) finished her homework, she went to bed. ② I knew the story because I had read the book. ③ I couldn't get in the room because I had forgotten my key. ⑤ He carried out all the responsibilities I had given to him.

11 (1) 이유를 나타내고 있으므로 Since (2) 상반되는 내용이므로 Though (3) 시간의 부사절을 이끄는 when이 적절하다.

12 각각 한 시제 앞선 일에 대한 것이므로 과거완료 시제로 쓰는 것이 적절하다.

13 첫 번째 문장에서는 예상한 것이 성취한 것보다 앞선 시제이므로 과거완료 had expected가 적절하다. 두 번째 문장에서는 다음에 어지는 절의 이유에 해당하므로 Since가 적절하다.

14 부정문에서 still은 부정어 앞에 위치한다. exactly가 was happening을 수식하는 것이 아니라 의문사 what을 수식하고 있고, 이런 경우에는, 의문사 바로 앞이나 뒤에 위치하는 것이 정상적인 어순이다.

15 머지않아 방 전체가 심하게 흔들리기 시작했다고 했으므로, 혼란스러움은 '공포'로 변했다고 하는 것이 적절하다. comfort: 안락, 편안

16 지진이 일어났을 때 필자의 동생이 무엇을 하고 있었는지는 대답할 수 없다. ① It occurred one night in February. ② No. ④ No. ⑤ No.

17 ⓐ in a few minutes: 몇 분 만에, ⓑ be prepared for: ~에 대비하고 있다

18 주어진 문장의 looked around에 주목한다. ②번 뒤에 주변을 둘러본 상황이 이어지고 있으므로 ②번이 적절하다.

19 이 글은 글쓴이가 지진을 겪은 뒤에 언제든 발생할 수 있는 다음 지진을 대비해야 한다는 것을 깨달았다는 내용의 글이므로, 주제로는 ④번이 적절하다. 예방은 치료약보다 낫다; 유비무환이다. (좋지 않은 일이 일어나기 전에 예방하는 편이 그 결과에 대처하는 것보다 쉽고 유효하다.)

20 '쓰나미'를 가리킨다.

21 near Haeundae Beach를 near Gwangalli Beach로 고쳐야 한다.

01 ②　　　02 ②　　　03 ⑤
04 (1) if　(2) whether　(3) whether　(4) will be
　　(5) can be　(6) will not be　(7) appear
　　(8) resemble
05 I don't know if she likes Italian food or not.
06 (1) if[whether]　(2) can be understood
　　(3) must be made
07 ③　　　08 ①　　　09 ③
10 The plan had to be postponed because of cost.
11 ①　　　12 ⑤　　　13 ④　　　14 ④
15 ②, ④
16 (1) Joan asked if[whether] I want to go to the
　　party.
　(2) It depends on whether it applies directly to
　　your job.
　(3) You'll have to choose whether to buy it or not.
　(4) The beautiful clothes will be put on right now.
　(5) Problems will occur as a result of human life.

01 ① I don't want to know if something happened. ③ Matthew asked Vivian if she wanted to go back home or not. ④ I'm not sure if Ted won the speech contest. ⑤ Let me know if she will bring some food.

02 This essay will have to be completely rewritten. 조동사가 있는 문장의 수동태는 '조동사+be+과거분사'의 형태로 나타낸다.

03 조동사가 있는 문장의 수동태는 '조동사+be+과거분사'의 형태로 나타낸다.

04 (1) 불확실하거나 의문시되는 사실을 나타내는 접속사 if가 적절하다. (2) 내용상 '~인지 (아닌지)'라는 의미의 접속사 whether가 적절하다. (3) 바로 뒤에 'or not'이 이어지고 있으므로 whether가 적절하다. (4) if가 명사절을 이끌고 있으므로 미래시제는 미래시제로 나타내야 한다. (5)~(6) 조동사가 있는 문장의 수동태는 '조동사+be+과거분사'의 형태로 나타내며, 부정문은 '조동사+not+be+과거분사'의 형태로 쓴다. (7) appear는 자동사이므로 수동태로 쓰이지 않는다. (8) resemble은 타동사이지만 상태를 나타내는 말로 수동태로 쓰이지 않는다.

05 '~인지 (아닌지)'라는 의미의 접속사 if가 나오므로 'I don't know'를 쓰고 'if+주어+동사'의 어순으로 쓴 후 'or not'을 문장의 마지막에 써야 한다.

06 (1) asked의 목적어를 이끄는 if나 whether가 적절하다. (2), (3) 조동사가 있는 문장의 수동태는 '조동사+be+과거분사'의 형태로 나타낸다.

07 첫 번째 빈칸에는 see의 목적어를 이끄는 if나 whether가 적절하다. 두 번째 빈칸에는 조동사가 있는 문장의 수동태의 부정문

은 '조동사+not+be+과거분사'의 형태로 나타내는 것이 적절하다.

08 조동사가 있는 문장의 수동태는 '조동사+be+과거분사'의 형태로 나타낸다.

09 불확실하거나 의문시되는 사실을 나타내는 접속사 if나 whether가 적절하며, 뒤에는 '주어+동사'의 절이 나와야 한다.

10 조동사가 있는 문장의 수동태는 '조동사+be+과거분사'의 형태로 나타낸다.

11 check의 목적어를 이끄는 if나 whether가 적절하며 whether는 'or not'이 바로 뒤에 나올 때 쓰일 수 있지만 if는 그럴 수 없다.

12 능동태를 수동태로 바꿀 때, 목적어를 주어로 쓰고, 주어는 'by+목적격'으로 쓰며(일반인의 경우 보통 생략함.), 동사는 조동사가 있는 경우 '조동사+be+과거분사'의 형태로 쓴다.

13 ④번은 뒤에 or not이 이어지므로 if는 들어갈 수 없고 whether가 들어가야 하지만 나머지는 모두 if나 whether가 들어갈 수 있다.

14 know의 목적어가 나와야 하는데 '~인지 (아닌지)'라는 의미로 사실의 여부를 확인하거나 불확실함을 나타내는 명사절을 이끄는 접속사 if가 적절하다.

15 ② Very little of the house may remain after the fire. remain은 자동사로 수동태로 쓰지 않는다. ④ Do you know if Cathy will come home soon? if절은 간접의문문을 이끄는 것이므로 '주어+동사'의 어순이 되어야 한다.

16 (1) 사실의 여부를 확인하거나 불확실함을 나타내는 명사절을 이끄는 접속사 if나 whether가 적절하다. (2) if는 전치사의 목적어로 쓰인 명사절을 이끌지 못하므로 if 대신에 whether로 써야 한다. (3) whether는 to부정사와 함께 쓰일 수 있지만 if는 그럴 수 없으므로 if 대신에 whether로 써야 한다. (4) The beautiful clothes가 주어이므로 수동태로 써야 하고, 조동사가 있는 문장의 수동태는 '조동사+be+과거분사'의 형태로 쓴다. (5) occur는 자동사이므로 수동태로 쓰이지 않는다.

01 (1) The final match may be watched by about a
　　million people.
　(2) The value of regular exercise should not be
　　underestimated (by us).
　(3) The robots can be made to work faster in the
　　future (by us).
　(4) This math problem can't be solved by anyone.
02 Ask her if[whether] she watches TV every night.
03 (1) if[whether] Jake draws a picture
　(2) will be taken
04 (1) if[whether] you like　(2) how I should respond

33

05 (1) I want to know if my study plans are effective.

(2) I want to check if I can view the content of the site.

(3) I am not sure if she runs fast enough.

06 (1) Whether I believe you or not is important.

(2) My heart raced, not knowing whether or not my son was alive.

(3) He seemed undecided whether to go or stay.

(4) My lost card might be used illegally.

(5) Ghosts can appear in visible form in the world of the living.

(6) The tree had to be sawn down.

07 (1) may be affected   (2) will be released

08 (1) He asked me if[whether] I saw his backpack.

(2) No one can tell if[whether] he is serious or not.

(3) Let's see if[whether] anyone lives in that house.

(4) The room won't be cleaned until 2 p.m.

(5) Their voices can be heard from here.

(6) He shall be missed by us all

01 (1), (2) 능동태를 수동태로 바꿀 때, 능동태의 목적어를 수동태의 주어로 쓰고, 주어는 'by+목적격'으로 문장의 뒤에 쓰며(보통 일반인의 경우 생략함.), 동사는 조동사가 있는 경우 '조동사+be+과거분사'의 형태로 쓴다. (3) 사역동사 make의 목적격보어로 쓰인 동사원형이 수동태에서 to부정사로 바뀌는 것에 주의한다. (4) No one이 수동태에서 not anyone으로 바뀌는 것에 주의한다. (by 이하가 일반인을 의미하므로 생략 가능한 문장인데, 부정의 뜻을 나타내야 하므로 no를 'not+any'로 보아 not을 앞으로 보내야 한다.)

02 목적어가 되는 명사절을 if[whether]로 시작하는 간접의문문으로 바꾼다.

03 (1) 명사절을 이끄는 if나 whether를 이용하여 '주어+동사'의 어순으로 쓴다. (2) 'some wonderful pictures'가 주어이므로 수동태를 이용하고 '조동사+be+과거분사'의 형태로 쓴다.

04 간접의문문에서 의문사가 없는 경우에는 'if[whether]+주어+동사'의 어순으로 쓰지만 의문사가 있을 경우 '의문사+주어+동사'의 어순으로 쓴다.

05 '~인지 (아닌지)'라는 의미의 접속사로 쓰이는 if를 이용하여 'if+주어+동사'의 어순으로 쓴다. if 뒤에 오는 절은 의문사가 없는 간접의문문이다.

06 (1) 문두에서 주어를 이끄는 역할을 하고 있으므로 If를 Whether로 고치는 것이 적절하다. (2) 바로 뒤에 or not이 나오고 있으므로 if를 whether로 고치는 것이 적절하다. (3) whether 다음에는 to부정사를 쓸 수 있지만 if는 쓸 수 없으므로 if를 whether로 고치는 것이 적절하다. (4) 조동사가 있는 문장의 수동태는 '조동사+be+과거분사'의 형태로 쓴다. (5) appear는 자동사이므로 수동태로 쓰이지 않는다. (6) The tree가 주어

이므로 수동태가 되어야 하고, had to가 있으므로 'had to be sawn'의 형태로 써야 한다.

07 Manufacturing processes와 The new model이 주어이므로 수동태로 써야 하고, 조동사가 있으므로 '조동사+be+과거분사'의 형태로 쓴다.

08 (1) if나 whether를 추가하여 'if[whether]+주어+동사'의 어순으로 쓴다. (2), (3) 'if나 whether를 추가하여 쓴다. (4), (5) 조동사가 있는 문장의 수동태는 '조동사+be+과거분사'의 형태로 쓰므로 be를 추가한다. (6) 수동태에서 행위자를 나타낼 때 쓰이는 'by+목적격'의 by를 추가한다.

교과서 Reading

확인문제 p.192

1 T 2 F 3 T 4 T 5 F

확인문제 p.193

1 T 2 F 3 T 4 F 5 T 6 F

확인문제 p.194

1 T 2 F 3 T 4 F 5 T 6 F

교과서 확인학습 A p.195~197

01 We Are All
02 coming up
03 Why don't you
04 No way
05 right person
06 thought about
07 Why not
08 Come on
09 special qualities
10 can be called
11 What
12 good leadership qualities
13 friendly, outgoing
14 get along
15 will be elected
16 good leadership qualities
17 has ever told
18 Why
19 trying to be
20 however
21 become a leader
22 don't know
23 a vision, to motivate others
24 any of those things
25 wonder if
26 wrong
27 other leadership qualities
28 do some research online
29 what
30 Builders
31 feels valued
32 positive environment

33 to talk to
34 Logical Analysts
35 reasoning skills
36 Analyze
37 achieve the team's goals
38 Hands-Off Managers
39 on their own
40 try to control
41 it is needed
42 Strict Directors
43 everyone's role
44 on time
45 each step
46 Quiet Supporters
47 by example
48 shine instead
49 Meet, needs
50 Creative Thinkers
51 Approach
52 Come up with
53 differently from
54 realized the reason
55 belong to, come up
56 call for
57 unique situation
58 different responsibilities
59 more confident
60 some of the qualities
61 pick me
62 let's try

교과서 확인학습 B

1 We Are All Leaders

2 Brian: The election is coming up.

3 Why don't you run for class representative, Yumi?

4 Yumi: No way.

5 I'm not the right person for that position.

6 I've never thought about running.

7 Brian: Why not?

8 Yumi: Come on, Brian.

9 Leaders have special qualities.

10 I don't think a person like me can be called a leader.

11 Brian: What do you mean?

12 I think you have very good leadership qualities.

13 You're really friendly and outgoing.

14 You also help people get along.

15 I have no doubt that you will be elected if you run..

16 Brian told me this afternoon that I have good leadership qualities.

17 No one has ever told me that before.

18 Why does he think so?

19 Maybe he was just trying to be nice.

20 When he said that to me, however, I started to think.

21 Can I really become a leader?

22 I don't know.

23 I think leaders should have a vision, clear goals, and the ability to motivate others.

24 I don't have any of those things.

25 Then I suddenly started to wonder if these are the only qualities that make a good leader.

26 Maybe I'm wrong.

27 Maybe there are other leadership qualities.

28 So I decided to do some research online.

29 Here's what I found!

30 GREEN LEADERS: "Team Builders"

31 Ensure that the team feels valued

32 Create a positive environment

33 Are friendly and easy to talk to

34 RED LEADERS: "Logical Analysts"

35 Have good reasoning skills

36 Analyze problems and situations

37 Think of the most effective ways to achieve the team's goals

38 PURPLE LEADERS: "Hands−Off Managers"

39 Allow others to work on their own

40 Do not try to control people

41 Give advice only when it is needed

42 ORANGE LEADERS: "Strict Directors"

43 Make everyone's role clear

44 Make sure everything is finished on time

45 Ensure each step is done properly

46 YELLOW LEADERS: "Quiet Supporters"

47 Lead by example

48 Let the team members shine instead

49 Meet the team members' needs

50 BLUE LEADERS: "Creative Thinkers"

51 Approach problems in new ways

52 Come up with fresh ideas

53 Deal with tasks differently from others

54 I was surprised that there are actually many different leadership styles, but soon I realized the reason.

55 We belong to many different groups, and many different situations can come up in our lives.

56 They all call for different leadership styles.

57 Each group's unique situation determines the best leadership style.

58 "I am a part of many different groups, and I have different responsibilities in each group."

59 After reading everything, I became more confident.

60 I discovered that I have some of the qualities of a "green leader."

61 If my classmates think a green leader would make our class better, they might pick me to be class representative!

62 Okay, let's try it!

35

01 (A) don't　(B) Why not　(C) if　　　02 ②

03 ④　　　　　04 ②　　　　05 I read

06 unique situation　　　　　07 ②

08 which → what

09 red leaders 또는 logical analysts

10 (A) on their own　(B) control　(C) it is needed

11 ④　　　　12 if[whether]　　　　13 ⑤

14 with　　　15 ②　　　16 to shine → shine

17 don't mind whether → make sure 또는 ensure

18 to　　　19 ③

20 (A) different leadership styles　(B) unique
　　(C) best leadership style

21 ⑤　　　　22 ③

23 a vision, clear goals, and the ability to motivate others

24 ③　　　25 be elected　　　26 ④

27 I'm not the right person for that position.

28 ③　　　29 Ensure　　　30 ④

31 (A) creative thinkers　(B) fresh ideas
　　(C) differently from

01 (A) '반 대표에 입후보하는 게 어때?'라고 해야 하므로 don't 가 적절하다. Why don't you 동사원형?: ~하는 게 어때?, (B) '왜 입후보하는 것에 대해 생각해 본 적이 없어?'라는 뜻이므로 'Why not'이 적절하다. (C) '만약 네가 입후보한다면'이라고 해야 하므로 if가 적절하다. whether: ~인지 아니지

02 ⓐ와 ③, ⑤: 경험 용법, ①, ④: 계속 용법, ②: 완료 용법

03 자기 같은 사람이 리더로 불릴 수 있다고 생각하지 않는다고 말한 사람은 '유미'이다. ① propose: 제안하다

04 call for = require = need = demand = want: 요구하다, ② stand for: ~을 상징하다, ~을 의미하다

05 reading을 '주어+동사'로 바꿔 쓰는 것이 적절하다.

06 각 집단의 '독특한 상황'이 최고의 지도력 유형을 결정한다.

07 녹색 리더는 팀이 반드시 가치 있다고 느끼게 하고 긍정적인 환경을 조성하고 친절하고 말을 걸기 쉬운 유형이므로 '팀 조직자'가 적절하다. ⑤ carefree: 근심 걱정 없는, 속 편한

08 선행사를 포함하는 관계대명사 what을 쓰는 것이 적절하다.

09 문제와 상황들을 분석하는 리더들은 '빨간색 리더' 또는 '논리적 분석가'들이다.

10 보라색 리더는 다른 사람들이 '스스로' 일하도록 해 주고, 사람들을 '통제하려고' 하지 않고, '필요할 때만' 조언한다.

11 앞에 나오는 내용과 상반되는 내용이 뒤에 이어지므로 however가 가장 적절하다. ② 게다가, 더욱이, ③ 뿐만 아니라, 더욱이, ⑤ 즉[말하자면]

12 의문사가 없을 때 접속사 if[whether]를 사용하여 간접의문문으로 고치는 것이 적절하다.

13 이 글은 '좋은 리더를 만드는 자질들이 무엇인가'에 관한 글이므로, 주제로는 ⑤번 '리더가 가져야 하는 자질들'이 적절하다.

14 ⓐ come up with: 찾아내다, 내놓다, ⓑ deal with: 다루다, 처리하다,

15 strict = severe = stern = rigid = rigorous: 엄격한, ② easy-going: 태평스러운, 안이한, 게으른

16 사역동사 let+목적어+원형부정사

17 주황색 리더는 모든 일이 제때 끝날 것을 '확실히 하는' 엄격한 감독관이다.

18 belong to: ~에 속하다

19 '한 번 해보자'라고 하는 이어지는 내용으로 보아 모든 것을 읽고 나서, 나는 더 '자신감'이 생겼다고 하는 것이 적절하다. confident: 자신 있는, ① 관대한, ② 겸손한, ④ 불안해 하는, 염려하는, ⑤ 이기적인

20 '서로 다른 지도력 유형들'을 요구하는 다른 많은 상황들이 우리 인생에서 발생할 수 있고, 우리가 속한 각 집단의 '독특한' 상황이 '최고의 지도력 유형'을 결정하기 때문이다.

21 이 글은 '각 집단의 독특한 상황이 최고의 지도력 유형을 결정한다.'는 내용의 글이므로, 제목으로는 ⑤번 '최고의 지도력 유형은 상황에 따라 다르다'가 적절하다.

22 주어진 문장의 'don't know'에 주목한다. ③번 앞 문장의 질문에 대한 답을 모른다는 것이므로 ③번이 적절하다.

23 '비전, 명확한 목표, 그리고 다른 사람들에게 동기를 부여할 능력'을 가리킨다.

24 '다른 지도력 자질들이 있는지도 모른다. 그래서 나는 온라인으로 조사해 보기로 결심했다'고 말했기 때문에 뒤에 올 내용으로는 '지도력 자질들에 대해 유미가 온라인으로 행한 조사'가 적절하다.

25 '당선될 것'이라고 해야 하므로, 수동태로 쓰는 것이 적절하다.

26 (A)와 ④: (특히 미국에서, 선거에) 출마[입후보]하다, ① (~에) 급히 가다, 달려가다(for, to), run for the doctor: 의사를 부르러 급히 가다, ② (탈것이) 달리다, (버스·배 따위의) 편이 있다, ③ ~을 경영하다, 관리하다, ⑤ (연극·영화의) 장기 공연[상영]

27 the right person: 적절한 사람

28 노란색 리더는 솔선수범하고 팀원들이 대신 빛나도록 해 주고 팀원들의 요구 사항을 충족시켜주므로 조용한 '지지자'라고 하는 것이 적절하다. ① 경쟁자, ② 상대, 반대자, ④ 도전자, ⑤ 경쟁자

29 make sure = ensure 반드시 ~하게 하다, 확실하게 하다

30 (B)와 ④: 단계, ① (발)걸음, ② 걸음걸이, ③ 밟다, 딛다, ⑤ 디딤판, 계단

31 파란색 리더는 새로운 방식으로 문제들에 접근하고 '신선한 아이디어'를 떠올리고, 그리고 다른 사람들과 '다르게' 일을 처리하는 '창조적 사상가'이다.

01 How[What] about   02 class representative

03 (A) special qualities   (B) class representative

04 (A) clear   (B) properly   (C) Approach

05 (A) Strict Directors   (B) on time   (C) properly

06 creative thinkers → quiet supporters   07 none

08 that → if[whether]

09 She thinks leaders should have a vision, clear goals, and the ability to motivate others.

10 Each group's unique situation determines the best leadership style.

11 green leader   12 representative

---

01 Why don't you+동사원형 ~?= How[What] about ~ing?: ~하는 게 어때?

02 '반 대표'를 가리킨다.

03 유미는 리더들은 '특별한 자질'을 갖추고 있고, 자신은 '반 대표'에 적합한 사람이 아니라고 말한다. suitable: 적합한

04 (A) 목적격보어에 해당 하므로 형용사 clear가 적절하다. (B) 동사 is done을 수식하므로 부사 properly가 적절하다. (C) approach는 타동사로 전치사 없이 목적어를 써야 하므로 Approach가 적절하다. approach = come up to

05 주황색 리더는 모두의 역할을 분명하게 해 주고, 모든 일을 '제 때' 끝날 것을 확실히 하고, 그리고 각 단계가 '적절히' 이행되도록 하는 '엄격한 감독관'이다.

06 노란색 리더는 솔선수범하고, 팀원들이 대신 빛나도록 해 주고, 그리고 팀원들의 요구 사항을 충족시켜 주는 '조용한 지지자'이다.

07 not ~ any는 '아무것도 ~ 아니다'라는 의미로 전체부정을 나타낸다. not과 any가 결합된 none을 써서 부정형을 나타내는 것이 적절하다.

08 that 뒤에는 확실한 내용이 나와야 하므로, '~인지 아닌지'의 의미를 가지는 접속사 if[whether]를 사용하여 wonder의 목적어에 해당하는 절을 이끌게 하는 것이 적절하다.

09 유미는 리더가 비전, 명확한 목표, 그리고 다른 사람들에게 동기를 부여할 능력을 가지고 있어야 한다고 생각한다.

10 the best leadership style: 최고의 지도력 유형

11 모든 것을 읽고 나서, 유미는 '녹색 리더'의 자질들 중 일부분을 가지고 있다는 것을 알게 되었다.

12 representative: 대표(자), 다른 사람이나 사람들의 집단을 대표하여 행동하거나 결정을 내리도록 선택된 사람

---

01 illogical   02 ⑤   03 ⑤

04 (1) in charge of   (2) take sides   (3) is good at

05 (1) She and I belong to different groups.

  (2) This work calls for a high level of knowledge.

  (3) I tried my best to meet their needs.

06 ④

07 (A) making the presentation materials

  (B) presentation materials

08 ⑤   09 take sides

10 ⓒ → misunderstanding   11 ③   12 ⑤

13 ②   14 ⑤   15 ⑤   16 ⑤

17 can be adopted   18 ①

19 ⓐ, ⓒ, ⓓ, ⓕ   20 ②

21 Why haven't you (ever) thought about running?

22 ②, ⑤

23 many different groups and situations

24 If my classmates think a green leader would make our class better

25 ①, ④   26 yellow   27 ④

28 아무도 재활용물품 분리를 원치 않을 때 유나가 그것을 분리했고, 글쓴이가 감명 받아서 그녀를 돕기 시작했다.

29 ③

---

01 주어진 단어는 반의어 관계를 나타낸다. logical: 논리적인, illogical: 비논리적인

02 '누군가나 무언가에 가까이 가다'를 가리키는 말은 approach(접근하다)이다.

03 outgoing: 외향적인

04 be in charge of: ~을 담당하다, take sides: 편을 들다, be good at: ~을 잘하다

05 belong to: ~에 속하다, call for: 필요로 하다, 요구하다, try one's best: 최선을 다하다

06 어떠한 문제가 있는지 묻는 질문에 도움이 많이 된다는 대답은 어색하다.

08 민수는 발표 자료를 만드는 것을 잘한다.

09 take sides: 편을 들다

10 전치사 뒤에 명사가 이어지므로 misunderstanding이 적절하다.

11 준수가 보기에 재우와 윤호는 그다지 대단하지 않은 일로 싸웠다.

12 주어진 문장은 수요일에 바쁜 Mandy를 위해 목요일에 만남을 제안하며 이에 대한 감사의 표현이 이어지는 ⓒ번이 가장 적절하다.

13 disappointed: 실망한, satisfied: 만족한, amused: 즐거운

14 대화를 통해 Mandy가 무슨 시험을 준비해야 하는지 알 수 없다.

15 ⑤번을 제외한 나머지는 모두 확실성을 나타낸다.

16 His case가 주어이고 next week이 있으므로 조동사 will이

있는 수동태로 'will+be+과거분사'의 형태가 적절하다.

17 조동사가 있는 수동태는 '조동사+be+과거분사'의 형태로 쓴다.

18 ①에는 to부정사가 바로 이어서 나왔으므로 whether가 적절하다. 나머지는 모두 if나 whether를 쓸 수 있다.

19 ⓑ that → if[whether] ⓔ forget → be forgotten

20 run for: ~에 입후보하다

21 '왜 입후보하는 것에 대해 생각해 본 적이 없어?'라는 뜻이다. not+ever = never

22 actually = in fact = as a matter of fact: 사실(은), ① 물론, ③ 게다가, ④ 대신에

23 '서로 다른 많은 집단과 상황들'을 가리킨다.

24 If: '만약 ~한다면'을 의미하는 조건을 나타내는 접속사

25 deal with = treat = handle: 다루다, 처리하다, ② ~을 돌보다, 시중들다, ③ 들고[데리고] 있다, 나르다, ⑤ ~을 매매하다

26 Chris는 '노란색' 유형의 리더에 해당한다.

27 파란색 리더들은 '새로운 방식으로' 문제들에 접근한다.

28 다음에 이어지는 일화를 소개하는 것이 적절하다.

29 ⓑ와 ③: 강조 용법, ①, ⑤: 재귀적 용법, talk to oneself: 혼잣말하다, ②, ④: 관용 용법, by oneself: 홀로, for oneself: 혼자 힘으로

단원별 예상문제
p.214~217

01 (1) properly (2) approaching (3) wonder
   (4) determines (5) confident
02 (E) → (C) → (A) → (D) → (B)   03 ⑤
04 ①   05 ⑤   06 ①   07 ③
08 He asked her to help him with his homework.
09 She was supposed to meet Nick to work on their presentation.
10 He suggested meeting on Thursday for their presentation.
11 ③   12 ④   13 ②
14 I don't have any of those things.
15 ③   16 ④   17 blue   18 ①
19 ②   20 ④
21 Because there are actually many different leadership styles.

01 approach: 접근하다, confident: 자신감 있는, determine: 결정하다, wonder: 궁금해하다, properly: 적절하게 potential: 잠재력, 가능성

02 (E) 각자 맡은 일 확인 → (C) 사진 담당 대답 → (A) 세진이 맡은 일 확인 → (D) 대답 및 Emma의 맡은 일 확인 → (B) 대답 및 준비 확인

---

03 주어진 문장은 역할을 바꾸자는 수진의 제안에 대한 반응으로 ⓔ번에 들어가기에 적절하다.

04 고민이 해결되었으므로 relieved(안심이 되는)가 적절하다.

05 수진이가 몇 번 발표를 했었는지는 알 수 없다.

06 주어진 문장 다음에 세 그룹에 대한 설명이 나와야 하므로 ⓐ가 적절하다.

07 (A) respond: 반응하다, responsible: 책임감 있는, (B) translate: 번역하다, transfer: 옮기다, (C) receive: 받다, send: 보내다

08 Mandy의 남동생은 이번 주 수요일에 숙제를 도와줄 것을 요청하였다.

09 Mandy는 도서관을 다녀온 후 발표 준비를 위해 Nick을 만나기로 되어 있었다.

10 Nick은 발표 준비를 위해 목요일에 만날 것을 제안했다.

11 첫 번째 문장에서는 '~인지 (아닌지)'라는 의미의 접속사로 불확실하거나 의문시되는 사실을 나타낼 때 쓰이는 if나 whether가 적절하다. 두 번째 문장에서는 조동사가 있으므로 '조동사+be+과거분사'의 형태로 쓴다.

12 ① They will check whether[if] stores in school zones sell unhealthy food to children. ② I was anxious about whether I failed the exam or not. ③ Try this product for a week and decide whether or not you want to buy it. ⑤ I wonder if[whether] you are going to attend the meeting.

13 'belong'은 자동사로 쓰이므로 수동태로 쓸 수 없다.

14 not ~ any는 '아무것도 ~ 아니다'라는 의미로 전체 부정을 나타낸다.

15 유미는 '내가 정말 리더가 될 수 있을까? 나는 모르겠다.'라고 했지만, '자신이 리더가 될 수 없다고 생각한다.'는 말은 언급되어 있지 않다.

16 ⓐ와 ④: (요구 따위를) 채우다, 만족[충족]시키다, ①, ⑤ 만나다, ② (길·강 등이) ~와 만나다, 교차하다, 합류하다, ③ (흔히 불쾌한 일을) 만나다[겪다]

17 Jennifer는 '파란색' 유형의 리더에 해당한다.

18 주황색 리더가 어떻게 모두의 역할을 분명하게 해주는지는 알 수 없다. ② They are orange leaders. ③ Yes. ④ It is "Creative Thinkers." ⑤ They approach problems in new ways.

19 주어진 문장의 They에 주목한다. ②번 앞 문장의 'many different groups and many different situations'를 받고 있으므로 ②번이 적절하다.

20 이 글은 '각 집단의 독특한 상황이 최고의 지도력 유형을 결정한다.'는 내용의 글이므로, 주제로는 ④번이 적절하다.

21 실제로 서로 다른 많은 지도력 유형들이 있기 때문이다.

28 should find, interested in

29 motivate one another

30 translate, sing together

31 Doing, things, improves   32 Follow, on social

33 post, messages, how, doing

34 with, messages, understand, easily

35 recommend watching, dramas

36 been watching, year

37 for help with listening

38 also, print out, subtitles

39 What Works

40 hundreds of, own way

41 what, motivated, enjoy learning

42 at first, much bigger

---

34 post, with the messages, more easily

35 recommend watching

36 I've been watching, for

37 Korean subtitles for help with listening

38 to print out the subtitles

39 Works for

40 hundreds of, their own way, learning

41 what keeps, motivated, enjoy learning

42 hard at first, make, much bigger

본문 TEST Step 2   p.12~14

01 a New Language, Find

02 Why, Learn Foreign Languages

03 learn, because of school requirements

04 others, for fun

05 In any case, ways to study

06 Let's, listen to their ideas

07 Love Soccer   08 a big fan, Spanish

09 understand interviews with

10 However, because, Spanish that well

11 How, improve my Spanish

12 The best way, to practice it

13 have changed the language, have been writing

14 most important is to become familiar with

15 suggest watching Spanish

16 will help, get used to   17 too fast, try watching

18 are used only, not

19 Learn, soccer vocabulary, memorize

20 why don't you try writing, in Spanish

21 will help, improve your writing skills

22 No More   23 is back

24 so excited, perform   25 just perfect

26 without subtitles, translations though

27 Any tips

28 should find, are interested in

29 motivate one another

30 translate, sing together

31 Doing, improves our Korean

32 Follow, on social media

33 post short messages, how, are doing

본문 TEST Step 3   p.15~17

1 새로운 언어를 배우고, 새로운 세상을 찾아라

2 왜 사람들은 외국어를 배울까?

3 많은 학생들이 학교 필수 수업이기 때문에 새로운 언어를 배운다.

4 다른 많은 이들은 재미를 위해 그것을 배운다.

5 어떤 경우에도, 모든 곳의 학생들은 새로운 언어를 공부하는 데 흥미로운 방법들을 찾아낸다.

6 이 학생들을 만나서 그들의 생각을 들어보자.

7 저는 축구를 정말 좋아해요!

8 전 스페인 축구 팀의 엄청난 팬이랍니다.

9 저는 제가 정말 좋아하는 선수들의 인터뷰를 이해하고 싶어요.

10 그런데 스페인어를 그렇게 잘 알지 못하기 때문에 그것이 쉽지 않아요.

11 어떻게 하면 제가 스페인어 실력을 늘릴 수 있을까요? – 오언, 16세

12 새로운 언어를 배울 수 있는 가장 좋은 방법은 그 언어를 매일 연습하는 것이랍니다.

13 저는 제 휴대 전화의 설정을 스페인어로 바꿨고, 제가 사야 할 목록을 스페인어로 적어 오고 있어요! – 줄리, 15세

14 가장 중요한 것은 우선 언어와 친해지는 것이에요.

15 나는 전 스페인 영화들을 자주 볼 것을 제안하는데요.

16 그것은 당신이 언어의 소리에 익숙해지도록 도울 거예요.

17 만약 사람들이 너무 빨리 말한다면, 어린이를 위한 스페인 영화들을 먼저 보는 것을 시도해 보세요. – 인호, 14세

18 어떤 단어들은 일상생활에서가 아니라 오직 축구에서만 쓰인답니다.

19 몇몇 축구 어휘들을 배우고 기억하세요.

20 또한, 스페인어로 경기에 대한 후기를 써 보는 건 어때요?

21 그것은 당신이 작문 실력을 향상하도록 도울 거예요. – 로한, 16세

22 더는 자막 없이!

23 DREAM4가 돌아왔어요!

24 저는 제가 정말 좋아하는 한국의 젊은 남성 밴드가 공연하는 것을 보는 게 너무 신이 나요.

25 그들의 노래와 춤은 정말 완벽하답니다.

26 그렇지만 자막이나 번역이 없이 그들의 노래를 이해하고 싶어요.

27 어떤 조언들이 있을까요? – 마리사, 14세

28 당신은 DREAM4에 관심이 있는 친구들을 찾아 모임을 시작해야 해요.

29 우리 모임에서 우리는 서로 동기를 부여한답니다.

30 우리는 함께 노래를 번역하고 노래해요.

31 이런 것들을 하는 것은 재미있고 정말로 우리의 한국어 실력을 향상해요! – 로리, 15세

32 소셜 미디어에서 DREAM4를 팔로우하세요.

33 그들은 종종 자신들이 어떻게 지내는지에 대해 한국어로 짧은 메시지를 올려요.

34 그들은 또한 메시지와 함께 사진들을 올려서 당신은 더 쉽게 게시물을 이해할 수 있어요. – 아이샤, 14세

35 저는 한국 드라마들을 볼 것을 추천해요.

36 저는 1년 동안 한국 드라마들을 시청해 왔고, 그것들은 정말 재미있어요!

37 듣기에 도움이 되도록 한국어 자막을 사용할 수 있고요.

38 맨 먼저 자막들을 출력해서 읽는 것도 좋은 생각이랍니다. – 브랜던, 16세

39 무엇이 당신에게 효과가 있는 걸까?

40 세상에는 수백 가지 좋은 조언들이 있지만, 모든 사람이 학습에 대한 그들만의 방법을 가지고 있다.

41 당신에게 계속 동기 부여가 되는 것을 찾아라, 그러면 당신은 학습을 더욱 즐길 것이다.

42 기억해라, 모든 언어는 처음에는 어렵지만, 새로운 언어가 당신의 세상을 더욱 넓혀줄 수 있다!

본문 TEST Step 4-Step 5

p.18~23

1 Learn a New Language, Find a New World

2 Why Do People Learn Foreign Languages?

3 Many students learn new languages because of school requirements.

4 Many others learn them for fun.

5 In any case, students everywhere have found interesting ways to study new languages.

6 Let's meet these students and listen to their ideas.

7 I Love Soccer!

8 I'm a big fan of a Spanish soccer team.

9 I want to understand interviews with my favorite players.

10 However, it's not easy because I don't know Spanish that well.

11 How can I improve my Spanish? – Owen, 16

12 The best way to learn a new language is to practice it every day.

13 I have changed the language of my phone to Spanish, and I have been writing my shopping lists in Spanish! – Julie, 15

14 What's most important is to become familiar with the language first.

15 I suggest watching Spanish movies often.

16 It will help you get used to the sound of the language.

17 If the people talk too fast, try watching Spanish children's movies first. – Inho, 14

18 Some words are used only in soccer, not in everyday life.

19 Learn some soccer vocabulary and memorize it.

20 Also, why don't you try writing a review of a match in Spanish?

21 It will help you improve your writing skills. – Rohan, 16

22 No More Subtitles!

23 DREAM4 is back!

24 I'm so excited to see my favorite Korean boy band perform.

25 Their singing and their dancing are just perfect.

26 I want to understand their songs without subtitles or translations though.

27 Any tips? – Marisa, 14

28 You should find friends who are interested in DREAM4 and start a club.

29 In my club, we motivate one another.

30 We translate songs and sing together.

31 Doing these things is fun and really improves our Korean! – Lori, 15

32 Follow DREAM4 on social media.

33 They often post short messages in Korean about how they are doing.

34 They also post pictures with the messages, so you can understand the posts more easily. – Aishah, 14

35 I recommend watching Korean dramas.

36 I've been watching Korean dramas for a year, and they're really interesting!

37 You can use Korean subtitles for help with listening.

38 It's also a good idea to print out the subtitles and read them first. – Brandon, 16

39 What Works for You?

40 There are hundreds of good tips out there, but everyone has their own way of learning.

41 Find what keeps you motivated; then you will enjoy learning more.

42 Remember, every language is hard at first, but a new language can make your world much bigger!

After You Read B

1. want to improve, have any tips
2. vocabulary which is related to
3. Watching, with Chinese subtitles, way to get better at
4. a lot

After You Read C

1. How to Learn
2. Interests, Spanish
3. To understand, interviews
4. Spanish every day
5. Become familiar with
6. soccer vocabulary, review, match in Spanish
7. what, motivated, enjoy learning more

Do It Yourself B

1. so excited to see, perform
2. without subtitles, translations though
3. tips

After You Read B

1. A: I want to improve my Chinese. Do you have any tips?
2. B: Learn vocabulary which is related to your interests.
3. C: Watching Chinese dramas with Chinese subtitles is a good way to get better at listening.
4. A: Thanks a lot!

After You Read C

1. How to Learn a New Language
2. Interests: Spanish soccer team
3. Wants: To understand the players' interviews
4. Useful Tips: • Practice Spanish every day.
5. • Become familiar with Spanish.
6. • Learn soccer vocabulary and write a review of a match in Spanish.
7. Find what keeps you motivated; then you will enjoy learning more.

Do It Yourself B

1. I'm so excited to see my favorite Korean boy band perform.
2. I want to understand their songs without subtitles or translations though.
3. Any tips? - *Marisa*

01 긍정적인	02 엄청난	03 유익한
04 편리한	05 비슷한	06 뇌
07 세포	08 손상을 주다	09 숙면
10 비교되는	11 호두	12 방해하다, 가로 막다
13 생강	14 위험	15 조사하다
16 진행과정을 추적하다		17 이득
18 포함하다	19 처리하다	20 단서
21 시력	22 증가하다	23 복합적인
24 주름	25 낮추다	26 반사하다
27 속이 빈	28 개선하다	29 감동받은
30 부정적인	31 민감한	32 화학물질
33 기능	34 생산적인	35 다양한
36 게다가	37 지금부터	38 적어도
39 반면에	40 생각이 떠오르다	
41 A뿐만 아니라 B도		42 ~로 나뉘어지다
43 A가 ~하지 못하게 하다		

01 cell	02 beneficial	03 process
04 hollow	05 walnut	06 negative
07 awesome	08 multiple	09 pillow
10 mirror	11 compared	12 positive
13 moved	14 damage	15 wrinkle
16 search	17 clue	18 function
19 vision	20 chemical	21 chew
22 ginger	23 productive	24 similar
25 increase	26 healthy	27 benefit
28 contain	29 brain	30 improve
31 prevent	32 lower	33 convenient
34 sensitive	35 from now on	36 work out
37 in addition	38 on the other hand	
39 keep -ing	40 a variety of	41 be divided into
42 not only A but also B		43 come to mind

1 thirsty, 목마른   2 hollow, 속이 빈   3 convenient, 편리한
4 vision, 시력   5 walnut, 호두   6 slice, 얇게 자르다
7 pillow, 베개   8 active, 활발한   9 wrinkle, 주름
10 brain, 뇌   11 risk, 위험   12 increase, 증가하다
13 improve, 개선하다   14 chew, 씹다   15 clue, 실마리
16 benefit, 이익

Listen & Talk 1 A

Have, heard, chewing, bad for, teeth / haven't Why / damage, make, sensitive

Listen & Talk 1 B

look tired, get enough / slept for over / When did, go to bed / went to bed, as usual / probably what, making, tired, Have, heard, when / Why, that / going to bed late, make, feel tired / other hand, improve, memory, productive, now on, try to, earlier

Listen & Talk 1 D-1

Have, heard, writing, good, health / really / improves, memory

Listen & Talk 2 A

smart, check, health information, smartphone / What kind of / how far, during, how well / surprised, small

Listen & Talk 2 B

What, doing, living room / doing yoga / working, by yourself / following, steps / Let, see, been watched, million times, surprised, have watched / programs, popular / convenient, don't have to, out, exercise / That's why, try, too

Listen & Talk 2 C

looks / magic, carry, everywhere / special about / awesome, to drink, every / surprised, talk / asks, like, thirsty / why, trying / drinking, increase, help, blood flow / buy

Do It Yourself A

hungry / Why don't, before / want, wait until / have, eating little, often, health / Really, eating three meals / waiting, eat, too, Eating little, often prevents, from eating / go eat, right now

Listen & Talk 1 A

B: Have you heard that chewing ice is bad for your teeth?

G: No, I haven't. Why is that?

B: It can damage your teeth. It can also make them too sensitive.

Listen & Talk 1 B

B: You look tired. Did you get enough sleep?

G: Yes, I did. I slept for over seven hours.

B: Okay. When did you go to bed?

G: I went to bed after midnight, as usual.

B: That's probably what is making you tired. Have you heard that when you go to bed is very important?

G: No, I haven't. Why is that?

B: Scientists say that going to bed late can make you feel tired the next day.

G: I didn't know that.

B: On the other hand, going to bed early can improve your memory and help you be more productive. From now on, try to go to bed earlier.

Listen & Talk 1 D-1

A: Have you heard that writing by hand is good for your health?

B: Oh, really?

A: Yes, it improves your memory.

Listen & Talk 2 A

G: What's this?

B: It's a smart band. It lets me check my health information on my smartphone.

G: What kind of information?

B: It shows how far I walk during the day and how well I sleep at night.

G: Interesting. I'm surprised that this small band can do all that.

Listen & Talk 2 B

B: What are you doing in the living room?

G: I'm doing yoga.

B: You're working out by yourself?

G: Yes, I'm following this online video. It shows me all the steps.

B: Let me see. Wow, it's been watched two million times! I'm surprised that somany people have watched this video.

G: I know! These kinds of programs are becoming popular right now.

B: It looks very convenient. You don't have to go out to exercise.

G: That's right. That's why I love these programs. You should try them, too.

Listen & Talk 2 C

B: What is that? It looks nice.

G: This is a magic cup. I carry it everywhere with me.

B: What's special about it?

G: It's awesome. It tells me to drink water every two hours.

B: Really? I'm surprised that it can talk to you.

G: It even asks me questions like "Aren't you thirsty?"

B: That's so cool! But why are you trying to drink more water?

G: Because drinking a lot of water can increase your energy and help your blood flow.

B: That's amazing. I should buy one!

Do It Yourself A

B: Oh, I'm so hungry.

G: Why don't you eat some snacks before dinner?

B: I don't want to. I'll wait until dinner.

G: Okay, but have you heard that eating little and often is good for your health?

B: Really? I thought eating three meals a day was fine.

G: If you keep waiting until dinner, you will eat too much and too quickly. Eating little and often prevents you from eating like that.

B: I see. Then I'll go eat an apple right now.

본문 TEST Step 1　　　　　　　p.33~34

01 Beneficial Foods, Bodies

02 containing, variety, keeps, healthy

03 which, good for, parts　　04 however, big clue

05 Look, following examples　06 not only, but, also

07 compare, with, heart　　08 that, look similar

09 multiple hollow spaces

10 that, chemicals that, are, blood

11 In addition, lower, disease

12 Look, shape, walnut　　13 notice anything

14 similar to, shape, brain

15 divided into, just like

16 wrinkles, which, brain

17 help, stay healthy, active

18 good, preventing, disease

19 slice, looks like

20 chemicals, which improves, vision

21 process, send, image, brain

22 if, healthy eyes

23 Cutting, because, makes, cry

24 try slicing, anyway　　25 looks a little like

26 which helps make, cells　27 move on to

28 comes to mind　　29 Doesn't, look like

30 taste, prevents, feeling, throwing

31 For, reason, good, stomach

32 amazing, mirror, that, good

33 many other such foods　34 as many, try, variety

본문 TEST Step 2　　　　　　　p.35~36

01 Beneficial, Bodies

02 that, containing, variety, keeps, healthy

03 are good for, body parts　04 however, a big clue

---

05 Look at, following

06 Each of, not only, but, also

07 Slice, compare, with　　08 that, look similar

09 multiple hollow spaces, are red

10 that, that, are, heart, blood

11 In addition, lower, heart disease

12 the shape, walnut　　13 notice anything

14 similar to, shape　　15 is divided into, like

16 wrinkles, which　　17 stay healthy, active

18 preventing, disease

19 A slice of carrot

20 that, which improves, vision

21 helps, process, send, to　22 if, healthy eyes

23 Cutting onions, because, makes you cry

24 try slicing, anyway

25 looks a little like, humam cell

26 contain, which helps make

27 move on to ginger　　28 comes to mind

29 Doesn't, look like

30 strong taste, come from, prevents, from feeling, throwing up

31 For this reason, be good for

32 Isn't, mirror, that

33 many other such foods

34 as many as you can, a variety of

본문 TEST Step 3　　　　　　　p.37~38

1 우리 몸에 이로운 음식

2 우리는 다양한 음식을 포함하는 식사가 우리의 몸을 건강하게 유지해 준다는 것을 알고 있다.

3 그러나 때때로 우리는 어떤 음식이 어떤 신체 부위에 좋은지 잘 모를 때가 있다.

4 하지만 자연은 우리에게 확실한 단서를 제시해 준다.

5 다음의 예들을 살펴보자.

6 각각의 이 음식들은 우리 신체의 특정 부분과 비슷해 보일 뿐만 아니라 그 신체 부위에도 좋다.

7 토마토 한 개를 잘라내서 그것을 사람의 심장과 비교해 보자.

8 당신은 그 둘이 비슷해 보인다는 것을 알게 될 것이다.

9 둘 다 여러 개의 빈 공간이 있고 붉은 색이다.

10 연구원들은 토마토를 붉게 만드는 화학 물질이 사람의 심장과 피에 유익하다고 한다.

11 게다가, 토마토를 먹는 것이 심장병에 걸릴 위험성을 낮출 수 있다.

12 호두의 모양을 살펴보자.

13 뭔가를 알아차릴 수 있는가?

14 그렇다, 호두의 모양은 인간의 뇌 형태와 매우 유사하다!

15 호두는 마치 인간의 뇌처럼 두 부분으로 나뉜다.

16 호두에는 또한 주름이 있는데, 이는 인간의 뇌에도 있는 것이다.

17 연구 결과는 호두가 사람의 뇌가 건강하고 활동적인 상태를 유지하는 데 도움을 준다는 것을 보여준다.

18 호두는 또한 알츠하이머병을 예방하는 데도 좋다.

19 썰어 놓은 당근의 모양은 사람의 눈과 비슷해 보인다.

20 당근에는 비타민 A를 만들 수 있는 화학 성분이 있는데, 그것이 시력을 개선한다.

21 비타민 A는 눈이 빛을 처리하여 뇌에 선명한 이미지를 보낼 수 있도록 돕는다.

22 그러므로 건강한 눈을 원한다면, 당근을 먹어라.

23 양파를 써는 것은 즐겁지 않은데 왜냐하면 그것이 당신을 울게 만들기 때문이다.

24 그렇지만 어쨌든 하나를 잘라 보아라.

25 당신은 양파의 내부가 약간 인간의 세포처럼 보인다는 것을 알 수 있다.

26 과학자들은 양파가 비타민 B를 함유하는데, 이 비타민 B가 새롭고 건강한 세포를 만들어 내는 데 도움이 된다고 주장한다.

27 이제 생강으로 넘어가 보자.

28 생강을 보면 몸의 어떤 부위가 생각나는가?

29 생강이 마치 위장처럼 생기지 않았는가?

30 당신은 어쩌면 생강의 강한 맛과 냄새를 좋아하지 않을지도 모르지만, 이러한 맛과 냄새는 복통과 구토를 예방하는 생강의 특별한 성분에서 나온다.

31 이러한 이유로 생강은 당신의 위장에 좋을 수 있다.

32 어떤 음식이 그 음식이 유익한 신체 부위의 생김새를 반영하고 있다는 점이 놀랍지 않은가?

33 흥미롭게도 그러한 음식은 상당히 많다.

34 가능한 한 그러한 음식을 많이 찾아서 다양한 음식을 먹도록 하라.

1 Beneficial Foods for Our Bodies

2 We all know that a diet containing a variety of foods keeps our bodies healthy.

3 But sometimes we are not sure which foods are good for which body parts.

4 Nature, however, gives us a big clue.

5 Look at the following examples.

6 Each of these foods not only looks like a certain body part but is also good for that body part.

7 Slice open a tomato and compare it with the human heart.

8 You will see that they look similar.

9 They both have multiple hollow spaces and are red.

10 Researchers say that the chemicals that make tomatoes red are good for your heart and blood.

11 In addition, eating tomatoes can lower your risk of heart disease.

12 Look at the shape of a walnut.

13 Do you notice anything?

14 Yes, it's very similar to the shape of the human brain!

15 A walnut is divided into two parts, just like the brain.

16 Walnuts also have wrinkles, which the brain has too.

17 Studies show that walnuts help our brains stay healthy and active.

18 They are also good for preventing Alzheimer's disease.

19 A slice of carrot looks like the human eye.

20 Carrots have some chemicals that can make vitamin A, which improves your vision.

21 It helps your eyes process light and send a clear image to the brain.

22 So if you want healthy eyes, eat carrots.

23 Cutting onions is not fun because it makes you cry.

24 But try slicing one anyway.

25 You can see that the inside looks a little like a human cell.

26 Scientists say that onions contain vitamin B, which helps make new, healthy cells.

27 Now, let's move on to ginger.

28 What body part comes to mind when you see it?

29 Doesn't it look like a stomach?

30 You may not like ginger's strong taste or smell, but these come from a special chemical that prevents you from feeling sick and throwing up.

31 For this reason, ginger can be good for your stomach.

32 Isn't it amazing that some foods mirror the body parts that they are good for?

33 Interestingly, there are many other such foods.

34 Find as many as you can and try to eat a variety of them.

Presentation Time

1. Have, heard, is good for

2. made a plan to go, every Tuesday, Thursday

3. sure, help us stay healthy

Wrap Up READING

Wrap Up READING

1. Be Healthier
2. healthy food that, recommend
3. like to talk about, are good for
4. with, protein, little fat
5. contain lots of
6. are good for the brain
7. why don't you try

Culture Link

1. in India
2. practice, to better understand, thoughts, emotions
3. to guide, to a healthier life

구석구석지문 TEST Step 2   p.44

Presentation Time

1. Have you heard that swimming is good for your back?
2. Our group made a plan to go swimming together every Tuesday and Thursday at World Sports Park.
3. We are sure it will help us stay healthy.

Wrap Up READING

1. Eat Chicken Sandwiches, Be Healthier
2. A chicken sandwich is a healthy food that I recommend.
3. I'd like to talk about some of its ingredients that are good for our health.
4. First, chicken breast is meat with a lot of protein and little fat.
5. Onions contain lots of vitamin B.
6. Also, walnuts are good for the brain.
7. So why don't you try a chicken sandwich this weekend?

Culture Link

1. Yoga in India
2. Indian people practice yoga to better understand their minds, bodies, thoughts, and emotions.
3. They use it to guide themselves to a healthier life.

단어 TEST Step 1   p.45

01 최근에	02 인식하는	03 초래하다
04 극심한 공포, 공황	05 붕괴되다, 무너지다	
06 세게 부딪치다	07 손상	08 나가다, 퇴장하다
09 피하다	10 심각한	11 들불, 산불
12 더 나쁜	13 제대로, 적절하게	14 흔한
15 영향을 주다	16 불안하게	17 실종된
18 지진	19 정확하게	20 파괴하다
21 폭우	22 전체의	23 기어가다
24 홍수	25 즉시	26 포함하다
27 자연 재해	28 언급하다	29 두들기다
30 혼란, 혼동	31 긴급하게	
32 (일ㆍ사건 등이) 일어나다, 발생하다		33 반응
34 격렬하게, 심하게	35 ~에 바탕을 둔	
36 역시 또한	37 할인을 받다	38 다양한
39 ~의 경우에	40 매우 많은	
41 넘어지다, 기울어지다		
42 길 한쪽으로 차를 대다		43 산산조각이 나다

단어 TEST Step 2   p.46

01 violently	02 cause	03 reaction
04 confusion	05 worse	06 properly
07 recently	08 destroy	09 common
10 damage	11 missing	12 chest
13 collapse	14 nervously	15 disaster
16 flood	17 earthquake	18 occur
19 crawl	20 smash	21 heat wave
22 panic	23 exactly	24 include
25 special effect	26 suddenly	27 exit
28 affect	29 tap	30 urgently
31 immediately	32 actually	33 heavy rain
34 serious	35 pull over	36 in the middle of
37 a variety of	38 tip over	39 in case of ~
40 based on ~	41 a large number of	
42 put in	43 roll off	

단어 TEST Step 3   p.47

1 exit, 나가다, 퇴장하다   2 curious, 호기심이 많은
3 properly, 제대로, 적절하게   4 common, 흔한
5 smash, 세게 부딪치다   6 collapse, 붕괴되다
7 wildfire, 산불, 들불   8 cause, 초래하다

9 flood, 홍수   10 include, 포함하다

11 earthquake, 지진   12 crawl, 기어가다

13 swing, 흔들리다   14 perform, 수행하다

15 destroy, 파괴하다   16 disaster, 재난

Listen & Talk 1 A

was, flood, hear about / floods, common, are, curious, how, happened / Let's, research

Listen & Talk 1 B

seem to be, natural disasters, these days / earthquake, south, storm / curious, which type of natural disaster, most damage / report, damage, each type, natural disaster, storms / guess, second / heavy, heavy snow / What / Based on, earthquakes, damage, been increasing, because, been happening / seems like, prepared, variety, natural disasters

Listen & Talk 1 C

hear about, fires / How serious / destroyed, number of houses, other buildings / Are, going on / actually, worse, living there / So do, curious about, leave / Actually more than, leave, homes, missing / terrible, somewhere safe

Listen & Talk 2 A

what else, need to put in, natural disaster survival kit / water, radio / Anything else / make sure, include batteries, radio

Listen & Talk 2 B

Performing, properly, save, Here, steps, proper, needs, Tap, Are, reaction, listen, feel for breathing, breathing, sure, place, hands in, chest, weight, harder, breaths, keep doing, until help arrives

Listen & Talk 2 D

In case of, what, do / Make sure, cover, wet cloth / else / Make sure that, exit, immediately

Do It Yourself A

hear, occurring, often, before / really, never felt / usually occur, southern, other places as well / curious, why, occurred, recently / Why don't, research / do / How about asking, help / Let's, find

Listen & Talk 1 A

B: There was a big flood in Europe. Did you hear about it?

G: No, I didn't. But floods aren't that common in winter, are they? I'm curious about how that happened.

B: Me too. Let's do some online research.

Listen & Talk 1 B

G: There seem to be many natural disasters in Korea these day.

B: I agree. There was an earthquake in the south last week. Also a storm is coming this week.

G: I'm curious about which type of natural disaster causes the most damage in Korea.

B: Actually I read a report yesterday about the damage from each type of natural disaster. Number on is storms.

G: I see. I guess earthquakes are second.

B: No, second is heavy rain, and third is heavy snow.

G: What about earthquakes?

B: Based on the report, earthquakes are fourth. But the damage from earthquakes has been increasing recently because they have been happening more often in Korea.

G: I see. It seems like we have to be prepared for a variety of natural disasters in Korea.

Listen & Talk 1 C

B: Hey, did you hear about the big fires in California?

G: No, I didn't. How serious are they?

B: They've destroyed a large number of houses and other buildings.

G: Are the fires still going on?

B: Yes, actually the wind has made the fires worse. I hope all the people living there are okay.

G: So do I. I'm curious about how many people had to leave their homes.

B: Actually more than 20,000 people had to leave their homes, and about 400 people are missing in that area.

G: That's terrible. I hope they're somewhere safe.

Listen & Talk 2 A

B: Mom, what else do we need to put in the natural disaster survival kit?

W: Well, we need water, some food, and radio.

B: Anything else, Mom?

W: Oh, make sure that you include batteries for the radio.

W: Performing CPR properly can save someone's life. Here are the steps for proper CPR. First, check that the person needs help. Tap the person and shout, "Are you okay?" If there's no reaction, call 119 for help. Second, listen, look, and feel for breathing. If the person's not breathing, begin CPR. Make sure you place your hands in the middle of the person's chest. Use your body weight to press harder on the chest. After 30 presses, give the person two breaths. Keep doing CPR until help arrives.

Listen & Talk 2 D

A: In case of a fire, what should I do?

B: Make sure that you cover your mouth with a wet cloth.

A: Anything else?

B: Make sure that you exit the building immediately.

Do It Yourself A

G: Did you hear that earthquakes are occurring more often in Korea than before?

B: Oh, really? I've never felt an earthquake in Korea.

G: They usually occur in the southern part of Korea, but now they are occurring in other places as well.

B: I didn't know that. I'm curious about why earthquakes have occurred so often in Korea recently.

G: Why don't we do some research to find out?

B: Sounds good, but where do we look first?

G: How about asking our science teacher first? I think she can help us.

B: Okay. Let's go and find her.

본문 TEST Step 1 — p.52~54

01 Waking Up, Earthquake

02 in, had gone, hit

03 woke up, because, shaking

04 thought, shaking, as, joke

05 heard, fall, break, pieces

06 what exactly was happening

07 whole, violently, turned, panic

08 shouted, earthquake, ran into

09 Since, experiencing, how, react

10 just kept saying

11 pulled, out of bed

12 ran, crawled under

13 swinging, falling, floor

14 dropped, covering, broke

15 tipped over, rolled off

16 Every second, something else

17 to worry, collapse

18 seemed to stop

19 crawling toward, door

20 At, moment, rang

21 coming home from work

22 shouted, stopped   23 Get out of

24 Take, stairs   25 Don't take

27 Where are

28 okay, asked urgently

29 answered, Don't worry   30 I'm okay

31 driving home, shaking

32 pulled over immediately

33 right now, going on

34 made, way down, outside

35 looked around

36 Parts, fallen, had smashed

37 open, avoid, falling pieces

38 could, have happened, few

39 Although, drills, thought, real

40 get scared, remember

41 forget, panic, felt, falling

42 take, drills seriously

43 realized, prepared, occur, time

본문 TEST Step 2 — p.55~57

01 Waking Up, Earthquake

02 in, had gone to bed, hit

03 was shaking

04 was shaking, as a joke

05 heard, fall to the floor, break into pieces

06 then, still didn't, what exactly was happening

07 to shake violently, confusion turned to panic

08 shouted that, ran into

09 my first time experiencing, how to react

10 kept saying

11 pulled, out of bed

12 ran to, crawled under

13 see, swinging violently, falling to

14 dropped, covering it broke

15 tipped over, rolled off

16 Every second, hear, break

17 to worry, collapse

18 shaking seemed to stop

19 crawling toward

20 At that moment, rang

21 coming home from work

22 shouted, It stopped

23 Get out of

24 Take, stairs   25 Don't take

26 Hurry   27 Where

28 okay, asked urgently

29 answered, Don't worry   30 okay

31 was driving home, shaking

32 pulled over immediately

33 right now, find out, going on

34 nervously made our way, outside

35 looked around

36 Parts of, had fallen, had smashed

37 to avoid, falling pieces

38 could, have happened, a few

39 Although, earthquake drills, experience a real earthquake

40 get scared, remember

41 can't forget the panic I felt, were falling to

42 After, take, drills seriously

43 realized, be prepared for, occur at any time

본문 TEST Step 3   p.58~60

1 지진에 눈을 뜨는 것

2 2월 어느 날 밤, 내가 잠자리에 든 후에 지진이 일어났다.

3 침대가 흔들렸기 때문에 나는 갑자기 잠에서 깼다.

4 나는 남동생이 장난으로 침대를 흔들고 있다고 생각했다.

5 하지만 그때 나는 내 책상 위에 있던 거울이 바닥으로 떨어져 산산조각이 나는 소리를 들었다.

6 그때 나는 남동생이 그런 것이 아니라는 것을 알았지만, 정확히 무슨 일이 일어나고 있었는지를 여전히 알지 못했다.

7 머지않아 방 전체가 심하게 흔들리기 시작했고 혼란스러움은 공포로 변했다.

8 엄마가 지진이라고 소리를 지르며 내 방으로 뛰어 들어왔다.

9 지진을 경험한 것이 처음이었기 때문에, 나는 어떻게 반응해야 할지 몰랐다.

10 나는 그저 "어떻게 해야 하지?"라는 말을 반복했다.

11 엄마는 나와 남동생을 침대 밖으로 잡아끌었다.

12 우리는 주방으로 달려가서 식탁 아래로 기어들어 갔다.

13 나는 전등이 심하게 흔들리는 것과 책이 바닥으로 떨어지는 것을 볼 수 있었다.

14 우리 가족 사진이 벽에서 떨어졌고 사진을 덮고 있던 유리가 깨졌다.

15 컵이 넘어지고 식탁에서 굴러 떨어졌다.

16 매 순간, 나는 아파트에 있는 다른 어떤 것들이 부서지는 소리를 들을 수 있었다.

---

17 나는 건물이 무너지지는 않을까 하는 걱정이 들기 시작했다.

18 그때 흔들림이 멈추는 것 같았다.

19 우리는 문으로 기어가기 시작했다.

20 그 순간, 엄마의 휴대 전화가 울렸다.

21 전화를 한 사람은 바로 아빠였는데, 직장에서 퇴근하던 중이었다.

22 아빠는 소리쳤다. "지진이 멈췄어요!

23 건물 밖으로 나와요!

24 계단을 이용해요!

25 엘리베이터를 타면 안 돼요!

26 서둘러요!"

27 "어디예요?

28 괜찮아요?"라고 엄마가 다급하게 물었다.

29 아빠가 대답했다. "걱정 말아요.

30 나는 괜찮아요.

31 진동이 시작할 때 운전해서 집으로 가던 중이었어요.

32 하지만 즉시 차를 길 한쪽에 댔어요.

33 무슨 일이 일어나는지 알기 위해 지금 라디오를 듣고 있어요."

34 우리는 초조한 마음으로 계단을 내려가서 밖으로 나갔다.

35 나는 주변을 둘러보았다.

36 건물의 일부분이 떨어져 나갔고 몇몇 차들은 박살이 났다.

37 우리는 추가적인 낙하물을 피하기 위해 공터로 갔다.

38 어떻게 이런 일이 몇 분 만에 일어날 수 있단 말인가?

39 비록 학교에서 많은 지진 대피 훈련을 해 왔지만, 내가 실제 지진을 겪으리라고는 전혀 생각해 보지 않았었다.

40 그날 밤을 기억하면 나는 여전히 두려워진다.

41 가구가 흔들리고 물건들이 바닥으로 떨어졌을 때 내가 느꼈던 공포심을 나는 잊을 수가 없다.

42 그날 밤 이후, 나는 지진 대피 훈련에 진지하게 임하기 시작했다.

43 나는 언제든 발생할 수 있는 다음 지진을 대비해야 한다는 것을 깨달았다.

본문 TEST Step 4-Step 5   p.61~66

1 Waking Up to an Earthquake

2 One night in February, after I had gone to bed, an earthquake hit.

3 I woke up suddenly because my bed was shaking.

4 I thought my brother was shaking my bed as a joke.

5 But then I heard the mirror on my desk fall to the floor and break into pieces.

6 I knew it wasn't my brother then, but I still didn't know what exactly was happening.

7 Soon the whole room began to shake violently, and my confusion turned to panic.

8 My mom shouted that it was an earthquake and ran into my room.

9 Since it was my first time experiencing an earthquake, I didn't know how to react.

10 I just kept saying, "What should I do?"

11 My mom pulled me and my brother out of bed.

12 We ran to the kitchen and crawled under the table.

13 I could see the light swinging violently and books falling to the floor.

14 Our family picture dropped from the wall and the glass covering it broke.

15 A cup tipped over and rolled off the kitchen table.

16 Every second, I could hear something else in the apartment break.

17 I started to worry that the building would collapse.

18 Then the shaking seemed to stop.

19 We started crawling toward the door.

20 At that moment, my mom's cell phone rang.

21 It was my dad, who was coming home from work.

22 He shouted, "It stopped!

23 Get out of the building!

24 Take the stairs!

25 Don't take the elevator!

26 Hurry!"

27 "Where are you?

28 Are you okay?" my mom asked urgently.

29 My dad answered, "Don't worry.

30 I'm okay.

31 I was driving home when the shaking started.

32 But I pulled over immediately.

33 I'm listening to the radio right now to find out what's going on."

34 We nervously made our way down the stairs and outside.

35 I looked around.

36 Parts of buildings had fallen and had smashed several cars.

37 We went to an open space to avoid more falling pieces.

38 How could all this have happened in a few minutes?

39 Although I had done many earthquake drills in school, I had never thought I'd experience a real earthquake.

40 I still get scared when I remember that night.

41 I can't forget the panic I felt when the furniture was shaking and things were falling to the floor.

42 After that night, I began to take earthquake drills seriously.

43 I realized that I should be prepared for the next earthquake, which can occur at any time.

After You Read B

1. when, earthquake occurred

2. began to, because, was shaking violently

3. How scary

4. all crawled, got us out of bed

5. happening at the moment

6. Lot's of, were falling, heard, break

7. did, realize

8. should be prepared for, can occur at any time

Think & Write Step 3

1. would like to tell

2. is set in, in

3. main character, pilot, missing, during

4. special effects used, disaster scenes

5. a little, at times

6. Go, watch it

After You Read B

1. R: How did you feel when the earthquake occurred?

2. W: I began to panic because the whole room was shaking violently.

3. R: How scary! What did you do next?

4. W: We all crawled under the table after my mom got us out of bed.

5. R: What was happening at the moment?

6. W: Lots of things were falling to the floor. I heard many things in the apartment break.

7. R: What did you realize after that night?

8. W: I realized that I should be prepared for the next earthquake. It can occur at any time!

Think & Write Step 3

1. I would like to tell you about the movie *San Andreas*.

2. This movie is set in Los Angeles and San Francisco in 2014.

3. The main character, a search-and rescue pilot, must search for his missing family during an earthquake.

4. The special effects used in the disaster scenes are very good.

5. The movie is a little sad at times, but the story is very interesting.

6. I give *San Andreas* four stars. Go and watch it!

Lesson **4**

단어 TEST Step 1 p.69

01 엄격한 02 성취하다, 이루다
03 반드시 ~하게 하다, 보장하다 04 지지자
05 추리, 추론 06 자신감 있는 07 분석하다
08 논리적인, 타당한, 사리에 맞는 09 오해
10 배달하다 11 긍정적인 12 나누다, 분리하다
13 편집하다 14 접촉 15 능력
16 장식하다 17 선거 18 해석하다
19 귀중한, 존중 받는 20 대표(자) 21 효과적인
22 통찰력, 비전, 시력 23 결정하다, 결심하다
24 접근하다 25 불간섭주의의, 자유방임의
26 분석가 27 동기를 부여하다
28 돌아오다, 반납하다
29 외향적인, 사교적인 30 발표
31 깨닫다 32 안심이 되는 33 바꾸다, 전환하다
34 조사, 연구 35 ~에 갇히다
36 솔선수범하다, 모범을 보이다
37 ~을 생각해 내다, 내놓다
38 ~을 담당하다, 책임지다 39 해결하다
40 잘 지내다, 사이좋게 지내다
41 ~을 필요로 하다, 요구하다 42 다루다, 처리하다
43 어울려 밖에서 시간을 보내다

단어 TEST Step 2 p.70

01 analyst 02 confident 03 positive
04 valued 05 deliver 06 approach
07 contact 08 misunderstanding
09 research 10 motivate 11 outgoing
12 supporter 13 switch 14 translate
15 relieved 16 divide 17 reasoning
18 edit 19 effective 20 ability
21 representative 22 prepare 23 achieve
24 presentation 25 run 26 election
27 determine 28 analyze 29 logical
30 goal 31 instead 32 strict
33 properly 34 vision 35 take sides
36 come up with 37 get along 38 let down
39 belong to 40 work on 41 take care of
42 be in charge of 43 deal with

단어 TEST Step 3 p.71

1 leadership, 지도력, 리더십 2 run, (선거에) 입후보하다
3 task, 일, 과업, 과제 4 ability, 능력
5 logical, 논리적인, 타당한 6 switch, 바꾸다, 전환하다
7 approach, 접근하다 8 edit, 편집하다
9 supporter, 지지자 10 motivate, 동기를 부여하다
11 analyze, 분석하다 12 confident, 자신감 있는
13 effective, 효과적인
14 hands-off, 불간섭주의의, 자유방임의
15 representative, 대표(자) 16 election, 선거

대화문 TEST Step 1 p.72~73

Listen & Talk 1 A
problem / matter / going to, right, just realized, on Saturday evening, What should I do / like, decision, Let's, with / miss, best friend's birthday

Listen & Talk 1 B
What's the matter / problem / happened / had a fight, stuck in, what to do / why, had a flight / big deal, some kind of misunderstanding / Why don't, listen to / friends of mine, can't take sides / works out

Listen & Talk 1 C
What's the matter / What to do, asked me to help him, things to do / have to / return some books, presentation, have to prepare for / do, a lot / seemed let down / how about meeting, instead, everything, help / help me out, understanding

Listen & Talk 2 A
Sports Day, help out / to take photos / good at taking photos, have no doubt that

Listen & Talk 2 B
divided, into, be responsible for, translate, into, edit, are printed, in charge of, I have no doubt that, who receive

Listen & Talk 2 C
excited, field trip / Let's check, in charge of / taking pictures / some research / write our field trip report / ready / have no doubt that, turn out

대화문 TEST Step 2 p.74~75

Listen & Talk 1 A
G: Mom, we've got a problem.
W: What's the matter?

G: We're going to have dinner with Grandma this Saturday, right? But I just realized that Sujin's birthday party is on Saturday evening. She's my best friend. What should I do?

W: That sounds like a difficult decision. Let's talk about it with your dad.

G: Okay, Mom. I'd love to see Grandma, but I don't want to miss my best friend's birthday party.

Listen & Talk 1 B

M: Junsu, are you okay? What's the matter?

B: Hello, Mr. Smith. I have a problem.

M: What happened?

B: You know Jaewoo, Yunho, and I are best friends, right? They had a fight, and now I'm stuck in the middle. I don't know what to do.

M: That sounds hard. Do you know why they had a fight?

B: Yes, but it doesn't sound like a big deal to me. I guess they had some kind of misunderstanding.

M: Why don't you all meet together and talk about it? I think they'll listen to you.

B: That's a good idea. They're both good friends of mine. I can't take sides.

M: I understand. I hope everything works out.

Listen & Talk 1 C

B: Hey, Mandy. What's the matter?

G: I don't know what to do, Nick. My brother asked me to help him with his homework this Wednesday, but I told him I can't. I have so many things to do that day.

B: What do you have to do this Wednesday?

G: I need to go to the library to return some books. Then I have to meet you to work on our presentation. After that, I have to prepare for an exam at night.

B: Oh, you do have a lot to do.

G: Yes. But my brother seemed let down, so I feel bad.

B: Well, then how about meeting on Thursday instead for our presentation? Then you can do everything and also help your brother on Wednesday.

G: That would help me out so much! Thanks for understanding, Nick!

Listen & Talk 2 A

G: Sports Day is coming. How do you want to help out?

B: I want to take photos for Sports Day.

G: That's great. You are really good at taking photos. I have no doubt that you will take some wonderful pictures.

Listen & Talk 2 B

B: In the Send Our Stories project, we are going to make a picture book for children in other countries. We've divided everyone into three groups. Each group will be responsible for a different task. Group A will translate a Korean story into English. Group B will make drawings for the book and edit it. After copies of the book are printed, Group C will be in charge of sending them to the children. It won't be easy, but I have no doubt that the children who receive these books will really enjoy them.

Listen & Talk 2 C

B: I'm so excited about our museum field trip.

G1: Me too. Let's check our tasks. Yen, what are you in charge of?

G2: I'm in charge of taking pictures.

G1: Okay. Sejin, are you going to do some research on the museum?

B: Yes, I am. Are you going to write our field trip report, Emma?

G1: That's right. I think we're ready.

G2: Good. I have no doubt that our project will turn out well.

본문 TEST Step 1   p.76~78

01 We, All Leaders
02 election, coming up
03 Why don't you run
04 No way
05 right person, position
06 never thought, running
07 Why not
08 Come on
09 special qualities
10 like, can be called
11 What, mean
12 good leadership qualities
13 really friendly, outgoing
14 also help, get along
15 no doubt, be elected
16 that, good leadership qualities
17 No, has ever told
18 Why, think so
19 just trying to be
20 When, however, think
21 Can, become, leader
22 don't know
23 vision, goals, ability, motivate
24 any of those things
25 suddenly, wonder if, qualities

26 Maybe, wrong

27 other leadership qualities

28 decided, do, research online

29 what, found　　　30 Team Builders

31 Ensure, feels valued

32 Create, positive environment

33 friendly, talk to　　　34 Logical Analysts

35 Have, reasoning skills　　　36 Analyze, situations

37 effective, achieve, goals

38 Hands-Off Managers　　　39 Allow, on, own

40 try to control

41 advice, when, needed

42 Strict Directors　　　43 Make, role clear

44 Make sure, on time

45 Ensure, step, properly　　　46 Quiet Supporters

47 by example

48 Let, shine instead

49 Meet, members' needs　　　50 Creative Thinkers

51 Approach, in, ways　　　52 Come up with

53 Deal with, differently from

54 surprised, different, realized, reason

55 belong to, come up　　　56 call for, styles

57 Each, unique situation determines

58 part, different responsibilities, group

59 After reading, more confident

60 discovered, some of, qualities

61 make, better, pick, representative

62 let's try

01 We Are All　　　02 election, coming up

03 Why don't you, representative

04 No way

05 right person, position

06 thought about running　　　07 Why not

08 Come on　　　09 special qualities

10 like, can be called　　　11 What, mean

12 good leadership qualities 13 friendly, outgoing

14 also help, get along

15 no doubt, will be elected

16 good leadership qualities 17 has ever told

18 Why, think so　　　19 trying to be

20 however, to think　　　21 become a leader

22 don't know

23 a vision, goals, to motivate others

24 any of those things　　　25 wonder if, qualities

26 wrong

27 other leadership qualities

28 do some research online

29 what, found　　　30 Builders

31 feels valued　　　32 positive environment

33 to talk to　　　34 Logical Analysts

35 reasoning skills　　　36 Analyze, situations

37 effective ways, achieve the team's goals

38 Hands-Off Managers　　　39 Allow, on their own

40 try to control　　　41 advice, it is needed

42 Strict Directors　　　43 everyone's role clear

44 Make sure, on time　　　45 each step, properly

46 Quiet Supporters　　　47 by example

48 shine instead　　　49 Meet, needs

50 Creative Thinkers

51 Approach, in new ways

52 Come up with

53 Deal with, differently from

54 realized the reason　　　55 belong to, come up

56 call for

57 unique situation determines

58 a part of, different responsibilities

59 more confident　　　60 some of the qualities

61 pick me, class representative

62 let's try

1 우리는 모두 리더들이다

2 Brian: "선거가 다가오고 있어.유지해 준다는 것을 알고 있다.

3 유미야, 반 대표에 입후보하는 게 어때?"

4 유미: "아니.

5 나는 그 자리에 적절한 사람이 아니야.

6 나는 입후보하는 것에 대해 생각해 본 적이 없어."

7 Brian: "왜?"

8 유미: "이봐, Brian.

9 리더들은 특별한 자질을 갖추고 있어.

10 나 같은 사람이 리더로 불릴 수 있다고 생각하지 않아."

11 Brian: "무슨 말이야?

12 내 생각에 너는 매우 좋은 지도력 자질들을 갖추고 있어.

13 너는 정말 친절하고 외향적이잖아.

14 또 너는 사람들이 어울리도록 도와주기도 해.

15 만약 네가 입후보한다면 당선될 거라고 믿어 의심치 않아."

16 Brian은 오늘 오후에 내게 내가 좋은 지도력 자질들을 갖추고 있다고 말했다.

17 이전에는 아무도 내게 그런 말을 한 적이 없었다.

18 왜 그는 그렇게 생각했을까?

19 아마도 그는 그저 친절하려고 했을 것이다.

20 그러나 그가 내게 그렇게 말했을 때, 나는 생각하기 시작했다.

21 내가 정말 리더가 될 수 있을까?

22 나는 모르겠다.

23 나는 리더가 비전, 명확한 목표, 그리고 다른 사람들에게 동기를 부여할 능력을 가지고 있어야 한다고 생각한다.

24 나는 그러한 것들 중 어느 것도 가지고 있지 않다.

25 그때 나는 갑자기 이것들이 좋은 리더를 만드는 유일한 자질들인지 궁금해하기 시작했다.

26 아마도 내가 틀린지도 모른다.

27 어쩌면 다른 지도력 자질들이 있는지도 모른다.

28 그래서 나는 온라인으로 조사해 보기로 결심했다.

29 여기에 내가 찾은 것이 있다!

30 〈녹색 리더〉 '팀 조직자'

31 팀이 반드시 가치 있다고 느끼게 한다

32 긍정적인 환경을 조성한다

33 친절하고 말을 걸기 쉽다

34 〈빨간색 리더〉 '논리적 분석가'

35 좋은 추론 기술을 갖고 있다

36 문제와 상황들을 분석한다

37 팀의 목표를 성취하는 가장 효과적인 방법들을 생각한다

38 〈보라색 리더〉 '방임적 관리자'

39 다른 사람들이 스스로 일하도록 해 준다

40 사람들을 통제하려고 하지 않는다

41 필요할 때만 조언한다

42 〈주황색 리더〉 '엄격한 감독관'

43 모두의 역할을 분명하게 해 준다

44 모든 일을 제때 끝날 것을 확실히 한다

45 단계가 적절히 이행되도록 한다

46 〈노란색 리더〉 '조용한 지지자'

47 솔선수범한다

48 팀원들이 대신 빛나도록 해 준다

49 팀원들의 요구 사항을 충족한다

50 〈파란색 리더〉 '창조적 사상가'

51 새로운 방식으로 문제들에 접근한다

52 신선한 아이디어를 떠올린다

53 다른 사람들과 다르게 일을 처리한다

54 나는 실제로 서로 다른 많은 지도력 유형들이 있어서 놀랐지만, 곧 그 이유를 깨달았다.

55 우리는 서로 다른 여러 집단에 속하고, 우리 인생에서 서로 다른 많은 상황들이 발생할 수 있다.

56 그것들은 모두 서로 다른 지도력 유형들을 요구한다.

57 각 집단의 독특한 상황이 최고의 지도력 유형을 결정한다.

58 "나는 서로 다른 많은 집단의 일부이고, 각 집단에서 각각 다른 책임을 갖고 있어."

59 모든 것을 읽고 나서, 나는 더 자신감이 생겼다.

60 나는 '녹색 리더'의 자질들 중 일부분을 가지고 있다는 것을 알게 되었다.

61 만약 나의 반 친구들이 녹색 리더가 우리 학급을 더 좋게 만들 거라고 생각한다면, 그들은 학급 대표로 나를 뽑을지도 모른다!

62 좋아, 시도해 보자!

본문 TEST Step 4-Step 5   p.85~90

1 We Are All Leaders

2 Brian: The election is coming up.

3 Why don't you run for class representative, Yumi?

4 Yumi: No way.

5 I'm not the right person for that position.

6 I've never thought about running.

7 Brian: Why not?

8 Yumi: Come on, Brian.

9 Leaders have special qualities.

10 I don't think a person like me can be called a leader.

11 Brian: What do you mean?

12 I think you have very good leadership qualities.

13 You're really friendly and outgoing.

14 You also help people get along.

15 I have no doubt that you will be elected if you run..

16 Brian told me this afternoon that I have good leadership qualities.

17 No one has ever told me that before.

18 Why does he think so?

19 Maybe he was just trying to be nice.

20 When he said that to me, however, I started to think.

21 Can I really become a leader?

22 I don't know.

23 I think leaders should have a vision, clear goals, and the ability to motivate others.

24 I don't have any of those things.

25 Then I suddenly started to wonder if these are the only qualities that make a good leader.

26 Maybe I'm wrong.

27 Maybe there are other leadership qualities.

28 So I decided to do some research online.

29 Here's what I found!

30 GREEN LEADERS: "Team Builders"

31 Ensure that the team feels valued

32 Create a positive environment

33 Are friendly and easy to talk to

34 RED LEADERS: "Logical Analysts"

35 Have good reasoning skills

36 Analyze problems and situations

37 Think of the most effective ways to achieve the team's goals
38 PURPLE LEADERS: "Hands-Off Managers"
39 Allow others to work on their own
40 Do not try to control people
41 Give advice only when it is needed
42 ORANGE LEADERS: "Strict Directors"
43 Make everyone's role clear
44 Make sure everything is finished on time
45 Ensure each step is done properly
46 YELLOW LEADERS: "Quiet Supporters"
47 Lead by example
48 Let the team members shine instead
49 Meet the team members' needs
50 BLUE LEADERS: "Creative Thinkers"
51 Approach problems in new ways
52 Come up with fresh ideas
53 Deal with tasks differently from others
54 I was surprised that there are actually many different leadership styles, but soon I realized the reason.
55 We belong to many different groups, and many different situations can come up in our lives.
56 They all call for different leadership styles.
57 Each group's unique situation determines the best leadership style.
58 "I am a part of many different groups, and I have different responsibilities in each group."
59 After reading everything, I became more confident.
60 I discovered that I have some of the qualities of a "green leader."
61 If my classmates think a green leader would make our class better, they might pick me to be class representative!
62 Okay, let's try it!

구석구석지문 TEST Step 1 p.91

Presentation Time Step 3

1. chose tasks to prepare for
2. will buy
3. will decorate the classroom
4. will play, party songs
5. no doubt that, will be a lot of

After You Read B

1. to lead my example, take care of others' needs
2. important thing, that, shine

3. enjoy approaching, in new ways
4. try my best, come up with
5. analyze, situations, look for, effective ways to achieve our goals

Do It Yourself B

1. Why don't you run
2. never thought about running
3. Why not
4. have special qualities
5. a person like, can be called
6. What do, mean
7. really friendly, outgoing
8. help people get along
9. no doubt, will be elected, run

구석구석지문 TEST Step 2 p.92

Presentation Time Step 3

1. Our group chose tasks to prepare for our class birthday party.
2. I will buy a cake.
3. Woojin and Taeho will decorate the classroom.
4. Yeji will play birthday party songs.
5. I have no doubt that our birthday party will be a lot of fun!

After You Read B

1. Hi, I'm Jennifer. I try to lead my example and take care of others' needs.
2. The important thing is that the members of my team shine.
3. Hello, I'm Heejin. I enjoy approaching problems in new ways.
4. I try my best to come up with new ideas.
5. Hi, I'm Chris. I analyze my team's problems and situations, and then I look for the most effective ways to achieve our goals.

Do It Yourself B

1. Brian: Why don't you run for class representative, Yumi?
2. Yumi: No way. I've never thought about running.
3. Brian: Why not?
4. Yumi: Leaders have special qualities.
5. I don't think a person like me can be called a leader.
6. Brian: What do you mean?
7. You're really friendly and outgoing.
8. You also help people get along.
9. I have no doubt that you will be elected if you run.

MEMO

◎ 선택형 문항의 답안은 컴퓨터용 수정 싸인펜을 사용하여 OMR 답안지에 바르게 표기하시오.
◎ 서술형 문제는 답을 답안지에 반드시 검정 볼펜으로 쓰시오.
◎ 총 30문항 100점 만점입니다. 문항별 배점은 각 문항에 표시되어 있습니다.

[서울시 강동구 ○○중]

1. 다음 빈칸에 한 번도 사용되지 <u>않</u>은 단어는? (3점)

- Water is a basic _____ of life.
- Carl didn't _____ for the night duty.
- I was asked to _____ a poem every week.
- She is a _____ speaker who always impresses the audience.

① mistake
② volunteer
③ confident
④ memorize
⑤ requirement

[서울시 양천구 ○○중]

2. 다음 단어의 영어 풀이가 옳지 <u>않</u>은 것은? (3점)

① motivate: to put something online for other people to see
② familiar: well-known; seen often in everyday life
③ translate: to change words into another language
④ review: to consider something carefully to see what is wrong with it or how it could be improved
⑤ perform: to do something like singing or acting to entertain people

[서울시 서초구 ○○중]

3. 다음 글의 문맥상 빈칸에 들어갈 단어로 옳지 <u>않</u>은 것은? (4점)

Travelling Becomes More Fun
When you visit a place and you start talking to them in their mother tongue, they become _____. You can learn a new language like Spanish and finally get to experience a deeper side of many different cultures through it.

① anxious
② kind
③ warm
④ friendly
⑤ hospitable

[전라북도 ○○중]

4. 다음 대화 중 <u>어색한</u> 것은? (2점)

① A: Would you like to have some bread?
   B: Yes. I'd like to.
② A: What do you want to do after school?
   B: I just want to go home and take a rest.
③ A: How did you like the play?
   B: I watched it with my friend.
④ A: What would you like to do this year?
   B: I'd like to learn how to play the violin.
⑤ A: How do you like the pizza here?
   B: It's so tasty.

[5-6] 다음 대화를 읽고 물음에 답하시오.

B: Hey, Suji! What are you holding?

G: Hi, Ben. It's a skateboard. I'm going skateboarding. (A)

B: Wow! I didn't know that you could skateboard. (B)

G: I joined a local skateboarding club last month.

B: I see. So how do you like it? (C)

G: It's really fun! It helps me make new friends, too. (D)

B: How? (E)

G: I go skateboarding with other members of the club, and we share tips with one another.

5. 위 대화의 흐름으로 보아, 주어진 문장이 들어갈 가장 알맞은 곳은? (3점)

How did you learn to skateboard?

① (A) ② (B) ③ (C)

④ (D) ⑤ (E)

6. 위 대화의 밑줄 친 부분의 의도로 알맞은 것은? (2점)

① 취미 묻기

② 계획 묻기

③ 이유 묻기

④ 선호에 대해 묻기

⑤ 만족이나 불만족에 대해 묻기

7. 다음 밑줄 친 ⓐ~ⓔ 중 문맥에 어울리지 않는 질문은? (4점)

A: What are you doing?

B: I'm writing a list of things that I want to do this year.

A: That's nice. ⓐWhat would you like to do this year?

B: First of all, I'd like to spend time volunteering with my friends during winter vacation.

A: That sounds great.

B: ⓑHow do you like it?

A: I'm thinking of going skateboarding regularly.

B: Wow, I didn't know you could skateboard. ⓒHow did you learn to skateboard?

A: I joined a local skateboarding club last month.

B: I see. ⓓDo you like it a lot?

A: Yes. It's really fun. It helps me make new friends, too.

B: How?

A: I go skateboarding with other members of the club, and we share tips with one another.

B: Then, ⓔwould you like to go skateboarding with me next Sunday?

A: That's really cool. I'd love to.

① ⓐ ② ⓑ ③ ⓒ

④ ⓓ ⑤ ⓔ

[8-9] 다음 대화를 읽고 물음에 답하시오.

A: Last year, I moved to Seoul.
B: How do you like (A)_____ in Seoul?
A: It's great! There are many thing to do. This year, I'd like to (B)_____.
B: That sounds fun!

8. 위 대화의 빈칸 (A)에 들어갈 적절한 말은?   (3점)

① live
② lived
③ living
④ live for
⑤ live with

9. 위 대화의 빈칸 (B)에 들어갈 적절한 말은?   (2점)

① go to a museum
② goes to a museum
③ went to a museum
④ going to a museum
⑤ were going to a museum

10. 다음 대화의 흐름상 (A)~(D)의 순서로 가장 적절한 것은?   (4점)

B: Hey, Suji! What are you holding?
G: Hi, Ben. It's a skateboard. I'm going skateboarding.
B: Wow! I didn't know that you could skateboard. How did you learn to skateboard?

(A) I see. So how do you like it?
(B) I joined a local skateboarding club last month.
(C) How?
(D) It's really fun! It helps me make new friends, too.

G: I go skateboarding with other members of the club, and we share tips with one another.

① (B)-(C)-(D)-(A)
② (D)-(C)-(B)-(A)
③ (B)-(A)-(D)-(C)
④ (D)-(A)-(C)-(B)
⑤ (B)-(C)-(A)-(D)

11. 다음 두 문장을 현재완료 진행형을 이용하여 한 문장으로 바꿔 쓰시오.   (4점)

I started listening to music two hours ago.
I am still listening to it.

정답 : _____

12. 다음 빈칸에 가장 잘 어울리는 것은?　(2점)

A: Did you make this shelf yourself? It's amazing!

B: Thanks. I began making furniture last year.

A: Cool! _____

B: It was hard at first, but now I love it.

A: That's great. I think you're really good at it.

① How are you doing?

② How do you like it?

③ Why did you learn it?

④ What would you like to do?

⑤ What's your favorite furniture?

13. 다음 중 밑줄 친 부분이 어법상 옳은 것은?　(3점)

① My friend thought <u>what</u> I knew the answer.

② I couldn't hear <u>that</u> he said to us.

③ <u>That</u> the cook baked was delicious.

④ She wanted to sweep the things <u>which</u> have fallen on the grass.

⑤ A baby sitter looks after children <u>who</u> parents both work.

14. 다음 두 문장을 각각 한 문장으로 바꿔 쓰시오. (5점)

(1) I started to write a diary. And I am still writing it.

→ _____

　(7단어)

(2) Sam started to swim. And he is still swimming.

→ _____

　(5단어)

15. 다음 밑줄 친 that 중 그 쓰임이 <u>다른</u> 하나를 고르면?　(3점)

① <u>That</u> red jacket is mine.

② I bought a bag <u>that</u> was made of leather.

③ Sue wears rainboots <u>that</u> I made for her.

④ The only thing <u>that</u> we have is a chocolate.

⑤ Ours is a cat <u>that</u> has gray eyes.

16. 다음 중 어법상 <u>어색한</u> 문장은?　(4점)

① I have an uncle, that works at an airport.

② Look at the mountain covered with snow.

③ The boy sitting next to Mina is my brother.

④ Do you know the man wearing a red shirt?

⑤ I bought a pair of shoes, which had scratches.

17. 다음 글을 읽은 독자의 반응으로 적절하지 <u>않은</u> 것은?
(4점)

Let's have a look at a few benefits of learning a foreign language.

It Boosts Your Brain

Learning a new language is a complex task. When you are learning new words, you are assigning another recognition pattern to everything you have ever known. Once you have learned a new language, your brain starts working faster and your problem-solving skills become sharp as well.

It Can Prove Good for Your Career

Having a foreign language on your CV is never a bad option. Not only does it tell your employer that you have the skill to learn another language, but it can also give you an advantage in certain scenarios. The entire world is connected digitally today and a lot of businesses make deals with foreign companies. If you are applying to a company that is in business with a foreign country whose language you have learned, then you will be their priority choice.

*assign 배정하다, 부과하다
recognition 인식

① Adela: There are advantages of learning new languages.
② Brian: It wouldn't be a disadvantage to have a foreign language on my CV.
③ Curtis: I would like to learn a new language to improve my problem-solving skills.
④ Justin: Once I learn a language, my recognition pattern would never change.
⑤ Daniel: There is a greater possibility for me to work for a Chinese company than a French company since I am fluent in Chinese and can't speak French.

18. 다음 글의 제목으로 가장 적절한 것은?
(3점)

What city do you want to go to in Korea? I want to go to Busan. In Busan, I want to try raw fish. I'd also like to go swimming at Haeundae beach and take pictures at Gamcheon culture village. Also, I want to visit Nampodong PIFF square. I'm sure these new experiences in Busan would help me understand Korea better.

*raw: 익히지 않은, 날것의

① What I Like About Korea
② What Keeps Me Surprised
③ What I Did in Busan Last Summer
④ What I Want to Experience in Busan
⑤ What I Want to Understand in Korea

[19~24] 다음을 읽고 물음에 답하시오.

> Why Do People Learn Foreign Languages?
>
> Many students learn new languages because of school requirements. Many others learn them for fun. In any case, students everywhere have found interesting ways to study new languages. Let's meet these students and listen to their ideas.
>
> I'm a big fan of a Spanish soccer team. I want to understand interviews with my favorite players. (A) However, it's not easy because I don't know Spanish that well. (B) How can I improve my Spanish?
>
> *Owen*, 16
>
> The best way to learn a new language is to practice it every day. I have changed the language of my phone to Spanish, and I have been writing my shopping lists in Spanish! (C)
>
> *Julie*, 15
>
> (가)<u>가장 중요한 것은 우선 언어와 친해지는 것이다</u>. I suggest watching Spanish movies often. (D) If the people talk too fast, try watching Spanish children's movies first.
>
> *Inho*, 14
>
> Some words are used only in soccer, not in everyday life. Learn some (나)_____ and memorize it. Also, why don't you try writing a review of a match in Spanish? (E) It will help you improve your writing skills.
>
> *Rohan*, 16

19. 위 글의 (A)~(E) 중 다음 문장이 들어갈 위치로 가장 알맞은 곳은? (4점)

> It will help you get used to the sound of the language.

① (A)　　　② (B)　　　③ (C)
④ (D)　　　⑤ (E)

20. 위 글의 내용과 일치하지 <u>않는</u> 것은? (3점)

① Many students learn new languages at school.
② Speaking new languages improves your speaking skill.
③ Owen really likes a Spanish soccer team.
④ Julie has been writing her shopping lists in Spanish.
⑤ Inho believes becoming familiar with the new language is very important.

21. 위 글 (가)의 해석을 읽고 〈보기〉의 단어를 바르게 배열하시오. (주어진 단어만 사용할 것) (5점)

> 보기
>
> to / most / familiar / important /
> is / with / what's / become

정답: _____ the
language first.

22. 위 글의 빈칸 (나)에 가장 알맞은 말은? (3점)

① player's names

② soccer vocabulary

③ good manners

④ safety tips

⑤ soccer skills

23. 위 글을 읽고 다음 질문에 대한 알맞은 답을 있는 대로 고른 것은? (3점)

> Q. What has Julie done to practice Spanish every day?

> ⓐ She has been learning some soccer vocabulary.
>
> ⓑ She has watched Spanish children's movies.
>
> ⓒ She has been writing shopping lists in Spanish.
>
> ⓓ She has changed the language of her phone to Spanish.
>
> ⓔ She has been writing a review of a soccer match in Spanish.

① ⓐ, ⓑ   ② ⓐ, ⓔ

③ ⓑ, ⓓ   ④ ⓒ, ⓓ

⑤ ⓒ, ⓐ

24. 위 글에서 스페인어를 향상시키기 위한 방법으로 언급되지 않은 것은? (3점)

① 스페인어 라디오 듣기 연습을 한다.

② 휴대전화의 언어 설정을 스페인어로 바꾼다.

③ 스페인어로 쇼핑 목록을 작성한다.

④ 스페인어로 된 영화를 자주 본다.

⑤ 축구 경기 후기를 스페인어로 써본다.

[25-30] 다음 글을 읽고 물음에 답하시오.

> ### <No More Subtitles!>
>
> DREAM4 is back! I'm so excited to see my favorite Korean boy band ⓐperform. Their singing and their dancing are just perfect. I want to understand their songs without subtitles or translations though. Any tips?
>
> *- Marisa*, 14
>
> You should find friends who are interested in DREAM4 and start a club. In my club, we motivate one another. We ⓑtranslate songs and sing together. Doing these things is fun and really ⓒimproves our Korean!
>
> *- Lori*, 15
>
> I recommend watching Korean dramas. They're really interesting! You can use Korean subtitles for help with listening. It's also a good idea to print out the subtitles and ⓓread them first.
>
> *- Brandon*, 16
>
> ⓔRemove DREAM4 on social media. They often post short messages in Korean about how they are doing. They also post pictures with the messages, so you can understand the posts more easily.
>
> *- Aishah*, 14
>
> **What Works for You?**
>
> There are hundreds of good tips out there, but everyone has their own way of learning. (A)당신에게 계속 동기 부여가 되는 것을 찾아라; then you will enjoy learning more. Remember, every language is hard at first, but a new language can make your world much bigger!

25. 다음은 위 글에 대한 요약 글이다. 빈칸에 들어갈 말로 바르게 짝지어진 것은? (4점)

> Marisa wants to understand a Korean boy band's songs without ⓐ_____. Lori suggests that she find friends who are interested in the boy band and start a club. They can ⓑ_____ one another to improve their Korean. Aishah suggests that she ⓒ_____ the boy band on social media because their short posts are easier to understand. Brandon suggests watching Korean dramas with Korean ⓓ_____.
> (가)_____

	ⓐ	ⓑ	ⓒ
①	subtitles	move	replace
②	reviews	motivate	expect
③	subtitles	motivate	follow
④	posts	perform	follow
⑤	messages	motivate	recommend

26. 위 글에 대한 주제문으로 빈칸 (가)에 들어갈 가장 적절한 것은? (4점)

① A language that can make your world bigger shouldn't be hard to learn.

② Find what gives you a reason to continue learning, and you will enjoy it more.

③ Posting pictures with messages in Korean on social media is most recommended.

④ Watching Korean dramas without translations is the most effective way to learn Korean.

⑤ Hundreds of tips on learning foreign languages make it difficult to find your own way of learning.

27. 위 글의 밑줄 친 (A)를 바르게 영작한 것은? (3점)

① Find how keeps you motivated

② Find why keeps you motivating

③ Find what keeps you motivated

④ Find when keeps you motivating

⑤ Find where keeps you motivated

28. 위 글의 밑줄 친 ⓐ~ⓔ 중 글의 내용과 어울리지 <u>않는</u> 것은? (4점)

① ⓐ   ② ⓑ   ③ ⓒ

④ ⓓ   ⑤ ⓔ

29. 위 글에서 Marisa의 고민으로 가장 알맞은 것은? (3점)

① 어떤 동아리에 가입해야 할지 모르겠다.

② 좋아하는 밴드의 공연 표를 구하기 어렵다.

③ 보고 싶은 공연 영상에 필요한 자막이 없다.

④ 자신의 한국어 실력을 향상하고 싶다.

⑤ 드라마를 보는 데 시간을 너무 많이 쓴다.

30. 위 글의 내용과 일치하는 것은? (3점)

① Marisa는 좋아하는 한국 보이 밴드의 노래를 자막 없이 잘 이해할 수 있다.

② Lori와 Marisa는 같은 동아리에 가입해 있다.

③ DREAM4는 한국어로 노래를 부르지 않는다.

④ Brandon은 Marisa에게 한국 드라마를 볼 것을 추천한다.

⑤ Aishah는 소셜 미디어에 종종 사진을 올린다.

3학년 영어 1학기 중간고사(1과) 2회

반		점수	
이름			

문항수 : 선택형(28문항) 서술형(2문항)　　20　.　.　.

◎ 선택형 문항의 답안은 컴퓨터용 수정 싸인펜을 사용하여 OMR 답안지에 바르게 표기하시오.

◎ 서술형 문제는 답을 답안지에 반드시 검정 볼펜으로 쓰시오.

◎ 총 30문항 100점 만점입니다. 문항별 배점은 각 문항에 표시되어 있습니다.

[서울시 송파구 ○○중]

1. 다음 문장의 빈칸 (A)~(C)에 들어갈 어휘로 알맞게 짝지어진 것은? (3점)

- He is getting (A)_____ to this new class schedule.
- It's important to be (B)_____ with the language first when learning a new language.
- You have a fever, dry cough, or loss of taste. In this (C)_____, you need to see a doctor.

	(A)	(B)	(C)
①	active	confident	case
②	used	familiar	case
③	used	confident	match
④	sensitive	familiar	match
⑤	sensitive	perfect	mistake

[전라북도 ○○중]

2. 다음 우리말과 같은 뜻이 되도록 빈칸에 알맞은 말을 고른 것은? (2점)

너는 올해 무엇을 하고 싶니?
→ What would you _____ to do this year?

① plan　　　　② like
③ have　　　　④ think
⑤ take

[전라북도 ○○중]

3. 다음 영영풀이의 내용이 어색한 것은? (4점)

① volunteer: to work to help others without being paid

② requirement: a necessary characteristic, quality, or skill

③ subtitle: text shown that is a story of a film's written dialogue

④ social media: websites and applications where users can create and share content or participate in social networking with other users

⑤ tradition: a custom or belief that has existed for a long time

[서울시 서초구 ○○중]

4. Which expression below should go in the blank? (4점)

B: _____ hiking yesterday morning?
G: It wasn't easy at all, but now I understand why not giving up is so important.

① Why did you go
② How about going
③ How did you like
④ What would you like
⑤ What did you think of

Jessy: What are you doing?
Brian: I'm writing a list of things that I want to do this year.
Jessy: That's nice. What would you like to do this year?
Brian: Well, first of all, ⓐI'd like to learn how to dance.
Jessy: That sounds great.
Brian: What about you? What would you like to do this year?
Jessy: I'm thinking of taking a writing class.
Brian: That's really cool.

[서울시 송파구 ○○중]

5. 위 대화의 밑줄 친 ⓐ와 바꿔 쓸 수 없는 것은? (3점)

① I'm willing to learn how to dance.

② I want to learn how to dance.

③ my wish is to learn how to dance.

④ I hope that you learn how to dance.

⑤ I wish to learn how to dance.

[서울시 송파구 ○○중]

6. 위 대화의 내용과 일치하는 것은? (4점)

① Brian is writing a list of plans for this year.

② Jessy is looking forward to learning dancing.

③ Brian wants to take a writing class this year.

④ Jessy is considering taking a writing class next year.

⑤ Brian and Jessy are talking about what they want to do next year.

Messi: Did you make this shelf yourself? It's amazing!
Son: Thanks. I started making furniture last year.
Messi: Cool! (A)_____
Son: It was hard at first, but now I love it.
Messi: That's great. I think you're really good at it.
Son: Thanks. I also think I'm good at making furniture. I think it's good to try new things.
Messi: Right. Having experiences lets us (B)_____.

[충청북도 ○○중]

7. 빈칸 (A)에 들어갈 말로 가장 알맞은 것은? (3점)

① How do you like it?

② When did you learn it?

③ Where did you start it?

④ Can I take a look at it?

⑤ Why do you make furniture?

[서울시 강동구 ○○중]

8. 빈칸 (B)에 들어갈 말로 가장 적절한 것은? (4점)

① enjoy our lives

② find new talents

③ change our jobs

④ think deeply and widely

⑤ understand other people

9. 다음 대화의 흐름상 빈칸에 들어갈 가장 알맞은 말은?
(2점)

G: What would you like to do this year?
B: I'd like to learn the guitar. I listened to the song "Cavatina," and I was struck by the sound of the guitar.
G: That's great. Where are you going to learn it?
B: My friend Jinsu _____. I'll ask him to teach me.

① is a very good guitar player
② was moved by the song "Cavatina"
③ is planning to play the song for you
④ wants to learn how to play the guitar
⑤ would like to learn the guitar this year

10. 다음 중 어법상 <u>어색한</u> 것은? (3점)

① What I cooked for dinner was chicken soup.
② Brian grows plants, that makes him feel relaxed.
③ We took the red bus, which took us to the museum.
④ He went to the flower shop, where he lost her wallet.
⑤ My uncle, who is a doctor, told me not to eat spicy food too often.

11. 다음 주어진 두 문장을 현재완료진행 표현을 이용하여 한 문장으로 쓰시오. (5점)

- My father started working at Walmart in 2015.
- He is still working there.

답: _____

12. 다음 중 밑줄 친 단어의 쓰임이 <u>다른</u> 하나는? (3점)

① Oh, that's <u>what</u> is keeping you up so late.
② <u>What</u> I want is to get an A in the final exam.
③ I wonder <u>what</u> the main topic of the lecture is about.
④ Never put off until tomorrow <u>what</u> you can do today.
⑤ <u>What</u> Jason wants to do after school is to play mobile games.

13. 다음 (A)와 (B)를 한 문장으로 바꿀 때 어법상 옳은 것은? (3점)

(A) It started raining two hours ago.
(B) It is still raining now.

① It had rained for two hours.
② It has been raining for two hours.
③ It had been raining for two hours.
④ It has been raining since two hours.
⑤ It had been raining since two hours.

14. 다음 중 '이 표현들은 우리가 어제 배운 것입니다.'를 바르게 영작한 것을 고르면? (3점)

① These expressions are what we learned yesterday.

② There are expressions what we learned yesterday.

③ These are what expressions we learned yesterday.

④ These are we learned what expressions yesterday.

⑤ These expressions are we learned what yesterday.

15. 다음 중 어법상 올바른 문장은? (4점)

① I bought a watch, that keeps good time.

② I'd like to make my own *hahoe* mask and learning how to dance the *talchum*.

③ I translated Kate's English letter from Korean.

④ I'm sure that these new experiences in Andong would help me to understand Korea better.

⑤ It is a meaningful experience because you will learn that cooking for others can make them happily.

16. 다음 대화의 흐름과 관계없는 것은? (3점)

> B: Hey, Suji! What are you holding?
> G: Hi, Ben. It's a skateboard. ⓐI'm going skateboarding.
> B: Wow! I didn't know that you could skateboard. ⓑHow did you learn to skateboard?
> G: I joined a local skateboarding club last month.
> B: I see. So do you like to skateboard?
> G: Yes. It's really fun! ⓒIt helps me make new friends, too.
> B: How? ⓓWhat's wrong?
> G: I go skateboarding with other members of the club, and ⓔwe share tips with one another.

① ⓐ   ② ⓑ   ③ ⓒ

④ ⓓ   ⑤ ⓔ

17. 다음 글 다음에 나올 내용으로 적절한 것은? (4점)

> Many students learn new languages because of school requirements. Many others learn them for fun. In any case, students everywhere have found interesting ways to study new languages. Let's meet these students and listen to their ideas.

① the reasons why students study English

② the importance of learning Spanish

③ how students can learn Spanish for fun

④ students' ideas about school requirements

⑤ students' interesting ways to study new languages

18. 다음 글을 쓴 목적으로 가장 적절한 것은? (4점)

Do you want to learn a new language? Here are some tips to help you learn a new language on your own. Firstly, listen to music in that language. Listening to music is a great way to learn common vocabulary. Read the lyrics while listening to the songs and try to memorize the words. You will become familiar with the language quickly. Secondly, read children's books in that language. It helps expand your vocabulary. It's a lot easier if you already know the story. Since you know what is happening in the story, you can easily guess the meaning of new words. Lastly, write all of the new words that you learn in a notebook. It's the best way to practice using your vocabulary. It will hard at first, but you will get better at expressing yourself over time. I hope these tips will hell you improve your language skills soon. Remember, practicing every day is the most important thing!

*lyrics 가사

① 노래의 가사를 이해하는 중요성을 홍보하려고
② 단기간에 단어를 암기하는 방법을 제공하려고
③ 새로운 언어를 배우는 것의 중요성을 알리려고
④ 동화책을 통한 새로운 언어 공부법을 소개하려고
⑤ 새로운 언어를 배우는 데 유용한 방법을 알려주려고

[19~24] 다음 글을 읽고 물음에 답하시오.

No More Subtitles!

DREAM4 is back! ⓐI'm so exciting to see my favorite Korean boy band perform. Their singing and their dancing are just perfect. I want to understand their songs without subtitles or translations through. Any tips?

Marisa, 14

ⓑYou should find friends who are interested in DREAM4 and start a club. In my club, we motivate one another. We translate songs and sing together. ⓒDoing these things is fun and really improves our Korean!

Lori, 15

(A)[Following / Follow] DREAM4 on social media. ⓓThey often post short messages in Korean about how they are doing. They also (가)post pictures with the messages, so you can understand the posts more easily.

Aishah, 14

I recommend watching Korean dramas. I've been (B)[watched / watching / to watch] Korean dramas for a year, and they're really interesting! You can use Korean subtitles for help with listening. It's also a good idea to print out the subtitles and read them first.

Brandon, 16

What Works for You?

There are hundreds of good tips out there, but everyone has (나)_____. Find (C)[that / what] keeps you motivated; then ⓔyou will enjoy learning more. Remember, every language is hard at first, but a new language can make your world much bigger!

19. 위 글의 밑줄 친 ⓐ~ⓔ 중 어법상 <u>어색한</u> 것은?

(3점)

① ⓐ   ② ⓑ   ③ ⓒ

④ ⓓ   ⑤ ⓔ

20. 위 글의 (A)~(C)에 들어갈 말로 알맞은 것은? (4점)

	(A)	(B)	(C)
①	Following	watched	what
②	Following	watching	that
③	Follow	to watch	what
④	Follow	watched	that
⑤	Follow	watching	what

21. 위 글의 밑줄 친 (가)와 같은 의미로 쓰인 것은? (3점)

① Did you open your <u>post</u>?

② The Chinese use green <u>post</u> boxes.

③ People can buy the stamps at a <u>post</u> office in Korea.

④ Students may play games or <u>post</u> photos on instagram.

⑤ Has the <u>post</u> arrived yet?

22. 다음 중 Lori가 한국어 학습을 위해 Marisa에게 한 조언으로 가장 적절한 것은?

(3점)

① watch Korean dramas

② read Korean movie subtitles

③ follow DREAM4 on social media

④ post short online messages in Korean

⑤ start a club with other DREAM4 fans

23. 위 글의 빈칸 (나)에 들어갈 말로 가장 적절한 것은?

(3점)

① their favorite boy band

② their own way of learning

③ their way of using translations

④ the interesting messages from teachers

⑤ their own social media for the best learning

24. 위 글의 내용과 일치하지 <u>않는</u> 것은?   (3점)

① Marisa는 노래 부르기와 춤추기를 좋아한다.

② Lori는 동호회를 시작하라고 추천한다.

③ Aishah는 소셜 미디어에서 DREAM4를 팔로우 하라고 말한다.

④ Brandon은 한국 드라마 보는 것을 추천한다.

⑤ 새로운 언어는 당신의 세상을 더욱 넓혀 줄 수 있다.

I'm a big fan of a Spanish soccer team. I want to understand interviews with my favorite players. (A) However, it's not easy because I don't know Spanish that well. (B) How can I improve my Spanish?

- *Owen*, 16

The best way to learn a new language is to practice it every day. I have changed the language of my phone to Spanish, and I have been writing my shopping lists in Spanish!! (C)

- *Julie*, 15

(가)_____ is important is to become familiar with the language first. (D) It (나)_____ the sound of the language. If the people talk too fast, try watching Spanish children's movies first.

- *Inho*, 14

Some words are used only in soccer, not in everyday life. Learn some soccer vocabulary and memorize it. Also, why don't you try writing a review of a match in Spanish? (E) It will help you improve your writing skills.

- *Rohan*, 16

[전라북도 ○○중]

25. 위 글의 (A)~(E) 중 다음 문장이 들어갈 위치로 가장 알맞은 곳은? (4점)

| I suggest watching Spanish movies often. |

① (A)   ② (B)   ③ (C)

④ (D)   ⑤ (E)

[전라북도 ○○중]

26. 위 글의 빈칸 (가)에 들어갈 알맞은 표현을 한 단어로 쓰시오. (3점)

→ _____

[충청북도 ○○중]

27. 위 글의 흐름상 빈칸 (나)에 들어갈 말로 가장 알맞은 것은? (4점)

① will you get used to help
② will help you get used to
③ will help you used to get
④ get used to help you will
⑤ get used to you will help

[인천시 ○○중]

28. 위 글의 내용과 일치하는 것은? (3점)

① Owen wants to interview his favorite soccer players.
② Inho doesn't like to watch Spanish movies.
③ Inho wants to talk to others in Spanish.
④ Rohan says that Owen doesn't have to learn soccer vocabulary.
⑤ Rohan tells Owen to try writing a review of a soccer match in Spanish.

[경기도 ○○중]

29. 위 글의 제목으로 가장 적절한 것은? (3점)

① How to Improve Spanish
② How to Interview in Spanish
③ The Benefits of Speaking Spanish
④ Let's Meet a Spanish Soccer Team
⑤ The Reason Why We Should Learn Spanish

[전라북도 ○○중]

30. 위 글에서 스페인어를 향상하기 위한 방법으로 언급되지 <u>않은</u> 것은? (3점)

① 전화기의 언어 설정을 스페인어로 바꾼다.
② 쇼핑 목록을 스페인어로 작성한다.
③ 스페인어로 된 어린이 영화를 자주 본다.
④ 축구 경기 후기를 스페인어로 써본다.
⑤ 빠른 속도로 원어민과 이야기하는 연습을 한다.

3학년 영어 1학기 중간고사(2과) 1회

문항수 : 선택형(27문항) 서술형(3문항)   20 . . .

반	
이름	
점수	

◎ 선택형 문항의 답안은 컴퓨터용 수정 싸인펜을 사용하여 OMR 답안지에 바르게 표기하시오.
◎ 서술형 문제는 답을 답안지에 반드시 검정 볼펜으로 쓰시오.
◎ 총 30문항 100점 만점입니다. 문항별 배점은 각 문항에 표시되어 있습니다.

[대구시 ○○중]

1. 다음 빈칸에 공통으로 들어갈 수 있는 단어는? (3점)

Min: My English speaking skill is not good. I want to _____ my speaking skill.
Jun: Hey, practice makes perfect. If you practice a lot, your skill will _____.

① memorize ② perform
③ post ④ improve
⑤ motivate

[경기도 ○○중]

2. 다음 중 영영 풀이가 바르게 연결되지 <u>않은</u> 것은? (3점)

① improve: to make something better
② bottom: the lowest part of something
③ talent: a natural ability to do something well
④ translate: to change words into another language
⑤ confuse: to put something online for other people

[전라북도 ○○중]

3. 다음 중 유감이나 동정을 나타내는 표현이 <u>아닌</u> 것은? (2점)

① That's a great idea.
② I'm sorry to hear that.
③ You must be worried.
④ That's a pity.
⑤ That's a shame.

[전라북도 ○○중]

4. 다음 친구의 문제에 관한 조언으로 적절한 것은? (2점)

The problem: My friend is upset with me. What can I do to apologize to her?

① You should not talk to her.
② How about a refund?
③ Why don't you go to the hospital?
④ How about texting her an apology?
⑤ You should talk to your homeroom teacher.

[서울시 양천구 ○○중]

5. 다음 ⓐ~ⓔ를 대화의 흐름에 맞게 배열한 것은? (4점)

M: You look tired. Did you get enough sleep?

ⓐ No, I haven't. Why is that?
ⓑ Okay. When did you go to bed?
ⓒ That's probably what is making you tired. Have you heard that when you go to bed is very important?
ⓓ Yes, I did. I slept for over seven hours.
ⓔ I went to bed after midnight, as usual.

M: Scientists say that going to bed late can make you feel tired the next day.

① ⓐ-ⓑ-ⓔ-ⓒ-ⓓ
② ⓐ-ⓒ-ⓓ-ⓑ-ⓔ
③ ⓓ-ⓑ-ⓔ-ⓒ-ⓐ
④ ⓓ-ⓒ-ⓐ-ⓑ-ⓔ
⑤ ⓓ-ⓔ-ⓒ-ⓐ-ⓑ

- 16 -

M: What are you doing in the living room?
W: I'm doing yoga.
M: You're working out by yourself?
W: Yes, I'm following this online video. It shows me all the steps.
M: Let me see. Wow, it's been watched two million times! I'm (A)_____ that so many people have watched this video.
W: I know! These kinds of programs are becoming popular right now.
M: It looks very convenient. You don't have to go out to exercise.
W: That's right. That's why I love these programs. You should try them, too.

[서울시 강남구 ○○중]

6. Which of the following fits in the blank (A)? (3점)

① relieved   ② surprised

③ confident   ④ confused

⑤ disappointed

[서울시 강남구 ○○중]

7. Which of the following is true according to the dialog? (3점)

① 이 동영상은 전세계적으로 판매된다.

② 이 동영상은 요가의 유래를 설명하고 있다.

③ 여자는 남자와 함께 동영상을 보며 요가를 하고 있다.

④ 요가 동영상을 올리는 것은 점점 인기가 많아지고 있다.

⑤ 여자는 동영상을 보며 운동하는 것이 운동하러 밖에 나가지 않아도 되기 때문에 좋아한다.

Boy: You look tired. Did you get enough sleep?
Girl: Yes, I did. I slept for over seven hours.
Boy: Okay. When did you go to bed?
Girl: I went to bed after midnight, as usual.
Boy: That's probably what is making you tired. (A)_____ that when you go to bed is very important?
Girl: No, I haven't Why is that?
Boy: Scientists say that going to bed late can make you feel tired the next day.
Girl: I didn't know that.
Boy: On the other hand, going to bed early can improve your memory and help you be more productive. From now on, try to go to bed earlier.

[인천시 ○○중]

8. 위 대화의 여자가 피곤해 보이는 이유는? (2점)

① 자다가 잠을 자주 깨서

② 잠을 7시간밖에 못 자서

③ 수면 자세가 좋지 않아서

④ 늦은 시간에 잠자리에 들어서

⑤ 자기 전에 음식을 많이 먹어서

[인천시 ○○중]

9. 위 대화의 빈칸 (A)에 알맞은 말은? (3점)

① Did you see

② Did you hear

③ Do you know

④ Have you heard

⑤ Are you hearing

10. 다음 대화 중 어색한 것은? (3점)

① W: Have you heard that chewing ice is bad for your teeth?

M: No, I don't. When is that?

② W: Why don't you eat some snacks before dinner?

M: I don't want to. I'll wait until dinner.

③ W: Why are you trying to drink more water?

M: Because drinking a lot of water can help the blood flow.

④ W: What are you doing in the living room?

M: I'm doing yoga.

⑤ W: Have you heard that eating little and often is good for your health?

M: Really? I thought eating three meals a day was fine.

11. 다음 대화의 빈칸에 들어갈 적절한 말은? (3점)

A: I'm always tired these days.
B: When do you go to bed?
A: Usually, I go to bed after midnight.
B: That's why you're tired! Have you _____ is important?

① heard of sleep

② hear that sleep

③ heard of sleeping

④ hearing that sleep

⑤ heard that sleeping

12. 다음 대화에서 문맥상 어색한 것은? (3점)

Minsu: What's this?
Aram: It's a smart band. ⓐIt lets me check my health information on my smartphone.
Minsu: What kind of information?
Aram: ⓑIt shows how far I walk during the day.
Minsu: Interesting.
Aram: ⓒDo you know who plays the guitar in the band? ⓓAlso it shows how well I sleep at night.
Minsu: I'm surprised that this small band can do all that.
Aram: ⓔYou can try it. Here it is.
Minsu: Really? You're so nice.

① ⓐ   ② ⓑ   ③ ⓒ

④ ⓓ   ⑤ ⓔ

13. 다음 글의 괄호 (A), (B), (C) 안에서 문맥에 맞는 낱말로 가장 적절한 것은? (4점)

We all know that a diet containing a variety of foods keeps our bodies (A)[health / healthy]. But sometimes we are not sure which foods are good for which body parts. (B)[However / In addition], nature gives us a big clue. Look at the following examples. Each of these foods not only (C)[looks / looks like] a certain body part but is also good for that body part.

	(A)	(B)	(C)
①	health	However	looks
②	health	In addition	looks
③	healthy	However	looks
④	healthy	In addition	looks like
⑤	healthy	However	looks like

14. 다음 중 밑줄 친 부분이 <u>어색한</u> 문장은? (3점)

① Look at the teacher <u>dancing</u> on the stage.

② The shop <u>selling</u> coffee beans became popular.

③ The men <u>giving</u> flowers are wearing sweatshirts.

④ We ate chocolate bread <u>baking</u> in the oven.

⑤ The little girl <u>holding</u> her mother's hand is laughing loudly.

15. 다음 괄호 안의 단어를 분사를 활용하여 알맞은 형태로 각각 쓰시오. (5점)

> a. The curry (A)_____ at this restaurant tastes good. (serve)
> b. The shop (B)_____ toy cars became popular. (sell)

정답 : (A) _____

　　　(B) _____

16. 다음 문장을 영어로 바르게 나열하시오. (4점)

> A: What is that?
> B: This is a magic cup.
> A: What's special about it?
> B: It tells me to drink water every two hours.
> A: <u>그것이 너에게 말을 할 수 있다니 나는 놀랍다.</u>
> (I / you / it / to / am / can / talk / that / surprised)

정답 : _____

17. 다음 중 어법상 옳은 문장은? (4점)

① She can read the poster writing in German.

② The person managed this store is not here now.

③ My family bought a house building in the 1970s.

④ They showed me the furniture making by their son.

⑤ Every dish served in this restaurant includes shrimps.

18. 다음 중 어법상 옳은 문장끼리 짝지어진 것은? (3점)

> ⓐ The woman you met yesterday works here.
> ⓑ That book 'Holes', that I was reading, is really good.
> ⓒ Do you know anyone, that speaks French and Spanish?
> ⓓ We stayed at the Grand Hotel, what Ann recommended to us.
> ⓔ The sun, what is one among millions of stars in the universe, provides us with heat and light.

① ⓐ　　　　　　　　② ⓐ, ⓓ

③ ⓑ　　　　　　　　④ ⓒ, ⓓ

⑤ ⓒ, ⓔ

A slice of carrot looks like the human eye. Carrots have some chemicals ⓐthat can make vitamin A, ⓑwhich improves your vision. It helps your eyes process light and send a clear image to the brain. So if you want healthy eyes, eat carrots.

Cutting onions is not fun because it makes you cry. But try slicing one anyway. You can see ⓒthat the inside looks a little like a human cell. Scientists say ⓓthat onions contain vitamin B, which helps make new, healthy cells.

Now, let's move on to ginger. What body part comes to mind when you see it? Doesn't it look like a stomach? You may not like ginger's strong taste or smell, but these come from a special chemical ⓔthat (A)_____ you from feeling sick and throwing up. For this reason, (B)_____.

Isn't it amazing that some foods mirror the body parts that they are good for? Interestingly, there are many other such foods. Find as many as you can and try to eat a variety of them.

[전라북도 ㅇㅇ중]

20. 위 글의 빈칸 (A)에 들어가기에 적합하지 <u>않은</u> 표현은? (두 개) (4점)

① stops

② keeps

③ prevents

④ protects

⑤ saves

[충청북도 ㅇㅇ중]

21. 위 글의 밑줄 친 ⓐ~ⓔ 중 생략할 수 있는 것을 <u>모두</u> 고른 것은? (3점)

① ⓐ, ⓑ, ⓒ   ② ⓐ, ⓒ

③ ⓑ, ⓒ, ⓔ   ④ ⓒ, ⓓ

⑤ ⓒ, ⓓ, ⓔ

[서울시 서초구 ㅇㅇ중]

19. 위 글의 제목으로 가장 적절한 것은? (4점)

① Several Types of Fruits

② Cooking a Variety of Foods

③ Beneficial Foods for Our Bodies

④ How to Make Our Bodies Healthy

⑤ How to Find a Diet Containing Vitamins

[경기도 ㅇㅇ중]

22. 위 글의 (B)에 들어갈 말로 가장 적절한 것은?(4점)

① many people like ginger

② people do not like to eat ginger

③ you should try not to smell ginger

④ I recommend ginger for headaches

⑤ ginger can be good for your stomach

23. 위 글의 내용과 일치하지 <u>않는</u> 것은?　　　(4점)

① Vitamin A is related to healthy eyes.

② Vitamin B is used to make new cells.

③ The inside of the onion is similar to a stomach.

④ A slice of carrot reminds people of human eye.

⑤ A special chemical of ginger keeps you from throwing up.

24. 위 글을 읽고 답할 수 <u>없는</u> 질문은?　　　(3점)

① What kind of vitamin helps improve our vision?

② How does vitamin A work for our body?

③ How do healthy cells make vitamin B?

④ Does ginger taste and smell strong?

⑤ What does a special chemical in ginger prevent?

[25-30] 다음 글을 읽고 물음에 답하시오.

We all know (A)<u>that</u> a diet (가)<u>contain</u> a variety of foods keeps our bodies healthy. But sometimes we are not sure which foods are good for which body parts. Nature, (a)_____, gives us a big clue. Look at the following examples. Each of these foods not only looks like a certain body part but is also good for (B)<u>that</u> body part.

Slice open a tomato and compare it with the human heart. You will see that they look similar. They both have multiple hollow spaces and are red. Researchers say that the chemicals (C)<u>that</u> make tomatoes red are good for your heart and blood. (b)_____, eating tomatoes can lower your risk of heart disease.

Look at the shape of a walnut. Do you notice anything? Yes, it's very similar to the shape of the human brain! A walnut is divided into two parts, just like the brain. Walnuts also have wrinkles, which the brain has too. Studies show that walnuts help our brains stay healthy and active. They are also good for preventing Alzheimer's disease.

Now, let's move on to ginger. What body part comes to mind when you see it? Doesn't it look like a stomach? You may not like ginger's strong taste or smell, but these come from a special chemical that prevents you from feeling sick and throwing up. For this reason, ginger can be good for your stomach.

25. 위 글의 제목으로 가장 알맞은 것은?　　　(3점)

① How to Lose Weight
② Many Ways to Cook Tomatoes
③ Beneficial Foods for Our Bodies
④ The Secret Chemicals in Nature
⑤ The Scariest Disease: Alzheimer's Disease

26. 위 글의 밑줄 친 (가)contain을 알맞은 형태로 바꾼 것은?　　　(3점)

① contain
② contains
③ containing
④ contained
⑤ to contain

27. 위 글의 흐름상 빈칸 (a)와 (b)에 들어갈 가장 알맞은 표현은?

　　　(4점)

	(a)	(b)
①	however	In addition
②	moreover	For example
③	in other words	Nevertheless
④	for this reason	On the other hand
⑤	similarly	Therefore

28. According to the passage above, what does a special chemical in ginger prevent? (Find and write in English in a full sentence.)　　　(4점)

답: It _____.

29. 위 글의 (A)~(C)의 that과 쓰임이 같은 것으로 알맞게 연결된 것은?　　　(3점)

ⓐ Why don't you buy that pencil?
ⓑ This is the country that I always want to visit.
ⓒ I'm not sure that he will come here.

① (A) - ⓐ　　　② (B) - ⓑ
③ (B) - ⓒ　　　④ (C) - ⓑ
⑤ (C) - ⓒ

30. 위 글을 읽고 알 수 없는 내용은?　　　(4점)

① 다양한 음식은 우리의 몸을 건강하게 해준다.
② 자연친화적인 환경에서 기른 음식은 몸에 좋다.
③ 음식들은 특정 신체 부분과 비슷해 보인다.
④ 토마토와 심장은 여러 빈 공간을 가지고 있다.
⑤ 토마토는 심장병을 예방하는 데 도움을 준다.

문항수 : 선택형(26문항) 서술형(4문항)   20 . . .

◎ 선택형 문항의 답안은 컴퓨터용 수정 싸인펜을 사용하여 OMR 답안지에 바르게 표기하시오.
◎ 서술형 문제는 답을 답안지에 반드시 검정 볼펜으로 쓰시오.
◎ 총 30문항 100점 만점입니다. 문항별 배점은 각 문항에 표시되어 있습니다.

[전라북도 ○○중]

1. 다음 빈칸에 들어갈 알맞은 단어는?   (3점)

Isn't it amazing that some foods _____ (반영하다) the body parts that they are good for?

① increase   ② measure

③ compare   ④ accept

⑤ mirror

[서울시 강남구 ○○중]

2. 다음 빈칸에 들어갈 단어의 영영 풀이로 알맞지 <u>않은</u> 것은?   (4점)

· You should ⓐ_____ your English grammar during the summer vacation.
· Good training can help to ⓑ_____ accidents.
· This drink doesn't ⓒ_____ any sugar.
· I will ⓓ_____ the prices of several digital cameras online.
· Some chemicals can ⓔ_____ your hair.

① ⓐ to make better

② ⓑ to stop something from happening

③ ⓒ to have something inside; to include

④ ⓓ to look at the similarities and differences between things

⑤ ⓔ to move one's body energetically in order to get fit and to remain healthy

[전라북도 ○○중]

3. 다음 빈칸에 공통으로 들어갈 한 단어를 쓰시오. (4점)

Eat _____ many healthy foods _____ you can.
(가능한 한 몸에 좋은 음식을 많이 먹어라.)

정답 : _____

[서울시 양천구 ○○중]

4. 다음 글의 문맥상 빈칸 어디에도 들어갈 수 <u>없는</u> 표현은? (대·소문자 관계 없음)   (4점)

Ms. Lee: Have you heard the term body image? It means "_____ your own body." A lot of teens have a negative body image. They think they're too fat or too thin compared to others. However, I want you to build a _____. Accept your body as it is and _____ every day. Remember, there is only one you, so don't _____ to others. _____ can make a big difference in your life.

① negative body image

② loving yourself

③ the way you see

④ give yourself praise

⑤ compare yourself

5. 다음 중 대화가 <u>어색한</u> 것은? (3점)

① A: Do I have to wear my school uniform?

B: No, you have to wear it.

② A: Do you remember the book I bought yesterday?

B: No, I don't.

③ A: Do you remember the singer that I liked?

B: Sure.

④ A: You know that we'll go on a field trip to Gongju on Friday?

B: Yes, I'm looking forward to going there.

⑤ A: What time do we meet Friday morning?

B: The bus leaves at 7:30. So be at the bus stop by seven.

6. 다음 대화를 자연스럽게 연결한 것은? (2점)

A: You look tired. Did you get enough sleep?

a. Okay. When did you go to bed?
b. I went to bed after midnight, as usual.
c. Yes, I did. I slept for over seven hours.
d. That's probably what is making you tired.

① b – a – c – d
② b – d – a – c
③ c – a – b – d
④ c – d – a – b
⑤ c – a – d – b

[7–8] 다음 대화를 읽고 물음에 답하시오.

B: You look tired. Did you get enough sleep?

G: Yes, I did. I slept for over seven hours.

B: Okay. When did you go to bed?

G: I went to bed after midnight, as usual.

B: (A) That's probably what is making you tired. Have you heard that when you go to bed is very important?

G: (B) No, I haven't. Why is that?

B: (C) Scientists say that going to bed late can make you feel tired the next day.

G: (D) I didn't know that.

B: (E) From now on, try to go to bed earlier.

*B: Boy, G: Girl

7. 다음 주어진 문장이 들어갈 가장 알맞은 곳은? (3점)

On the other hand, going to bed early can improve your memory and help you be more productive.

① (A)   ② (B)   ③ (C)

④ (D)   ⑤ (E)

8. According to the dialog, which one is correct? (3점)

① The boy did not sleep well.

② Sleeping enough is very important.

③ The girl hardly goes to bed after midnight.

④ Sleeping habit isn't related with feeling tired.

⑤ The boy suggests the girl should sleep earlier.

9. 다음 대화의 내용과 일치하는 것을 〈보기〉에서 모두 고른 것은? (4점)

M: Hey Emma, what are you doing in the living room?
W: Oh, Ryan, I'm doing yoga.
M: You're working out by yourself?
W: Yes. I'm following this online video. It shows me all the steps.
M: Let me see. Wow, it's been watched two million times! I'm surprised that so many people have watched this video.
W: I know! These kinds of programs are becoming popular right now.
M: It looks very convenient. You don't have to go out to exercise.
W: That's right. That's why I love these programs. You should try them, too.
M: Okay, I'll try.

보기

ⓐ The online video helps Emma to learn yoga alone.
ⓑ Emma has watched the online video two million times.
ⓒ Ryan will try exercising by himself using online video programs.
ⓓ Many people are interested in working out by themselves these days.
ⓔ Ryan likes to work out at home while Emma does not.

① ⓐ, ⓑ, ⓔ   ② ⓐ, ⓒ, ⓓ
③ ⓑ, ⓒ, ⓓ   ④ ⓑ, ⓓ, ⓔ
⑤ ⓒ, ⓓ, ⓔ

10. 다음 빈칸에 들어갈 말로 가장 알맞은 것은? (2점)

Jin: What is that? It looks nice.
Hoon: This is a magic cup. I carry it everywhere with me.
Jin: What's special about it?
Hoon: It's awesome. It tells me to drink water every two hours.
Jin: Really? _____

① Let's talk together.
② Would you like some water?
③ I think that's not a problem.
④ You should see a doctor then.
⑤ I'm surprised that it can talk to you.

[11~12] 다음 대화를 읽고 물음에 답하시오.

Seungmin: (a)_____ that chewing ice is bad for your teeth?
Jua: No, I haven't. Why is that?
Seungmin: It can damage your teeth. It can also make them too sensitive.

11. 위 밑줄 친 부분 (a)에 들어갈 알맞은 표현은? (3점)

① Have you heard
② Do you know
③ Did you hear
④ Is it true
⑤ Do you think

12. What does Seungmin believe? (3점)

① Chewing ice can damage Jua's teeth.

② Chewing ice prevents Jua from having a heart disease.

③ People should brush their teeth every day.

④ Brushing teeth can damage teeth.

⑤ Brushing teeth makes teeth too sensitive.

14. 다음 괄호 안의 단어를 알맞은 형태로 바꾸어 문장을 완성하시오. (6점)

(1) She can read the poster _____ in German. (write)

(2) I interviewed an actor _____ for human rights. (work)

(3) Every dish _____ in this restaurant includes shrimp. (serve)

13. 다음 중 어법이 옳은 것만을 있는 대로 고른 것은? (3점)

ⓐ Is that what you want?
ⓑ I don't believe what you told me.
ⓒ This cake is that I ate yesterday.
ⓓ What I need these days is more sleep.
ⓔ You can borrow the book what I have.
ⓕ I like the gift that my friend gave me.
ⓖ The thing what surprised me at the festival was his performance.

① ⓐ, ⓓ, ⓔ
② ⓐ, ⓑ, ⓓ, ⓕ
③ ⓐ. ⓒ, ⓓ, ⓖ
④ ⓑ, ⓒ, ⓓ, ⓕ
⑤ ⓑ, ⓒ, ⓔ, ⓕ, ⓖ

15. 다음 괄호 안의 문장을 문맥에 맞게 바르게 나열하시오. (3점)

Have you heard the term body image? It means "the way you see your own body." A lot of teens have a negative body image. They think they're too fat or too thin compared to others. However, I want you to build a positive body image. Accept your body as it is and give yourself praise every day. Remember, there is only one you, so don't compare yourself to others. (Loving / difference / your / make / big / a / yourself / in / can / life).

정답 : _____

16. 다음 빈칸에 들어갈 말로 알맞은 것끼리 짝지어진 것은? (4점)

> • This is very (A)_____ work.
> • I was busy hearing her (B)_____ story.
> • She was (C)_____ when she heard that.

	(A)	(B)	(C)
①	tired	boring	shocking
②	tiring	boring	shocked
③	tired	bored	shocking
④	tiring	boring	shocking
⑤	tiring	bored	shocked

17. 다음 주어진 글을 읽고 잘 이해한 학생은? (3점)

> The phrase "Candy will rot your teeth" has probably been drilled into your head since you were a kid. But there are many foods out there that are worse for your dental hygiene than candy, like crackers. That's because acid － not sugar － is the major cause of tooth decay.

① Stella: The worst factor for tooth decay is sugar.

② Lizzy: Eating crackers is good for your dental health.

③ Jason: I think eating candies is the number one factor for our tooth decay.

④ Chloe: I'm sure eating crackers is not worse for our teeth than eating sweets.

⑤ Zach: There is something more harmful than sugar for your teeth.

18. 다음 중 어법상 적절하지 <u>않은</u> 것은? (3점)

① I like those K-pop idols dancing on the stage.

② I will go to the tower built in 1903.

③ This is my car repaired yesterday.

④ Are you wearing the pants given by me?

⑤ Do you know the man worn sunglasses?

[19–20] 다음 글을 읽고 물음에 답하시오.

> *La Dolce Vita*
>
> *La Dolce Vita* is a lovely Italian restaurant ⓐ<u>serving</u> fresh pizza, pasta, and other delicious Italian dishes. This is one of the most popular restaurants ⓑ<u>locating</u> in the heart of the city. It has a large dining room with a high ceiling ⓒ<u>decorating</u> in gold and red. Don't miss out on this amazing place ⓓ <u>known</u> for its high quality dishes. The menu is large, the food is good, and the service is excellent. There's also a small café ⓔ<u>selling</u> coffee and tea.
>
> ○ 11:00-21:30 daily
> ☎ 01 3524 5323

19. 위 글의 내용과 일치하지 <u>않는</u> 것은? (3점)

① *La Dolce Vita* is an Italian restaurant, which is famous for its high quality dishes.

② You can eat fresh pizza, pasta, and other delicious Asian food.

③ You can find *La Dolce Vita*, the Italian restaurant, in the heart of the city.

④ The restaurant has a large dining room, which has a high ceiling.

⑤ A small café, which is inside the restaurant, sells coffee and tea.

[21~22] 다음 글을 읽고 물음에 답하시오.

Cheer yourself up and put a smile on your face by eating a banana. The popular fruit contains a protein called tryptophan. Once it has been digested, tryptophan then gets converted in a chemical neurotransmitter called serotonin. This is one of the most important mood-regulating chemicals in the brain and most anti-depressant drugs work by adjusting levels of serotonin production. Higher levels are associated with better moods.

Finally my study provides you a message that there are many things or articles which resemble some or the other things in nature and they may have specific (A)_____ on them. This doesn't mean each and every article will resemble another and it has role on it. It's just in some cases. Just it is not a (B)_____ belief; it's a (C)_____ proved truth.

*convert 전환시키다 / regulate 조절하다
/ resemble 닮다, 유사하다 / adjust 조절하다
/ neurotransmitter 신경전달물질

20. 위 글의 밑줄 친 ⓐ~ⓔ 중 어법상 옳은 것을 있는 대로 고른 것은? (3점)

① ⓐ, ⓑ, ⓓ

② ⓐ, ⓓ, ⓔ

③ ⓑ, ⓒ, ⓔ

④ ⓑ, ⓓ, ⓔ

⑤ ⓑ, ⓒ, ⓓ, ⓔ

21. 위 글의 빈칸 (A)~(C)에 들어갈 표현을 알맞게 고른 것은? (4점)

	(A)	(B)	(C)
①	object	scientific	superstitiously
②	object	superstitious	scientific
③	function	scientific	superstitiously
④	function	superstitious	scientific
⑤	function	superstitious	superstitiously

22. 위 글의 내용과 일치하는 것은? (3점)

① All things in nature resemble each other.

② Tryptophan can be converted into serotonin.

③ Higher levels of serotonin production are not associated with better moods.

④ Most anti-depressant drugs work by adjusting levels of tryptophan production.

⑤ A banana contains tryptophan, which is one of the most important chemicals in the brain.

[23-24] 다음 글을 읽고 물음에 답하시오.

Look at the shape of a walnut. Do you notice anything? Yes, it's very similar to the shape of the human brain! ⓐ호두는 두 부분으로 나뉘어진다, just like the brain. Walnuts also have wrinkles, (A)_____ the brain has too. Studies show that walnuts help our brains (B)_____ healthy and active. They are also good for (C)_____ Alzheimer's disease.

23. 위 글의 밑줄 친 ⓐ의 뜻이 되도록 〈보기〉의 단어를 배열하시오. (3점)

┌─ 보기 ─────────────────────────┐
│ is / divided / two / a walnut / into / parts │
└────────────────────────────────┘

정답: _____

24. 위 글의 빈칸 (A), (B), (C)에 들어갈 형태로 가장 적절한 것은? (4점)

	(A)	(B)	(C)
①	who	stayed	prevent
②	who	stay	prevent
③	which	stayed	prevent
④	which	stay	preventing
⑤	which	stayed	preventing

[25-30] 다음 글을 읽고 물음에 답하시오.

(가)

(A)We all know that a diet contained a variety of foods keeps our bodies healthy. But sometimes we are not sure which foods are good for which body parts. Nature, however, gives us a big ⓐclue. Look at the following examples. (B)Each of these foods not only look like a certain body part but is also good for that body part.

Slice open a tomato and ⓑcompare it with the human heart. You will see that they look similar. They both have ⓒmultiple hollow spaces and are red. Researchers say that the chemicals that make tomatoes red are good for your heart and blood. In addition, eating tomatoes can lower your risk of heart disease.

Look at the shape of a walnut. Do you notice anything? Yes, it's very similar to the shape of the human brain! A walnut is divided into two parts, just like the brain. (C)Walnuts also have wrinkles, that the brain has too. Studies show that walnuts help our brains stay healthy and ⓓactive. They are also good for preventing Alzheimer's disease.

(나)

A slice of carrot looks like the human eye. Carrots have some chemicals that can make vitamin A, which improves your vision. It helps your eyes process light and send a clear image to the brain. So, if you want healthy eyes, eat carrots.

Cutting onions is not fun because it makes you cry. But try slicing one anyway. You can see that the inside looks a little like a human cell. Scientists say that onions ⓔcontain vitamin B, which helps make new, healthy cells.

Now, let's move on to ginger. What body part comes to mind when you see it? Doesn't it look like a stomach? You may not like ginger's strong taste or smell, but (D)these come from a special chemical that prevent you from feeling sick and throwing up. For this reason, ginger can be good for your stomach.

Isn't it amazing that some foods mirror Ⓐ _____ _____ _____ _____ _____ _____ _____? Interestingly, there are many other such foods. (E)Find as many as possible and try to eat a variety of them.

26. 위 글의 밑줄 친 ⓐ~ⓔ 중 〈보기〉의 빈칸에 들어갈 단어로 가장 <u>어색한</u> 것은? (4점)

> **보기**
> • There are only _____ choice questions on the test.
> • I always _____ prices before I buy things.
> • Your _____ participation is needed in my class.
> • I practiced hard to _____ my English speaking skills.
> • The police officer found an important _____ to solve the case.

① ⓐ   ② ⓑ   ③ ⓒ

④ ⓓ   ⑤ ⓔ

27. 위 글의 문맥상 Ⓐ의 빈칸에 들어갈 표현을 〈보기〉의 단어들을 모두 사용해서 완성할 때 네 번째 오는 단어는? (3점)

> **보기**
> for / parts / the / are / body / they / good

① the   ② they

③ are   ④ parts

⑤ body

25. 위 글의 (A)~(E) 중 어법상 옳은 문장은? (3점)

① (A)   ② (B)   ③ (C)

④ (D)   ⑤ (E)

28. 위 글의 (가)에서 언급되지 <u>않은</u> 것은? (3점)

① The name of nutrients that walnuts have

② The foods that keep our bodies healthy

③ The foods that mirror the human brain

④ The thing that lowers the risk of heart disease

⑤ The benefit of the chemicals which make tomatoes red

29. 위 글의 (가), (나)의 내용과 일치하는 것은? (3점)

① The outside of carrots is similar to the human eye.

② Though cutting onions is enjoyable, it makes you cry.

③ Only a few foods have a special chemical to heal your body.

④ Not ginger's taste but its smell is beneficial for your stomach.

⑤ You can especially get vitamin A and vitamin B from certain foods.

30. 위 글의 (가)와 (나)를 읽고 나누는 대화로 적절하지 <u>않은</u> 것은? (4점)

① Julia: There are lots of beneficial foods for our bodies. I didn't know that there are foods that look like a certain body part. Isn't amazing?

② Apple: Yes, right. I'm surprised that the inside of the tomato is similar to the human heart, and even eating tomatoes is beneficial for our heart.

③ Julia: You can say that again. Such foods mirror the body parts they are helpful to. The shape of walnut resembles our brain, so it prevents you from getting brain disease.

④ Apple: Yes, so I will recommend my parents to eat walnuts every day. Lately, my eyes are too tired, so I need to take vitamin B, and my sister drinks a cup of ginger tea, which is good for her stomach.

⑤ Julia: Wow, you really care for your health. I will also try to find out many healthy foods and eat a variety of foods.

◎ 선택형 문항의 답안은 컴퓨터용 수정 싸인펜을 사용하여 OMR 답안지에 바르게 표기하시오.
◎ 서술형 문제는 답을 답안지에 반드시 검정 볼펜으로 쓰시오.
◎ 총 30문항 100점 만점입니다. 문항별 배점은 각 문항에 표시되어 있습니다.

[충청북도 ○○중]

1. 다음 중 단어의 뜻이 잘못 연결된 것은? (2점)

① storm - 폭염

② disaster - 재난

③ heavy rain - 폭우

④ earthquake - 지진

⑤ process - 처리하다

[서울시 송파구 ○○중]

2. 다음 빈칸 ⓐ～ⓔ에 들어갈 어휘로 가장 적절한 것은? (3점)

· The class ⓐ_____ and broke.
· We left early to ⓑ_____ heavy traffic.
· The wind blew more and more ⓒ_____.
· He ⓓ_____ deeply before speaking again.
· She showed me the ⓔ_____ way to use the machine.

① ⓐ pulled over

② ⓑ breathe

③ ⓒ violently

④ ⓓ occurred

⑤ ⓔ confusion

[인천시 ○○중]

3. 다음 중 밑줄 친 부분이 어색한 것은? (3점)

① He changed a lot <u>as</u> he got older.

② I have breakfast <u>before</u> I go to school.

③ <u>Although</u> she was full, she refused to eat.

④ You must do this <u>even if</u> you don't want to.

⑤ Jenny can't watch TV <u>unless</u> she finishes her homework.

[4-5] 다음 대화를 읽고 물음에 답하시오.

John: Hey, did you hear about the big fires in California?
Lilly: No, I didn't. (A)_____ serious are they?
John: They have destroyed a large number of houses and other buildings.
Lilly: Are the fires still going on?
John: Yes, actually the wind has made the fires worse. I hope all the people living there are okay.
Lilly: So do I. I'm curious (B)_____ how many people had to leave their homes.
John: Actually more than 20,000 people had to leave their homes, and about 400 people are missing in that area.
Lilly: That's terrible. I hope (C)_____ somewhere safe.

[서울시 송파구 ○○중]

4. 위 대화의 빈칸 (A)～(C)에 들어갈 말로 알맞게 짝지어진 것은? (4점)

	(A)	(B)	(C)
①	Why	at	we're
②	Why	from	they're
③	How	about	you're
④	How	at	you're
⑤	How	about	they're

5. 위 대화의 내용과 일치하는 것은?   (3점)

① Lilly는 이미 캘리포니아의 화재에 대해 알고 있
   었다.

② 다행히 큰 불은 잡혔다.

③ 바람이 화재를 악화시켰다.

④ 많은 사람들이 안전한 곳으로 대피하였다.

⑤ 약 400명의 사람이 그 지역에서 숨졌다.

6. 다음 대화를 읽고 Jisu와 Minsu의 재난 대비 비상 장비
에 들어 있을 물건을 빠짐없이 고르면?   (4점)

> Minsu: Jisu, what do we need to put in the
> natural disaster survival kit?
>
> Jisu: Well, we need some drinks and food,
> but not something that tastes too sweet.
>
> Minsu: I got it. Oh, can we put my laptop in
> the survival kit? It is very important to me.
>
> Jisu: I don't think we have enough space for
> it.
>
> Minsu: Well, you're right. What about a
> radio?
>
> Jisu: Good point. Oh, but make sure that you
> include batteries for it. It will be useless
> without batteries.

보기

> ⓐ batteries   ⓑ coke   ⓒ protein bars
> ⓓ Minsu's laptop   ⓔ water   ⓕ a radio

① ⓐ, ⓑ, ⓒ, ⓔ

② ⓐ, ⓑ, ⓓ, ⓕ

③ ⓐ, ⓒ, ⓔ, ⓕ

④ ⓑ, ⓒ, ⓓ, ⓕ

⑤ ⓒ, ⓓ, ⓔ, ⓕ

7. 다음 대화의 빈칸에 들어갈 적절한 말은?   (3점)

> A: Did you know there was a big flood in
> Gangneung?
> B: Really? I didn't know that. I'm curious
> about _____ it happened.
> A: It happened in 2002.

① why   ② what

③ when   ④ how

⑤ who

8. 다음 대화의 흐름에 맞게 ⓐ~ⓒ를 배열하면? (3점)

> A: This is a fire drill!
>
> ⓐ Taking the elevator is very dangerous.
> Make sure you don't take the elevator in
> a real fire.
> ⓑ You're right. Let's take the stairs!
> ⓒ Why don't we take the elevators?

① ⓐ → ⓑ → ⓒ

② ⓐ → ⓒ → ⓑ

③ ⓑ → ⓐ → ⓒ

④ ⓒ → ⓐ → ⓑ

⑤ ⓒ → ⓑ → ⓐ

9. 다음 대화의 문맥상 밑줄 친 (A)에 들어갈 문장으로 알맞은 것은? (3점)

> Jane: There was a big flood in Europe. Did you hear about it?
> John: No, I didn't. But floods aren't common in winter, are they?
> Jane: (A)_____
> John: Me, too. Let's do some online research.

① I'm curious about how that happened.

② Have you ever experienced a flood?

③ Why don't you help people in Europe?

④ Do you know how to react when a flood happens?

⑤ Natural disasters are so scary.

10. 다음 대화의 흐름상 (A)~(E)의 배열이 가장 자연스러운 것은? (4점)

> G: Did you hear that earthquakes are occurring more often in Korea than before?
>
> (A) Why don't we do some research to find out?
> (B) I didn't know that. I'm curious about why earthquakes have occurred so often in Korea recently.
> (C) Sounds good, but where do we look first?
> (D) They usually occur in the southern part of Korea, but now they are occurring in other places as well.
> (E) Oh, really? I've never felt an earthquake in Korea.
>
> G: How about asking our science teacher first? I think she can help us.

① (A) - (E) - (D) - (C) - (B)

② (B) - (D) - (A) - (C) - (E)

③ (D) - (C) - (E) - (B) - (A)

④ (E) - (C) - (A) - (B) - (D)

⑤ (E) - (D) - (B) - (A) - (C)

11. 다음 빈칸 ⓐ~ⓒ에 들어갈 동사의 형태를 순서대로 바르게 짝지은 것은? (3점)

We nervously made our way down the stairs and outside. I looked around. Parts of buildings had fallen and had smashed several cars. We went to an open space to avoid more falling pieces. How could all this have happened in a few minutes?

Although I ⓐ_____ many earthquake drills in school, I had never thought I'd ⓑ_____ a real earthquake. I still get scared when I remember that night. I can't forget the panic I felt when the furniture was shaking and things were falling to the floor. After that night, I ⓒ_____ to take earthquake drills seriously. I realized that I should be prepared for the next earthquake, which can occur at any time.

	ⓐ	ⓑ	ⓒ
①	had done	- experienced	- begin
②	has done	- experienced	- was begun
③	had done	- experience	- began
④	did	- experience	- was begun
⑤	has done	- experience	- began

12. Which is grammatically correct? (정답 2개)(4점)

① Elly has not started yet when Tom arrived.

② Jake had never taught French before he came Korea.

③ His mother gave him a watch before he had lost it.

④ I had seen the movie three times if I see it once again.

⑤ We stayed in the hotel which we had booked on a website.

13. 다음 빈칸에 알맞은 말은? (2점)

I asked him who _____ the window.
(나는 그에게 누가 창문을 깼는지 물어봤다.)

① break

② has broken

③ had broken

④ will break

⑤ was breaking

14. 다음 글의 빈칸 (A)~(C)에 들어갈 말로 알맞게 짝지어진 것은? (3점)

Last weekend, my sister and I (A)_____ to go on a picnic, but we changed our plans since the yellow dust was really bad. (B)_____ we couldn't go outside, we had a good time. (C)_____ we finished dinner, we watched a movie together.

	(A)	(B)	(C)
①	had plan	Unless	After
②	had plan	Unless	While
③	had planned	Although	After
④	had planned	Unless	If
⑤	had planning	Although	If

15. 다음 우리말의 뜻과 어법에 맞게 주어진 〈보기〉의 단어를 모두 이용하여 빈칸을 완성하시오. (필요시 형태를 바꿀 것) (5점)

나는 다음 지진에 대비해야 한다는 것을 깨달았고, 다음 지진은 언제라도 발생할 수 있다.

―보기―
be, which, occur, prepare, should, can

정답: I realized that I _____ _____

_____ for the next earthquake,

_____ _____ _____ at any

time.

16. 다음 글의 빈칸 (A)와 (B)에 들어갈 알맞은 형태는? (3점)

We nervously made our way down the stairs and outside. I looked around. Parts of buildings had (A)_____ and had smashed several cars. We went to an open space to avoid more (B)_____ pieces. How could all this have happened in a few minutes?

	(A)	(B)
①	fall	fell
②	fallen	falling
③	fell	falling
④	fallen	fell
⑤	fell	fallen

17. 다음 ⓐ~ⓕ 중 어법상 올바른 것을 <u>모두</u> 고른 것은? (3점)

ⓐ I asked him who had broken the window.
ⓑ Kate has studied very hard before she watched TV.
ⓒ I had lost my keys, so I couldn't got into my room.
ⓓ She had teach English for 20 years before she retired.
ⓔ I had been sick for two weeks before I seen a doctor.
ⓕ When I got to the restaurant, my family had finished dinner.

① ⓐ, ⓔ　　　　② ⓐ, ⓕ
③ ⓑ, ⓔ　　　　④ ⓒ, ⓓ
⑤ ⓓ, ⓕ

[18-19] 다음 글을 읽고 물음에 답하시오.

My mom pulled me and my brother out of bed. We ran to the kitchen and ⓐcrawled under the table. I could see the light ⓑswinging violently and books ⓒto fall to the floor. Our family picture dropped from the wall and the glass ⓓcovering it broke. A cup tipped over and rolled off the kitchen table. Every second, I could hear something else in the apartment ⓔbreak. I started to worry that the building would collapse.

18. 위 글의 밑줄 친 ⓐ~ⓔ 중 어법상 <u>어색한</u> 것은? (3점)

① ⓐ　　　② ⓑ　　　③ ⓒ
④ ⓓ　　　⑤ ⓔ

19. 위 글의 글쓴이가 묘사하고 있는 상황과 관계가 <u>없는</u> 것은? (3점)

① 전등이 심하게 흔들리고 있었다.

② 책이 바닥으로 떨어지고 있었다.

③ 가족사진이 벽에서 떨어졌다.

④ 컵이 엎어져 식탁에서 굴러떨어졌다.

⑤ 아파트의 유리창이 모두 깨어졌다.

20. 다음 안내의 내용과 일치하는 것은? (4점)

> Performing CPR properly can save someone's life. Here are the steps for proper CPR. First, check that the person needs help. Tap the person and shout, "Are you okay?" If there's no reaction, call 119 for help. Second, listen, look, and feel for breathing. If the person's not breathing, begin CPR. Make sure you place your hands in the middle of the person's chest. Use your body weight to press harder on the chest. After 30 presses, give the person two breaths. Keep during CPR until help arrives.

① You can save someone's life even if you don't do CPR properly.

② You should not do anything before you call 119.

③ You must put your hands in the middle of the person's chest.

④ Using your body weight when you perform CPR is not recommended.

⑤ Keep doing CPR for 30 minutes.

21. 다음 중 표의 내용과 일치하지 <u>않는</u> 문장은? (3점)

Jimin's Day	
1:20 p.m.	Jimin bought some popcorn and drinks.
1:35 p.m.	The movie *Avengers* started.
1:50 p.m.	Jimin's friend Rachael arrived at the movie theater.
4:36 p.m.	The movie *Avengers* finished.
...	...
5:15 p.m.	Jimin and Rachael got to the restaurant.
5:30 p.m.	Rachael's birthday party started.
8:00 p.m.	Rachael's birthday party finished.
8:20 p.m.	Jimin's brother Jiho arrived at the restaurant.

① Jimin had bought some popcorn and drinks before the movie *Avengers* started.

② The movie hadn't started when Rachael arrived at the movie theater.

③ Rachael and Jimin had a birthday party after the movie had finished.

④ Jiho got to the restaurant but Rachael's birthday party had already finished.

⑤ Jiho missed the birthday party because he had arrived at the party too late.

22. 다음 (A)에 들어갈 말로 가장 적절한 것은? (3점)

> Although I had done many earthquake drills in school, I had never thought I'd experience a real earthquake. I still get scared when I remember that night. I can't forget the panic I felt when the furniture was shaking and things were falling to the floor. After that night, (A)_____. I realized that I should be prepared for the next earthquake, which can occur at any time.

① I became afraid of earthquake drills more.

② I began to take earthquake drills seriously.

③ I totally forgot the earthquake I had experienced.

④ I came to know how to remove an earthquake.

⑤ I wondered how many people were hurt on the street.

23. 다음 우리말 뜻에 맞게 빈칸을 완성하시오. (4점)

> 나는 어릴 때 만화책을 읽곤 했다.
> → When I was young, I _____ _____ read comics.

[24~30] 다음 글을 읽고 물음에 답하시오.

> One night in February, (A)_____ I had gone to bed, an earthquake hit. I woke up suddenly because my bed was shaking. I thought my brother was shaking my bed as a joke. But then I heard the mirror on my desk fall to the floor and break into pieces. I knew (가)it wasn't my brother then, but I still didn't know ⓐwhich exactly was happening.
>
> Soon the whole room began ⓑto shake violently, and my confusion turned to panic. My mom shouted ⓒthat it was an earthquake and ran into my room. (B)_____ it was my first time experiencing an earthquake, I didn't know how to react. I just kept saying, "What should I do?"
>
> My mom pulled me and my brother out of bed. We ran to the kitchen and crawled under the table. I could see the light swinging violently and books falling to the floor. Our family picture dropped from the wall and the glass covering it broke. A cup tipped over and rolled off the kitchen table. Every second, I could hear something else in the apartment ⓓto break. I started to worry that the building would collapse.
>
> Then the shaking seemed to stop. We started crawling toward the door. At that moment, my mom's cell phone rang. It was my dad, who was coming home from work.
>
> He shouted, "It stopped! Get out of the building! Take the stairs! Don't take the elevator! Hurry!" "Where are you? Are you okay?" my mom asked urgently. My dad answered, "Don't worry. I'm okay. I was driving home when the shaking started. But I pulled over immediately. I'm listening to the radio right now ⓔto find out what's going on."

24. 위 글의 "I"가 겪은 일을 시간 순서대로 나열했을 때 (a)~(e) 중 네 번째 올 사건은? (4점)

(a) The mirror fell from my desk to the floor.
(b) The shaking seemed to stop.
(c) My dad called my mom to tell us to get out of the building.
(d) The glass covering our family picture broke into pieces.
(e) My mom, brother, and I took the stairs to escape from the building.

① (a)　　　　② (b)　　　　③ (c)

④ (d)　　　　⑤ (e)

26. 다음은 지진을 경험한 필자를 인터뷰한 내용이다. 주어진 글의 내용과 일치하지 않는 것으로 짝지어진 것은? (4점)

R: What was the first thing that happened when the earthquake hit?
W: ⓐMy bed was shaking suddenly. But I didn't notice it was an earthquake at first.
R: How did you feel when the whole room was shaking violently?
W: ⓑMy confusion turned to panic because the building just began to collapse.
R: How crazy! What did you do next?
W: ⓒWe all crawled under the table after my mom pulled us out of bed.
R: What was happening at that moment?
W: ⓓA lot of things were falling to the floor.
R: What was the most difficult thing when the earthquake occurred?
W: ⓔWhen I didn't know how to react even though I'd experienced earthquakes before.

① ⓐ　　　　　　　　　② ⓐ, ⓑ

③ ⓑ, ⓔ　　　　　　　④ ⓑ, ⓒ, ⓔ

⑤ ⓒ, ⓓ, ⓔ

25. 위 글의 내용과 일치하지 않는 것은? (3점)

① The earthquake hit in February when I was sleeping at night.

② When the mirror on my desk fell to the floor and broke into pieces, I knew what my brother was shaking.

③ When the books were falling to the floor in the kitchen, I was under the table with my mom and brother.

④ As the earthquake stopped shaking, we began crawling toward the door.

⑤ My dad, who was coming home from work, called my mom.

27. 위 글의 빈칸 (A), (B)에 들어갈 접속사를 올바르게 짝 지은 것은? (3점)

	(A)	(B)
①	before	Although
②	after	Since
③	if	Since
④	after	Although
⑤	before	Unless

29. 위 글의 밑줄 친 ⓐ~ⓔ 중 문법적으로 <u>어색한</u> 것은? (2개) (4점)

① ⓐ   ② ⓑ   ③ ⓒ

④ ⓓ   ⑤ ⓔ

28. 위 글의 밑줄 친 (가)it이 가리키는 것은? (3점)

① pulling her out of bed

② the meaning of a serious joke

③ the reason why her bed was shaking

④ the shout for help after the earthquake hit

⑤ the fault of breaking the glass covering our family picture

30. 위 글의 I의 심경으로 가장 적절한 것을 고르면? (4점)

① scared   ② ashamed

③ bored   ④ excited

⑤ pleased

◎ 선택형 문항의 답안은 컴퓨터용 수정 싸인펜을 사용하여 OMR 답안지에 바르게 표기하시오.
◎ 서술형 문제는 답을 답안지에 반드시 검정 볼펜으로 쓰시오.
◎ 총 30문항 100점 만점입니다. 문항별 배점은 각 문항에 표시되어 있습니다.

[충청북도 ○○중]

1. 다음 빈칸에 들어갈 말로 가장 알맞은 것은? (2점)

_____ it was snowing heavily, I stayed home all day.

① If   ② After   ③ Since
④ Although   ⑤ In any case

[서울시 송파구 ○○중]

2. 다음 중 밑줄 친 어휘가 올바르지 않은 것은? (3점)

① If something is done underline{immediately}, it is done slowly.
② To shake means to move back and forth quickly.
③ To collapse means to fall down because something is weak.
④ If you smash something, you break it into many pieces.
⑤ If you are in panic, you feel so frightened or worried that you cannot act or think normally.

[서울시 송파구 ○○중]

3. 다음 우리말을 영어로 바르게 옮긴 것은? (3점)

• 그는 나이가 들어감에 따라 많이 바뀌었다.

① He changed a lot as he got older.
② He changed a lot if he got older.
③ He got older unless the changed a lot.
④ Although he changed a lot, he got older.
⑤ Even though he changed a lot, he got older.

[4-5] 다음 대화를 읽고 물음에 답하시오.

B: Hey, did you hear about the big fires in California?
G: No, I didn't. How serious are they?
B: They've destroyed a large number of houses and other buildings.
G: Are the fires still going on?
B: Yes, actually the wind has made the fires worse. I hope all the people living there are okay.
G: So do I. (A)I'm curious about how many people had to leave their homes.
B: Actually more than 20,000 people had to leave their homes, and about 400 people are missing in that area.
G: That's terrible. I hope they're somewhere safe.

[인천시 ○○중]

4. 위 대화의 밑줄 친 (A)와 바꾸어 쓸 수 있는 것은? (2점)

① I know
② I'm sure
③ I wonder
④ I'm interested in
⑤ I'm worried about

5. 위 대화를 읽고 답할 수 없는 질문은? (2점)

① What is the cause of the fire?

② How many people are missing?

③ Why are the fires still going on?

④ How serious are the big fires in California?

⑤ How many people had to leave their homes?

6. 다음 대화에 따르면 한국에서 두 번째로 큰 피해를 입히는 자연재해는 무엇인가? (3점)

A: I'm curious about which type of natural disaster causes the most damage in Korea.

B: Actually I read a report yesterday about the damage from each type of natural disaster. Number one is storms.

A: I see. I guess earthquakes are second.

B: No. Second is heavy rain, and third is heavy snow.

A: What about earthquakes?

B: Based on the report, earthquakes are fourth. But the damage from earthquakes has been increasing recently because they have been happening more often in Korea.

A: I see. It seems like we have to be prepared for a variety of natural disasters in Korea.

① storms

② earthquakes

③ heavy snow

④ heavy rain

⑤ tsunamis

7. 다음 대화의 흐름상 빈칸에 들어갈 말로 알맞지 않은 것은? (3점)

A: There was a big flood in Europe. Did you hear about it?

B: No, I didn't. But floods aren't that common in winter, are they? _____ how that happened.

A: Me too. Let's do some online research.

① I'm curious about

② I have heard

③ I'm wondering

④ I'd like to know

⑤ I want to know

8. 자연스러운 대화가 되도록 〈보기〉에 이어질 문장을 순서대로 배열한 것은? (4점)

보기

David: Susie, this is a fire drill! Let's go!

Susie: Okay! The guidelines say that we have to get in line quickly.

ⓐ Right. Remember to lower your body while you're walking.

ⓑ We're going to the meeting place, right?

ⓒ No. Make sure you don't take the elevators in a real fire. It's very dangerous.

ⓓ I got it. Hey, why don't we take the elevators? They're faster than the stairs.

① ⓐ - ⓑ - ⓒ - ⓓ

② ⓑ - ⓐ - ⓓ - ⓒ

③ ⓑ - ⓒ - ⓓ - ⓐ

④ ⓒ - ⓓ - ⓐ - ⓑ

⑤ ⓓ - ⓐ - ⓑ - ⓒ

9. 다음 대화에서 밑줄 친 부분의 의도로 가장 알맞은 것은? (3점)

> Son: Mom, what else do we need to put in the natural disaster survival kit?
> Mom: Well, we need water, some food, and a radio.
> Son: Anything else, Mom?
> Mom: Oh, <u>make sure</u> that you include batteries for the radio.

① 궁금증 표현하기
② 당부하기
③ 설명 요청하기
④ 걱정 표현하기
⑤ 놀람 표현하기

11. 다음 주어진 단어를 활용하여 아래의 우리말을 〈조건〉에 맞게 영작하시오. (4점)

조건

- 필요하면 어형을 변화할 것
- 빈칸에 들어갈 부분만 답지에 적을 것
- 의미에 맞게 과거와 과거완료 시제를 모두 사용할 것

> 우리는 그가 그 돈을 어디에 감추었었는지 알지 못했다.

→ We (1)_____ where he (2)_____ the money. (know / hide)

10. 다음 문장의 밑줄 친 부분이 서로 의미가 같은 것끼리 짝지어진 것은? (4점)

① Don't speak <u>while</u> you're eating.
  <u>While</u> I like her paintings, I don't like her personality.

② I saw Mr. Jackson <u>as</u> I took a walk with my dog.
  <u>As</u> she has no money, she can't buy the medicine.

③ It has been two months <u>since</u> he left us.
  <u>Since</u> she lives alone, she doesn't need a big house.

④ I'd liked to know <u>if</u> he will come.
  <u>If</u> you don't have any special plan, let's go camping together.

⑤ <u>Although</u> Mina knew the right answer, she didn't let us know.
  We were still worried <u>although</u> everything had turned out well.

12. 다음 글의 문맥과 어법에 맞게 빈칸 (A), (B), (C)에 들어갈 가장 알맞은 것은? (4점)

> Then the shaking seemed to stop. We started crawling toward the door. At that moment, my mom's cell phone (A)_____. It was my dad, (B)_____ was coming home from work.
> He shouted, "It stopped! Get out of the building! Take the stairs! Don't take the elevator! Hurry!" "Where are you? Are you okay?" my mom asked (C)_____. My dad answered, "Don't worry. I'm okay. I was driving home when the shaking started.

	(A)	(B)	(C)
①	ring	which	lovely
②	rang	who	quietly
③	ring	which	hopefully
④	rang	who	urgently
⑤	rung	which	kindly

13. 다음 글의 문맥에 맞게 빈칸에 들어갈 알맞은 접속사를 〈보기〉에서 찾아 쓰시오. (3점)

Last weekend, my sister and I had planned to go on a picnic, but we changed our plans (A)_____ the yellow dust was really bad. (B)_____ we couldn't go outside, we had a good time. (C)_____ we finished dinner, we watched a movie together.

보기
although / after /since

(A)_____

(B)_____

(C)_____

15. 다음 우리말과 일치하도록 주어진 두 문장을 조건에 맞게 한 문장으로 쓰시오. (4점)

조건
1. 접속사 when을 사용할 것.
2. 과거완료 시제를 포함할 것.

The movie *Avengers* started, and then I got to the movie theater.

→ _____

(내가 영화관에 도착했을 때, 영화 Avengers는 시작했었다.)

14. Which sentence is not grammatically correct? (3점)

① I had taught history for 10 years before I left this school.

② I've finished my science project yesterday.

③ The shop had already closed when we arrived there.

④ He has been reading a novel since this afternoon.

⑤ She had never eaten Burrito until she visited Mexico last month.

16. 다음 글의 흐름상 주어진 문장이 들어갈 곳으로 가장 적절한 곳은? (3점)

When I arrived at school, class had already begun.

Today everything went wrong. First, I got up late. (A) I quietly sat down at my desk. (B) Soon I realized that I had left my report at home. (C) Suddenly my teacher asked me to read my report. (D) I had never been in such a situation, so my face got really red. (E) I want to forget everything about today!

① (A) ② (B) ③ (C)
④ (D) ⑤ (E)

[17–18] 다음 글을 읽고 물음에 답하시오.

Performing CPR properly can save someone's life. Here are the ⓐsteps for proper CPR. (A) First, check that the person needs help. ⓑTap the person and shout, "Are you okay?" (B) Second, listen, look, and feel for ⓒbreathing. If the person's not breathing, begin CPR. (C) Make sure you ⓓplace your hands in the middle of the person's chest. (D) Use your body weight to ⓔpress hard on the chest. (E) After 30 presses, give the person two breaths. Keep doing CPR until help arrives.

[충북 청주시 ○○중]

17. 위 글의 (A)～(E) 중 다음 문장이 들어갈 위치로 가장 알맞은 것은? (3점)

If there's no reaction, call 119 for help.

① (A) ② (B) ③ (C)

④ (D) ⑤ (E)

[충북 청주시 ○○중]

18. 위 글의 밑줄 친 ⓐ～ⓔ 중 그 뜻이 잘못 연결된 것을 고르면? (3점)

① ⓐsteps - 단계

② ⓑTap - 간지럽히다

③ ⓒbreathing - 호흡

④ ⓓplace – 두다, 놓다

⑤ ⓔpress - 누르다

[19–21] 다음 글을 읽고 물음에 답하시오.

We nervously ⓐ계단으로 내려가서 and outside. I looked around. Parts of buildings had fallen and ⓑ차 몇 대를 박살냈다. We went to an open space to avoid more falling pieces. How could all this have happened in a few minutes?

Although I had done many earthquake drills in school, I had never thought I'd experience a real earthquake. I still get scared when I remember that night. ⓒ그 공포를 잊을 수 없다. I felt when the furniture was shaking and things were falling to the floor. After that night, I ⓓ지진 대피 훈련을 진지하게 받기 시작했다. I realized that I should be prepared for the next earthquake, ⓔ언제라도 일어날 수 있는

[서울 강동구 ○○중]

19. 위 글의 밑줄 친 ⓐ～ⓔ를 영어로 옮긴 것 중 어색한 것은? (4점)

① ⓐ made our way down the stairs

② ⓑ had turned over several cars

③ ⓒ I can't forget the panic

④ ⓓ began to take earthquake drills seriously

⑤ ⓔ which can occur at any time

[전북 익산시 ○○중]

20. 위 글의 글쓴이에 대한 설명으로 알맞지 않은 것은? (3점)

① 학교에서 지진 대피 훈련을 했었다.

② 지진은 언제라도 일어날 수 있다고 생각해 왔다.

③ 지진이 일어났던 밤의 공포를 잊을 수가 없다.

④ 다음에 있을 지진에 대비해야 한다고 생각한다.

⑤ 지진을 겪은 후에 지진 대피 훈련에 진지하게 임하고 있다.

21. 위 글의 글쓴이 가족이 공터로 나간 이유를 우리말로
쓰시오. (15자 내외)   (4점)

답: _____

22. 위의 주어진 글 (A)에 이어질 내용을 순서에 맞게 배
열한 것으로 가장 적절한 것은?   (3점)

① (B) - (D) - (C)

② (C) - (B) - (D)

③ (C) - (D) - (B)

④ (D) - (B) - (C)

⑤ (D) - (C) - (B)

[22~26] 다음 글을 읽고, 물음에 답하시오.

(A) My mom pulled me and my brother out
of bed. We ran to the kitchen and crawled
under the table.

(B) ⓐThen the shaking seemed stopping. We
started crawling toward the door. At that
moment, my mom's cell phone rang. ⓑIt
was my dad, that was coming home from
work. He shouted, "It stopped! Get out of
the building! Take the stairs! Don't take
the elevator! Hurry!"

(C) "Where are you? Are you okay?" my
mom asked urgently. My dad answered,
"Don't worry. I'm okay. ⓒI was driving
home when the shaking started. But I
pulled over immediately. ⓓI'm listening to
the radio right now to find out what's
going on."

(D) I could see the light swinging violently
and books falling to the floor. ⓔOur
family picture dropped from the wall and
the glass covered (가)it broke. A cup tipped
over and rolled off the kitchen table. ⓕ
Every second, I could hear something else
in the apartment break. I started to worry
that the building would collapse.

23. 위 글의 밑줄 친 (가)it이 가리키는 3단어를 찾아 쓰시
오.   (3점)

답: _____

24. 위 글의 내용과 일치하지 않는 것은?   (3점)

① 전등이 세차게 흔들렸다.

② 책이 바닥으로 떨어졌다.

③ 사진이 벽에서 떨어졌다.

④ 컵이 엎어져서 굴러 떨어졌다.

⑤ 건물이 무너지기 시작했다.

25. According to the passage, which action didn't
the writer and the writer's family do when the
earthquake occurred?   (4점)

① 주인공의 가족은 부엌 식탁 밑으로 기어들어 갔다.

② 지진이 멈춘 것 같았을 때, 주인공 가족은 걸어서
문 쪽으로 갔다.

③ 아버지는 계단을 통해 건물 밖으로 나오라고 했다.

④ 아버지는 지진이 시작되자 바로 자동차를 길가에
세웠다.

⑤ 주인공은 건물이 무너질까봐 걱정했다.

26. 위 글의 ⓐ~ⓕ 중에서 어법상 <u>어색한</u> 곳 3군데를 찾아 문장 번호를 쓰고 〈보기〉와 같이 고치시오.　(6점)

> **보기**
> I enjoyed to play the piano.
> [to play] → [playing]

문장 번호 - 어색한 형태 - 바르게 고친 형태

답: (1)＿＿＿＿　＿＿＿＿＿＿ → ＿＿＿＿＿＿＿

　　(2)＿＿＿＿　＿＿＿＿＿＿ → ＿＿＿＿＿＿＿

　　(3)＿＿＿＿　＿＿＿＿＿＿ → ＿＿＿＿＿＿＿

28. 위 글의 괄호 (A), (B), (C) 안에서 문맥에 맞는 표현으로 가장 적절한 것은?　(4점)

	(A)	(B)	(C)
①	after	use	Since
②	after	but	Since
③	after	but	Although
④	before	but	Although
⑤	before	because	Since

[27~30] 다음 글을 읽고 물음에 답하시오.

> One night in February, (A)[before / after] I had gone to bed, an earthquake hit. I woke up suddenly because my bed was shaking. I thought my brother was shaking my bed as a joke. But then I heard the mirror on my desk fall to the floor and break into pieces. I knew it wasn't my brother then, (B)[because / but] I still didn't know what exactly was happening.
>
> Soon the whole room began to shake violently. My mom shouted that it was an earthquake and ran into my room. (C)[Since / Although] I had never experienced the earthquake before, (가)＿＿＿＿＿＿＿＿＿.
> I just kept saying, "What should I do?"

29. 위 글의 상황에서 주인공이 느꼈을 심경의 변화로 가장 적절한 것은?　(4점)

① bored → excited

② lonely → satisfied

③ nervous → relieved

④ thankful → regretful

⑤ confused → frightened

27. 위 글의 내용으로 보아 (가)에 들어갈 문장으로 가장 적절한 것은?　(3점)

① I knew what to do

② I didn't know how to react

③ I told my mom when to leave

④ I told my mom where to hide

⑤ I didn't know when to wake up

30. 위 글의 내용과 일치하지 <u>않는</u> 것은?　(3점)

① 2월의 어느 날 밤에 지진이 일어났다.

② 나는 침대가 흔들려서 잠에서 깼다.

③ 나는 개가 침대를 흔드는 줄 알았다.

④ 나는 거울이 책상에서 떨어져 산산조각이 나는 소리를 들었다.

⑤ 지진을 처음 겪어 어떻게 반응해야 할지 몰랐다.

◎ 선택형 문항의 답안은 컴퓨터용 수정 싸인펜을
사용하여 OMR답안지에 바르게 표기하시오.
◎ 서술형 문제는 답을 답안지에 반드시 검정볼
펜으로 쓰시오.
◎ 총 30문항 100점 만점입니다. 문항별 배점
은 각 문항에 표시되어 있습니다.

[충북 청주시 ㅇㅇ중]

1. 다음 중 단어와 주어진 뜻이 서로 일치하는 것은?
(3점)

① election: to reach a goal by working hard
② analyze: to make sure that something happens
③ approach: to move toward or closer to something
④ achieve: to study or think about something in a careful way
⑤ ensure: the process of choosing a person for a position by voting

[경기도 ㅇㅇ중]

2. 다음 주어진 단어들 중 빈칸에 들어갈 수 없는 것은?
(3점)

as / if / after / since / although

• _____ he was hungry, he refused to eat.
• _____ she was tired, she went to bed early.
• _____ we had lunch, we ate cake for dessert.
• I'll clean my place today _____ my parents will visit me tomorrow.

① as　　　　　　② if
③ after　　　　　④ since
⑤ although

[전라북도 ㅇㅇ중]

3. 다음 문장을 수동태 문장으로 바꾸시오. (by + 행위자
는 생략 가능)　　　　(4점)

You must finish this project today.

답 : _____

[서울시 강남구 ㅇㅇ중]

4. 다음 짝지어진 대화가 어색한 것은?　　　(2점)

① A: I think we're ready for our project.
　 B: Good. I bet that it will turn out well.
② A: I want to make a student contact information list.
　 B: That sounds good. I doubt that it will be very helpful.
③ A: Can we really make a picture book for children in other countries?
　 B: It won't be easy, but I'm certain that we can make it.
④ A: I want to take photos for Sports Day.
　 B: That's great. You're really good at taking photos. I'm 100% sure that you'll take some wonderful pictures.
⑤ A: I don't think a person like me can be called a leader.
　 B: What do you mean? You're really friendly and outgoing. I'm positive that you'll be elected if you run.

Brian: The election is coming up. Why don't you run for class representative, Yumi?

Yumi: No way. I'm not the right person for that position. (가)(running / thought / never / have / about / I)

Brian: Why not?

Yumi: Come on, Brian. Leaders have special qualities. I don't think a person like me can be called a leader.

Brian: What do you mean? I think you have very good leadership qualities. You're really friendly and outgoing. You also help people get along. I have no doubt ⓐ _____.

[전라북도 ㅇㅇ중]

5. 위 대화의 단어 영영풀이가 <u>잘못된</u> 것은? (3점)

① election: the process of choosing someone for a position by voting

② representative: somebody who has been chosen to speak on behalf of a group

③ quality: a distinctive feature

④ outgoing: rarely meeting and talking to other people

⑤ get along: to be friendly with

[전라북도 ㅇㅇ중]

6. 위 대화의 괄호 (가) 안의 문장을 문맥에 맞게 바르게 나열하시오. (3점)

답 : _____

[충북 청주시 ㅇㅇ중]

7. 위 대화의 흐름이 자연스럽도록 빈칸 ⓐ에 들어갈 가장 알맞은 말은? (3점)

① that I will elect her if she runs

② that you will be elected if you run

③ that I will elect him if Brian runs

④ you will elect some people if they run

⑤ you will be elected if he doesn't run

[충북 청주시 ㅇㅇ중]

8. 위 대화에 나타난 Yumi와 Brian의 태도로 가장 알맞은 것은? (4점)

	Yumi	Brian
①	sociable	critical
②	arrogant	neutral
③	outgoing	negative
④	uncertain	supportive
⑤	confident	encouraging

[충북 청주시 ㅇㅇ중]

9. 위 대화의 내용과 가장 일치하는 것은? (3점)

① Yumi would like to nominate herself to be class representative.

② Yumi has thought about running for class representative before.

③ Brian thinks leaders have special qualities that Yumi doesn't have.

④ Brian is just trying to be nice to Yumi when he compliments her.

⑤ Brian bets that Yumi will be chosen as class representative.

10. 다음 글의 내용과 일치하지 <u>않는</u> 것은? (3점)

In the Send Our Stories project, we are going to make a picture book for children in other countries. We've divided everyone into three groups. Each group will be responsible for a different task. Group A will translate a Korean story into English. Group B will make drawings for the book and edit it. After copies of the book are printed, Group C will be in charge of sending them to the children. It won't be easy, but I have no doubt that the children who receive these books will really enjoy them.

① 다른 나라 아이들을 위한 그림책을 만들 계획이다.

② 그룹 A는 영어를 한국어로 번역할 것이다.

③ 그룹 B는 책에 그림을 그릴 것이다.

④ 그룹 C는 아이들에게 책을 보낼 것이다.

⑤ 필자는 아이들이 그림책을 좋아할 것이라고 확신한다.

[11~12] 다음 대화를 읽고 물음에 답하시오.

Yoongyum(Y): Taehyun, are you okay? What's the matter?

Taehyun(T): Hello, Yoongyum. I have a problem.

Y: What happened?

T: You know Jaewoo, Yunho, and I are best friends, right? They had a fight, and now I'm stuck in the middle. I don't know what to do.

Y: That sounds hard. Don't you know why they had a fight?

T: Yes, but it doesn't sound like a big deal to me. I guess they had some kind of ⓐ _____.

Y: Why don't you all meet together and talk about it? I think they'll listen to you.

T: That's a good idea. They're both good friends of mine. I can't take sides.

Y: I understand. I hope everything goes well.

11. 위 대화의 내용과 일치하지 <u>않는</u> 것을 고르면?(4점)

① Taehyun, Jaewoo, and Yunho are best friends.

② Taehyun doesn't know what to do between Jaewoo and Yunho.

③ Taehyun doesn't know why Jaewoo and Yunho had a fight.

④ Yoongyum advises Taehyun to meet all together and talk about the problem.

⑤ Yoongyum hopes Taehyun's problem works out well.

12. 위 대화의 문맥상 ⓐ에 들어갈 단어로 적절한 것은?
(3점)

① debate

② goal

③ leadership

④ misunderstanding

⑤ material

13. 다음 대화의 빈칸에 들어갈 말로 알맞은 것은? (2점)

Sana: Hey, Momo. _____

Momo: I don't know what to do, Sana. Hee-chul asked me to help him with his homework this evening, but I told him I can't. I have so many things to do today.

① What's the matter?

② How do you like it?

③ Where have you been?

④ How was your weekend?

⑤ Can you tell me what to do?

14. 다음 두 문장을 접속사 if를 이용하여 한 문장으로 쓰시오.
(4점)

1. Please let me know.
2. Do you like me?

답 : _____

15. 다음 대화를 올바르게 이해하지 못한 사람들로 짝지어진 것은?
(3점)

B: Mom, we've got a problem.

W: What's the matter?

B: We're going to have dinner with Grandma this Saturday, right? But I just realized that Sujin's birthday party is on Saturday evening. She's my best friend. What should I do?

W: That sounds like a difficult decision. Let's talk about it with your dad.

B: Okay, Mom. I'd love to see Grandma, but I don't want to miss my best friend's birthday party.

*B: Boy, W: Woman

David: "The boy's family planned to have dinner with his grandma this Saturday."

Smith: "Sujin is the boy's best friend."

Robert: "The boy hasn't decided yet what to do this Saturday."

Ramsey: "His father will let him go to the party."

James: "The boy doesn't have a good relationship with his grandmother."

① Robert, James

② Ramsey, James

③ Smith, Ramsey

④ David, Smith

⑤ David, Robert

16. 다음 두 문장을 한 문장으로 바꿔 쓸 때, 빈칸에 들어갈 말로 알맞은 것은? (3점)

I'm wondering. + Is Faker going to come to the PC room?
→ I'm wondering ＿＿＿＿ ＿＿＿＿ ＿＿＿＿ going to come to the PC room.

① Faker is if
② if is Faker
③ Faker if is
④ if Faker is
⑤ is Faker if

17. 다음 중 어법상 옳은 문장은? (3점)

① This problem must solved now.
② The song will play by our band.
③ This artwork may be not touched.
④ All animals should treat with respect.
⑤ This job must be done by tomorrow.

18. 다음 대화를 통해 빈칸에 들어갈 알맞은 말을 영어로 쓰시오. (4점)

A: Will you go to Jimin's birthday paty?
B: 나는 내가 거기에 갈 수 있을지 없을지 확실하지 않아.
A: Why? What is your problem?
B: Because I have to prepare the exam.

→ I am not sure ＿＿＿＿ or not ＿＿＿＿ ＿＿＿＿ ＿＿＿＿ there.

19. 다음 밑줄 친 부분의 쓰임이 나머지 넷과 <u>다른</u> 하나는? (3점)

① I want to know <u>if</u> you are interested in music.
② I am not sure <u>if</u> I'll be able to do it.
③ She asked me <u>if</u> I could go to the party.
④ We'll go to the picnic <u>if</u> it's sunny tomorrow.
⑤ I'm not sure <u>if</u> we can use this machine.

20. 다음 중 어법상 <u>어색한</u> 것은? (3점)

① The letter will be sent by Tim tomorrow.
② Their voices can't be heard from here.
③ Should the button be pushed right now?
④ Some diseases can be cured medicine.
⑤ She will be called Snow White.

ⓐI was surprised that there are actually many different leadership styles, but soon I realized the reason.

ⓑWe belong to many different groups, and many different situations can come up in our lives. They all call for different leadership styles. ⓒEach group's unique situation determine the best leadership style.

After reading everything, I became more confident. ⓓI discovered that I have some of the qualities of a "green leader." (A)If my classmates think a green leader would make our class better, ⓔthey might pick me to be class representative! Okay, let's try it!

22. 위 글의 ⓐ~ⓔ 중 어법상 어색한 것은? (3점)

① ⓐ　　　　② ⓑ　　　　③ ⓒ

④ ⓓ　　　　⑤ ⓔ

23. 위 글의 제목으로 가장 적절한 것은? (4점)

① The Most Unique Leadership Type

② Tips for Becoming a Great Leader

③ Different Groups, Different Leadership

④ The Qualities of Class Representative

⑤ How to Be a Green Leader in Your Class

21. 위 글을 쓴 목적으로 가장 적절한 것은? (4점)

① 자신이 원하는 리더를 홍보하려고

② 무수히 많은 리더십의 종류를 설명하려고

③ 적합한 리더가 되기 위한 노력을 공유하려고

④ 훌륭한 사람만이 리더가 되어야 함을 주장하려고

⑤ 고유한 상황에 맞는 리더가 필요함을 알려주려고

24. 위 글의 밑줄 친 (A)와 쓰임이 같은 것은? (4점)

① I will buy the book if you need it.

② I wonder if you like the food.

③ The judge is going to decide if he is guilty.

④ Joan asked me if I want to go to the party.

⑤ The boy wanted to check if the monster was alive or dead.

GREEN LEADERS: "Team Builders"
· Ensure that the team feels valued
· Create a positive environment
· Are friendly and easy to talk to

RED LEADERS: "Logical Analysts"
· Have good reasoning skills
· Analyze problems and situations
· Think of the most effective ways to achieve the team's goals

PURPLE LEADERS: "(A)_____"
* Allow others to work on their own
* Do not ⓐtry to control people
* Give advice only when it ⓑis needed

ORANGE LEADERS: "(B)_____"
* Make everyone's role ⓒclearly
* Make sure everything ⓓis finished on time
* Ensure each step ⓔis doing properly

YELLOW LEADERS: "Quiet Supporters"
* Lead by example
* Let the team members ⓕshine instead
* Meet the team members' needs

26. 위 글의 ⓐ~ⓕ 중 올바르지 않은 어법의 개수는?

(3점)

① 0개   ② 1개   ③ 2개

④ 3개   ⑤ 4개

25. 위 글의 빈칸 (A)와 (B)에 들어갈 알맞은 말은?

(4점)

    (A)   (B)

① Logical Analysts - Creative Thinkers

② Creative Thinkers - Hands-Off Managers

③ Creative Thinkers - Strict Directors

④ Hands-Off Managers - Strict Directors

⑤ Hands-Off Managers - Logical Analysts

27. 위 글의 내용과 일치하지 않는 것은? (4점)

① GREEN LEADERS make sure the team feels valued.

② PURPLE LEADERS advise team members only when they need advice.

③ ORANGE LEADERS ensure that all tasks are done on time.

④ YELLOW LEADERS directly lead the team to the team's goals.

⑤ RED LEADERS have good reasoning skills.

Brian told me this afternoon that I have good leadership qualities. (A) No one has ever told me that before. Why does he think so? Maybe he was just trying to be nice. (B) Can I really become a leader? I don't know. I think leaders should have a vision, clear goals, and the ability to motivate others. (C) I don't have any of those things.

(D) Then I suddenly started to wonder (가)if these are the only qualities that make a good leader. (E) Maybe I'm wrong. Maybe there are other leadership qualities. So I decided to do some research online.

Here's ⓐ_____ I found!

28. 위 글의 흐름상 다음 문장이 들어가기에 가장 적절한 곳은? (4점)

When he said that to me, however, I started to think.

① (A) ② (B) ③ (C)

④ (D) ⑤ (E)

29. 위 글의 빈칸 ⓐ에 들어갈 알맞은 관계대명사는?
(3점)

답 : _____

30. 위 글의 밑줄 친 (가)if와 쓰임이 <u>다른</u> 것은? (4점)

① I will stay home <u>if</u> it rains tomorrow.

② I don't know <u>if</u> she likes Italian food.

③ Please let me know <u>if</u> you like it or not.

④ Joan asked me <u>if</u> I wanted to go to the party.

⑤ The boy wanted to check <u>if</u> the monster was alive.

3학년 영어 1학기 기말고사(4과) 2회

반		점수	
이름			

문항수 : 선택형(27문항) 서술형(3문항)   20 . . .

◎ 선택형 문항의 답안은 컴퓨터용 수정 싸인펜을
  사용하여 OMR답안지에 바르게 표기하시오.
◎ 서술형 문제는 답을 답안지에 반드시 검정볼
  펜으로 쓰시오.
◎ 총 30문항 100점 만점입니다. 문항별 배점
  은 각 문항에 표시되어 있습니다.

[전라북도 ○○중]

**1. 다음 대화의 흐름상 빈칸에 들어갈 단어가 가장 알맞게
짝지어진 것은?**   (3점)

A: Mom, we've got a problem.
B: What's the (A)_____?
A: We're going to have dinner with Grandma
   this Saturday, right? But I just realized
   that Sujin's birthday party is on Saturday
   evening. She's my best friend. What should
   I do?
B: That sounds like a difficult (B)_____.
   Let's talk about it with your dad.
A: Okay, Mom. I'd love to see Grandma, but
   I don't want to miss my best friend's
   birthday party.

	(A)	(B)
①	matter	decision
②	wrong	division
③	matter	division
④	wrong	decision
⑤	problem	doubt

[서울시 강남구 ○○중]

**2. 다음 주어진 단어를 활용하여 〈조건〉에 맞게 학교 규칙
을 완성하시오.**   (5점)

조건
• 필요하면 단어를 추가하거나 어형을 변형할 것.
• 답안지에는 빈칸에 들어갈 말만 쓸 것.

Back to School with Covid-19 Rules
(1) Hands _____ regularly with
    safe water and soap. (should / wash) (3단어)
(2) Masks _____ all the time.
    (must / wear) (3단어)
(3) Close physical contact between students
    _____.(will / allow) (4단어)

[충북 청주시 ○○중]

3. 다음 중 대화가 어색한 것은?   (2점)

① A: These two pairs of shoes are on sale!
     Which do you like better?
   B: I prefer the white shoes to the black ones.
② A: I want to straighten my hair. Can you
     recommend a good place?
   B: Sure. I know two places, Styles Studio
     and Hair Castle.
③ A: I should prepare for an exam this
     Thursday, but I also have to go to band
     practice.
   B: Oh, you have a lot to do. It seems you
     must choose between the two.
④ A: Let's check out tasks. Are you in charge
     of taking pictures?
   B: Yes. I have no doubt that you will take
     some wonderful pictures.
⑤ A: In my opinion, the Special Sandwich is
     the healthier choice.
   B: But it's much more expensive than the
     Classic Sandwich.

4. Which of the following does NOT fit in the blank (A)? (3점)

> Nick: Hey, Mandy. (A)_____?
> Mandy: I don't know what to do, Nick. My brother asked me to help him with his homework this Wednesday, but I told him I can't. I have so many things to do that day.

① What's wrong?

② What's the matter?

③ Is there any problem?

④ What's bothering you?

⑤ What makes you say that?

[5-6] 다음 대화를 읽고 물음에 답하시오.

> Wonho: I'm so excited about our museum field trip. We are going to make a picture book about the museum for children in other countries. I'm excited about that too.
> Gahyun: Me too. Let's check our tasks. Minju, what is your group in charge of?
> Minju: We're in charge of taking pictures, and making drawings for the book.
> Gahyun: Okay. Sejin, are your group members going to do some research on the museum?
> Sejin: Yes, we are. What is your group in charge of, Wonho?
> Wonho: We're writing the book. Also, we will translate Korean into English. Gahyun's group will print the copies of the book. What else is your group in charge of, Gahyun?
> Gahyun: After the books are printed, we are sending them to the children. It won't be easy, but I have no doubt that the children who receive these books will really enjoy them. I think we're ready.
> Minju: Good. Each group will be responsible for a different task. I have no doubt that our project will @turn out well.

5. 위 대화의 내용과 일치하지 <u>않는</u> 것은? (3점)

① Wonho can't wait to go on a museum field trip.

② Minju and her group members will draw pictures for the book.

③ Sejin's group will do some research on the museum.

④ They haven't decided whose group will print the books.

⑤ Minju is sure that they will do well on their project.

6. 위 대화의 밑줄 친 @의 뜻으로 알맞은 것은? (4점)

① to happen unexpectedly

② to need or request something

③ to deeply study every piece of something to understand it

④ to want to know more about something you aren't sure of

⑤ to develop or end in a particular way; to have a particular result

7. 다음 대화의 흐름상 빈칸 (A)에 들어갈 가장 알맞은 말은? (3점)

A: I'm so excited about our museum field trip.
B: Me too. Let's check our tasks. Yen, what are you in charge of?
C: I'm in charge of taking pictures.
B: Okay. Sejin, are you going to do some research on the museum?
A: Yes, I am. Are you going to write our field trip report. Emma?
B: That's right. I think we're ready.
C: Good. (A)_____ that our project will turn out well.

① I'm not certain
② I don't think
③ I was surprised
④ I'm not positive
⑤ I have no doubt

8. According to the dialog above, why doesn't Yumi want to run for the election? (3점)

① Because Yumi has bad character.
② Because Yumi thinks difficult to be elected.
③ Because Yumi thinks she has no special qualities.
④ Because Yumi is the only one not running fast.
⑤ Because Yumi doesn't take care of others' feeling.

9. 위 대화의 ⓐ~ⓔ 중 흐름상 어색한 것은? (3점)

① ⓐ   ② ⓑ   ③ ⓒ
④ ⓓ   ⑤ ⓔ

[8-10] 다음 대화를 읽고, 물음에 답하시오.

Brian: The election is coming up. ⓐWhy don't you run for class representative, Yumi?
Yumi: No way. I'm not the right person for that position. I've never thought about running. ⓑCan you be my running mate?
Brian: Why not?
Yumi: Come on, Brian. ⓒLeaders have special qualities. ⓓI don't think a person like me can be called a leader.
Brian: What do you mean? I think you have very good leadership qualities. ⓔYou're really friendly and outgoing. You also help people get along. 만약 네가 입후보한다면, (A) 네가 우리의 리더가 될 거라고 믿어 의심치 않아.

10. 위 대화에서 밑줄 친 (A)의 우리말과 같은 뜻이 되도록 상자 안의 단어를 바르게 배열하여 영작하시오. (단, 필요에 따라 단어의 형태는 변형 가능) (4점)

leader, that, you, have, our, I, no, be, doubt, will

답: _____ if you run.

11. 다음 글의 괄호 (A), (B), (C) 안에서 글의 흐름과 어법에 맞는 것을 고르면? (3점)

After 3 month school break, I've finally come back to my classroom. I met my friends who I missed so much. Once I saw them, they asked me a lot of questions.

Seulki wondered **(A)**[how / if] I was. Irene, who always studies hard, asked me, "**(B)**[Do / Be] you have any plans for the final exam?" Also, one of my best friends Wendy asked me to help her study English. She always wants to get better grades, but she doesn't know how to.

Most of my friends were happy to see each other again, but not all of them liked coming to school. Hyoung was not sure **(C)**[whether / that] she is glad to be back to school.

	(A)	(B)	(C)
①	how	Do	whether
②	if	Be	that
③	how	Be	whether
④	how	Do	that
⑤	if	Do	whether

12. 다음 중 어법상 어색한 것은? (4점)

① I don't know whether to go or not.

② I wonder whether it was raining or snowing.

③ It doesn't matter if or not the dog is on a leash.

④ I'm not sure if we can use this coupon.

⑤ How can you tell whether the machine is working?

13. 다음 빈칸 ⓐ, ⓑ, ⓒ에 들어갈 말이 알맞게 짝지어진 것은? (4점)

A: That injured man can't walk and has to ⓐ_____.

B: Yes, the situation is serious. We must ⓑ _____ something before it's too late.

A: I called 911, but why isn't the ambulance coming? The medical decision will not ⓒ_____ until we move him to the hospital.

B: Let's wait. It will come soon.

	ⓐ	ⓑ	ⓒ
①	carry	do	be made
②	be carried	be done	be made
③	carry	be done	make
④	be carried	do	be made
⑤	be carried	do	make

14. 다음 밑줄 친 if의 용법이 다른 것은? (2점)

① <u>If</u> I have some free time, I'll go to the park.

② <u>If</u> it rains, I will stay at home.

③ I will get angry <u>if</u> the student tells a lie.

④ Please give her this note <u>if</u> you see her.

⑤ I asked him <u>if</u> he got married.

15. 다음 대화가 자연스럽게 이어지도록 (A)~(E)를 바르게 배열한 것은? (3점)

Smith: What happened?
Junsu: You know Nick, Yunho, and I are best friends, right? They had a fight, and now I'm stuck in the middle. I don't know what to do.

(A) Yes, but it doesn't sound like a big deal to me. I guess they had some kind of misunderstanding.
(B) That's a good idea. They're both good friends of mine. I can't take sides.
(C) Why don't you all meet together and talk about it? I think they'll listen to you.
(D) I understand. I hope everything works out.
(E) That sounds hard. Do you know why they had a fight?

① (C) - (B) - (E) - (D) - (A)
② (C) - (D) - (E) - (A) - (B)
③ (E) - (A) - (C) - (B) - (D)
④ (E) - (B) - (C) - (A) - (D)
⑤ (E) - (C) - (A) - (D) - (B)

16. 다음 글의 주어진 우리말과 일치하도록 빈칸에 알맞은 낱말을 영어로 쓰시오. (4점)

Jamil's Online Store
Dear Mr. Steve
We are sorry that the item you ordered is out of stock. 이 물건은 다른 상점에서 배송될 것입니다. We hope you will get it in five days.

→ This item _____ _____ _____ from another store.

[17-20] 다음 글을 읽고 물음에 답하시오.

GREEN LEADERS: "Team Builders"
· Ensure that the team feels valued
· Create a positive environment
· Are friendly and easy to talk to

RED LEADERS: "(A)_____"
· Have good reasoning skills
· Analyze problems and situations
· Think of the most effective ways to achieve the team's goals

PURPLE LEADERS: "(B)_____"
· Allow others to work on their own
· Do not try to control people
· Give advice only when it is needed

ORANGE LEADERS: "Strict Directors"
* Make everyone's role clear
* Make sure everything is finished on time
* Ensure each step is done properly

YELLOW LEADERS: "Quiet Supporters"
· Lead by example
· Let the team members shine instead
· Meet the team members' needs

BLUE LEADERS: "(C)_____"
· Approach problems in new ways
· ⓐ_____
· Deal with tasks differently from others

17. 각 학생의 리더십 유형이 잘못 짝지어진 것은? (3점)

① Glen: I come up with new ideas to solve the problem. - Blue Leader

② Dale: I lead by example and take care of others' needs. - Yellow Leader

③ Rick: I don't control people and let others work on their own. - Purple Leader

④ Shane: I think it's important to make sure everything is finished on time. - Red Leader

⑤ Maggie: I create a positive environment and make sure everybody feels respected. - Green Leader

18. 위 글의 ⓐ에 들어갈 말로 가장 적절한 것은? (2점)

① Come up with fresh ideas

② Are friendly and easy to talk to

③ Ensure that the team feels valued

④ Ensure each step is done properly

⑤ Make sure everything is finished on time

19. 위 글의 내용과 일치하는 것은? (3점)

① 보라색 리더는 항상 팀원들에게 충고한다.

② 노란색 리더는 팀원들이 솔선수범하게 한다.

③ 파란색 리더는 기존의 방식으로 문제를 해결한다.

④ 노란색 리더는 팀원들의 요구를 충족하려고 노력한다.

⑤ 보라색 리더는 팀원들에게 맡겨진 일만 하도록 감독한다.

20. 위 글의 (A)~(C)에 들어갈 말로 바르게 짝지어진 것은? (3점)

① (A) Creative Thinkers
   (B) Logical Analysts
   (C) Hands-Off Managers

② (A) Logical Analysts
   (B) Hands-Off Managers
   (C) Creative Thinkers

③ (A) Creative Thinkers
   (B) Hands-Off Managers
   (C) Logical Analysts

④ (A) Logical Analysts
   (B) Creative Thinkers
   (C) Hands-Off Managers

⑤ (A) Hands-Off Managers
   (B) Logical Analysts
   (C) Creative Thinkers

21. 다음 글에서 전체 흐름과 관계 없는 문장은? (4점)

I was surprised that there are actually many different leadership styles, but soon I realized the reason. ⓐWe belong to many different groups, and many different situations can come up in our lives. ⓑThey all call for different leadership styles. ⓒPeople want strong leadership styles all the time. ⓓEach group's unique situation determines the best leadership style. ⓔI am a part of many different groups, and I have different responsibilities in each group.

① ⓐ   ② ⓑ   ③ ⓒ

④ ⓓ   ⑤ ⓔ

[22-25] 다음 글을 읽고 물음에 답하시오.

Brian told me this afternoon that I have good leadership qualities. (A) No one has ever told me that before. Why does he think so? (B) Maybe he was just trying to be nice. When he said that to me, ⓐ_____, I started to think. (C) Can I really become a leader? I don't know. I think leaders should have a vision, clear goals, and the ability to motivate others. I don't have any of those things. (D) Maybe I'm wrong. Maybe there are other leadership qualities. (E) ⓑ_____ I decided to do some research online.

*I: Yumi

23. 위 글 바로 다음에 이어질 내용으로 가장 적절한 것은? (4점)
① different leadership styles
② ways to become a leader
③ different ways to motivate others
④ qualities that the writer has as a leader
⑤ qualities of the most popular leadership

24. 위 글의 빈칸 ⓐ, ⓑ에 들어갈 말이 바르게 짝지어진 것은? (4점)

	ⓐ	ⓑ
①	however	Thus
②	therefore	In fact
③	by the way	Instead
④	for instance	In short
⑤	on the other hand	Otherwise

22. 위 글의 (A)~(E) 중 주어진 문장이 들어갈 곳으로 가장 적절한 것은? (3점)

Then I suddenly started to wonder if these are the only qualities that make a good leader.

① (A)   ② (B)   ③ (C)
④ (D)   ⑤ (E)

25. 위 글의 내용과 가장 일치하는 것은? (3점)
① The election has already finished.
② Yumi wants to be a leader.
③ Brian is not sure that Yumi will be elected.
④ Everyone tells Yumi that she has leadership.
⑤ Yumi does not think that she can motivate others.

I was surprised ⓐthat there are actually many different leadership styles, but soon I realized the reason.

We belong to many different groups, and many different situations can come up in our lives. They all call for different leadership styles. Each group's unique situation ⓑdetermine the best leadership style.

After ⓒreading everything, I became more confident. I discovered that I have some of the qualities of a "green leader." ⓓIf my classmates think a green leader would make our class better, they might pick me ⓔto be class representative! Okay, let's try it!

28. 위 글을 쓴 목적으로 가장 적절한 것은?　(4점)

① 자신이 원하는 리더를 홍보하려고
② 적합한 리더가 되기 위한 노력을 공유하려고
③ 무수히 많은 리더십의 종류를 설명하려고
④ 고유한 상황에 맞는 리더가 필요함을 알려주려고
⑤ 훌륭한 사람만이 리더가 되어야 함을 주장하려고

26. 다음 글의 요지로 가장 알맞은 것은?　(3점)

① 교실에는 그린 리더의 자질이 필요하다.
② 여러 가지 지도력 유형을 갖추어야 한다.
③ 지도자는 집단과 상황을 변화시킬 수 있다.
④ 집단과 상황에 따라 다른 지도력 유형이 필요하다.
⑤ 지도력 유형을 이해하면 책임감 있는 지도자가 될 수 있다.

29. 위 글의 ⓐ~ⓔ 중 어법상 어색한 것은?　(4점)

① ⓐ　　　　② ⓑ　　　　③ ⓒ
④ ⓓ　　　　⑤ ⓔ

27. 위 글의 내용과 일치하지 않는 것은?　(3점)

① 글쓴이는 학급 회장 선거에 도전해 보기로 했다.
② 글쓴이는 지도력의 유형이 다양하다는 사실을 잘 몰랐었다.
③ 다양한 지도력에 대해 알게 된 후 글쓴이는 자신감을 가지게 되었다.
④ 글쓴이는 학교에서 요구되는 최고의 지도력인 그린 리더의 자질을 가지고 있다.
⑤ 다양한 지도력이 필요한 이유는 사람들이 다양한 집단과 상황에 속해있기 때문이다.

30. 위 글의 표현의 뜻으로 옳지 않은 것은?　(4점)

① belong to – ~에 속하다
② confident – 자신 있는
③ call for – ~을 요구하다
④ determine – 결정하다
⑤ come up – 나타나다

MEMO

정답 및 해설

Lesson 1 (중간) 1회

01 ① 02 ① 03 ① 04 ③ 05 ② 06 ⑤ 07 ②
08 ③ 09 ① 10 ③
11 I have been listening to music for two hours.
12 ② 13 ④
14 (1) I have still been writing a diary.
　 (2) Sam has still been swimming.
15 ① 16 ① 17 ④ 18 ④ 19 ④ 20 ②
21 What's most important is to become familiar with
22 ② 23 ④ 24 ① 25 ③ 26 ⑤ 27 ③ 28 ⑤
29 ④ 30 ④

01 위에서부터 순서대로 requirement(필요한 것), volunteer(자원하다), memorize(외우다, 암기하다), confident(자신감 있는)가 들어가는 것이 문맥상 적절하다.

02 motivate는 '동기 부여하다'라는 뜻을 가진 단어이다. '어떤 것을 다른 사람이 볼 수 있게 온라인에 올리다'라는 영영 풀이가 가리키는 것은 post(게시물을 올리다)이다.

03 위 글의 흐름상, 어떤 장소를 방문할 때 그곳의 언어로 이야기하면 사람들이 더 친절해진다는 내용이다. 따라서 ① anxious(불안한, 걱정하는)라는 단어는 빈칸에 적절하지 않다.

04 연극이 어땠냐는 A의 질문에 대해 그것을 친구와 봤다고 대답하는 B의 답변은 대화의 흐름상 자연스럽지 않다.

05 '스케이트보드 타는 건 어떻게 배운 거야?'라는 질문은 스케이트보드 클럽에 가입했다는 내용의 질문으로 적절하므로 (B)에 오는 것이 알맞다.

06 How do you like ~?은 '~은 어때?, ~가 마음에 드니?'라는 뜻으로 상대방에게 어떤 대상에 대한 만족 여부를 물을 때 사용하는 표현이다.

07 "How do you like it?"은 "그것은 어떠니?"라는 뜻으로 어떤 경험이나 일이 어떻게 느껴졌는지 물어보는 표현이다. 따라서 새해에 무엇을 할 것인지에 대해 이야기를 나누고 있는 위 대화의 흐름상 적절하지 않다.

08 "How do you like ~?"은 "~은/는 어떠니?"라는 뜻으로 어떤 경험이나 일에 대해 어떻게 느끼는지 물어보는 표현이다. 따라서 위 대화에서는 서울에 사는 것은 어떠냐고 물어보는 표현인 ③ living이 들어가야 어법상 자연스럽다.

09 "I'd like to ~"는 "I would like to ~"의 줄임말로, "~하기를 원한다"는 의미이다. 따라서 빈칸 (B)에 들어갈 표현으로 가장 적절한 것은 ① go to a museum(박물관에 가다)이다.

10 B가 G에게 스케이트보드 타는 법을 어떻게 배웠냐고 묻자, G는 지난달에 지역의 스케이트보드 동아리에 가입했다고 대답한다. 이에 B가 그것은 어떠냐고 물어보고, G는 재밌고 새 친구를 사귈 수 있게 도와준다고 말한다. 이에 B가 어떻게 도와 주냐고 묻자 G가 마지막 문장에서 다른 회원들과 스케이트보드를 타러 가고 서로 조언을 나눈다고 말하는 순서로 이어지는 것이 대화의 흐름상 가장 적절하다.

11 'have been -ing'는 과거의 어느 시점에서부터 현재까지 '~해오고 있다'라는 현재완료진행의 표현이다.

12 대화의 흐름상 빈칸에는 A가 B에게 가구를 만드는 것은 어떠냐고 묻는 표현인 ② How do you like it?(그것은 어떠니?)가 들어가야 가장 적절하다.

13 ① that / ② what / ③ What / ⑤ whose로 고쳐야 어법상 적절한 문장이 된다.

14 'have/has been -ing'는 과거의 어느 시점에서부터 현재까지 '~해오고 있다'라는 뜻으로, 현재완료진행의 표현이다.

15 ①That은 '저, 저것의'라는 뜻의 한정사이다. 나머지 문장에서 that은 모두 관계대명사로 쓰였다.

16 관계대명사 that은 계속적 용법으로 사용할 수 없다. 따라서 이 경우 관계대명사의 계속적 용법으로 문장을 만들 땐, who를 쓰는 것이 어법상 적절하다.

17 본문에 You develop much better cognitive thinking이라고 언급되어 있다.

18 위 글에서는 화자가 부산에 가서 하고 싶은 경험들에 대해서 이야기하고 있다. 따라서 제목으로 가장 적절한 것은 ④ What I Want to Experience in Busan(내가 부산에서 경험하고 싶은 것)이다.

19 '그것은 당신이 그 언어의 소리에 익숙해질 수 있도록 도와준다'라는 문장이 들어가기에 가장 적절한 곳은 스페인어를 배우고 싶으면 스페인어로 된 영화를 보라고 조언하고 있는 곳인 (D)이다.

20 새로운 언어로 말하는 것이 말하기 능력을 향상시켜 준다는 문장은 위 글에서 언급되어 있지 않다.

21 become familiar with ~에 친숙해지다

22 마지막 문단에서는 축구를 좋아한다면 축구에서 쓰이는 단어를 배워서 그걸 외우라고 조언해 주고 있다. 따라서 빈칸

에 들어갈 말로 가장 적절한 것은 ② soccer vocabulary (축구 어휘)이다.

23 두 번째 문단에 언급되어 있듯이, Julie가 스페인어를 매일 연습하기 위해 한 일은 쇼핑 목록을 스페인어로 작성하고 핸드폰의 언어를 스페인어로 바꾼 것이다.

24 스페인어 라디오 듣기 연습을 하라는 내용은 위 글에서 언급되어 있지 않다.

25 ⓐ subtitles 자막 ⓑ motivate 동기를 부여하다 ⓒ follow 팔로우하다

26 위 글의 마지막 문단에서 'There are hundreds of good tips out there, but everyone has their own way of learning.'(수많은 조언들이 있지만, 모든 사람들은 자신만의 학습 방법이 있다.)라고 언급한 바 있다.

27 what은 '~하는 것'이라는 뜻으로 'the thing(s) which~'의 의미이다. 따라서 ③ Find what keeps you motivated가 가장 적절하다.

28 좋아하는 남자 그룹의 노래를 번역이나 자막 없이 듣고 싶다는 Marisa에게 그 남자 그룹을 소셜 미디어에서 지워라 (Remove)라는 조언은 위 글의 문맥상 자연스럽지 않다.

29 Marisa는 좋아하는 남자 그룹의 노래를 번역이나 자막 없이 듣고 싶다고 언급한 바 있다.

30 Brandon은 "I recommend watching Korean dramas."라고 조언한 바 있다.

Lesson 1 (중간)

2회

> **01** ② **02** ② **03** ③ **04** ③ **05** ④ **06** ① **07** ①
> **08** ② **09** ① **10** ②
> **11** My father has been working at Walmart since 2015.
> **12** ③ **13** ② **14** ① **15** ④ **16** ④ **17** ⑤ **18** ⑤
> **19** ① **20** ⑤ **21** ④ **22** ⑤ **23** ② **24** ① **25** ④
> **26** What **27** ② **28** ⑤ **29** ① **30** ⑤

01 (A) get used to ~에 익숙해지다 (B) familiar 익숙한 (C) in this case 이 경우에

02 would like to ~하고 싶다

03 subtitle은 '자막'이라는 뜻을 갖는 단어이다.

04 위 대화의 흐름상 빈칸에는 어제 아침에 등산한 것은 어땠냐고 물어보는 표현이 들어가야 한다.

05 "I'd like to ~"는 "~하기를 원한다"라는 뜻이다.

06 Brian은 대화 초반에 "I'm writing a list of things that I want to do this year."라고 언급했다.

07 대화의 흐름상 빈칸에는 Messi가 Son에게 가구를 만드는 것은 어떠냐고 묻는 표현인 ① How do you like it? (그것은 어떠니?)이 들어가야 가장 적절하다.

08 위 대화에서는 가구를 만드는 Son과 Messi가 새로운 것을 시도하고 경험하는 것이 새로운 재능을 발견할 수 있게 해 준다고 이야기하고 있다. 따라서 빈칸에 들어갈 말로 가장 적절한 것은 ② find new talents이다.

09 B가 기타를 배우고 싶다고 말하자 G가 어디서 기타를 배울 것인지 묻는다. 따라서 B는 친구 진수가 기타를 잘 치기 때문에 진수한테 가르쳐 달라고 부탁할 것이라고 대답한다.

10 관계대명사 that은 계속적 용법으로 사용할 수 없다. 따라서 이 경우 관계대명사의 계속적 용법으로 문장을 만들 때, which를 쓰는 것이 어법상 적절하다.

11 'have/has been ~ing'는 과거의 어느 시점에서부터 현재까지 '~해오고 있다'라는 뜻으로, 현재완료진행의 표현이다.

12 ③ what은 의문사로 쓰였다. 나머지는 모두 what이 관계대명사로 쓰인 명사절 문장이다.

13 과거의 어느 시점에서부터 현재까지 '~해오고 있다'를 표현할 때 현재완료진행형인 'have/has been ~ing'을 쓸 수 있다.

14 관계대명사 what은 '~한 것'이라는 뜻으로, 'the thing(s) which ~' 대신 쓸 수 있다.

15 ① that → which / ② learning → learn / ③ from → into / ⑤ happily → happy로 고쳐야 어법상 적절한 문장이 된다.

16 "What's wrong?"은 "무슨 일이니?"라는 뜻으로, 스케이트보드 동아리의 좋은 점에 대해서 이야기하고 있는 위 대화의 흐름상 적절하지 않다.

17 위 글의 마지막에, 학생들을 만나 새로운 언어를 배우는 것에 대한 그들의 생각을 알아보자고 이야기하고 있다. 따라서 위 글 다음에 나올 내용으로 적절한 것은 ⑤ students' interesting ways to study new languages(학생들의 새로운 언어를 공부할 수 있는 흥미로운 방법들)이다.

18 위 글의 초반부에 'Here are some tips to help you learn a new language on your own.'(여기 스스로 새로운 언어를 배울 수 있게 도와주는 팁들이 있다.)라고 글의 목적을 말하고 있다.

19 ⓐ exciting을 excited로 바꿔야 어법상 적절한 문장이 된다.

20 (A) Follow 팔로우하다
(B) have been watching ~을 보아 왔다

(C) what ~한 것

21 (가)post는 '(온라인에 게시물을) 올리다'라는 뜻으로 사용되었다. 이와 같은 뜻으로 사용된 문장은 ④ Students may play games or post photos on instagram.(학생들은 게임을 할 수도 혹은 인스타그램에 사진을 올릴 수도 있다.)이다.

22 Lori는 남자 그룹의 노래를 자막과 번역 없이 듣기 위해 한국어를 배우고 싶어하는 Marisa에게 다른 팬들을 찾아서 그들과 소통하라고 조언하고 있다.

23 위 글에서는 새로운 언어를 배울 수 있는 여러 조언들에 대해서 이야기하고 있지만, 그럼에도 불구하고 각자 자신만의 방법이 있다고 말하고 있다.

24 Marisa가 노래 부르기와 춤추기를 좋아한다는 내용은 위 글에서 언급되지 않았다.

25 '난 스페인어로 된 영화를 자주 보는 것을 추천해.'라는 표현이 들어가기에 가장 적절한 곳은 스페인어 영화를 자주 보는 것이 스페인어 소리에 익숙해질 수 있도록 도와준다고 말하고 있는 (D)이다.

26 관계대명사 what은 '~한 것'이라는 뜻으로, 'the thing(s) which ~' 대신 쓸 수 있다.

27 help + 목적어 + get used to ~: ~에 익숙해질 수 있도록 도와주다

28 마지막 문단에서 Rohan은 'why don't you try writing a review of a match in Spanish?'라고 조언한 바 있다.

29 위 글에서는 스페인어를 배우고 싶어하는 Owen에게 다른 학생들이 스페인어를 배울 수 있는 팁에 대해서 조언을 해 주고 있다. 따라서 제목으로 가장 적절한 것은 ① How to Improve Spanish(스페인어 능력을 향상시킬 수 있는 방법)이다.

30 빠른 속도로 원어민과 이야기하는 연습을 한다는 내용은 위 글에서 언급 되어 있지 않다.

Lesson 2 (중간) 1회

01 ④	**02** ⑤	**03** ①	**04** ④	**05** ③	**06** ②	**07** ⑤
08 ④	**09** ④	**10** ①	**11** ⑤	**12** ③	**13** ⑤	**14** ④

15 (A) served (B) selling
16 I am surprised that it can talk to you.

17 ⑤	**18** ①	**19** ③	**20** ④, ⑤		**21** ④	**22** ⑤
23 ③	**24** ③	**25** ③	**26** ③	**27** ①		

28 prevents you from feeling sick and throwing up
29 ④ **30** ②

01 위 대화의 흐름상 빈칸에 공통으로 들어가기에 가장 적절한 단어는 ④ improve(향상시키다, 향상하다)이다.

02 confuse는 '혼란스럽게 하다'라는 뜻을 가진 단어이다. '다른 사람을 위해 온라인에 무언가를 올리다'라는 영영풀이가 가리키는 것은 post(온라인에 게시물을 올리다)이다.

03 ① That's a great idea.는 "좋은 생각이다."라는 뜻으로 유감이나 동정을 나타내는 표현이 아니다.

04 친구가 화가 나 있어서 그녀에게 사과하고 싶다는 화자에게 해 줄 수 있는 조언으로 가장 적절한 것은 ④ How about texting her an apology?(문자 메시지로 사과를 하는 건 어때?)이다.

05 M이 A에게 충분히 잤냐고 묻자, A는 7시간 이상 잤다고 대답한다. M은 다시 A에게 몇시에 잤냐고 묻자 A는 보통 때처럼 12시 이후에 잤다고 대답하고 M은 그것 때문에 피곤한 것이라고 말하면서, 언제 자는지가 중요하다는 걸 들어보았냐고 질문한다. 이에 A가 이유를 묻자 M이 늦게 잠드는 것은 다음날 피곤함을 느끼게 한다고 과학자들이 말했다고 대답하는 순서로 이어지는 것이 대화 흐름상 가장 자연스럽다.

06 위 빈칸 (A)에 들어가기에 가장 적절한 것은 놀라움을 나타내는 표현인 ② surprised(놀라워 하는)이다.

07 여자는 남자의 말("You don't have to go out to exercise.")에 대해 "That's why I love these programs."(그게 내가 이 프로그램을 좋아하는 이유야.)라고 대답했다.

08 평소처럼 12시 이후에 잠을 잤다는 여자의 말에 대해 남자가 "그게 너를 피곤하게 만드는 거야."("That's probably what is making you tired.")라고 언급했다.

09 "~를 들어본 적 있니?"라고 물어볼 때 "Have you heard ~?"라는 표현을 쓸 수 있다.

10 얼음을 씹어 먹는 것이 치아 건강에 나쁘다는 것을 들어보았냐는 여자의 질문에 대해 '아니, 안 들어. 그게 언제니?'라고 대답하는 남자의 대답은 대화 흐름상 자연스럽지 않다.

11 "수면이 중요하다는 걸 들어본 적 있니?"라고 질문할 때, 상대방의 어떤 사실을 들어본 적 있는지 물어보는 표현인 "Have you heard ~?"라는 표현을 쓸 수 있다.

12 위 대화에서는 건강을 체크하게 도와주는 스마트 밴드에 대해서 이야기하고 있다. ⓒDo you know who plays the guitar in the band?(누가 밴드에서 기타를 연주하는지 아니?)라는 질문은 대화 흐름상 적절하지 않다.

13 (A) keep+목적어+healthy ~가 건강을 유지하게 하다

(B) however 그러나, 하지만

(C) look like ~처럼 생기다

14 ④baking을 baked로 고쳐야 어법상 적절한 문장이 된다.

15 관계대명사로 이어진 문장에서 '주격 관계대명사+be동사'는 생략 가능하다. '주격 관계대명사+be동사+현재분사(~ing)' 또는 '주격 관계대명사+be동사+과거분사(~ed)'의 형태로 쓰인 문장에서 생략될 경우, 각각 현재분사와 과거분사가 선행사를 수식하게 된다. (A)에는 선행사가 The curry이므로 served가, (B)에는 selling이 들어가야 어법상 적절하다.

16 "I'm surprised that ~."은 "난 ~해서 놀랐다"라는 의미로 that 이하의 문장에 대해 놀랐음을 나타내는 표현이다.

17 ① writing → written / ② managed → managing / ③ building → built / ④ making → made로 고쳐야 어법상 적절한 문장이 된다.

18 ⓑ that I was reading → which I was reading / ⓒ that → who / ⓓ what → where / ⓔ what → which로 고쳐야 어법상 적절한 문장이 된다.

19 위 글에서는 우리 몸에 도움이 되는 당근, 양파, 생강과 같은 음식들에 대해서 설명하고 있다. 따라서 위 글의 제목으로 가장 적절한 것은 ③ Beneficial Foods for Our Bodies(우리 몸에 이로운 음식들)이다.

20 생강의 아프거나 토하는 것을 막게 해주는 특별한 화학물질이 냄새와 맛을 좋아하지 않을 수도 있다는 내용이다. 따라서 빈칸에 적절하지 않은 것은 ④ protects(보호하다)와 ⑤ saves(구하다)이다.

21 ⓒthat와 ⓓthat은 모두 두 문장을 연결해 주는 접속사로 사용되었기 때문에 생략 가능하다.

22 생강의 특별한 화학 물질이 토하거나 아프게 되는 것을 막아준다고 이야기하고 있다. 따라서 빈칸에 들어갈 말로 가장 적절한 것은 ⑤ ginger can be good for your stomach이다.

23 위(a stomach)와 비슷하게 생긴 음식으로 언급된 것은 양파가 아니라 생강이다.

24 ③ How do healthy cells make vitamin B?(건강한 세포가 어떻게 비타민B를 만드는가?)에 대해서는 언급되어 있지 않다.

25 위 글에서는 우리 몸에 도움이 되는 토마토와 호두와 같은 음식들에 대해서 설명하고 있다. 따라서 위 글의 제목으로 가장 적절한 것은 ③ Beneficial Foods for Our Bodies(우리 몸에 이로운 음식들)이다.

26 contain이 포함된 문장은 '주격 관계대명사+be동사'인

'which is'가 생략된 문장이다. 따라서 현재분사 ③ containing이 가장 적절하다.

27 (a)의 앞 문장과 뒷문장의 내용이 반대되기 때문에 however(그러나)가, (b)의 뒷문장에서 앞 문장의 내용이 추가되고 있으므로 In addition(게다가)이 들어가는 것이 적절하다.

28 마지막 문단에 'these come from a special chemical that prevents you from feeling sick and throwing up.'이라고 언급되어 있다.

29 (A)that은 접속사, (B)that은 한정사(저, 저것의), (C)that은 관계대명사로 쓰였다. ⓐ는 한정사, ⓑ는 관계대명사, ⓒ는 접속사로 쓰였다.

30 자연친화적인 환경에서 기른 음식은 몸에 좋다는 내용은 위 글에서 언급 되어 있지 않다.

Lesson 2 (중간) 2회

01 ⑤	02 ⑤	03 as	04 ①	05 ①	06 ③	07 ⑤
08 ⑤	09 ②	10 ⑤	11 ①	12 ①	13 ②	

14 (1) written (2) working (3) served

15 Loving yourself can make a big difference in your life.

16 ②	17 ⑤	18 ⑤	19 ②	20 ②	21 ②	22 ②

23 A walnut is divided into two parts. **24** ④ **25** ⑤

26 ⑤	27 ②	28 ①	29 ⑤	30 ④

01 mirror는 '반영하다'라는 의미로 사용되었다.

02 ⓐimprove, ⓑprevent, ⓒcontain, ⓓcompare, ⓔbenefit가 들어가는 것이 문맥상 적절하다.
⑤는 'exercise'를 가리키는 영영 풀이이다.

03 as many+명사+as you can: 가능한 한 많은 ~

04 위에서부터 순서대로, the way you see, positive body image, give yourself praise, compare yourself, Loving yourself가 들어가는 것이 적절하다.

05 교복을 입어야 하느냐는 A의 질문에 대해, "아니, 넌 교복을 입어야 돼."라는 B의 대답은 대화의 흐름상 자연스럽지 않다.

06 A가 B에게 충분히 잤냐고 묻자, B는 7시간 이상 잤다고 대답한다. A는 B에게 몇 시에 잤냐고 묻자 B는 평소처럼 12시 이후에 잤다고 대답하고 A는 그것 때문에 피곤한 것이라고 말하는 순서로 이어지는 것이 대화 흐름상 가장 자연스럽다.

07 '다른 한편으로, 잠을 일찍 자는 것은 기억력을 향상시키

고 당신을 더욱 생산적이 되도록 도와줄 수 있다.'라는 문장이 들어가기에 가장 적절한 곳은 잠을 일찍 자라고 조언하는 곳인 (E)이다.

08 남학생은 일찍 잠드는 것의 장점을 이야기하면서 여학생에게 "From now on, try to go to bed earlier."라고 조언했다.

09 ⓑEmma가 온라인 영상을 20만번 본 것은 아니다. ⓔ Emma는 집에서 운동하는 것을 좋아한다고 언급했다.

10 "I'm surprised that ~."은 "난 ~해서 놀랐다"라는 의미로 that 이하의 문장에 대해 놀랐음을 나타내는 표현이다.

11 "~를 들어본 적 있니?"라고 물어볼 때 "Have you heard ~?"라는 표현을 쓸 수 있다.

12 승민이는 대화 후반부에 얼음을 씹어 먹는 것이 치아에 손상을 주고 치아를 민감하게 만든다고 언급하고 있다.

13 ⓒ that → what / ⓔ, ⓖ what → that으로 고쳐야 어법상 적절한 문장이 된다.

14 위 문장들은 '주격 관계대명사+be동사'가 생략된 문장이다. 이때 선행사가 사물/사람이냐에 따라 과거분사/현재분사가 쓰일 수 있다.

15 동명사가 주어로 쓰일 경우 동사는 단수형 동사가 되는 것에 주의한다. / make a difference 차이를 만들다

16 (A) tiring 피곤하게 하는, (B) boring 지루하게 하는, (C) shocked 충격을 받은

17 위 글에서는 설탕보다 치아 건강에 더 해로운 음식이 많이 있다고 이야기하고 있다.

18 ⑤ worn을 wearing으로 고쳐야 어법상 적절한 문장이 된다.

19 위 글에 따르면 피자와 파스타, 그리고 다른 맛있는 이탈리아 음식(serving fresh pizza, pasta, and other delicious Italian dishes)을 제공한다고 언급되어 있다.

20 ⓑ locating → located / ⓒ decorating → decorated로 고쳐야 어법상 적절한 문장이 된다.

21 (A) function 역할, (B) scientific 과학적인, (C) superstitiously 미신으로

22 바나나에 함유되어 있는 트립토판이 두뇌 활동에 있어 가장 중요한 감정 조절 화학 물질 중 하나라고 언급되어 있다.

23 be divided into ~로 나뉘어 지다

24 (A) 선행사가 사물이므로 which가, (B) help의 목적보어이므로 동사원형인 stay가, (C) 전치사 for가 쓰였으므로 동명사형인 preventing가 들어가는 것이 어법상 적절하다.

25 (A) contained → containing
(B) look like → looks like

(C) that → which
(D) prevent → prevents로 고쳐야 어법상 적절한 문장이 된다.

26 위에서부터 순서대로, ⓒmultiple, ⓑcompare, ⓓactive, improve, ⓐclue가 들어가는 것이 문맥상 적절하다.

27 글의 문맥상, the body parts they are good for가 된다.

28 호두가 가진 영양분의 이름은 언급되지 않았다.

29 비타민 A와 비타민 B는 각각 당근과 양파에서 얻을 수 있다고 언급되어 있다.

30 비타민 B는 새로운 세포를 만드는 데 도움을 준다고 언급되어 있다.

Lesson 3 (기말) 1회

01 ①	02 ③	03 ③	04 ⑤	05 ③	06 ③	07 ③
08 ④	09 ①	10 ⑤	11 ③	12 ②, ⑤		13 ③
14 ③	15 should be prepared / which can occur					
16 ②	17 ②	18 ③	19 ⑤	20 ③	21 ②	22 ②
23 used to		24 ③	25 ②	26 ③	27 ②	28 ③
29 ①, ④		30 ①				

01 storm은 '폭풍', '폭풍우'라는 뜻을 갖는 단어이다.

02 pull over 차를 세우다 / breathe 숨쉬다, 호흡하다 / violently 난폭하게 / occurr 발생하다 / confusion 혼란

03 Although는 '~이긴 하지만, ~임에도 불구하고'라는 뜻을 갖는 접속사이다. 문맥상 접속사 Because를 쓰는 것이 적절하다.

04 (A) How serious 얼마나 심각한지 (B) be curious about ~에 대해 궁금해하다 (C) 화재로 인해 집을 잃은 캘리포니아 사람들이 안전했으면 좋겠다는 의미이므로 they're가 들어가는 것이 자연스럽다.

05 John의 말에 "actually the wind has made the fires worse."라고 언급 되어 있다.

06 위 대화에 따르면, 생존 키트에는 마실 것과 음식이, 특히 달지 않은 먹을 것들이 필요하다고 했다. 또한 노트북 컴퓨터는 넣을 자리가 없지만 라디오와 배터리를 챙긴다고 이야기했다. 따라서 ⓐ batteries, ⓒ protein bars, ⓔ water, ⓕ a radio가 재난 대비 생존 키트에 들어갈 물품들이다.

07 B의 질문에 대한 A의 대답이 강릉의 큰 홍수가 2002년에 발생했다는 것이었다. 따라서 빈칸에 들어갈 의문사로 가

장 적절한 것은 ③ when이다.

08 A가 화재 훈련이라고 말하자, B는 엘레베이터를 이용해 나가자고 제안한다. 이에 A가 화재 발생시 엘레베이터를 타는 것은 위험하며 진짜 화재 발생시에는 엘레베이터를 타지 않도록 주의하라고 말한다. 이에 B가 동의하며 계단으로 내려가자고 말하는 순서로 이어지는 것이 대화 흐름상 가장 자연스럽다.

09 Jane이 유럽에서 발생했던 큰 홍수에 대해서 들어보았냐고 물었고 John은 듣지 못했다고 말하면서 홍수는 겨울에는 흔한 현상이 아니냐고 되묻는다. John이 온라인으로 조사를 해보자고 대답했으므로 빈칸에 들어갈 Jane의 말로 가장 적절한 것은 ① I'm curious about how that happened.(난 그것이 어떻게 발생했는지 궁금해.)이다.

10 G가 한국에서 지진이 예전보다 자주 일어난다는 사실을 들어보았냐고 묻자, B는 한국에서 지진을 느낀 적이 없다고 대답한다. G가 한국 남부에서는 지진이 자주 일어났는데 최근에는 다른 곳에서도 지진이 자주 발생한다고 말해주자, B는 왜 한국에서 예전보다 자주 지진이 발생하는 건지 궁금하다고 말한다. 이에 G는 그걸 알아내기 위해 조사를 하자고 제안한다. B는 어디서부터 살펴봐야 하는지 물어보자 G가 과학 선생님께 물어볼 것을 제안하는 순서로 이어지는 것이 대화의 흐름상 가장 자연스럽다.

11 ⓐ 문장 전체의 시제인 과거완료시제에 따라 had done이 적절하다. ⓑ 조동사 would가 사용되었으므로 experience가 적절하다. ⓒ 글의 전반적인 시제인 과거 시제인 began이 들어가야 문맥상 적절하다.

12 ① has → had / ③ His mother gave him a watch before he had lost it. → His mother had given him a watch before he lost it. / ④ had seen → will have seen으로 고쳐야 어법상 적절한 문장이 된다.

13 위 글에서 창문을 깬 일은 화자 I가 그에게 물어본 일보다 더 과거에 일어난 일이다. 따라서 빈칸에 들어갈 말로 가장 적절한 것은 과거완료시제인 ③ had broken이다.

14 (A) 소풍을 계획한 일은 계획을 바꾼 일 보다 더 과거의 일이므로 과거 완료 시제인 had planned가 되어야 한다. (B) Although ~이긴 하지만 (C) After ~한 후에

15 관계대명사의 계속적 용법은 관계대명사를 이용해 추가적인 정보를 계속 제공하고 있는 절을 쓰는 것을 의미한다. 따라서 선행사로 쓰이는 명사 다음에 콤마(,)를 쓰고 which나 who와 같은 관계대명사를 쓸 수 있다. 주의할 것은 관계대명사 that은 사용할 수 없다.

16 (A) 과거완료시제가 사용되었으므로 과거분사인 fallen이 들어가야 한다. (B) falling 떨어지는

17 ⓑ has studied → had studied ⓒ got → get ⓓ had teach → had taught ⓔ seen → saw로 고쳐야 어법상 적절한 문장이 된다.

18 지각동사 see를 쓰고 있고, 목적어 book을 꾸며주는 목적보어에 위치해 있으므로 ⓒto fall은 falling이 되어야 한다.

19 아파트의 유리창이 모두 깨졌는지에 대해서는 위 글에서 언급된 바 없다.

20 심폐소생술을 시행할 때에는 심폐소생술을 받는 사람의 가슴 중앙에 손을 올려 놓아야 한다고('Make sure you place your hands in the middle of the person's chest.') 언급되어 있다.

21 위 도표에 따르면, Rachael이 극장에 도착한 것은 1시 50분으로, 영화는 이미 1시 35분에 시작되었다.

22 과거에 진짜 지진을 겪고 난 후, 지진이 언제든지 일어날 수 있음을 알게 됐다는 내용이므로 빈칸에 들어갈 말로 가장 적절한 것은 ② I began to take earthquake drills seriously.(지진 대비 훈련을 진지하게 받기 시작했다.)이다.

23 'used to ~'는 과거의 일정 기간 동안 어떤 일을 했지만 현재는 하고 있지 않은 일을 나타낼 때 쓰는 표현으로 '~하곤 했다'라는 의미를 갖는다.

24 위 글에 따르면, 화자 I가 겪은 일을 시간 순서대로 나열하면 (a) - (d) - (b) - (c) - (e)이다.

25 위 글의 첫 문단에 따르면, 화자 I는 거울이 바닥에 떨어지고 산산조각 났을 때에 무슨 일이 일어나는지 몰랐다고 언급한 바 있다.

26 ⓑ건물은 무너지지 않았으며, ⓔ글쓴이는 이전에 지진 대비 훈련을 하기는 하지만 지진을 직접 겪어본 적은 없다고 언급되어 있다.

27 (A) after ~한 후에 (B) Since ~ 때문에

28 위 글의 문맥상, 화자는 침대를 흔드는 것이 남동생이라고 생각했지만 남동생이 아니라 지진이었다. 따라서 (가)it이 가리키는 내용은 ③이다.

29 ⓐ which → what, ⓓ to break → break[breaking]로 고쳐야 어법상 적절한 문장이 된다.

30 위 글에서 화자 I는 지난 2월에 겪었던 지진에 대해서 회상하고 있다. 따라서 I의 심경으로 가장 적절한 것은 ① scared(두려워하는)이다.

Lesson 3 (기말)

2회

01 위 문장에서는 눈이 많이 오고 있었기 때문에 하루 종일 집에 있었다는 의미이다. 따라서 빈칸에 들어갈 말로 가장 적절한 것은 접속사 ③ Since(~때문에)이다.

02 immediately는 '곧', '즉시'라는 뜻을 갖는 단어이다.

03 as: ~함에 따라

04 'I'm curious about ~'은 '~에 대해 궁금하다'라는 의미로, 어떤 일에 대한 궁금증을 나타낼 때 쓸 수 있는 표현이다.

05 위 대화에서 화재의 원인에 대해서는 언급되어 있지 않다.

06 위 대화에 따르면, 가장 피해를 주는 자연 재해는 폭풍이고 그 다음은 폭우("Second is heavy rain,")라고 언급되어 있다.

07 위 대화에서는 유럽에서 발생했던 홍수에 대해서 이야기하고 있다. A가 온라인으로 조사해 보자고 대답했다. 따라서 빈칸에 들어갈 B의 말로 가장 적절하지 않은 것은 ② I have heard(~에 대해 들은 적 있다)이다.

08 Susie가 화재 대비 훈련에 있어서 줄을 빠르게 서야 한다고 말하자, David는 집합 장소에 가는 것이냐고 묻는다. 이에 Susie는 맞다고 대답하면서 걸어갈 때 몸을 낮추는 것을 잊지 말라고 말한다. David는 계단보다 빠른 엘레베이터를 타자고 제안하지만 Susie는 화재가 났을 때 엘레베이터를 타는 것은 위험하다고 말하는 순서로 이어지는 것이 대화의 흐름상 가장 자연스럽다.

09 'make sure to/that ~'은 '반드시 ~해라', '확실하게 ~해라'라는 뜻으로 어떤 일에 대해 당부할 때 쓰는 표현이다.

10 while ~하는 동안에; 반면에 / as ~할 때; ~ 때문에 / since ~ 이래로; ~ 때문에 / if ~인지; 만약 ~라면 / although ~이긴 하지만

11 (1) 과거형 문장이므로 didn't know가 되어야 한다. (2) 돈을 숨긴 것은 그 사실을 알지 못했던 일보다 더 이전의 과거이므로 과거완료시제인 had hidden이 되어야 어법상 적절하다.

12 (A) 글의 시제가 과거이므로 ring의 과거형인 rang이 적절하다. (B) 관계대명사의 계속적 용법이 사용되었는데, 이때 관계대명사절이 아버지를 수식하므로 who가 들어가야 한다. (C) urgently 급박하게

13 (A) since ~ 때문에 / (B) although ~이긴 하지만, ~임에도 불구하고 / (C) after ~한 후에

14 ②는 어제 과학 숙제를 끝마쳤다는 의미의 문장이므로 현재완료시제가 아니라 과거시제인 finished가 오는 것이 어법상 적절하다.

15 주어진 문장에 따르면, 영화관에 도착한 것보다 영화가 시작한 것이 더 먼 과거이므로 과거 완료 시제를 이용해 'When I got to the movie theater, the movie *Avengers* had started'라고 표현할 수 있다.

16 '내가 학교에 도착했을 때, 수업은 이미 시작해 있었다.'라는 문장이 들어가기에 가장 적절한 곳은 늦게 일어나 학교에 가서 조용히 자리에 앉았다는 곳인 (A)이다.

17 '반응이 없다면, 119에 도움을 요청하세요.'라는 문장이 들어가기에 가장 적절한 곳은 쓰러진 사람의 의식을 확인한 후인 (B)이다.

18 ⓑTap은 '가볍게 두드리다'라는 뜻으로 사용되었다.

19 ⓑturn over는 '뒤집다', '뒤집히다'라는 뜻을 가진 숙어이다.

20 글쓴이는 자신이 지진 대비 훈련을 해왔지만 지진이 언제라도 일어날 수 있다고 생각한 것은 지진을 겪고 난 후라고 언급했다.

21 첫 문단에 'We went to an open space to avoid more falling pieces.'라고 언급되어 있다.

22 지진이 발생해서, 엄마가 남동생과 주방에 가서 테이블 밑으로 들어간 후, 지진으로 물건들이 떨어지는 것을 목격하면서 건물이 무너질까 걱정했지만(D), 흔들림이 멈춰서 문 쪽으로 나갈 때 아버지로부터 전화가 왔고(B), 어머니가 아버지와 통화(C)하는 순서로 이어지는 것이 글의 흐름상 가장 자연스럽다.

23 대명사 it은 앞에서 언급된 단수 명사를 가리키는 것으로, 이 문장의 경우에는 Our family picture를 가리킨다.

24 건물이 무너질 것 같이 보였지만 흔들림이 멈추고 건물은 무너지지 않았다.

25 지진이 발생했을 때 화자와 화자의 가족은 걸어서가 아니라 기어서 문 쪽으로 갔다.

26 ⓐ seem to ~한 것처럼 보이다 ⓑ 관계대명사의 계속적 용법에서 that은 사용할 수 없다. ⓒ 능동의 의미이므로 현재분사 covering을 써야 한다.

27 위 글의 내용상, 이전에 지진을 겪어 보지 않았기 때문에 지진에 어떻게 반응해야 할지를 몰랐다는 문장인 ② I didn't know how to react가 가장 적절하다.

28 (A) after ~한 후에 (B) but 그러나 (C) Since ~ 때문에

29 위 글에서는 화자 I가 잠자리에 들었을 때 침대가 흔들렸고 무슨 일이 일어나는지 몰랐다가 엄마가 지진이 일어났다고 소리친 후 어찌할 바를 몰라 무서워했다고 회상하고 있다. 따라서 화자의 심경의 변화로 가장 적절한 것은 ⑤ confused → frightened이다.

30 화자는 개가 아니라 남동생이 침대를 흔드는 줄로 생각했다고('I thought my brother was shaking my bed as a joke.') 언급되어 있다.

Lesson 4 (기말)

> **01** ③ **02** ② **03** This project must be done today.
> **04** ② **05** ④
> **06** I have never thought about running.
> **07** ② **08** ④ **09** ⑤ **10** ② **11** ③ **12** ④ **13** ①
> **14** Please let me know if you like me.
> **15** ② **16** ④ **17** ⑤ **18** whether / I can go **19** ④
> **20** ④ **21** ⑤ **22** ③ **23** ③ **24** ① **25** ④ **26** ③
> **27** ④ **28** ② **29** what **30** ①

01 election 선거 / analyze 분석하다 / approach 접근하다 / achieve 성취하다 / ensure 보장하다

02 위에서부터 순서대로 although, as, after, since가 들어가는 것이 문맥상 자연스럽다.

03 수동태는 '주어+be동사+동사의 과거분사+by+행위자'의 형식을 가지며 '…에 의해 ~되다[당하다]'라는 의미로 주어가 동사가 나타내는 행위를 당하거나 행동의 영향을 받는 것을 나타낸다. 수동태 문장의 주어 자리에는 능동태 문장의 목적어가 오고, by 다음에는 능동태 문장의 주어를 쓴다. 누가 그 동작을 했는지 중요하지 않거나 잘 모를 때, 수동태 문장으로 표현한다. 수동태는 현재, 과거, 미래 시제로 쓸 수 있고, 'be동사+동사의 과거분사'에서 be동사로 시제를 표현한다.

04 A가 학생 연락처를 만들고 싶다고 말하자, 좋은 생각이라고 말하면서 그건 도움이 되지 않을 거라는 B의 대답은 대화의 흐름상 자연스럽지 않다.

05 outgoing은 '외향적인', '사교적인'이라는 뜻을 갖는 단어이다.

06 '~에 대해서 생각해 본 적 없다'라는 문장을 만들 때 'I have never thought about ~'이라는 표현을 쓸 수 있다.

07 'I have no doubt that ~'은 that 이하의 문장에 대해 확신한다라는 의미를 지닌 구문으로 'I'm sure that ~'으로 바꿔 쓸 수 있다.

08 Brian은 유미에게 학급 반장 선거에 나갈 것을 제안하고 있고, 유미는 반장 선거에 나가는 것에 대해 확신이 없는 상태이다.

09 대화 후반부에 Brian은 유미가 학급 반장을 뽑힐 것이라고 확신하고 있다고 언급한 바 있다.

10 그룹 A는 한국어로 된 이야기를 영어로 번역할 것이라고 언급되어 있다.

11 태현이는 재우와 윤호가 싸운 이유를 알고 있다고 언급했다.

12 misunderstanding: 오해

13 위 대화의 내용에 따르면, 모모는 희철이가 숙제를 도와달라고 했지만 할 일이 많아서 도와줄 수 없는데 도와줄 수 없다고 말을 못했다고 설명한다. 따라서 빈칸에 들어갈 내용으로 가장 적절한 것은 ① What's the matter?(무슨 일이니?)이다.

14 접속사 if는 '~인지 아닌지'라는 의미로 whether와 바꿔 쓸 수 있다.

15 대화 속 소년의 아버지가 소년을 친구의 생일 파티에 가게 해 줄 것이라고 언급된 바 없으며, 소년이 한 말 "I'd love to see Grandma."로 미루어 볼 때, 할머니와는 좋은 관계에 있다고 유추할 수 있다.

16 '~인지 아닌지 궁금해'라는 표현은 "I'm wondering if ~"라고 쓸 수 있다. 이때 if 이하에는 의문문이 아니라 평서문을 쓴다.

17 ① must solved → must be solved / ② will play → will be played / ③ may be not → may not be / ④ should treat → should be treated로 고쳐야 어법상 적절한 문장이 된다.

18 '~인지 아닌지'라는 표현은 접속사 whether가 이끄는 절을 쓸 수 있다.

19 ④의 if는 조건절을 이끄는 접속사로 '만약 ~라면'이라는 뜻으로 사용되었다. 나머지는 모두 '~인지 아닌지'라는 표현으로 사용되었다.

20 ④ medicine → by medicine으로 고쳐야 어법상 적절한 문장이 된다.

21 위 글에서는 우리 모두가 각자 다른 집단에 속하며 그러므로 각자 다른 스타일의 리더가 필요하다고 이야기하고 있다.

22 Each group's unique situation은 단수 취급한다. 따라서 ⓒ determine은 determines로 고쳐야 어법상 적절한 문장이 된다.

23 위 글에서는 우리 모두가 각자 다른 집단에 속하며 그러므로 각자 다른 스타일의 리더가 필요하다고 이야기하고 있다. 따라서 위 글의 제목으로 가장 적절한 것은 ③ Different Groups, Different Leadership(다른 집단, 다른 리더십)이다.

24 (A)if는 조건절이 쓰인 문장이다. 이와 쓰임이 같은 문장은 ① '네가 필요하다면 난 그 책을 살게.'이다.

25 위 글에 따르면, 퍼플 리더는 다른 사람들을 통제하려고 하지 않기 때문에 Hands-Off Managers(불간섭하는 관리자)가 적절하다. 오렌지 리더는 사람들의 역할을 명확하게 하고 모든 일이 제시간에 끝날 수 있도록 하기 때문에 Strict Directors(엄격한 감독관)가 적절하다.

26 ⓒclearly → clear / ⓔis doing → is done으로 고쳐야 어법상 적절한 문장이 된다.

27 옐로 리더가 팀을 목표에 직접적으로 이끈다는 이야기는 언급되어 있지 않다.

28 '그러나, 그가 그걸 내게 말했을 때, 나는 생각하기 시작했다'란 문장이 들어가기에 가장 적절한 곳은 Brian의 말로 인해 자신이 좋은 리더인지에 대해서 생각하게 된 (B)이다.

29 관계대명명사 what은 '~한 것'이라는 의미로, the thing(s) which와 바꿔 쓸 수 있다.

30 (가)if는 '~인지 아닌지'라는 의미로 쓰였다. 따라서 이와 쓰임이 다른 것은 ① I will stay home if it rains tomorrow.(내일 비가 온다면 내일 집에 있을 것이다.)이다.

Lesson 4 (기말) 2회

01 ①
02 (1) should be washed (2) must be worn
(3) will not be allowed
03 ④ **04** ⑤ **05** ④ **06** ⑤ **07** ⑤ **08** ③ **09** ②
10 I have no doubt that you will be our leader
11 ① **12** ③ **13** ④ **14** ⑤ **15** ③
16 will be delivered **17** ④ **18** ① **19** ④ **20** ②
21 ③ **22** ④ **23** ① **24** ① **25** ⑤ **26** ④ **27** ④
28 ④ **29** ② **30** ⑤

01 (A) What's the matter? 무슨 일이니? (=What's wrong?) (B) decision 결정, division 분배

02 수동태 문장의 주어 자리에는 능동태 문장의 목적어가 오고, by 다음에는 능동태 문장의 주어를 쓴다. 수동태는 현재, 과거, 미래 시제로 쓸 수 있고, 'be동사+동사의 과거분사'에서 be동사로 시제를 표현한다.

03 사진 찍는 걸 담당하냐는 A의 질문에 대해 그렇다고 대답하면서 '네가 좋은 사진을 찍을 것이라고 확신해.'라는 B의 대답은 대화 흐름상 적절하지 않다.

04 Nick의 질문에 대해 Mandy가 자신이 처한 일에 대해서 털어놓고 있다. 따라서 빈칸에 들어갈 말로 적절하지 않은 것은 ⑤ What makes you say that?(왜 그렇게 생각하니?)이다.

05 원호와 민주는 가현이네 그룹이 책을 인쇄하기로 했다고 이야기했다.

06 ⓐturn out은 '~인 것으로 밝혀지다'라는 뜻을 가진 단어이다.

07 'I have no doubt that ~'은 that 이하의 문장에 대해 확신한다라는 의미를 지닌 구문으로 'I'm sure that ~'으로 바꿔 쓸 수 있다.

08 유미가 학급 반장 선거에 나가고 싶지 않은 이유는 자신이 특별한 자질을 갖고 있다고 생각하지 않기 때문이다.

09 유미가 자신은 학급 반장으로 생각하지 않고 있다고 했으므로 ⓑ "나의 러닝 메이트가 될 수 있니?"라는 문장은 흐름상 자연스럽지 않다.

10 'I have no doubt that ~'은 that 이하의 문장에 대해 확신한다라는 의미를 지닌 표현으로 'I'm sure that ~'으로 바꿔 쓸 수 있다.

11 (A) how I was 내가 어떻게 지냈는지 (B) Do you have any plans for ~? ~를 위한 계획이 있니? (C) whether ~인지 아닌지

12 ③ if → whether로 고쳐야 어법상 적절한 문장이 된다.

13 ⓐ 부상 입은 사람이 실려가는 것이므로 수동형인 be carried가 적절하다. ⓑ 조동사 must가 쓰였으므로 do가 적절하다. ⓒ 의학적 결정이 주어이므로 수동태형 동사인 be made이 적절하다.

14 ⑤if는 '~인지 아닌지'라는 뜻으로 사용되었다. 나머지는 모두 '만약 ~라면'이라는 뜻으로 사용되었다.

15 준수의 두 친구가 싸워서 어떻게 해야 할지 모르겠다고 말하자, Smith는 그들이 왜 싸웠는지 아냐고 물어보고(E) 준수는 알고 있고 둘 사이에 오해가 있는 것 같다고(A) 대답한다. Smith는 다같이 만나서 이야기해 보라고 제안하고(C) 준수는 좋은 생각이라고 대답한다(B). 이에 Smith

는 일이 잘 됐으면 좋겠다고(D) 말하는 순서로 이어지는 것이 흐름상 가장 자연스럽다.

16 물건이 배송되는 것이므로 수동태인 will be delivered 가 쓰여야 어법상 적절하다.

17 Shane이 말한 모든 것이 제시간에 끝날 수 있게 하는 것이 중요하다고 생각하는 리더는 레드 리더가 아니라 오렌지 리더이다.

18 블루 리더의 자질로 가장 적절한 것은 새로운 방법으로 문제에 접근하고 '신선한 아이디어를 떠올리며', 다른 사람과 다르게 문제를 해결하는 것이다.

19 노란색 리더는 팀원들의 요구를 충족하려고 노력한다 (Meet the team members' needs)고 언급되어 있다.

20 (A) 좋은 추리 능력을 갖고 있고 팀의 목적을 위해 가장 효과적인 방법을 생각한다고 나와 있으므로 Logical Analysts가 가장 적절하다. (B) 다른 사람이 스스로 일을 하게 하고 사람들을 통제하려고 노력하지 않는다고 했으므로 Hands-Off Managers가 적절하다. (C) 새로운 방식으로 문제에 접근하고 다른 사람과 다르게 문제를 해결한다고 했으므로 Creative Thinkers가 가장 적절하다.

21 위 글에서는 다른 집단에는 다른 리더십이 필요하다고 이야기하고 있다. 따라서 ⓒPeople want strong leadership styles all the time.(사람들은 항상 강한 리더십을 원한다.)는 문장은 글의 흐름과 관련이 없다.

22 '그리고 나서 나는 갑자기 이것들만이 좋은 리더를 만드는 자질들인지 궁금해하기 시작했다'라는 문장이 들어가기에 가장 적절한 곳은 좋은 리더의 자질들을 이야기하고 있는 (D)이다.

23 위 글의 후반부에서는 다른 리더십의 자질들에 대해서 온라인으로 조사를 해본다고 언급했다. 따라서 위 글에 이어질 내용으로 적절한 것은 ① different leadership styles이다.

24 ⓐ의 앞 부분과 뒷부분의 내용이 반대되므로 however가 적절하다. ⓑ 화자가 다른 리더십의 자질들이 있는지 궁금해서 온라인으로 조사를 한다는 내용이므로 Thus(그러므로)가 가장 적절하다.

25 위 글에서 유미는 자신이 리더의 자질이 있는지 잘 모르겠다고 언급한 바 있다.

26 위 글에서는 다른 집단에는 다른 리더십이 필요하다고 이야기하고 있다. 따라서 위 글의 요지로 가장 적절한 것은 ④ '집단과 상황에 따라 다른 지도력 유형이 필요하다.'이다.

27 글쓴이는 그린 리더의 자질을 갖고 있다고는 했지만 그것이 학교에서 요구되는 최고의 지도력이라고는 언급되지 않았다.

28 위 글에서는 다른 집단에는 다른 리더십이 필요하다고 이야기하고 있다. 따라서 위 글의 목적으로 가장 적절한 것은 ⑤ '고유한 상황에 맞는 리더가 필요함을 알려주려고'이다.

29 주어 Each group's unique situation은 단수 취급한다. 따라서 ⓑdetermine은 determines가 되어야 어법상 적절하다.

30 come up은 '(해답 등)을 떠올리다'라는 뜻을 갖는다.

MEMO

MEMO

적중 1○○ + 특별부록

Plan B

우리학교
최신기출

능률 · 김성곤 교과서를 배우는

학교 시험문제 분석 · 모음 · 해설집

전국단위 학교 시험문제 수집 및 분석
출제 빈도가 높은 문제 위주로 선별
문제 풀이에 필요한 상세한 해설

중3-1
영어

능률 · 김성곤

값 6,000원

53370

ISBN 979-11-337-1605-0